NEW SOUTH AFRICAN REVIEW 1

NEW SOUTH AFRICAN 1 REVIEW

2010: DEVELOPMENT OR DECLINE?

EDITED BY JOHN DANIEL, PRISHANI NAIDOO,
DEVAN PILLAY AND ROGER SOUTHALL

WITS UNIVERSITY PRESS

Published in South Africa by:

Wits University Press
1 Jan Smuts Avenue
Johannesburg
2001
http://witspress.wits.ac.za

First published 2010

ISBN 978-1-86814-516-4

Cover image: Africa Media Online – Terry February – Cape Town Stadium

Project managed by Monica Seeber
Cover design and layout by Hothouse South Africa
Printed and bound by Ultra Litho (Pty) Ltd.

Contents

PART 2: STATE, POLITICS AND POLICY

PART 3: EDUCATION, HEALTH AND LAND

PART 4: CRIME AND SEX

Preface

In producing this, the first edition of the *New South African Review*, its editors seek to follow that tradition of critical scholarship established so firmly by the seven volumes of the *South African Review* which appeared in the 1980s and 1990s. They provided invaluable insights into the apartheid state's strategies and the popular responses and struggles of those troubled and difficult years. Now, fifteen years into the making of South Africa's democracy, the issues which face our society are very different, albeit bearing the heavy imprint of the country's divided and unequal past. Since 1994, the successive governments headed by ANC presidents Mandela, Mbeki, Motlanthe and Zuma have not only had to assume the normal burdens of state but also to confront massive challenges of transformation across the political, economic, social and international spheres.

In retrospect, there have been considerable achievements. Yet, again, there have been many wrong moves, many downright failures and many disappointments, even though we should, perhaps, be humble enough to recognise that, with its particular legacies, South Africa is not an easy country to govern. Thus it is that the objective of the *New South African Review* is to provide a forum for reflection upon achievements, problems and challenges, and to stimulate debate between divergent positions held upon a wide range of issues. It is intended to be accessible to a wide range of readership, and to draw upon authors from well beyond academia. Its objective is to be informative, discursive and, at times, to be downright provocative. It is not intended to be an annual review of events, although it will seek to provide contemporary comment, and it will engage with (indeed, seek out) current controversies.

The *New South African Review* is housed in the Department of Sociology at the University of the Witwatersrand. We should like to acknowledge, with thanks, financial support from the Konrad Adenauer Foundation and from the Faculty Research Committee of the Faculty of Humanities at Wits. Neither of those bodies is responsible for any of the views expressed in any chapters of this volume, but both have kindly provided the material means whereby workshops and editorial meetings have been held, and peer review of all chapters conducted. Without their encouragement and backing this project would never have got going. Our thanks must also go to our authors for having more or less behaved themselves in submitting and revising chapters more or less according to a tight schedule, and for accepting our editorial harrying with a good grace. Finally, we should like to thank Doreen Atkinson, Jackie Cock, Mark Colvin, Simon Dagut, Emily Delap, Bill Freund, Leah Gilbert, Ruth Hall, Catherine Jenkins, Duncan Innes, Don Lindsay, Helene Perold, Maxine Reitzes and Christopher Saunders for making valuable comments upon different chapters in the peer review process.

John Daniel (School of International Training, Durban), Prishani Naidoo, Devan Pillay and Roger Southall (all based at the Department of Sociology, University of the Witwatersrand).

May 2010

South Africa 2010:
From short-term success
to long-term decline?

Roger Southall

For a decade and a half following the arrival of democracy, South Africa enjoyed its longest period of uninterrupted economic growth since the mid-1960s, 'the golden age of apartheid'. Even if it is going far too far to suggest that the fifteen odd years after 1994 amounted to a 'second golden age' (Abedian 2009), crude economic indicators demonstrate positive annual growth throughout the period, an increase in per capita incomes (at year 2000 prices) from R20 214 in 1994 to R25 897 in 2008, and a decline in the proportion of people living in absolute poverty[1] from 4.2 per cent in 1996 to 1.4 per cent in 2008 (SAIRR 2008-09: 92 and 302).

Further, even though the fruits of growth were highly unevenly shared and public service provision in key areas seriously attenuated, the extent of poverty was leavened by a substantial increase in transfer payments made by the state to the old, disabled, unemployed, for child support, and so on. Although these gains left much to be desired, it is nonetheless wise to locate them against the background of South Africa's overall economic decline from around 1980 until 1994 and a period of near calamitous collapse during the uncertain years of the political transition. Meanwhile, this extended period of growth was accompanied by South Africa's movement from racial authoritarianism to a democracy which, whilst incomplete, has provided a framework for political stability. Compared to the grim picture which the country projected in 1990, South Africa in 2010 is 'another country'. Only a democratic South Africa, and one with a relatively advanced and stable economy, would have won the dubious honour of the right to host soccer's World Cup in 2010 (Cornellison below).

Numerous critics have decried these achievements as seriously flawed: economically as failing to provide for socially just and sustainable development; politically by providing for a
hollowed out democracy in which the constitution is under constant threat from the ruling
African National Congress (ANC); and socially for a marked failure to ground aspirations
towards collective welfare in an efficiently functioning state. Indeed, in this volume, we present
a series of chapters which query the logic and performance of the present trajectory, outlining
variously how its pursuit has led to deindustrialisation (Mohamed), persistent and unremit-
tingly high levels of unemployment (Makgetla), and how it is running up against underlying
resource constraints (Pillay, Swilling, Muller). Certainly, it is in the nature of the social sciences
to provide critiques of the existing world against the imagination of utopias (even if, as Vale
argues below, current state policies discourage such unbounded thinking). However, the role
of the social sciences is also to compare existing reality against what might have been, whether
for better or for worse. From this perspective, post-apartheid South Africa can lay claim to
having been something of a success during the first two decades of democracy. The present
outcome was by no means an historical inevitability, and accordingly critics of an imperfect
present need to recognise that matters might have turned out a lot worse. Even so, it would
seem that the foundations of this success over the short-term are today under threat; that this
may be heralding a long-term decline; and that there is serious reason for South Africans to be
worried about the direction in which their country is headed. This volume is devoted to exploring key dimensions of this possibility; and this introduction to sketching out its dynamics.

THE FOUNDATION OF SOUTH AFRICA'S SHORT-TERM SUCCESS

There is a substantial literature which has sought to address the nature of South Africa's
democratisation, ranging from celebrations of a 'miracle' through to sharp criticisms of an
'elite transition'. Suffice it to say here that what, in retrospect, needs emphasising is how the
political transition (an agreement by the then white controlled government to concede a non-
racial democracy backed up by assurances of the entrenchment of a 'constitutional state')
was complemented by an economic deal, largely forged behind the scenes, in which business
built political and economic alliances with elements of the incoming ANC elite (later to be
formalised as Black Economic Empowerment or BEE), while the ANC committed itself to
market economics and abandoned plans for nationalisation. This had the makings of what
Scott Taylor (2007) terms a 'reform coalition'.

Taylor refers to reform coalitions as alliances of public and private sector interests that are
found in developed and developing contexts and which take joint action to exploit a comple-
mentarity of interest via economic reform. They are best institutionally organised in forums
which bring business and the state together, and are sites of negotiation and bargaining in
which private and public partners may be of highly unequal strength. Where they work, they
require give and take, for just as the state is not necessarily capable of taking wise decisions
about the economy, business is likely to be more concerned with its immediate interests than
the general welfare of society. Reform coalitions thus occur when the interests of business

and state converge to enact, modify or implement growth-promoting policies that both parties expect will foster investment and increases in productivity, exemplifying what Peter Evans has referred to as the 'embeddedness' of state and society. By contrast, business-state relationships that privilege either a bureaucratic state bourgeoisie and/or particular corporate elites at the expense of growth-producing policies fall outside the definition of a reform coalition. For instance, where state power is relatively unconstrained, policies and practices may be implemented that negate the conditions which business requires for investment; or where business backs budget deficits which drastically reduce social welfare expenditure without making provision for alternative safety nets, the outcome can be debilitating in economic as well as social and moral terms.

Taylor and others argue that these characteristics have been substantially lacking in most sub-Saharan African countries (Brautigam *et al* 2002). Typically, the private sector has remained weak due to colonial inheritance, post-colonial policy and an outsized economic role for the state; business associations have been weak; and personalised rule has resulted in state predation, facade-like bureaucracies, clientelism and corruption. In post-apartheid South Africa, however, a reform coalition underpinned the political transition. Critically, fearing nationalisation, key business actors (notably from the mining and financial sectors) combined to convince leading elements of the ANC to adopt a liberalising economic framework which, they argued, was the only sure way to attract investment, spur growth and create jobs. This culminated in the ANC leadership's adoption of the Growth, Employment and Redistribution (GEAR) strategy even though it was contrary to the party's election manifesto (the Redistribution and Development Programme), and even though it was at cost of the exclusion from policy-making of both smaller business interests and the party's partners, the Congress of South African Trade Unions (Cosatu) and the South African Communist Party (SACP) (Bassett 2008). Although this clearly privileged the interests of big business, Taylor (2007: 189) opines that 'it is not at all clear that alternative coalitions would have produced wider social and economic benefit for South Africa and prevented wider political instability during a very fragile period ... Business and the emergent ANC-state *needed* each other; each conferred legitimacy upon the other'. Broadly, the coalition that emerged endured because it continued to provide utility to either side: 'profitability, new trade opportunities, public-private partnerships, the preservation of ANC political dominance, and not insignificantly, the enrichment of erstwhile ANC elites through BEE' (Taylor 2007: 190).

Taylor acknowledges that investment and employment levels and overall economic performance ('low but positive') were to fall far short of neoliberal expectations, and admits the need for a wider dialogue between business and the state which would lead to adoption of a more comprehensive range of strategies productive of more socially inclusive growth. Nonetheless, he insists that business remains 'indispensable to South Africa's future', and argues that as long as the state can 'placate labour and the left, it will continue its relationship with predominantly white capital while witnessing the steady expansion of black empowerment companies' (Taylor 2007: 191).

An immediate critique of Taylor is that he systematically underplays the important role which organised labour (Cosatu) played in facilitating the forging and functioning of the reform coalition. Nonetheless, his overall projection of South Africa's 'low but positive' growth as an outcome of balance between business and the state after 1994 is broadly convincing, not least because the counterfactual cannot be determined. However, although it is also arguable that the conditions for the viability of the reform coalition are changing for the worse, to argue this is to necessitate an exploration of the wider context of any such coalition. This, it is proposed, was constituted in South Africa of three major dimensions.

The first aspect of this wider context was agreement not only that the government would pursue market economics, but that the capital market would be progressively internationalised. The key literature places heavy emphasis upon the manner in which successful 'growth coalitions' have centred around business-government relations which cohere around reform projects embracing trade liberalisation, export-friendly policies, engagement with the global economy and macroeconomic policies which will attract foreign capital and backing by international financial institutions such as the International Monetary Fund (IMF) and World Bank (WB). This has been replicated in most surveys of the reform project in South Africa. Thus although it is recognised that, given its racial profile, direct pressure by business had contradictory effects, the ANC leadership became exposed to a wide variety of international and domestic influences which pushed it towards the adoption of conservative measures designed to shore up local and international business confidence. It was not just that the ANC elite became convinced of the need to accommodate the international investment market, but also that it had to do so in the face of the 'dismal record of economic governance' elsewhere on the continent. 'In a post-Cold War world, there appeared to be few alternatives to the fiscal rectitude and other policies endorsed by Washington' (Handley 2005: 222).

The second dimension was the ANC's determination, expressed at its Mopani summit with black business in October 1993, that its assumption of control over the state would be complemented by processes of BEE. At the time of the transition, big business was uncomfortably aware of the need to narrow the huge political gulf that was separating it from the incoming government by indicating a willingness to alter its racial profile. The South Africa Foundation (SAF) – the grouping of the sixty-plus largest and most influential companies, domestic and international, whose principal purpose was to represent the interests of the private sector to government – was a 'bastion of traditional white capital', and was urgently aware of the need for firms to recruit black executives, and for business as a whole to show itself 'proactive on the issues of particular political importance to the ANC, such as black empowerment and, more narrowly, jobs and wealth creation' (Taylor 2007: 171–2). Initially, BEE was unprogrammatic and took the form of the direct recruitment of individuals, usually with strong links to the ANC, to high positions in large firms or on to boards of directors as well as the sale of aspects of their operations to black entrepreneurs. Subsequently, after the delivery of the Black Economic Empowerment Commission (which was largely driven by the demands of black business) to government in 2001, BEE became a major plank in the Mbeki administration's programme, culminating in the passage of the BEE Act of 2003 (Southall 2003).

Less noticed, but perhaps more important, was the use made by the ANC of the parastatals as avenues for black advancement. Overall, by 1999, the parastatals – dominated by the big four (Transnet, Eskom, Telkom and Denel) – accounted for around 15 per cent of GDP, 86 per cent of state-owned enterprise (SOE) turnover, 94 per cent of SOE income, and 77 per cent of SOE employment. Historically, they had been used by the NP to promote Afrikaner empowerment, and now they were to become platforms for black empowerment; first, as a means for increasing direct black control over the economy; second, as a training ground for blacks who were later to shift to the private sector. In retrospect, it is scarcely surprising that although GEAR formally espoused neoliberal mantras, the privatisation that took place concerned largely 'non-core' assets of the parastatals (with their sale being used to promote empowerment ventures). There was, to be sure, a rather disastrous exception in the form of the partial privatisation of Telkom in 1997, which by 2003 had led to a major empowerment group losing substantial amounts of capital after a collapse in the share price. But overall, despite the undoubted commitment of the government to commercialising the public sector, its enthusiasm for selling it off was distinctly muted. Indeed, by the time of the 2004 election, the government had drawn back from any serious talk about privatisation, and had committed itself rather to the 'restructuring' of the major SOEs so that they could serve 'developmental' purposes (Cassim 2006; Southall 2007).

The third major support of the 'reform coalition' was the assumption that the ANC as government would provide for the social and political conditions in which private capital could operate. After all, it was the steady erosion of the capacity of the NP government to maintain control over the subordinated black majority of the population from the mid-1970s which had led to the equally steady withdrawal of the support of large-scale capital for continued white rule from the early 1980s (as indicated *inter alia* by the succession of meetings, some of them clandestine, between business leaders and the exiled ANC in a variety of foreign locations). In broad terms, large-scale business underwrote the political transition because it came to recognise that only the ANC (which during the 1980s had called for South Africa to be rendered 'ungovernable') had the popular legitimacy which could provide for a restoration of political stability; and only a democratic settlement could provide that political stability, which by the early 1990s, had itself become a pre-condition for economic liberalisation. This is not to say that large-scale business had much faith in the ability of the ANC to run the affairs of state extending beyond economic policy through to the running of the education, health, legal, policing and defence systems *et cetera* efficiently. (This was to be indicated by the extent to which better off whites – notably the corporate community – withdrew into privatised spheres of social life, from private healthcare through to gated communities). Nonetheless, there was overall recognition by large scale business that political stability could only be attained by the prospect of a 'triple transition', that is, the formal extension of social as well as economic and political citizenship rights to blacks as well as to whites (Webster and Omar 2003).

In sum, the 'reform bargain' which facilitated South Africa's success was underpinned by the new government's commitment to providing the opportunity for large-scale business to internationalise; by capital accepting, at least rhetorically, the social and economic imperative of black empowerment; and by the widespread recognition of the necessity of a 'triple transition'. However, it can be argued that, even if the superstructure of the reform bargain still largely holds, its support system is beginning to give way.

THE CONTRADICTIONS OF INTERNATIONALISATION

The central argument of domestic business, foreign investors, the international financial institutions and the major foreign governments (notably the US and UK) backing the political
transition was that the level of economic growth required by post-apartheid South Africa
could only be attained through engagement with the global economy and the access this would
give to continually advancing high technology (Habib *et al* 1998: 106). Yet the reality is that
the opening up of the economy has had highly contradictory outcomes; first, the economy
has become far more subject to short-term global financial influences without; second, an
accompanying level of diversification; third, while access to new technology has improved,
South Africa's technological advance is shaky; and fourth, critically, the disappointingly low
level of economic growth which has been achieved has been grossly insufficient in providing
for the employment needs of the country while being accompanied by high levels of inequality.
These are all in themselves huge topics, but briefly:

The internationalisation and financialisation of South African capital

It is well-known that the apartheid era provided the conditions for the concentration and consolidation of capital, as the major mining houses diversified into manufacturing, as finance
capital diversified into both, and as English-speaking and Afrikaner capital steadily merged
their interests with each other and foreign capital. A further development was a greater inter-
penetration of private capital and the parastatals. By 1981, over 70 per cent of the total assets
of the top 138 companies in South Africa were controlled by state corporations and eight private conglomerates spanning mining, manufacturing, construction, transport, agriculture and
finance (Davies *et al* 1984: 58). Yet greater concentration was to come as, with the mounting
political crisis, foreign companies disinvested and sold their assets locally. By 1990, just three
conglomerates – Anglo-American, Sanlam and Old Mutual – controlled a massive 75 per cent
(R425bn) of the total capitalisation (R567bn) of the Johannesburg Stock Exchange (JSE)
(McGregor *et al* 2009). However, a dramatic change was to sweep through the capital market
thereafter. First, the conglomerates chose to 'realise shareholder value' by an extensive process
of 'unbundling'; second, the opening up of the economy encouraged major South African
corporations to go global alongside a (limited) inflow of foreign capital (see Mohamed below).

The post-1994 liberalisation of the economy was critical. By December 2008, although the
market capitalisation of the big three had increased to R1.1 trillion, this represented no more
than 24.4 per cent of the total capitalisation of the JSE. Unable to invest widely abroad under
apartheid, the conglomerates had invested their excess capital by buying local assets which
were often far distant from their core business. But from the early 1990s they had responded
to lobbying by their own shareholders to unbundle by selling their non-core assets.

Their non-core assets were largely taken up by institutional investors, both public (for
example the Public Investment Corporation) or private (pension funds), as well as by new
BEE players who were, in turn, backed by the banks and the institutional investors themselves.[2]
Meanwhile, unbundling had a major effect upon the big three (and the other former conglomerates) themselves. In 1990, Sanlam controlled sixty-four JSE listed companies with

interests across food, clothing, mining and construction. By 2008, it had slimmed down to become a financial services company, having in excess of 25 per cent ownership in only four companies on the JSE. Similarly, whereas in 1990 Old Mutual had a controlling stake in seventy-four JSE-listed companies, by 2008 it had stakes exceeding 25 per cent in only two companies (Nedbank and Mutual & Federal). Yet the most remarkable transformation took place at Anglo-American. In 1992, Anglo controlled some eighty-six JSE-listed companies which had interests across the economy, yet by 2008 it had become a more focused miner with holdings of more than 25 per cent in only four JSE companies: AngloGold Ashanti, AngloPlatinum, Kumba and Tongaat Hulett (McGregor *et al* 2009).

Unbundling was accompanied by rapid internationalisation. Major South African corporations had invested overseas even under apartheid (through both legal and illegal means), yet they had faced myriad restrictions and controls in doing so. From 1994, however, the situation eased considerably, notably by the scrapping of the Financial Rand, the grant by government of exchange control exemptions to major corporations, and a reduction in controls on the outward flow of capital. Most particularly, from 1997, the government granted permission for some of the largest South African companies – notably Billiton, South African Breweries, Anglo-American, Old Mutual and Liberty Life – to move their primary listings from the JSE to London, thereby facilitating their evolution into major multinationals. This development was accompanied by a massive outflow of South African investment capital (McGregor *et al* 2009). In short, the transition provided the conditions under which significant segments of domestic capital could exit South Africa and foreign capital would come in, facilitated by Johannesburg's rapidly moving to become the continent's primary financial centre for global capital..

Much has been made of the extent to which South African capital has moved into the wider continent since the early 1990s, and indeed this is remarkable, not least because it has been a movement which has been so broad-based, across virtually every sector of industry, and because South Africa has become the foremost source of new foreign investment in Africa. Even so, in 2006, Africa absorbed only 6.4 per cent of South Africa's outward foreign investment, compared to Europe which took 66 per cent (R82.45bn) and the Americas 24 per cent (R29.62bn) respectively (Daniel and Bhengu 2009: 142). However, whilst domestic capital has moved out, foreign investors have moved in to purchase assets from the unbundling conglomerates: for instance, Toyota, First Bowring and SA Motor Corporation from Anglo, Trek Petroleum and Mobil Oil, Carlton Paper and Gencor (now BHP Billiton) and Blue Circle from Sanlam. Yet the group that has gained most from these unbundlings is composed of anonymous investors represented by institutional investors guided by fund managers. Indeed, by the end of 2007, foreign shareholders held 45 per cent of the JSE's issued shares, up from just 18.9 per cent a year earlier (Hasenfus 2009).

Overall, these various developments add up to the massively increased exposure of the economy to global market 'sentiment'. As argued by Adam *et al* (1997: 162-3):

> 'Defiance of global expectations that was possible with the relatively isolated semi-colonial outpost in 1948 is now immediately penalised by currency fluctuations, higher interest rates on loans or capital outflows and refusal of investments ... the ANC has to prove constantly that it is worthy of outside support ...'

To be fair, South Africa avoided the immediate effects of the financial meltdown which afflicted the global economy, most noticeably in the West, from 2008. A fortuitous combination of the apartheid legacy of control and post-apartheid macroeconomic stringency had ensured that the financial sector had remained quite tightly regulated. Hence the excesses of deregulation and over-lending that brought many major financial institutions to their knees in the West were not repeated in South Africa. No banks collapsed. Unlike what happened in the United States, the United Kingdom and elsewhere, the financial sector received no sudden and major injection of public money to stave off a downward spiral. Nonetheless, as Mohamed indicates, South Africa has become dramatically exposed to international currency flows, as 'hot money' moves in or out of the economy. Rapid outflows of foreign currency (as in 2001) lead to depreciation of the rand against major global currencies, a rise in inflation, and hikes in interest rates; returning inflows of currency (as during 2004–2006) raise the value of the rand internationally, knock exports, increase imports and lead to current account deficits and balance of payments difficulties. In short, South Africa's increased global exposure has made government policy become increasingly responsive to the short-term demands of what Trevor Manuel once termed the 'amorphous market' rather than being able to pursue long-term strategies of development. This is in considerable part because internationalisation and financialisation have tended to reinforce the commodity basis of the economy.

Reinforcing the minerals-energy complex

South Africa's economic trajectory from the late nineteenth century saw a shift away from an agrarian to a minerals-exporting country. Even though the expansion of mining stimulated wider industrialisation from the beginning of this transformation; even though from the 1920s onwards, nationalist governments implemented protective strategies which encouraged manufacturing; and even though by the 1960s the major mining houses had moved beyond their base in gold, diamonds, coal or whatever to become huge conglomerates spanning finance and industry as well as minerals, the economy remained dominated by what Fine and Rustomjee (1996) have identified as the minerals-energy complex (MEC). To be sure, the direct contribution of mining to GDP declined from 12.1 per cent in 1951 to 9.5 per cent in 2008. In contrast, that of manufacturing remained static (18.1 per cent in 1951 to 18.8 per cent in 2008), whilst that of finance grew from 9.3 per cent to 21.7 per cent (SAIRR 2008-09: 139). Nonetheless, although South African industry has achieved considerable capacity and success, the economy continues to bear the heavy imprint of the MEC. Most importantly, broad sectors of manufacturing, energy supply, construction and transport remain intimately connected with, if not dependent upon, mining and servicing its needs: 'technical linkages between the two broad sectors have been significant and account for a substantial proportion of non-MEC manufacturing' (Fine and Rustomjee 1996: 245). Further, as Nattrass (1981: 269) remarked nearly three decades ago, 'South Africa remains heavily dependent upon the successful export of relatively few items and the composition of her exports largely reflects her natural resource endowment'. By 1990, manufacturing accounted for 80.2 per cent of exports and 96.7 per cent of imports, while mining accounted for 15.3 per cent of exports and just 1.64 per cent of imports. However, by 2008, manufacturing accounted for only 58.3 per cent of exports and 78.2 per cent of imports, while mining accounted for 37.9 per cent of exports and 20.3 per cent of imports (the latter figure obviously including oil) (SAIRR 2008/09: 139). Suffice it to say here that globalisation would seem to have enhanced South Africa's dependence upon the MEC rather than encouraged a wider diversification of the economy. This might not matter so much except that the long-term trend is for the MEC to become increasingly capital intensive and to provide declining opportunities for employment.

Meanwhile, the liberalisation of the economy may well have intensified dependence upon foreign knowledge production rather than advancing it domestically, for the internationalisation of South African industry has probably rendered it more feasible for firms to draw on knowledge and research from global supply chains (which may themselves often be embedded in multinational company structures) (Lorentzon 2006: 195). While there is nothing wrong with exploiting foreign sources of knowledge, there is plenty wrong if this is not built upon by a concerted national system for industrial innovation. Such a system in South Africa remains in its infancy, due in considerable part, according to some authors, to the country's lack of an integrated industrial policy (Morris *et al* 2006).

Employment, unemployment and inequality

There is little point in belabouring the well known fact that the post-apartheid economy is characterised by a crisis of unemployment. Debate continues about the contribution made towards this by the post-apartheid labour regime, which through the Labour Relations Act of 1995 and the Basic Conditions of Employment Act of 1997 provides significant protections for formally employed labour. Concession to this regime was crucial to incorporating Cosatu into the transitional deal, but a standard criticism of many commentators is that it has unduly privileged organised labour, acts as a major disincentive to employment creation (particularly by small business) and has encouraged employers to duck regulation by shifting towards 'flexible' employment patterns. Even so, deeper structural and technological changes have encouraged greater capital intensity which, in combination with the legacy of apartheid policies in education (and a failure to address it), has forged a labour market which remains heavily segmented along racial lines and which displays socially disastrous levels of unemployment. Unemployment is particularly high amongst the unskilled, and disproportionately affects the African population (McCord and Bhorat 2003: 113; Webster and von Holdt 2005). As explored by Makgetla below, these broad patterns have been exacerbated by the impact of the present global crisis upon the South African economy, which in 2009 resulted in the loss of nearly one million jobs.

Even if these job losses were to be reasonably rapidly reversed, this would be totally inadequate for addressing long-term employment needs. A study by a working group convened from representatives of government, business and labour, orchestrated by Miriam Altman of the Human Sciences Research Council, indicates that even if unemployment were to be halved to 13 per cent, by 2014 (the target set by the government), 35 per cent of the population would continue to live below the poverty line of R2 500 a month unless they were to be rescued by receipt of social grants. This reflects the fact that not only are wages for unskilled workers low, relative to the cost of living, but wage earners in poor households support, on average, six people. Yet even this scenario rests upon attainment of an average 6 per cent growth rate between 2004 and 2014, a goal which is highly unlikely to be achieved. More likely are lower growth scenarios which will see a rise in the proportion of the 'working poor' and those living in poverty.

In many African countries, the poor and unemployed can draw support from agriculture. In South Africa, however, African peasant production was long ago destroyed by the appetites of the mines for labour and of settler agriculture for land, and today the former homeland areas are agriculturally devastated, land reform has stalled[3] and rural African communities are heavily reliant on financial inputs from urban areas. In practice, this has substantially increased pressure on the post-apartheid state to expand its financial support not merely for the unemployed but for the poor generally through an array of social benefits ranging from old age pensions to disability grants. As a result, while the aspirations of South Africa to become a 'welfare state', inclusive of contemporary proposals for a national health system (Reynolds below), are morally commendable, there are numerous questions regarding the extent to which they are affordable over the long-term.[4] Critics point out that the growth in numbers of grant recipients (13.9 million in 2010 rising to sixteen million by 2013) is not matched by a similar increase in the number of direct taxpayers (six million) (*Business Report*, 22 February 2010).

The immediate answer to unemployment, argues Altman, is an expansion of the public service, recording a shift towards the hiring of teachers, nurses, and police as well as, importantly, entry level workers. Increasing the number of publicly funded low-skilled jobs would make the most immediate impact upon the level of unemployment, yet because low-skilled public sector workers earn twice to three times more than they are paid in the private sector, the government cannot afford to hire them at present pay levels, and it is not likely that public sector unions will easily accept the idea of a reduced wage, even for new job entrants. Even more problematic is the fact that, 'While the size of the public service has been growing in recent years, its capacity to do its job hasn't' (Paton 2007:43).

If the crisis of unemployment appears recalcitrant, its social impact is made worse by the extent and nature of social inequality. In 2008, while the richest 10 per cent of the population received 53.1 per cent of income and the richest 20 per cent received 70 per cent of total national incomes, the poorest 10 per cent received just 0.57 per cent and the poorest 20 per cent just1.6 per cent (RSA 2009: 22). These proportions have not changed significantly since the early 1990s, despite some modest shift of the overall proportion of national income going to blacks,[5] demonstrating the deeply structural nature not just of poverty but of the inequality of distribution. Politically, its impact is severely worsened by three features of the contemporary scene; first, the alacrity with which corporate executives in both the private and parastatal sectors have fastened on to global trends in 'top people's' remuneration, claiming massive benefits in terms of share options, retainers, bonuses and restraint of trade agreements on top of huge salaries; second, the apparently insatiable greed of elements of the new black elite, and the entrenchment of a culture of entitlement based upon corrupt access to state tenders; and third, the preference of South African elites for highly conspicuous consumption in terms of extravagant lifestyles, clothing, cars, mansions and 'bling' (all of which is stoked by the popular media's obsession with celebrity).

BLACK EMPOWERMENT: Politically necessary, but economically costly?

BEE has increasingly come to have a bad name, reflecting what *Business Report* (5 February 2010) records as 'the country's deep disenchantment with the empowerment process, which has come to be seen as a means of instant wealth for people with political connections and influence, while ordinary people have largely continued to live in poverty. Generally speaking, BEE is taken as having created a small group of 'BEE-llionaires' without having had a significant impact on the white domination of industry. This story is variously presented, but notably as white capital having sought self protection by forging deals with the incoming ANC elite, of the politically connected gaining preferential access to state tenders, and of blacks 'fronting' for white companies to obtain contracts from government (Bassett 2008). Meanwhile, despite heavy emphasis on the expansion of a black middle class, there is widespread suspicion voiced by the more assertive BEE protagonists that the empowerment process continues to be undermined by white resistance to black upward mobility throughout much of industry and the professions.

The reality is that the progress (or otherwise) of BEE in industry is highly complicated and multidimensional, its interpretation rendered difficult by a paucity of reliable data. On the one hand, too little is made of some of the achievements of BEE. For a start, for all the limitations of the process, black inroads have been made into ownership and management of industry despite a general lack of black capital and of education and training. There are today a small number of black majority-owned major companies (for instance, Shanduka and Mvelaphanda), more smaller such companies (of which we know rather little), and overall – depending upon broader market conditions – considerable upward momentum in the number of BEE deals. Likewise, although white faces continue to predominate in the boardroom and management, the number of blacks in senior corporate positions is steadily increasing.

According to the Presidency, 'the total value of BEE transactions as a percentage of total mergers declined between 1996 and 2002 and rose sharply from 5.1 per cent in 2002 to 31.1 per cent in 2004. However, lower growth rates have been achieved since then, averaging 19.5 per cent in 2008. This indicates progress in embracing and responding to the principles of the Broad Based Economic Empowerment Bill No. 53 of 2003' (RSA 2009a: 17). Similarly, the Presidency reports that the number of black senior and top managers in private industry increased from 18.5 per cent in 2000 to 32.5 per cent in 2008. Notwithstanding that different data sets vary considerably, the broad thrust of these figures is that the demographic profile of the private sector in South Africa has changed considerably since 1994. This was both a political necessity if the transition was to be underpinned by visible 'transformation' and a demographic one given the limited supply of white skills and the wastage of black talent under apartheid.

Nonetheless, there are substantial grounds for fearing that many BEE gains are hollow.

For a start, the commitment of business has been questionable, the government having systematically appeased large-scale capital by making major concessions over BEE targets and compliance in pursuit of economic growth (Tangri and Southall 2008). Second, even leaving aside the suspicion that (an unknown) proportion of deals are the product of politically connected 'tenderpreneurship' rather than of Weberian-style enterprise and risk taking, BEE deals have overwhelmingly been funded by debt. This, of course, is far from unusual in merger and acquisitions activity but it has consistently meant that BEE firms have been particularly exposed when they have encountered difficult market conditions, as occurred most notoriously in 1997 (when many black investors fell foul of that year's plunge in share prices) but more pertinently as a result of the current global crisis, with empowerment analysts reporting that black investors in BEE deals have been left with a huge debt burden, and that the deals are having to be restructured by the banks in order to save them from collapse (*Business Report*, 6 January 2010). Meanwhile, although criticism of established firms doing major deals only with a small number of 'usual suspects' has moved them towards more broadly based shareholdings, the large majority of BEE deals involve South African companies only, with multinational investors holding back: thus in 2009, only four out of twenty BEE deals in the mining sector were initiated by foreign investors (*ibid*). Two (albeit tentative) conclusions would seem to follow: first, given the perils for black investors of investment on the open market, the advantages of seeking deals with the state which offer political protection from market fluctuations are likely to be enhanced. Second, given the increasing dependence of South Africa upon foreign investment and the increased weight of foreign firms on the JSE, the government may find it necessary to relax further the conditions and implementation of BEE.

Meanwhile, pursuit of black empowerment has exacerbated a growing crisis within the parastatals. For the ANC, the state owned enterprises (SOEs) have a vital role to play in promoting growth and are viewed as key instruments of a 'developmental state'. Formally, they are governed by boards which, although appointed by the government as the 'shareholder', operate at arm's length and are relatively autonomous from political authority. In practice, the balance between the government setting broad parameters versus intervention for political reasons has proved difficult to achieve. The most notable instance has been the government's ignoring of advice in the late 1990s that the country needed more power stations, which culminated in a major power crisis in 2008, widespread power shortages and the mining industry having to cut production to work with rationed supply. It is difficult to avoid the conclusion that the welcome upward mobility of blacks within the parastatals has been unduly politicised through the penetration of political influences into what should more properly be internal human resources processes, the suspicion being that who obtains senior positions may influence the allocation of tenders to external actors (Williams 2010).

The outcome has been a parastatal sector which is constantly having to be bailed out with unbudgeted public funding, has earned an unenviable reputation for inefficiency, and is often held hostage to political fortune. Recent indicators have been major controversies around suspensions, dismissals and resignations of CEOs and aspirants to their jobs from most major parastatals, and ferocious battles around their leadership as different factions within the ANC have lobbied hard for the appointment of their favoured candidates to top positions,[6] this apparently linked to networks of 'tenderpreneurship' geared to securing contracts from state bodies. By early 2010, Transnet, SAA, Eskom, Armscor and a key section of Denel and Saab Aerostructures, were all being led by acting CEOs, with the authority of the new minister of public enterprises, Barbara Hogan, undermined by ANC infighting (Ensor 2010). Such political contestation has inevitably intruded upon long-term strategic planning, with Eskom, for instance, apparently wedded to a business model which, *inter alia*, is tied to reckless expansion of dirty and dangerous (coal-fired and nuclear) technologies at the cost of engagement with more environmentally friendly alternatives; dangerously compromised by its relationship with Chancellor House (an ANC owned company) which together with Hitachi is contracted to supply generation systems for new coal-fuelled power stations; and has secured approval for price increases to overcome capital shortages which may make South Africa's electricity among the most expensive in the world (Ashton 2010; Pillay, this volume).

Some parastatals' functioning may be more performance oriented than is presented by screaming headlines in the media (for example, Wells 2010) but even so, the image of a public enterprise sector that is simultaneously inefficient and expensive makes a nonsense of the government's commitment to the pursuit of a developmental state and contradicts its own desire to attract foreign investment, promote growth and create jobs.

FRAYING AT THE EDGES? The ANC's declining control of society

The ANC provided an absolutely necessary condition for the success of South Africa's 'reform bargain': the political legitimacy of the state and government in a country where both had been under bitter attack for decades. Today it continues to have no effective challenger, and in 2009 again demonstrated its capacity to win elections on a playing ground which, whilst tipped in its favour (notably by its access to massive financial resources), nonetheless allows ample scope for opposition party mobilisation. However, there are numerous indications that the ANC's hegemonic hold over its original liberation constituency is declining: apart from its loss of the Western Cape provincial election to the Democratic Alliance and the decline of its proportion of the vote in all provinces except KwaZulu-Natal, the 2009 elections continued a constant trend whereby the ruling party is still winning elections but with the support of a declining proportion of eligible voters, and its support is increasingly drawn from Africans (Daniel and Southall 2009). As Butler points out below, this is against a background of declining popular trust in key political institutions. The converse is the ANC's declining capacity to shape and control society. Three aspects are highlighted here: division and dissent within the ruling party itself; the crisis in education; and popular protests at perceived failures in 'delivery' by provincial and local government.

Division within the ANC

Butler outlines how the divisions within the ANC which erupted in the ousting of Mbeki as ANC president and the election of Zuma at Polokwane in December 2007 have continued into the Zuma government. Unlike under Mbeki, differences within the party are increasingly open, yet contestation is often ill-mannered, supposed debate about policies is often really about personal and factional advantage, and the party is increasingly riven by struggles for office, patronage and resources, with Zuma balancing one faction off against another while, simultaneously, Xhosas are replaced by Zulus in key locations, notably the intelligence services. So desperate is this struggle that in some provinces and municipalities it is waged with violence,

killings and assassination. Reference has already been made to how ANC politics have penetrated the parastatals, but factional struggle has also entered the public service, and various
ministries have become host to political networks which seek diversion of public resources to
private pockets. As Hoag demonstrates below with regard to a single department, Home
Affairs, this administrative disorder results in enervation, fear, corruption and 'comfortable
underperformance'. This endangers projects of institutional reform, and under Zuma, is
widely perceived to have rendered the government rudderless. Meanwhile, although labels of
right and left are of dubious utility (Julius Malema of the ANC Youth League punts nationalisation of the mines while the South African Communist Party rejects it), Zuma's opting for
broad continuity in fiscal policy under the finance minister, Pravin Gordhan, has alienated
Cosatu and the SACP and placed major strain on the coalition of support which brought him
to power. Indeed, partly resulting from his own personal indiscretions which have caused the
party acute embarrassment, but more particularly because he appears to be distancing himself
from the organised left, Zuma's own position has now become a matter of debate, and the
party may well be plunged into a succession struggle well before he is required to seek
re-election as leader at the party's next scheduled national conference in 2012.

Zuma's ascendancy to the presidency has been widely interpreted as having presented a
threat to constitutionalism. The decision by the National Prosecuting Authority (NPA) to
drop the corruption charges against Zuma before the 2009 election; the abolition of the
Scorpions, the prosecuting authority within the NPA which was pressing charges against him;
the appointment of an apparent Zuma loyalist as national prosecutor; and a series of judicial
appointments which have been much criticised within the legal fraternity have all been widely
represented as a threat to judicial independence and the separation of powers which is formally
embedded in the constitution. More widely, the penetration of ANC political battles into the
public service presents a major long term-threat to capacity as well as to the rule of law.

The crisis in education

There is a broad consensus that South Africa's public educational system is simply not working
and that this adversely effects the supply of skills needed by the economy (Bloch 2009). Despite
a massive increase in expenditure on education since 1994 (so that, today, the level of public
expenditure on education matches if not exceeds that of leading industrialised states),[7] the
results remain dismal. The pass rate for final year at high school has dropped for five consec-
utive years, falling from 73.3 per cent in 2003 to 60.62 per cent in 2009 (SAIRR 2008/09: 420;
Serrao, 2010) and a large percentage of schools lack adequate staffing, facilities and equipment.[8] The entry of insufficiently prepared students into universities and other institutions
of higher education has led to a dismally low completion rate (only 15 per cent of students
who entered higher education in 2002 graduated in the next five years). The performance of
the country's students in key areas such as mathematics and the sciences is particularly poor:
whereas only 47 per cent of first year students entering university in 2009 were found to be
'academically literate', just 25 per cent were found to be 'quantitatively literate', and a mere 7
per cent were found to be proficient in maths (SAIRR 2008-09: 368). Although significant
steps have been taken to address racial inequalities, educational achievement continues to

reflect the apartheid racial hierarchy, with students from minority racial communities (notably whites and Indians) regularly outperforming coloureds and Africans in key areas such as engineering and the physical sciences (see Lewins below). Not surprisingly, the education deficit translates into a lack of engineers, technicians and other skilled personnel, with employers consistently complaining about the educational levels of many of those who have successfully graduated from the universities (Benjamin 2010).

Perhaps even more alarming is the high dropout rate from schools which reflects the dynamics of class as well as race. As many as 58 per cent of children who entered the school system in 1998 had dropped out by the time that their fellows had reached Grade 12 in which they took the matric exam in 2009; overwhelmingly, the majority of these will be Africans who will in all probability face a life of unemployment, Meanwhile, parents with money are increasingly turning to private education. For all that the government is strongly committed to addressing backlogs and poor outcomes, its capacity to do so appears limited. Not least of its problems, according to informed commentators, is a demoralised and ill-disciplined teaching profession (notably in schools serving poor black communities), and the overwhelming determination of the South African Democratic Teachers' Union, the largest teacher trade union, to protect teacher interests at the expense of a more rounded commitment to the educational system.

Protest at incapacity

Recent years have been characterised by numerous and highly publicised protest actions against governments at provincial and local levels, choreographed in much of the media as protests against lack of 'service delivery'. Far too often for comfort, these have become interlaced with outbursts of popular violence against perceived community outsiders, usually characterised as 'xenophobia'. In many such cases, violence against persons is compounded with violence against property, often public facilities such as schools, libraries or municipal offices. Protest is therefore often dismissed by officialdom as stoked by malcontents who have oppositional political motives, or by wider society as irrational and primitive. Social protest is, however, a highly complex phenomenon. Amongst the factors that would seem to be involved are feelings of relative deprivation, high levels of inequality within an increasingly consumerist society, the failures of the educational system, high unemployment among blacks (notably young men), a lack of entrepreneurship and capital among South African black urban dwellers which is often visibly exposed by more successful foreign migrants, resentments against perceived corruption in government, and the lack of accountability of politicians and arrogance of officials. Lack of regard for the law (in significant part an inheritance of apartheid) combined with inadequate law enforcement creates a context in which protests often turn violent, a tendency fuelled by resort to violent methods of crowd control by the police. In turn, violent protests are themselves a collective manifestation of the wider violence in South African society, reflective of the lack of social coherence in a society still highly divided along lines of class, race, ethnicity, gender and geography (Bruce below; RSA 2009b).

Tales about the failures of provincial governments and municipalities to deliver services and of a decline in standards are legion, and are often interspersed with indications of considerable corruption and cronyism. Such narratives represent more than post-colonial melancholy, for there is evidence enough that all is not as it should be: for instance, provincial and municipal delivery failure is often matched by inability to spend annual budgets. Numerous municipalities, including some metros, are effectively bankrupt and in total financial disarray. Nonetheless, although there is substantial indication of incompetence and incapacity at levels of government which most immediately affect ordinary citizens, there is simultaneously clear evidence of substantial improvements in the access of poorer communities and households to services ranging from housing to running water and electricity. In addition, through its social grants network, the government now contributes the greatest single source of income to a third of all African households, while as much as a quarter of the population receives monthly grants from the state (Cronje 2009). So why, we may ask, are the poor so damned ungrateful?

The answer is beyond disaggregation here. However, what it adds up to is a striking loss of the ANC's authority and control over society – especially over the working class – and an emergent underclass of deprived and unemployed South Africans.

Hitherto, the revolt of the underprivileged has not taken a coherent political form (although Zuma's rise to power, backed by majority elements within Cosatu and the SACP, undoubtedly had a significant class dimension). However, ironically, analysts of both the left (Pillay 2009) and the right (Cronje 2009) combine in projecting a strong possibility of growing levels of protest leading to Cosatu and the SACP breaking with the Alliance and linking up with social movements to threaten the ANC's political hegemony. This is scarcely the prospect envisaged by white capital in 1994. Nor is any resulting scenario – an erosion of governmental control of the townships akin to the NP's experience in the 1980s; growing anti-capitalist protest and class warfare culminating in an electoral victory of a new left party over the ANC; or continuing rule by the ANC, but with reduced moral and political authority and greater reliance on patronage and coercion – promising to the continued survival of a 'reform bargain', especially one increasingly reliant upon infusions of foreign investment.

SLIDE TOWARDS MEDIOCRITY?

There is need to maintain perspective. According to the World Economic Forum's Global Competitiveness Index for 2009/10, South Africa performed relatively well in a context of global economic crisis.[9] South Africa was rated the 45th most competitive country out of 134 internationally, the highest rated country in Africa. Furthermore, South Africa jumped to 5th place overall with regard to trust in its banking system, and came in at 24th regarding intellectual property protection, 5th for accountability of private institutions, and 36th for business sophistication. Likewise, according to the Economist Intelligence Unit, South Africa was identified as the fourth most favoured site for investment amongst sixty-six 'emerging markets'. In other words, the economy is internationally regarded as having considerable strengths, and will doubtless continue to be regarded as a gateway to the wider continent. In addition, South Africa remains a major player internationally in terms of its mining industry, and demand for its mineral resources will be sustained by global demand for commodities, especially from China.

Overall, therefore, it would be absurd to suggest that South Africa is about to undergo an apocalyptic decline. However, it can be argued that the country could be on the verge of a long-term descent towards mediocrity, largely because of issues of governance (political and economic) and human development. Worryingly, South Africa is slipping in terms of international rankings concerning corruption (55th out of 180 rated by the WEF in 2009, one place lower than a year earlier)[10] and was ranked 90th in terms of labour market efficiency and 121st in terms of labour-employee relations. South Africa also did exceptionally badly with regard to perceptions of the health of its workforce (127th), and the business costs of crime and violence (133rd), with there being little confidence in the ability of the police to provide protection (106th).

Although global competitive indicators reflect the views of international business, the latter set of rankings lend support to the notion that the foundations of the reform bargain are subsiding, for they indicate that South Africa's two worlds – of rich and poor, capital and labour – remain as divided as ever. To put it another way, how long can South African industry continue to compete globally if the economy is unable, simultaneously, to make major inroads into the highly inter-related issues of unemployment, poverty and violence? And will not failure to successfully address these challenges undermine democracy?

The very posing of such questions points to the urgent need for an alternative to the present economic trajectory. We may highlight four major challenges.

First, there is a need for a reshaping of the 'reform bargain'. Taylor's formulation of the original bargain revolved around business getting most of what it wanted in terms of market reforms and access to international opportunity in exchange for the ANC's getting most of what it wanted politically. Yet the terms of the bargain were somewhat paradoxical, for the more that South African capital gained access to the international market, the more capital in South Africa has become internationalised. In other words, to secure 'growth', the government is increasingly dependent upon acceding to the whims of 'the market' which, in reality, is composed of foreign financial institutional investors and multinational corporations which have little interest in the conditions of South African society except insofar as they impinge directly upon short-term profitability. Thus the outcome has been continued white domination of the private sector and an investment pattern that has failed to match growth to jobs, to compensate for which the government and ANC have turned to the mantra of the developmental state which, willy-nilly, implies the need for greater state intervention in the economy. Now, while the present shift towards devising 'industrial strategy' records a welcome nod to long-term thinking, transformation of South Africa into a developmental state implies a state (and human resources) capacity (for picking 'winning strategies' and implementing them) which the country seems not to have. Reviving the 'reform bargain' in these circumstances is therefore very difficult, but it would seem to involve, at a minimum, business committing much more seriously than hitherto to meaningful empowerment and to job creation in exchange for commitment by government to providing market security. While some progress has been made towards BEE becoming more 'broadly based', far greater effort needs to be made by large scale capital to the processes of sharing ownership with employees, skilling the work force, procurement and serious engagement with small companies, and promoting employment. Similarly, land reform, hitherto pretty much a dismal failure, is only likely to be made to work through the forging of a genuine partnership between government and commercial agriculture if the dangers of 'Zimbabweanisation' are to be averted (Atkinson below).

Second, there is urgent need for large-scale capital to join with government, labour and civil society in addressing the appalling levels of social inequality. It may well be that the starting point for such a societal commitment will come from appeal to common sense, the notion that the social conditions for production, inclusive of safety of persons and property, cannot be secured unless the drift to widening inequality is reversed. Pragmatically, there is much that could be done. After all, if South Africa is as relatively attractive to international investment as the global competitiveness ratings cited above indicate, there would seem to be considerable scope for government to drive harder bargains with business to promote employment: if business won't hire more people directly, then corporations can cough up more to enable government itself to launch employment schemes and, in turn, this may require the union movement to re-think its opposition to greater labour market flexibility. (Gordhan's 2010 budget made a useful start here with proposals for lower paid temporary employment for first time job seekers.) Yet more than pragmatism is required, for 'the disposition to admire and almost to worship, the rich and the powerful, and to despise, or, at least, to neglect persons of poor and mean condition ... is ... the great and most universal cause of the corruption of our moral sentiments'. These words of Adam Smith (cited by Judt 2010) indicate the need for a vigorous collective commitment to realising the moral, as well as the economic, value of social justice. The social coherence that South Africa lacks flows ultimately from poorer citizens' sense of social exclusion from the fruits of democratic society.

Achieving greater social equality will require, third, a move away from the political economy of 'entitlement' and easy money. The debate about entitlement has hitherto focused almost entirely upon the notion that, because of the racial inequality embedded in South Africa's past, (many) blacks feel 'entitled' to company ownership, high salaries, good jobs, and public assets, with such feelings promoted by policies of 'demographic representivity'(Johnson 2009). However, the debate about entitlement needs to be seriously widened. Nothing has been more damaging to capital's reputation than the revelations of the obscene salaries and benefits claimed by CEOs, supposedly justified by their market worth, alongside exposure of market collusion by companies in anti-competitive practices that ramp up prices for the poor. Yet equally damaging to the cause of democratic politics has been the sense of entitlement which numerous politicians have exhibited by plunder of public funds compounded by displays of arrogance to the people who have elected them. Much is made (although apparently little achieved) in contemporary South Africa of making both business and government more accountable. Fortunately, there are some signs that public disgust with excess is causing constituencies in both sectors to re-think. But at root is the far, far more difficult exercise of challenging the broader paradigm whereby we live.

The path pursued by South African since 1994 has been an unashamedly capitalist one which has equated 'growth' with 'development', substituted 'deracialisation' for greater social quality, and fostered private consumption over public welfare. In this, South Africa has followed international neoliberal trends far more than the socially egalitarian ethos which is at the heart of the historical mission of the ANC. Ever more, the outcomes look disastrous. As argued here, the country's initial success is based on shaky foundations and, increasingly, there is evidence that the present trajectory is becoming unsustainable. Most obviously, this relates to the careless disregard which the active legacy of the minerals-energy complex and the present growth pattern have on the economy. Just as the present existing form of global capitalism is rapidly reaching its ecological limits, so South Africa's failure to rein in the mining industry's abuse of the environment (notably the country's limited water resources) and to commit seriously to moving away from dirty energy (Eskom's recalcitrance compounded by the government's passivity) points to a developing crisis of survival whose parameters are almost unimaginable to the present generation.

The economic crash and the global environmental crisis are two sides of the same coin, prompting growing struggles and debate about the future of capitalism itself. Whatever the future, South Africa's bid to adapt to changing global necessities and popular demands requires an imaginative response. South Africa made one such leap in 1994: can it make another in the near future?

NOTES

1   Defined by the international measure of living on less than US$1 a day.

2   Thus, for instance, Sanlam gave birth to three significant BEE groups, with Pamodzi taking over from what was Fedfood, Royal Bafokeng from Impala Platinum, and Tsebo Outsourcing from Fedics. Tokyo Sexwale's Mvelaphanda was to buy a large stake in Old Mutual's Benguela Concessions, while Brimstone (a Cape based empowerment company) now owns clothing firm Rex Trueform. Anglo's unbundling has provided a basis for various empowerment deals with, for instance, Cyril Ramaphosa's Shanduka now having a 5 per cent stake in Anglo's Scaw Metals.

3   But see Kariuki below for an optimistic perspective on present developments.

4   According to the Annual Surveys of the South African Institute of Race Relations (SAIRR), (1994-95: 400; 2008-09: 166), the proportion of the budget spent on 'social security and welfare' was 6.9 per cent in 1990-91 and 9.3 per cent in 1995-95. By contrast, the National Treasury estimates that 'social protection' will amount to 15.9 per cent of budget expenditure in 2010. Although these figures may not be directly comparable, the sharp upward trend is unmistakeable.

5   Annual total disposable income for whites dropped from 44.3 per cent of the total in 1998 to 40.3 per cent in 2008 (SAIRR 2008-09: 288).

6   The principal examples in 2009 were highly publicised battles over the suspension for alleged disciplinary offences by the Transnet board of Siyabonga Gama, the head of Transnet Freight Rail, who received vigorous backing from elements within the ANC and Cosatu in his bid to become CEO of Transnet, and the forced resignation of Jacob Maroga as CEO of Eskom, who similarly had strong support from within the ANC, in a messy battle which culminated in the subsequent resignation of Bobby Godsell, former CEO of Anglo-Gold Ashanti, as chairman of the board following, apparently, lack of backing by President Jacob Zuma.

7   Public expenditure as a proportion of GDP and as a proportion of total government expenditure for South Africa in 2007 was 5.4 per cent and 17.45. Comparative figures for Germany were 4.5 per cent and 9.7 per cent. For the UK they were 5.5 per cent and 12.5 per cent. For the US: 5.7 per cent and 13.7 per cent (SAIRR 2008/09: 379).

8   A few basic statistics can illustrate the problems: in 2006, 4 per cent of public schools had no toilet facilities whatsoever, and only 31.6 per cent had flush toilets; 10 per cent of schools had no water

supply; only 23.1 per cent had a laboratory, and only 10 per cent of these were adequately stocked; 14.7 per cent had no electricity supply; and only 23.15 per cent had a computer centre; and, horrifically, only 21.1 per cent had a library (SAIRR 2008/09: 407-415 citing figures from the Department of Education's National Education Infrastructure Management System).

9   The Index is conducted by the World Economic Forum in partnership with 'leading academics and a global network of research institutes' and calculates its rankings 'from publicly available data and an annual poll of over 12 000 business leaders worldwide'. See http://www.southafrica. info/busines/economy/competitiveness2009.htm.

10   World Bank Governance Indicators saw South Africa's control of corruption decline from 75.7 out of 100 in 1996 to 66.7 in 2007 (SAIRR 2008-09: 726).

REFERENCES

Abedian I (2009) Worms in the bud of post-apartheid boom. *Business Report*, 18 January.

Adam H, F van Zyl Slabbert and F Moodley (1997) *Comrades in Business: Post-liberation Politics in South Africa.* Cape Town: Tafelberg.

Ashton G (2010) Eskom is an enemy of progress. *The Star*, 29 January.

Bassett C (2008) South Africa: Revisiting capital's 'Formative Action', *Review of African Political Economy* 35 (116): 184–202.

Benjamin C (2010) Receiving an education for unemployment. *Business Day*, 5 January.

Bloch G (2009) *The Toxic Mix: What's Wrong with South Africa's Schools and How To Fix It.* Cape Town: Tafelberg.

Brautigam D, L Rakner and S Taylor (2002) Business associations and growth coalitions in sub-Saharan Africa. *The Journal of Modern African Studies* 40 (4): 519–548.

Cassim R (2006) South Africa's first wave of economic reforms. In Padayachee V (Ed) *The Development Decade? Economic and Social Change in South Africa, 1994-2004.* Cape Town: HSRC Press: 55–85.

Cronje F (2009) How South Africa's protest movement may develop. http://sairr.org.za/sairr-today/news_item.2009-07-23.5748727460//searchterm=None.

Daniel J and N Bhengu (2009) South Africa in Africa: Still a formidable player. In Southall R and H Melber (Eds) *A New Scramble for Africa? Imperialism, Investment and Development.* Pietermaritzburg: UKZN Press: 139-164.

Daniel J and R Southall (2009) The national and provincial electoral outcome: Continuity with change. In Southall R and J Daniel *Zunami! The 2009 South African Elections.* Johannesburg: Jacana: 232–269.

Davies R, D O'Meara and S Dlamini (1984) *The Struggle for South Africa: A Reference Guide to Movements, Organizations and Institutions.* London: Zed Books.

Ensor L (2010) Parastatals: Hogan's stress test. *Business Day*, 21 January.

Habib A, D Pillay and A Desai (1998) South Africa and the global order: The structural conditioning of a transition to democracy. *Journal of Contemporary African Studies* 16 (1): 95–115.

Handley A (2005) Business, government and economic policymaking in the new South Africa. *The Journal of Modern African Studies* 43 (2): 211–240.

Hasenfus M (2009) JSE in foreign hands. http://www.fin24.com/articles/default/display_article.aspx?ArticleId=1518-24_2298835.

Johnson R (2009) *South Africa's Brave New World: The Beloved Country Since the End of Apartheid.* London: Allen Lane.

Judt T (2010) What is living and what is dead in social democracy? *New York Review*, 14 January.

Lorentzen J (2006) The *noledge* of numbers: S&T, R&D and innovation indicators in South Africa. In Padayachee V (Ed) *The Development Decade? Economic and Social Change in South Africa, 1994-2004.* Cape Town: HSRC Press: 183–189.

McGregor A, R Rose and S Cranston (2009) Power-shift. *Financial Mail*, 23 January.

Morris M, G Robbins and J Barnes (2006) The role of government in fostering clusters: the South African automotive sector. In Padayachee V (Ed) *The Development Decade? Economic and Social Change in South Africa, 1994-2004.* Cape Town: HSRC Press: 201–223.

Nattrass J (1981) *The South African Economy: Its Growth and Change.* Cape Town: Oxford University Press.

Pillay D (2009) COSATU, the SACP and the ANC Post-Polokwane: Looking Left but does it feel Right? *Labour, Capital and Society* 41(2): 4–37.

Republic of South Africa (RSA) (2009a) *Development Indicators 2009.* http://www.info.gov.za/other-docs 2009/developmentindicators2009.

RSA (2009b) Parliament of the Republic of South Africa: A Report on the Current 'Service Delivery Protests' in South Africa. Commissioned by the House Chairperson Committees, Oversight and ICT.

Serrao A (2010) SA's trillion rand education scandal. *The Star*, 23 February.

South African Institute of Race Relations *South Africa Survey.* Various Years. Johannesburg: South African Institute of Race Relations.

Southall R (2004) The ANC and black capitalism in South Africa. *Review of African Political Economy* 31 (100): 313–328.

Southall R (2005) Black empowerment and corporate capital. In Buhlungu S, J Daniel, R Southall and J Lutchman (Eds) *State of the Nation: South Africa 2004-2005.* Cape Town: HSRC Press: 455–478.

Southall R (2007) The ANC, black economic empowerment and state owned enterprises: a recycling of history? In Buhlungu S, J Daniel, R Southall and J Lutchman (Eds) *State of the Nation: South Africa 2007.* Cape Town: HSRC Press: 201–225.

Tangri R and R Southall (2008) The politics of black economic empowerment in South Africa. *Journal of Southern African Studies* 34 (3): 699–716.

Taylor S (2007) *Business and State in Southern Africa: The Politics of Economic Reform.* Boulder: Lynne Rienner Publishers.

Webster E and R Omar (2003) Work restructuring in post-apartheid South Africa. *Work and Occupations* 30 (2) : 194–213.

Webster E and K von Holdt (2005) *Beyond the Apartheid Workplace: Studies in Transition.* Pietermaritzburg: UKZN Press.

Wells C (2010) Transnet may be disrupted but performance is robust and finances sound. *Sunday Independent*, 21 February.

Williams D (2010) State owned enterprises: End of the road. *Financial Mail*, 19 February.

ECONOMY, ECOLOGY AND SUSTAINABILITY

South Africa and the eco-logic of the global capitalist crisis

Devan Pillay

———

South Africa has been severely affected by the global financial crisis. Despite a return to growth in 2010, the crisis will come back as long as its fundamental roots are not addressed. Indeed, we need to ask whether the crisis is a purely 'financial' one, or multidimensional. Is it of recent origin, or something that began with the market liberalisation of the late 1970s – or does it go right back to the origins of capitalism as a world system, of which South Africa is a microcosm?

Despite the fact that SA's financial sector was much better regulated than at the centres of the global system, the financial crisis has deepened an already severe socio-economic crisis. As the chapters that follow show, it accelerated declining manufacturing output or the deindustrialisation of the economy, partly because of a decline in global demand and partly because of the rand's rise against the British pound and US dollar. Most severely, up to one million jobs were lost in 2009, in a context of massive unemployment (unofficially close to 40 per cent of economically active citizens), rising social inequality and persistent poverty. To take two telling indices: over one-third of the population is food insecure, and a quarter of children under six years of age is malnourished (Human Sciences Research Council, cited in Andrews 2008).

At a fundamental level, there are increasing indications that the country's growth trajectory faces a crisis of 'sustainability' in both senses of the word – sustainable growth that creates decent jobs and rising living standards for all, as well as sustainable growth that protects the natural environment and leaves the earth with sufficient resources for future generations.

This crisis is rooted in the structure of the South African economy, which was inherited from the colonial past.

In South Africa, racial capitalism emerged as a result of a minerals-energy complex (Fine and Rustomjee 1996) – a synergy between the mining industry and fossil energy systems that sustain it, as well as a financial sector that grew out of it. This minerals-energy-financial complex remains central to South African capitalism, subordinating all other economic activities, including manufacturing. It rests on the exploitation of fossil fuels and risky mining operations that have seen the death of tens of thousands of people over the last century. A slowly deracialising minority experiences the only tangible benefits, whilst the (mainly black) majority live in conditions of underdevelopment in the predominantly rural former homelands, or in polluted slums and townships in the urban areas.

Efforts to move out of this dependence have been half-hearted. The only strategy the state has so far embarked on is a combination of limited redistribution (mainly poverty alleviation through grants), an incoherent land redistribution programme, short-term public works programmes, repeated attempts at an industrial policy and a gradually visible but hitherto lame 'sustainable development' effort. These are undermined by a logic of accumulation that maintains at its centre the minerals-energy-financial complex – as well as a culture of consumerism that rests on ever-expanding, unsustainable wants, fuelled by a sales effort (the advertising/media industry) that is essential to the production/accumulation process.

This logic of uneven (or enclave) capitalist development is, in many ways, a microcosmic expression of global capitalist development. The crisis of sustainability is integrally linked to the global economic/ecological crisis, and can only be fully understood in relation to the global context. This contribution discusses the dimensions of the poly-crisis in historical perspective, and asks whether capitalism has reached both its natural and its social limits. Is the answer a 'green capitalism' (or for some a 'green new deal') or does capitalism need to be completely transcended (a form of 'eco-socialism')? It ends with a consideration of South African responses to the crisis, as discussed in the chapters that follow, as well as other responses within government and civil society.

THE GLOBAL POLY-CRISIS

The notion of 'crisis' can take on different meanings, depending on which discipline one is located in. It seems appropriate, therefore, to begin with a commonplace definition. According to the *Chambers 21st Century Dictionary* (1999), a crisis is either, on the one hand, a time of 'difficulty or stress' (or an 'emergency'); or, on the other, a 'turning point' (a crucial or 'decisive' moment). In the first sense, a crisis can come and go, leaving the system largely intact. In the second sense, a crisis can dramatically alter, even overthrow, the system, bringing forth a fundamentally altered state of being. In either case a crisis can be short-term and dramatic, or long-term and gradual, with dramatic eruptions from time to time.

A crisis is usually deemed a crisis by those in the midst of it, experiencing its effects. The poor, hungry and exploited majority of the world's (and South Africa's) population, it could be argued, have been in crisis for much of the twentieth century – stripped of their land and means of subsistence, and forced to sell their labour (if they are lucky) or beg and steal to eke out an existence, often in health-threatening working and living environments deliberately placed close to the polluting waste of industry. From an ecological perspective, the natural world or ecosystem (including other living creatures) has been in various stages of crises as industrial development crowds out non-human animals, forcing them into fenced-off parks and zoos, hunted and sought for trophies, while the destruction of forests, pollution and emissions threaten the very existence of earth as we know it. The latter has only become a concern for the privileged and powerful when it threatened their own system of production and consumption – but only grudgingly, and partially. Many are still in denial.

However, when there is a crisis of profitability, such that the wealth of the rich and powerful is directly threatened, only then is a 'crisis' truly proclaimed. This is even more so when the rich and powerful at the centre of global capitalism – in North America and Western Europe – are affected, which is the case today.

The financial crisis has had a direct impact on the real economy, with low consumer demand leading to a crisis in manufacturing, and millions of job losses throughout the world. This crisis, which began in 2007 and has grabbed the headlines since then, rapidly displaced the ecological crisis gripping the world a few months previously (particularly when oil prices began to approach the US$200 a barrel level). The run-up to, and aftermath of, the December 2009 Copenhagen conference on climate change temporarily put the natural limits to growth back on the global agenda, but with relatively low oil prices (around US$70 a barrel), the minds of the world's governments were insufficiently focussed to produce a binding commitment to lowering carbon emissions and move decisively towards a non-nuclear renewable energy regime.

High oil prices, the threat of depleted fossil fuels (particularly oil) to run the modern economy, oil spills, the destruction of rain forests, the displacement of millions of rural dwellers for the building of dams to supply industry, the rapid decline of biodiversity, rampant carbon emissions and pollution such as acid rain and acid mine drainage (which endanger the health of both humans and the eco-system) and natural disasters caused by climate change – all of these and many other ecological disasters are rarely or weakly linked to the economic/financial crisis, and the socio-political consequences of both.

In other words, when we speak of a 'global crisis', it is necessary to conceptualise the interconnected economic, ecological and socio-political crises, as well as a looming food crisis that arises out of them (Roberts 2008). Indeed, as Foster (1999: 195) observes, the word 'ecology', coined by Ernst Haeckel in 1866, has the same Greek root *oikos* for household, out of which grew the word 'economy'. Neoclassical economics, as Karl Polanyi (1944) argued, have sought to dis-embed economics from society, as well as nature, to produce what the political economist Ben Fine[1] has called economics imperialism – the subordination of society and nature to a narrow, mathematised and dismal pseudo-science. The poly-crisis points to the necessity to re-embed and subordinate the economy to society and nature.

These crises are rooted in a centuries-long process of what David Harvey (2005), following Rosa Luxembourg, calls 'accumulation by dispossession' – the dispossession of people's land and livelihoods, of the commons, of the natural environment. We are witnessing, in South

Africa and globally, the commodification of all that is valued, where wealth is measured not in terms of the intrinsic value of things and relationships, or for Karl Marx their 'use-value', but in terms of their exchange value (what they can be bought and sold for – that is, for money).

This process began as merchant capitalism in fourteenth century medieval Europe (Mielants 2007) and, through the dispossession and plunder of people and resources in Africa, the Americas and Asia, wealth was accumulated in Western Europe, providing the capital for the industrial revolution of the seventeenth century. This, of course, required further waves of colonial plunder and dispossession in the search for cheap labour, resources and markets for an ever-expanding global regime of accumulation.

Capitalism, in other words, is characterised not merely by the marvels of innovation, entrepreneurship, modernisation, higher standards of living and increasing consumer choice. This is only one side of the coin, which the insiders (like readers of this volume) enjoy. More accurately, capitalism is a system of uneven or *enclave* development – namely a world system comprising islands of privilege and power, surrounded by seas of alienated poverty, pollution and plundered resources. The promise of 'modernisation' and its 'neoliberal' or free market variant, that expanded growth will eventually bring 'development' to all the world's population, has proven to be more myth than reality. Instead, poverty and inequality between and within nations has increased significantly (Bieler *et al* 2008). Capitalism, as Marx once said, develops *and* destroys. It simultaneously enriches (the few), and impoverishes (the many). The development of Europe and later North America (the core countries) rested to a significant extent on the underdevelopment of the rest of the colonised world (the peripheral or semi-peripheral countries) (Wallerstein 1979; Frank 1966).

The current capitalist crisis has evoked a variety of responses: from the very narrow, one dimensional approaches (free market and Keynesian-lite) which see the crisis purely as a financial one, to broader Marxist (and Keynesian-Marxist) approaches which conceptualise the crisis as economic, rooted in the stagnation of the real economy (particularly the manufacturing falling rate of profit), to the very broad, multidimensional eco-Marxist approaches which see the crisis as a complex interaction between economic, ecological and social crises that has its roots in a pattern of industrialisation that relies on the exploitation of fossil fuels – what Altvater (2006) calls 'fossil capitalism'.

In Marxist terms, an economic crisis refers to deep-seated, system-threatening breakdowns in the accumulation process. They can be short-term (for example the Asian crisis of 1997) or long-term (the Great Depression of the 1930s). The current financial crisis is not financial in origin, but has its roots in the stagnation of the real economy (Foster and Magdoff 2009; Brenner 2009; Arrighi 2007). This is due to the falling rate of profit, as a result of two things:

Firstly, the *struggles of subordinate classes*, including the working class at the workplace, as well as the working class and other classes in society at large, to extract as much of the surplus produced as possible, either directly from the employers through higher wages and benefits, or indirectly from the state through higher taxes to fund a higher social wage (in the form of public health care, education, subsidised transport, subsidised food, welfare benefits and other social services).

The second factor, closely interrelated to the first, is *inter-firm competition*, both at the national and the international levels. Rising costs make firms uncompetitive in relation to their competitors, unless they are subjected to the same rising costs. Increased competition spurs on innovation and the accumulation process, giving rise to a crisis of 'over-production', which drives down the unit price of commodities. This exacerbates the crisis of profitability, forcing firms to cut back and leading to the under-utilisation of productive capacity. Firms go bankrupt, workers are laid off, and stronger firms take over weaker ones, leading to the monopolisation of capital[2] (Baran and Sweezy 1968).

One way out of the cycle of declining profitability, at least temporarily, is to find cheaper sources of labour elsewhere, cheaper raw materials and new markets for excess products. Drawing on David Harvey, Beverly Silver (2004) identifies various 'fixes' that capitalism uses to navigate its way out of continuous crises of profitability. These include the spatial fix, where capital moves to cheaper and cheaper locales of production; the product fix, where capital moves from one niche product to another, chasing increased profitability (for example, from textiles to automobiles to information technology); and the technology fix, where through innovation labour-saving technology increases the productivity of labour. These fixes, however, only partially or temporarily address the accumulation crisis.

As in the past, a crisis in profitability in manufacturing boosts the financialisation of capitalism. This time, however, with a more globalised economy and new computer technology at their disposal, investments in 'fictitious' capital to increase profit rates rapidly overtook investments in the real economy. In the USA, the heart of global capitalism, the percentage of financial profits over total domestic profits in 2007 was just below 40 per cent, compared to well below 20 per cent in the early 1980s and below 15 per cent in the 1960s (Foster and Magdoff 2009: 93). By contrast, manufacturing profits steadily declined from over 50 per cent of domestic profits in the late 1960s to less than 15 per cent in 2005 (Foster and Magdoff 2009: 55).

To cut a long and complex story short, the financialisation of capitalism is not the *cause* of the capitalist crisis, but was itself *a response* to the crisis of the 1970s (Brenner 2009; Arrighi 2007). This is what Beverly Silver (2004) calls the financial fix. Inherently crisis-ridden, this 'fix' spawned a number of short-term crises in different parts of the world over the past two decades, including the US savings and loan crisis (1989-91), the Japanese asset price bubble collapse (1990), the Scandinavian banking crisis (early 1990s), the European exchange rate crisis (1992-3), the Mexican debt crisis (1994-5) the East Asian crisis (1997), the Russian crisis (1998), the Argentinian meltdown (2001), and the dot com bubble burst (2001). The current financial crisis, which hit the core developed countries directly, is the deepest since the Great Depression.

Foster and Magdoff (2009), in an extension of the Sweezy and Baran analysis, characterise the new stage of capitalism as monopoly-finance capitalism. It is based on ever-increasing concentrations of capital, under the rule of mega-financial institutions that straddle the globe, where manufacturing firms are intermeshed with financial firms and investments. Despite the anger against these institutions for 'causing' the financial crisis, governments in the USA and Europe are reluctant to take decisive action against them, regarding them as 'too big to fail'. Indeed, executives of these institutions continue to pay themselves enormous salaries and bonuses, with much talk but little action against them. This is unsurprising, given the fact that core government elites are themselves part of what David Rothkopf (2009) calls the 'superclass' – six thousand people in a planet of six billion who, in addition to powerful governments and international finance, also run transnational corporations and global media houses (Rothkopf also includes world religions and underground criminal and terrorist empires).

Fossil capitalism is a system of accumulation based on mass consumerism (the creation of everlasting wants), but because of rising global inequality and stagnant or declining real wages, these new wants cannot be satisfied because potential consumers do not have the means to purchase the commodities produced. The only way out is increased indebtedness – household debt in the USA has increased from 62 per cent of GDP in 1997 to 92 per cent of GDP in 2005 (Foster and Magdoff 2009: 47). Consumer debt as a percentage of disposable income increased from 62 per cent in 1975 to 127 per cent in 2005 (Foster and Magdoff 2009: 29). This mirrors the increased indebtedness of the US economy as a whole, as it borrows on the financial markets to maintain its position as global hegemon – by fuelling its war machine (a form of military Keynesianism), preserving its legitimacy through social and internal security spending, continuing to provide subsidies to threatened industries (particularly agriculture) and, of course, bailing out the banking system.

ACCUMULATION, 'AFFLUENZA' AND THE RISE OF THE 'AMERICUM'

The end result of over two centuries of 'accumulation by dispossession' is a system of uneven development, with rising inequality at both the national level, in general, and at the global level. According to noted African economist Samir Amin (2008), the proportion of 'precarious and pauperised' members of the working classes (broadly defined to include formal and informal workers and the unemployed) has over the past fifty years risen from less than one quarter to more than one half of the global urban population.

Economic globalisation has, since the 1980s, simultaneously enlarged the periphery within the core countries (within increased informalisation of work and unemployment, and a declining social wage), as well as enlarged the core within the periphery and particularly within the semi-periphery (countries such as Brazil, South Africa and India, and increasingly China), as capital moves around globally. However, with a few exceptions such as the now 'developed' status of east Asian countries like South Korea, the overall global picture of uneven, enclave development remains intact, at least for the foreseeable future. This is despite ostentatious claims by national elites, such as in India, that their country will be 'fully developed' within the next thirty to fifty years – conveniently ignoring that 95 per cent of its workforce is informalised labour (Bieler et al 2008), while in the rural areas 'development' has deepened immiseration, causing a massive increase in farm suicides and the rapid rise of Maoist groups championing the cause of the rural poor (Perry 2010).

These islands of privilege are, of course, modelled on western patterns of consumption – particularly that of the USA. Thomas Friedman (2008) warns about 'too many Americans' in the world today – meaning too many hyper-consumers, influenced over the past decades by American mass media (particularly films, advertising, television shows and magazines) that celebrate the 'American dream' of unsustainable consumption based on the creation of incessant wants (as opposed to real needs). Friedman, a short while ago a celebrant of economic globalisation based on spreading growth everywhere (see Friedman 1999 and 2005) now warns against 'America's affluenza', '*an unsustainable addiction to growth*' (2008:54, my emphasis).

Friedman (2008: 56) quotes Tom Burke of the NGO 3GE (Third Generation Environmentalism), who coined the term 'Americum' – a unit of 350 million people with an income above US$15 000 and a 'growing penchant for consumerism', particularly American-style energy-sapping living spaces, cars, fast foods and levels of unrecycled garbage. According to Burke, current growth and consumption trends suggest that by 2030 the number of Americums will have increased from two to eight or nine – at least a fourfold increase within the space of between thirty and forty years: in other words, from 700 million people to over 3 billion – half the current world population. Of course the total population will also have grown (some say to about 7–8 billion by 2030).

If the crisis of accumulation is temporarily arrested, and global growth and 'prosperity' increases as suggested, these carbon copies of American consumerism will threaten the very foundations of that prosperity. It will inevitably run into the natural limits of growth – what Jeff Wacker of the Electronic Data Systems (quoted in Friedman, p 57) calls the 'eco-logic of capitalism' which, says Friedman, has become 'an important, if not the most important, restraint on growth'. The expansion of Americum production and consumption will require the colonisation of three more planets, because, argues Friedman (2008: 55), 'we are going to make planet earth so hot, and strip it so bare of resources, that nobody … will be able to live like Americans one day'.

Friedman concedes that it would be arrogant for Americans like himself to urge developing countries not to grow, implying that they should remain poor. He quotes an Egyptian cabinet member:

> It is like the developed world ate all the *hors d'oeuvre*, all the entrees, and all the desserts and then invited the developing world for a little coffee 'and asked us to fit the bill'. That is not going to happen. The developing world will not be denied (Friedman 2008:55).

The solution, he argues, is partly for the rest of the world to leapfrog unsustainable technologies and develop on a green basis (which China is beginning to do, albeit inconsistently, given its rising addiction to private cars and carbon-intensive power plants). Ultimately, he suggests, this will only happen if America itself undergoes a green revolution, and radically re-orients its patterns of production and consumption – so that when others copy America, they will not be carbon copies, but *green* copies.

GREEN CAPITALISM OR ECO-SOCIALISM?

The above analysis from within the very heart of the US establishment – the *eco-logic* of capitalism – resonates to some extent with the emerging eco-Marxist or eco-socialist school of thought (Foster 2009; Burkett 2005; Altvater 2006; Albo 2006; Lowy 2006; Kovel 2002). The ecological consequences of hyper-accumulation include, in the words of John Bellamy Foster (2002: 12):

… global warming, the destruction of the ozone layer, removal of tropical forests, elimination of coral reefs, overfishing, extinction of species, loss of genetic diversity, the increasing toxicity of our environment and our food, desertification, shrinking water supplies, lack of clean air, and radioactive contamination – to name a few. The list is very long and rapidly getting longer, and the spatial scale on which these problems manifest themselves are increasing.

If the socio-economic and ecological crises have a common origin – industrial capitalism – can a solution to these crises be found *within* capitalism, or does the very nature of capitalism need to be *transcended* for solutions for all of humanity, in harmony with the natural environment, to be found?

The answer to this question depends on the paradigm used. Clapp and Dauvergne (2005) give us four basic paradigms that try to make sense of the current crisis, namely the market liberal, institutionalist, bioenvironmentalist and social green approaches. Of these the first two, which fit broadly into the ecological modernisation frame, do not question the logic of capitalism, based on heightened economic growth, but differ on the degree of state involvement in addressing the problems. Market liberals believe the market will solve environmental problems, while institutionalists believe in the necessity of global (and national) regulation. The last two, by contrast, tend to be more critical of the subordination of the environment and society to economic growth, with bioenvironmentalists placing the natural environment (and population growth) at the centre of concern, while social greens (including Marxist as well as non-Marxist eco-socialists) place human society at the centre, in harmony with the natural environment.

The obvious attempts at 'greenwashing', namely using 'sustainable development' as a public relations ploy, is arguably the dominant practice of corporations throughout the world, promoted by global institutions such as the World Bank and World Trade Organisation (Peet 2003; Bruno and Karliner 2004; Bakan 2004; Harris-White and Harris 2006; and Rogers 2006). Friedman (2008) argues for a 'green revolution' within the logic of regulated capitalism. However, he is critical of the tepid greenwashing that passes for sustainable development and makes a strong case for a fundamental reorientation of our economies, where *state regulation* and *standards* need to be imposed in order to spur on innovation towards green solutions to our energy. As such, his approach has shifted from a market liberal to an institutionalist perspective, and is a challenge to those on the eco-socialist left who argue that, because capitalism is the source of the energy crisis, any solution that benefits the entire globe, and not enclaves of privilege, must transcend capitalist relations of production.

Foster (2009) directly engages with Friedman, criticising his devotion to nuclear power and unproven 'clean coal' technology, which are also part of US President Obama's green strategy. Instead, he asserts:

Yet the more radical ecological solution that seeks an immediate closing down of coal-fired plants and their replacement by solar, wind, and other forms of renewable power – coupled with alterations on the demand-side through the transformation of social priorities – is viewed by vested interests as completely undesirable (Foster 2009: 21).

A 'transformation of social priorities' that addresses enclave development and ecological destruction at the national and global levels would have to take on those vested interests – implying a class struggle between the power elite at the top of the pyramid, and the subordinate classes at the bottom. The difference between traditional twentieth century Marxist-Leninist (or social democratic) socialist struggles and a new form of twenty-first century 'eco-socialist' struggle is that while the former is state-centric, and facilitated by a hierarchical (vanguardist or mass based) political party, the latter is society-centric, and facilitated by mass participatory democracy. The form of struggle has a direct bearing on the outcome, following the Gandhian principle 'be the change you want to see'. This is a long-term battle that is already taking shape in discussions and activism, for example, at the World Social Forum, as well as in places where the subordinate classes have actually taken power, as in Bolivia and Kerala, India (Williams 2008).

In the wake of the global crisis that has delegitimised the certainties of neoliberal economics, there is a growing literature on what the content of shifted social priorities entails (for example Ransom and Baird 2009; Korten 2009; Eisler 2009; Patel 2009). According to Bolivian president Evo Morales (2009: 168):

> It is nothing new to live well. It is simply a matter of recovering the life of our forbears and putting an end to the kind of thinking that encourages individualistic egoism and the thirst for luxury. Living well is not living better at the expense of others. We need to build a communitarian socialism in harmony with Mother Earth.

What this actually means in practice is a work in progress, a feeling-around for policies and practices that build social solidarity in harmony with nature. It includes, at minimum, the extension of the commons, or public social goods, including basic services such as water, electricity, education, health, communication and transportation as human rights, not commodities to be bought and sold (Morales 2009). It means using renewable forms of energy that preserves the earth for future generations, based on the principle of sufficiency (Kovel 2002) and not endless growth pivoted on endless wants.

There is an emphasis on local and regional economies to, amongst other things, maximise democratic participation, and minimise carbon footprints caused by long-distance trade, particularly in fresh produce (or what some term 'food miles'). For example, Cuba has achieved universally recognised success in getting local communities to produce organic fruit and vegetables in urban food gardens, for consumption by local communities themselves (Barclay 2003). The Bolivarian Alliance for the Americas (ALBA), which brings together a range of Latin American countries, including Cuba, Venezuela, Bolivia, Ecuador and Nicaragua, offers a radical reconceptualisation of trade relations based on fair trade, social solidarity and meeting human needs – as opposed to the cut-throat competition embedded in 'free' trade (Hattingh 2008). In the longer-term, an eco-socialist vision means shorter working time (which can substantially address the problem of unemployment, provided that it rests on a substantial social wage in the form of free or heavily subsidised public services, funded by, for example, global taxation), and more leisure time to pursue creative and socially useful activities. Frigga Haug (in Bullard 2009), drawing on Marx's vision of communism, offers the fourfold challenge:

- Four hours on wage labour (production)
- Four hours on reproductive work (cooking, cleaning, gardening, caring for families)
- Four hours on creative work (music, art, poetry, sport)
- Four hours on political work (community organising).

Whether one adopts a green 'new deal' perspective, or a more radical eco-socialist perspective,[3] both pose fundamental challenges to capitalism's growth-at-all-costs tendencies. As the chapters in this section suggest, South Africa, like most countries in the world, has to deal with powerful vested interests if it wants to wean itself off the minerals-energy-financial complex, which is central to the accumulation-production-consumption treadmill that perpetuates massive social inequality, poverty and environmental degradation.

SOUTH AFRICA'S RESPONSES

I have argued that the current crisis cannot be separated from a broader crisis of capitalist growth that many argue is rooted in a manufacturing crisis of profitability, the enduring social crisis experienced by the majority of the world's (and South Africa's) population, as well as an ecological crisis of multiple dimensions (including resource depletion, pollution of various kinds and climate change) that threatens the very existence of the earth as we know it.

As indicated at the outset, South Africa is in many ways a microcosm of the world crisis, given its history of plunder, exploitation and enclave (or bifurcated) development. The wealth of the few is dialectically interlinked with the poverty of the many – a notion that sits uncomfortably with those who dominate the ideological discourse in the country and the world. Instead of the dominant view that separates the 'alleviation of poverty' of the majority from the 'accumulation of wealth' of the few, or the 'economic' from the 'social' and 'ecological', it is necessary to take a more holistic view of the poly-crisis at the global level, in order to understand its impact at the national or local levels. In this sense, the *alleviation of wealth* becomes a central pre-condition to the *eradication* of poverty (Sachs 2001).

Articles in this section address aspects of this crisis as it affects South Africa. Seeraj Mohamed and Neva Makgetla directly address the impact of the financial crisis on South Africa's economy. Mohamed shows how South Africa's immersion in the global economy after 1994, and its adoption of neoliberal macroeconomic policies, accelerated the financialisation of capital with devastating consequences for industrial development and employment creation. He underlines the view that South Africa was in crisis long before the recent financial crisis, through rising unemployment, deindustrialisation, debt-driven consumption, and the outsourcing and informalisation of labour. These features of the country's higher growth path, which was also driven by the growth in private security services (as the upper and middle class enclaves shield themselves from rising crime arising out of increased social dislocation) may very well have been the 'wrong' kind of growth.

Mohamed shows how the corporate sector speculated in financial markets more than in fixed investment, further weakening the country's fragile industrial base, and entrenching its reliance on the mineral-energy complex. The post-apartheid period was characterised by massive capital flight, and a rash of mergers and acquisitions, which served to further stifle diversification of the economy. Economic liberalisation, low inflation and high interest rates, in keeping with global practice, was explicitly designed to attract foreign investment – but what South Africa attracted in the main was increased speculation and 'hot' money. The heightened role of services in the economy is not a sign of maturation, but 'is due to the withdrawal of capital from the economy and the misallocation of capital towards financial speculation, housing price booms and exuberant consumption instead of productive investment' (p60 in this volume).

Neva Makgetla continues this line of argument with a focus on the impact of the recent financial crisis on employment in the country. South Africa's already high unemployment (officially at 26 per cent but unofficially up to 40 per cent of economically active citizens) worsened significantly during 2009. She shows a loss of almost a million jobs, at a far higher rate than the drop in GDP. Makgetla, however, acknowledges that government's short-term countercyclical fiscal policy response and substantial industrial investment, unlike in the late 1990s downturn, seem to have moderated the impact of declining growth, investment and jobs. While revenues dropped by 9 per cent in 2009, Treasury maintained expenditure growth at 9 per cent, increasing the budget deficit to almost 8 per cent of GDP. On the other hand, microeconomic responses were too little too late, she argues, and the rapid appreciation of the rand has slowed the recovery significantly.

Along with Mohamed, Makgetla argues that the recent crisis underlines the need for a re-think of traditional approaches to industrial policy, which is still oriented towards exports, to the neglect of domestic and regional demand and the creation of employment, while also increasing living standards.

Scarlett Cornelissen unpacks the economic costs and benefits of hosting the football world cup. As she shows, South Africa's headlong rush into hosting this spectacle, to showcase the country as a desirable tourist and investment destination, may cost the country dearly. Inflated job and incomes projections belie the real costs of building stadiums that will probably end up as white elephants. While the country may benefit in terms of increased national unity, and by showing the world that we can be as capable of hosting a multi-billion dollar event as any developed country, it is becoming clearer that instead of addressing our problems of underdevelopment and inequality, the event might in fact worsen them.

For many the World Cup, like the recent Miss World beauty pageant which cost the City of Johannesburg millions of rand for little return, is indicative of the misplaced priorities of the enclave elite, which are out of sync with the interests of the increasingly restless impoverished outsiders.

Finally, Mark Swilling and Mike Muller introduce the concept of 'decoupling', whereby economic development is decoupled from negative environmental impacts and resource extraction.[4]

Swilling's comprehensive overview of government policies and initiatives argues explicitly for a 'green new deal', in contrast to South Africa's continued reliance on a 'resource-intensive economic growth path', which has led to the rapid depletion and degradation of our natural resources. Swilling identifies a range of impressive policy interventions in recent years, to shift the country towards a greener development path, but laments the fragmented and incoherent nature of these shifts. Tellingly, South Africa's recent World Bank loan for a carbon-intensive power plant, its pursuit of nuclear power alternatives and the continued embrace of a minerals-energy economic growth path at the macro-economic level, underlines the country's persistent subordination of 'sustainable development' to traditional growth imperatives.

Muller is more positive about decoupling with respect to water resources, arguing that state planning (together with ongoing interaction with major water uses and other stakeholders) has been critical. From his past experience as South Africa's director general for water affairs, Muller believes that South Africa has already been successful in decoupling socio-economic development from water availability. He gives a detailed description of South Africa's water resource planning system, but warns that while effective legislation is in place, the institutions and knowledge base that underpin decoupling remain weak – and this includes the effectiveness of broader development institutions and municipalities.

CONCLUSION

Ecological issues, as integral parts of the social and economic spheres, are increasingly being placed on the world's agenda, particularly in parts of Latin America. For example, the 2010 election campaign in Colombia placed an explicitly Green candidate, Anatanas Mockus, the former mayor of Bogota, in a strong position to become the first Green Party president in the world (*Financial Times* 30 May 2010). Radical attempts to transcend capitalism are being embraced in countries like Bolivia under Evo Morales, who is pursuing an explicit green socialist development strategy (Morales 2009). The financial and ecological crisis has spurred on greater awareness about the need for fundamental alternatives among activists in social movements and trade unions around the world (Ransom and Baird 2009; Angus 2009).

In South Africa, a new mood is slowly awakening as it becomes clear that the ANC's 'national democratic revolution' (NDR) is little more than a 'national tender revolution' (NTR), where new or aspiring members of the black elite fight furiously among themselves for the spoils of state patronage in the form of state tenders at local, provincial and national levels. Black economic empowerment, instead of tackling the roots of class power and social inequality, is designed to facilitate the entry of black elites into the world of white economic power and hyper-consumption.

Nevertheless, there are countervailing tendencies in government. In May 2010, the government convened the Green Economy Summit, attended by a range of ministries and the presidency, and driven in large part by the new minister of economic development and former unionist Ebrahim Patel. It seems that much was achieved to address criticism that government efforts have been *ad hoc*, piecemeal and incoherent across government. According to Mark Swilling, who attended the gathering 'this Summit reflects a significant sea change…There [was] unprecedented cooperation between several ministries and the presidency on the need for a green economy and a resource-perspective on future growth'.[5] Whether this positive development translates into meaningful action, whereby powerful vested interests within government and the minerals-energy-financial complex are tackled head-on, remains to be seen.

Even though the biggest labour formation, the Congress of South African Trade Unions

(Cosatu) is enmeshed in the NDR/NTR through its alliance with the ruling party, it is increasingly posing critical questions related to corruption, social inequality, growth priorities and, amongst some affiliates, the ecological limits to growth. There are also signs of such shifts in thinking within the South African Communist Party (SACP) (Cronin 2009 and Bond 2009). Outside the ANC-SACP-Cosatu alliance, there are embryonic moves to build an alternative pole of attraction, through the Conference for a Democratic Left (comprising former ANC and SACP leaders, as well as Cosatu members and activists from a broad spectrum of left groups around the country). The CDL explicitly pose the possibility of a 'grassroots democratic, eco-socialist, feminist political programme' (CDL 2010:2) as an alternative to the crisis of fossil capitalism. The hope is that, sooner rather than later, Cosatu as the leading component of the labour movement will finally realise that the Alliance is a dead end of false promises, and will break away to help build a counterhegemonic alternative that places eco-socialism firmly on the agenda. Such an alternative envisions a society-centric notion of a democratic developmental state, based on a mobilised and empowered civil society, as opposed to the state-centric versions that are vulnerable to capture by dominant elites.

While not necessarily embracing eco-socialist alternatives, the following chapters nevertheless point to the necessity of South Africa's moving out of its reliance on the minerals-energy-financial complex in order to create jobs on a sustainable basis – socially as well as ecologically. A genuine, coherent and effectively pursued green new deal, given the vested interests lined up against it, would be a radical departure from the country's current trajectory. Even if it may not address the root causes of the crisis, it could be a stepping stone towards more fundamental options in the longer-term.

The alternative to a green new deal and to eco-socialism is either the earth's destruction as we know it, or a new form of eco-fascist 'enclivity', where a small gated minority enjoys the benefits of green technology, secure employment and comfortable lifestyles, while the majority is locked out through repressive force, to live in polluted squalor. Can the emerging counter-movement, globally and in South Africa, prevent such an outcome? Only time will tell.

NOTES

1   These remarks were made at a Global Labour University workshop in Johannesburg, October 2009.
2   The regular emergence of new competitors to challenge existing dominant firms (or, in South Africa's case, the break-up of monopolies such as the Anglo-American Corporation during the post-apartheid era), and hence reduce monopolisation, does not contradict the underlying trend towards monopolisation, as new competitors either become absorbed by, or themselves absorb, the dominant firms – or firms such as South Africa's banks and cellphone service companies collude to keep prices high (hence the need for state regulation, often ineffective, to enforce competition).
3   Ransom and Baird's *People First Economics* (2009), contains alternative perspectives that straddle the New Deal and eco-socialist spectrum.
4   A critique of decoupling is offered by Foster (2002: 22-24), who calls it the 'myth of dematerialisation'. He quotes *The Weight of Nations* (World Resources Institute, 2000) that concludes, 'efficiency gains brought about by technology and new management practices have been offset by [increases in] the scale of economic growth'.
5   E-mail to author, 2 June 2010.

REFERENCES

Andrews M (2008) Land hunger feeds food hunger, *Amandla* No 2, June/July: 13–15.

Aguiar J (2007) Capital and nature: An interview with Paul Burkett, *Monthly Review* April.

Albo G (2006) The limits of eco-localism: Scale, strategy, socialism. In *Socialist Register 2007*. New Delhi: Leftword Books.

Altvater A (2006) The social and natural environment of fossil capitalism. In *Socialist Register 2007*. New Delhi: Leftword Books.

Amin S (2008) Preface, In Bieler A, I Lindberg and D Pillay (Eds) *Labour and the Challenges of Globalisation: What Prospects for Transnational Solidarity?* London: Pluto.

Angus I (Ed) (2009) *The Global Fight for Climate Justice: Anticapitalist Responses to Global Warming and Environmental Destruction*. London: Resistance Books.

Arrighi G (2007) *Adam Smith in Beijing*. London: Verso.

Bakan J (2004) *The Corporation: The Pathological Pursuit of Profit and Power*. London: Constable.

Baran P and P Sweezy (1968) *Monopoly Capitalism*. Harmondsworth: Penguin.

Barclay E (2003) Cuba's Security in Fresh Produce. *Environmental News Network*, September 12.

Bieler A, I Lindberg and D Pillay (Eds) (2008) *Labour and the Challenges of Globalisation: What Prospects for Transnational Solidarity?* London: Pluto.

Bond P (2009) Comments on the current financial crisis and possibilities for the left by Jeremy Cronin. http://www.ukzn.ac.za/ccs/default.asp?2,68,3,1681 [Accessed 15 June 2010]

Brenner R (2009) Overproduction not financial collapse is the heart of the crisis: the US, East Asia, and the world (Interview with Jeong Seong-jin) *The Asia-Pacific Journal*, 6 May 2009.

Bruno K and J Karliner (2004) *Earthsummit.biz: The Corporate Takeover of Sustainable Development*. Oakland: Food First Books.

Bullard N (2009) To live well. In Ransom D and V Baird (Eds) (2009) *People First Economics*. Oxford: New Internationalist Publications.

Burkett P (2006) *Marxism and Ecological Economics*. Leiden: Brill.

Clapp J and P Dauvergne (2008) *Paths to a Green World*. New Delhi: Academic Foundation.

Cock J (2007) *The War Against Ourselves: Nature, Power and Justice*. Johannesburg: Wits University Press.

Conference of the Democratic Left (CDL) (2009) Unite to make another South Africa and world possible! (pamphlet issued by the National Convening Committee, Yeoville, Johannesburg).

Cronin J (2009) The current financial crisis and possibilities for the left. Joe Slovo Memorial Lecture, Chris Hani Institute, 28 January. http://www.ukzn.ac.za/ccs/default.asp?2,68,3,1681 [Accessed 15 June 2010]

Desai M (2004) *Marx's Revenge: The Resurgence of Capitalism and the Death of Statist Socialism*. London: Verso.

Eisler R (2009) *The Real Wealth of Nations: Creating a Caring Economics*. San Francisco: Berrett-Koehler.

Everest L (2004) *Oil, Power and Empire*. Monroe: Common Courage Press.

Fine B and Z Rustomjee (1996) *The Political Economy of South Africa: From Minerals-Energy Complex to Industrialisation*. Boulder: Westview Press.

Foster J B (1999) *Marx's Ecology*. New York: Monthly Review Press.

Foster J B (2002) *Ecology Against Capitalism*. New York: Monthly Review Press.

Foster J B (2009) *The Environmental Revolution*. New York: Monthly Review Press.

Foster J B and F Magdoff (2009) *The Great Financial Crisis*. New York: Monthly Review Press.

Frank A G (1966) *The Development of Underdevelopment*. New York: Monthly Review Press.

Friedman T (1999) *The Lexus and the Olive Tree*. London: Allan Lane.

Friedman T (2005) *The World is Flat*. London: Allan Lane.

Friedman T (2008) *Hot, Flat and Crowded*. London: Allan Lane.

Gramsci A (1971) *Selections from Prison Notebooks*. London: Lawrence & Wishart.

Harriss-White B and E Harris (2006) Unsustainable capitalism: the politics of renewable energy in the UK. In *Socialist Register 2007*. New Delhi.

Harvey D (2005) *The New Imperialism*. Oxford: Oxford University Press.

Hattingh S (2008) ALBA: Creating a Regional Alternative to Neo-liberalism? mrzine.monthlyreview.org/2008/hattingh070208.html (downloaded 2 June 2010).

Korten D C (2009) *Agenda for a New Economy: From Phantom Wealth to Real Wealth*. San Francisco: Berrett-Koehler.

Kovel J (2002) *The Enemy of Nature: The End of Capitalism or the End of the World?* London: Zed Books.

Lowy M (2006) Eco-socialism and democratic planning. In *Socialist Register 2007*. New Delhi: Leftword Books.

Mielants E H (2007) *The Origins of Capitalism and the 'Rise of the West'*. Philadelphia: Temple University Press.

Morales E (2009) How to save the world, life and humanity. In Ransom D and V Baird (Eds) *People First Economics*. Oxford: New Internationalist Publications.

Patel R (2009) *The Value of Nothing: How to Reshape Market Society and Redefine Democracy*. London: Portobello Books.

Ransom D and V Baird (Eds) (2009) *People First Economics*. Oxford: New Internationalist Publications.

Roberts P (2008) *The End of Food: The Coming Crisis in the World Food Industry*. London: Bloomsbury.

Rogers H (2006) Garbage capitalism's green commerce. In *Socialist Register 2007*. New Delhi: Leftword Books.

Peet R (2003) *The Unholy Trinity: The IMF, World Bank and WTO*. Johannesburg: Wits University Press.

Perry A (2010) *Falling off the Edge: Globalization, World Peace and Other Lies*. (2nd Edition). London: Pan Books.

Polany K (1944) *The Great Transformation*. Boston: Beacon Press.

Rothkopf D (2009) *Superclass: How the Rich Ruined our World*. London: Abacus.

Sachs W (Ed) (2001) *The Jo'burg-Memo: Memorandum for the World Summit on Sustainable Development*. Johannesburg: Heinrich Böll Foundation.

Silver B (2004) *Forces of Labour*. Cambridge: Cambridge University Press.

Wallerstein I (1979) *The Capitalist World-Economy*. Cambridge: Cambridge University Press.

William M (2008) *The Roots of Participatory Democracy: Democratic Communists in South Africa and Kerala, India*. New York: Palgrave.

CHAPTER 1

The state of the South African economy

Seeraj Mohamed

The South African economy was in a state of crisis before the recent global financial crisis.

The official unemployment rate has remained at well over 20 per cent over the past decade. Employment has declined in manufacturing, indicating deindustrialisation of the economy. Though employment in services has grown, this was not in productive services but instead seems to have been driven by acceleration in debt-driven consumption, outsourcing and growth in private security services; as a result, recent relatively high levels of economic growth could very well have been the 'wrong' kind of economic growth for South Africa.

The South African gross domestic product (GDP) grew at around 5 per cent or more per annum from 2004 to 2007, and although this growth was accompanied by increased employment and investment, not all growth in GDP, investment and employment is good for a country. This chapter argues that an important lesson of this short period of relatively high economic growth in South Africa is that one has to consider the quality of economic growth and the type of employment and investment associated with it. In other words, we have to examine the causes of economic growth and the types of investments made and of jobs created. When we move beyond the assumption that all economic growth is good for an economy we can begin to understand that an economy growing at 5 per cent per annum can be performing poorly. The South African economy was in a crisis, even though GDP grew at around 5 per cent per annum from 2004 to 2007.

Figure 1: Annual percentage changes in GDP and GDP per capita (2000 prices)

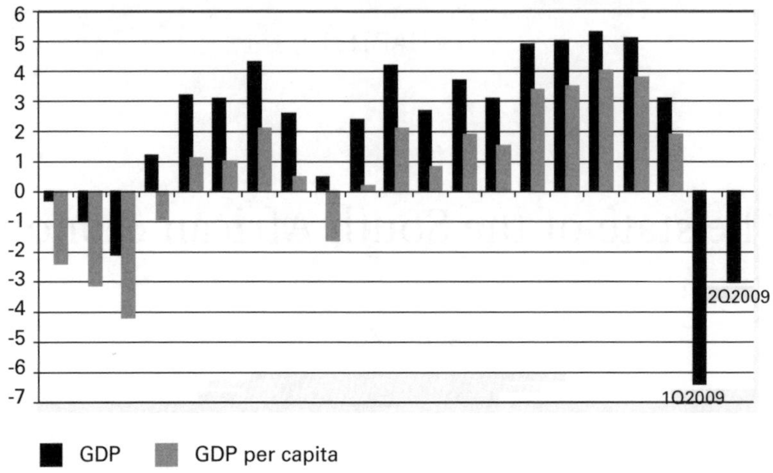

Source: SARB

The global financial crisis and economic recession meant that the growth rate declined to 3.1 per cent in 2008 and there was a recession in 2009. According to Statistics South Africa's quarterly labour force survey, there was an employment decrease of 770 000 people (5.6 per cent) from the third quarter of 2008 to the third quarter of 2009. During this period, the number of people classified as 'not economically active' increased by almost 1.1 million and more than half (0.56 million) were classified as 'discouraged work-seekers'. Manufacturing production decreased by nearly 20 per cent from April 2008 to April 2009, while services sectors, particularly retail trade, declined and lost jobs.

Estimates by companies such as Auction Alliance put home foreclosures at around 300 a month during late 2008 and early 2009. In May 2009, Rael Levitt of Auction Alliance projected that mortgage stress (homeowners two months in arrears on bond repayments) would shoot up from 125 000 in the first quarter of 2009 to close to 200 000 in the second quarter of 2009. He added 'We also are projecting that severe mortgage stress (four months in arrears on bond repayments) will shoot up from 55 000 homeowners in the first quarter to 85 000 in the second quarter' (*Business Day* 14 May 2009).[1]

ABSA Bank reported that car repossessions peaked at 7 000 a month during 2008 and expected similar levels during the first half of 2009 (*Business Day* 1 April 2009).[2] The National Credit Regulator (NCR) reported in September 2009 that it expected 150 000 consumers to be under debt review by Christmas 2009, that there were about 100 000 consumers undergoing debt counseling in September 2009, and that these 100 000 consumers owed R20 billion, of which R12 billion was in home mortgages.[3] Therefore, the average debt for consumers under review in September 2009 was R200 000. Clearly, most of the people entering debt review are middle class, since a large proportion of poor South Africans do not have access to credit from the large financial institutions and if they did they would not be allowed that level of debt.[4] It is also worth keeping in mind that the figures reported by the NCR are only for people undergoing debt counselling and do not show the true extent of middle class indebtedness in the country.

So how did the economy manage to sink so low so fast? The Ten Year Review put out by the Presidency in October 2003 sounded an optimistic note, saying that government's economic policies had saved the economy from a fiscal crisis and put it on a path towards more investment and economic growth. 'South Africa has achieved a level of macroeconomic stability not seen in the country for forty years. These advances create opportunities for real increases in expenditure on social services, reduce the costs and risks for all investors, and therefore lay the foundation for increased investment and growth' (Presidency 2003, p.33).

Figure 2: Official unemployment rates

Total unemploymenr rate drawing on revised LFS 2000-7 and QLFS 2008-9 (Percentages)

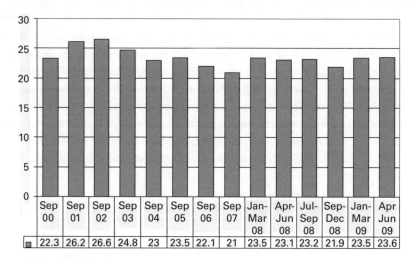

	Sep 00	Sep 01	Sep 02	Sep 03	Sep 04	Sep 05	Sep 06	Sep 07	Jan-Mar 08	Apr-Jun 08	Jul-Sep 08	Sep-Dec 08	Jan-Mar 09	Apr-Jun 09
■	22.3	26.2	26.6	24.8	23	23.5	22.1	21	23.5	23.1	23.2	21.9	23.5	23.6

Source: StatsSA, drawing on their revised LFS 2000-07 and QLFS 2008-09

That the drafters of the Ten Year Review believed that there was macroeconomic stability in the economy during 2003 shows that they had adopted a neoliberal perspective towards economic policy. Within this perspective, macroeconomic stability is defined as maintaining a low government budget deficit (or preferably a surplus) and low levels of inflation. The authors of the Ten Year Review seem to have forgotten the currency crisis during 2001 when the rand depreciated by 35 per cent against the US dollar and the South African Reserve Bank (SARB) responded by pushing up interest rates by 4 per cent within a year. The impact of the increase in interest rates was increased unemployment: the official, narrow measure of unemployment grew from 23.3 per cent in September 2000 to 26.2 per cent in September 2001 and 26.6 per cent in September 2002. GDP annual growth dropped from 4.2 per cent in 2000 to 2.7 per cent in 2001, recovered to 3.7 per cent in 2002 and declined to 3.1 per cent in 2003. The authors of the Ten Year Review had let their neoliberal ideological blinkers blind them to all that recent macroeconomic instability.

The early 2000s was also a remarkable time because of the volatility in global financial markets as a result of the dotcom crisis. Capital fled equity markets in the US and went in search of high returns in real estate, subprime and securitised debt markets to set up conditions for the next financial crisis. The impact of the dotcom bubble was felt in South African markets; the 2001 currency crisis, referred to above, was caused by huge foreign investment portfolio outflows during 2000 that grew into a flight of capital in 2001 and the volatility in the South African economy was a result of largely uncontrolled movement of short-term capital flows into and out of the economy. The massive depreciation of the rand against the US dollar had a huge impact on the inflation rate because of the higher rand cost of imports, such as oil. The SARB responded with interest rate hikes and unemployment grew.

Uncontrolled flows of short-term capital (often referred to as hot money) were also important contributors to the relatively high levels of economic growth from 2004 to 2007. There was a massive recovery in foreign portfolio investment inflows to South Africa from 2004, and by 2006 net portfolio flows to South Africa were 7.4 per cent of the size of GDP. The impact of such large flows of the economy was huge; they caused the rand to strengthen, which had a negative impact on exports but a huge stimulatory effect on imports, and as a result, the negative balance on the current account as a percentage of GDP grew rapidly from -3.4 per cent of GDP in 2004 to -7.3 per cent of GDP in 2007 notwithstanding the large increase in global demand for minerals commodities and the large price increases for key South African exports such as platinum, coal and gold. The large current account deficit was a huge risk to the South African economy and its ability to maintain its balance of payments. In other words, the risk of a currency and financial crisis increased significantly.

Figure 3: Household debt to disposable income (ratio)

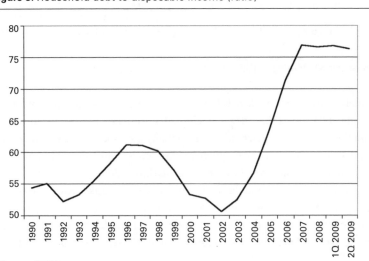

Source: SARB

The large and rapid growth in short-term capital flows is also associated with increased liquidity in the South African financial sector and increased extension of credit to the private sector. This increased credit was not used for long-term productive investment but instead was associated with increased debt-driven consumption and speculation in financial and real estate markets. The huge increases in household debt and the increased investment and employment in the retail and wholesale services sector were due to the increased credit extension made possible by increased hot money flows into the economy.

One of the consequences of the process of global financialisation was that events in financial markets shaped developments in the real sector. The debt-driven, consumption-led economic growth in South Africa was driven by increased inflows of short-term capital. At the same time, the South African financial sector was emulating the behaviour of its US counterpart (which boosted leverage and loosened lending conditions) and increasingly securitising debt and extending more debt for mortgages, car finance and consumption. There was very rapid growth in derivatives markets. The large South African corporations had also become increasingly financialised and seemed to follow the global trend whereby increasing product market competition caused many corporations to earn a larger share of their revenues and profits from financial activities and speculating in financial assets. The South African Reserve Bank's flow of funds data shows that the South African corporate sector was speculating in financial markets more than it was investing in fixed investment (see figure 11 below).

The broader context for these economic events in South Africa are the industrial structural weaknesses of the economy and massive changes in corporate structure that have occurred in the economy since the end of apartheid. The industrial structural weaknesses stemmed from the development of the economy around mining and minerals or the minerals and energy complex (MEC), as argued by Fine and Rustomjee (1996). Much of the change in corporate structure occurred because of the responses of big businesses to democracy. The global context of increasing financialisation of nonfinancial corporations led to a massive global corporate restructuring and increased concentration of the global economy, and this process influenced the change in South African corporate structure. The global process of concentration entrenched and deepened the existing global division of labour between the rich countries of the North and the developing countries of the South. In general, rich countries controlled global economic value chains and the design, engineering, branding and distribution of products while the developing countries were, in the main, involved in either assembly manufacturing or providing low cost agricultural or minerals inputs into the global value chains. The corporate restructuring in South Africa began a reversal of previous industrialisation, leaving the economy more concentrated and more dependent on the mining and minerals sectors. These developments had a significantly negative impact on workers in South Africa.

The short period of growth at around 5 per cent per annum from 2004 to 2007 blinded many South African economists and economic policy makers to the crisis that was unfolding. The current financial crisis provides an excuse for the poor performance and high job losses in the economy but on the whole, this short period of high growth from 2004 to 2007 left the economy poorer. The decisions to adopt neoliberal economic policies, particularly macroeconomic and financial policies, have had a hugely negative impact on South Africa by allowing short-term financial flows to create macroeconomic instability that destroys industry and jobs. They have directed the misallocation capital towards speculation and bubbles in financial and real estate markets, and away from long-term job-creating productive investment. The relatively little fixed investment that has occurred is largely in services sectors linked to increased speculation in financial and real estate markets and the growth in debt-driven consumption.

INDUSTRIAL STRUCTURAL WEAKNESSES AND CORPORATE RESTRUCTURING

South African economic development occurred around the mining and minerals sectors, and the state and mining industry supported growth of manufacturing sectors with strong links to the MEC, the formation of which, according to Fine and Rustomjee (1996), was a result of the political compromise between large English mining interests and the large Afrikaner business and political establishment. It was also shaped by the politics of oppression of black South Africans and the strict control over black workers.

Most manufacturing sectors with weaker connections to the MEC have remained weak and have not received strong state support and adequate investment from the large mining finance houses that had dominated the South African economy until the 1980s. With the exception of a few sectors, such as automobiles and components, manufacturing remains dominated by sectors with strong links to the MEC. These, with the exception of engineering and capital equipment, are capital- and energy-intensive process industries, such as electricity generation, minerals beneficiation (iron and steel, aluminum) and the Sasol oil from coal process and its chemicals byproducts. Downstream, value-added manufacturing sectors have not been adequately developed and manufacturing remains relatively undiversified. The structure of the economy underwent further change with the transition to democracy in South Africa and was shaped by changes in the global economy.

Many leaders of big business were uncomfortable with the democratic transition in South Africa,[5] as the change in government was accompanied by massive restructuring of the South African corporate sector. I argue here that the transition to democracy is one reason for the corporate restructuring, the shape of which was influenced by important changes in the global economy. The 1990s saw the rise to prominence of institutional investors and the shareholder value movement.[6] The growth to prominence of institutional investors and the shareholder value movement was part of the process of financialisation that had started in the 1970s. Crotty (2002) says that the rise of institutional investors in the US led to a situation where on average US stocks are held for just one year and, in addition, an increasing share of industrial company revenues is from financial nonproductive assets. The second change was the surge in merger and acquisition activity during the 1990s. There are a number of reasons for this global restructuring that concentrated global businesses and caused them to focus on core businesses. The prominence of institutional investors and the shareholder value movement was central to this restructuring because institutional investors demanded simpler structures. Much of the funds for the new global giants were sourced from institutional investors, who invested mostly in big companies that have familiar brands, large market share, high R&D (research and development) spending and focus on their core activities. Both these changes to the global economy had profound impacts on the structure of the South African corporate sector.

Since 1994 the South African corporate sector has engaged in the following activities:
- conglomerate unbundling and restructuring;
- consolidation within sectors by conglomerates as part of ensuring stronger focus and better strategic direction, which has also increased concentration;
- internationalisation, mostly outward, by firms which moved their primary listing overseas, and foreign acquisitions by South African listed firms; and
- black economic empowerment deals, first, through special purpose vehicles for financing and second, more recently, in areas where government policy has provided a specific impetus.

Figure 4: South African mergers and acquisitions (M&A) (Rbn, current prices)

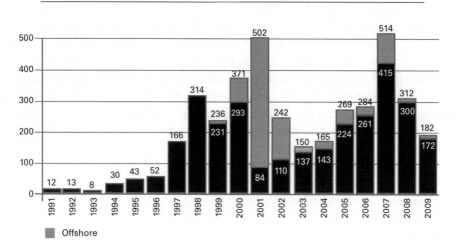

Source: Ernst and Young M&A, 2010

Nolan (2003) points out that total global merger activity grew from over US$150 billion in 1992 to over US$2000 billion in 1998, when eight of the world's ten largest mergers took place. By 2000 it had peaked at over $3.4 trillion. Large South African companies were caught up in this process of global restructuring, and the offshore listing of major South African corporations from 1997 can be seen within the context of this merger frenzy. The result was a spectacular growth in M&A activity in South Africa. According to Ernst & Young data there was an increase from 136 M&A deals in 1994 to a peak of 605 in 1998; from 1999 to 2002 there was an average of 530 M&As. According to Ernst & Young, in 1991 South African M&A activity was R12 billion and by 2001 M&A activity peaked to R502 billion (see figure 2).

Most of the pyramid structures, which were at the centre of the MEC as a system of accumulation and were used by the powerful families to control most of the South African economy, were restructured and disentangled. Global markets were restructured and market share was reapportioned – the wealthy and powerful in South Africa did not want to be left out of this process. They wanted to ensure not only that they got their share of the international market in minerals by internationalising their operations, but also to consolidate and secure the viability of their South African assets.

At the same time, South Africa was undergoing a transition from apartheid to democracy and there was argument about the future economic policy of the country. The changes in South Africa meant that many of the wealthy and the large corporations wanted to move their assets out of reach of the new government. The restructuring of global assets and the transition to democracy provides important reasons for the decision of a number of large corporations to move their primary listings – studies show that capital flight continued to be high throughout the 1990s, indicating that wealthy South Africans wanted to increase their wealth offshore.[7] A company that moved its primary listing offshore would be able to move a large amount of capital out of South Africa legally because it would not be bound by exchange control restrictions on residents, and thus large amounts of capital could leave the country in the form of dividends or other payments.

A number of large South African corporations have moved their primary listings offshore to the London Stock Exchange since the late 1990s. This move has turned former South African corporations into foreign investors into South Africa. Some have opted for joint listings on the JSE and developed country stock markets; common reasons provided for these delistings by the 'delisters' are that they allowed the companies to be valued in a hard currency, reduced the risk premium for changes in the value of the rand, and improved their expansion capability. In the process they have also modified the conglomerate structure to clear up cross-holdings.

Companies that moved their primary listings include:
- Billiton (formerly Gencor and now part of BHP Billiton)
- SAB (now part of SAB Miller)
- Anglo American Corporation
- Old Mutual
- Liberty

The primary listings in London were supposed to allow the conglomerates to raise capital to fund investments in South Africa, and they have managed to raise a large amount of funds in foreign markets, but they have not invested in South Africa. There has been a much more striking pattern of outward acquisition and investments. For example, Anglo American embarked on an extensive drive to increase international investments in mining while SAB, Sasol, Sappi, and Kumba have been involved in acquisitions of firms in Europe, South America, Australia and China. The offshore listings have allowed the captains of industry who live and work as businessmen in both the global North and South Africa to change their power relationship with the new South African state: they are able to control the South African assets that they wish to control but they also have more control over the movement of their capital. The South African state did not interfere in these companies because it feared losing credibility with other potential investors and financiers.

The changes also meant that the shareholder value movement in the North (including flighty institutional investors) and the business media that claim to present their views have gained more influence over the major corporations operating in South Africa and in the future direction of the economy. At the same time, the South African government has become hesitant about implementing progressive economic policies that could address unemployment and poverty for fear that these policies would drive down share prices and create a negative view of South African policies in international financial markets and business media. The result of the offshore listings was that many large South African corporations were no longer South African and that they were investing capital produced in South Africa over the past 150 years to expand their internationalised corporations. It is worth remembering that much of that capital was generated in exploiting the non-renewable mineral wealth of South Africa and harsh exploitation of South African workers. Many of the businesses that listed offshore and become global corporations had been involved in extensive merger and acquisition activity through which their South African assets have decreased as a proportion of their total assets. They have diluted their South African identities and concequently the size of their supposed responsibilities towards the new South Africa and development there.

These corporations strenuously advocated lifting exchange controls and argued for their right to list offshore, the central point of these arguments being that they would then be able to raise capital more easily to invest in South Africa. Clearly, the opposite was true. As Roberts *et al* (2003, p.15) correctly argue, 'In five of the last ten years outward direct investment has in fact exceeded inward FDI. Major foreign investments have largely been limited to the acquisition of stakes in state-owned utilities (Telkom and South African Airways) and the re-entry of firms such as Toyota and General Motors which had exited under sanctions, although specific examples exist of sectors where foreign companies have contributed to the resumption of growth.'

The unbundling of the conglomerates and the 'rebundling' should be considered in the context of the political and global factors affecting these businesses. The combination of the unease of white business with the changes in South Africa, and the understanding of the leaders of big business that they had to signal a willingness to share future business activities with black people, put two types of pressure on big business to restructure: The first was restructuring for political expediency; the second was directly linked to withdrawing from the South African economy. In other words, big business had adapted to the political changes by reducing its risk within the South African economy by internationalising operations. They have also accepted a political compromise to maintain their control over much of the South African economy by sharing a portion of ownership with black businesses.

Goldstein's (2000, p.15) interpretation of this process is:

> While the refocusing on core business has followed from the need to ensure competitiveness against the background of the opening of the domestic economy to world competition and weaker gold and commodity prices, voluntary unbundling has been an expedient strategy to appease the possible rise of nationalization sentiments. In order to build up a black capitalist constituency, it was important to conclude highly visible and large-scale deals. The first such deal was Sanlam's sale of Metropolitan Life (METLIFE), an insurance company, to New Africa Investment Ltd (NAIL). In 1996 Anglo broke up its majority-owned sub-holding JCI (Johannesburg Consolidated Investment) into platinum (Amplats), a homonymous mining subsidiary, and an industrial arm, Johnnic.

Goldstein recognises that global and domestic factors shaped the behaviour of South African big business. His research indicates that the boom in mergers and acquisitions in South Africa during the 1990s was different to those in other countries and he shows that there were particularly South African characteristics to the M&As: the restructuring in South Africa was more about dismantling pyramid structures than increasing the competitiveness of industrial sectors. Goldstein says, 'Of the twenty largest South African deals reported in 1992-98, 75 per cent corresponds to the simplification of the corporate structure; 10 per cent to consolidation in the financial industry; 10 per cent to foreign acquisitions; and only one deal – TransNatal's acquisition of Rand Coal to form Ingwe Coal in 1994 – is a "genuine" South African merger (p.17).' He makes the important point that it is remarkable that South African conglomerates have not made any large acquisitions in their own country, pointing out that this lack of acquisition is true even in sectors such as utilities and internet related investments '… where family-controlled business groups in OECD countries have been active even while refocusing their portfolios on the core business' (*ibid*).

The South African context for mergers and acquisitions was one where the MEC continued to stifle investments into diversifying the industrial base of the South African economy. Instead, the concern of big businesses that dominated the MEC was to restructure in order to appear more attractive to investors speculating in the markets where they had relisted.

FINANCIALISATION OF THE SOUTH AFRICAN ECONOMY

The South African financial system had developed along similar lines to that of the English and US systems and can be described as market-based rather than bank-based (Roux 1991). In other words, South African businesses that require finance for long-term investment use retained earnings or seek finance in securities markets. The state-owned Industrial Development Corporation does provide some industrial finance but on the whole its lending is a very small share of total lending in the country and its main customers have been large, capital intensive projects in the mining and minerals sectors (Roberts 2008). The banks and other monetary institutions largely provided business with short-term operating capital and serviced the credit card, home mortgage, vehicle lease and finance and other short-term lending for consumption.

Figure 4 shows that during the period 1990 to 2008 this form of credit allocation continued in the economy. One can see the growth in mortgage advances from 2003 to 2008 which supported the growth of a housing price bubble in the relatively more affluent real estate market in South Africa. House price increases in South Africa were higher than in the US during the period 2003 to 2007, when US subprime lending was rampant. For the period 1990 to 2008, investment was a relatively very small share of total private sector credit extension.

An important phenomenon in the global economy and South Africa is that the size and influence of the financial sector grew from the 1980s, when financial markets and cross-border capital flows were liberalised. The market-based banking system and banking deregulation by the apartheid state during the 1980s supported the growth of the South African financial sector. Further, the political changes, the decline in MEC investments and trade liberalisation led to greater private sector interest in financial assets from the mid-1990s. Figure 5 shows that value added by the finance and insurance services sector increased rapidly during the 1980s when economic growth and investment as a percentage of GDP declined significantly. The contribution of the finance and insurance sectors to GDP grew even more rapidly from 1994 to 2007, while overall investment levels remained relatively low. An improvement in investment levels from 2003 included the impact of government's infrastructure investments from 2006, increased services sector investment linked to financial sector growth, increased household consumption and more household construction and purchase of automobiles. In short, the growth of the financial sector and its increased share of GDP were not associated with higher levels of investment.

Figure 5: Private sector credit extension by all monetary institutions by type (percentages of total)

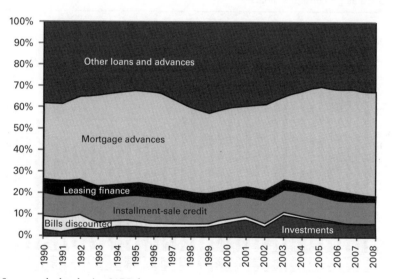

Source: calculated using SARB data

An important aspect of the financialisation of the South African economy during the post-apartheid period was increased capital inflows, particularly short-term portfolio flows from developed countries. These short-term flows signalled not only the end of apartheid financial isolation but, more importantly, a change in sentiment about South Africa by global financiers, after they had ignored South Africa subsequent to its 1985 debt crisis. The slow liberalisation of exchange controls by the South African government from 1996 may also have affected this sentiment but the more important reason for the increased flows to South Africa was the huge increase in global liquidity that was accompanied by large movements of short-term portfolio flows into certain developing countries in Asia, Latin America and South Africa in Africa.

I argued in 2006 that the surge in net short-term capital flows to South Africa increased macroeconomic instability with more volatility in exchange rates, interest rates and inflation associated with changes in capital inflows (see Mohamed 2006). A stark illustration of this volatility and instability was the sharp drop in the rand to dollar exchange rate of 35 per cent in 2001, which could be defined as a currency crisis. This was caused by a rapid decline in net portfolio flows in 2000 which turned sharply negative in 2001 (see figure 6). During this period, inflation increased sharply as a result of the weaker rand. The South African Reserve Bank, which follows an inflation targeting policy, increased interest rates by 4 per cent. Net portfolio capital flows began recovering in 2002 and turned positive in 2003. They grew over the next few years to peak at nearly 8 per cent of GDP. This recovery in portfolio flows was accompanied by rapid reductions in interest rates that contributed to the house price and financial asset bubble from 2003 to 2007.

Figure 6: Gross fixed capital formation and finance and insurance sector value added as percentages of GDP

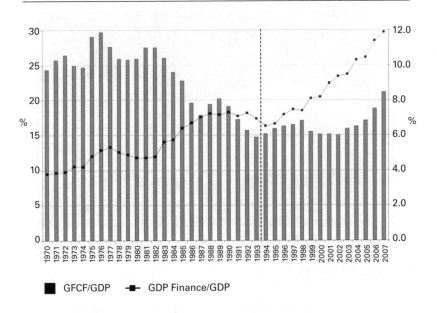

Source: Quantec

In an examination of the period up to 2002, I argue that the surge in portfolio capital flows to South Africa and the related increased extension of credit to the private sector during the 1990s was not associated with increased levels of fixed investment but with increased household consumption, financial speculation and capital flight.

Figure 6 compares the trends of total fixed capital formation, private business fixed capital formation, total domestic credit extension and total credit extended to the private sector all as percentages of GDP for South Africa for the period 1990 to 2007. Figure 7 shows that credit extension to the private sector increased about 22 per cent from 2000 to 2008 but that private business investment increased by only 5 per cent during that period. What can also be inferred from Figure 7 is that a part of the increase in capital formation from 2006 may not be due to private business capital formation but to state investment in infrastructure. The increase in private capital formation from 2003 to 2008 is due to investments spurred on by increased financial speculation and debt-driven consumption, not long-term investment in productive investment. Long-term productive investments are required to redress the structural industrial weaknesses of the South African economy. I explain the process, which I describe as misallocation of finance, below.

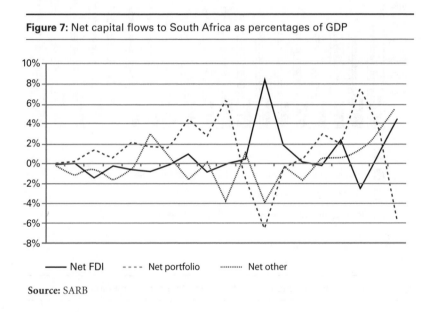

Figure 7: Net capital flows to South Africa as percentages of GDP

Net FDI   - - - - Net portfolio   ·········· Net other

Source: SARB

Figure 8 draws on data from the SARB's flow of funds data to provide a trend of capital formation after depreciation by sector. We see that the foreign sector has very low levels of net fixed investment. Net investment by the South African financial institutions (the banks and insurers) in fixed capital formation turned negative from 2003. Figure 9 shows that there has been a huge increase in corporate business enterprise net investment, from about R30 billion in 1999 to almost R130 billion in 2007. There has also been large growth in government and household net capital formation over that period.

Figure 9 shows calculations for trends of net acquisitions of financial assets by sector calculated from the SARB flow of funds data. The first stark difference between figure 8 and figure 9 is the scale of the different charts. The Y-axis on figure 8 goes up to R140 billion and that of figure 9 to R450 billion. The next stark difference is that every sector in figure 9, except for general government, had large and increasing net acquisition of financial assets, whereas in figure 8 we noted that it was only government, household and corporate business enterprises that showed large increases in net capital stock. There was rapid growth in acquisition of financial assets in all the financial categories. The other monetary institutions category, which includes the commercial banks, had huge growth in acquisition of financial assets, which nearly tripled from just over R150 billion in 2003 to nearly R430 billion in 2007.

Figure 8: Credit extension and investment as percentages of GDP

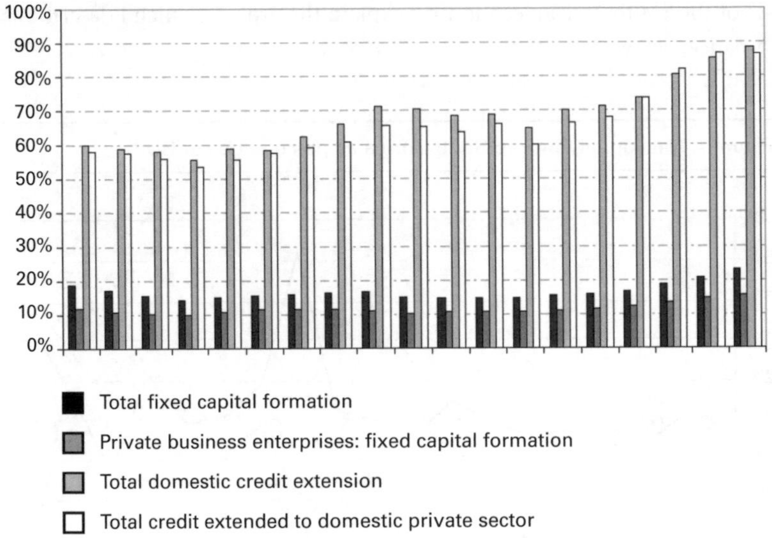

■ Total fixed capital formation

▧ Private business enterprises: fixed capital formation

▧ Total domestic credit extension

□ Total credit extended to domestic private sector

Source: calculated using SARB data

Figure 9: Capital allocated to capital formation by sector, Rbillions

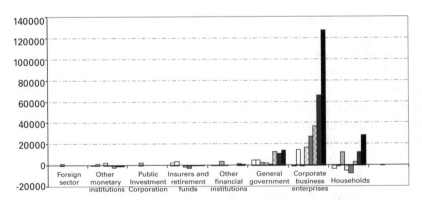

□1993 ▫1995 ▪1997 ▪1999 ■2001 ▪2003 ▪2005 ■2007

Source: calculated from SARB flow of funds data

Household net capital formation in 2007 at around R30 billion was a fraction of their net acquisitions of financial assets, which more or less doubled to R200 billion in 2007 from about R100 billion in 2005. The trend in acquisition of financial assets by corporate business enterprises increased until the financial crisis (and the dotcom crisis) in 2001 and then declined until 2005. However, it had a sudden surge and by 2007 had grown, from the 2001 peak of about R100 billion, to over R170 billion.

Figure 10 highlights an important fact about corporate business' net acquisition of financial assets relative to net fixed capital formation for the period for which we have SARB flow of funds data (1993 to 2007): corporate business enterprise net capital formation (that is, gross capital formation less depreciation) was lower than net capital formation for all years between 1994 and 2007 except for 2004 and 2005. Corporate saving was low for the period and turned negative in 2006-7. Many of the studies of financialisation in the US economy focus on the increasing financialisation of nonfinancial corporations (NFCs). One aspect of this financialisation is the increased share of income and profits of NFCs from involvement in financial markets and investment in financial assets. The flow of funds data on use of capital by corporate business enterprises in South Africa seems to support the notion that there has been financialisation of NFCs in South Africa.

Figure 10: Capital allocated to financial assets, Rbillions

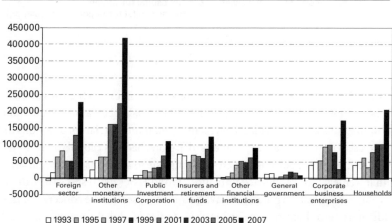

☐ 1993 ▦ 1995 ▨ 1997 ■ 1999 ■ 2001 ■ 2003▨ 2005 ■ 2007

Source: calculated from SARB flow of funds data

A number of recent studies show that financialisation of nonfinancial corporations was associated with lower levels of investment by nonfinancial corporations. This literature focuses on developed countries, particularly the US. Aglietta and Breton (2001) argue that the greater influence of financial markets on nonfinancial corporations and their demands for higher returns influenced executives of nonfinancial corporations to increase their dividend payments and to use share buybacks to raise share prices. They were left with less capital for investment.

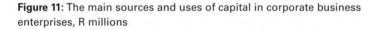

Figure 11: The main sources and uses of capital in corporate business enterprises, R millions

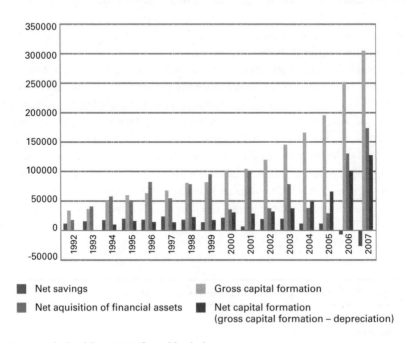

- Net savings
- Net aquisition of financial assets
- Gross capital formation
- Net capital formation (gross capital formation – depreciation)

Source: calculated from SARB flow of funds data

As Crotty (2002) explains, nonfinancial corporations have increased the sizes of their financial subsidiaries and have become involved in more financial speculation. Duménil and Lévy (2004) show that interest and dividend payments from nonfinancial corporations to financial markets increased: nonfinancial corporations, therefore, had less capital to invest in their own activities. Stockhammer (2004) uses regression analysis to show that financialisation is associated with lower levels of capital accumulation. Froud *et al* (2000) show the extent to which executives of nonfinancial corporations have become focused on the concerns of the financial markets for short-term high returns, using case studies of global corporations to show how this sensitivity to financial markets has created dysfunctional behaviour in large corporations, and arguing that the narrative provided by CEOs of large corporations to financial markets is not supported by examination of the financial statements of those companies. Orhangazi (2007) uses firm level data in the US to show a negative relationship between real investment and financialisation. He argues that financialisation of nonfinancial corporations may have caused a change in the incentives of management that caused them to direct capital towards financial investments.

Much more research is required to understand the impact of financialisation of NFCs on the South African economy and on developing countries in general. Given the available evidence

I argue that the largest South African corporations have become more sensitive to the demands of the financial sector, particularly the shareholder value movement. Recent corporate restructuring and the content of annual reports of these giant corporations are indications of this sensitivity. Lazonick and O'Sullivan (2000) argue that the predominance of the shareholder value approach to corporate governance has been accompanied by a shift from patient to impatient capital – in other words, the increased influence of financiers and the shareholder value movement over corporate executives has caused a shift in management behaviour. Investors and management are less concerned with building and nurturing businesses over a long period of time, and have become focused on short-term returns. This behaviour is even more marked where big business has moved capital out of South Africa and increased its efforts to internationalise. Crotty (2002) says that this shift to impatient capital has led to management treating their subsidiaries not as long-term investments but as part of portfolios of assets. We have seen former South African giant corporations unload a huge number of South African businesses that they have decided are not part of their core businesses and increase their investments abroad. Froud et al (2007) argue that this increased focus on short-term financial returns in NFCs is bad for labour because decreasing employment is good for increasing profits in the short-run even if losing experienced workers may be detrimental to these NFCs in the long-run. South Africa requires capital that will make a long-term commitment to employment and building the skills of their workforces. Financialisation increases short-term motives, and therefore firms are less likely to invest in long-term skills development.

THE SOUTH AFRICAN ECONOMIC CRISIS: Financialisation and deindustrialisation

The process of financialisation occurred on top of an industrial structure dominated by the MEC where the manufacturing sector was inadequately developed and diversified. The infrastructure and institutions of the economy, developed to support the MEC, were not geared towards supporting diversified industrial development. Economic policy choices did not support investments in industry but supported a preference for liquid, financial investments. The inflows of short-term capital to the economy from the mid-1990s led to increased private sector access to credit but this increase was associated with increased debt-driven consumption by households and speculation in real estate and financial asset markets.

Figure 12 shows that acceleration in household consumption from the mid-1990s speeded up even more from 2003. Increased short-term capital flows and increased access to private debt were an important influence on household consumption. Obviously, the trade deficit was negative for years when net flows were positive but we also see a large increase in the trade deficit from 2005 which grew to over 7.5 per cent of GDP in 2008. Household debt to disposable income grew from about 60 per cent in the mid-1990s to almost 80 per cent in 2008 while household savings turned negative in 2005 and remained negative through 2008. It is worth noting that a large proportion of South Africans do not have access to credit and so the average debt to disposable income numbers reported by the SARB may well underestimate the level of indebtedness of more affluent South Africans.

The impact of growth in net acquisition of financial assets and the increased level of household debt-drive consumption are shown in the next few charts. Investment and capital formation has been concentrated in the financial services sector and the services sectors have benefited from increased consumption.

Figure 12: Trends in household consumption, government consumption, investment and trade, 1970-2007 (Real 2000, Rmillions)

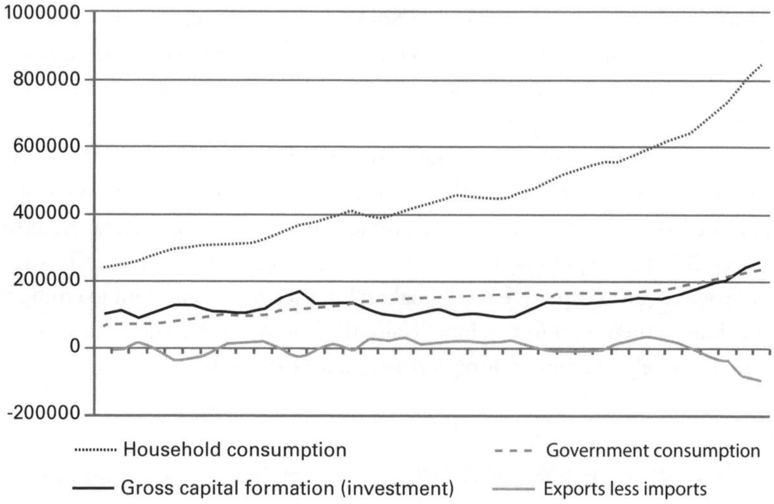

Household consumption
Government consumption
Gross capital formation (investment)
Exports less imports

Source: SARB

Figure 13 shows the top ten sectors by size of investments for 2006 to 2008. The first of these was an important year for increased debt-driven consumption, increasing minerals commodity prices and the growing house and financial asset price bubbles. During 2006, services sectors dominated investment. The other mining sector, largely platinum mining, makes it into the top ten investment sectors, as do two manufacturing sectors, automobiles and components and coke and refined products (investments into Sasol the formerly state-owned company that produces oil from coal). The automobiles and components sector was supported by increased private sector credit that led to a large growth in car sales. Manufacturing sectors do not make it into the top ten investment sectors in 2008 as a result of the declining investment in manufacturing owing to the impact of the global economic crisis.

Figure 14 shows changes in capital stock from 2000 to 2006 for all sectors of the South African economy. The change in capital stock is important to consider because there was an increased level of depreciation write downs during the period (see figure 10). The period from 2000 to 2006 was chosen to show the impact of the 2001 currency crisis and the recovery from 2003; 2007 is excluded because investment performance was affected by the start of the financial crisis. Figure 13 shows that the sectors that benefitted from investment and that had growth in capital stock were services sectors. The largest capital stock growth after general government services was finance and insurance services. Almost all manufacturing sectors had relatively low growth in capital stock or negative capital stock growth. The motor vehicles, parts and accessories sector was the only manufacturing sector that had relatively large growth in capital stock – which occurred because automobiles and components was the only manufacturing sector where government had implemented an industrial policy. It was also supported by the increased access to private credit by households.

Figure 13: Top ten investment sectors for 2006 and 2008

2006 Top 10 sectors by investment (as a % of total investment)

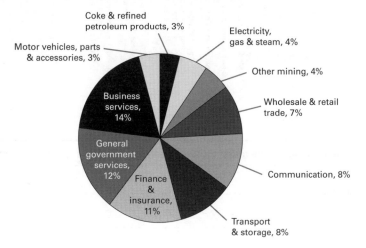

2008 Top 10 sectors by investment (as a % of total investment)

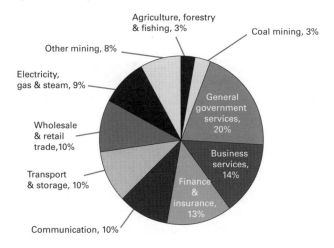

Source: Quantec

Figure 14: Change in capital stock from 2000 to 2006 for all economic sectors (Real 2000 prices, Rmillions)

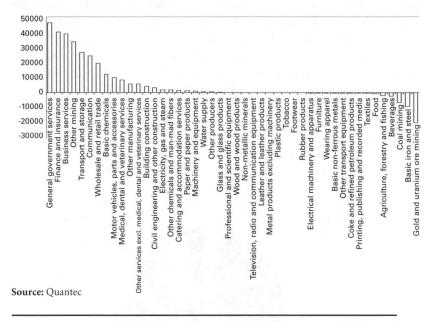

Source: Quantec

Figure 15: Derivative market futures contracts (Rbillions, current prices)

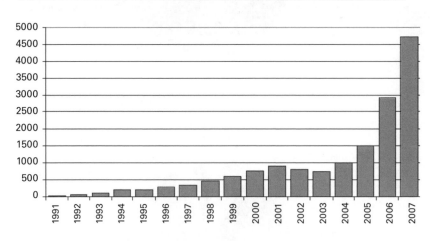

Source: SARB

The South African economy has not only emulated the increased levels of debt, house prices and household consumption in the US economy – our financial sector has also copied the behaviour of its US counterparts by increasing debt and by increasing securitisation of debt. Figure 15 shows the rapid growth of the derivatives market (futures contracts) in South Africa from 2003. There was also huge growth in US and global derivatives markets during this period. Even though the South African financial sector has not had significant direct losses related to the collapse of the subprime market in the US, the South African financial sector could well have been headed towards creating the conditions for a domestic financial collapse.

IMPACT ON WORKERS

During the 1980s, after the new Labour Relations Act (1981) was passed, the black trade union movement had won significant ground in asserting the rights of black workers and had forced significant change to workplace organisation by challenging apartheid workplace forms of control and discipline (Von Holdt 2003, Omar and Webster 2004). The ANC government, on the one hand, implemented neoliberal economic policies set out in GEAR (the Growth, Employment and Redistribution programme adopted by government in 1996), such as inflation targeting, deficit cutting and trade and financial liberalisation. On the other hand, they implemented a progressive new labour relations regime. A number of statutes were adopted once the ANC took power:

- The National Economic Development and Labour Council (NEDLAC) Act of 1994
- The Labour Relations Act of 1995 (LRA)
- The Basic Conditions of Employment Act of 1997 (BCEA)
- The Skills Development Act of 1998
- The Employment Equity Act of 1998
- The Social Plan Act of 1998

These statutes were influenced by the progressive trade union movement's advocacy for high road labour relations that rejected neoliberal notions that South Africa's global competitiveness could be enhanced by lowering wages and increasing labour market flexibility.[8]

The effect of these changes instituted by the new government is summarised by Omar and Webster (2004, p.208):

> The removal of political apartheid has severed the link between the state and racial despotism in the workplace, changing the dynamic between race and class. Indeed, the post-apartheid state is no longer bolstering the racial division of labor. It is intervening through legislation to break down the apartheid workplace regime.

In beginning to address apartheid institutions of control and discipline in the workplace, the democratically elected govenment weakened the power of capital relative to workers. The new legislation indicated that the relationship between the state and business would be different in a democratic South Africa, and that pressure by the trade unions, the majority of the electorate (who are black) and democratic standards would shape institutions in the workplace and labour markets. Unfortunately, the shift to neoliberal economic thinking within the state created a situation where macroeconomic and financial policies favoured big business. Labour may have won the battle for progressive legislation but they seemed to have lost the war for progressive economic policies.

The high level of concentration in the South African economy has not changed as a result of the corporate restructuring of the 1990s and the surge in international mergers and acquisitions (Roberts *et al* 2003). In South Africa, most sectors are dominated by one or two firms that are often vertically integrated. A few large corporations still dominate the economy. On the whole, control of the commanding heights of the South African economy remains in the hands of white capitalists. Since the end of apartheid these capitalists have become more accepted into the global economy and have increased the integration of their businesses with global business.

South African capital adapted to changes in labour relations and its relative loss of power since 1994. Although there has been restructuring of the workplace and improvements for black workers in the largest enterprises, many capitalists have also moved production offshore, limited new investment in the economy, resorted to capital flight, listed on overseas stock exchanges, shed jobs and chosen more capital intensive production methods – and have generally been unwilling to create new jobs.

Business has resisted unions' attempts to democratise firm level decision-making and other efforts to increase worker power. Instead, the unions sought to undermine central bargaining and to bypass the national industry bargaining councils. They increasingly entered into agreements at enterprise level and introduced individualised performance management and reward systems. There has also been an increase in contracting out of services and 'non-core' activities by businesses and they increasingly casualised jobs that had been full-time. In many sectors, including business services, retail services, transport services and footwear and clothing production, there has been growing informalisation.[9]

Outsourcing has been a major strategy for South African big business to address its changing power relationship with capital. Services have been a major contributor to economic growth in South Africa. The shares of finance and business services, trade, catering and accommodation, and transport, storage and communication services have all increased over the past fifteen years. This predominance of services has been interpreted by some commentators in a positive light – as a sign of the maturing of the South African economy and its move to a post-industrial development phase. While services tend to be more labour absorbing, and thus provide a better answer to the high levels of unemployment than an industry-oriented development path, Mohamed and Roberts (2007) argue that the rise in employment in services has been in extremely low-wage activities such as security and cleaning services, meaning that average remuneration has fallen as employment has increased. We argue: '… some of these jobs are a result of the change in classification as such activities are outsourced by, for example, manufacturing firms to independent businesses and are now classified under services' (p.9). Our view is that the increasing role of services in the South African economy is not a sign of economic maturation and is not good for labour. The growth in the importance of services is due to the withdrawal of capital from the economy and the misallocation of capital towards financial speculation, housing price booms and exuberant consumption instead of productive investment.

Tregenna (2008) developed a methodology to analyse outsourcing and related shifts in the sectoral structure of employment. Her rigorous quantitative analysis supports our arguments.

She says:

> The analysis confirms that significant intersectoral outsourcing has taken place in South Africa over the last decade. The focus here is on the outsourcing of cleaners and security guards, away from manufacturing and from the public sector and towards private services. Employment in these two occupations has become increasingly concentrated in the 'other business services' subsector of services in particular, which is where companies that provide services such as cleaning and security to firms across the economy are generally classified (Tregenna 2008, p.33).

Increasing outsourcing of manufacturing and mining jobs has left many more workers with precarious employment, harsher and less safe working conditions, lower wages and reduced benefits.

CONCLUSION

Big business worked closely with the apartheid state to prop up the economy during the politically turbulent 1980s, when community and labour struggles were advancing and international pressure and economic isolation of the economy intensified. The economy was dominated by diversified conglomerates. These large groups bought up the assets of foreign companies that left South Africa. In fact, there seems to have been a reversal of capital flight during this period (Mohamed and Finnoff 2005). After democracy there was huge restructuring of the South African corporate sector, many of the largest conglomerates embarking on a process to increase their international operations and to reduce their South African businesses. In line with the demands of the shareholder value movement, they simplified their corporate structures and increasingly focused on core business activities when they restructured. In short, much of big business had diversified its businesses to reduce their exposure to the South African economy after 1994. At the same time, South Africa had a weak industrial structure focused around a minerals and energy complex because of the political, economic and historical processes that shaped its industrialisation. The corporate restructuring further weakened the industrial structure of the economy.

The economic policies of the new democratic government were aimed at attracting and appeasing foreign finance and investment. It was probably believed that foreign investment would pour into the new South Africa and reshape and modernise the industrial landscape. The economic policies were deliberately neoliberal because it was believed that foreign investors would be attracted to a country where the government was willing to show its credibility by ensuring low inflation and low budget deficits. The government did not adopt or implement an industrial policy to address the industrial structural weaknesses because of the fiscal implications and because their neoliberal policies favoured less state intervention in the economy.

The neoliberal macroeconomic and financial policy choices of the government proved disastrous. The policy choices left them unable to deal with the effects of financialisation and the corporate restructuring and deindustrialisation crisis in the economy. These policy choices further integrated the economy into the global economy and opened it to relatively uncontrolled hot money flows. The surges of hot money into and out of the economy led to volatility in macroeconomic variables such as exchange rates and interest rates and had a huge impact on liquidity in financial markets. The effect of this volatility was to exacerbate the declining interest in long-term, productive industrial investment and instead there was a misallocation of capital towards speculation in real estate and financial markets and debt-driven consumption.

The integration into global financial markets has increased the risk of financial crisis and the vulnerability to contagion from financial problems elsewhere. The weak industrial structure and continued dependence on mining and minerals exports creates a balance of payments risk because imports for consumer goods and capital equipment for mining and infrastructure investment have increased. The large corporations and wealthy South Africans with their liquid and mobile capital are able to respond to macroeconomic volatility and the risk of financial crisis in South Africa by moving their money abroad. The government's policies have made this capital flight easier. Poor South Africans are forced to bear the brunt of the poor economic policy choices of their government. They have lost their jobs or have had the quality of their jobs reduced through outsourcing. They have become more dependent on government grants, such as child support and old age pensions. Unless there is a huge effort to address the industrial decline in South Africa and new economic policies implemented to support industrial growth and transformation, the majority of South Africans will face an increasingly bleak economic future.

NOTES

1   The quote is from the article 'Defaults hit upmarket mortgages', in *Business Day*, 14 May 2009 (available online at http://www.businessday.co.za/Articles/Content.aspx?id=71123). For another report on the state of the property market in 2008 and early, 2009 see 'Auctions reveal the immediate truth and nothing but the truth' published in *Property: The Property Magazine*, available online at http://www.thepropertymag.co.za/pages/452774491/Auctions/09/April/auctions.asp.

2   'Consumers struggle to hold onto their cars', in *Business Day*, 1 April 2009, available online at http://www.businessday.co.za/Articles/Content.aspx?id=62152.

3   '150 000 Consumers under debt review by Christmas', in *Business Day*, 1 September 2009, available online at http://www.businessday.co.za/Articles/Content.aspx?id=80240.

4   The NCR said in November 2009 that on average 80 per cent of new mortgages provided during June 2008 to June 2009 were to people whose gross income was over R15 000 a month.

5   See Terreblanche (2002) for an account of the response of white people and big business to the political changes.

6   For an interesting discussion on the growing influence of institutional investors and the emergence of maximising shareholder value as a 'new ideology for corporate governance' see Lazonick and O'Sullivan (2000, p.13). It is worth noting that the growth in importance of the business media industry and their influence over business structure and executive behaviour is also significant.

7   Mohamed and Finnoff (2005) show that capital flight from South Africa was higher during the period after the democratic elections (1994 to 2000) than it was before the election (1980 to 1993). They argue that mis-invoicing of trade made up a significant share of capital flight, indicating that it was probably big businesses with large export and import volumes involved in mis-invoicing of trade.

8   The central place of workers' struggles in the liberation struggle meant that the demands of the workers for labour relations reform were high on the agenda throughout the negotiations period and when the ANC took control of the government. The labour relations reforms were passed very quickly and by the time GEAR and more conservative policies were accepted, many within the ANC and the new state were giving a sympathetic ear to business when it complained about inflexible labour markets.

9   Omar and Webster (2004) examine the responses of management to changes in labour markets. They draw their conclusions from sociological studies of workplace and managerial changes in the mining industry, footwear manufacturers and call centre operators.

REFERENCES

Aglietta M and R Breton (2001) Financial systems, corporate control and capital accumulation. *Economy and Society* 30 (4).

Business Day newspaper (various editions).

Crotty J (2002) The effects of increased product market competition and changes in financial markets on the performance of nonfinancial corporations in the neo-liberal era. Working Paper no. 44. Amherst: Political Economy Research Institute, University of Massachusetts.

Duménil G and D Lévy (2004) *Capital Resurgent*. Cambridge, MA: Harvard University Press.

Epstein G (2005) Introduction: Financialization and the world economy. In Epstein G (Ed) *Financialization and the World Economy*. Cheltenham and Northampton: Edward Elgar.

Ernst & Young (2006) Mergers and acquisitions: A review of activity for the year 2005. Ernst & Young South Africa (available online at http://www.ey.com/ZA/en/Home).

Fine B and Z Rustomjee (1996) *The Political Economy of South Africa: From Minerals-Energy Complex to Industrialization*. Boulder: Westview Press.

Froud J, C Haslam, S Johal and K Williams (2000) Shareholder value and financialization: consultancy promises, management moves. *Economy and Society* 29 (1): 80-110.

Froud J, S Johal, A Leaver and K Williams (2007) *Financialization and Strategy: Narrative and Numbers*. New York: Routledge.

Goldstein A (2001) Business governance in Brazil and South Africa: How much convergence to the Anglo-Saxon model? *Revista Brasileira de Economia Politica* 21 (2): 3-23.

Lazonick W and M O'Sullivan (2000) Maximizing shareholder value: a new ideology for corporate governance. *Economy and Society* 29 (1): 13–35.

Mohamed S (2006) Capital flows to the South African economy since the end of apartheid. Presented at the Annual Conference for Development and Change, Brazil, December 2006.

Mohamed S (2009) Financialisation, the minerals and energy complex and South African labour. Presented at the Global Labour University Conference, Tata Institute of Social Sciences, Mumbai, India, February 2009.

Mohamed S and K Finnoff (2005) Capital flight from South Africa: 1980-2000. In Epstein G (Ed) *Capital Flight and Capital Controls in Developing Countries*. Cheltenham and Northampton: Edward Elgar.

Mohamed S and S Roberts (2007) Questions of growth, questions of development. *New Agenda: South African Journal of Social and Economic Issues* 28: 37–46.

Nolan P (2003) Industrial Policy in the early 21st century: The challenge of the global business revolution. In Chang H-J (Ed) *Rethinking Development Economics*. London: Anthem Press.

Omar R and E Webster (2003) Work restructuring in post-apartheid South Africa. *Work and Occupations* 30 (2): 194–213.

Orhangazi O (2005) Financialization and capital accumulation in the non-financial corporate sector: A theoretical and empirical investigation. Working Paper 149. Amherst, MA: Political Economy Research Institute, University of Massachusetts.

Presidency, Government of South Africa (2003) Towards a Ten Year Review: Synthesis report on imple-
    mentation of government programmes. Pretoria: Policy Coordination and Advisory Services, The
    Presidency.
Roberts S (2005) Industrial development and industrial policy in South Africa: A ten year review.
    Presented at conference South African Economic Policy Under Democracy – A Ten Year Review,
    Stellenbosch, 28 and 29 October 2005.
Roberts S (2008) Patterns of industrial performance in South Africa in the first decade of democracy:
    the continued influence of minerals-based activities. In *Transformation: Critical Perspectives on
    Southern Africa* 65: 4-35.
Roberts S, N Chabane and J Machaka (2003) Ten Year Review: Industrial structure and competition
    policy. Unpublished mimeograph.
Roux A (1991) Financing economic development in South Africa. Unpublished mimeograph.
Stockhammer E (2004) Financialization and the slowdown of accumulation. *Cambridge Journal of
    Economics* 28 (5): 719-741.
Terreblanche S (2002) *A History of Inequality in South Africa: 1652 – 2002*. Pietermaritzburg: University
    of Natal Press.
Tregenna F (2008) Sectoral engines of growth in South Africa: An analysis of services and manufacturing.
    Working Papers RP2008/98, World Institute for Development Economic Research (UNU-WIDER).
Von Holdt K (2003) *Transition from below: Forging trade unionism and workplace change in South
    Africa*. Pietermaritzburg: University of Natal Press.

CHAPTER 2

The international economic crisis and employment in South Africa

Neva Seidman Makgetla

The international economic crisis had a significant impact on South Africa, with a drop in the GDP and an even larger decline in employment from the end of 2008 through the third quarter of 2009. The impact was greatest in low-income, marginalised sectors – informal, domestic and agricultural workers – and for young adults.

Two aspects made the employment losses particularly harmful. First, South Africa has long faced unusually high joblessness by international standards. Second, the strong decline in employment in low-income sectors aggravated already deep inequalities.

Government's short-run response, which included a counter-cyclical fiscal policy and substantial infrastructure investment, moderated the drop in investment and growth and presumably the loss of jobs. But it did not prevent a significant fall in employment or provide support directly to the self-employed informal and domestic workers who lost their incomes. A central weakness was the failure to address international capital flows, which recovered long before the world economy and propped up emerging economy currencies like the rand. That, in turn, undermined the competitiveness of the economy as a whole, slowing the overall recovery.

More broadly, the crisis pointed to the need to re-think traditional approaches to industrial policies, which still largely shaped South African economic policies. In particular, the space for growth on the basis of expanding exports of manufactures, always quite narrow for South Africa, seemed likely to shrink with the structural changes in the global economy associated with the crisis.

The first section of this paper reviews trends in employment for the year from the end of 2008. The second section describes the context – the high levels of joblessness and inequality that persisted even when the economy was growing relatively strongly before 2008. Section three describes the government response to the crisis as well as the available indications of its impact. The final section reflects on some of the implications for longer-term development strategy.

THE IMPACT OF THE GLOBAL ECONOMIC CRISIS ON EMPLOYMENT

The global economic crisis led to a sharper fall in South Africa's employment than in the GDP. Moreover, the pattern of employment losses tended to deepen inequalities, with a particularly severe impact on marginalised and lower level workers and consequently on Africans and youth.

The international downturn affected South Africa directly through the constraints on the export sectors – mostly the mining value chain, the auto industry and the wood/paper sector – and the higher cost of international credit. As the following chart shows, after a decline of around 3 per cent in the GDP between the last quarter of 2008 and the second quarter of 2009, the economy grew by 1 per cent in the second half of 2009.[1]

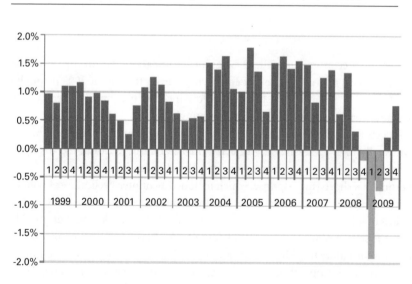

Table 1. Quarterly GDP growth, first quarter 1994 to fourth quarter 2009

Source: Calculated from series on quarterly seasonally adjusted annualised GDP in constant (2005) rand. Statistics South Africa. GDP in excel spreadsheets. Downloaded from www.statssa.gov.za in April 2010.

The percentage drop in employment was significantly larger than the decline in GDP. Moreover, in the third quarter of 2009, while the GDP rose, job losses accelerated, especially in the formal sector. As table 2 shows, employment fell by around a million, or 6 per cent, between the fourth quarter of 2008 and the third quarter of 2009. Half of all job losses, and most of those in the formal sector, occurred in the third quarter of 2009.

Table 2. Employment losses in 2009

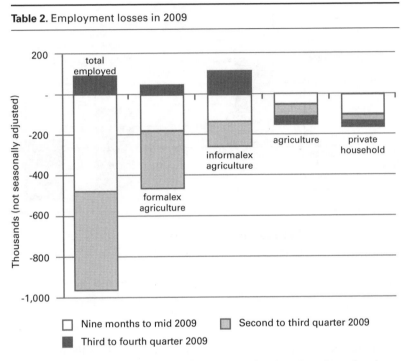

Source: Calculated from Statistics South Africa. *Quarterly Labour Force Survey* for relevant quarters. Table 2. Pretoria. Downloaded from www.statssa.gov.za in April 2010.

In the last quarter of 2009, employment increased by 89 000 or 0.7 per cent, which probably reflected the return to economic growth. The figures were not seasonally adjusted, however, and employment typically increases in December in any case; thus, the increase in employment, while welcome, probably did not herald a strong recovery.[2]

Taken together, informal, agricultural and domestic work contributed only 30 per cent of total employment. That meant job losses in these industries were proportionately far larger than in the rest of the economy, with a decline of more than 10 per cent overall. It appears that many formal employers cut hours and incomes from the start of the recession, although most avoided retrenchments at least until the third quarter of 2009. That, in turn, reduced demand for goods and services from (largely self-employed) informal and domestic workers.

Within the formal sector, job losses affected lower level, low-wage workers most heavily, further adding to the burdens on poor households and communities. As the following table shows, production and elementary workers lost around 10 per cent of all employment, with the steepest decline in the third quarter of 2009.

Table 3. Percentage change in formal employment by occupation, fourth quarter 2008 to third quarter 2009

Fourth quarter 2008 to second quarter 2009
Second quarter 2009 to third quarter 2009

Source: Calculated from series on occupations in Statistics South Africa. Quarterly Labour Force Survey from fourth quarter 2008 to third quarter 2009. Database in SPSS format. Downloaded from www.statssa.gov.za in November 2009.

The crisis had a differentiated impact on the provinces. Gauteng bore the brunt of job losses, accounting for almost half of the decline although it contributed just a third of total employment (with around a fifth of the national population). By contrast, the Western Cape saw relatively low employment losses, especially in manufacturing. This trend presumably arose because manufacturing in Gauteng was largely linked to the mining value chain – refining and smelting downstream, and production of structural steel products and capital goods upstream – while the Western Cape housed light industry and petroleum refineries.

The overall pattern of job losses aggravated racial inequalities. From the fourth quarter of 2008 to the third quarter of 2009, Africans lost 9 per cent of all employment opportunities, while other groups[3] lost 4 per cent.

In part, this trend reflected the relatively high level of African employment in the informal sector and agriculture, which saw particularly sharp employment losses. Only 63 per cent of all employed Africans had formal jobs in the third quarter of 2009, compared to 86 per cent of other groups. Even within formal employment, however, Africans lost 6 per cent of jobs, twice the percentage job losses for other workers. That situation arose for two reasons: on the one hand, production and elementary workers were predominantly African and suffered the largest employment falls, while on the other, more than two thirds of employed people in the Western Cape, which came off comparatively lightly, were non-African.

Table 4. Formal employment loss by race and occupation, fourth quarter 2008 to third quarter 2009

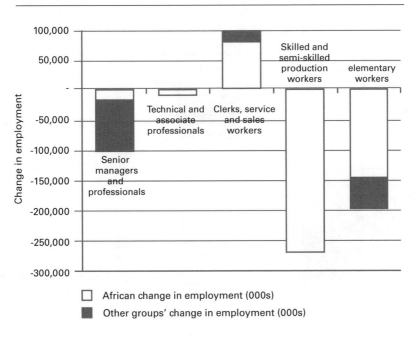

Source: Calculated from series on occupations in Statistics South Africa. Quarterly Labour Force Survey from fourth quarter 2008 to third quarter 2009. Database in SPSS format. Downloaded from www.statssa.gov.za in November 2009.

Women generally fared better than men in terms of employment losses. Some 3 per cent of women lost paid positions between the fourth quarter of 2008 and the third quarter of 2009, compared to 6 per cent for men.

This discrepancy did little to moderate the generally disadvantaged position of black women in the labour market. In the third quarter of 2009, women comprised just 45 per cent of all paid employment, making up only 41 per cent of formal workers and 34 per cent of agricultural workers, but 79 per cent of domestic and 46 per cent of informal workers. Domestic work accounted for 20 per cent of employment for African women.

In the current crisis, the heavy job losses in domestic work had a huge impact especially on younger African women, but they were offset by lower employment losses for women than for men in other sectors. That is partially explained by women's historically weak representation in mining, heavy manufacturing and construction, which were hard hit, and their strong participation in the public services, which did not shed jobs.

Younger workers suffered particularly heavy employment losses. That trend harboured significant risks for social cohesion and for longer-term social and economic development. As table 5 shows, despite job gains in the final quarter, workers under twenty-five saw one employment opportunity in eight disappear in 2009. That compared to around one in twenty jobs lost for older workers.

Table 5. Percentage change in employment by age, fourth quarter 2008 to fourth quarter 2009

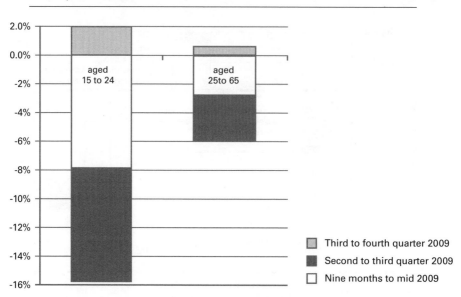

Source: Calculated from Statistics South Africa. *Quarterly Labour Force Survey.*
Relevant quarters.

Heavy job losses among younger workers reflected various factors: the relatively low levels of youth employment in the public sector, which did not lose any jobs; a very sharp drop in paid domestic jobs for workers under thirty; and the general principle in the formal sector of retrenching workers with the shortest service first.

In short, the job losses that resulted from the global economic downturn from the end of 2008 to the end of 2009 generally aggravated the deep inequalities that already characterised the South African economy. They had the deepest impact on low-income workers, especially in marginalised sectors, which in turn meant African communities suffered the harshest impact. In addition, the very high levels of job loss amongst young workers had particularly negative implications for social cohesion and long-term development.

THE CONTEXT: Extraordinarily low levels of employment

Effective strategies to address the job losses resulting from the economic downturn in 2008/9 must be rooted in a broader understanding of the high levels of joblessness that South Africa inherited from apartheid. Unusually high unemployment rates by world standards go hand in hand with low pay for many of those who do find work.

The most common figure used to track joblessness, the unemployment rate, reports the share of working age people who are currently actively looking for income-generating employment as a percentage of both workseekers and the employed. However, where unemployment proves persistently high, as in South Africa, that may understate the actual need for paid employment since many people simply stop looking for work. This section therefore starts by analysing the share of employed people as a percentage of working age adults – which the International Labour Organisation (ILO) calls the employment ratio and Statistics South Africa the absorption rate – which is a more objective indicator of the need for employment.

In the mid-2000s, the employment ratio in South Africa was far lower than the international norm. As the following chart shows, less than half of South African adults had some kind of income-generating employment, compared to two thirds for the world as a whole.

Table 6. The employment ratio in South Africa compared to the international norm.

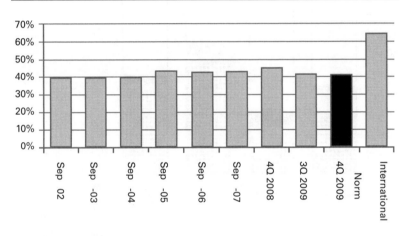

Source: Employment ratio for South Africa calculated from data on employment status in, Statistics South Africa, Labour Force Surveys and Quarterly Labour Force Surveys for the relevant periods. International norm from ILO, '3. Employment Indicators (KILM 2-7)', in *Key Indicators of the Labour Market.* Sixth Edition manuscript. 2009. Downloaded from www.ilo.org in September 2009. No page numbers.

The ILO reported that South Africa ranked among the ten countries in the world with the worst employment ratios. Half of these ten countries were in the Middle East and North Africa, where women were effectively excluded from the labour market. The other countries with employment ratios similar to South Africa were Armenia, Macedonia, Guadeloupe and Puerto Rico (ILO 2009, Section 3, KILM 2).

As table 6 shows, the employment ratio in South Africa improved modestly through the mid-2000s, as economic expansion was associated with a relatively rapid rise in employment. Data before the introduction of the Labour Force Survey[4] (replaced by the Quarterly Labour Force Survey in 2008) are unreliable, so we can only analyse trends from 2002. The downturn in 2008/9 returned the employment ratio to levels last seen in 2004.

The employment ratio reflected inequalities and economic marginalisation associated with race and gender, as the following table shows. In the third quarter of 2009, only 33 per cent of African women had income-generating employment of any kind, compared to 44 per cent of African men and 58 per cent of people in other groups. Moreover, only one in five African women had formal non-agricultural employment, compared to almost a third of African men and half of other people.

Table 7. Employment status by race and gender, third quarter 2009 (figures in parentheses are the employment ratios)

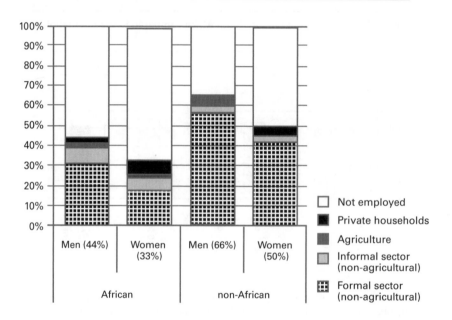

Source: Calculated from data on population group, gender and employment status in Statistics South Africa. Quarterly Labour Force Survey, Third Quarter 2009. Database downloaded from www.statssa.gov.za in December 2009.

Statistics South Africa publishes two figures for the unemployment rate. The 'narrow' or 'official' unemployment rate counts as unemployed only those workers who say they have actively looked for work over the past week. The 'broad' unemployment rate includes people who want income-generating employment but are too discouraged to look for it. As table 8 shows, both the broad and narrow unemployment rates declined through the boom years of the mid-2000s, but increased in 2008/9 as employment levels dropped. The broader rate jumped from 34.2 per cent in the fourth quarter of 2008 to 40.1 per cent in the third quarter of 2009, while the narrow rate climbed from 22.3 per cent to 24,5 per cent. The fourth quarter of 2009 saw only modest improvements.

Table 8. The unemployment rate and the employment ratio, September 2002 to fourth quarter 2009.

Source: Calculated from data on employment status in, Statistics South Africa, Labour Force Surveys and Quarterly Labour Force Surveys for the relevant periods·

Table 9. The unemployment rate by age, September 2002, fourth quarter 2008 and third quarter 2009

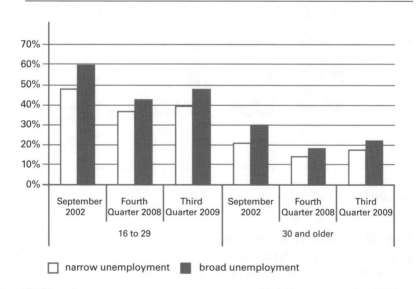

Source: Calculated from data on employment status and age in Statistics South Africa, Labour Force Survey 2002 and Quarterly Labour Force Survey Fourth Quarter 2008 and Third Quarter 2009. Databases downloaded from www.statssa.gov.za in December 2009.

The unemployment rate is more useful than the employment ratio for analysing joblessness among younger people, since it effectively differentiates between students and those who actually want income-generating work. As the following chart shows, the broad unemployment rate for those aged sixteen to twenty-nine dropped from 48 per cent in September 2002 to 37 per cent in the fourth quarter of 2008, but rose to 39 per cent in the third quarter of 2009. The narrow unemployment rate showed similar trends.

Between 2002 and 2008, 3.3 million paid employment opportunities emerged outside mining and agriculture, which shrank. Most of the expansion took place in the tertiary sector. Public and private services, construction and retail together accounted for 78 per cent. Of these sectors, only retail saw substantial job losses in the downturn from the end of 2008 to the third quarter of 2009.

Table 10. Employment by sector, September 2002, second quarter 2008 and third quarter 2009.

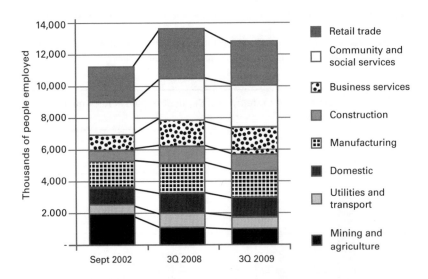

Source: Calculated from data on employment by sector in Statistics South Africa, Labour Force Survey 2002 and Quarterly Labour Force Survey Third Quarter 2008 and Third Quarter 2009. Databases downloaded from www.statssa.gov.za in December 2009.

Most of the employment creation in the mid-2000s also occurred in the formal sector. As a result, informal employment dropped from 18 per cent in 2002 to 16 per cent in the third quarter of 2008, and to 15 per cent in the third quarter of 2009.

The low employment ratio went hand in hand with very low pay in some major sectors, notably agriculture, domestic work, parts of business services and the informal sector. As Table 11 shows, in the third quarter of 2008, some 26 per cent of all workers earned under R1 000 a month.

Table 11. Share of workers earning under R1 000 a month by sector in third quarter 2008

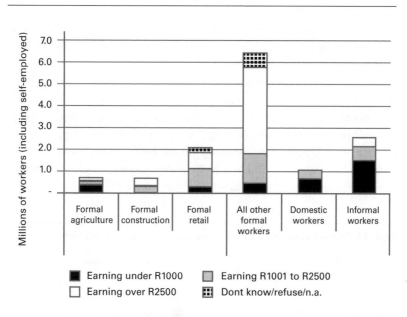

Source: Calculated from data on income groups by sector in Statistics South Africa, Quarterly Labour Force Survey, third quarter 2008. Database downloaded from www.statssa.gov.za in December 2009.

The share of working people earning under R1 000 a month had dropped from almost 40 per cent in 2002, a reflecting real wage growth as well as inflation, in large part due to the introduction of minimum wages in agriculture and domestic work at around R1 000 a month in the mid-2000s. Unfortunately, Statistics South Africa stopped publishing wage data in the Quarterly Labour Force Survey after the third quarter of 2008, so the impact of the crisis on incomes cannot be tracked.

The high levels of joblessness and low incomes for many of those who found work meant that the sharp drop in employment from the end of 2008 had a particularly strong social impact. A major concern was that the bulk of employment loss occurred amongst the working poor, who had the fewest buffers against income loss. Moreover, as discussed below, most of the government's response to the crisis aimed at protecting formal manufacturing and mining employment, with relatively little to assist those in more marginal sectors.

THE NATIONAL RESPONSE

From late 2008, the government responded to the international crisis through a combination of countercyclical fiscal decisions and efforts to support companies and retrenched workers in collaboration with social partners. The evidence available to date suggests that the macro-economic measures were effective in ameliorating the impact of the crisis. In contrast, the microeconomic measures were implemented only after long delays and on far too small a scale to address the unemployment crisis directly. Moreover, the government did not deal effectively with the rapid appreciation of the rand from early 2009, which seemed likely to slow the economic recovery significantly.

The commitment to a countercyclical fiscal policy emerged from the decision to maintain growth in expenditure despite the slowdown in revenues. In the 2009 fiscal year, revenues dropped by 9 per cent but nonetheless, the Treasury maintained expenditure growth at 9 per cent (Treasury 2010) and as a result, the budget deficit reached almost 8 per cent of the GDP.

The adoption of a countercyclical strategy contrasted with the experience in the last severe downturn. In the late 1990s, the Treasury had cut expenditure, which probably aggravated the slowdown as well as causing significant difficulties for the major public services.

Table 12. Change in national expenditure and revenues in real terms (a), 1998 to 2009

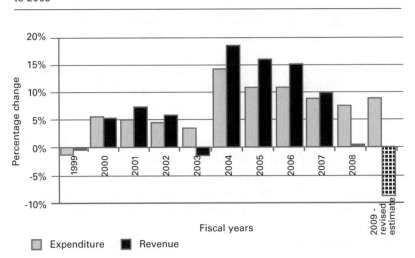

Note: (a) Expenditure and revenues are deflated using CPI. Since the CPI series has changed twice over the period, the figures should be treated as estimates. Source: Data for expenditure and revenue for 1999 to 2008 from Treasury, Budget Reviews, relevant years, Table 1. Data for CPI downloaded from www.statssa.gov.za in 2005 and January 2010. Data on anticipated revenue drop in 2009 from Treasury, *Statement of the National Revenue, Expenditure and Borrowing as at 28 February 2010, Issued by the Director General: National Treasury.* Tables on revenue and expenditure. Downloaded from www.treasury.gov.za in April 2010.

The Treasury called South Africa's fiscal response to the crisis 'among the biggest in the world' (Treasury 2009a, p. 6) but the rapid expansion in spending could not be sustained unless the economy, and revenues, picked up fairly soon. Even so, in order to shrink the budget deficit to 4 per cent of the GDP by 2012, the Treasury planned to increase expenditure by only 1 per cent a year in real terms for the next three years. That contrasted with an average growth in spending of 9 per cent a year in 2006 to 2009 (Treasury 2009a, p. 38).

The risk, in South Africa as around the world, was that the lack of fiscal space after 2010 could limit government's ability to accelerate the recovery or address any renewed downturn. Internationally, this situation may cause a double-dip recession, with a further decline in the global economy as stimulus packages wind down in the course of 2010.

The fiscal response to the crisis centred on carrying out infrastructure investment plans initiated in the mid-2000s. South Africa benefited from the fact that these programmes were planned before the recession started. Expenditure from 2009 to 2011 was expected to split almost evenly between general government and state-owned enterprise, mostly Eskom and Transnet. Altogether, public investment was expected to total almost R270 billion in 2010, and around R300 billion in each of the next two years (Treasury 2009a, p. 44).

As the following table shows, in the year to the third quarter of 2009, a sharp jump in public investment contrasted with a steep decline in private investment. As a result, total gross fixed capital formation climbed 2 per cent in the nine months to mid-2009, although it then fell 1 per cent in the third quarter of 2009. It peaked at 23.7 per cent of GDP in the first quarter of 2009, before the drop in private investment pushed it back down to 22.5 per cent in the third quarter of that year (SARB 2010, p. S-150).

Table 13. Gross fixed capital formation by type of organisation, 1999 to 2009, in constant 2005 prices, annualised and seasonally adjusted

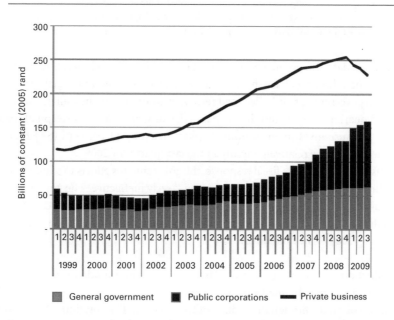

Source: Data on gross fixed capital formation by type of organisation in South African Reserve Bank. Zipped data files on national accounts for the Quarterly Bulletin No 254, December 2009. Downloaded from www.reservebank.co.za in January 2010.

The impact of the expansionary fiscal policy was reflected in GDP and employment trends by sector. Value added in general government and construction combined climbed by almost 5 per cent in 2009, while the rest of the economy shrank by 3 per cent.

Table 14. Change in value added by sector, 2009

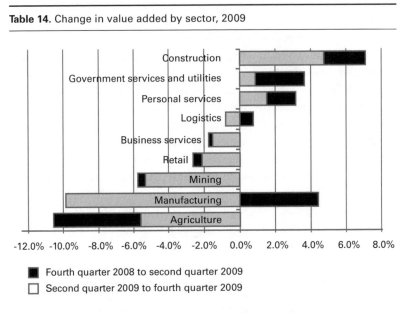

■ Fourth quarter 2008 to second quarter 2009
□ Second quarter 2009 to fourth quarter 2009

Source: Calculated from data on seasonally adjusted value added by industry in constant (2005) prices in Statistics South Africa. GDP data to fourth quarter 2009. Excel spreadsheet downloaded from www.statssa.gov.za in April 2010.

The employment data also pointed to the impact of the stimulus package, although less unambiguously. As the following chart shows, employment in utilities and social services, which were largely in government hands, declined relatively little between the fourth quarter of 2008 and the third quarter of 2009, and then expanded. Construction saw a steep fall for most of 2009, largely because investment in housing plummeted by 11 per cent (SARB 2010, p. S-120). But the sector grew relatively rapidly in the last quarter of 2009.

In contrast to the large scale fiscal response, the government's efforts to support companies and individuals affected by the downturn seemed largely ineffective. The government agreed these measures with organised business, labour and community representatives under the auspices of the National Economic, Development and Labour Council (NEDLAC) in February 2009 (NEDLAC 2009). They included:

- Introduction of a 'training layoff', using sector training funds to support retrenched workers while they obtained a qualification;
- Provision of funds through the Industrial Development Corporation (IDC) to companies facing hardship because of the economic downturn;
- Strategies targeted at stressed sectors;

- Tightening up on illegal imports of consumer goods;
- Encouraging local procurement by government departments and companies; and
- Growth in the national public employment scheme, the Expanded Public Works Programme (EPWP).

Government estimates indicated that these programmes, taken together, created or saved a total of around 100 000 full-time employment opportunities (Zuma 2009) – that is, about 10 per cent of all the opportunities lost by the third quarter of 2009.

Table 15. Change in employment by sector, third quarter 2008 to third quarter 2009

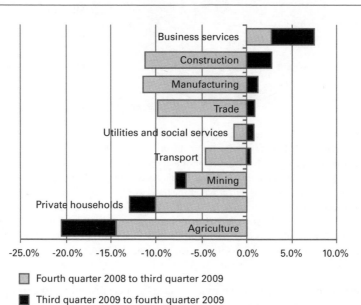

Source: Calculated from data on employment by main industry in Statistics South Africa. Quarterly Labour Force Survey. Third quarters 2008 and 2009. Databases downloaded from www.statssa.gov.za in December 2009.

The IDC set aside R6 billion for the three years from 2009 to 2011, which was supplemented by R2 billion from the Unemployment Insurance Fund. By November 2009 it had extended around R1.5 billion in loans to thirty companies, largely in mining (Nkwinti 2009). In December, the government reported that the IDC had thirty-three applications in the pipeline, for a total of R2 billion, and that it had saved an estimated 7 700 jobs (Zuma 2009). By this estimate, each job saved had cost the IDC around R130 000.

Ensuring local procurement of inputs by the state could potentially compensate companies for the decline in private demand, but in the event, efforts to implement the government commitment in this area proved halting. Attempts to encourage local procurement of inputs for the infrastructure investment programme were burdened by short lead times on many tenders

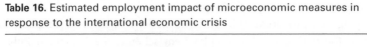

Table 16. Estimated employment impact of microeconomic measures in response to the international economic crisis

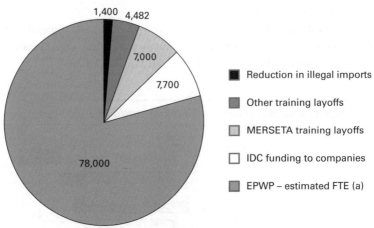

Notes: (a) The EPWP created some 224 000 short-term employment opportunities. The estimate given here reflects past estimates by the programme of the ratio between full-time employment equivalents (FTE) and employment opportunities in the programme. Source: For employment data, President JG Zuma, 'Media statement by President JG Zuma following the report back by the leadership group of the framework response to the economic crisis, Presidential Guesthouse, Pretoria, 3 December 2009'. Downloaded from www.gov.za in January 2010; the ratio between FTE and employment opportunities estimated from Department of Public Works, 'EPWP Report for the Period from April 2008 to March 2009', Annexure A, downloaded from www.epwp.gov.za in January 2010.

as well as the strong rand – factors that made it hard for local producers to gear up to compete. Only in December 2009 did the government officially propose that departments set aside points in the tender process for local procurement (Zuma 2009). Even then, as of early 2010 no formal communication had been sent to departments by the Treasury.

The government also created low level employment opportunities directly through the EPWP. In the first half of 2009, it created 225 000 employment opportunities, the equivalent of about 78 000 full-time jobs. That meant it provided around four out of five of all full-time equivalent positions created under the micro-economic measures in the national response to the crisis. The EPWP was expected to grow to 610 000 full-time equivalents by 2013/4 (EPWP 2010). That target equalled around 10 per cent of all unemployed plus discouraged work-seekers in the third quarter of 2009.

The government response was notable for its failure to address a looming problem: the appreciation of the rand. In the NEDLAC document, the state agreed with the main economic stakeholders on the importance of a competitive currency (NEDLAC 2009, p. 8). Yet in late 2009, the rand was stronger against a trade-weighted basket of currencies than at any time since 2006, although it did not reach the historically strong levels of 2004 and 2005 (SARB

2010, p. S-103). The value of the currency had recovered by about 20 per cent from the beginning of 2009. That, in turn, made it harder for South African producers to compete with imports and on international markets.

Table 17. Trade-weighted value of the rand, monthly average, 2004 to 2009

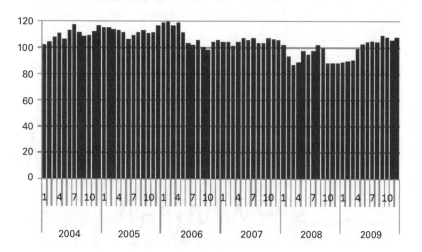

Source: For data through October 2009, series on trade-weighted value of the rand from South African Reserve Bank. Zipped data files for the Quarterly Bulletin No 254 – December 2009. Downloaded from www.reservebank.co.za in January 2010. For data from October 2009, South African Reserve Bank. *Quarterly Bulletin, March 2010.* Page S-78. Downloaded from www.reservebank.co.za in April 2010.

The rise in the rand was mimicked in other emerging markets. It apparently reflected the efforts of the central banks of the global North to stimulate their economies by pumping funds into their economies and restraining interest rates. Institutional investors from the industrialised economies responded by looking to short-term equity and bond holdings in middle-income countries. In the case of South Africa, after an outflow of R5 billion in the third quarter of 2008, inflows climbed to R41 billion in the third quarter of 2009. In nominal terms, that was higher than all except two quarters in the previous twenty years. Inflows fell back to R23 billion in the following quarter – still substantial compared to previous years.

In response to the appreciation in the rand, in late October 2009 the Treasury relaxed some exchange controls. The argument was that this would foster an outflow of capital to offset inflows from the rest of the world (Treasury 2009a, p. 9). As of January 2010, this strategy had not visibly affected the value of the rand, although the trade-weighted data were not yet available. More important, even if it succeeded, South Africa would have traded national resources for short-term, unreliable foreign inflows into stocks and bonds. That outcome seemed likely to make it more difficult in future to mobilise national savings to support developmental investments.

In contrast to the South African strategy, Brazil imposed a 2 per cent tax on investment in equity and bonds, explicitly to deter short-term inflows that were propping up its currency (Silverblatt 2009). In effect, the Brazilian government found that sustained economic growth required a stable and weaker currency more than increased imports fuelled by short-term portfolio investments from abroad.

Table 18. Quarterly capital flows (balance on financial account), first quarter 1990 to third quarter 2009.

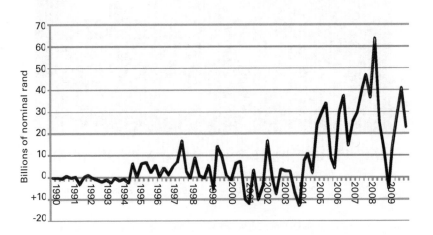

Source: For data through the third quarter of 2009, series on quarterly change in financial account from South African Reserve Bank. Zipped data files on balance of payments for the Quarterly Bulletin No 254 – December 2009. Downloaded from www.reservebank.co.za in January 2010. For the final quarter of 2009, South African Reserve Bank. *Quarterly Bulletin, March 2010.* Page S-103. Downloaded from www.reservebank.co.za in April 2010.

THE CRISIS AND SOUTH AFRICA'S DEVELOPMENT STRATEGY

The international crisis was associated with far-reaching structural changes in the world economy. That, in turn, has implications for South Africa's longer-term development strategy (see Makgetla 2009). In particular, profound shifts in international markets made it seem even less likely that South Africa could grow on the basis of manufactured exports, although that remained the official core of government's industrial policy.

The emphasis on exporting manufactured goods largely shaped the discourse on industrial policy worldwide and in South Africa (see Hausman *et al* 2007). It largely reflected the belief that the rapid economic growth in East Asia from the 1960s was rooted in vigorous industrial policies to support manufacturing for markets mostly in Europe and the US. In South Africa, the Department of Trade and Industry (dti) argued that 'long-term increases in employment – in all sectors of the economy – needs to be underpinned by higher growth in the production sectors of the economy, led by manufacturing', with a strong focus on encouraging tradable goods production in particular (dti 2010, p. 6).

This view of East Asian industrialisation neglected three factors that enabled effective industrial policy there. First, East Asian countries generally enjoyed relative equality and social cohesion (see Campos and Root 1998), which meant both capital and workers were more likely to agree on economic growth as a social panacea. In particular, measures to raise productivity prove more acceptable in economies with high levels of low-wage employment than in economies with low employment, where growth through rising productivity in export sectors actually limits employment creation. Second, the United States provided extraordinary levels of support because it saw the East Asian countries until the 1990s as a bulwark against communism. Finally, over the past half century the region as a whole gradually developed logistics infrastructure and market institutions that vastly reduced the cost of exporting to and communicating with the global North. Obviously, none of these factors applied in South Africa.

The international economic crisis laid bare a fourth obstacle to a growth strategy based on manufactured exports. That strategy explicitly assumed virtually unlimited demand in the global North, and in particular the US. If countries could produce competitively, they would be assured of adequate demand. Yet the downturn of the late 2000s could be understood as a crisis of inadequate demand resulting on the one hand from deepening inequalities in much of the North and on the other from the suppression of wages to support continued exports in much of East Asia, including China, as well as some European countries.

The growing imbalance in demand was reflected in the huge balance of payments surpluses enjoyed by the rapidly growing economies of East Asia. The recycling of those surpluses laid the basis for the credit bubble that led to the financial crisis of late 2008. Once the credit bubble burst, demand for imports by the global North contracted sharply.

The prospects for resuming export-led growth remained unclear at the end of 2009. While economic expansion resumed in China and other Asian economies, exports remained far below the levels of 2008. To replace foreign demand, these countries embarked on extensive programmes to stimulate domestic sales, including subsidies for purchasers of consumer durables as well as huge investments in infrastructure.

These developments had significant implications for South Africa's longer term prospects. Essentially, South Africa participated in the boom of the 2000s by exporting mining products to world markets since the relatively strong rand of the mid-2000s largely blocked manufactured exports (see Hausman *et al* 2007). As noted above, employment growth occurred rather in the services and construction, essentially to meet the needs of the small high-income group and state infrastructure and redistributive programmes. The new international conditions meant that exports of consumer and capital goods faced even higher obstacles than during the boom.

This situation called into question the basic thrust of South Africa's industrialisation policy, embodied as of 2010 in the first and second Industrial Policy Action Plans (IPAP) published by the Department of Trade and Industry (dti 2007 and 2010). For most of the period from 1994, the dti's industrial policy centred on supporting manufactured exports. The first IPAP contained virtually no projects to meet domestic or regional demand or to create employment while raising living standards. The auto industry enjoyed by far the largest subsidies of any industry, with tax relief used mostly to encourage exports. (Barbour 2005) The second IPAP paid greater attention to industries that would meet local demand, both for wage goods and for the infrastructure build programme, but it still maintained a strong emphasis on export-oriented and knowledge-based industries.

In the event, the industrialisation policy proved singularly ineffective. As the second IPAP pointed out, that reflected in part inadequate resourcing and inconsistent implementation. The share of total government spending going explicitly to support agriculture, mining, manufacturing and construction fell from 4 per cent in the mid-1990s to 3 per cent in the mid-2000s.[5] In the 2000s, moreover, the economy's growing dependence on short-term capital inflows led to appreciation of the rand. In these circumstances, exports from the mining value chain, including refined but not fabricated base metals, continued to dominate.

Table 19. Mining in the economy, 1998 to 2008

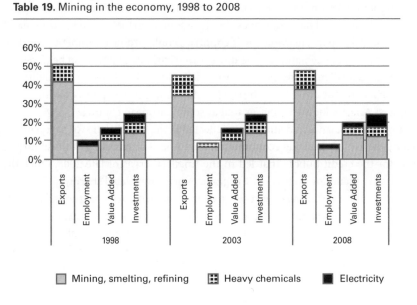

Source: Calculated from standardised industry data in Quantec EasyData. Downloaded from www.quantec.co.za in September 2009.

The structural issues laid bare by the global economic crisis pointed to the need for more innovative approaches to development. A viable growth strategy should focus more on meeting needs in the domestic and regional market, including basic consumer goods and infrastructure effectively funded through the state. In addition, it would have to ensure effective measures to enhance the overall efficiency and inclusiveness of the economy by continuing to improve core economic infrastructure; addressing the serious problems with general education systems serving most black communities; and reducing the cost of living for working people, especially for food, public transport and healthcare. Finally, as the second IPAP noted, it would need to include institutional changes to mobilise domestic resources to fund priority investments while reducing dependence on short-run inflows of financing through the stock and bond markets.

This relatively modest growth strategy might seem second-best to establishing a world-class modern industrial economy. Given the emerging constraints on global demand, however, it was more likely to succeed in laying the basis for sustained growth than a classical export-oriented industrial strategy. Moreover, it would do more to generate opportunities for the majority of southern Africans in the short to medium term, helping to overcome the employment backlogs that the international economic crisis aggravated.

NOTES

1   The media generally reported annualised quarterly falls in GDP, which look significantly larger than the actual drop.
2   The database for the Quarterly Labour Force Survey for the fourth quarter of 2009 was not available at the time of writing, so some elements of the analysis here only go up to the third quarter of 2009.
3   In the third quarter of 2009, the QLFS reported that 9 per cent of South Africans did not report their race, compared to none in the fourth quarter of 2008 and the second quarter of 2009. The increase appears to reflect almost exclusively a decision by whites and to a lesser extent Coloureds and Asians, mostly in relatively senior positions, not to declare their race. Thus, the share of Africans in the total population was reported at 79 per cent for all three quarters, while the share of Coloureds and Asians dropped from 12 per cent in the earlier two quarters to 9 per cent in the third quarter of 2009, and the share of whites dropped from 9 per cent in the earlier quarters to 3 per cent. In addition, the category that did not give race in the third quarter of 2009 had an employment profile similar to that of non-Africans: the employment ratio was 56 per cent, compared to 48 per cent for declared non-Africans; the share in formal employment was 93 per cent, compared to 79 per cent for all non-Africans and 92 per cent for whites; the share employed as senior managers and professionals was 40 per cent, compared to 27 per cent for whites, and 11 per cent for Coloureds and Asians. The employment by industry was not as good a match, however. The non-declared category had a larger share in community, business and financial services and a lower share in manufacturing than non-Africans who gave their race.
4   The survey was piloted in 2001, and can be relied on from September 2002.
5   Data on expenditure by sector from 1995 kindly provided by the national Treasury in 2008.

REFERENCES

ANC (1994) The Reconstruction and Development Programme: A Policy Framework. Downloaded from www.policy.org.za in July 2001.
Barbour P (2005) An assessment of South Africa's investment incentive regime with a focus on the manufacturing sector. London: Overseas Development Institute. Downloaded from www.odi.org.uk in August 2006.
Campos JE and H Root (1996) The Key to the Asian Miracle: Making Shared Growth Credible. Washington DC: Brookings Institute.
Chang HJ (2002) Kicking Away the Ladder: Development Strategy in Historical Perspective. London: Anthem Press.

Department of Trade and Industry (2007) Industrial Policy Action Plan (IPAP). Downloaded from www.dti.gov.za in January 2010.

Department of Trade and Industry (2010) 2010/11 – 2012/13 Industrial Policy Action Plan. Pretoria.

Hausman R *et al* (2007) Final recommendations of the International Panel on ASGISA. Pretoria: Treasury.

International Labour Organisation (2009). 3. Employment Indicators (KILM 2-7). In *Key Indicators of the Labour Market*. Sixth edition manuscript. Downloaded from www.ilo.org in September 2009. No page numbers.

Makgetla N (2009) The International Economic Crisis and South Africa. *New Agenda* No. 36.

National Economic Development and Labour Council (2009) Framework for South Africa's response to the international economic crisis. Downloaded from www.info.gov.za in January 2010.

Nkwinti G (2009) Briefing notes for the economic sectors and employment cluster Programme of Action (PoA) media briefing by Minister of Rural Development and Land Reform, G Nkwinti. 10 November 2009. Downloaded from www.gov.za in January 2010.

South African Reserve Bank (2010) *Quarterly Bulletin December 2009*. Downloaded from www.reserve-bank.co.za in January 2010.

Silverblatt R (2009) Brazil to Tax Foreign Investors. *Fund Observer*, 20 October. Downloaded from www.usnews.com in January 2010.

Treasury (2009a) Medium-Term Budget Policy Statement 2009. Downloaded from www.treasury.gov.za in October 2009.

Treasury (2009b) Budget Review 2009. Downloaded from www.treasury.gov.za in February 2009.

Zuma JG (2009) Media statement by President JG Zuma following the report back by the leadership group of the framework response to the economic crisis, Presidential Guesthouse, Pretoria, 3 December 2009. Downloaded from www.gov.za in January 2010.

CHAPTER 3

The economic impact of South Africa's 2010 World Cup:
Ex ante ambitions and possible *ex post* realities

Scarlett Cornelissen

———•———

The significance of South Africa's hosting of the nineteenth Fédération Internationale de Football Association (FIFA) World Cup in mid-2010 extended far beyond the fact that it would be the first time that this mega-event would be hosted on the African continent. It was rather that the World Cup, because of its size and the capital investments that were required to host it, held a number of long-term implications for economic and social development in South Africa. Over the years many expectations had been raised by the country's leaders of the event's effects on employment and growth; concomitantly, extensive financial commitments had already been made by public authorities. The central question is therefore how such investments and the infrastructural developments that were undertaken for the World Cup were consonant with broader economic processes in the country, and what the legacies of the tournament would be for South Africa's political economy. What lessons, in this regard, could be taken from similar sport mega-events hosted in other locations? This chapter evaluates the *ex ante* projections and potential *ex post* impacts of the tournament against the practices, experiences and principles derived from the study of sport mega-events in other parts of the world. It reviews the main economic and sectoral changes that have been made in recent years for the hosting of the World Cup and considers what some of their long-term economic legacies – and their related socio-political fall-outs – may be.

The first part of the chapter is conceptual in nature. It contextualises both the nature and the economic dimensions of sport mega-events in the contemporary era and reviews the varied legacies – infrastructural, economic and sectoral – of such events. It gives an overview of the various scholarly perspectives on the measurement of impact and considers some of the methodological and other drawbacks in established impact assessment practice. The second part of the chapter reviews the projections that have been made about the 2010 World Cup's likely impacts and the macroeconomic, infrastructural and sectoral investments which were undertaken. A concluding section considers some of the principal prospects and challenges that the World Cup posed for South Africa.

SPORT MEGA-EVENTS AND THEIR LEGACIES

The FIFA World Cup is an archetypal first-order mega-event: that is, it is a large-scale and prestigious sports competition among elite athletes held on a regular and rotational basis in different locations across the world. Sport mega-events are marked by the high levels of interest they evoke internationally; the resultant high levels of spectatorship they draw; and the volumes of corporate investments – and revenues – that they can command. In terms of revenue, the FIFA World Cup is the largest sport mega-event, closely matched by the Olympic Games. The World Cup differs from the Olympics in that it is a multi-site (or multi-city) tournament. Both are however global media festivals with major economic importance for sport and non-sport stakeholders. The 2004 Summer Games in Athens drew an estimated television audience of 3.9bn viewers and a cumulative audience of 40bn (Horne 2008). The 2006 FIFA World Cup hosted by Germany, by contrast, had a cumulative television audience of 26.3bn (FIFA 2006). As an indication of the extended 'mediatising' of sport mega-events in recent years, the sale of global television rights for the 2006 FIFA World Cup generated US$1.97bn in revenue for FIFA, six times the value of television receipts for the World Cups hosted in the 1990s (Horne 2008). Television sales for the 2010 World Cup were worth just over US$2bn, causing it to be the most profitable tournament thus far for the FIFA federation.

It is not only the commercial scope, but also the size of sport mega-events that has grown over the years. Seven new sports were added to the Summer Olympics, for instance, between 1980 and 2000, so that the programme of the Games today consists of twenty-eight different sports.[1] A decade ago the number of national teams participating in the FIFA finals was expanded from twenty-four to thirty-two, extending not only the geographical representation but also international interest in, and the reach of, the tournament. The programme and format of the FIFA tournament was concomitantly broadened, so that since 2002 sixty-four matches are played over a four-week period.

Sport mega-events are defined by their scale and the opportunities they present to hosts and corporate sponsors for profiling and promotion. There has been growing enthusiasm over the past number of decades to host such events – which has much to do with the desire by public (particularly urban) authorities to catalyse local regeneration through the expansion of service-led consumer-based industries. It is notable therefore that many of the recent hosts of the Olympic Games (such as Barcelona, Atlanta, Sydney and Athens) and the smaller-order Commonwealth Games (in particular Manchester and Melbourne) have aligned their hosting of the event with other infrastructural and sectoral developments aimed at stimulating, variably, local culture industries, sports tourism economies or local business (also see Euchner 1999; Harvey 1989). Strategies toward re-imaging or re-branding are generally a key part of cities' mega-event campaigns (see A Smith 2005 and Smith & Fox 2007).

It is worth noting that the ambition to use mega-events to rejuvenate urban economies is also common to hosts from the developing world. Cape Town's bid for the 2004 Olympic Games, for instance, intended to use the city's staging of the event as a platform to stimulate development across the city, to help foster physical integration by means of new transportation and other infrastructure linkages, and to boost foreign and domestic tourism (see Swart and Bob 2004). Kuala Lumpur, host to the 1998 Commonwealth Games, sought to use its staging of the event *inter alia* to advance the diffusion of technology in the city (Dobson and Sinnamon 2001). However, there are some significant differences in the motives for holding a mega-event between aspiring hosts from the developing world, and those from the developed world, that can influence how they view and design events. In the cases of the 2008 Beijing and 1988 Seoul Olympics, for example, the Games were as much aimed at displaying the host city's features to the outside world as they were intended to demonstrate national achievements. To a significant extent the Beijing 2008 Games were designed to represent 'the shop window for a Chinese economy that is experiencing record growth rates and one that seeks international recognition for its relatively recent re-entry into the world economic system' (Poynter 2006: 6). While an important concern for the Chinese authorities, boosting Beijing's local economy was not the prime motivation for their staging of the Games (also see Brownell 2008). The city nonetheless benefited by new and upgraded infrastructure, most prominently the newly built Olympic stadium, the refurbished international airport and the new rapid rail connection to the neighbouring city of Tianjin.

In general, therefore, hosts from the developing world seek to use mega-events to stimulate local economic development (mostly coupled with wider national objectives which could range from boosting macroeconomic growth to providing dynamism to national tourism economies) or to achieve greater exposure for the nation-state and its foreign policy (also see Black 2008). Host cities from the developing world also differ from their counterparts in the developed world in that they aim for widespread development, rather than targeted regener-ation of specific, dilapidated local areas (such as London's aim to regenerate its impoverished East End with the staging of the 2012 Olympics). These nuances in economic ambitions and the way they shape developing and developed countries' and cities' hosting of mega-events, or the extent to which these influence economic legacies, have not yet been studied in system-atic detail (Cornelissen 2009a).

Although contexts may differ and there are local variations among hosts it is possible to identify a number of common legacies from sport mega-events. These include tangible and intangible impacts which may be grouped into primary and secondary legacies in terms of the short-, medium- and long-term consequences of events on aspects such as infrastructure, design, image and tourism, and governance structures. Primary legacies relate to the effects on a given city or region which could be directly attributed to its hosting of an event. These generally refer to the development of event-specific infrastructure such as competition venues, stadiums and event tourist lodgings and other facilities to accommodate visitors. Secondary legacies are the indirect and induced effects that stem from wider infrastructural investments made in anticipation of, or contingent on, the event and that provide the substance to subsequent development trajectories in the host location. These could include changes in infrastructure, including transportation networks and nodes; alterations in the design of a city; changes to the built and physical environment; and the establishment of new sporting venues that have the potential for post-event utilisation (see for example Cashman 2006). Stimulation of tourist arrivals after the event could also be classed as secondary legacies. The two kinds of legacies are of course interwoven. By the nature of urban economies, for instance, infrastructural development of any kind has an impact on the wider economy. This is even the case for stadiums or other sporting venues, for they lock into the particular infrastructure matrix that exists in the host city (Bale and Moen 1995). Similarly, transportation is a basic infrastructure, which means that even if transport links are developed for the specific purposes of an event, they will have ramifications for the wider urban or regional setting.

Poynter (2006) provides further breakdown of the secondary legacies of mega-events stemming from investments that are not exclusively event-related. Such investments include infrastructure development (transport, telecommunications, sport facilities), environmental improvement (decontamination, water usage, parklands), housing, parks, and the contribution to what has been termed the 'urban culture' (which includes leisure, entertainment and recreation facilities).

Measuring event legacies

If there is general consensus among researchers that hosting a mega-event can leave a range of material, spatial and symbolic legacies, there is less agreement on the factors determining whether such legacies are of a positive or negative nature, or on their duration. In part this is due to the unique character of these events. They are spatially and temporally highly distinct from other forms of sports consumption (such as participant-driven, amateur or more regular sporting competitions) or other types of spectacles (such as exhibitions) from which economic income may be derived. Wright (2007: 346) aptly distinguishes mega-events from sporting contests organised on a more permanent, albeit smaller, scale by declaring that '(e)ssentially, they are based specifically on what is happening as opposed to what is available'. First, mega-events are once-off occurrences, and planning for them has to be tailored to a deliberate point of closure. Second, the time limit placed on not only the hosting, but also activities related to infrastructure development or the design of key sites is often used as rationalisation by event authorities for circumventing statutory procedures or evading consultation with affected communities (Horne and Manzenreiter 2006). That events are essentially 'owned' by the sports federations in whose name they are staged lessens the influence event authorities have over central aspects of organising, but can also cause those authorities to take hasty and opaque decisions. Far from yielding to long-term developmental visions, the limited time frames involved in the hosting of a mega-event tend to encourage swift and centralised decision-making that may deviate from long-existing growth programmes in a host city or country (Owen 2002). Fitting event planning into established urban or macroeconomic programmes has been a challenging enterprise for many hosts (see for example Hiller 2000).

Finally, mega-events are in spatial terms relatively fixed occurrences. Although elite-level competitions may be held in different sites across one city or country, such sites are spatially well contained, with mobility in and around the venues highly regulated. As spaces of consumption, and sites where economic activity can be stimulated, competition venues generally involve the limited and controlled circulation of capital extra to that generated by the sponsors and corporations aligned with the proprietor sports federation. The spatially concentrated nature of mega-events can also affect the long-term sustainable prospects of a host area, since positive, but also detrimental, effects can remain geographically focused (Frey, Iraldo and Melis 2007).

Three additional challenges in mega-event legacy appraisal relate to the variety of methodologies that are often used to measure impacts; the lack of agreement among researchers about which forms of investments should be considered part of an event's costs and which as part of its revenues; and the way in which different economic sectors are differently affected and therefore manifest different legacies.

The variation in the sectoral legacies of mega-events is well illustrated in the case of the tourism sector. It is generally assumed that tourism stands to gain most from the hosting of a sport mega-event. This stems from the nature of the tourism sector itself, which is composed of numerous different industries including industries central to tourism activities, such as (air and overland) transport, accommodation and tour operator sectors, and those which are not central to, but support or are affected by tourism activities, most notably construction, retail and other leisure industries. The compound composition of tourism is generally thought to be an important asset of the tourism sector, since it means that the potential for generating income is heightened and that the effects filter through to all core and related industries – the so-termed multiplier effect of tourism (Mathieson and Wall 1982; Smith 2000). However, numerous commentators have noted that negative effects – such as visitor displacement – can also emanate from the hosting of a major event. An oft-cited example is the 2002 FIFA World Cup hosted by Japan and South Korea, where tourist arrivals declined in the year of the tournament (Horne and Manzenreiter 2004). Indeed, Lee and Taylor (2005) suggest that arrivals to South Korea may have fallen short by more than one-third of pre-event predictions. The 2006 FIFA World Cup held in Germany drew a great number of spectators (3 407 000, outranked in this only by the number of visitors to the 1992 FIFA World Cup in the USA where stadiums were of a larger capacity (FIFA 2006)) but there are some indications that major markets within Germany's overall tourism economy, such as business tourism, saw a decline during the tournament year (Preuss, Kurscheidt and Schütte 2007: 8).

The potential deflation of established tourism markets during a major sports tournament stems in part from a common failure by event planners or their consultants to adequately profile prospective visitors and to sufficiently tailor tourism development plans towards what amounts to a very specific type of tourist market. Instead, the inclination has been to view sports tourist arrivals to major events as incidental or additional consumers. This is problematic for two reasons. First, it pre-empts a more precise assessment of the tourism impact of a given event. Crompton (2001) notes how the methodological practice to include in event impact studies all tourist visitation during a sports tournament, instead of only that stimulated by the event itself, is a habitual but inaccurate one, leading to routine impact over-estimation. Second, the travel behaviour and consumption patterns of sports tourists are often very different from those of other tourist markets. Such tourists, for whom sport is the primary motivation for travel, may have little interest in making use of other tourist facilities or attractions beyond their own needs (Higham 2005). In the main therefore, while the tourism flow generated by sport mega-events can be substantial, can prompt new infrastructure to arise, and can induce the development of new markets which can be nurtured over the longer term, it can also be offset by its selective nature. Even though events may create net tourism benefits for a host, this often accrues some years after the event was hosted. Few pre-event assessments take this time lag into account (see for instance Cashman 2006).

In terms of assessing the overall economic impacts of sport mega-events, pre-event appraisals used during bid campaigns often wittingly or unwittingly overestimate a given event's potential economic consequences. This is often the case where bid campaigners have an interest in highlighting an event's benefits above possible costs, and is often caused by the methodologies used: economic multipliers tend to be inflated; gross economic output is wrongly equated with event impacts; and the legacy footprint of an event is projected to extend over an implausibly large geographical area (Crompton 1995; Matheson 2008). Often too, pre-event impact studies either underplay or miscalculate the costs associated with the hosting of an event, commonly neglecting to include aspects such as expenses incurred from the start of bid processes (Gibson 1998). Many other hidden costs may surface during an event itself, or in its immediate aftermath, leading to significant mismatches between *ex ante* projections and *ex post* assessments. Frequently, the reason is that public authorities regard capital investments on infrastructure as a benefit and not a cost. While it is the case that newly constructed roads and upgraded transport systems can help bolster wider economic production, it is often not understood that these infrastructural developments represent capital deviated from other projects, or increases in government borrowing which in the absence of the mega-event would not have been incurred. More thorough assessments of event expenditures should therefore try to calculate the implications of such opportunity costs for the macroeconomy, the consequences of the possible reduction of tax bases, and the costs that servicing an event place on local economies.

Ideally, the effects, benefits and costs of events should be assessed during four phases: the bid preparation and process period (which in the case of the Olympics and the FIFA finals could range between two and four years); the five- to seven-year period during which preparations towards the event take place; the short period (two to four weeks) during which the event is held; and the more extensive post-event period. Preuss (2004) suggests that in the case of the Olympic Games secondary legacies are influenced by the scale and extent of pre-event infrastructure investments: where the period of investment is longer, the period of impact is extended, in Preuss's assessment for up to eighteen years. Even so, the condition of the wider national economy can promote or brake positive stimulatory impacts on the host economy. Preuss provocatively contends that a prolonged period of impact could also have negative repercussions for a host city and the national economy, in the case of rapidly expanding economies contributing to rising property prices in the long run.

Mega-events have also been associated with other negative social and environmental legacies (Waitt 2003) including forced evictions, particularly of poorer, inner-city residents in some

North American cities, the redirection of public funds from programmes such as housing delivery, and the over-securitisation of host cities (see for example CORHE 2007; Lenskyj 2008).

In all, it is a serious indictment of sport mega-events that most credible *ex post* and longitudinal studies show that their effects on employment and wages are limited and of a temporary nature, and that they are of negligible consequence for hosts' macroeconomies (see for example Allmers and Maennig 2008; Baade and Matheson 2004; Preuss 2004; Szymanski 2002). Indeed, many economists consider sport mega-events poor stimulants to economic development (see Coates and Humphreys 2002; Porter 1999). At worst, an event could leave long-term deficits and public debt from which hosts could only emerge several years after the event has come to an end (the most notorious example is the 1976 Olympic Games, which left the authorities of Montreal with a debt which they only managed to repay thirty years later). Possibly one of the strongest predictors of how a host could be affected in the future relates to the set of governance relationships that exists there, and the management structures that are set up to stage an event. In this regard Poynter (2006) notes that in those cases where greatest positive legacy has been achieved – such as Barcelona from its hosting of the 1996 Summer Games – the city bid 'related to an existing urban development plan' (Poynter 2006). Greatest success therefore stems from using events to fit into previously developed programmes, and not 'retrofitting' programmes into event objectives.

THE 2010 FIFA WORLD CUP: Projections, preparations and prospects

South Africa's hosting of the 2010 FIFA World Cup should be understood within the emergent international political economy of sport mega-events and in terms of the relationship between sport and politics in the country in the post-apartheid era. As suggested, there has been the stronger commercialisation of large-scale sports events over the years, which in turn helped place an economic premium on the hosting of such events for national and urban governments across the world. Against this background, it is useful to regard South Africa's hosting of the World Cup as the culmination of an extended strategy by the government to use sports events to position the country more prominently in the international arena. This was mostly aimed at drawing foreign direct investment and enhancing the country's status as a tourist destination. Indeed, since the end of apartheid, South Africa had bid for a significant number of high profile sports events. In 1992 the city of Cape Town put in a bid to host the 2004 Olympic Games. The city failed in its Olympic bid, but there has been speculation that another South African city, Durban, may bid for the 2020 Games. In 1995, South Africa hosted the Rugby World Cup and in 1996 the country provided the venue for the biennial continental football championship, known as the Africa Cup of Nations. Then, in 1999, South Africa hosted the All Africa Games and two further world championships in 2003 – the International Cricket Council's World Cup, and the Women's World Cup of Golf. However, securing the rights to host the 2010 FIFA World Cup was a particular victory for South Africa's bid campaigners, since this presented a unique opportunity to showcase the country on the world stage (for reviews see Cornelissen and Swart 2006).

But the pursuit to host sports events has also been underpinned by a second rationale on the part of South Africa's leaders, which relates to the powerful connection which has historically existed between sport and politics in the country and the role that sport plays in the socio-cultural imaginary. Since the political symbolism that has surrounded the Springboks' victory of the 1995 Rugby World Cup, sport has gained significance as a means of helping to overcome racial differences and as a vehicle for redress in the post-apartheid era. This has been a strong and consistent element of the government's pronouncements on the 2010 World Cup. As an illustration, Makhenkesi Stofile, the minister of sport stated that:

> (T)he awarding of the 2010 World Cup host to South Africa by FIFA is a legacy on its own. For South Africa and the rest of Africa, the memory of that tournament will be a lasting legacy. But we cannot end there … (We) believe that preparations for the 2010 World Cup must leverage the fast-tracking of some elements of our transformation agenda … (We) must use this opportunity to level the proverbial playing grounds, both in respect of infrastructure and otherwise (Stofile 2007).

Macroeconomic projections

An economic argument about the potential effects of the World Cup was an important part of political leaders' efforts to gain domestic support for the bid. Since the launch of the initial bid a number of years ago, estimations of the likely effects of the 2010 tournament on the South African national economy were to see some significant revision. In 2003, Grant Thornton, the consulting company contracted by the South African 2010 Soccer World Cup Bid Company to appraise the World Cup's long-term consequences, produced a study on the event's potential economic legacy. The company assessed direct expenditure by four sources: spend at the event by domestic and international spectators; trip spend by spectators, teams and their entourages, the media, sponsors and FIFA office bearers; other spend on merchandising and concessions; and capital expenditure on infrastructure and stadiums. Using cost-benefit analysis, the company projected that the tournament would produce direct expenditure by spectators of R12.7bn, that it would contribute R21.4bn to the gross domestic product and create an additional R7.2bn in government taxes, and that the event would generate the equivalent of 159 000 annual jobs (although it was unspecified how many of those jobs would be permanent or temporary/seasonal and at which levels they would be created). The study anticipated that the direct cost of the World Cup, mainly arising from expenditure on the upgrade of stadiums and infrastructure, would be (a rather modest) R2.3bn (see Grant Thornton 2003).

In 2008 and again in 2010, shortly before the start of the tournament Grant Thornton updated the initial forecasts based on revised data, their more recent analyses showing some significant variation from preliminary assessments (see Grant Thornton 2008; 2010). Table 1 details projected costs and benefits from the studies.

From the table it is clear that expectations for 2010's macroeconomic impacts were to rise significantly, with national income anticipated from the tournament subsequently becoming more than double the volume projected in initial assessments. Yet there were some major deficiencies in these projections. The most important related to the identification and balancing of costs versus benefits. The cost-benefit methodology used by Grant Thornton is widely used in mega-event impact studies and because of its relatively easy and saleable format disseminates well in pro-event and political circles. This methodology has however been criticised by many sports economists for its potentially flawed assessment of the true costs of hosting an event, in particular its predisposition to consider money spent on infrastructure improvement (including development of stadiums) as a form of income, rather than a cost. As suggested above, construction costs for the development of infrastructure related to a sport mega-event can variously place additional strain on a national or regional economy, can drain resources from surrounding areas and, if materials or labour need to be imported, may constitute a source of revenue leakage. As such, while they may have obvious benefits, infrastructure upgrades are more appropriately considered an opportunity cost and should be factored in to impact assessments in that way (see Matheson 2008 for a lucid discussion).

From table 1 it is evident that the Grant Thornton study did not do this, projecting for instance in 2008 potential total impact of R55bn from the World Cup (which was revised upward to R93bn in their 2010 study). This is based on the misleading inclusion of expenditure

Table 1. Changes in official projections of impacts of 2010 World Cup

	2003	2008
Benefits (income)		
Contribution to GDP	R21.4bn	R55bn
consisting of:		
➢ stadium & infrastructure upgrade		➢ R33bn
➢ sale of match tickets		➢ R6bn
➢ trip spend by spectators		➢ R8bn
➢ sponsorship		➢ R750m
Additional tax income	R7.2bn	R19bn
Costs		
Upgrade of stadiums and infrastructure	R2.3bn	R33bn
Other impacts		
New employment	159 000	415 000
Foreign (overseas) tourist arrivals (number)	235 000	480 000
➢ consisting of African tourists (number)	45 300	150 000
Tourism receipts		R8.5bn
International media presence (number)	10 500	18 000
Major development projects (unspecified and unquantified)		

Source: Grant Thornton 2003; 2008

on stadium upgrades (R33bn) as part of the event's contribution to GDP and was therefore an inflated estimate of the event's income potential. If anything, escalation in stadium construction costs was to become one of the more worrisome features of World Cup preparations. By the end of 2008, for instance, budget overruns for stadium construction – caused by a variety of factors, including high international prices for construction material such as cement – was estimated at R3.2bn (*Business Day* 2 December 2008). By the time the FIFA tournament took place, expenditure on the upgrade and construction of stadiums was considerably more than the money initially committed by the national government as part of its World Cup investments.

Two additional problems with the Grant Thornton estimations are first, the anticipated fiscal and employment contributions of the World Cup, and second, the projected tournament tourist visitation. In an earlier critique, Bohlmann (2006) cautioned that the impact and employment multipliers used by Grant Thornton tended to be over-optimistic in comparison with other impact studies carried out for similar events. It was also not specified in the Grant Thornton studies whether the projected employment stimulated by the tournament would be long- or short-term or how the jobs would be affected by seasonal variation in demand. From other studies it has been shown that, while revenues may increase in specific sectors (such as accommodation) for the short period during which a tournament takes place, wages remain the same or – since there is often a sharp rise in casual employment in that time – may fall. Employment multipliers used in many *ex ante* studies often do not take these processes into account and therefore tend to be exaggerated (Matheson 2008). No comprehensive study has yet been done on the leakage and income attrition effects of construction for the 2010 tournament on the national economy. Notably, however, early post-event assessments suggest that employment in the construction sector fell sharply – by more than 10 per cent – after the completion of World Cup infrastructure (Sapa 22 June 2010).

Finally, there was to be much dispute about whether the 2010 World Cup would draw the numbers of tourists estimated by South Africa's tourism authorities (see for example Cornelissen 2009b). By the close of the tournament, over one million foreigners had visited South Africa during the four-week period, representing a year-on-year increase of 25 per cent (or 200 000) additional tourists, but still significantly short of the close to half-million foreign visitors initially projected. No systematic study was conducted by the authorities that profiled World Cup visitors in terms of football spectators' specific travel habits, nor did broad projections of expected tourist arrivals take possible displacement or crowding-out effects adequately into account.

In expectation of the World Cup's projected economic effects, the national government undertook to spend more than R400bn over the four-year period between 2006 and 2010, as part of a much larger capital investments programme to develop infrastructure, upgrade ports of entry, roads and railway lines and secure the provision of energy (Manuel 2007; and see table 2). At the end of the tournament, public investments stood at around R600bn. Although only R21.6bn of this (R11.8bn for the development of transport and other infrastructure and R9.9bn for the construction and improvement of the competition venues) was regarded by the government as its direct expenditure on the World Cup, it should be kept in mind that these investments would not have been made in the absence of the tournament. As such, the R600bn should properly be viewed as part of the World Cup expenditure legacy.

Table 2. Spending commitments by the national government relevant to the World Cup, 2006-2010

World Cup specific spending	Value
Infrastructure	
➤ Stadium upgrades and construction	R8.4bn
➤ Transport and other infrastructure	R9bn
Non-infrastructure investments	
➤ Volunteer, social/community development & sport development	R379m
➤ World Cup opening & closing ceremonies	R150m
➤ Security surveillance & deployment/training of security personnel	R666m
➤ Upgrade of telecommunications & improvement of emergency medical services	Unspecified
Capital investments not directly related to the 2010 World Cup	
comprising construction and upgrade of national road networks; airports; harbours; energy supply	R400bn+

Source: Manuel 2007 & www.sa2010.gov.za/en/funding.

The positive aspect of this is that, as part of World Cup preparations, public investment was made on much needed infrastructural programmes. A significant portion of the R400bn+, for instance, was dedicated to the upgrade of South Africa's dated road network (of which the South African National Roads Agency was the principal beneficiary) and the improvement of public transport. Other investments concerned the extensive upgrading of all international and some regional airports (which tally in excess of R19bn). Yet these investments constituted approximately one-tenth of South Africa's annual gross domestic product (estimated at purchasing power parity), and represent, over the longer term, a substantially higher cost for the tournament than what was spent by the German authorities for the 2006 World Cup (approximately R72bn). By way of further comparison, the 2008 Beijing Olympic Games cost about R196bn and was the most expensive Summer Games ever hosted in the history of the modern Olympics.

While the intention of South Africa's authorities therefore was to use the 2010 World Cup to stimulate new large-scale developments in the country, it came at a prohibitive cost, and was made without guarantee that the tournament would deliver on many of the projected economic spin-offs.

Infrastructural and urban costs, impacts and legacies

While the national government was the principal shareholder and investor in the World Cup preparations, provincial and urban authorities also held major stakes in the tournament. Indeed, many of the costs for stadium upgrades and World Cup specific transport were borne by host cities and their provincial governments.

For the 2010 World Cup much emphasis was placed on the timely development or preparation of three types of infrastructure: the competition venues and stadiums; transportation; and tourist accommodation. Of the ten stadiums that were used for World Cup matches, six were newly built or refurbished (in the host cities of Cape Town, Durban, Johannesburg (Soccer City stadium), Port Elizabeth, Nelspruit and Polokwane), while four existing stadiums – the majority of them rugby venues – were upgraded. The upgraded stadiums were located in the cities of Bloemfontein, Johannesburg (Ellis Park stadium), Pretoria and Rustenburg.

Because stadiums are the singular 'showpiece' of mega-events, most hosts invest large volumes of resources in the construction and design of sites that are unique and could be used to support the brand – existing or new – of the city. In this way, although primary event infrastructure, stadiums could feed into the secondary legacies of mega-events. Nonetheless, there is much dispute among researchers about the potential positive and negative legacies of stadiums and event competition venues. There are many examples of underutilised or unused Olympic villages or stadiums across the world, with the worst examples probably being Montreal and various cities in Japan and South Korea. There has been a general move to avoid the construction of 'white elephants,' and international sports organisations such as the International Olympic Committee and the Commonwealth Games Federation have included a demonstrable post-event infrastructure legacy as a required section in bidding cities' bid books (see Smith and Fox 2007). There is a general consensus among researchers that the best way to achieve this is through the development of multifunctional and multipurpose competition venues which help to stimulate or support community sport usage or sports tourism (Higham 2005).

Many of South Africa's larger cities, secure with the prospects of hosting higher order matches in the 2010 tournament, proceeded to invest a great deal of resources on the development of flagship stadiums, but development of some of the more prominent (and expensive) ones was marked by unfettered cost escalation. For example, Johannesburg's Soccer City, refurbished to increase its seating capacity to 94 700, and host to the headquarters of FIFA and the South African Football Association before and during the tournament, had by 2010 drawn cost overruns of about R1bn, meaning that its total cost was likely to be in the range of R3.2bn (*The Guardian* 3 March 2010). It was estimated that the construction of Cape Town's stadium would cost R4.5bn, substantially more than the R2.4bn initially projected for it (*Mail & Guardian* 15 December 2009).

Similarly, some of the major transport developments related to the World Cup witnessed delays in schedule and excessive rises in cost. The Gautrain rapid rail system, at times linked by the Gauteng provincial government to the World Cup and at times detached by them from their wider tournament preparations, is probably most emblematic of this, with construction costs rising by the end of 2009 in excess of R25bn. But other host cities also saw delays in the development of new transport systems. The launch of Cape Town's 2010 Integrated Rapid Transport System was delayed by several months and its costs more than tripled (*Cape Times* 9 November 2009). To alleviate some of the transport pressure in host cities during the tournament, a number of cities developed plans for Bus Rapid Transit Systems (BRT). The City of Johannesburg launched its own BRT in August 2009 amid threats of strikes and violence by the local taxi industry.

South Africa's authorities regarded the tournament as a major international marketing and (re)branding opportunity for tourism. Indeed, the country's early bid campaign for the World

Cup was in part motivated by the prospect of dovetailing the hosting of the sports event with some international re-imaging, and boosting the tourism sector. In the post-apartheid era, tourism has developed as a major economic sector, with South Africa ranked as the top international tourism destination in Africa. Currently, the country's annual international tourism market stands close to eight million arrivals.

Yet early on during the preparations for the World Cup, assessments by South Africa's tourism authorities were to show that the country had a significant accommodation deficit, with the shortfall most marked in cities such as Johannesburg and Durban (DEAT 2005). During the lead-up to the Cup, host cities endeavoured to ensure that there was a sufficient supply of accommodation for visitors and spectators, but less than a year before the start of the tournament, some high-ranking FIFA officials voiced concern that this might not be the case. For instance, Jerome Valcke, FIFA's secretary general, stated in an interview that, 'I am not worried about ticket sales but instead about accommodation for the fans. It is our concern that every fan in the world who has bought a ticket also gets a flight and a room … We need enough accommodation for the guests and a high and secure transport capacity'.[2]

Not surprisingly, therefore, questions of infrastructural development and capacity were to be uppermost in the discussions about South Africa's state of preparedness for the 2010 tournament. Reporting in the international media meanwhile reflected a deep-seated sense of international scepticism over the country's ability to host an event of that magnitude. As such, 'getting it right' as far as infrastructural developments for the tournament was concerned, was as essential for the long-term socio-economic legacies such developments could leave as it was for a successful tournament and positive assessments of the World Cup.

Added to this, the implementation of an appropriate World Cup security plan presented another challenge – and cost – to South African authorities. This is because in addition to the standard security measures that need to be undertaken for a tournament of this kind – directed against hooliganism and the prevention of potential terror attacks – authorities also needed to take measures against crime. South Africa has gained international notoriety for the depth of crime and social violence in the country (see the chapter by David Bruce in this volume); indeed, this reputation has widely been regarded as a deterrent to potential foreign visitors to the tournament. To a significant extent, therefore, the 2010 World Cup security plan also had to consist of an effective communication strategy to counter negative international perceptions of the country. Drawing on, *inter alia,* assistance from Germany and international bodies such as Interpol, the security blueprint for the tournament had to be approved by FIFA.

During June 2009 South Africa hosted the Confederations Cup which, although smaller in scale than the World Cup, was regarded as the dry run for the bigger tournament. It became clear during the Confederations Cup that the country's World Cup security plans were in need of improvement. A few days before the start of the Cup, for instance, the Local Organising Committee (LOC) had failed to appoint a security company, necessitating the hasty deployment of an additional number of officers from the South African police force. A few incidents of crime occurred against Confederation Cup visitors (mainly robberies), which were widely reported in the international media. The LOC consequently indicated that they would deploy 41 000 new security staff and that the police force would provide 700 officers to patrol World

Cup venues during 2010. Yet South Africa had much to do to counter widespread cynicism about the ability of overstretched security and policing infrastructure to deliver an effective World Cup anti-crime strategy. It is unclear, however, what the long-term financial implications of this would be.

CONCLUDING REMARKS

In the contemporary era sport mega-events have come to be regarded by many governments – increasingly those in the global South – as a critical pathway to development. In truth, however, the temporal and spatial characteristics of mega-events significantly determine the kinds of short- and long-term effects these events could have. In this, mega-events pose some major tests to the standard precepts of conventional development theory: extensive in scale, sectorally focused and concentrated in duration, these events clash with what are today widely accepted notions of inclusive and broad-based development. With reference to the Olympic Games, for instance, Frey *et al* (2007:2) note that:

> (A)ctually, the high concentration implied by the Games in terms of time (a two-week event), space (one host city only, or even specific areas within the city) and investment (the operating and infrastructure costs of the Games are in billions) seems to conflict with the concept of sustainable development, that calls for the distribution and sharing of environmental, social and economic impacts across time and space for spreading benefits and minimising negative effects on the whole society.

There was much anticipation both within and beyond South Africa over the legacies of the 2010 FIFA World Cup and what South Africa's hosting of the event could mean for a country in which levels of social inequality, violence and deprivation are high. While the event might leave an important political legacy, it was less clear what its long-term economic effects would be.

Further, in a gloomy current international economic environment, and given the fact that national growth prospects have been adversely affected by the country's energy supply deficit, it is reasonable to expect that by the time the final totting-up has been done it will be found that the South African government ended up spending much more on the 2010 World Cup than it had initially anticipated, even though some might regard that as already exorbitant. On the other hand, some economists argued that the World Cup did have positive stimulatory effects which could help offset the deflationary path which the economy is expected to undergo over the next few years.

In the lead-up to the World Cup, the government of President Jacob Zuma had had to contend with growing social unrest, municipal strikes and demands for improved service delivery. Social protest had progressively grown in scale and violence during the course of 2009. While it was not directly related to the World Cup, it is noteworthy that there was an increasing spontaneous tide of civic action that questioned what the real benefits of the event would be. An illustrative case is a violent demonstration in late October 2009 in the township bordering the

Soccer City stadium, during which residents vowed that 'there will be no 2010' because they had no houses and no jobs. The government is 'pouring money into 2010...why are they not pouring money into housing?' (*The Times*, 22 October 2009).

To a significant extent the World Cup and its legacy threatens to become part of South Africa's broader politics of class contestation, as there is an increasing demand that the event should have benefited not only major businesses and the affluent, but also the country's poor. A hidden aspect of South Africa's obvious construction boom, for example, is the extent to which the commercial opportunities linked to this expansion was absorbed by only a few dominant construction firms (for reviews of the politics of stadium construction, see for instance Alegi 2007).

These aspects present a number of challenges to the national government, which not only had to deliver a well prepared and safe tournament that satisfies international scrutiny, but also had to respond to an increasingly restive domestic constituency. Given the experience of previous sports events hosted by South Africa, the 2010 World Cup had the potential to foster racial reconciliation and nation building, even if that was short-lived. This was to depend, however, on how successful the event was judged to have been by the international community, and on whether people in South Africa believe that the tournament brought them real material benefits. Ultimately, it may well turn out that the World Cup created economic benefit for only a handful.

NOTES

1   In reality, the expansion of the Summer Games programme has been more extensive since each sport has a number of different disciplines and involves competitions for men and women.
2   Cited in 'Sorge um Unterkünft in Südafrika,' www.sportal.de/sportal/generated/.../14293300000.html

REFERENCES

Alegi P (2007) The political economy of mega-stadiums and the underdevelopment of grassroots football in South Africa. *Politikon* 34 (3): 315-331.

Allmers S and W Maennig (2008) South Africa 2010: Economic scope and limits. *Hamburg Contemporary Economic Discussions* 21: 1-33.

Baade R and V Matheson (2004) The quest for the Cup: Assessing the economic impact of the World Cup. *Regional Studies* 38 (4): 341-352.

Bale J and O Moen (Eds) (1995) *The Stadium and the City*. Keele: Keele University Press.

Black D (2008) Dreaming big: The pursuit of second order games as a strategic response to globalisation. *Sport in Society* 11 (4): 467-480.

Bohlmann HR (2006) Predicting the economic impact of the 2010 FIFA World Cup on South Africa. University of Pretoria Department of Economics Working Paper Series: 2006–11.

Brownell S (2008) *Beijing's Games: What the Olympics Mean to China*. Lanham, MD: Rowman & Littlefield.

Business Day (2008) 2010 stadiums R3.2bn over budget, 2 December 2008.

Cape Times (2009) Cape Town contingency plan for 2010, 9 November 2009.

Cashman R (2006) *The bitter-sweet awakening: The legacy of the Sydney 2000 Olympic Games*. Petersham: Walla Walla Press.

Centre on Housing Rights and Evictions (COHRE) (2007) Fair play for housing rights: mega-events, Olympic Games and housing rights. Geneva: COHRE.

Coates D and B Humphreys (2002) The economic impact of post-season play in professional sports. *Journal of Sports Economics* 3 (3): 291–299.

Cornelissen S (2009a) A delicate balance: major sport events and development. In R Levermore and A Beacom (Eds) *Sport and international development*. New York: Palgrave.

Cornelissen S (2009b) Sport, mega-events and urban tourism: exploring the patterns, constraints and prospects of the 2010 FIFA World Cup. In Pillay U, R Tomlinson,and O Bass (Eds) *Development and Dreams: Urban Development Implications of the 2010 Soccer World Cup*. Cape Town: HSRC Press.

Cornelissen S and K Swart (2006) The 2010 World Cup as a political construct: the challenge of making good on an African promise. *Sociological Review* 54 (2):108–123.

Crompton J (1995) Economic impact analysis of sports facilities and events: eleven sources of misapplication. *Journal of Sport Management*. 9: 14–35.

Crompton J (2001) Public subsidies to professional team sport facilities in the USA, in Gratton C and P Henry (Eds) *Sport in the City: The Role of Sport in Economic and Social Regeneration*. London: Routledge.

Department of Environmental Affairs and Tourism/South African Tourism (2005) 2010 Soccer World Cup Tourism Organising Plan. Pretoria: DEAT.

Dobson N and RA Sinnamon (2001) A critical analysis of the organisation of major sports events. In Gratton C and I Henry (Eds) *Sport in the city: the role of sport in economic and social regeneration*. London: Routledge.

Euchner C (1999) Tourism and sports: The serious competition for play. In Judd DR and SS Fainstein (Eds) *The Tourist City*. London: Yale University Press.

FIFA (2006) The FIFA Marketing Report 2006 FIFA World Cup™. Zurich: FIFA.

Frey M, F Iraldo and M Melis (2007) The impact of wide-scale sport events on local development: an assessment of the XXth Torino Olympics through the Sustainability Report. RSA Region in Focus? International Conference, Lisbon, 2-5 April 2007.

Gibson HJ (1998) Sport tourism: a critical analysis of research. *Sport Management Review* 1: 45–76.

Government of South Africa (2010) Fact sheet – government preparations for the 2010 FIFA World Cup™, www.sa2010.gov.za.

Grant Thornton (2003) An evaluation of the economic impact of the 2010 FIFA World Cup on the South African economy. Johannesburg: Grant Thornton Kessel Feinstein.

Grant Thornton (2008) South Africa the good news. 27 November 2008. 2010 World Cup set to contribute R55bn to SA's GDP. http://www.sagoodnews.co.za/countdown_to_2010/2010_world_cup_set_to_contribute_r55bn_to_sa_s_gdp_.html [Accessed 12 November 2008].

Grant Thornton (2010) Updated economic impact of the 2010 FIFA World Cup. Media release, 21 April 2010.

The Guardian (2010) South African World Cup final venue Soccer City goes $133m over budget, 3 March 2010.

Harvey D (1989) *The Condition of Postmodernity: An Enquiry into the Origins of Cultural Change*. Oxford: Blackwell.

Higham J (Ed) (2005) *Sport Tourism Destinations: Issues, Opportunities and Analysis*. Oxford: Elsevier Butterworth Heinemann

Higham J and T Hinch (2009) *Sport and Tourism: Globalization, Mobility and Identity*. Elsevier: Butterworth Heinemann

Hiller H (2000) Mega-events, urban boosterism and growth strategies: an analysis of the objectives and legitimations of the Cape Town 2004 Olympic Bid. *International Journal of Urban and Regional Research* 24 (2): 439–458.

Horne J (2008) The four 'cs' of sports mega-events: capitalism, connections, challenges and contradictions. Keynote address delivered at 'Mega-events and civil societies' conference, Queen Mary, University of London, 26-27 June 2008.

Horne J and W Manzenreiter (2004) Accounting for mega-events: forecasts and actual impacts of the

2002 Football World Cup Finals on the host countries Japan/Korea. *International Review for the Sociology of Sport* 39 (2): 187–203.

Horne J and W Manzenreiter (Eds) (2006) *Sports Mega-Events: Social Scientific Analyses of a Global Phenomenon.* Oxford: Blackwell Publishing.

Lee C and T Taylor (2005) Critical reflections on the economic impact assessment of a mega-event: the case of 2002 FIFA World Cup *Tourism Management* 26: 295–603.

Lenskyj H (2008) *Olympic Industry Resistance: Challenging Olympic Power and Propaganda.* New York: State University of New York Press.

Mail & Guardian (2009) Cape Town stadium 'complete', 15 December 2009.

Manuel T (2007) Budget speech 2007 by Minister of Finance Trevor A Manuel MP, http://www.info.gov.za/speeches/2007/07022115261001.htm#1 [Accessed 23 February 2007].

Matheson V (2008) Mega-events: The effect of the world's biggest sporting events on local, regional and national economies. In: Howard D and B Humphreys (Eds) *The Business of Sports.* Connecticut: Westport.

Mathieson A and G Wall (1982) *Tourism: Economic, Physical and Social Impacts.* London: Longman.

Owen K (2002) The Sydney 2000 Olympics and urban entrepreneurialism: local variations in urban governance. *Australian Geographical Studies* 40 (3) : 563–600.

Porter P (1999) Mega-sports events as municipal investments: A critique of impact analysis. In Fizel J, E Gustafson and L Hadley (Eds) *Sports Economics: Current Research.* Westport, CT: Praeger Press.

Poynter G (2006) From Beijing to Bow Creek: Measuring the Olympics effect. University of East London, London East Research Institute Working Papers in Urban Studies.

Preuss H (2004) *The Economics of Staging the Olympics – A Comparison of the Games 1972-2008.* Cheltenham: Edward Elgar.

Preuss H, M Kurscheidt and N Schütte (2007) *Konomie des Tourismus durch Sportgroßveranstaltungen: Eine empirische Analyse zur Fußball-Weltmeisterschaft 2006.* Köln: Sport und Buch Strauss.

South African Press Agency (Sapa) (2010) Employment falls as Cup projects end, 22 June 2010.

Smith A (2005) Conceptualizing city image change: The 're-imaging of Barcelona *Tourism Geographies,* 7 (4): 398–423.

Smith A and T Fox (2007) From 'event-led' to 'event-themed' regeneration: The 2002 Commonwealth Games Legacy. *Urban Studies,* 44 (5/6): 1125–1143.

Smith S (2000) Measurement of tourism's impact. *Annals of Tourism Research* 27 (2) : 530–531.

Stofile M (2007) Opening address by Sport and Recreation Minister M Stofile at the International Year of African Football and 2010 World Cup workshop, Pretoria, 7 March 2007. Pretoria: Government Communication and Information System.

Swart K and U Bob (2004) The seductive discourse of development: The Cape Town 2004 Olympic bid. *Third World Quarterly* 25 (7): 1311–1324.

Szymanski S (2002) The economic impact of the World Cup. *World Economics* 3 (1): 169–177.

The Times (2009) Riverlea residents demand 2010 employment, 22 October 2009.

Waitt G (2003) The social impacts of the Sydney Olympics. *Annals of Tourism Research* 30 (1): 194–215.

Wright RK (2007) Planning for the great unknown: The challenge of promoting spectator-driven sports event tourism. *International Journal of Tourism Research* 9: 345–359.

CHAPTER 4

Growth, resource use and decoupling:
Towards a 'green new deal' for South Africa?[1]

Mark Swilling

The 1994 democratic transition heralded unprecedented change. Virtually every facet of policy and practice in the emergent democratic state was reviewed and revised. A bill of rights forms part of the new constitution and specifically guarantees the right of all South Africans to have the environment protected for the benefit of present and future generations. More pertinently, section 24 (b) of the constitution obliges stakeholders, in civil society and government, to 'secure ecologically sustainable development'. But reconciling complex and sometimes conflicting relationships between poverty, economic development and protection of environmental assets is a major challenge. In particular, the dominant economic growth and development paradigm fails to address a wide range of underlying resource constraints that can rapidly undermine the preconditions for the kind of developmental growth that is required to reduce inequalities and poverty over time. Remarkably, although the South African government has systematically increased financial support for scientific research because it is believed that scientific knowledge reinforces development, this self-same community of scientists is generating research that raises very serious doubts about whether South Africa's resource-intensive economic growth path can continue in light of the rapid depletion and degradation of the country's natural resources (see Burns and Weaver 2008).

This gathering scientific consensus (made possible by significant increases in state funding for scientific research almost exclusively in the natural sciences) has had limited impact on economic policy making and virtually no impact on the underlying theories of economic growth that inform the thinking of the economic policy-making community. Government either needs to listen to the scientists and change the economic model, or explain why it chooses to ignore the science.

GLOBAL CONTEXT

There is a broad global consensus that we face the unprecedented twin challenge created by interlinked economic and environmental crises. As the economic and environmental crises mutually reinforce one another, decision-makers across the public, private and nonprofit sectors in both the developed and developing world intensify demands for practical solutions. A succession of global mainstream assessments over the past decade have together raised very serious questions about the sustainability of a global economic growth model that depends on material flows that have reached – or soon will reach – their natural limits (Barbier 2009; Gleick 2006; Intergovernmental Panel on Climate Change 2007; United Nations Environment Programme 2007; United Nations 2005; Watson *et al* 2008; World Resources Institute 2002; World Wildlife Fund 2008).

The crisis of resource depletion and the negative economic implications of climate change have even been recognised by mainstream reviews such as the Stern Report (Stern 2007) which estimated the economic costs of climate change, and the International Energy Agency, which finally acknowledged in 2008 that 'the era of cheap oil is over' (International Energy Agency 2008).

Unfortunately, the scientific consensus reflected in the assessments cited above has had a very limited impact on mainstream economic policy-makers connected in World Bank/IMF networks. This is most clearly evident in the institutional economics of the so-called 'post-Washington consensus' as reflected in the Growth Report published by the Growth and Development Commission that brought together the most eminent actors in these networks (including Trevor Manuel). For this group of economists, the only constraints to accelerating traditional modes of economic growth are institutional (Commission on Growth and Development 2008).

Resource limits are ignored, except for a distracted reference to the Stern Report and the Fourth Assessment Report of the IPCC. However, there is a growing realisation that economic policy-making needs to respond to the severity of the global ecological crisis: Europe, China, South Korea, various progressive Latin American countries and the USA since Obama have adopted what are generally referred to now as 'green economy' policies and strategies. In 2009, the G20 adopted resolutions supporting the idea of a 'global green new deal'. Nobel prizewinners Joseph Stiglitz and Amartya Sen headed a commission initiated by French president Sarkozy that recommended in 2009 that GDP is no longer an adequate measure of progress, suggesting that it be replaced by a happiness index (Stiglitz *et al* 2009).

This, combined with the European Union's 'green growth' approach, is resulting in significant shifts. In October 2008, the Seventeenth National Congress of the Communist Party of China endorsed President Hu Jintao's call for the building of a new 'ecological civilisation' which, according to vice premier of the State Council Li Keqiang, the Party has defined as the 'summary of physical, spiritual and institutional achievements of human beings when they develop and utilise natural resources while taking initiative to protect nature' (Keqiang 2009). This has become the cornerstone of China's 'green development' strategy, which is the strategic focus of China's massive economic recovery package. Unfortunately, in his medium term budget policy statement in October 2009, South Africa's new finance minister, Pravin Gordhan, ignored the global scientific consensus about the ecological limits to growth and explicitly endorsed the Growth Report. This position effectively disconnects South Africa from the $100–$200 billion worth of investments in low carbon development and contradicted South Africa's negotiating position at the Copenhagen Climate Change Conference of December 2009.

The key dimensions of the 'polycrisis' (Morin 1999) are now being recognised, as global discussion of a 'green new deal' gathers momentum. Attention is increasingly on the intersections between global warming, ecosystem breakdown, resource depletion, the global economic crisis, persistent poverty and accelerating urbanisation (without adequate investments in urban infrastructure). Global warming by a minimum of two degrees centigrade, exacerbated by the 70 per cent increase in GHG emissions between 1970 and 2004 described in the Fourth Assessment Report of the IPCC, is both an outcome of an unsustainable economy and the most significant catalyst for change (Intergovernmental Panel on Climate Change 2007). As the Stern Report made clear, poorer countries will suffer 'first and most' from the consequences of global warming even though they have 'contributed least' to global warming (Stern 2007). The global economic crisis will exacerbate this suffering as the global economy shrinks, with recovery projected to take anything between three and ten years. According to the International Labour Organisation, the number of unemployed in developing countries may rise by the end of 2009 by between eighteen and fifty-one million people over 2007 levels (cited in Barbier 2009). When food prices rose by almost 60 per cent during the first half of 2008, the number of people living in poverty increased by between 130 and 155 million (cited in Barbier 2009).

The International Energy Association predicted in 2008 that demand for oil will increase by 45 per cent by 2030, without any evidence that it will be possible to find this amount of oil at affordable prices as the costs of extraction across the world's oil fields rise as the quality and quantity of reserves decline, thus further undermining traditional drivers of economic recovery. Its 2008 World Energy Outlook report concluded that the 'the era of cheap oil is over' (International Energy Agency 2008).

It is therefore unsurprising that oil prices have tended to rise over the past year despite recessionary conditions. Predictions that oil could rise to US$180 a barrel in the relatively near future are now quite common (Barbier 2009).[2] The Millennium Ecosystem Assessment found that fifteen out of twenty-four key ecosystem services are degraded or used unsustainably, often with negative consequences for the poor – 1.3 billion people live in ecologically fragile environments located mainly in developing countries, half of whom are the rural poor (United Nations 2005). At the same time, as the world's population grows from the current six billion to eight billion by 2030, a massive urbanisation wave is underway – what the 2006/7 State of the World's Cities report called the 'second wave of urbanisation' – that has already pushed us across the 50 per cent urbanised mark (United Nations 2006). The inevitable result is the unprecedented expansion and creation of new cities as the number of urbanites in the developing world increases from

309 million in 1950 to a staggering 3.9 billion by 2030. African and Asian cities will absorb the additional two to three billion people that are expected to be living on the planet by 2050, even though they are the least equipped to handle this challenge (United Nations 2006).

It has been estimated that the combined value of the fiscal stimulus packages assembled by the G20 in 2009 is between US$2 and US$3 trillion, or 3 per cent of global GDP (Barbier 2009). If these stimulus packages focus exclusively on economic recovery and ignore global warming, ecosystem breakdown, the end of cheap oil and global poverty, the outcomes will contradict the original recovery intentions. Even in the USA it has been recognised that economic recovery investments must be coupled to investments in more sustainable use of resources: of the US$827 billion to be spent by the US government, US$100 billion has been allocated to green investments.

South Korea has an ambitious green new deal investment package worth US$36 billion which comprises the bulk of its recovery package, and China has earmarked 38 per cent of its recovery package (equal to four trillion yuan) for green technology investments. These examples demonstrate that the causes of the current crisis are being recognised and are far more complex than merely short-term economic factors. They are also investments that will drive unprecedented rates of innovation as governments and private sector players strive to convert these investments into competitive advantages within the global economy. This logic was reflected in a shift in global ideological discourse expressed most clearly by the British prime minister, Gordon Brown, when he wrote in *Newsweek*:

> There can be little doubt that the economy of the twenty-first century will be low-carbon. What has become clear is that the push toward decarbonisation will be one of the major drivers of global and national economic growth over the next decade. And the economies that embrace the green revolution earliest will reap the greatest economic rewards … Just as the revolution in information and communication technologies provided a major motor of growth over the past thirty years, the transformation to low-carbon technologies will do so over the next. It is unsurprising, therefore, that over the past year governments across the world have made green investment a major part of their economic stimulus packages. They have recognised the vital role that spending on energy efficiency and infrastructure can have on demand and employment in the short term, while also laying the foundations for future growth (*Newsweek*, 28 September 2009).

Although Brown recognises here that a new industrial growth path is required, his government continues to support the continued financialisation of the British and global economy which is, ultimately, about debt-driven consumption of goods produced in low-wage regions that, in turn, require very cheap natural resource inputs. This is not the kind of model that can deliver a 'green revolution'.

This argument has been confirmed by the work of a new UNEP Panel established in the wake of the Fourth Assessment Report of the IPCC, the United Nations Environment Programme. The International Panel for Sustainable Resource Management (IPSRM) has highlighted the crucial role of material resource flows and associated environmental impacts (see http://www.unep.fr/scp/rpanel/biofuels.htm). By resource flows, we mean primarily the metabolic flow of fossil fuels, biomass, minerals and metals through the global economy. The focus is on the extraction and domestic use of materials quantified in tons and the aim is to analyse the relationship between economic growth and resource use. Material Flow Analysis (MFA) is the methodological tool that is used to conduct this analysis. MFA has matured over the past five years and has become an established method for assessing the sustainability of local, national and global economies (Bringezu and Schutz 2001; Bringezu and Bleischwitz 2009; Bringezu *et al* 2004; Fischer-Kowalski 1998; Fischer-Kowalski 1999; Haberl *et al* 2004; Krausman *et al* 2008; see Krausmann *et al* forthcoming).

Using MFA, it has been possible to compute global material flows for the first time. These flows include fossil fuels, biomass, minerals and metals. Over the period of accelerated globalisation and financialisation since 1980, the total extraction of all these resources has increased by 36 per cent, from forty billion tons in 1980 to fifty-five billion tons in 2002.

Figure 1. Global used resource extraction by material category (in billion tons)

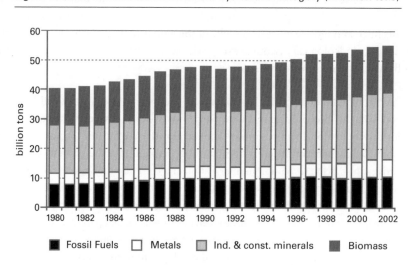

(**Source:** Behrens *et al* 2007)

Increased resource extraction has not, however, resulted in greater equity. The 1998 United Nations Human Development Report demonstrated that by the end of the 1990s the richest 20 per cent of the world's population was responsible for 86 per cent of consumption expenditure, whereas the poorest 20 per cent were responsible for only 1.3 per cent of consumption expenditure (United Nations Development Programme 1998).

In other words, as total domestic consumption shot over the fifty billion ton per annum mark in the late 1990s, 20 per cent of the world's population had the means to purchase 86 per cent of this harvest. This, in turn, was made possible by declining real prices of primary resources, with negatives consequences for Africa's resource-rich resource-exporting countries.

Indeed, a World Bank report estimated that these prices were lower than the real value of the resources, which means that many African countries (including South Africa) have experienced a decline in their gross national incomes (which includes the value of financial, human and natural capital) as exports of primary resources have increased (World Bank 2005).

The IPSRM developed three 2050 scenarios (assuming that there will be nine billion people on the planet by this time), comparing them to the year 2000 'baseline scenario' of fifty-five billion tons of extracted material (Swilling *et al* 2009). It was demonstrated that the current metabolic rate is between eight and a half and ten tons of materials per capita. The average rate in industrialised countries is double this rate, with rates going up to twenty-five and forty tons per capita in low density developed economies like the USA and Australia. The metabolic rate of almost two-thirds of the world population who also live in developing countries is five to six tons. Three scenarios were evaluated. The first is a business-as-usual scenario that will take the global economy from the current fifty-five billion tons of extracted materials per annum to 140 billion tons. There is no scientific evidence that the resources exist (fossil fuels, metals, biomass) to sustain this business-as-usual scenario. The second and third scenarios are more sustainable, arriving at seventy-five billion and fifty-five billion tons respectively per annum. Scenario two (seventy-five billion tons per annum) is in line with the gradual change scenario envisaged by the IPCC, while the third scenario is more in line with radical changes suggested by ecosystem science, which presumes that a global agreement is reached to stabilise at the current level of extraction and material use.

The IPSRM brings together two well consolidated intellectual traditions: industrial ecology and ecological economics. These traditions, which agree with those of institutional economists, are crucial but go further by emphasising the ecological constraints to growth. They share the view that a new economic theory is required that makes it possible to conceptualise the economic modalities of a 'green economy', that is, an economy that grows by reducing rather than increasing resource consumption, or what in the literature is referred to as 'dematerialisation'. The core concept at the centre of this work is 'decoupling'. The notion of decoupling opens up a new way of thinking about the relationship between the rate of economic growth and the rate of resource consumption and its associated impacts. This implies two types of decoupling: 'resource decoupling' (decoupling growth rates from resource extraction) and 'impact decoupling' (decoupling growth rates from environmental impacts). It is also possible to make a distinction between 'relative decoupling' and 'absolute decoupling': the former implies slower rates of resource use and impacts relative to economic growth rates, while the latter refers to negative rates of growth of resource consumption and related impacts. Policy and strategic decisions can be made to foster the relative/absolute decoupling of both resource use and impacts in contextually specific ways that reduce the significance of resource limits as a constraint to growth (Swilling *et al* 2009). The inevitable result will be the redefinition of growth, or what the Latin American ecological economist Gilberto Gallopin has called 'non-material growth', which he distinguishes from the European notion of 'zero growth' (Gallopin 2003).

Decoupling makes it possible to think about the connections between economic growth, improved well-being through development and sustainable resource use in ways that open up more creative options for innovation than has hitherto been the case. After the Club of Rome report in the early 1970s, there was a pervasive assumption that growth was the cause of environmental destruction and therefore sustainable development would only be achieved through zero growth strategies. This conception was only tenable because economic growth and resource use were seen to be directly proportional to one another. For the Brundtland Commission Report, the focus was on how best to 'sustain' development (conventionally defined), and the only limits that mattered were institutional and technological factors, not natural resource constraints. The intersubstitutability of different forms of capital that Brundtland legitimised effectively reduced the conceptual space for decoupling and the result is that both developed and developing countries have been allowed to validate resource intensive growth paths to eliminate poverty. These are now coming up against the natural resource limits that have hitherto not received significant attention.

Both resource and impact decoupling are necessary – one without the other will prove ineffective when it comes to realising sustainability goals. By decoupling resource use from economic growth, our understanding of economic growth also changes. Instead of seeing economic growth as inevitably driven only by value derived from an increasing quantity of material goods and assets, so-called 'non-material growth' (or prosperity or well-being) is driven by knowledge intensity and associated investments in culture, livability, education, improved health, environmental quality, safety, a sense of place and (individual and collective) capabilities for enhancing well-being and freedom.

Developing countries should not regard the call for sustainable resource management as a threat to development and poverty eradication. On the contrary, sustainable resource management offers new opportunities for investments in innovations that could stimulate endogenous growth strategies in developing economies. These could be more effective in eradicating poverty than traditional strategies that depend on primary exports or exports of cheap manufactured goods underpinned in both cases by resource depletion and/or environmental degradation. As oil prices rise, long distance trading regimes will be forced to restructure and the sooner developing countries prepare for this eventuality, the better off they will be when it happens. Unfortunately, most developing countries think that sustainable resource management refers only to costly impact decoupling. Resource decoupling is where the economic opportunities for developing countries lie, and impact decoupling reinforces adaptation with major benefits for millions of poor people who depend on the ecological sustainability of ecosystem goods and services (such as fishing, indigenous forests, good soils and stable climates and their associated predictable rains).

LIMITS OF RESOURCE INTENSIVE GROWTH[3]

It is becoming increasingly apparent that key ecological thresholds in South Africa are being breached by its prevailing approach to growth and development, and that this is resulting in dysfunctional economic costs. It is this condition of rising costs caused by a new set of material, ecologically driven constraints that sets the context for new ways of thinking about the country's economic growth model and poverty reduction strategies.

After the first democratic elections in 1994, South Africa experienced an unprecedented growth period that came to an end towards the end of 2008. As a resource-rich resource-exporting country, South Africa benefitted from the rise in commodity prices over the past decade, but suffered as they collapsed temporarily during 2008 as a result of the global financial crisis. Figures 2 and 3 demonstrate this growth period, and how economic growth has correlated with employment growth, which is a key strategy for the reduction of poverty.

Figure 2. Real GDP growth 1983–2004

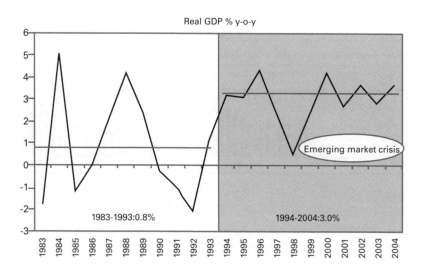

(**Source:** Republic of South Africa: National Treasury 2006)

Figure 3: GDP and employment growth 1983–2004 (non-agricultural sectors)

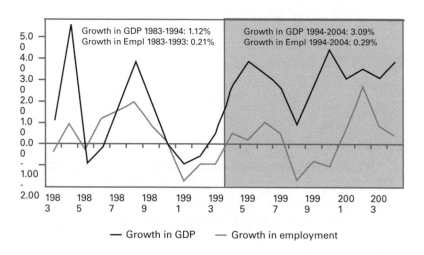

(**Source:** Republic of South Africa: National Treasury 2006)

South African economic growth has been driven by a combination of expanded domestic consumption financed by rising levels of household debt (securitised against residential properties) and exports of primary resources which entrenched the hegemony of the so-called 'mineral-energy complex'. The manufacturing sector has, unfortunately, declined relative to other sectors in response to a vigorous strategy to lower import tariffs and liberalise the capital markets (thus favouring investments in liquid assets rather than long-term fixed investments). Figures 4 to 6 below reveal the rise in consumption spending and the relative decline in the growth of the manufacturing sector.

Figure 4: Growth in demand 1990–2005

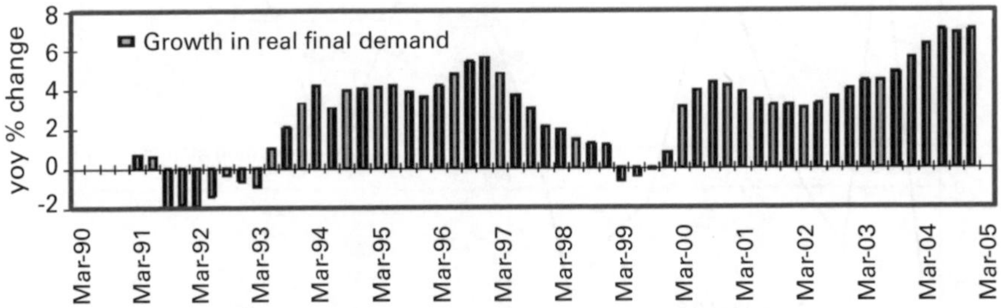

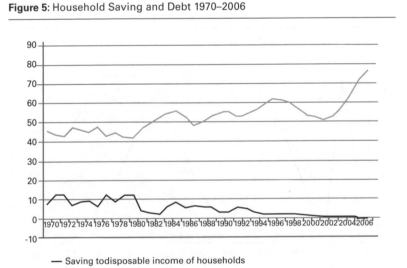

(**Source:** Republic of South Africa: National Treasury 2006)

Figure 5: Household Saving and Debt 1970–2006

— Saving todisposable income of households
— Household debt to disposable income of households

(**Source:** Mohamed 2008)

The growth in final real demand is shown in figure 3, but when read against rising debt levels and the declining contribution of manufacturing relative to mining and natural resource industries as reflected in figure 5, it is clear that debt-financed consumption has been the driver of consumer demand for an increasing quantity of imported products, while growth has shifted to an *increasing* reliance on the extraction and export of natural capital. The balance of payments pressures this created was at first mitigated by the beneficial effects of rising commodity prices, but with the global economic crisis, easy credit to drive consumption and high commodity prices both came to an end, although it is clear that commodity prices are steadily rising as China and a few other industrialising developing countries continue to grow at much higher rates than the global average. This dependence on the mineral-energy complex and debt-financed consumption-driven growth is quintessentially the core structural problem at the heart of the South African economic crisis (see Mohamed in this volume and Fine and Rustomjee 1996).

South Africa's dependence on its rich endowment of natural wealth is reflected below:

Figure 6: Increase in economic value per sector in R'm, 1970–2007 (at year 2000 prices).

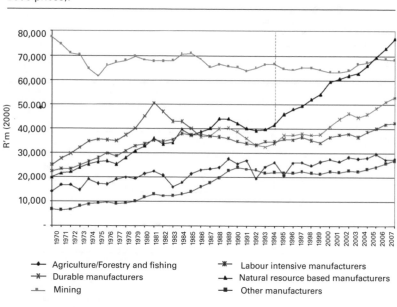

- Agriculture/Forestry and fishing
- Durable manufacturers
- Mining
- Labour intensive manufacturers
- Natural resource based manufacturers
- Other manufacturers

(**Source:** Quantec RSA Standardised Industry Database)

Figure 7 reveals the significance of ore extraction, although it has declined since 1980. At the same time, coal extraction has increased to fuel the coal-based electricity generation industry, which supplies the cheapest electricity in the world to South Africa's economy. The low price coal and mineral policy has resulted in limited diversification of the economy and high levels of inefficiency.

Despite the dependence on ore and coal extraction, there is also evidence of decoupling in the twenty years leading up to 2000, as revealed in figure 8.

Figure 7: Domestic extraction in millions of tons, 1980–2000

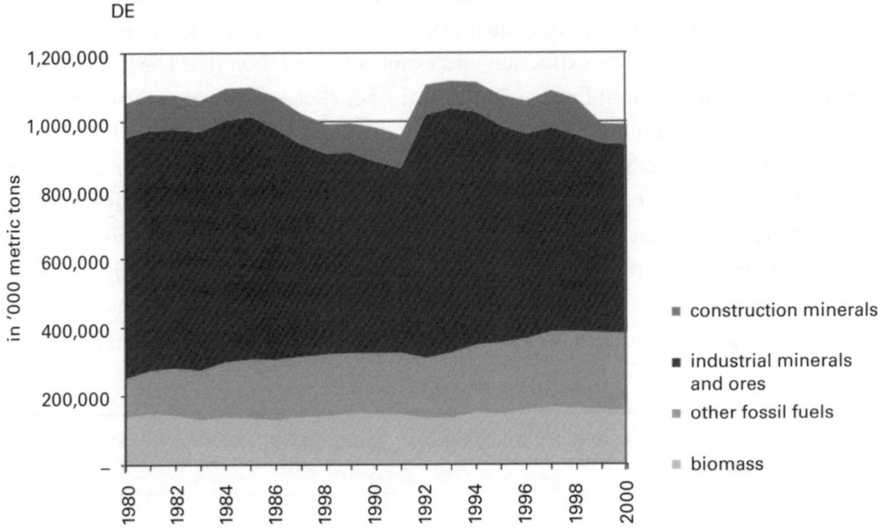

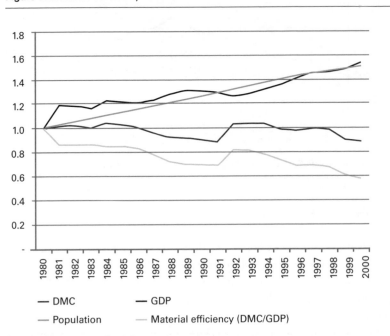

(**Source:** Krausman *et al* 2005)

Figure 8: Material efficiency 1980–2000

(**Source:** Krausman *et al* 2005)

Although based on a limited study, Figure 8 does suggest that a relatively minor level of decoupling is taking place – domestic material consumption (DMC) of primary materials[4] has declined while population growth and GDP have grown. Figure 8 reveals the significance of exports of primary resources for the economy. South Africa's economy is still dominated by the mineral-energy complex which, in turn, has managed to convince government that economic growth by selling off natural capital (coal and ores) at very low prices makes economic sense. This led to the strategically senseless decision to sell ISCOR to Mittal Steel with a back-to-back agreement that Mittal could buy South African iron ore for cost plus 3 per cent forever, which is why Mittal could testify at the Competition Tribunal that its South African operations are the most profitable compared with the rest of its global operations. Workers, in the end, paid the price as steel prices pegged to the international price of steel increased the costs of production thus placing downward pressures on wages, and increased the costs of construction thus making housing and infrastructure delivery more expensive.

Figure 9: Primary material exports 1980–2000

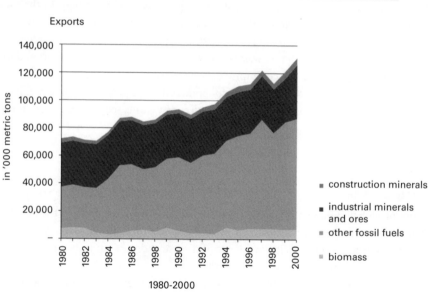

(**Source:** Krausman *et al* 2005)

In short, South Africa is a good example of an economy caught up in the financialisation of a globalised economy, with debt-driven consumption as the key driver of growth. This has undermined manufacturing as tariff barriers have been lowered and cheap imports from Asia have risen. It has also resulted in debt-financed consumption spending, and increased dependence on revenues from exported primary resources at low prices. The unsustainability of this growth strategy is partially recognised by the government and key stakeholders, and various interventions are being considered by a wide range of state institutions, including the

Department of Environmental Affairs, National Treasury, Department of Trade and Industry, Department of Human Settlements, Department of Energy, Department of Water Affairs, Department of Transport and key financial institutions such as the Industrial Development Corporation (IDC) and and Development Bank of Southern Africa (DBSA). However, South Africa is a robust constitutional democracy with three layers of government (national, regional and local) that are, in turn, relatively independent from one another. This has resulted in very low levels of intragovernmental coordination, each sector responding to the sustainability challenges in their own ways. What is lacking is a government-wide approach that connects industrial policy, resource management strategies and the protection of ecosystem services.

2010 is slated as a key year for consolidating the green economy policy framework, which could become the focus of the newly established National Planning Commission. In February 2010, the cabinet approved a department of environmental affairs document entitled Proposals on Green Jobs – A South African Transition. This will be followed up by a comprehensive strategy document, the National Green Economy Strategy, which will be considered at the Cabinet Legotla in July 2010 – fairly soon after the Green Economy Summit planned for 19–21 May. The IDC and the DBSA are working with the Department of Environmental Affairs to work out detailed financial plans for implementing the green economy strategy. In the meantime, the Gauteng government has adopted what it calls a 'developmental green economy strategy' that is heavily focussed on decoupling by targetting investments in renewable energy, water efficiency, recycling of solid and liquid wastes, moving people into public transport and massively increasing locally produced food to improve food security and create jobs.

Whether these initiatives amount to a coherent, effective policy outcome and implementation strategy remains to be seen. A consideration of various sectoral responses follows.

RESOURCE LIMITS

Climate change[5]

The use of global climate models has predicted the following changes to the South African climate within the next fifty years, with drastic impacts on national water availability, food and biomass production capacity, incidence of disease and the country's unique biodiversity:

- continental warming of between 1 and 3°C;
- broad reductions of approximately 5 per cent to 10 per cent of current rainfall;
- increased summer rainfall in the north east and south west, but reduced duration of summer rains in the north east;
- nominal increases in rainfall in the north east during the winter season;
- increased daily maximum temperatures in summer and autumn in the western half of the country;
- extension of the summer season characteristics.

Carbon dioxide (CO_2) emissions are South Africa's most significant greenhouse gas (GHG), contributing more than 80 per cent of its total GHG emissions for both 1990 and 1994. The main source of CO_2 emissions is the energy sector, which generated 89.7 per cent of total

CO_2 in 1990 and 91.1 per cent in 1994. These high emission levels relate to the high energy intensity of the South African economy, which depends on large scale primary extraction and processing, particularly in the mining and minerals beneficiation industries. Although still a developing economy, its energy intensive nature and its dependence on coal-driven energy sources results in an extremely high carbon emission level per unit of GDP, compared to the rest of the world:

Table 1: Comparative carbon emissions, 2004

Area	Population (million)	GDP per capita	Carbon Footprint (CO2 emissions per capita (tons))	Carbon Intensity (CO2 emissions per unit of GDP)
South Africa	46.6	$ 10,715	9.8	0.99
Sub-Saharan Africa	781.3	$ 1,945	1.0	0.57
USA	293.6	$ 40,971	20.6	0.57
OECD	1160.5	$ 28,642	11.5	0.45
World	6389.3	$ 9,348	4.5	0.55

(**Source**: UNDP 2008)

In July 2008, the Cabinet adopted a document generally known as the long term mitigation scenario (LTMS) which was commissioned by the Department of Environmental Affairs and Tourism and compiled mainly by a group of University of Cape Town researchers. This report produced two primary scenarios, the 'growth without constraints scenario' and the 'required by science scenario'. The first models the long-term implications of current economic policy, and concludes that emissions will grow from 440 megatons of CO_2-eq in 2004 to 1 600 megatons of CO_2-eq by 2050. This would involve rising fuel consumption by 500 per cent, building seven new coal-fired power plants or sixty-eight integrated gassification plants, constructing nine conventional nuclear and twelve pebble bed modular reactor (PBMR) plants, and introducing five new oil refineries. Renewable energy will play a negligible role. The 'required by science scenario' envisages very radical interventions to position South Africa in a post-carbon world. The result would be a 30 per cent to 40 per cent reduction of CO_2-eq emissions by 2050 from 2004 levels. The LTMS 'required by science scenario' views this ambitious programme of extreme decoupling as necessary, but the LTMS authors admit that it cannot be reliably costed as the required technologies must still mature. The LTMS document was adopted by Cabinet in July 2008, with a commitment to the 'required by science scenario' as the preferred option. Although this has major implications for economic and development policy, there is limited evidence that these implications have been registered. The 2009 medium-term policy framework acknowledged the need to address this issue, but there was no reference to the drastic structural changes required and the intellectual adherence to the logic of the Growth Report means that climate change policy has not been understood by the Treasury.

Oil resources[6]

Imported oil meets approximately 16 to 20 per cent of South Africa's energy needs. Table 2 illustrates that if demand for liquid fuels in South Africa (essentially the hydrocarbons petrol, diesel and jet fuel) is driven by current transport demand patterns and transport modes, even modest growth rates of 3 per cent and 6 per cent per year would lead to increases of 1.8 and 3.2 times present (2004) volumes.

Table 2: Past and projected consumption of transportation fuels (million litres/year)

											Low Growth Rate (3%)	High Growth Rate (6%)
Year	1995	1996	1997	1998	1999	2000	2001	2002	2003	2004	2024	2024
Petrol	10153	10566	10798	10883	10861	10396	10340	10335	10667	10985	19840	35230
Diesel	5432	5759	5875	5959	5993	6254	6488	6831	7263	7679	13869	24628
Jet Fuel	1368	1601	1777	1877	1995	2020	1924	1967	2099	2076	3749	6658

(**Source**: Cairncross 2005)

Current macroeconomic policy documents do not address the challenge of peak oil. There is no estimate of the rate of increase of the oil price, nor is there an assessment of the potential impact if oil prices continue to rise, as they inevitably will. The combination of growing demand and rising prices will severely undermine economic growth and poverty reduction measures. It follows that either growth rates must be revised downwards, or massive investments are required to substantially reduce consumption of imported hydrocarbons.

Energy[7]

Just over 70 per cent of South Africa's energy is derived from coal – a long-term trend that will more than likely continue well into the future. The remaining 30 per cent is derived from oil (20 per cent), gas (1.5 per cent), nuclear (3 per cent) and biomass (5.1 per cent). Significantly, coal-to-liquid and gas-to-liquid technologies account for 30 per cent and 8 per cent respectively of the total liquid fuel supply.

Cheap energy (possibly the cheapest in the world), and abundant coal supplies, have made it possible to build an energy intensive economy. Table 3 reveals how resource intensive the South African economy is, compared with other parts of the world.

The biggest future challenge for the energy sector is the rapid growth in electricity demand without a clear plan to increase generation capacity. Expanding access to electricity by poor households and the imperatives of a growing economy put increasing pressure on supply. Peak demand started to outstrip supply in 2006/2007, resulting in rolling blackouts across the country with negative economic consequences.

Up to the present, policy makers have paid little attention to large-scale energy efficiency (EE) and renewable energy (RE) interventions. The White Paper on Renewable Energy

(November 2003) identified an RE target of 4 per cent by 2013 and a 12 per cent reduction in energy consumption by 2014. Scenario building exercises have provided evidence that up to 50 per cent of South Africa's future energy supply could stem from RE by 2050, although for this to be realised, planning and investments need to proactively focus on this long-term trend. In other words, there is agreement that the energy sector must be dematerialised, but no agreement on how far this should go, or on the balance between RE and EE.

In the short term, immediate electricity generation needs will be met by re-commissioning old coal-fired power stations and by escalating Research and Development support for the controversial pebble bed modular reactor.[8] But the long-term financial viability and security of nuclear power remains uncertain. Short-term high impact investments in proven wind and solar power technologies could rapidly create the basis for a long-term supply of renewable energy. The fact remains that investments so far in the PBMR technology could have supplied a free solar hot water heater to every household in South Africa (a solar hot water heater effectively removes 50 per cent of the demand for electricity, thus halving the demand for coal-fired electrical power). A simple cost benefit analysis will demonstrate the wisdom of such an investment, not to mention the new value chains and associated job creation in a labour intensive industry that would ensue. As many other countries now realise, the cost of hydrocarbons will inevitably rise over the next three decades while the cost of renewable energies will inevitable decline as the technologies improve.[9]

Table 3: South Africa's total primary energy supply in comparative perspective

	TPES/capita	TPES/GDP	TPES/GDP	Elec. consumption per capita (national average)
	Toe/capita	Toe/ 000 1995 US$	Toe/ 000 PPP 1995 US$	kWh/capita
South Africa	2.51	0.63	0.29	4,533
Africa	0.64	0.86	0.32	503
South Korea	4.10	0.31	0.30	5,901
Indonesia	0.69	0.70	0.25	390
Non-OECD	0.96	0.74	0.28	1,028
OECD	4.78	0.19	0.22	8,090
World	1.67	0.30	0.24	2,343

Key: TPES = total primary energy supply, toe = tones of oil equivalent, PPP = purchasing power parity (that is, adjusted to remove distortions of exchange rates), GDP = Gross domestic product.

Water and Sanitation[10]

With an average annual rainfall of 497 mm, South Africa is a dry country, and 98 per cent of available water resources have already been allocated. This means that 'South Africa simply has no more surplus water and all future economic development (and thus social well-being)

will be constrained by this one fundamental fact that few have as yet grasped' (Turton 2008: 3). The country therefore has no further 'dilution capacity' when it comes to absorbing effluents in its water bodies. The Johannesburg-Pretoria complex, South Africa's most significant urban-economic conurbation, is located on a high altitude watershed which means that out-flows of waste water pollute the downstream water resources on which Gauteng depends for its water supplies and the result is that South Africa's national water resources contain some of the highest (after China) toxin levels, in particular mycrocystin, for which no remedy currently exists. Cyanobacteria blooms, caused by end-of-pipe nitrogen-phosphorus-potassium (NPK) loads, threaten national water security. Inter-basin water transfers have degraded the ecological integrity of aquatic systems, and radionuclides, heavy metals and sulphates from mining activities have polluted valuable water resources. In short, the combination of low average rainfall, over-exploitation and re-engineered spatial flows have led South Africa to an imminent water crisis in quantity as well as quality.

According to the Department of Water Affairs, in 2000 there was still surplus capacity of around 1.4 per cent. Recent models indicate that very serious water shortages can be expected by as early as 2013. Significantly, it is in the urban and domestic sector where consumption increases are set to triple:

Table 4: Historical consumption and projected water requirements for 2030 per sector.

Sector	m3/annum	
	1996	2030
Urban and domestic	2 171	6 936
Mining and industrial	1 598	3 380
Irrigation and afforestation	12 344	15 874
Environmental	3 932	4 225
Total	20 045	30 415

Table 4 graphically represents the resource use crisis that will be generated by economic growth and poverty eradication if existing water management systems and processes remain unchanged.

There is scope for major water saving in two sectors – urban and domestic use, and the agricultural sector. Recycling urban waste water is an urgent priority. For example, between 40 per cent and 50 per cent of all water piped into households is used to flush toilets, yet it is technically possible to flush toilets from on-site grey water flows (in particular for large middle class homes), or through neighbourhood-level closed loop systems that recycle water back to households. Rainwater harvesting and grey water supplies for irrigation also have potential. The second major water-saving priority is in agriculture, especially in combination with organic farming methods that simultaneously rebuild the biological capacity of soils and moisture retention capacity in the top layers.

The government is aware of these severe water supply constraints. In her 2007 budget speech, the minister of water affairs and forestry dedicated considerable space to her water efficiency campaign, with apparent emphasis on regulations and tighter controls. But unless more immediate and drastic action is taken, economic growth will soon be undermined by water shortages and related dysfunctionalities (such as salinisation of aquifers). The research results are clear: available physical extra capacity in 2000 was at most 1.7 per cent higher than existing requirements, while growth in water demand could be as much as 25 per cent higher than available yield by 2025. Even if demand only increases by 1 per cent a year, by 2014 the economy will already be facing severe shortages on a number of fronts and by 2019 water shortages will have pulled the economy into a downward spiral of low growth and growing socio-economic inequalities, with associated 'mini resource wars' over water supplies.

Sophisticated modelling work by University of Pretoria researchers shows that a combination of physical, fiscal, institutional and technological interventions could turn this potential disaster into a major opportunity for effective sustainable resource use (Blignaut 2006). However, for this to occur, water resources need to be seen as a 'binding constraint', and government must seriously invest in the sustainable resource use approach advocated by all leading researchers and policy managers in the water resource sector.

Solid Waste[11]

Solid waste includes all municipal and industrial waste. As of 2005, the solid waste system managed the disposal of 20 Mt[12] of municipal solid waste (MSW), 450 Mt of mining related wastes and 30 Mt of power station ashes. MSW quantities are growing faster than the economy in many cities[13] (the typical daily average of 2 kg per person is three to four times that in many European cities). Both the quantity and nature of solid waste differs considerably across the socio-economic spectrum. People in informal settlements generate on average 0.16 kg a day, whereas over 2 kg a day is not unusual in affluent areas. Food and green waste makes up 35 per cent of waste in affluent households, compared with 20 per cent for poor households. In Cape Town 60 per cent of industrial waste is recycled, compared to only 6.5 per cent of residential and commercial waste (among the lowest in the world), and there is no reason to believe that the situation is much different in other South African cities.

While many countries have moved away from 'disposal-to-landfill' as the primary means of solid waste management, in South Africa the large bulk of MSW is disposed of in landfill sites spread out across the country. Although national costs have not been calculated, they are probably similar to those in Cape Town, where the cost of managing landfills – and related dumping – doubled between 2000 and 2004.

Growth in the minerals and coal-based energy sector leads directly to increased industrial wastes with limited productive recycling and re-use – a clear example of the way unsustainable resource use is coupled to growth and poverty reduction. Yet technologies and processes for decoupling waste from growth and poverty eradication are simple, low cost and extensively used throughout the world.

Waste recycling represents one of the most immediate, tangible and low cost investments in dematerialisation available. It saves on capital costs, creates jobs, and forces the middle classes to take greater responsibility for the resources they throw away. It is also normally a highly competitive sector, with sophisticated value chains for resources such as used engine

Figure 10: Past and projected consumption of transportation fuels (million litres per year)

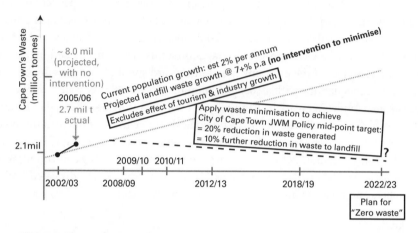

Effect/implication of waste minimisation
Roll-out/implementation must:
• Create infrastructure;
• Educate, make all aware:
• Encourage public/industry participation;
• Facilitate creation of recycling market through partnerships (industry, NGOs, CBOs);
• Enable job creation through recycling rather than clean-ups;
• Enforce stricter standards

(**Source**: City of Cape Town 2007)

oil, used vegetable oils, a wide range of plastics, building rubble, organic matter for composting, glass, cans, paper, and so on. Numerous studies confirm that recycling has very positive economic benefits for job creation, manufacturing and technology and innovation – and waste recycling also has significant export potential.

The National Integrated Waste Management Act adopted by Parliament in 2009 will force every local government to prepare an integrated waste management plan with defined targets for recycling, thus paving the way for a recycling revolution. The stage is now set to move South Africa decisively into a post-disposal approach with respect to MSW, with a special focus on middle and high income consumers. The Mineral and Petroleum Resources Development Act (2002) makes specific provision for waste management and pollution control in the mining sector and, together with the emerging MSW approach, provides the basis for the emergence of a vast decentralised network of market-driven and community-based recycling businesses. In addition the national cleaner production strategy is being beefed up, establishing incentives and legal requirements to stimulate cleaner production systems (CPS) in the business sector – particularly in mining and construction – with a special focus on investments in recycling enterprises.

Soils[14]

South Africa falls within the so-called third major soil region typical in mid-latitudes on both sides of the equator. The result is that South Africa is dominated by very shallow sandy soils with severe inherent limitations for agriculture; only 13 per cent of the land is arable and a mere 3 per cent is high potential land. The result is overexploitation and the use of inappropriate farming methods as we try to exceed the capacity of our soils to meet growing food requirements. All this has resulted in far-reaching nationwide soil degradation.

Water erosion remains the biggest problem, causing the loss of an estimated 25 per cent of the nation's topsoil in the past century and continuing still. Other factors include: wind erosion affecting 25 per cent of soils; soil compaction owing to intensive mechanised agriculture; soil crusting caused by overhead irrigation systems; acidification of more than five million hectares of arable land, caused by poor farming practices particularly incorrect fertilizer and inadequate lime applications; soil fertility degradation resulting from annual net losses of the three main plant nutrients (nitrogen, phosphorous and potassium); soil pollution caused by various human practices; and urbanisation often spreading across high value arable land on the outskirts of cities.

Once land is degraded, there is little potential for recovery and therefore areas where degradation is limited must be prioritised so that efforts can be focussed on prevention through appropriate farming practices. Reversing the above trends will require locally trained soil scientists who recognise that our soil conditions are highly unusual (because they are 'third major soil region' soils) and therefore we cannot copy solutions generated in countries with a different soil profile. Location-specific technical solutions are required, as blanket solutions have proved unworkable, and locally trained soil scientists must work together with local leader farmers using horizontal learning practices. This has worked in India, Cuba and many other places in the developing world, and is urgently required in South Africa.

Biodiversity[15]

South Africa is globally recognised as the third most biologically diverse country in the world, yet its diversity is one of the most threatened on the planet. Significantly, this concerns not just the prevalence of plant and animal species, but also critical ecosystems that provide vital services to human society.

Although South Africa has invested enormous public, private and community resources into expansion of protected areas, conservation areas and reserves, innovative partnerships will in future be required to ensure that the burden for all this is not carried entirely by the fiscus. To this end, the Protected Areas Act offers a unique opportunity: it provides for any land, including private or communal, to be declared a formal protected area, co-managed by the landowner(s) or any suitable person or organisation. This means that formal protected area status is not limited to state-owned land, and that government agencies are not the only organisations that can manage protected areas, and opens the way for a range of innovative arrangements not previously possible. A related challenge is to forge the links between protected area development, sustainable tourism and benefits to surrounding communities, who should be key stakeholders in protected areas.

The National Environmental Management Act provides for a comprehensive regulatory framework for protecting crucial environmental resources. The core instrument used to give

Table 5: Key threats to South Africa's ecosystems

	Officially classified as threatened	Main issues and causes
Terrestrial ecosystems	34 per cent	• degradation of habitat • invasion by alien species
Freshwater ecosystems • *Wetlands destroyed* • *Fish threatened*	82 per cent *50 per cent* *36 per cent*	• pollution • over-abstraction of water • poor water course condition
Marine ecosystems • *Estuaries endangered*	65 per cent *62 per cent*	• climate change • unsustainable marine harvesting • seabed destruction by trawling • coastline urbanisation • marine pollution

effect to this Act is the environmental impact assessment (EIA). Although development projects must be subjected to an EIA, the focus is on costs of pollution and environmental impacts, and not on resource inputs and prices. This does not provide a sufficient basis for decoupling over the long-run.

POLICY RESPONSES

Recent years have witnessed an emerging trend in South Africa's national policy discourse: the call for more responsible use of natural resources. Growing numbers of policy statements acknowledge that the country's economic growth and development path is too resource inten-sive and that this needs to change. However, this way of thinking is by no means a dominant paradigm in policy-making circles. Section 24(b) of South Africa's new constitution commits the state to 'secure ecologically sustainable development and use of natural resources while promoting justifiable economic and social development'. This provides the point of departure for the national framework for sustainable development (NFSD) adopted in June 2008 (Republic of South Africa. Department of Environmental Affairs and Tourism 2007).

During the course of 2009, the Cabinet mandated the Department of Environmental Affairs to transform this policy framework into a more binding 'strategy', hence the commencement of the complex process of formulating the national strategy for sustainable development. However, key macroeconomic policy documents make no reference to section 24(b) of the constitution, the LTMS and the NFSD.

Macroeconomic policy versus section 24(b) of the constitution

In line with an ideological shift since 2002 away from neoliberalism towards a more 'develop-mental state' approach, the accelerated and shared growth initiative for South Africa (ASGI-SA) was adopted in 2006 as the official economic policy framework. Its focus is on specific 'binding constraints' that must be dealt with by concerted state-coordinated interventions that run contrary to traditional neoliberal prescriptions. ASGI-SA lists the following binding constraints: currency volatility; cost, efficiency and capacity of the logistics and transport system; shortage of skilled labour; barriers to entry and limits to competition; regulatory environment; and state capacity.

In 2007, Cabinet adopted the national industrial policy framework (NIPF) (Republic of South Africa. Department of Trade and Industry 2007). The NIPF lists four preconditions for effective industrialisation through industrial sector interventions:
- stable and supportive macroeconomic environment
- adequate skilled labour supply supported by appropriate education infrastructure
- existence of traditional and modern infrastructure[16]
- innovation capabilities to foster development of domestic technologies and systems.

Neither ASGI-SA nor NIPF makes any reference to section 24(b) of the constitution. Natural resources and ecosystem services are not identified as 'binding constraints', suggesting that no action is required to prevent further degradation. A viable set of ecosystems and long-term supply of natural resources are not regarded as preconditions for successful industrialisation; the implicit assumption appears to be that natural systems, within which the socio-economic system is embedded, are intact and durable. In short, contrary to all the scientific evidence, the natural resource base is taken for granted.

National framework for sustainable development (NFSD)

The NFSD was adopted by Cabinet in June 2008. In sharp contrast to macroeconomic policy, it explicitly acknowledges the growing stress on environmental systems and natural resources from economic growth and development strategies, and maps out a vision and five 'pathways' to a more sustainable future:
- enhancing systems for integrated planning and implementation
- sustaining our ecosystems and using resources sustainably
- investing in sustainable economic development and infrastructure
- creating sustainable human settlements
- responding appropriately to emerging human development, economic and environmental challenges.

The NFSD commits South Africa to a long-term programme of resource and impact decoupling. The government has resolved that the NFSD will be converted into a full-blown national *strategy* for sustainable development by the end of 2010 that will include specific targets, commitments and budget allocations under the above headings.

Ad hoc policy shifts

Because resource constraints and negative environmental impacts are material realities, they show up in all sorts of unanticipated ways. Although some of these unanticipated consequences are reflected in prices that, in turn, loop back into production costs and consumption prices, others are deeper and more long-term, with consequences that get reflected in less material things like the quality of life, the wealth of future generations and unemployment. What is interesting is that there is a wide range of policy shifts over the last few years that reveal that government and stakeholders are responding in *ad hoc* ways to these underlying resource constraints and environmental impacts. Examples include the following:

- the passing of the National Integrated Waste Management Act in 2009 that provided for the introduction, for the first time, of the globally recognised '3R' framework (reduce, recycle and re-use);
- the National Environmental Management Air Quality Act of 2004 was a response, albeit lacking in several respects, to the declining quality of the air that we breathe, in particular in urban areas, which results in rising health costs for the treatment of respiratory diseases;
- the introduction by the Department of Agriculture of a 'land care' programme aimed at finding ways of rehabilitating the quality of our soils, even though virtually no funds are allocated to this task – contrast this to Cuba and China, the former making soil rehabilitation by organic farming methods a top security priority after the fall of the Soviet Union in 1990, and the latter deciding to incentivise organic farming methods as a key element of its rural development programme that targets the 600 million rural Chinese who produce the bulk of China's food. Unfortunately, South Africa's 2009 rural development strategy (a cornerstone of the Zuma government's political strategy) makes no mention of the need to rehabilitate South Africa's soils even though it assumes millions will make a living cultivating these soils;
- the national water resource strategy has been a focus of the Department of Water Affairs (DWA) for a number of years, but a greater sense of crisis is evident in the work that is going into the water for growth and development strategy which acknowledges that South Africa has a limited water supply that will negatively affect future growth and development strategies. However, practical implementation radically to change water management systems at municipal level has yet to materialise and there is doubt that DWA has the capacity to implement a sustainable water resource strategy;
- the introduction of the renewable energy feed-in tariff that makes it possible for investors to establish renewable energy plants that will feed energy into the national grid in return for payments from ESKOM. This follows global trends, but ESKOM sneakily included a regulation that only it can buy this power – which means nothing will happen because ESKOM has made it clear that it does not intend concluding contracts to do this in the near future. Furthermore, it has decided to halt its own investments in renewable energy, and will consider building a concentrated solar power plant only because the World Bank insisted on it as a condition of its loan for building a coal-fired power station;
- the introduction by the Department of Human Settlements of a national programme to introduce sustainable resource-use criteria into the design of the settlement projects and houses that it subsidises across the country, with special reference to things such as densities, orientation of buildings, roof overhangs and insulation, installation of solar hot water heaters, and sustainable use of water and waste resources;
- the inclusion of carbon taxes in the 2007 and 2008 budgets. This was smart because the transition to a low-carbon economy can best be achieved by a slow and gradual decrease in the carbon intensity of the economy through taxes and incentives that increase the price of

carbon in ways that can capture the revenues generated for re-investment in low-carbon technologies;

- the adoption by the Department of Science and Technology of the global change grand challenge policy framework which provides for a ten year investment in the kind of science that will develop for South Africa the skills sets and knowledge base for designing and implementing more sustainable production and consumption systems;
- that big shift within the transport sector in favour of large-scale investments in public transportation systems that will, one hopes, gradually lead to much more aggressive measures to retard the growth of private car consumption and use;
- the adoption by Cabinet in 2008 of the LTMS and the NFSD already mentioned;
- the significant moves emanating from the Cabinet's economic cluster to formulate a 'green economy' approach, including the green jobs and industries for South Africa initiative (known as 'Green-JISA');
- section 12.2 of the much praised industrial policy action plan released in February 2010 by the minister of trade and industry refers specifically to the need for 'green and energy-saving industries' because rising energy costs 'render our historical capital and energy-intensive resource processing based industrial path unviable in the future'.
- the Treasury has promised to release its carbon tax discussion document in mid-2010;
- in the slow and painful process of formulating and adopting a national climate change policy framework, largely driven by the need to position South Africa globally as a player in the global climate negotiations leading up to the Copenhagen Conference in December 2009, the national climate change response strategy is promised for 'mid-2010';
- the Department of Energy has agreed to start the process of revising the integrated resources plan in April 2010, and in late 2009 it appointed consultants to write the long awaited renewable energy white paper;
- in December 2009, the Department of Energy released the solar hot water framework that promises to ensure the delivery of one million solar hot water heaters;
- as far as our key ecosystem services are concerned, significant progress has been made, including the passing of the National Environmental Management Biodiversity Act (NEMBA), the National Environmental Management Protected Areas Act (NEMPAA) in 2004, and the National Environmental Management Integrated Coastal Management Act in early 2009;
- connections between sustainable resource use and livelihood creation are recognised in programmes such as Working for Water, Working for Wetlands, LandCare, Coast Care and the Integrated Sustainable Rural Development programmes.

All these initiatives can be traced in one way or another to resource constraints and the negative implications for both growth and development. Unfortunately, macroeconomists and industrial strategists are not reading the clear signals of these *ad hoc* responses, a strategic blind spot that is rooted in the dualistic nature of our science, which does not equip development economists with knowledge of natural resources and ecosystems. As a result the responses are *ad hoc* in nature, rather than part of structural change in recognition of global and local resource constraints. It is hoped that the national strategy for sustainable development, set for adoption by Cabinet in 2010, will integrate these emerging trends into an overarching long-term development vision for South Africa. But unless the National Planning Commission is mandated to drive the NSSD it will fail to provide a framework for integration that helps South Africa catch up with many leading developed and developing nations that have realised that sustainable resource use holds the key to innovation-led growth and development.

Growing influence of sustainability thinking

In July 2008, the South African Cabinet endorsed the outcomes of the long term mitigation scenario (LTMS) process, which explored options for climate change mitigation in a multi-stakeholder exercise. Reinforcing the NFSD, the LMTS recommended the 'required by science scenario' that envisages a 30 per cent to 40 per cent reduction in South Africa's emissions by 2050. In April 2006, the Treasury published for comment a remarkable document entitled 'A Framework for Considering Market-Based Instruments to Support Environmental Fiscal Reform in South Africa'. It defines an environmental tax as a *'tax on an environmentally-harmful tax base'* (Republic of South Africa. National Treasury 2006ii [emphasis in original]) and examines all existing environmental taxes, charges and levies,[17] which, combined, account for approximately 2 per cent of GDP and just under 10 per cent of total tax revenue. The report suggests that in light of the sustainable development challenge, tax shifting is required so that taxes levied on 'bads' (such as pollution) can be increased and taxes on 'goods' (such as labour) reduced. This, the report argued, is the 'double-dividend hypothesis' – 'minimising the burden of environmentally-related taxes on the affected sectors, whilst creating the required behavioural incentives to achieve certain environmental outcomes' (Republic of South Africa. National Treasury 2006v). Put differently, taxes from unsustainable practices should increase, and should be reinvested in more sustainable practices.

It is noteworthy that the Treasury perspective described above is effectively a *command and control* perspective focussed on impacts and different from 'upstream' interventions that focus on primary resource inputs and prices. Nevertheless, this report, plus the gathering influence of the NFSD, did lead to the following statement by the minister of finance during his budget vote speech in 2008:

> We have an opportunity over the decade ahead to shift the structure of our economy towards greater energy efficiency, and more responsible use of our natural resources and relevant resource-based knowledge and expertise. Our economic growth over the next decade and beyond cannot be built on the same principles and technologies, the same energy systems and the same transport modes, that we are familiar with today. (Minister of Finance, Parliament, 20 February 2008).

Although this is the clearest and most radical statement so far by a senior South African politician about the need for far-reaching measures to decouple rates of growth from rates of resource consumption, this way of thinking has been abandoned by the new finance minister in the Zuma administration for reasons that were left unexplained. Nevertheless, other ministers have responded to resource constraints in their respective sectors by emphasising the need for sustainable resource use approaches. They include the minister of water affairs and forestry, who has admitted that by 2013 South Africa will face severe water shortages if alternatives are not implemented; the minister of energy, who has finally acknowledged that South Africa needs a rapidly expanding renewable energy sector;[18] and the minister of housing, who wants to see all low-income housing settlements subsidised by government to include sustainable design elements such as correct orientation, insulation, public transport links, recycling, energy efficient and supply with renewable energy. Significantly, the minister of science and technology has called for a ten-year science investment plan that will include a strong focus on innovations for sustainability, with decoupling referred to as a specific goal for innovation research and incentives. The Department of Environmental Affairs has completed the national cleaner production strategy, which lays down the framework through which different stakeholders (government, industry and civil society) will participate to ensure that South Africa achieves her goals on sustainable production and consumption (DEAT 2005b).

These policy shifts all reflect the fact that underlying resource constraints are forcing South Africa to adapt in an *ad hoc* manner, thus undermining the opportunities for innovation and new investment that they offer. While China, Europe, South Korea, Brazil, India and (even) the USA realise that resource depletion creates opportunities for innovation and investment, South Africa's economists seem to have disregarded Trevor Manuel's call to 'shift the structure of our economy'. Instead, the values and logic of the mineral-energy complex remain hegemonic.

DECOUPLING – OPPORTUNITIES FOR ACTION

Perhaps the most significant prospect for decoupling in South Africa is the massive injection of public and private investment funds to drive a vast multi-year infrastructure investment programme worth nearly R800 billion. A cornerstone of the government's long-term growth strategy, this national programme offers a unique opportunity to advance towards a more sustainable future. There is no doubt that public investment in infrastructure is a powerful way to ensure that growth sets up the conditions for meaningful poverty reduction. But there are two key questions.

The first is whether these investments address the challenges discussed above. There are some obvious positive investments, such as in public transport, upgrading of the rail infrastructure, and sustainable approaches to housing. These are already government priorities. There are also some obvious gaps, for example investments in soil rehabilitation, sustainable water and sanitation, air quality and renewable energy on a big scale.

The second question is less about *what* is being built, but more about *how* it will be built. There is an enormous opportunity to design and build low-carbon infrastructures and buildings that could contribute significantly to decoupling. Furthermore, the way infrastructures and buildings are developed on a big scale could be the single biggest catalyst we may ever have to drive a long-term commitment to sustainable resource use that, in turn, frees up resources for poverty eradication. Finally, doing things in new ways opens up a wide range of new value chains that could be exploited by new entrants into the sector with major employment creation opportunities. In its response to the global economic crisis, government has accepted that 'green collar jobs' will play a role.

Box 1 provides an overview of perfectly feasible and affordable strategic measures, following the priority headings used in the ASGI-SA policy document to prioritise investment focus areas.

Box 1: Decoupling opportunities

Energy
- Increase energy efficiency by 20 per cent to 30 per cent: boost demand-side management fund and remove it from ESKOM control; establish efficient decision-making system.
- Increase renewable energy supply to 30 per cent of national requirements, from large-scale wind, solar, wave and biomass plants by independent power producers using feed-in tariffs, and incorporate solar energy into all residential developments.
- Promote solar roof tops: co-finance one million new houses with solar roof tiles and water heaters.
- Create financial incentives and terminate disincentives through price mechanisms for investment in energy efficiency innovations.

Water and sanitation
- Switch from building dams to sustainable ground water exploitation and management (including storage and aquifer replenishment).
- Invest in reducing water loss from leakages to below 10 per cent.
- Reduce domestic water consumption by 40 per cent by mandatory use of water efficient household fittings, grey water recycling and rainwater harvesting.
- Build neighbourhood-level plants that recycle grey water for toilet flushing, capture methane gas for energy generation and capture nutrients for re-use in food production and greening.
- Invest in technology innovations to reverse the qualitative degradation of national water resources.

Transport and logistics
- Increase investments in urban public transportation systems, especially bus-rail-transit (BRT).
- Shift long distance freight transport from road to rail.
- Reduce dependence on oil through shift to electric cars, hydrogen and ecologically sustainable biofuels.

Housing and social infrastructure
- Eliminate housing backlog by construction of five million low-income houses with sustainable design and close to centres of employment.
- Increase densities from fifteen to twenty dwelling units per hectare to a minimum of thirty-five to forty-five dwelling units perhectare through smaller plot sizes, multistory living, and neighbourhood designs that minimise private vehicle transportation.
- Implement municipal 'green house' regulations governing all private, public and social infrastructure.

LED infrastructure
- Substantial investment in institutional development for LED as envisaged in the LED framework for South Africa (2006), but with a strong focus on payments for ecosystem services, waste recycling and re-use, and investments in sustainability innovations (for instance local manufacture and installation of solar energy systems).

CONCLUSION

The dominant economic paradigm in post-apartheid South Africa has so far failed to address a wide range of underlying resource constraints that will almost certainly undermine many preconditions for growth and development. The body of evidence that has emerged over the past decade at the global level and within South Africa clearly demonstrates that there are very serious material resource and ecological limits to the type of growth and poverty eradi-cation policies proposed by economic policy think-tanks like the Growth and Development Commission (that the minister of finance so admires). With significant exceptions, growth models have not emphasised the need for decoupling growth rates from rates of resource con-sumption and associated declining quality of the environmental systems that we depend on for things like clean air, productive soils and clean water. Reversing this trend will require pol-icy frameworks and interventions that are currently absent from national economic policy documents but which are slowly starting to emerge, with 2010 clearly set to be a watershed year. It is one thing, however, to formulate policy, and it is a very different matter when it comes to implementation through inter-institutional coordination, budget reform and regulatory interventions. Like many other policy realms, the South African state's capacity to formulate policies is not matched by its capacity to implement them.

There is broad consensus around two economic and social challenges for South Africa's second decade of democracy:
- how to boost growth to 6 per cent and ensure a more equitable distribution of wealth; and
- how to eradicate poverty, with special reference to the millennium development goals.
   The sustainability perspective means there now is a third challenge, and through the adoption of the NFSD and LTMS, this is being recognised:
- how to decouple growth rates and poverty eradication from rising levels of natural resource use and waste.

Many of South Africa's leading scientists have for some time been saying that economic growth policies are premised on incorrect assumptions about the health and durability of our natural resources and ecosystem services. Aligning economic policy with section 24 (b) of the consti-tution is not simply about preserving the environment. As other countries have experienced, it is also about preventing wasteful expenditure on avoidable system failures. But, above all, it can also be about the creation of new opportunities for driving non-material forms of growth that improve quality of life for all, forever.

NOTES

1   This case study is based on a report entitled Growth, Sustainability and Dematerialisation: Resource Use Options for South Africa by Mark Swilling, commissioned by the Presidency, South African Government, presented at the Workshop on Scenarios for South Africa in 2019, Presidency, Pretoria, July 2007 (Swilling 2007).
2   There is a significant difference between the notion that 'the era of cheap oil is over' and the notion that we have reached, or are about to reach, 'peak oil'. The latter notion is based on the assumption that there will be a decline in the total production of oil, whereas the former is more

concerned with the implications of rapidly rising oil prices for a global economy that depends on oil to meet 60 per cent of its energy needs.

3   This section is based primarily, but not exclusively, on background research materials commissioned to inform the writing of the National Framework for Sustainable Development that was adopted by Cabinet in June 2008. The materials were circulated publicly and most are available on www.deat.gov.za. The commissioned research papers are referenced in the sub-headings that follow, and additional research integrated where necessary. Because this section relies quite heavily on these papers, they are not specifically referenced in detail. The supporting research and back-up references can be found in these commissioned papers.

4   Domestic material consumption is the sum of domestic extraction of primary resources, plus imported primary resources, minus exported primary resources.

5   Based on the work of the Scenario Building Team (2007), Department of Environmental Affairs and Tourism, (2005a).

6   Based on the work by Jeremy Wakeford (2007).

7   Based on AGAMA Energy (2005).

8   Although towards the end of 2009 there were confirmed reports that Government was considering shelving the PBMR.

9   For example, concentrated solar power plants, which are already 60 per cent efficient, can be connected to salt batteries that can store energy for twelve to fourteen hours; this effectively means that solar power can contribute to the base load, which has been the key obstacle so far.

10   This section relies on the following documents: Ashton & Turton (2008); Department of Water Affairs and Forestry (2006); Republic of South Africa. Deparment of Water Affairs and Forestry (2004); Republic of South Africa. Department of Water Affairs and Forestry (2002); Turton (2008).

11   Based on Von Blottnitz (2005).

12   Mt =1 million metric tonnes or 1 billion kg.

13   For example, in Cape Town MSW is growing by 7 per cent a year.

14   Based on Laker (2005).

15   Based on Driver et al (2005).

16   Traditional infrastructure includes transport, electricity and water, while modern infrastructure refers to wireless, satellite, broadband, fixed line and mobile telecommunication networks.

17   Transport fuel levies (general fuel levy, road accident fund levy, equalisation fund levy, customs and excise levy); vehicle taxation (ad valorem customs and excise duty, road licensing fees); aviation taxes (aviation fuel levy, airport charges, air passenger departure tax); product taxes (plastic shopping bags levy); electricity (NER electricity levy; local government electricity surplus); water (water resource management charge, water resource development and use of water works charge, water research fund levy), and waste water (waste water discharge charge system – proposed).

18   A renewable energy feed-in tariff was introduced in 2009, as well as a new Air Quality Management Act.

REFERENCES

Ashton PJ & AR Turton (2008) Water and security in sub-Saharan Africa: Emerging concepts and their implications for effective water resource management in the Southern African Region. In Brauch HG, J Grin, C Mesjasz, H Krummenacher, NC Behera, B Chourou, UO Spring, PH Liotta and P Kameri-Mbote (Eds) *Facing Global Environmental Change: Environmental, Human, Energy, Food, Health and Water Security Concepts, Volume IV*. Berlin: Springer-Verlag.

Barbier EB (2009) A Global Green New Deal: Report prepared for the Economics and Trade Branch, Division of Technology, Industry and Economics, United Nations Environment Programme.

Behrens A, S Giljum, J Kovanda and S Niza (2007) The material basis of the global economy: Worldwide patterns of natural resource extraction and their implications for sustainable resource use policies. *Ecological Economics* 64: 444–453.

Blignaut J (2006) Macro-perspectives on water supply and demand: Implications of the 6 per cent economic growth rate. Presentation to National Environmental Advisory Forum: Pretoria, 3 October.

Bringezu S & R Bleischwitz (2009) *Sustainable Resource Management: Global Trends, Visions and Policies*. Germany: Wuppertal Institute.

Bringezu S & H Schutz (2001) *Material use Indicators for the European Union, 1980-1997. Economy-Wide Material Flow Accounts and Balances and Derived Indicators of Resource Use*. Luxembourg: Eurostat.

Bringezu S, H Schutz, S Steger and J Baudisch (2004) International comparison of resource use and its relation to economic growth: The development of total material requirement, direct material inputs and hidden flows and the structure of TMR. *Ecological Economics*. 51 (1/2): 97-124.

Burns M and A Weaver (2008) *Exploring Sustainability Science: A Southern African Perspective*. Stellenbosch: Sun Press.

Cairncross EK (2005) Air Quality. Cape Town: Unpublished paper commissioned by the Department of Environmental Affairs and Tourism.

City of Cape Town (2007) Report to the Chairperson: Utility Services Portfolio Committee Solid Waste Management. Department Sector Plan for Integrated Waste Management and Service Delivery in Cape Town. Cape Town: City of Cape Town, unpublished document.

Commission on Growth and Development (2008) *The Growth Report: Strategies for Sustained Growth and Inclusive Development*. Washington, DC: World Bank.

Department of Water Affairs and Forestry (2006) South Africa's Water Sources: 2006. Pretoria.

Fine B and Z Rustomjee (1996) *The Political Economy of South Africa: From Minerals-Energy Complex to Industrialization*. Boulder: Westview Press.

Fischer-Kowalski M (1998) Society's metabolism: The intellectual history of materials flow analysis, Part I, 1860–1970. *Journal of Industrial Ecology*. 2 (1): 61–78.

———- (1999) Society's metabolism: The intellectual history of materials flow analysis, Part II, 1970–1998. *Journal of Industrial Ecology*. 2 (4): 107–136.

Gallopin G (2003) *A Systems Approach to Sustainability and Sustainable Development*: Project NET/00/063. Santiago: Economic Commission for Latin America.

Gleick P (2006) *The World's Water (2006-2007): The Biennial Report on Freshwater Resources*. Washington, DC: Island Press.

Haberl H, M Fischer-Kowalski, F Krausman, H Weisz and V Winiwarter (2004) Progress towards sustainability? What the conceptual framework of material and energy flow accounting (MEFA) can offer. *Land Use Policy* 21: 199–213.

Intergovernmental Panel on Climate Change (2007) *Climate Change 2007*. Geneva: United Nations Environment Programme.

International Energy Agency (2008) *World Energy Outlook*. Paris: International Energy Agency.

Keqiang L (2009) Keynote Speech to the Annual General Meeting of the China Council for International Cooperation on Environment and Development. Beijing, 11–13 November 2009.

Krausmann F, N Eisenmenger, J Braunsteiner-Berger, M Deju, V Huber, L Kohl, A Musel, ML Nussbaum, S Rechnitzer and H Reisinger (2005) *MFA for South Africa*. Vienna: Institute for Social Ecology.

Krausmann F, H Schandl, M Fischer-Kowalski and N Eisenmenger (2008) The global socio-metabolic transition: Past and present metabolic profiles and their future trajectories. *Journal of Industrial Ecology* 12: 637–656.

Krausmann F, S Gingrich, KH Eisenmenger, H Haberl and M Fischer-Kowalski, forthcoming. Growth in global materials use, GDP and population during the 20th century. *Ecological Economics* 68 (10): 2696–2705.

Mohamed S (2008) Financialization and accumulation in South Africa. Unpublished PowerPoint presentation, 7 April 2008. Johannesburg: Corporate Strategy and Industrial Development, University of the Witwatersrand.

Morin E (1999) *Homeland Earth.* Cresskill, NJ: Hampton Press.

Republic of South Africa. Deparment of Water Affairs and Forestry (2004) National Water Resource Strategy. Pretoria: Department of Water Affairs and Forestry.

Republic of South Africa. Department of Environmental Affairs and Tourism (2007) People Planet Prosperity. A Framework for Sustainable Development in South Africa. [Online: retrieved 24 February 2008]. Department of Environmental Affairs and Tourism: Pretoria: 24 February 2008. Available from: www.sustainabilityinstitute.net.

Republic of South Africa. Department of Trade and Industry (2007) A National Industrial Policy Framework. Pretoria: Department of Trade and Industry.

Republic of South Africa. Department of Water Affairs and Forestry (2002) The Development of a Sanitation Policy and Practice for South Africa. Pretoria: Department of Water Affairs and Forestry.

Republic of South Africa. National Treasury (2006) A Framework for Considering Market-Based Instruments to Support Environmental Fiscal Reform in South Africa. Pretoria: Government Printer.

Republic of South Africa: National Treasury (2006) Accelerating Economic Growth – A Diagnostic Scan. Unpublished PowerPoint Presentation. Pretoria: National Treasury.

Stern N (2007) *Stern Review: Economics of Climate Change.* Cambridge: Cambridge University Press.

Stiglitz J, A Sen and JP Fitoussi (2009) *Report by the Commission on the Measurment of Economic Performance and Social Progress.* Report Commissioned by President Sarkozy, French Government.

Swilling M, E van Weiszaecker, M Fischer-Kowalski, A Manalang, R Yong, Y Moriguchi and W Crane (2009) Decoupling and Sustainable Resource Management: A Review – Draft 1.6. Paris: International Panel for Sustainable Resource Management, United Nations Environment Programme.

Turton AR (2008) Three strategic water quality challenges that decision-makers need to know about and how the CSIR should respond. Keynote Address: Science Real and Relevant: Pretoria. Centre for Scientific and Industrial Research, 18 November 2008.

United Nations (2005) *Millenium Ecosystem Assessment.* New York: United Nations.

United Nations (2006) *State of the World's Cities 2006/7.* London: Earthscan & UN Habitat.

United Nations Development Programme 1998. Human Development Report 1998. [Online: retrieved October/22/2006]. United Nations Development Programme: New York: 5 November 2006. Available from: http://hdr.undp.org/reports/global/1998/en/.

United Nations Environment Programme 2007. *Global Environment Outlook GEO 4: Environment for Development.* Nairobi: United Nations Environment Programme.

Von Blottnitz H (2005) Solid Waste. Cape Town: Unpublished paper commissioned by the Department of Environmental Affairs and Tourism.

Wakeford J (2007) Peak Oil and South Africa: Impacts and Mitigation. Cape Town: Association for the Study of Peak Oil and Gas – South Africa.

Watson RT, J Wakhungu and HR Herren (2008) International Assessment of Agricultural Science and Technology for Development (IAASTD).

World Bank (2005) *Where is the Wealth of Nations? Measuring Capital for the Twenty-First Century.* Washington, DC: World Bank.

World Resources Institute (2002) *Decisions for the Earth: Balance, Voice and Power.* Washington, DC: World Resources Institute.

World Wildlife Fund (2008) *Living Planet Report 2008.* Gland, Switzerland: World Wildlife Fund.

CHAPTER 5

Planning for sustainable living with limited water

Mike Muller

The development of our society, our growing population, and the legitimate demands of the disadvantaged majority for access to that most crucial natural resource - water - have placed new demands on what is, although renewable, a limited resource that can easily become polluted or over-used. There is only so much water that falls on our land every year. Unless we wish to begin to remove the salt from our vast resources of sea water (a very expensive process that requires enormous amounts of energy) we have to live within our means
(Department of Water Affairs and Forestry 1997: p.2 [emphasis added])

INTRODUCTION: Water as a 'lead sector' in planning for sustainability

In 1998, water resources in South Africa were effectively nationalised. This went largely unremarked, save for a cursory mention by the Free Market Foundation (Harris 2002). It was in part because the measure was carefully designed and expressed as a deprivation of property rights, through regulation in the execution of a public trust, rather than an outright expropriation. The intention was to ensure that, given the limited availability of a natural resource essential for diverse social, economic and environmental purposes, it would be available for use in the public interest. Nonetheless, what had been permanent property rights were transformed by legislation into temporary use rights with a maximum term of forty years.

An important dimension of the general public interest argument was that this policy created the formal framework for adaptation to future environmental changes which, in the face of climate change and other pressures, is increasingly recognised as vital for the achievement of sustainable development. The public interest requirements of achieving environmental sustainability were highlighted as a key justification for what otherwise could have been considered a 'taking' of property:

'It is submitted that these statutory powers contained in the NWA are suitably formulated to comply with the constitutional protection of property rights, if they are delicately exercised to reasonably balance property rights with the public interest, where the scarcity of water, the environmental requirement of sustainable use and the socio-economic requirements are the factors which contribute to the determination of the public interest in water resources management' (Uys 2009).

To understand the implications and broader relevance of this approach, it is useful to consider the concept of 'decoupling', which has been developed as a framework for addressing the goal of sustainability[1] in the face of multiple environmental challenges. Decoupling implies breaking the link between levels of resource use and 'development', however that is defined. But it is imprecise and needs to be better defined in order to become a useful framework for societies which seek to achieve the goal. The challenges faced in the management of water illustrate this well.

South Africa is a relatively water-scarce country (ranking thirtieth out of 180 countries in terms of available water per capita) (UNESCO-WWAP 2006). It is already 'water-stressed' and is approaching a state of water scarcity as commonly defined, which is based on the amount of water a country requires to maintain self-sufficiency in food (Falkenmark 1986). Yet water availability has not generally constrained economic development (Chenoweth 2008). Nor, while water scarcity limits local development options, can it be said to have constrained overall social and economic development since there is evidence that, where water-based development opportunities exist, take-up has been constrained by other factors (Muller 2009).

Indeed, it can be argued that in the water domain South Africa has already been relatively successful in decoupling its development from water availability, although environmental interests would argue that the environment has paid a price for that.

Decoupling in the water sector is thus not a theoretical construct or policy proposal but a current practice occurring within a relatively well-defined policy framework and institutional arrangements. 'Living within our means' lies explicitly at the heart of the national approach to this particular natural resource, as illustrated in the extract from the introduction to the 1997 National Water Resource Policy White Paper cited above.

To the extent that it has been successful, it is important to consider how this has been achieved while, where there have been failures, lessons need to be drawn.

Historically, the state has played a variety of roles in managing water resources. In the first instance, it invested in extensive public infrastructure to increase the amount of water that is reliably available for users. But it also established a regulatory framework to discipline water use and to manage conflicts between users. Finally, however, it has played an overarching planning role which has directed both the investment and regulatory interventions. It is suggested that the role of the state has been and remains pivotal through both formal and informal processes.

In the context of current discussions about the role of planning in a developmental state and the need for a developmental state to include environmental sustainability among its broad goals, this paper seeks to outline the role that planning processes, broadly interpreted, have had in the past and continue to have in the present in achieving a sustainable set of development outcomes in the water-related sectors. This discussion requires a more nuanced interpretation of the objectives and process of planning and is particularly relevant to current discussions about a new approach to strategic planning in government (Presidency 2009).

Whatever the precise mechanisms, the outcome is that on many measures, development has proceeded while water availability has remained constant. It is argued that, through the support and guidance of planning processes, decoupling has been achieved. In this sense, water resources are a lead sector in South Africa's quest for genuine sustainability.

Decoupling an improving quality of life from growing environmental impacts

The fundamental challenge of sustainability is to ensure that human activities do not overwhelm the capacity of the earth's natural systems to support them. This objective obviously clashes with the desire of most peoples for an improved quality of life, which is often benchmarked against the examples of 'developed' countries such as the USA and Western Europe. In the popular discourse, it is tritely pointed out that it would require the resources of four or five earths to support the world's current population at that standard of living with today's production systems (see for example, Cascio 2008 or, for a more technical discussion, *Nature* 2009).

This in turn gives rise to the concept of decoupling: improvements in the quality of life have to be achieved in different ways which do not impose such pressure on the natural environment: they have to be decoupled from the use of limited natural resources – such as water.

The countries of the OECD have formalised decoupling as an objective and an indicator to be monitored by member countries:

> The term decoupling refers to breaking the link between 'environmental bads' and 'economic goods.' Decoupling environmental pressures from economic growth is one of the main objectives of the OECD Environmental Strategy for the First Decade of the 21st Century, adopted by OECD Environment Ministers in 2001 (OECD 2008: p.1).

However, in understanding the concept of decoupling as it has been used, there are a number of different interpretations that need to be considered.

One group of '*radical decoupling*' strategies would seek to reverse the processes of globalisation and, through re-localisation, to encourage a delinking of regional or sub-regional African economies, or sectors of them, from the global market (see for example Amin 1990 and Amin 2009). While this may be perceived of as a radical step, it in fact reflects current practice in communities from Europe and Japan to India and the USA where, in the immediate interests of key social groups, sectors of the economy are regulated and protected from external competition (Potter and Burney 2002) and reflects a significant trend in development planning. It has also been advocated as an approach for the future (Friedman 1993). But this is essentially a political, social and economic strategy rather than an environmental one. For developing countries, to the extent that it constrains access to relevant technologies, it could result in increased environmental impacts; for instance if deforestation continued as a source of domestic energy in the absence of renewable energy sources.

A second form of decoupling addresses another set of interests and could be called parochial or '*cosmetic decoupling*' or 'greenwashing' since it involves distancing one community from its environmental impacts by exporting them to other locations. Many of the post-industrial societies of Europe and North America have done this by exporting physical production activities to developing countries and focusing their domestic economies on lower-impact service activities while still enjoying the fruits of resource-intensive consumption. Indeed, the Chinese growth path has been driven by this transfer of mass production activities and, as a resource-based economy, South Africa's relatively high energy consumption is a direct reflection of this process. To see through this kind of cosmetic decoupling, measures such as 'footprinting' seek to measure the overall impact of a set of production or consumption activities (Wackernagel and Rees 1996) although they have limited application in water resource assessment given its local nature; the impact of using water in the Amazon states of Brazil will be different to that in the arid nations of the Middle East.

For the purpose of this discussion, however, the interest is in promoting a path of social, economic and environmental development that allows a steady global improvement in peoples' quality of life without further compromising the environment, a *developmental decoupling*.

In this context, it is important to clarify that decoupling does not imply that there will be no further impacts on the natural environment. The ideology of 'no further environmental degradation' is strongest in the 'developed' countries whose natural environment has been totally transformed – as for instance in the destruction of European forests or the annihilation of North American wildlife. But it does imply that further development will occur within an envelope of impacts that is sustainable over the long term.

Planning for development – its evolution from normative allocation to social process

Development planning, when divorced from its real estate/urban development context, is still associated with the failed socialist experiments of the USSR and Eastern Europe. In this context, planning lay at the core of economic policy and management and policy directions and decision-making about investments, production volumes and in many cases, consumption allocations were transmitted through the centralised planning process.

There is wide consensus that such centralised planning cannot successfully be used to direct the workings of a modern economy and society (or any large and complex organisation) in situations of uncertainty and limited information. But there remains a need for a process to assist such organisations to achieve their desired objectives, to initiate actions in the present reality that move the organisation towards that future desire.

So, almost in parallel with the decline in interest in central planning, there has been a growth in interest in strategic planning, notably from the corporate sector, although this is often so far removed from traditional planning processes that it is considered simply to be a 'strategy' process rather than planning *per se* (Stiglitz 1998). And this exists, formally or informally, wherever large organisations have established (or been given) clear objectives, and are not simply driven by generic opportunistic goals such as finding a niche where it is possible to generate increasing profits.

Practitioners of this new generation planning have emphasised that the planning process is as much about establishing common mindsets within organisations, 'a change in the way managers view their world' as in projecting the evolution of business activities (Wack 1985).

South Africa's renewed interest in strategic development planning is a good example and, to the extent that it identifies specific time-bound actions to be undertaken by government as well as a process of interaction with the wider community, it is not inaccurate to describe it as a planning process. After sixteen years of national democracy, it is becoming evident that key societal goals of 'a better life for all' are not being achieved through current policies. Racial disparities remain stark, inequality is at record levels and levels of participation in the economy have stalled, leaving many working age people dependent on social grants.

As a result, there is political pressure to introduce approaches which can address these failures. The establishment of the role of a minister in the Presidency for national planning, with responsibility for establishing a national planning commission is a response to the pressures and evidence of the belief that a planning process is needed to achieve what are essentially transformational goals in a complex and difficult context (Presidency 2009).

Given the challenges, there are many sceptical voices although, in deference to the relative novelty of the initiative and not less to the individual tasked with undertaking it, these are still relatively muted. 'Wait and see' perhaps characterises the majority of responses. This is why it is relevant and indeed important to demonstrate that such processes can help to achieve overarching societal goals, such as sustainability. It is this, it is argued, that the water sector has been doing.

The changing goals of water resource management: decoupling formalised as an objective

The formal acknowledgement that South Africa had entered a necessary transition from water development to water management, that future social and economic growth had to be achieved without a growth in the availability of water, came in the 1996 white paper on a national water policy for South Africa (Department of Water Affairs and Forestry 1997).

This chose to depart from the traditional goal of government, which had been ' ... to ensure that water is available in sufficient quantity, quality and reliability for the development and well-being of the nation', as expressed in the first draft of the water law principles. Instead, it was stated that the goal of 'managing the quantity, quality and reliability of the nation's water resources is to achieve optimum long term social and economic benefit for society from their use'.

This carried with it a range of implications. In the past, reconciliation between the demand of water and its supply had usually been achieved by the simple expedient of increasing the supply through infrastructure development. In the future, the management of demand, increasing water use efficiency and the reallocation of water between uses would become more important as described in the introductory quotation.

This was further elaborated in a discussion about the objectives of and approach to water resource management:

> Since much of the accessible resource has been developed ... the task is increasingly to manage within the constraints that are given us by nature ... The challenge of water management in the 21st century is to ensure that the society develops in a way that can function successfully within the constraints of its resource base. It is to treat the development, use and protection of our water as a common endeavour in the interests of all ... (Department of Water Affairs and Forestry 1997 p.16).

From infrastructure development to reconciliation and management: the planning framework

It needs to be emphasised that the focus here is not on the water supply and sanitation services that lucky citizens enjoy and of which less fortunate ones dream. It is on the natural resource and the extent to which demands upon it – including its use as a source of domestic water and as a 'sink' for the disposal of waste water – can be sustained into the future.

Once the proportion of available water resources abstracted reaches a critical level (60 per cent is widely considered to be such a threshold: see International Water Management Institute 2007) the assurance of supply of sufficient water at an adequate level of reliability and the maintenance of its quality at usable levels requires ongoing, active management, particularly in a highly variable climatic regime. Planning is an important component of this and has a number of dimensions which are discussed below.

However, before addressing planning as a mechanism to achieve the desired reconciliation between the supply of water and its availability, it is necessary to consider the obvious alternative: the use of market mechanisms.

The limits to the market approaches in water management

One approach often proposed to guide the allocation of natural resources and keep their use within sustainable limits is to establish effective markets. However, there is limited evidence that markets, by themselves, can achieve the desired objectives in the water sector. Indeed, the assertion that market solutions will alone achieve appropriate allocation decisions for water resources finds little empirical support.

The best documented case is that of Chile where, in the 1970s, the right-wing government of General Pinochet introduced text book free-market economic reforms which included the water sector. As one commentator has said,

> After more than 20 years, Chile's experience with a narrow and free-market approach to water rights has shown that this approach has some important economic benefits, but that these benefits are closely associated with serious problems and costs (Bauer 2005).

The problem, says Bauer, is that the framework established has failed to address some key issues. Specifically, it has proved to be

> ... incapable of handling the complex problems of river basin management, water conflicts, and environmental protection. These more complex problems, of course, are precisely the fundamental challenges of integrated water resources management. In addition, peasants and poor farmers have for the most part not received the economic benefits, which indicates that social equity is another weak point of the current framework *(ibid)*.

The reasons for this include the nature of the 'good' – it has extensive social and environmental dimensions which are difficult to price and, once priced, difficult to trade. The externalities of market based decisions are difficult to identify and quantify. In South Africa, the archetypal case would be the social and economic impact of a Northern Cape fruit farmer selling up his irrigation allocation to an upstream mine or city, leaving a destitute rural community and sunken public investments in infrastructure.

But there are also important physical limits to tradeability. The fact that water can be accessed in one place does not mean that the same quantity can be accessed at another, even on the same river or in the same irrigation scheme. This adds significant complexity to any attempt at a system-wide market-based solution to the challenge of reconciling supply and demand. The very nature of the 'water right' is elusive. It is rarely a right to a guaranteed, fixed quantity of water at a specified time. Invariably, it is more or less preferential access to what water may be available at a given time; the reliability of the supply is often more important than the volume and may be more or less precisely defined. 'Dry rights' are common in stressed environments, including South Africa.

Similarly, in relation to quality issues, what the water resource provides is a dilutive disposal capacity which varies almost daily. But 'waste loads' cannot easily be transferred from one 'user' of this capacity to another since water quality impacts are highly site-specific. This is not to say that setting a price for a water supply or for the use of waste disposal capacity is not an important signal, offering a useful regulatory instrument for resource managers. But it is not strictly a market price.

As the Chilean example demonstrates, while market mechanisms may be useful in addressing resource allocation between economic users of the resource, they are not particularly useful in achieving the broader environmental and social objectives that characterise water resource management. Indeed, the dominant paradigm of integrated water resource management (IWRM), is portrayed as an approach which seeks to achieve a balance between the social, environmental and economic objectives of different societies, recognising that they differ from place to place and from time to time.

Thus within the IWRM paradigm, economic instruments are just one element of a much larger toolbox, the dominant elements in which are the instruments of governance, of which planning is part. Reviewing successful examples where good water resource management had contributed to the achievement of broader development objective, co-author Roberto Lenton and I noted that, in all the cases:

A very similar basic approach was applied, which recognised:
- the unitary nature of the water resource;
- the physical interventions that could be adopted to manage it;
- the limits to those physical interventions; and
- the need for an institutional framework that:
- brought stakeholders together in an equitable manner that gave voice to the weak as well as to the powerful;
- sought to achieve a balance of interests between them and, within this;
- recognised the value and importance of the waters concerned,
- identified the environmental dimension of water management either explicitly as a separate 'use' or as a desirable outcome; and
- developed organisations able to promote the overall approach.

And we concluded that:

> Societies will use their own practices of governance to determine the appropriate balance between social, economic and environmental goals, which will change over time (Lenton and Muller 2009).

Planning is an important part of that governance mix.

WATER RESOURCE SECTOR PLANNING PROCESSES

Water resource planning in South Africa has often been characterised as a process of reconciliation between supply and demand. This may be considered narrowly, as a process to forecast needs and then to identify infrastructure developments that can meet them. Physical resource assessment together with infrastructure planning defines an envelope of reliably available water. However, as available resources are used, the reconciliation process must necessarily focus increasingly on the demand side and identify interventions that can reduce demand, meet it from non-traditional sources or 'trade-off' one set of uses against others.

To achieve this requires significant technical capacity to identify and monitor water uses as well as to characterise and monitor the water resource itself. Over nearly a century, the national administration, currently the Department of Water Affairs, has built a capacity to do this. While this technical work is essential for effective planning, it should not be conflated with the planning process.

Before 1998, the planning processes were not codified but the National Water Act, 1998 specified a planning process, which is outlined below. However, the informal technical and institutional mechanisms that evolved prior to this have continued to be effective. These included catchment management forums, non-statutory organisations that brought together the major water users in areas where water stress was growing, to discuss approaches to resolve them.

A key consideration is the extent to which formal and informal mechanisms have worked together to produce the desired results and one lesson that can be drawn from this experience is about the interaction between formal and informal processes.

National Water Resource Strategy

Within the framework established by the 1998 National Water Act, the National Water Resource Strategy (NWRS) is intended to play a central role. The Act requires the National Water Resource Strategy to '… set out the strategies, objectives, plans, guidelines and procedures of the minister and institutional arrangements relating to the protection, use, development, conservation, management and control of water resources …'

The first NWRS was published in 2004, after two years of consultation; it includes analysis of the water balance in the nineteen water management areas (WMAs) into which the country is divided, with specific proposals for achieving reconciliation including both new infrastructure, connections with water surplus WMAs and demand management interventions.

The predecessor of the NWRS was the Management of the Water Resources of South Africa, published by DWA in 1986. This had already begun to address many of the issues tackled in the 1996 White Paper, the 1998 National Water Act and the NWRS. Even at a time when governance in South Africa was fractured and divided, the notion that common approaches were needed for the management of the limited resource, and that consultation with users, was important to ensure a coherence of approach.

Catchment management strategies

Catchment management strategies are subsidiary to the NWRS. They provide the framework for water resources management within a specified WMA, which were established to follow the natural boundaries of river basins. The NWRS provides the framework within which all catchment management strategies will be prepared and implemented in a manner that is consistent throughout the country. The Act stipulates that a catchment management strategy must not be in conflict with the NWRS. But the interaction is not simply top down. It is explicitly stated in the NWRS 'that insights and information gathered during the development of catchment management strategies will inform the regular review of the NWRS, enabling it to remain relevant to local conditions and circumstances' (Department of Water Affairs and Forestry 2004, p.9).

In the absence of formally established and function CMAs, the DWA has continued to produce 'strategic perspectives' for each catchment which cover the same key dimensions.

Water service development plans

The 'top-down/bottom-up' mechanism is repeated at more local levels. In terms of the Water Services Act, 1997, which regulates water supply and sanitation, water services development plans have to be prepared by all metropolitan and district municipalities, as well as by those local municipalities which are authorised to fulfil the role of a water services authority. These plans should include projections of water resource requirements to meet projected needs as well as approaches adopted to provide sanitation services and safely dispose of the wastes.

The National Water Act requires catchment management strategies to take account of these development plans in determining water allocations to a municipality and issuing licences. Data from these plans will be incorporated into the national water resources information system, thereby contributing to national water resources planning.

The water service development plans are also supposed to include details of water demand management and conservation measures. When preparing its water services development plan, a water services authority must refer to the relevant catchment management strategy for information about the availability of water to support proposed water services targets, the source of the water, and the requirements for the quality of waste water that is to be returned to the water resource after use.

It is at this level that the informal mechanisms that pre-dated the National Water Act are most evident. As a matter of course, major municipalities made estimates of their water requirements and sought to identify appropriate sources for them. This required interaction with the national department which in turn used these demand projections to guide its regional and catchment planning approaches.

Other sectoral processes (agricultural and industrial development)

While the coordination with water services as a water resource user sector is the area that is most explicitly developed, formal planning processes exist with other sectors, as illustrated below:

Figure 1: Water-related planning in the national planning framework

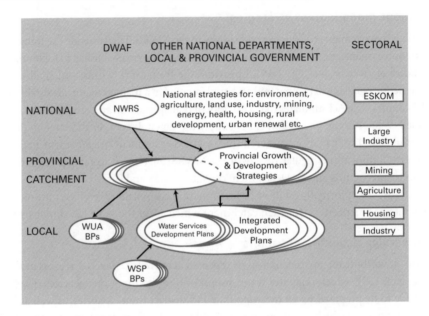

(CMS - catchment management strategy; WUA - water user association; WSP - water services provider; BP - business plan)
(**Source**: Department of Water Affairs and Forestry, 2004)

Thus, irrigation policy was developed jointly with the Department of Agriculture, although that delayed the process substantially. The policy on managing the impacts of mining on water resources was developed in consultation with the Minerals and Energy Department as well as with the Chamber of Mines, which represents the mining industry.

Water to support electricity generation and the production of liquid fuels is specifically prioritised as a national strategic issue in the NWRS:

> Much of the country's economic activity, as well as its social stability, depend on a sufficient and reliable supply of electrical power. The abstraction and storing of water for use at power station operated by Eskom, as the organisation entrusted with generating the bulk of the country's electricity, is therefore regarded as being water use of strategic importance. All water that is taken from a water resource or stored for whatever purpose at Eskom power generation facilities will therefore be authorised by the Minister.

Water use designated as being of strategic importance will, however, be subject to the same efficiency criteria and water demand management requirements as is applied to other uses. Dry-cooling of power stations should be applied where feasible when new generating capacity is built (Department of Water Affairs and Forestry 2004 p.52).

Finally, while water resource management is an environmental management activity in its own right, the policy-makers recognised that the approaches taken had to be consistent with the overarching approach to environmental management. To this end, joint work was undertaken with the Department of Environmental Affairs and Tourism so that, notwithstanding the inevitable bureaucratic boundary disputes, overall approaches were coherent and there was cooperation and coordination in their implementation.

Again, prior to any formal requirement for interaction, industries and the national Department were in regular contact to ensure that needs were understood and appropriate approaches were planned to meet them.

THE LINKAGES BETWEEN WATER AND BROADER STRATEGY AND PLANNING

Managing water is about achieving goals which are often implicit or poorly defined through effective management of uncertainty and ambiguity. That is why it is such a useful metaphor for other dimensions of sustainability in a world in which uncertainty is a dominant factor. But water resource planning cannot happen in isolation – it needs effective engagement with a range of stakeholders, not just the major water users but also communities that are affected by water and water management decisions.

This cannot occur only in a water focused context; indeed, one of the general challenges of development planning is to promote cross sectoral coordination. To achieve this, a generic planning system is required within which there must be an effective interface with water planning.

The context in which South Africa's constitution was negotiated ensured that the roles and functions of different levels of government would be clearly defined. Indeed, the terminology of levels was replaced by 'spheres' to emphasise the autonomy of the local domain, a key objective of minority groups who had hoped to retain some degree of self-government. The challenges of managing a system with relatively extreme decentralisation and devolution of power has given rise to a complex (and often dysfunctional) system in cooperative governance. However, in the planning area at least, the formal instruments are clearly defined.

Local government integrated development plans

The formal linkage between water resources planning and broader development planning is strongest at the local level. Although the Water Services Act preceded the establishment of municipalities and local government and the associated legislation, water services development plans were explicitly designed to form part of the integrated development plans that municipalities must prepare in terms of the Municipal Systems Act, 2000 (No. 32 of 2000).

Provincial government growth and development strategies

Provincial governments are also expected to promote coordinated development and, to achieve this, to prepare provincial growth and development strategies. Covering economic development areas, these focus on areas such as agriculture, mining and other industries which are particularly relevant to the water sector. However, since water resources are a national government competence, the sector is not formally represented in provincial planning meetings unless specially invited. Where this has been done, excellent alignment has been achieved, as illustrated by the Limpopo case (see below).

National spatial development perspective

Water is recognised as an important constraint for development. The national spatial development perspective, up to now the overarching national planning instrument, has highlighted that 'the dominant pattern of settlement and economic activity in South Africa is largely out of line with water availability' (Presidency 2003: p.13).

However, while the objective of water resource management has been explicitly stated in South Africa's policy as 'optimal benefit', it is not always obvious how this 'optimality' will be determined. What it has meant in the past is that development decisions involving water, or water development proposals, have been considered on an *ad hoc* basis through inter-ministerial consultations or Cabinet discussions.

National Planning Commission

The proposed establishment of a national planning commission is intended to address the *ad hoc* nature of decision making across society; water and its use has been explicitly identified as one of the cross-cutting issues that need to be addressed by the Commission.

> A long-term plan has to be informed by breaking down the country's high level aspirations into focused strategies. These would deal with such issues as economic development, human resource development, building a developmental state, enhancing regional stability and so forth. A plan has to take into account environmental factors such as the global economy, climate change, demographic trends and regional peace and stability. Long-term cross cutting issues such as food, energy and water security would also have to be factored in (Presidency 2009: p.4).

International perspectives

Many of South Africa's major rivers are shared with neighbouring countries and their use is subject to agreements with those countries. The National Water Act provides for water to be 'reserved' in terms of international treaties for use by neighbours and this is detailed in the NWRS. The bilateral and multilateral agreements and institutional arrangements (mainly technical committees) between the countries provide a basis for joint planning and joint studies to assess the resource and identify potential development opportunities.

There has been pressure from donor countries with influence on policy in neighbouring countries to establish autonomous river basin commissions to undertake management of shared rivers. However, although a number have been established, they have not functioned particularly effectively. In a planning context, their obvious defect is that, as autonomous regional institutions, they are isolated from the administration of other sectors in the partner countries

WATER RESOURCE PLANNING IN PRACTICE: Some exhibits

It is not possible in a single chapter to provide detailed examples of the assertion that the planning processes, broadly understood, have contributed to achieving decoupling and sustainability. However, through a range of examples, key elements of the operation and outcome of the planning process can be illustrated.

Water for electricity

One of the earliest demonstrations of decoupling in practice has been the change in the water intensity of electricity generation. This followed the recommendation by a 1970 commission of enquiry that, because electricity is generated in water stressed areas (close to coal deposits), efforts should be made to reduce water consumption (Government of South Africa 1970).

Between 1980 and 2006, Eskom reports that it has decreased its water use from 2.85 l/kWh to approximately 1.32 l/kWh in 2006. This was largely achieved by the use of dry cooling rather than water cooling for its inland power stations. 'Matimba Power Station near Lephalale in the Limpopo Province is claimed to be the largest direct-dry-cooled station in the world, with an installed capacity greater than 4000 megawatts ... Water consumption is in the order of 0.1 litres per kWh of electricity sent out, compared with about 1.9 litres on average for the wet-cooled stations' (Eskom 2009).

Dry cooling carries a significant cost penalty but this is considered to be acceptable given the limited water resource availability. (This example illustrates the interconnectedness of natural resource decoupling issues – since dry cooled power stations are less efficient than water cooled ones, their hydrocarbon fuel use is greater and their CO_2 emissions are greater; a balance thus needs to be struck between water efficiency and CO_2 emissions.)

Price setting reflects relative scarcity

One outcome of an effective planning process is that it should give appropriate signals to guide development. For large commercial users, it would be desirable for water prices to reflect water scarcity. However, most municipal water services providers aim to meet the needs of existing and future consumers within their area of jurisdiction. In these circumstances, the transmission of signals about scarcity may be impaired.

The nature of the price setting mechanism in water necessarily involves interactions between the water services providers (municipal level), regional bulk suppliers (water boards in many areas) and the national Department of Water Affairs which acts as custodian of the resource and provides and operates infrastructure to achieve reliable supplies for major users, including municipalities. All three levels have specific price setting responsibilities and for most metropolitan and large urban areas, water prices are built up from resource charges, bulk charges and local service charges.

In inland areas, there are clear constraints on increasing water supplies; where augmentation is possible, the marginal cost is invariably much higher than current costs. On the other hand, in coastal cities there is essentially an infinite supply of water available from desalination of sea water.

It is thus significant that the cost of water to industrial users inland and at the coast is different. Inland prices tend to be set at the top end of domestic charges, generally set to reflect the marginal cost of augmenting water supplies; at the coast, the prices reflect the mean domestic charge, which correlates closely with the emerging cost of desalination. Although it is not formal policy to set tariffs according to these criteria, the interaction between providers about opportunities for augmentation does appear to have influenced the price setting process (Muller 2007).

Limpopo changes its development strategy

One demonstrable success of the interaction between the formal water planning system and the provincial development strategy is provided by the experience of the Limpopo province. The 2004 draft Limpopo GDS focused on expansion of agriculture, mining and tourism as key economic and job creating sectors. Unfortunately, all depend on the availability of water which is in very short supply in the province. When this was drawn to the attention of the province, the result was a much more nuanced GDS which recognised that there were constraints on expansion of agriculture if the other sectors were to be allowed to develop (Muller 2009).

After identifying key development 'clusters', the strategy noted that:

> ... all these clusters are faced with one major development constraint, namely water. Water is a scarce resource in South Africa and more so in the Limpopo province. ... The formation and promotion of the cluster development, however, has to go hand in hand with a water resource and management strategy to ensure optimal use. All effort should be made to use the existing water in the best possible way. This includes implementing water demand-side and conservation strategies. Continuous research to improve water use efficiency is therefore of the utmost importance (Limpopo Provincial Government 2004: p.25).

The platinum rush and responses to supply constraints in the Olifants basin

A more detailed example of the effective functioning of the planning system follows from the experience in the Limpopo province where rapid expansion of platinum mining is occurring. In a repeat of the experience of the emergence of gold mining in Gauteng, the platinum deposits lie in a water-stressed part of the Limpopo river basin, a region in which there is already significant competition for limited water supplies.

Water supply was identified as a constraint on the development of the platinum mines in the early 2000s as part of regional planning in which the Limpopo province played a leading role. Partly at the instigation of the provincial government, the national department and a consortium of most of the mining companies active in the area initiated a programme to identify opportunities to address the requirements of the expansion. A range of opportunities were considered, including taking water from agricultural use and building storage infrastructure to enable new supplies to be taken from the limited surplus available in the area (Department of Water Affairs and Forestry 2004; *Engineering News* 2008).

The resulting programme identified key infrastructure investments and a decision was taken to retain agricultural allocations as far as possible. Since approximately seven years was required for the new infrastructure to come on stream, other interventions were required to meet supply requirements in the interim. One response was for the mining companies to 'rent' unused agricultural water from farming schemes which had fallen into disrepair; the revenue was earmarked to fund their rehabilitation. The other was for the mining companies to collaborate with municipalities to purify and re-use urban wastewater for process purposes. While the construction of the infrastructure is still underway, it is notable that water supply constraints have not unduly hampered the industry, although they have guided the phasing and location of its expansion.

Accommodation of competing demands on the Komati and Pongola/Maputo shared rivers

One concern about planning processes which involve collaborative processes between a range of participants is the asymmetry between the actors. This is well illustrated in the Komati River basin where major corporate users such as Eskom and Sappi compete for use of the limited resource with municipalities, commercial farmers, nature conservation in the form of the Kruger National Park and, since 1994, with small-scale black farmers in the former homeland of KaNgwane.

The different users have come together in sometimes fractious discussions to share the available water. Through the intermediary of water user associations, available water is shared between white commercial farmers and their black neighbours who farm on a smaller scale. The farmers, in turn, have engaged with municipalities and industry – including power utility Eskom which takes water out of the catchment to supplement its cooling water supplies in power stations in the Vaal catchment. Pollution from Sappi's pulp and paper plant at Ngodwana, which was affecting farmers on a tributary to the Komati, has been addressed through major corporate investments in process upgrading. And the conservation authorities actively monitor users and the state of the resource.

The need for cooperation and consensus on the use of water is not limited to the territory of South Africa and there has also been structured engagement across the border with both Mozambique and Swaziland regarding the two shared rivers, the Komati and the Pongola/Maputo. During times of limited flow, members of user communities on both sides of the border have met under the umbrella of the three country technical committee which oversees relations. Again, while these meetings have sometimes been difficult, the users have ensured that sufficient water is supplied to what are agreed are key users in all three countries.

The consequence of these interactions is not just that operational peace and equilibrium has been achieved. As important are trans-national planning processes, conducted under the aegis of a tripartite technical committee, which have facilitated a substantial expansion of irrigation in Swaziland while Mozambique's future requirements for urban supplies have been 'reserved'.

Gauteng and Vaal system: 'Thieving farmers' or optimal use?

Perhaps the most impressive example of the development-oriented reconciliation process is that of the supply of water to the economic heartland of the country, the province of Gauteng and surrounding areas. It is estimated that approximately 60 per cent of the country's GDP is generated in this area which is also home to 50 per cent of the country's population.

Situated high in the catchment on the watershed dividing the basin that drains to the Limpopo river and discharges in the Indian Ocean, and that of the Orange river which drains to the Atlantic, this is not an optimal location from a water management perspective. It is estimated that less than 10 per cent of current activity and population could be supported from the natural resource of the local Vaal and Crocodile basins, which are tributaries to the Orange and Limpopo respectively. Nevertheless, through a combination of water resource development projects typical of the 'hydraulic mission' stage of water development, the region receives a reliable supply. Indeed, in recent times, bulk water supply has been more reliable than electricity despite the fact that its sources are far more variable and unpredictable than those for electricity.

This has been achieved through a dynamic planning and development process involving a number of informal administrative forums convened by, amongst others, DWA and Rand Water, and drawing in the major municipalities in the region as well as mining and other industries. The most recent development was the completion of Phase 1B of the Lesotho Highlands project which diverts additional water from the Orange River to its Vaal tributary (from whence much is further diverted, after use, to tributaries of the Limpopo as purified waste).

Since infrastructure projects of this nature are 'lumpy' there is a period during which demand falls short of the increased supply. During this period, additional sub-economic uses can be allowed without detriment to other users; this has been happening informally as farmers riparian to the diverted waters expand their irrigation.

With the limits of the current tranche of increase now in sight (additional water, or stabilisation of demand, may be required as early as 2017), this informal use is being highlighted and efforts are starting to bring it under control as well as to enhance water conservation in urban areas supplied by the system. This is an appropriate response, both on the part of opportunistic farmers, but also in the timing of the response of the authorities and indicates that the monitoring (if not yet the enforcement) is still effective.

But is there decoupling? An important indicator of changing patterns of use is also the reduction in water use per household. While this is in large measure due to the changing character of households (both in size, income and important dimensions such as plot size, all of which affect water consumption), water policy has supported these other drivers to achieve a reduction in unit consumption as the population served has increased.

How eThekwini put its World Cup at risk

It would be incorrect to suggest that the planning process always works effectively and one reason for this is over-estimation of the ability to manage 'soft' institutional interventions and demand management. One example of (relative) failure is the water supply to the eThekwini metropolitan area (the Durban area). Water is relatively plentiful on the eastern seaboard, although the growth of South Africa's second largest conurbation has already required a number of coastal rivers to be tapped and for water to be imported from further afield. The Umgeni Water Board, responsible for bulk supplies had, together with DWAF, identified the need for augmentation of supplies before 2010, to meet growing demand. However, in their planning meetings, they had not convinced the eThekwini metro municipality that this investment was necessary – in part because the metro had had experiences of over-investment by Umgeni in the past which had contributed to higher than necessary tariffs for a number of years. They also hoped to reduce the demand, both through the promotion of water conservation and by implementing water re-use schemes (*Daily News* 2009a).

Thus, although studies showed the need to start construction on schemes to augment supplies, this was delayed. Unfortunately, the demand management alternatives did not achieve the results desired and as a result the metropolitan area will be at risk of supply constraints until the completion of the Spring Grove dam, currently scheduled for 2012. This highlights one of the vagaries of water resource management: the risk of a supply shortfall is based on hydrological analysis and there is a better than one in twenty chance that rainfall will be insufficient to meet the full demand. That is not a comfortable position to be in during an *el Niño* event[2] and it has been officially recognised that eThekwini will be 'at risk' for the next two years (*Daily News* 2009b).

What is relevant in this case is that one of the parties to the planning process chose to use an alternative strategy; it was the failure of this strategy that has placed the city at risk rather than a failure of the planning system *per se.*

Development opportunities forgone

Another failure of the system relates to the need for other sectors and agencies of government to respond to opportunities that may be identified through the water sector's planning processes. The mere existence of a development potential does not necessarily translate into a development intervention, whether because of coordination failures (failure to transmit the information from one sector to the other) or implementation failures (inability to act on the potentials identified). Thus in the 2004 NWRS, six opportunities for irrigation and afforestation were identified in different parts of the country. However, despite sectoral efforts to promote these opportunities, little development has occurred.

CHALLENGES

In all the cases described above, what is notable is that detailed investment and regulatory interventions were not decided upon and implemented by a single central body. The process was rather to engage with all spheres of government as well as civil society actors, to identify options and to encourage different agencies to implement the appropriate responses.

Essentially, the process created a common understanding of the issues and a common vision of how best they could be addressed. While that carries risks (as in the case of eThekwini) it has the advantage that the institutions most affected by the decisions are often those that have to take the action. In addition, it means that the decisions will tend to be supported by all concerned which is critical since, as in Gauteng, the investment costs in Lesotho are incurred by the national department but have to be funded from municipal and industrial consumers, through intermediaries such as bulk supplier Rand Water. This requires a high level of alignment between institutions which is achieved through regular, structured engagements between the national department, Rand Water and key municipal and industrial water users guided by systematic modelling of both supply and demand parameters.

It would be premature to suggest that the planning processes introduced in the water sector have achieved decoupling across the sector that is likely to be sustainable in the long-term. Extensive challenges remain which, in turn, reflect the broad challenge of achieving sustainable development.

Decentralisation

Effective decentralisation is necessary if bottom-up processes are to effectively complement those operating top-down. This requires local institutions with the financial and technical capacity, and the social mandate, to engage. Current South African experience is that this has not yet been achieved. Widespread municipal failure has affected the water resource sector both through failure to manage and predict the use of water (through water conservation activities and local resource planning) and by its failure to manage the impacts of waste water on the resource. Failure of these operational functions may undermine the efficacy of planning decisions taken at higher levels.

There has also been failure in the water sector to formally decentralise its institutions. Only a handful of a potential nineteen catchment management agencies have been established and their functionality is limited; most have not produced a catchment management strategy, which is supposed to provide the foundation for their activities as well as for their interaction with national planning processes.

Social coherence and stakeholder engagement

Linked to the issues of decentralisation is the broader question of the relationship of institutions of governance with their communities. The challenge is most acute with services at household level, which requires consensus about approaches to service provision for the effective and sustainable functioning of network services. However, similar considerations apply to the relations between management institutions and users in the management of the water resource.

While there is evidence of effective engagement of large users (Eskom, Sasol, large mining companies, metro municipalities and organised agriculture), this is less evident at a local level where many specific issues have to be resolved. There are many challenges around the use of shared groundwater resources, as well as over specific surface water resources relating to the failure of collective action, which could undermine the overall goals of water resource management.

Groundwater: The less visible commons

The management of underground water is a technical challenge because it is more difficult to assess and monitor than surface supplies. This often leads to an underestimation of its potential contribution to meeting the needs of users. Conversely, it also frequently results in gross over-exploitation of the resource in which one set of users extracts more water than can sustainably be provided, at the expense of other users.

Less visible water uses

A particular challenge in arid countries like South Africa is to understand the impact of activities that are not traditionally thought of as water-using activities, on the water resource. South Africa is an international leader in some aspects of this, notably the recognition of the water used by plantation forestry as well as of water use by alien vegetation.

However, there are other dimensions which are likely to become increasingly important in the future. There is growing recognition that the overall water resource available to a country includes all rainfall, rather than only that which runs off into streams, rivers and percolates underground. This is leading to proposals to 'harvest' rainwater more intensively, whether through household infrastructure or new agricultural techniques as well as to boost the recharge of underground reservoirs. While this approach is attractive, it will often have an impact on the surface water resource, potentially to the detriment of other water users.

South Africa has already regulated the construction of small dams in certain sensitive catchments reflecting hydrological analysis which has demonstrated that the impact of such construction simply reduces the total available water in a catchment by virtue of increased evaporation and the interruption of stream flows. However, under pressures from climate change and intensification of agriculture, new approaches might be adopted which could affect the delicate balance that has been achieved between different components of the resource and its different users.

The dimension of quality

It is increasingly recognised that the quality of water is as important as its quantity for the achievement of development goals. This is graphically demonstrated by the availability along the coast of large volumes of seawater which can only be used after expensive desalination treatment. However, the management of water quality adds to the complexity of water management. It imposes another set of objectives and constraints and requires another dimension of technical expertise to monitor and assess quality parameters.

The current policy and legislation recognise the challenge and it is taken into account in planning processes. Although there have been many successes, notably a proliferation of shared ventures between different users to re-use municipal wastewater in industrial processes, the evidence is still that water resource quality is deteriorating, particularly in the inland areas.

CONCLUSIONS

This detailed description of the water resource planning system and a selection of mainly positive outcomes suggests that structured strategic development planning processes and related informal engagements are making a significant contribution to the achievement of society's broader sustainability goals. There is evidence of significant decoupling of water use from social and economic development, often expressed by an explicit recognition of the imperative of 'living within our means' in government policy and the framework for implementing that policy. One (legal) authority went further and placed the water sector's reforms squarely in terms of the sustainability focus on future generations:

> It is this writer's opinion that the incorporation of the public trust doctrine was a viable alternative to the downright nationalisation of water rights. If state administration is efficient and uncorrupted the implementation of the doctrine will be hailed by generations yet to be born! (Pienaar and van der Schyff 2007).

Some caveats remain. In the water sector, the institutions and knowledge base to underpin them remain weak. This is particularly the case in respect of technical challenges such as the use of underground water resources. More generally, the success of the water sector's approach is inherently dependent on the effectiveness of the broader development institutions which is still in question. The role of municipalities as the institutional focus of local development is critical.

It is also evident from the case studies presented that the formal planning activities have been only part of the overall process. However, the generic approach followed in less formal contexts, involving systematic ongoing interaction between major water users and other stakeholders, including local, provincial and national government, follows closely the approach formalised in legislation.

The implication is that planning processes can and do contribute to decoupling and the achievement of sustainability. They do this, however, not through formalisation but largely by engagement and cooperation between interested parties driven, if not by common interests, by common understanding leading to a sense of collective responsibility to achieve optimum outcomes in constrained situations. In the water sector, the achievement of the formal policies and legislation is as much to build this collective approach as to enforce normative decisions. This highlights what is increasingly widely recognised to be the main purpose of planning processes, the construction of a common framework within which diverse actors can move coherently towards common goals.

NOTES

1   The concepts of sustainability and sustainable development are widely used, often without great precision. For the purposes of this paper, sustainability is a state which can be sustained into the future. Sustainable development describes a process of socio-economic improvement that is sustainable; it can usefully be contrasted with other kinds of sustainability, such as 'sustainable poverty' which has proved to be pernicious in many parts of the world. For a broader discussion of these and related concepts such as resilience, see Gallopin and Raskin, 2002.

2   El Niño is a global climatological phenomenon associated with drought periods in southern Africa, although the el Niño increases the probability of low rainfall and is not an absolute predictor.

REFERENCES

Amin S (1990) *Maldevelopment Anatomy of a Global Failure.* London: Zed Books.

Amin (2009) A critique of the Stiglitz report. *Pambazuka News,* No. 446. (Accessed at http://pambazuka.org/en/category/features/58453, September 2009).

Bauer C (2005) In the image of the market: the Chilean model of water resources management, *International Journal of Water* 3 (2): 160.

Cascio J (2008) How many earths? Hartford, USA: IEET. (Accessed at http://ieet.org/index.php/IEET/more/2454/).

Chenoweth J (2008) A re-assessment of indicators of national water scarcity. *Water International* 33: 1,5–18.

Daily News (2009a) Stalled dam hikes water costs. *Daily News,* 11 March 2009.

Daily News (2009b) Durban water system is stressed. *Daily News,* 28 September 2009.

Department of Water Affairs and Forestry (1997) National Water Policy. White Paper, Pretoria.

Department of Water Affairs and Forestry (2004) National Water Resource Strategy (first edition). Pretoria.

Department of Water Affairs and Forestry (2004) Olifants Water Management Area: Internal Strategic Perspective, draft, February 2004, Pretoria.

Engineering News (2008) State Limpopo miners sign water scheme agreement. *Engineering News,* 26 May 2008.

Eskom (2009) Reduction in Water Consumption. (Accessed at http://www.eskom.co.za/live/content.php?Item_ID=2785).

Falkenmark M (1986) Fresh water – time for a modified approach. *Ambio,* 15, 192–200.

Friedman J (1993) Toward a non-Euclidian model of planning. *Journal of the American Planning Association* 482, Autumn 1993.

Gallopin GC and PD Raskin (2002) *Global Sustainability: Bending the Curve.* London and New York: Routledge.

Government of South Africa (1970) Commission of Enquiry into Water Matters. Pretoria.

Government of South Africa (1998) National Water Act, Act no 36 of 1998. Pretoria.

Harris J (2002) The onrushing train of minerals nationalisation is almost upon us. Johannesburg: Free Market Foundation.

International Water Management Institute (2007). *Water for Food, Water for Life: A Comprehensive Assessment of Water Management in Agriculture.* London: Earthscan.

Lenton R and M Muller (2009) *Integrated Water Resource Management in Practice: Better Water Management for Development.* London: Earthscan: 289.

Limpopo Provincial Government (2004) Limpopo Growth and Development Strategy 2004-2014, Polokwane.

Muller M (2007) Administered prices study on economic inputs – water sector. Nedlac Fund For Research Into Industrial Development, Growth And Equity (FRIDGE), Nedlac/HSRC.

Muller M (2009) Attempting to do it all: How a new South Africa has harnessed water to address its development challenges. In Lenton R and M Muller (Eds) *Integrated Water Resource Management in Practice: Better Water Management for Development.* London: Earthscan.

Nature (2009) Earth's boundaries? (editorial). *Nature* 461, 447-448 (24 September 2009) doi:10.1038/461447b; Published online 23 September 2009.

OECD (2008) Indicators to measure decoupling of environmental: Pressure from economic growth. Paris: OECD.

Pienaar GJ & E van der Schyff (2007) The reform of water rights in South Africa. *Law, Environment and Development Journal,* p. 179, available at http://www.lead-journal.org/content/07179.pdf.

Potter C & J Burney (2002) Agricultural multifunctionality in the WTO – legitimate non-trade concern or disguised protectionism? *Journal of Rural Studies,* Vol 18, 1, January 2002.

Presidency of South Africa (2003) National Spatial Development Perspective. Pretoria.

————- (2009) Green Paper: National Strategic Planning. Pretoria.

Stiglitz J (1998) *Towards a New Paradigm of Development*. Geneva: United Nations.

UNESCO-WWAP (2006) Water – a shared responsibility. United Nations World Water Development Report 2, (UNESCO-WWAP Table 4.3). Paris: United Nations Educational, Scientific and Cultural Organization (UNESCO).

Uys M (2009) South African Water Law Issues. Report to the Water Research Commission. Pretoria: WRC June 2009.

Wack P (1985) Scenarios: Uncharted water ahead, scenario planning. *Harvard Business Review*, Sep/Oct 1985: 73–89.

Wackernagel and W Rees (1996) *Our Ecological Footprint: Reducing Human Impact on the Earth*. Canada: New Society Publishers.

STATE, POLITICS AND POLICY

2

The politics and challenges of delivery

John Daniel

These [apartheid] laws may have disappeared from the statute books, but their effects are still felt across the country. Freedom imposes on us a responsibility to work together in the process of changing such conditions. And we must do this fast, because in four year's time we will have been free for twenty years. We will not have much sympathy for any reasons advanced to explain the failure to make a difference in the lives of our people.
(President Jacob Zuma, Freedom Day address, 27 April 2010)

This section begins with a sweeping overview of the radically changed South African political landscape post-Polokwane. It is followed by three chapters looking at different aspects of that landscape that either bedevil or deeply affect the state's priority to deliver a better life to all South Africans. Closing the section is the only chapter in the entire volume with a foreign policy dimension, a void which we intend to fill in the next edition of the *Review*. This void does, however, speak to the much lower foreign policy profile of the Zuma administration in contrast to the hectic jet-setting years of the two Mbeki governments. That was a time when the actual physical presence of the president *in* the country sometimes evoked comment, and it would not be far-fetched to suggest that the priority Thabo Mbeki accorded to South Africa's diplomatic role in Africa and the wider world cost him dear at home. Only someone with his eye 'off the ball' could have failed to notice how, by his second term, he had alienated his once adoring party constituency and even imagined that they would amend the party's rules and grant him a third term as its leader.

By stark contrast, to Jacob Zuma and his government the domestic terrain comes first. It is the political coal face, the frontline. He and his political team understand all too well that its political fate will be determined not at the African Union or in the UN Security Council but in the dusty and pot-holed township streets occupied by an increasingly impatient lumpen army of the poor. To distort the slogan once employed by former US President Bill Clinton, 'it's delivery, stupid'; hence the quote at the head of this chapter.

Respected University of the Witwatersrand academic and *Business Day* political columnist, Anthony Butler, examines the state of the African National Congress (ANC) under Jacob Zuma's leadership. His chapter is developed in five parts. It opens with a discussion of Thabo Mbeki's legacy. To summarise a deeper discussion, Butler argues that where Mbeki failed (as over AIDS policy and Zimbabwe) 'he created fertile ground for discontent' and where he succeeded (as in the creation of a black economic elite) he 'generated antagonisms'. But his greatest organisational failure, Butler argues, was to allow the party's internal machinery, its branch structure, to atrophy and to create a structural vacuum on the ground which his 'left' opponents in the Communist Party and Cosatu, as well as elements in black business, in some marginalised provincial structures and in formations like the Youth and Women's Leagues, exploited brilliantly to rebuild – seemingly unnoticed by the Mbeki-ites and their dozy intelligence structures – a vast branch network which controlled the floor at Polokwane and which swept the Zuma ticket to power.

This ascendancy of the coalition around Zuma is examined in some detail in the second part of the chapter. It examines how some of the failures of Mbeki's policies, such as the hardships imposed on the poor by the implementation of GEAR and the growing dysfunctionality of the municipalities and their failure to deliver, were used by this coalition to deliver at Polokwane 'a decisive defeat for Mbeki – but a less clear-cut victory for Zuma'.

The third part looks at how the new Zuma-aligned ANC leadership adroitly managed the inevitable political fall-out from the routing of the Mbeki-ites and how they were able to ensure that many of its most significant individual casualties – notably Trevor Manuel, Naledi Pandor, S'bu Ndebele and Joel Netshitenzhe – did not defect to the opposition in what ultimately became the Congress of the People (COPE).

Section four examines Jacob Zuma's finest hour, the brilliant ANC election campaign of 2009, which saw the party blunt the COPE challenge and sweep back to state power with only a slightly reduced parliamentary majority. Its only setback was its loss of the Western Cape to the Democratic Alliance (DA), something which, given the ineptitude and racial insensitivity of the Cape's Africanist-oriented provincial leadership, would have happened even if Thabo Mbeki had still been the ANC's leader.

Finally, Butler looks at the current ANC government under Zuma and notes that it has been characterised by both continuity and change – continuity in policy and change in style. Gone is the lofty and stern 'know-it-all' attitude of the Mbeki-ites, replaced by a much more 'folksy'common touch. Where Mbeki once preached, Zuma often sings and chats. But when it comes to policy, and particularly economic policy, it's business as usual. Trevor Manuel, now in the guise of Pravin Gordhan, still rules – to the chagrin of the Polokwane left forces. The result is renewed tension within the Tripartite Alliance. But, as Butler notes, other class forces are emerging within the ANC which talk the left talk of nationalisation but which largely despise the Alliance and see the mining sector, for example, as a site of personal wealth accumulation. Riding the BEE wave, this new social force has a solid base in the ANC Youth League which, in Butler's words, practices a 'muscular and irreverent style of politics', one which has 'adopted the language of the left for non-left purposes'.

Butler concludes with some thoughts on the future of the Zuma presidency and the president himself. About the latter he detects a political vulnerability occasioned by his own behavioural lapses and by the fracture of the coalition that brought him to power. The ANC is now a house badly divided ideologically and Butler suggests that Zuma may become a victim of the in-fighting that is ongoing and will intensify as the 2012 ANC elective conference nears. While he does not say as much, one could conclude from Butler's analysis that a key question now is not whether Zuma will win a second term as ANC president, but whether he will complete his first.

So-called 'service delivery' street protests are a pervasive feature of political life in South Africa today. Not so ten or more years back, although they were not unknown. When they did occur they were normally around basic services issues such as the provision of water and electricity to poor communities and the attempts by municipalities to get the new consumers to pay for them. Witwatersrand University sociologist Prishani Naidoo has spent years researching the ANC government's efforts to cater for the needs of the growing black urban poor as well as to get them to behave in a certain way – as paying consumers.

Having adopted the GEAR neoliberal policy framework in 1996, the government had little choice, Naidoo argues, but to wrap its service delivery package within a cost-recovery frame-work. This has sparked a contestation more than a decade long, with groups representative of the poor, particularly in and around Soweto and the massive Orange Farm informal settlement (the largest such area in South Africa) located on the East Rand.

In this article, Naidoo charts the resistance of the poor and the various devices municipalities have employed to counter the opposition. Naidoo dubs these schemes – which have involved propaganda blitzes like the Masakhane campaign which sought to instill in the citizenry a culture of payment – attempts at indigent management. The Masakhane campaign failed among the urban and peri-urban poor and gave way to coercion in the form of water and electricity cut-offs. This, in turn, generated ever more intense protests and was in any event, circumvented by the extraordinary ability of the poor to reconnect both water and electricity supply systems illegally. Then came pre-paid meters but they too have been widely resisted. The introduction of monthly quotas of free water and power has likewise not stemmed the resistance of the poor, who claim that they amount to too little.

Naidoo focuses her analysis of the state's attempts at indigent management through a case study of the City of Johannesburg whose policy formulators have, she suggests, at least made an attempt to take on board the objections of community groups. The result has been a tar-getted policy model which attempts to separate the 'can't pays' from the 'won't pays'. For those identified as being in the former category, the city has developed a special cases policy which tops up the free basic provision of water and electricity with subsidies for refuse removal and sanitation. For the latter, it has involved a series of measures aimed at getting them to change their behaviour, to become responsible citizens and to pay up. With little effect, it should be said.

Naidoo's sentiments, it would be fair to suggest, are with the resisters. She was herself active in the Anti-Privatisation Forum for many years and she has spent a long time documenting the resistance as part of her doctoral research. The result is a detailed account of an area of contestation which goes to the heart of the post-apartheid state's dilemma. How does a new government with limited resources and in the context of hideous socio-economic inequalities deliver on its policy promises and constitutional obligations to the masses of the poor without some form of fiscal return? Why should some not pay while others assume an ever increasing burden of delivery charges? And if some cannot, who decides, and how? And how does one change an entrenched but self-serving culture of non-payment into one of responsible citizenship? What is the alternative to indigent management along the lines developed by the City of Johannesburg? These are some of the questions not addressed by Naidoo in this chapter. Perhaps in a future *Review* she will rise to that challenge. It would be an important contribution to a vital debate.

Any national survey of South Africa's top ten hates would likely find two entities on virtually every list – taxi drivers and the Department of Home Affairs (DoHA). For DoHA, this may be a little unfair. It is probably not the post-apartheid state's worst performer, for Education and Correctional Services would be strong contenders in any race for the bottom. So why is it that it is DoHA that everyone loves to hate? In his chapter, Colin Hoag suggests it is because absolutely everyone in South Africa, even the rich and the powerful, has to deal with it. They can avoid National Education by going the private school route, and the rich and powerful rarely go to prison even when they are guilty. But at some point in their lives, even the rich need new passports or identity documents. So, even they have to venture into the dingy dens which seem be the norm when it comes to DoHA's offices, and there they too must stand … and stand some more … waiting to reach that glass portico only to find that the face behind it has gone to lunch. As Hoag notes, everyone has his or her own Home Affairs horror story.

Since 1994, DoHA has been subjected to a number of turnaround strategies but to little detectable effect. Acquiring those essential documents still takes an unacceptable length of time, assuming, that is, that they do not get lost in the process. Why is this the case? This is what Hoag sets out to answer in this the first detailed analysis of DoHA's workings I have come across. Hoag argues that there is on the one hand, too little acknowledgement of the sheer weight of the department's burden: vital official documents 'including birth, marriage, death certificates, national identity documents, passports, and work and visitor permits'. Then, on the other hand, it must deal with the seemingly never-ending flood of Asian and African migrants into this country since 1994. It is DoHA which must determine who deserves asylum and who of the others can stay or must be deported. To do these tasks well, Hoag argues, would require a skills level, technical resources and leadership abilities of the highest order, which DoHA simply does not possess.

But the problem, Hoag argues, is deeper. At the root, he suggests, is a debilitating organisational culture which both fosters and derives from an antagonistic relationship with both clients and senior management. This culture has two main aspects: fear and enervation. What Hoag argues is that the average DoHA bureaucrat lives with a constant fear of displeasing someone – clients, managers, lawyers – and the result is a tendency to play safe, something which runs parallel with enervation which leaves officials 'often reluctant to do anything, much less to think independently and act decisively'. Space does not allow a detailed examination of this culture but Hoag's chapter, too, is a detailed and original piece of analysis. Clearly, it will take more than larger budgets, better technology and sophisticated turnaround strategies to get DoHA 'up to speed'; those will help but without a paradigm shift to the Department's working practices and the relationships between staff and management, any gains will be limited. DoHA will remain firmly ensconced on that top ten hate list.

As noted above, among DoHA's multiple burdens are the many millions of refugees and undocumented migrants who have entered South Africa since 1994. They are the subject of the chapter by Loren Landau, Tara Polzer and Aurelia Wa Kabwe-Segatti, all of whom are affiliated to the Southern African Migration Project (SAMP), the country's authoritative think-tank on regional migrant flows. Southern Africa, like much of the global South is a region on the move and it is heartening to learn in this chapter that SAMP has been commissioned by Nkosazana Dlamini-Zuma, minister of Home Affairs and former minister of Foreign Affairs, to undertake a review of South Africa's laws governing international mobility. If any member of the Zuma cabinet has a clear understanding of the need for a change of policy on migration matters, it is this respected public official. In selecting SAMP to undertake this review she has done well.

Landau *et al* make a number of important points in their chapter. They open by noting that democracy in 1994 generated two significant migrant currents. One was internal in that it opened South Africa's hitherto 'forbidden cities' to poor black South Africans confined by apartheid to barren rural reserves. The second was external in the form of non-South African Africans seeking 'profit, protection and onward passage', a flow bloated by the early 2000s implosion of the Zimbabwe state. Unmentioned, however, is a third current in the form of Asian (primarily Indian, Pakistani and Bangla Deshi) and mainland Chinese migrants whose numbers may well match those of the African inflow although they disappear more easily into established Asian communities with a greater capacity and/or opportunity for self-help and trade than, it seems, the African migrants possess. Finally and importantly, they note that there is no accurate or authoritative figure for the actual number of African migrants/refugees in South Africa now, but intimate that it is substantially fewer than the popular press suggests and that the inflow to our cities from internal migrants outnumbers those from beyond our borders.

That said, Landau *et al* argue that the external African inflow is a growing internal stress factor in that it has significantly increased the state's delivery burden while also containing within it the possibility or threat of xenophobic violence. Migration, they conclude, is an issue that will not go away and cannot be ignored, and 'without a coherent and shared perspective within government and between government and the general public' little can be achieved.

This section ends with a chapter that looks at a service being given by South Africans rather than the perils posed to the state by those services perceived as not being delivered – the role and impact of South African women peacekeepers in some of Africa's worst 'hot' spots. One of the hallmarks of South Africa's post-1994 foreign policy has been its engagement with Africa. Largely driven by Thabo Mbeki's vision of an African renaissance and of the need for Africa to solve its own problems, South Africa has become, as Maxi Schoeman *et al* note, the thirteenth biggest troop-contributing country to international peace missions, but the largest in regard to the number of women troops deployed to these various missions, and only one of a handful that deploys women in combat positions.

Schoeman *et al* discuss how this situation has emerged as a consequence of decades of feminist activism culminating in the UN Security Council's Resolution 1325 of 2000 which drew attention to the role and position of women in conflict and which called for gender mainstreaming in all UN peace operations. In this chapter, Schoeman *et al* report on the basis of extensive interviewing on the experiences of South Africa's women peacekeepers in the

Democratic Republic of Congo (DRC) and of their male counterparts' perceptions of those roles. Unsurprisingly, it is not the most progressive of pictures; the South African women peacekeepers are seen largely as support persons, confined to base and not routinely deployed to combat situations. Women soldiers, they found, occupy the lower ranks in the military hierarchy, with barely a senior officer amongst them. Gender mainstreaming, they discovered, is an ill-understood concept, and one usually seen as something that applies to women and not to men.

The authors conclude by noting that deep social change in regard to gender is needed if the South African Defence Force is to meet fully its obligations to women – but they argue that this will take time. It is not something which will happen overnight or at the behest of a UN resolution.

CHAPTER 6

The African National Congress under Jacob Zuma[1]

Anthony Butler

———•———

Jacob Zuma has been president of the African National Congress (ANC) since December 2007 and state president of South Africa since April 2009. His rise to these offices was accompanied by some of the most turbulent politics that the liberation movement has experienced since the transitional upheavals of the early 1990s.

Zuma's personal journey to the state presidency was an extraordinary one (Gordin 2008). As many of his supporters quickly came to recognise, however, he is a leader with serious political and personal limitations. The thrilling tale that ended at Polokwane was more enthralling – and will perhaps prove more historically significant – than Zuma's troubled incumbency in the Union Buildings.

This chapter is divided into five main sections. First, it surveys the legacy of former ANC and state president Thabo Mbeki, an activist leader whose administrations significantly shaped both the character of the ANC as a liberation movement and the nature of the contemporary South African state. The rise of Zuma – and the challenges he now confronts – cannot be understood in isolation from the actions and plans of his controversial predecessor. Where Mbeki failed, he created fertile ground for discontent. When he succeeded, he nevertheless generated antagonisms.

Secondly, the chapter explains Zuma's ascendancy within the ANC. It explores the fault lines created during Mbeki's presidency and demonstrates how the former president's actions, in trying to manage the ANC and state successions, created opportunities for Zuma to build a coalition of support. The struggle between Mbeki's incumbent faction and Zuma's disparate alliance culminated at the ANC's tumultuous fifty-second national conference at Polokwane in December 2007 with a decisive defeat for Mbeki – but a less clear-cut victory for Zuma.

In a third section, the chapter traces the trajectory of the ANC after Polokwane. Although the incoming senior leadership compared favourably to the outgoing 'top six', the uneven overall composition of the National Executive Committee (NEC) was quite widely, if not particularly astutely, criticised. The new leaders rapidly and quite successfully limited the damage caused by personal and factional rifts, and managed the ramifications of breakaway politics for the unity of the movement.

Fourth, we explore the culmination of this process of healing in the general election campaign of 2009. The ANC's resounding victory under Zuma's leadership – directed by a new campaign team and dominated by Zuma's personal campaigning style – helped the movement to reconstitute itself behind its new leader. This section also traces the significance of the new opposition party, the Congress of the People (COPE), and evaluates the Democratic Alliance's (DA's) achievement in seizing control of the Western Cape.

A fifth part of the paper looks at the ANC in government since April 2009. Although it is still relatively early days, the implications of Zuma's institutional innovations and Cabinet appointments are becoming clearer. He promised both continuity and change. This section argues that continuity has marked most institutions and policies, whereas change has been confined primarily to matters of style. There are, nevertheless, new dynamics in the ANC and the tripartite alliance: the ANC's partners, the Congress of South African Trade Unions (Cosatu) and the South African Communist Party (SACP), have become more vocal and have achieved a small degree of policy leverage.

The paper closes with some thoughts about the future. Predictions of a 'move to the left' vastly overstated the power of Cosatu and the SACP. These were powerful forces at Polokwane but in the post-conference environment they were increasingly sidelined. A more conservative social policy, and a continued pragmatism around the economy, seems to be the most likely policy outcome. Thabo Mbeki's ANC governed during an unprecedented period of international economic expansion and at the height of a global commodity boom. Zuma and his successors will not enjoy these favourable external conditions. Zuma's ANC, moreover, is weighed down by the negative legacies of Mbeki's rule: poor public services, deep political antagonisms, a mature AIDS epidemic, a seemingly intractable unemployment crisis, a dysfunctional state, and the spread of extensive patronage systems linking politics and the state with business.

THE MBEKI LEGACY

For most of the second half of the twentieth century the ANC was an exile organisation. Although this picture must be qualified (Suttner 2009), the Lusaka-based ANC pursued its quasi-military and diplomatic struggle largely in isolation from domestic anti-apartheid forces. The township revolutions of the 1980s, and the trade union and United Democratic

Front (UDF) formations that emerged domestically, were largely autonomous from – and only belatedly endorsed by – the exile movement.

It is still too early to place the leadership of Thabo Mbeki in historical perspective. His rise to the presidency of the ANC is now quite well understood (Gumede 2005: 31–52; Gevisser 2007: 631–50), and some aspects of his political philosophy have been examined in detail (Roberts 2007: 130–51, 242–64). While assessments of the role of his personal leadership must at this stage remain tentative, it is likely that the significance of his historical agency has been exaggerated. In the ANC's first major post-apartheid conference in 1991, elements from the exile SACP leadership, the UDF and Cosatu achieved an unexpected but brief ascendancy. Mbeki and Zuma were among the many conservative exiles swept aside during this first false dawn for the left (Butler 2007: 252–5). Mbeki was merely the most prominent figure in the counter-reaction that re-established conservative and exile control of the movement during the first half of the 1990s. By 1994, he was in a position to advise President Nelson Mandela on his Cabinet appointments (Mandela 2007).

By 1997, he was chair of key Cabinet committees and heir apparent, but this was by no means a purely personal achievement – a rising group of political and business families, many of them from the Eastern Cape, accompanied Mbeki in his ascent. Ross (2008: 217) has described Mbeki as merely 'the most prominent of a ruling class of upwardly mobile black professionals, many schooled in the struggle'.

As ANC president, Mbeki both empowered and diminished the liberation movement in which he had been formed. He insisted that the ANC must remain the ultimate strategic centre of political authority yet he emasculated the key office of the secretary general and used the ANC presidency to gain control of party and state appointments.

The ANC's internal organisational and educational systems atrophied under Mbeki's leadership and the lacklustre secretary-generalship of Kgalema Motlanthe. Branch formation became disorderly and political education ground to a halt. The ANC nevertheless became a remarkably effective electoral machine, securing majorities in national elections of 63 per cent in 1994, 66 per cent in 1999, 70 per cent in April 2004, and 66 per cent in the difficult election year of 2009 (Lodge 2005; Butler 2009a).

Mandela's ANC, and then Mbeki's, could also point to impressive accomplishments. Mandela's government came to power in difficult circumstances in 1994, confronting deeply entrenched social and economic problems. It worked with the Inkatha Freedom Party (IFP) to curtail political violence in KwaZulu-Natal (KZN). Under Mbeki, the ANC viewed the rule of law as an instrument of the 'national democratic revolution' rather than as an obstacle to it (Roberts 2007: 130–51). The ANC was also a serious and deliberative policy-maker that presented carefully crafted policy priorities to electors (Lodge 2005) and used incremental institutional innovations, particularly in the national administration and the cabinet system, to increase the effectiveness of policy implementation (Butler 2009b).

Proposals for the reconfiguration or abolition of the provincial tier of government were formulated late in Mbeki's second term. In general, however, Mbeki was not an aggressive institutional or constitutional reformer. Instead, his administrations centralised power within existing institutions, using a combination of ANC and state mechanisms to bring recalcitrant provincial and regional barons into line. One constant feature, year on year, was an expansion of the reach of the power of the presidency although this was by no means an arbitrary or despotic power because his office grew side by side with an effective cabinet system and a powerful national Treasury (Butler 2009b).

Mbeki's ANC also championed a new and powerful black business class (Butler 2010) while simultaneously creating a massive system of social grants to mitigate the worst effects of poverty. The ANC was successful in promoting a distinctive racial transformation agenda but without encouraging the racial and ethnic conflict that could have been a natural consequence of the country's political history. The movement promoted and practised nonracialism, while ethnic balance continued to be a central consideration in party lists and the appointment of office holders. Such balance – although never without controversy – was accompanied by an uneven commitment to gender representivity (Hassim 2009).

THE RISE OF ZUMA

There was one key exception to the movement's deliberative approach in the Mbeki period that helps to explain his later crucifixion. It concerns economics, where the conservative policy framework known by the acronym GEAR (Growth, Employment, and Redistribution) was imposed on the liberation movement after only perfunctory deliberation. The so-called '1996 class project' that allegedly motivated GEAR later became a rallying point for leftist antagonists of the Mbeki government.

The burden of structural change associated with GEAR was placed primarily on the already poor. GEAR, however, was an understandable product of its time and circumstances. Despite its controversial character, it was eminently defensible as an economic stabilisation programme (Maphai and Gottschalk 2003). It was always compatible with the microeconomic interventionism favoured by leftists but never fully developed by them in policy terms. Those leftists who did not shoulder the burdens of office complained correctly, but largely irrelevantly, that GEAR did little to change South Africa's underlying economic pathologies (Hirsch 2005, 65–108).

The broader failure of many of government's other front-line social and economic policies began to emerge during Mbeki's second term. An early symptom of these underlying system crises was the deterioration in the quality of democratic politics as citizens despaired of formal avenues of accountability. Although the ANC secured significant victories in national elections, these wins were achieved on the basis of a declining proportion of eligible voters. In 2004, 39 per cent of eligible voters actually supported the ANC as against 54 per cent in 1994 (Schulz-Herzenberg 2007, 2009). Falling turnouts were accompanied by growing distrust in key political institutions (Roberts 2008).

Increasingly pervasive street protests were at times reminiscent of the protests of the 1980s in their intensity and destructiveness (Atkinson 2007). Although the causes of these protests remained complicated, and they were mostly local in origin, the broader problem to which they pointed was a gulf between citizens and their political representatives (who were all too evidently looking after themselves). The low-hanging fruit of post-apartheid reconstruction and development had been quickly picked. Thereafter, the provision of basic household services at affordable prices proved to be beyond the capabilities of local governments and parastatals.

The municipal meltdown began to develop a relentless quality after 2004. Local government provides essential public services such as water, sanitation, electricity, roads, recreation facilities, and the settlements in which people must make their lives. Small communities across the country faced electricity cut-offs, overflowing sewers, sub-standard housing projects and endemic corruption.

While Mbeki's ministers introduced palliative measures to restore ailing municipal administrations to health, these initiatives – most famously Project Consolidate – did not move beyond symptoms to address the underlying causes of the local government crisis (DPLG 2007). Meanwhile, ministers made further unreasonable demands upon municipal systems, delegating to them responsibilities for the provision of public services for which they lacked the necessary human and financial resources.

Where they had ever existed, the management systems of many small towns and district municipalities began to collapse. It became increasingly rare for a local authority to be staffed with an autonomous municipal manager, an experienced chief engineer and a qualified financial officer. The numbers of engineers fell, while the tasks they were called upon to perform grew dramatically, and by the end of Mbeki's rule a mere three civil engineering professionals were serving every 100 000 people, as against twenty-one in the late 1980s. Municipal engineering departments ran down artisan training programmes, sewerage and water systems moved towards crisis, poor roads increasingly cut citizens off from schools and clinics, and long-term planning and investment in economic infrastructure all but evaporated (Lawless 2005, 2007).

A paralysing politicisation, and associated corruption, of municipal administration lay at the heart of this still unresolved crisis. The Municipal Systems Act allows a mayor to govern in secret with a hand-picked executive committee. The ANC allowed its local political leaders to make full use of this dangerous mechanism. A decade ago, old-school town managers were cast as the enemies of transformation, preoccupied only with maintaining municipal services for whites. Elected ANC mayors meanwhile laboured under intense pressure to deliver houses, water and sanitation to communities who had nothing. The exclusion of municipal managers and engineers from key decisions for a decade, however, has now resulted in a devastating neglect of bulk services, maintenance, and infrastructure investment (Lawless 2007).

The white diehards were soon dispatched but executive mayors continued to drive out skilled black and white municipal managers and engineers and to replace them with compliant youngsters unable to resist councillors' abuses of power. Politicians quickly dominated official committees, often only to rig tenders to their own benefit. Despite government's 2004 restoration of the sole power to adjudicate tenders to officials, councillors circumvented controls and redoubled their efforts to drive noncompliant officials from their fiefdoms.

The municipal crisis under Mbeki was a failure of the liberation movement itself, as the ANC has begun to recognise (ANC 2009c; DPLG 2007). The ANC was unable and unwilling to force its own local leaders to heed the advice of professional managers, finance officers and engineers.

But it was not just municipal services that were in crisis. In the health sector, South Africa's maturing HIV/AIDS epidemic began to have major economic and political repercussions.

Few ANC leaders would today claim that government's response to the epidemic in the Mbeki era was optimal, and some have recently been sharply critical of it. It remains unclear why national leaders such as Thabo Mbeki and Kgalema Motlanthe were so hostile to the provision of antiretroviral medications and whether 'denialism' is a useful analytic category for understanding their actions (Butler 2005a, compare Geffen and Cameron 2009).

The rapid infection phase came as early as 1998 when there were perhaps 800 000 new infections in one year. The high point of HIV prevalence did not occur until a decade later, when HIV began 'running out of people to infect' and deaths began outstripping new infections. Shortly before Mbeki's departure, the number of people infected with HIV began to level off at the extraordinary level of six million, and the country was heading for an extended surge in AIDS deaths that would test its social and political fabric (Marais, this volume).

South Africans in rural areas and former Bantustans were more or less totally excluded from ARV programmes, and treatment reached just 30 per cent of those who needed it. Under Mbeki, a continuous diet of obfuscation and evasion from the government persuaded advanced HIV-infected citizens that a quiet death was preferable to the stigma of testing and declaration. The AIDS crisis was part of a wider health system crisis under Mbeki that encompassed skills flight, corruption in provincial administrations, hospital mismanagement, and private insurance that benefitted seven million at the cost of 60 per cent of financial resources. The public school system was another under-performer with massive expenditures making little impact on consistently lamentable outcomes (Chisholm 2005; Carter 2008; Bloch 2008).

Such major failures of government under Mbeki were initially forgiven by citizens on the grounds that government had inherited apartheid's legacies. The ANC remained visibly (if intermittently) sensitive to the suffering of ordinary people. It was a highly unusual political party in that it successfully managed the transition from party of exile to a mass movement (Lodge 2005: 111) and then to an effective campaigning vehicle. The rigorous organisation of exile proved useful for effective electoral competition even as the ANC became 'catch-all' in character, stressing competence above ideology and trying to appeal to many sectors of society.

The ANC's ability to secure consensus in a complex and class-divided society turned on its organisation and ideology. Organisationally it required a wide support base to secure its electoral ascendancy, and its system of alliances, most notably the tripartite alliance with Cosatu and the SACP, was used adroitly to secure the allegiance of activists.

Ideologically, ANC leaders explained their struggle to achieve a more just society as the pursuit of a 'national democratic revolution' (NDR). This conception of democracy had its origins in the SACP's efforts to link the anti-apartheid struggle with a wider anti-capitalist revolution (ANC 1969, Slovo 1988) and NDR is 'a process of struggle that seeks the transfer of power to the people', whose 'strategic objectives' include the creation of 'a non-racial, non-sexist, democratic and united South Africa where all organs of the state are controlled by the people' (Netshitenzhe 2000; Cronin 1996). The ambiguity in this formulation has allowed the ANC to remain ostensibly unified around a common project – while different class components of the ANC in reality pursue their class and personal interests. NDR's various phases have been manipulated to deflect conflict by conflating principles with tactics and immediate goals with ultimate social outcomes (Butler 2005b, Netshitenzhe 2000). Ultimately, NDR allowed Mbeki's ministers to defer, for too long, honest debates over the feasible character of South African social democracy in contemporary international conditions.

The possibility of wider dialogue was hampered by ANC arrogance and various forms of political centralisation. The exile ANC cherished an exceedingly non-participatory conception of public service 'delivery' that demobilised communities and civil society organisations. When provincial administrations failed, the instinctive response of the national leadership was to assert central control. Meanwhile, at national level, the presidency became an intrusive presence in the cabinet system, taking upon itself the role of ultimate arbiter of intergovernmental conflicts. There is no doubt that the expanding presidency was in part a response to failures of government service delivery. However, it also aggrandised the occupants of the presidency, and the president himself, to such an extent that they began to think of themselves as irreplaceable. Succession problems became inevitable as ANC factions came to see the presidency as the one big prize that no significant grouping could allow to fall into the hands of others.

Inside ANC structures, the interventions of Luthuli House – and in particular of a heavy handed ANC presidency – became deeply resented. Although Mbeki had a legitimate responsibility to neutralise ethnic mobilisation, factionalism and patronage networks, his own faction (which did not view itself as such) was perceived to be using these roles to justify prohibitions on legitimate debate, competition for office, and the interrogation of national office holders.

Jacob Zuma, as Thabo Mbeki's deputy president, was more than a minor player in these unfolding dramas. But the central dynamic of the politics of Mbeki's second term concerned his faction's sense of indispensability, its access to resources, and its consequent determination to secure for itself a longer-term control of the liberation movement and the state, and this factional project became public knowledge in 2007 when Thabo Mbeki allowed his supporters to put his name forward for a third term as president of the ANC. This proposal for a third term was advanced in the spirit of necessity, on the grounds that there was no other suitable candidate available. Zuma's role, it became clear, was to act as the unthinkable alternative candidate whose accession to the ANC and state presidencies must be stopped at all costs.

Victory for Mbeki at Polokwane would have allowed him to control the state presidency succession and to act as the long-term power behind the throne. In one view, he was destined to become life president of the liberation movement, 'safeguarding' the revolution and retaining veto powers in politics and business. In another interpretation, he might even be obliged to serve a third term as state president to avert the alleged problem of 'two centres of power' in the state and ANC.

Mbeki's faction was well positioned in 2007–2008 to bring its project to fruition as a result of criminal charges then pending against Zuma by the National Prosecuting Authority (NPA). Zuma, like many of his peers, was vulnerable to prosecution. Unlike them, however, he was subjected to an extensive series of investigations. His financial advisor Schabir Shaik was convicted of fraud in June 2005 and the judge commented on the 'mutually beneficial symbiosis' between the two. Then, after twelve days of media speculation about Zuma's future, Mbeki relieved him of his duties as deputy president. The president told a joint sitting of parliament that 'in the interest of the honourable deputy president, the government, our young democratic system and our country, it would be best to release the honourable Jacob Zuma from his responsibilities as deputy president of the republic and member of the Cabinet' (Vasagar 2005). Zuma was soon formally charged with corruption by the NPA.

Zuma's fight back from this low point is an extraordinary tale. His first supporters were elements in Cosatu and the SACP who had endured a decade of struggle with Mbeki's administration and its '1996 class project' – although both Cosatu and the SACP remained deeply divided over the succession issue. If these champions were motivated by Zuma's supposed sympathy for leftist causes, an equally big factor in his favour was his growing appeal among black businesspeople. He was able to play on discontent about the allocation of business opportunities in Mbeki's ANC and unhappiness about the alleged hold on national power and wealth of prominent families from the Eastern Cape establishment.

Mbeki faced vehement opponents in provincial ANC structures. Some of them had been rightly marginalised for creating patronage systems and looting provincial coffers. Zuma's own complaint that he was being victimised, however, was echoed across the country by ANC barons who used money to buy power and power to amass money. Support for Zuma was even greater in municipalities where patronage opportunities had been monopolised by incumbents now labelled as Mbeki loyalists. Mbeki was also vulnerable to ethnic mobilisation. Activists in KZN complained that the succession of a Zulu was being wilfully obstructed and the perceived Xhosa ascendancy was resented elsewhere in the country.

Mbeki and Zuma were both weak candidates for the ANC and state presidencies. Many ANC leaders with no particular attachment to either man calculated that a Zuma presidency was a necessary price to pay to stop the Mbeki faction's arrogant march towards perpetual power.

The Polokwane conference, when it finally arrived in late December 2007, was every bit as exciting as anticipated. It witnessed the defeat of incumbent ANC president Thabo Mbeki – but this was only the beginning. The preferred Zuma list of candidates for the top six offices swept aside Mbeki's candidates. The NEC elections saw the eviction of long-established and respected ANC leaders. It seemed that a permanent revolution in ANC politics might be in the making.

AFTER POLOKWANE

The changes to the ANC leadership were shocking and disorienting – and not just within the ANC. DA leader Helen Zille complained that the ANC had been 'irreversibly captured by populists, careerists and convicted criminals' (Zille 2008). Opposition leaders and the news media largely failed to register that the eviction of an incumbent factional leader seeking a third term was a major step forward for the entrenchment of democracy in South Africa.

Besides President Jacob Zuma and Deputy President Kgalema Motlanthe (who had both been part of the outgoing top six) the new senior office holders were a credible and even distinguished team. Treasurer Mathews Phosa and Secretary General Gwede Mantashe were independent thinkers with significant constituencies of their own and in no respect beholden to the movement's new president. The new NEC as a whole (ANC 2009a) brought the arguably glorious variety of the ANC's regional political cultures to the movement's centre.

When the National Working Committee was elected by the NEC on 8 January 2009, its composition changed for the better. Arrivals included important members of provincial executive councils such as Collins Chabane, Tina Joemat-Pettersson, Angie Motshekga, Maite Nkoana-Mashabane and Dina Pule who had experience of government away from the centre. Finally, the NWC could begin to take decisions about policy in more complete awareness of the tumultuous nature of the regions in which they had to be implemented (ANC 2009b).

When this NWC elected the chairs of NEC policy committees in the next step of ANC post-conference protocols, a sober commitment to continuity was evident in the retention of the chairs of the most important of these bodies. In the policy and economic transformation committees, Jeff Radebe and Max Sisulu remained at the helm. Former UDF activist Valli Moosa and businessman Cyril Ramaphosa were other independent forces elected to head NEC committees.

Polokwane's effects on the composition of Cabinet were less significant than they initially appeared. The conference rightly punished unsuccessful ministers such as Ngconde Balfour, Charles Nqakula, Thoko Didiza and Geraldine Fraser-Moleketi. Some of those who departed – Ronnie Kasrils, Ivy Matsepe-Casaburri, Manto Tshabalala-Msimang and Essop Pahad – were of advanced years and already destined for retirement. Of more concern than ministerial turnover was the wave of instability at lower levels of government that led to the 'recall' or destabilisation of perceived Mbeki loyalists – in reality variously aligned incumbents labelled as Mbeki loyalists to ease their removal – around the country.

These inevitable political upheavals unfortunately coincided with a set of unprecedented social and economic crises. In January 2008, long-developing problems in power generation resulted in a temporary shutdown of the mining industry, major residential supply interruptions ('load shedding'), and significant long-term damage to the investment climate for energy-intensive industries.

Soon after the load shedding debacle began, an outbreak of 'xenophobic violence' in May 2008 resulted in the deaths of more than sixty people, many of them South African citizens from the north of the country (Hassim *et al* 2008). This violence exacerbated fears about a resurgence of racial and ethnic politics and confirmed the ineffectuality of the ANC leadership when confronted by large-scale popular protest.

But the fall-out from the leadership struggle fortunately turned out to be less serious than initially expected. Activists with no special affection for Zuma participated in the expulsion of Mbeki's faction. Influential figures were on both Mbeki and Zuma 'lists' with the consequence that the two 'factions' were not really mutually exclusive. A significant ANC 'centre' remained in place to execute damage limitation exercises and to restore stability to the movement.

Damage control began on the floor of the Polokwane conference as Mbeki loyalists were on the verge of being purged from the NEC. The new leadership lobbied hard at the eleventh hour to ensure the re-election of figures associated with Mbeki such as Finance Minister Trevor Manuel, Education Minister Naledi Pandor, Presidency Policy head Joel Netshitenzhe, and KZN Premier S'bu Ndebele (ANC 2009a).

Conflict nevertheless continued throughout 2008 between the transformed NEC and a Cabinet that was Mbeki's creation, and tension was exacerbated by Mbeki's continued occupancy of the Union Buildings and by the unabated pursuit of Zuma on fraud and racketeering charges. In the end, it was a legal judgement concerning alleged political interference in the prosecution of Zuma that provided a pretext for the September removal or 'recall' of Mbeki from office on the instructions of the NEC.

This decision sparked fears of renewed turmoil but in reality it stabilised the ANC. It led almost immediately to the creation of an opposition party that eventually adopted the name Congress of the People (COPE). The succession contest had created deep divisions between individuals and groups, and COPE's creation provided a home for some of the most reviled Mbeki loyalists. It also made it easier for many Mbeki loyalists to remain in the ANC because desertions to the new party were now electorally dangerous. Purges and recalls came to a halt and the ANC's candidate list process moved ahead more smoothly. Discipline was restored and the movement was able to plan systematically for the fast approaching 2009 elections.

Polokwane had, however, taken a toll on popular support for the ANC. As the election moved closer, the movement's leadership focused on rebuilding party unity and restoring stability to regional structures.

THE 2009 GENERAL ELECTION

In 2009, the ANC returned to its campaigning strengths. The person of the ANC president, Jacob Zuma, was the focus of the ANC campaign. Unlike previous elections, in which the ANC had kept the temperature of campaigns low in order to starve opposition parties of the oxygen of media coverage, the 2009 campaign was upbeat.

When it came to candidate selection, Zuma's assorted backers were looking for personal advancement and for a cull of the Mbeki faithful. Their hunger for post-Polokwane change, however, had to be set against the needs to retain experience and to avert mass defections to COPE. This purported defection threat helped secure an inclusive outcome. The national list process was presided over by the ANC deputy president, Kgalema Motlanthe, who faced down critics of his inclusive and consensual style (Butler 2009a). With the exception of the Eastern Cape, where the withdrawal of COPE benefitted the left, the SACP and Cosatu remained poorly represented at the top echelons of national and provincial lists from where key office-holders were normally selected.

The manifesto steered clear of divisive issues and identified five key challenges: in unemployment, health, education, rural development, and crime and corruption. The campaign was bolstered by the unprecedented mobilisation prior to Polokwane and by consequently high membership numbers. ANC finances were unusually healthy as a result of business donations, contributions by foreign political parties, and indirect transfers of parastatal resources.

The ANC destroyed the COPE challenge in the new party's Eastern Cape heartlands by launching its manifesto in East London. Addressing activists a few days before the launch, NEC policy head Jeff Radebe insisted that 'Amathole belongs to the ANC [and] the Eastern Cape is the heartland of the ANC'. He revealed that the movement had hired 300 buses, 100 minibus taxis and three trains to bring 75 000 supporters to the launch (*Pretoria News* 7 January 2009).

The ANC's door to door campaigning style once again paid dividends. The party also targeted key constituencies, regions and issues. Among the most important targets were religious leaders, professionals, traditional leaders, black businesspeople and young people. Zuma was an effective campaigner among church leaders, especially in the fast-growing African churches. He was also an asset in his meetings with traditional leaders and black businesspeople. Where Zuma was weaker, among the youth, a role was forged for the new president of the ANC Youth League, Julius Malema, who galvanised young people in colleges and universities where COPE had posed a potential challenge.

There were some negative aspects for the ANC to the overall election results. The success of the DA in seizing the Western Cape was, in particular, a heavy blow. The neutralisation of the COPE challenge and the restoration of stability to the ANC itself, however, were significant victories. Although South Africa has a semi-parliamentary system in which citizens vote only for a party and not for a president, Zuma had secured the closest thing available to a mandate to rule.

ZUMA'S ANC IN GOVERNMENT

As soon as Jacob Zuma was inaugurated, the country's problems closed in around his administration. A wave of strikes and community protests erupted almost immediately and quickly dashed hopes of a political honeymoon. Zuma's ministerial appointments, particularly in the economic sphere, were nevertheless greeted as tactically adroit. The left was seemingly accommodated, while the Treasury maintained its status as the most powerful department. In the presidency, a planning commission and new monitoring capabilities were initiated under Trevor Manuel and Collins Chabane.

Zuma quickly changed the tone of national politics by allowing ministers and officials to openly debate corruption, HIV/AIDS, crime and the crisis in the education system. The new president adopted the guise of an amiable outsider recently arrived in Pretoria. The *Mail & Guardian* newspaper even graced a story with the headline 'Zuma presses government over service delivery', as if the composition and actions of the cabinet had nothing whatsoever to do with him. Zuma's public relations entourage surrounded him with an aura of avuncular good cheer – a good strategy for retaining personal popularity, but an advantage he failed to convert into political momentum.

Zuma proclaimed education as his priority and expressed a wish to meet every school principal in the land, but he showed no stomach for bringing teacher unions into line. He supposedly championed fiscal prudence but facilitated public sector pay settlements that placed government budgets under severe strain. He likewise encouraged debate over elite enrichment and corruption, but seemed unlikely to countenance action against his own allies.

The unexceptional priorities of the ruling party, which formed the government's programme of action, centred around health, education, the fight against crime, rural development, land reform, and creating decent work. Beyond these specific areas of focus, three key issues have dominated analysis of Zuma's ANC in government.

The first has concerned a supposed 'shift to the left' in ANC economic policy. Liberal intellectuals spent much of the early post-Polokwane period bemoaning an impending shift towards a socialist state. Such a shift, however, has not occurred, nor does it seem likely to do so. Many of the key struggles in which the society is engaged – over corruption, AIDS, education, and a functional public service – are not much illuminated by the application of left-right categories, and to the degree that they are society seems to be moving right, not left.

Finance Minister Pravin Gordhan's first major speech explained the constraints on fiscal policy in an era of slower global growth. His first budget speech, in February 2010, confirmed that an orthodox economic policy framework would remain in place. He offered Cosatu only sleight of hand concessions concerning the reserve bank's inflation-targeting mandate. He insisted that public sector pay rises had to be brought under control. He torpedoed the national health insurance scheme, and announced public-private partnerships in hospitals. Finally, he failed to act against labour brokers while introducing proposals for a two-tiered labour market (Treasury 2010).

The finance minister joined what appeared to be an orchestrated campaign against ANC Youth League president Julius Malema's ostentatious consumption in order to retain the sympathy of the left, arguing that 'lifestyle audits' and tax data would play a wider role in government's anti-corruption drive.

Curbs on waste, corruption and mismanagement, essential though they are, are insufficient in themselves to finance a 'pro-poor' budget or to protect priority programmes in crime reduction, employment, AIDS, rural development and education. The economic environment will no longer allow scope for leftist experimentation or the pouring of national resources into supposedly 'strategic' parastatals. Gordhan's words cannot guarantee fiscal prudence, but they indicate that populism and patronage spending, rather than leftist experimentation, are now widely recognised as the key challenges to sustainable fiscal policy.

Rather than a shift to the left, we have seen a reassertion of economic orthodoxy accompanied by a fitful shift towards social authoritarianism. When out campaigning, Zuma expressed cynically populist views on the constitution, pregnant children, gays and capital punishment. He also offered a conservative interpretation of the institution of traditional leadership. There is every prospect that Zuma will drift right under the influence of his own prejudices and a need to court South Africa's socially conservative electorate. What is distinctive about a potential new era of social conservatism is that it might include a fully fledged model of selective citizenship in which poor people in rural areas, and particularly women, might come to enjoy the dubious benefits of traditional leadership across the full range of community and collective services.

Former president Mbeki's faction set the country on a dangerous course with its steady centralisation of authority. Mbeki's administration, however, moved in this direction haphazardly, stifling cabinet deliberation and parliamentary autonomy gradually, and incrementally increasing its abuses of the security and criminal justice systems. Zuma's administration, by contrast, seems to have started out with a road map for centralisation. Former intelligence operatives, Zuma's personal associates, have been appointed to positions of particular sensitivity in the justice cluster and intelligence organisations.

A second key issue has been corruption and patronage. Critics complain that Zuma's rise has changed the composition and not the ugly character of the increasingly predatory elite.

The SACP and its Cosatu allies have argued for greater regulation of public representatives' behaviour, the banning of external directorships, and the closing of revolving doors between public and private sectors. The left has also insisted that public representatives must not accept gifts from companies that benefit from their relationships with government.

Zuma has responded with a series of nondecisions and stalling stratagems which suggest that he is personally unwilling to alienate his support base with draconian controls on the elite's abuse of state power – although lively debates within the Alliance, the NEC and parliament indicate that vigorous action may emerge despite him.

Gwede Mantashe complained to a January 2010 NEC meeting about the predominance of 'lobbying and positions' in ANC politics: 'The influence of money in our processes is having the biggest potential to change the character of the movement', he claimed. The ANC is moving from being 'people-driven' to a formation in which 'power is wielded by a narrow circle of those who own and/or control resources … An emerging perception is that daggers are always out and there is no political life other than vying for positions in the ANC' (IOL 2010). In February 2010, soon after the budget speech, Mantashe announced a new register of ANC members' business interests that will be managed by his own office.

The third source of interest in the new administration has concerned institutional reform. Zuma's set-piece speeches for the first three months of his presidency outlined his supposed motivation for increasing the number of government departments and reconfiguring the cabinet subcommittee (or 'cluster') system. A new planning commission, headed by former finance minister Trevor Manuel, will guide cabinet on long-range planning issues. A monitoring and evaluation ministry will attempt to monitor government departments' achievements of specified policy outcomes.

Despite these potentially valuable innovations, however, Zuma has threatened to erode the political status and institutional power of the key state institution, the national Treasury. The relationship between the head of government and the finance minister is the most important one in any administration, yet Zuma has played political poker at the expense of Treasury credibility. Government's strategy to put the public finances back on a sustainable path requires unpopular decisions to be taken about priorities. Zuma has mostly pretended that expenditures on public sector pay, social grants, national health insurance and the security sector can be declared 'untouchable'.

Zuma's team has peddled the idea that the Treasury is becoming a 'normal' department. Yet the Treasury is uniquely and structurally in antagonism with other departments. Government departments cannot help but generate poorly considered and opportunistic expenditure proposals, for ministers need to generate spoils for their constituencies, officials have empires to build and business people want easy profits. As political scientists first observed of the US 'military-industrial complex', the resulting 'iron triangles' of politicians, state agencies and private companies work together to boost government spending (Adams 1981).

The private interests of politicians and officials make matters worse. Kickbacks, revolving doors and resource gifts for personal networks all encourage departments to spend. Although this is not a left-right issue, ideological arrogance and wishful thinking can also encourage big spending. 'Strategic investment' and 'industrial policy' can be used to justify a relaxation of Treasury controls even when the state is in reality vulnerable to severed losses. Treasury officials have hitherto formed a thin but fragile barrier against imprudent expenditure.

Ministers should doubtless change the policy frameworks that underpin budgets, in particular by developing sector strategies and public sector investment programmes. Specific expenditure decisions nevertheless need to be justified according to their merits, however those merits may be defined. Whatever its flaws may be – and there are many – the only institutional mechanism that South Africa possesses for maintaining such a system of justification is the Treasury.

Zuma has brought into the centre of government a disdain for this culture of justification. The announcement by the Presidency in late 2009 that the finance minister would no longer sit on all ministerial cluster committees was accompanied by the warning that 'the clusters of the Forum of South African Directors General are being reconfigured accordingly' (Presidency 2009). Pravin Gordhan's predecessor, Trevor Manuel, sat on all ministerial cluster committees. No policy proposal reached Cabinet without an agreed statement of anticipated financial implications signed off by the Treasury.

The point of Treasury justification is that demands on the public purse should all be interrogated robustly. Ministers proposing 'strategic' investments and grandees from powerful families should be obliged to provide reasoned justifications for their proposals. Under Zuma, there is a danger that bad habits from the provinces will establish themselves in Pretoria. Big-spending directors general and ministers may soon be able to propel proposals through the Cabinet committee system without Treasury support. If such demands reach full Cabinet, decisions as to their merits or demerits will be taken by volatile coalitions of ministers and party barons.

THE FUTURE OF THE ANC

The defeat of Thabo Mbeki and the rise of Jacob Zuma are sometimes celebrated as a return to a golden age. The 'perversions' of Mbeki's rule, we are told, have been put behind the liberation movement. Zuma, it is claimed, will rule by consensus like Nelson Mandela before him. This fanciful interpretation of recent events underestimates the strong commonalities between the ruling elite under Mbeki and the emerging leadership under Zuma. The elite's objectives and the context in which they must govern remain fundamentally unchanged. To the degree that Polokwane has taken the ANC in new directions, these are far from being unambiguously positive.

It would be desirable for the ANC to be disciplined by an effective opposition. However, the ANC still dominates national politics, and the countervailing power of opposition parties is in some respects more limited than ever. COPE offered a feeble challenge to the ANC; the business elite associated with former president Thabo Mbeki provided both funding and a sense of purpose to this pseudo-party, but COPE failed comprehensively to achieve its objectives in the 2009 elections. Even the financiers' imposition of Mvume Dandala as presidential candidate did not propel the party to government in Eastern Cape or to the balance of power in Western Cape. This left it with no real leverage over the new ANC leadership and little patronage to dispense beyond the allocation of seats in Parliament and the provincial legislatures. COPE's business backers have now deserted it, desperate to rejoin the ANC and so to re-establish their umbilical connection to the empowerment state. The rising leadership of the ANC, with its centre of gravity in KZN, Gauteng, Limpopo and Mpumalanga, has no interest in an early resolution to the political crises of the Eastern Cape. The survival of COPE, by presenting the ANC with an eminently defeatable enemy, has been politically convenient for these new leaders. They will be weakened if the disarray within COPE results in the reincorporation of many of its members into the ANC.

Meanwhile, the Inkatha Freedom Party (IFP) is facing meltdown. The ANC cannot directly absorb the IFP in the way it digested the party of the Afrikaners, the National Party. Newly-created state instruments for disbursing money to traditional leaders, however, may ease the pain of a withdrawal from politics. As long as the ANC pays apparent homage to Zulu royalty, to traditional leaders, and to Buthelezi himself, it can now open or close the taps of patronage to modulate the speed at which the IFP's electoral base crumbles.

Even the DA is vulnerable. Under Helen Zille, it has increasingly become a regional party of the Western Cape. Disappointing election results elsewhere, and the patronage opportunities of government, have made the Cape the place to develop a DA career. The DA, moreover, cannot build effective alliances with parties like COPE or the IFP, because these potential allies remain mesmerised by ANC money and power. Selectively targeted laws to promote 'trans-parency' and 'accountability' in party funding, together with the development of new ANC mechanisms for milking business and parastatal donors, may one day soon cripple the DA's finances while leaving the ANC relatively unscathed.

In the management of racial and ethnic issues, the ANC appears to be running into intractable difficulties, some of which concern the movement's largely incomprehensible, if admirable, doctrine of nonracialism. The ANC's pursuit of racial, ethnic and regional balance has heavily influenced appointments to senior government positions since 1994. The move-ment was broadly successful in this balancing act, although complaints surfaced about the over-representation of whites, a scarcity of non-Nguni Africans, and the abundance of Xhosa speakers in former president Thabo Mbeki's second administration.

Zuma's Cabinet appointments seemed to respect the imperative of balance, and he signally made amends for the historical under-representation of leaders from Limpopo, KwaZulu-Natal and Mpumalanga in the highest offices. His own elevation to the presidency helped to end a protracted monopolisation of the highest offices by leaders from the Eastern Cape.

National appointments, however, quickly became mired in controversy. When Zuma announced that Gill Marcus would become Reserve Bank governor, analyst Duma Gqubule complained that the prevalence of 'minority' incumbents in economic portfolios, such as Trevor Manuel (planning commission), Pravin Gordhan (finance), Ebrahim Patel (economic development), Rob Davies (trade and industry), and Barbara Hogan (public enterprises) demonstrated the ANC's 'lack of confidence' in 'blacks of African descent'. The theme was quickly picked up by the president of the ANC Youth League, Julius Malema, who launched a sustained attack on the dominance of 'minorities' in the economic portfolios. In the eyes of Zuma's defenders, Malema underestimated how severely apartheid had depleted the pool of

African financiers and economists available for promotion. For all these qualifications, though, the ANCYL leader was right to insist that there is something seriously wrong with Zuma's pattern of appointments. When it comes to the economic portfolios, African politicians and officials can eventually establish a track record with the markets, as Tito Mboweni and Jabu Moleketi demonstrated. Nevertheless whites, and perhaps Indians, have less need to prove their competency.

Mboweni and Manuel endured long and harrowing inductions by the markets. In his later years at the ministry of finance, when Manuel had become a paragon of fiscal virtue, a *Financial Times* correspondent tellingly claimed he was white. Zuma's appointments are arguably a step backwards because they amount to a concession to the racial misconceptions of market actors. The racialisation of conflicts around parastatal appointments continued in 2009 in extended sagas over the appointment and resignation of Transnet and Eskom senior managers. Such incendiary conflicts open to question the ability of the ANC to maintain its doctrine of nonracialism in the face of orchestrated exhibitions of purported racial solidarity, and Youth League president Malema has been misrepresenting the ANC's historic doctrines in order to suggest that Africans, in particular, must be the beneficiaries of state advancement and empowerment largesse.

The spectre of ethnic mobilisation has also not gone away with the departure of Mbeki's alleged 'Xhosa nostra'. When Zuma chose the KwaZulu-Natal safety and security MEC, Bheki Cele, as the new national police commissioner, the KZN leader of COPE, Siyanda Mhlongo, denounced the 'Zulufication of the security, intelligence and judiciary organs' (*PoliticsWeb* 2009). Mhlongo's unease presumably derived from the rise of others of Zulu descent to security-related portfolios: Nathi Mthethwa (police), Siyabonga Cwele (state security), Jeff Radebe (justice), Vusi Mavimbela (presidency director general), Nkosazana Dlamini-Zuma (home affairs), and Siphiwe Nyanda (communications).

Zuma partisans could claim with some justification that the breakaway party was mistaking benign regional power shifts for malign ethnic favouritism. The organic growth and electoral achievements of the ANC in KZN naturally resulted in activists moving up to Pretoria, where the province has long been under-represented. Any new president, moreover, surrounds himself with trusted lieutenants, and many of those with whom Zuma was most closely associated – in the south Natal underground, in ANC intelligence, or in exile – happen to be of Zulu or Indian descent, as a result of the places and times at which he was politically active.

A shift in the ANC's centre of gravity has occurred and the likely continued debilitation of Eastern Cape structures may leave a united KZN as the movement's unchallenged primary power block. The real concern that Zuma's justice and security sector appointments raise, however, lies in the personal affiliations of appointees to the president. This is not because, as by COPE's account, many of them are Zulus, but because they are among the president's closest political allies.

When Thabo Mbeki packed security and justice offices with trusted lieutenants at the start of his second term, it was a precursor to the abuse of executive power. The potential for a small group of closely associated politicians and officials to manipulate the police, the directorate of priority crime investigation, the prosecuting authority, and even the courts, is all too real. Such institutions should build procedural autonomy and rigid rule compliance, rather than be falling into a comradely interdependence. Cronyism in the justice sector threatens to undermine the ANC's responses to perhaps the most urgent problem it faces, that of corruption.

THE FUTURE OF JACOB ZUMA

After his landslide victory at Polokwane in 2007, and his success as a campaigner in the 2009 elections, there was every reason to believe that Jacob Zuma would be a two-term president. Despite his advanced age, it seemed improbable that the movement would dare re-open succession wounds by permitting another leadership contest as early as 2012.

The coalition that helped Zuma to defeat Thabo Mbeki did not, however, survive into his new administration. The first signs of difficulty lay in conflicts over economic policy between the organised left and the leadership. Then, late in 2009, rumours began to circulate that the deputy police minister and former president of the Youth League, Fikile Mbalula, would challenge Gwede Mantashe for the office of ANC secretary general in 2012.

The office of 'S-G' has a special significance in the movement. Its incumbents since 1991 – Cyril Ramaphosa, Kgalema Motlanthe and now Gwede Mantashe – have all persuasively claimed an organic relationship with ordinary working people. However controversial their political positions might sometimes have been, these men have continued to draw upon deep reservoirs of respect. The very idea that an immature creature of youth politics might tout himself for S-G has been unthinkable for many ANC activists. Mantashe's position as lynch pin of the left, and key anti-corruption campaigner in the movement, made his attempted removal all the more controversial. Commenting on Julius Malema's role in promoting Mbalula for the office, National Union of Metalworkers of South Africa (Numsa) general secretary Irvin Jim asked, 'Why did the president (Jacob Zuma) keep quiet when his party's secretary general was being attacked? The ANC is not run by *tsotsis* who would sit in shebeens and decide to put their friends as leaders' (*Daily Dispatch* 22 February 2010). Many Cosatu affiliates believe Mantashe's attempted removal has been motivated by business interests chasing tenders, and by factions seeking ANC office to facilitate wealth accumulation. Such individuals, Numsa observed, 'clearly regard the secretary general as not amenable to such an accumulation strategy'.

Zuma also suffered renewed personal troubles when a major national newspaper reported that the president had 'fathered a love child with Sonono Khoza, daughter of (soccer boss) Irvin Khoza, a man six years his junior' (*Sunday Times* 31 January 2010). Misreading the public mood, Zuma delayed his apology for more than a week and then limped, politically damaged, into a mediocre state of the nation address. The personal difficulties in which Zuma has found himself are not accidental, in that Thabo Mbeki probably endorsed Zuma's elevation to the ANC deputy presidency in 1997 precisely because of Zuma's intrinsic and multi-dimensional vulnerability to selective prosecution, smear, and public ridicule.

Zuma's dependency on the KZN ANC to maintain him in office may also be a fatal weakness. He rose to the ANC presidency at a time when its internal factional politics were already beginning a historic transformation. The politics of the ANC have largely been conducted at regional or provincial level, and even exile politics were underpinned by a parallel ethnic factionalism. A secure power base in either the Eastern Cape or Natal was a pre-requisite for building a successful leadership coalition. Only upon such a foundation could a wider alliance, incorporating labour, the youth, minorities, and smaller regional groupings, be constructed. It is for these reasons that the ANC presidency has historically alternated (with occasional short intermissions) between leaders of Xhosa and Zulu descent.

Zuma's presidency, assisted by the decline of the Inkatha Freedom Party and by continued disarray in the Eastern Cape, might normally have marked the beginning of a Natal ascendancy, since the presence of a substantial new KZN contingent in Pretoria, notably in the justice and security cluster, testifies to the provincial machine's determination to secure a foothold in national politics. This old pattern of ANC politics, however, is being challenged by the emergence of a powerful class dimension. As we have noted, Cosatu and the SACP together played a major role in Zuma's rise to the ANC and state presidencies. Left activists are not happy to perpetuate a Zuma presidency dedicated to social authoritarianism, patriarchy, and the interests of KZN business and political elites.

The growth of black business power, and the emergence of the black middle classes, have each meanwhile introduced new sets of interests into ANC internal politics. The movement's rising business elites, concentrated in Gauteng, are able to send relatively few delegates to ANC conferences but their money can be used to build alliances and patronage networks through which to buy the voting power of poor but populous provinces.

The ANC's factional politics are fluid and multi-dimensional, and the interaction of distinct provincial and regional structures across the country will continue to play a crucial role in determining who controls national positions and institutions. The power of the KZN ANC, and its ability to maintain Zuma across two terms, should not be underestimated. However, there are two class-based national factions in play, the first of which is associated with the Youth League and with Tokyo Sexwale, human settlements (housing) minister and former Gauteng premier. Sexwale's presidential aspirations are widely recognised, and there is speculation that he does not wish to wait until 2019, when a KZN succession may have been engineered or fresh challengers may have emerged.

The organised left, fronted by ANC secretary general Gwede Mantashe, is also approaching a major crossroads. Both Cosatu and the SACP were severely weakened by the purges that were part of the Polokwane struggle. The former faces an internal power struggle between currently dominant industrial and mineworkers' unions and emerging public sector federations, while the latter will soon confront painful generational transitions. Their time for concerted action, if ever, is now.

Although the tripartite alliance has not split, and the ANC continues to accommodate a wide range of class interests and ideologies, the politics of class will inevitably play an increasingly decisive role in the internal strugles of the movement. Jacob Zuma may yet be their first victim.

NOTES

1   Parts of this chapter first appeared in different form on the pages of *Business Day* in 2009 and 2010.

REFERENCES

Adams G (1981) *The Iron Triangle: The Politics of Defense Contracting.* New York: Council on Economic Priorities.

ANC (1969) Strategy and Tactics of the ANC. April–May, available at http://www.anc.org.za/ancdocs/history/stratact.html [accessed 27 October 2004].

ANC (2009a) ANC National Executive Committee. Johannesburg: African National Congress. Available at http://www.anc.org.za/show.php?doc=lists/ancnec.html [accessed 30 November 2009].

ANC (2009b) ANC National Working Committee. Johannesburg, African National Congress. Available at http://www.anc.org.za/show.php?doc=lists/nwc.html&title=NWC+Members [accessed 30 November 2009].

ANC (2009c) Statement of the National Executive Committee of the ANC on the occasion of the 97th anniversary of the ANC. Johannesburg, 8 January.

Atkinson D (2007) Taking to the streets: Has developmental local government failed in South Africa? In Buhlungu S, J Daniel, R Southall and J Lutchman (Eds) *State of the Nation: South Africa 2007.* Cape Town: HSRC Press.

Bloch G (2008) Complexity of systems change in education, in Maile S (Ed). *Education and Poverty Reduction Strategies.* Cape Town: HSRC Press: 125–35.

Butler A (2005a) South Africa's HIV/AIDS policy, 1994–2004: How can it be explained? *African Affairs* 104: 417, 591–614.

Butler A (2005b) How democratic is the African National Congress? *Journal of Southern African Studies,* 31(4): 719–36.

Butler A (2007) *Cyril Ramaphosa.* Johannesburg: Jacana.

Butler A (2009a) The ANC's National Election Campaign of 2009: *Siyangoba.* In Southall R and J Daniel (Eds) *Zunami: The 2009 South African Elections.* Johannesburg: Jacana.

Butler A (2009b) *Contemporary South Africa.* 2nd edition. New York: Palgrave Macmillan.

Butler A (2010) Black economic empowerment since 1994. In Shapiro I and K Tebeau (Eds) *After Apartheid.* Charlottesville: University of Virginia Press.

Carter J (2008) Education in South Africa: Some points for policy coherence. In Maile S (Ed) *Education and Poverty Reduction Strategies.* Cape Town: HSRC Press: 19–38.

Chisholm L (2005) The state of South Africa's schools. In Daniel J, R Southall and J Lutchman (Eds) *State of the Nation: South Africa 2004–2005.* Cape Town: HSRC Press: 201–26.

Cronin J (1996) Thinking about the concept National Democratic Revolution, *Umrabulo* 1 (4th Quarter). http://www.anc.org.za/show.php?doc=ancdocs/pubs/umrabulo/umrabulo1.html#art2 [Accessed 2 June 2010].

DPLG (2007) National Capacity Building Framework for Local Government. Pretoria: Department of Provincial and Local Government.

Geffen N and E Cameron (2009) The deadly hand of denial: Governance and politically-instigated AIDS denialism in South Africa. Centre for Social Science Research, University of Cape Town: Working Paper 257.

Gevisser M (2007) *The Dream Deferred: Thabo Mbeki.* Johannesburg: Jonathan Ball.

Gordin J (2008) *Zuma: A Biography.* Johannesburg: Jonathan Ball.

Gumede WM (2005). *Thabo Mbeki and the Battle for the Soul of the ANC.* Cape Town: Zebra.

Hassim S (2009) Godzille and the witches: Gender and the 2009 elections. In Southall R and J Daniel (Eds) *Zunami: The 2009 South African Elections.* Johannesburg: Jacana.

Hassim S, T Kupe and E Worby (Eds) (2008) *Go Home or Die Here: Violence, Xenophobia and the Reinvention of Difference in South Africa.* Johannesburg: Witwatersrand University Press.

Hirsch A (2005) *Season of Hope: Economic Reform under Mandela and Mbeki.* Scottsville: UKZN Press.

IOL (2010) Money threatens ANC – Mantashe. Independent Online, 25 January. Available at http://www.iol.co.za/index.php?art_id=vn20100125044012647C955923 [Accessed 22 February].

Lawless A (2005) Numbers and needs: Addressing imbalances in the civil engineering profession. Johannesburg: South African Institute of Civil Engineers.

Lawless A (2007) Numbers and needs in local government: Addressing civil engineering – the critical profession for service delivery. Johannesburg: South African Institute of Civil Engineers.

Lodge T (2005) The African National Congress: There is no party like it; Ayikho Efana Nayo. In Piombo J and L Nizjink (Eds) *Electoral Politics in South Africa: Assessing the first democratic decade*. New York: Palgrave Macmillan: 109–28.

Mandela, Nelson (2007) Foreword. In O'Malley P *Shades of Difference: Mac Maharaj and the Struggle for South Africa*. London: Penguin Books.

Maphai V and K Gottschalk (2003) Parties, politics and the future of democracy. In Everatt D and V Maphai (Eds) *The Real State of the Nation*. Johannesburg: Interfund: 51–74.

Netshitenzhe J (2000) The NDR and Class Struggle: An Address to the Executive Committee of COSATU, *The Shop Steward* 9 (1), available at http://www.cosatu.org.za/shop/shop0901/ shop0901-06.html [Accessed 28 October 2004].

Presidency (2009) Ministerial clusters reconfigured to improve coordination and delivery. Pretoria, 19 October. Available at http://www.thepresidency.gov.za/show.asp?type=pr&include=president/ pr/2009/pr10191458.htm&ID=1813 [Accessed 30 November 2009].

Roberts Ben (2008) Between trust and scepticism: Public confidence in institutions. *HSRC Review* 6 (1): 10–11.

Roberts RS (2007) *Fit to Govern: The Native Intelligence of Thabo Mbeki*. Johannesburg: STE Publishers.

Ross R (2008) *A Concise History of South Africa*. 2nd edition. Cambridge: Cambridge University Press.

Schulz-Herzenberg C (2007) A silent revolution: South African voters, 1994-2006. In Buhlungu S, J Daniel, R Southall and J Lutchman (Eds), *State of the Nation: South Africa 2007*. Cape Town: HSRC Press: 114-145.

Schulz-Herzenberg C (2009) Trends in party support and voter behaviour, 1994–2009. In Southall R and J Daniel (Eds) *Zunami. The 2009 South African Elections*. Johannesburg: Jacana.

Slovo J (1988) The South African Working Class and the National Democratic Revolution. Umsebenzi Discussion Pamphlet. South African Communist Party, available at http://www.sacp.org.za/ docs/history/ndr.html [Accessed 28 October 2004].

Suttner R (2008) *The ANC Underground in South Africa*. Johannesburg: Jacana.

Treasury (2010) National Budget Speech, 17 February. Pretoria, National Treasury. Available at http://www.Treasury.gov.za/documents/national%20budget/2010/ [Accessed 22 February 2010].

Vasagar J (2005) Mbeki fires deputy in corruption scandal. *The Guardian*, 15 June.

Zille H (2008) Battle for SA's soul begins. PoliticsWeb, 9 January. Available at http://www.politicsweb. co.za/politicsweb/view/politicsweb/en/page72308?oid=85178&sn=Detail&ccs_clear_cache=1 [Accessed 14 November 2009].

CHAPTER 7

Indigent management:
A strategic response to the struggles of
the poor in post-apartheid South Africa[1]

Prishani Naidoo

... The United Democratic Front (UDF) rejects the current government policies of privatisation of housing, which fail to cater for the housing needs of 80 per cent of the black population in South Africa. The UDF believes that all the people of South Africa deserve more than third-class housing in the form of site and service schemes. The UDF believes strongly that the state has a centrally important role to play in the provision of land, services and houses for all South Africans. The UDF commits itself to a process of serious negotiations towards the establishment of new land and housing policies that can begin to solve the problems of landlessness and homelessness ... There can be no justification for the continuation of landlessness and homelessness, for the lack of clean water, electricity, water-borne sewerage and other basic facilities, and the government must move rapidly to rectify the situation. Constitutional negotiations and a political settlement in South Africa will be rendered useless if urban areas continue to be inaccessible to the poor and the homeless.

(United Democratic Front, Memorandum to Hernus Kriel,
then minister of planning and provincial affairs, 16 August 1990)

People should stop being dependants of government because it will destroy them. Going through free schooling, then under-performing to a point where they don't qualify for bursaries and loans or even pass matric, then falling pregnant and depending on social grants to raise these children and waiting for RDP houses similar to those they grew up in is not right ... That's why, during housing protests, you see young people – who can study and work – instead of old people. We need to instil morals in our children because solutions for the housing backlog relate to education, poverty and moral regeneration.

(Nomvula Mokonyane, then MEC for housing,
now premier of Gauteng, *City Press* 18 November 2007)

These two quotes, seventeen years apart, speak to similar problems faced by both the apartheid and the African National Congress (ANC) governments – how to cater to the needs of the growing urban black poor and how to manage the growing numbers of poor black people claiming their place in urban areas and refusing forms of control over their ways of living.[2] While the ANC set itself apart from the apartheid regime, winning the first democratic elections in 1994 on the promise of a better life for all, it assumed the responsibility for fulfilling the historical promise of liberation in a context in which neoliberalism had become a dominant force globally, its own approaches to transforming the state, and its relationship to its citizens coming to be defined by this paradigm.[3] With the adoption of neoliberal policies, fulfilling the historical promises of liberation came to be portrayed as the responsibility of the state and individual citizens working together in a 'partnership' that recognised the changed context in which government would unfold. In the words of Nomvula Mokonyane, an ANC leader, we see the mobilisation of a new language of morality targeted at poor citizens demanding that the ANC government take responsibility for addressing their unequal and inferior standards and quality of life created by the apartheid government and continuing into the post-apartheid era. This increasing mobilisation of notions of morality in service of neoliberal approaches to the economy and governance by the ANC has been noted by several commentators (Barchiesi 2006; Everatt 2008; Marais 2007; Naidoo and Veriava 2005, Veriava 2009), particularly in calls made by state and party officials since the mid-1990s aimed at discouraging South Africans from becoming dependent on state 'handouts' (in the form of social grants and free basic services such as water and electricity).

As the ANC government has adopted neoliberal policies, the role of the state has come to be viewed and portrayed as that of 'enabling' individual citizens to become 'self-reliant' and active in the production of their own well-being, primarily through the state providing only the most basic means by which, it is argued, the individual will be able to become economically productive. Franco Barchiesi (2006) shows how the policy of developmental social welfare, set out in the 1997 White Paper on Social Development, outlines these changed roles for the state and citizens. Several speeches and statements from ANC leaders enforce the view that the state's role can go no further than facilitating access to those very basic necessities required for the individual citizen to take on the responsibility of making 'a better life' for himself or herself (Mandela 1995; Mbeki 2008). In such characterisations, poor people come to be imagined and represented as 'deserving' or 'undeserving' (Everatt 2008; Hart 2007). The former are understood as those who are willing to assume responsibility for their own well-being, working hard in whatever jobs they can find and/or becoming small-scale entrepreneurs to be able to pay for basic services and therefore deserving minimal assistance from the state. The latter are those of the poor who continue to make demands of the state for increased assistance (handouts), refusing to help themselves out of their poverty traps. Mokonyane's words assume, then, that the state is meeting its end of a partnership in which the individual citizen also has a responsibility which, in this case, she laments, is not being met.

While recent developments in the ANC alliance have led some individuals to question whether possibilities might now be opened up for a change in macroeconomic policy (Everatt 2008;

Pillay 2008) with, for example, the adoption of more 'pro-poor' measures by the state (Everatt 2008) such as the provision of a universal basic income grant (BIG),[4] the evolution of munic-ipal policy with regard to basic services suggests that this is not the case. If one considers that the ANC's Polokwane conference (which for these commentators marks the opening up of these possibilities for shifts away from neoliberal policies within the ruling party) took place in 2007, the most recent indigent management policy introduced by the City of Johannesburg in July 2008 (*Siyasizana*, explored in much greater detail below) signals a cementation of neoliberal forms of rule. While there might now be talk of changes at national level about some aspects of macroeconomic policy, at municipal level it would seem that the enforcement of the principle of cost recovery through technologies that encourage individual conservation, self-restraint and self-discipline among those unable to pay for services, continues in ever more rigorous (and sophisticated) ways. This pursuit of indigent management at municipal level would also suggest that the role of the state continues to be imagined by those in power as providing only very basic resources to its most vulnerable citizens so as to encourage their self reliance and responsibility for making better lives for themselves.

As the rest of this chapter will show, strategies that move away from creating universal forms of access to decommodified services towards more targeted interventions that provide such access incrementally according to an individual's ability to pay, while being portrayed as 'pro-poor', actually work towards moulding the behaviours of that population group in ways that further entrench inequality and differentiated standards of living.

This chapter will explore some of the contestations that have emerged over what constitutes state and individual responsibility in struggles for the delivery of basic services, focusing particularly on how contestation comes to focus on what 'basic needs' are and to whom in society the state should provide the resources necessary for these needs to be met. In particular, it will look at how indigent management policies came to be revived and reshaped in the struggle between the state and poor people over the enforcement of the duty to pay for basic services, contributing to the further technicisation of the realm of politics and the latter's increasing reduction to contestation over 'the necessities for life'.[5]

Through the experience of struggles for basic services and the shaping of municipal policy in the City of Johannesburg post-1996, indigent management will be shown to emerge as a strategy, in the first instance, of cost recovery and 'responsibilisation' (making people into good citizens as defined by the neoliberal state) rather than as a 'pro-poor' intervention. In the context of 'the poor' mobilised as a political identity by new social and community move-ments and drawing attention to the need for the state to take stock of the effects of its cost-recovery policies, the mobilisation of indigent management seems strategic on the part of the state. It is as if the state is pressed to prove that it has not strayed from its promises to restruc-ture its role in the social contract and to enforce – among that particular population group identified as 'the poor' – certain ways of relating ('responsibly') to 'the necessities of life' and to the state. This chapter will try to understand the effects of the strategic mobilisation of an identity of the poor, by those most negatively affected by the introduction of neoliberal policies on state policy, on movements and on individuals.

ENFORCING A 'CULTURE OF PAYMENT' – FROM MASAKHANE TO INDIGENT MANAGEMENT

As the ANC prepared to govern, it needed to reorient its membership and constituency – away from the culture of protest that had come to define the liberation movement and towards more responsible forms of citizenship. In the sphere of basic services, as cost recovery became a priority in framing delivery, individual civic responsibility came to be portrayed as paying for services consumed, and conserving and consuming only according to one's ability to pay. Against the backdrop of the payment boycotts of rent and service charges in the 1980s and 1990s in South African townships (resulting in what many have called a 'culture of non-payment'), and the expectation reflected in the quoted UDF memorandum for the state to meet its responsibility and provide for the needs of its citizens, the newly-elected ANC government undertook a campaign entitled *Masakhane* ('we are building'), aimed specifically at encouraging the individual responsibility of each citizen in the project of nation building.

On 20 January 1995, the Department of Constitutional Development launched the campaign as 'part of a drive to normalise and improve relations of governance and to focus on rights and responsibilities of citizens and government' (Department of Constitutional Development 1996: 1). Central to this campaign was the encouragement of citizens to pay for their basic services. *Masakhane* encouraged citizens to view this act of payment as part of their responsibility in a partnership with the state for development and delivery, and to understand the limited position of the state as a result of its alleged increased financial constraints and need for fiscal discipline.[6]

But the re-education imperatives of *Masakhane* had little effect on levels of payment,[7] and within a year of its launch more punitive strategies for preventing non-payment were encouraged (Moosa 1997). The practice of cut-offs (physically putting an end to the supply of water and/or electricity to an individual household) became the preferred strategy of service providers.[8] But, in a context of growing instability of income, as unemployment continued to rise and the nature of work shifted to more informal and flexible types, cut-offs did not induce the intended response of payment for services. Instead, numbers of those unable to pay rose in protest against being denied access to the necessities of life, coming together as affected communities and, over time, as social movements, drawing attention to the exclusion and marginalisation of poor people from development and the nation building project (Pithouse 2009).

Individuals and movements began to adopt new strategies and tactics of resistance such as illegal reconnections to water and electricity supplies. It is this contest, between social movements and the state, that the remobilisation of indigent management as a strategy for dealing with the criticism that the poor have been excluded is first encountered. It emerges in the experimentation with various technologies for enforcing the duty to pay for services, primarily through separating the 'can't pays' from the 'won't pays'. Ironically, then, it is in response to demands made on the state by groups identifying themselves as the poor that such strategies of indigent management emerge, seemingly answering the call for the state to understand and answer the problems of its poorest citizens, for whom it is said to hold some moral responsibility, understood historically.

Since the first protests against water and electricity cut-offs and evictions, recorded in Eldorado Park, Johannesburg, followed by Secunda (Mpumalanga) and Butterworth (Transkei) in 1997 (Bond 2000a), through those of 1998 in the townships of the East Rand and 1999 and 2000 in Cape Town (McDonald and Smith 2004), Durban (Desai 2002) and Johannesburg (Naidoo and Veriava 2005), to the wave of uprisings starting again nationwide in 2004, and the most recent acts of community resistance that have come to be called 'service delivery protests', the state – broadly at a national level, and more concretely at a local (municipal) level – has experimented with a number of strategies aimed at entrenching the principle of payment for basic services, and accompanying logics of conservation and self-restraint.

After the failure of *Masakhane* and cut-offs, state provision of free basic services became the next means attempted to enforce the duty to pay. Free basic services were portrayed as representing a dramatic shift in governmental policy when they were introduced by President Thabo Mbeki in 2000 (Mosdell 2006: 283; Ruiters 2005) after sustained protest action, particularly against water cut-offs, water privatisation, and the outbreak of cholera in a rural part of KwaZulu-Natal (Madlebe) in which prepaid water meters had been experimented with as a strategy of cost recovery (Cottle and Deedat 2002). While much has been written about the evolution of a national free basic services policy (Bond 2008; Mosdell 2006; Ruiters 2005), what is important here is that the underlying aim of the attempt to develop it has been that of ensuring cost-effectiveness and cost-efficiency through enhancing mechanisms for collecting payment for services and preventing non-payment.

For Greg Ruiters, the free basic water policy speaks to a much deeper shift in forms of government, in which the provision of free basic services is tied to means by which recipients are encouraged to 'take greater care of and "ownership" of services'; and is separated into individual, metered 'consumer units' at the level of the household. He also argues that the crafting of a free basic services policy allows for the longer-term registration of those 'truly deserving of assistance', 'the poor' in the form of indigent registers, through which targeted assistance could be provided in a restricted and regulated manner. In this way, Ruiters argues, state managers come to see the free basic water policy as 'a strategy', 'an innovative approach that will enable us to separate the "can't pays" from the "won't pays"' (Muller 2001, quoted in Ruiters 2005: 7 and Veriava 2009).

Implementation of the national free basic services policy at a municipal level has taken different forms, each geared towards ensuring that individuals live within their means – that is, according to how much they are able to pay for over and above the free monthly household allocations.[9] These have included the installation of 'tricklers' in taps to restrict the flow of water in order to reduce consumption and regulate the usage of the free 6 kl, and forcing poor customers to agree to a 10 amp supply of electricity (known to cause tripping and to restrict usage) in order to access the free allocation of electricity (Ruiters 2007: 494). Such mechanisms, beyond the physical restriction of the flow of services, were also, it is argued, aimed at encouraging self-control, self-restraint, and self-discipline of consumption (*ibid*; Coalition Against Water Privatisation *et al* 2006; Veriava 2009). One of the most restrictive technologies, one that has come under much criticism, particularly in struggles of communities in Orange Farm and Soweto since 2002, is that of the prepaid meter (Coalition Against Water Privatisation *et al* 2003; Harvey 2005; Ngwane and Veriava 2004; Veriava 2009).

Prepaid meters were first introduced by Eskom in the mid-1990s as part of its initiative to electrify black townships,[10] and prepaid water meter projects were rolled out in 1998 (in Khutsong, Hermanus, Modderspruit, Koffiefontein and rural parts of the Eastern and Northern Cape (Ruiters 2005: 11), as well as in Mogale City (previously Krugersdorp)), but it was not until 2002 and the rollout of a campaign called Operation *Gcin'amanzi* to install prepaid water meters in Soweto (preceded by a pilot project in Orange Farm) that the perniciousness of prepaid technology was confronted in the mainstream. This was through protests led by residents in Orange Farm and Soweto, supported by affiliates of the Anti-Privatisation Forum (APF), in particular the Orange Farm Water Crisis Committee (OWCC) and the Soweto Electricity Crisis Committee (SECC).

While the state and private companies argued that prepaid technology allowed for individuals to better manage their consumption of services over and above their free allocations, whilst facilitating the delivery of these free allocations, groups such as the APF asserted that the monthly allocations were insufficient for the basic needs of large township households, and represented a curtailment in the basic rights of all citizens to the necessities for life. The prepaid meter, unlike a cut-off, which worked retroactively to punish after consumption, prevented any use of a service beyond the free allocations until after payment. In this way, there was no room for debts or arrears to be incurred, and the service provider was saved the bother of negotiation with non-paying customers and/or the ordeal of cutting services. More importantly, activists pointed out how the prepaid meter functioned to encourage certain ways of living amongst poor residents, in particular encouraging self-discipline, conservation and self-restraint in the consumption of basic services. In the words of Trevor Ngwane and Ahmed Veriava (2004: 130):

> The meter is the most profound symbol of neoliberalism. It brings together its two most important characteristics, the commodification of the basics for life and the development of new forms of control. Through the prepaid meter, life is turned into a site of accumulation, and people cut themselves off. This is our brave new world!

In Johannesburg, where prepaid water meters were introduced in a multi-million rand campaign billed as reducing water wastage and losses in Soweto and increasing conservation and efficient consumption by residents, movements including the Phiri Concerned Residents' Forum (PCRF), the SECC, the OWCC and the APF[11] have waged serious battles (sometimes violent) against Johannesburg Water[12] workers, police, and other authorities, in order to physically prevent the installation of pipes and meters in their yards. While this chapter cannot do justice to the complexities and nuances of the Phiri struggle, it is nevertheless important to acknowledge its effects on the evolution of municipal policy for the delivery of basic services in the City of Johannesburg. For it is in response to these struggles, and the demands made by people involved in them, that a comprehensive indigent management strategy has been crafted, in which the provision of free basic services becomes the means by which prepaid meters can be imposed on those identified as the poor, and a whole series of governmental techniques can be introduced in the management of this population group. Contrary to suggestions that the adoption of more targeted approaches or indigent management policies could reflect a move away from neoliberal policies because they offer a means for those areas without access to services to gain access, and because they have been tied to debt write-offs (Everatt 2008; Von Schnitzler 2008), the experience of the City of Johannesburg clearly reflects the further enforcement of neoliberal prescriptions of individual responsibility, self-restraint, conservation, and payment for services through indigent management. While the language adopted increasingly includes the term 'pro-poor', the provision of differentiated levels of service to, and the encouragement of particular forms of behaviour among, those identified and targeted as the poor reinforce inequality and the principle that access to higher levels of services and a better quality of life should be restricted to those able to pay.

While the next section of this chapter takes up the experience of Johannesburg, it is important to reflect on how closely related municipal and national experience and policy formulation processes are, with experiments at local level feeding into strategies evolving at national level. As the City of Johannesburg began to look towards indigent management in its strategising from 2002 onwards, in the midst of protests, with dedicated processes of research culminating in 2004 and the beginning of the process of drafting a social package, processes at a national level also began to explore different mechanisms for addressing the ongoing crisis in the delivery of basic services.

In 2003, noting government's commitment to providing free basic services 'to address the needs of the masses of impoverished citizens of South Africa' and its constitutional obligation to provide a 'basic level of service' to all citizens, as well as the numerous 'difficulties' in the provision of basic services, the Department of Provincial and Local Government (DPLG) undertook a study into the provision of free basic services in the country. Consisting of a quantitative survey of all 284 municipalities, interviews with a national sample of municipalities (twenty-eight), and interviews with identified stakeholders in the sphere of free basic service delivery (for example Eskom and the Department of Water Affairs and Forestry), the study found that 67 per cent of municipalities had undertaken some formal process to identify households qualifying for free basic services. This represents 'an interest to develop a record of indigents' in several municipalities (DPLG 2003: iii). The report also found, however, that a number of problems were being experienced by municipalities with regard to developing their own indigent management policies.

The document mentions throughout the need for the development of guidelines for municipalities about their approach to the indigent. The report showed how a targeted approach, such as that of an indigent register and policy, would make more sense for municipalities with regard to cost-effectiveness, 'efficiency', and the ability to monitor the interventions made by government. While the report recognised that municipal managers interviewed in the study had expressed reluctance at adopting such policies because of their perceived administrative burden, it nevertheless made a strong case for the development of national guidelines for the implementation of indigent management policies at municipal level. Significantly, the report stated:

> Free basic services was intended to service the poorest of the poor, by providing a basic
> level of service to people who would not otherwise be able to afford this. However, results
> of both the pilot study, and the survey of municipalities undertaken as part of this study,

suggest that a high percentage of free basic service implementation is being provided on a broad basis and not in a targeted manner. Free basic services are being provided to all people currently listed on the municipalities' billing system. The implication of this is that a substantial amount of free basic services are being provided to people who are not entitled to this service (according to the national indigent policy) but who are easy to locate i.e. they already appear on the billing system (DPLG 2003: 71).

In language markedly different from that in the times of *Masakhane* and cut-offs, state and party officials began acknowledging that certain sections of the population were unable rather than unwilling to pay for basic services. For example, Father Smangaliso Mkhatshwa, then chairperson of the South African Local Government Association (SALGA) made the following public statement in 2004:

> At today's meeting in Kempton Park the SALGA Consultative Assembly agreed to a campaign to register the poor throughout our country in the war against poverty. The aim of the campaign is to ensure that the most marginalised of our people – the poorest of the poor – receive a subsidy from their municipalities for basic services. This will go a long way to ensure service delivery to the poor, who are deprived of a basic amount of water sanitation services and electricity because they are too poor to pay for these services rather than unwillingness to pay for services (South African Local Government Association (SALGA) media release, 16/6/2004, [my emphasis]).

In June 2005, in a period of heightened struggles in the sphere of basic services, the DPLG released a draft framework for a national indigent policy, designed to assist municipalities with the establishment of their own frameworks for indigent management. Interestingly, the entire proposed indigent policy hinged on the provision of free basic services or, at least, the provision of those services necessary for life. The proposed policy framework states:

> Indigent people have in common the need to access affordable basic services that will facilitate their productive and healthy engagement in society (DPLG 2005a).

In a September 2005 discussion document fleshing out this framework, it is stated: 'The term "indigent" means "lacking the necessities of life"' (DPLG 2005b: 3). The document goes on to describe these necessities, in line with the South African constitution, as being sufficient water, basic sanitation, refuse removal, environmental health, basic energy, health care, housing, food and clothing, stating that 'anyone who does not have access to these goods and services is considered indigent' (*op cit*: 3-4). It describes itself in the following way:

> This policy is aimed at including those currently excluded from access to basic services, through the provision of a social safety net. What poor people in South Africa have in common is the need to access affordable basic services that will facilitate their productive and healthy engagement in society (*op cit*: 2).

Importantly, the document makes a distinction between an 'essential package of services', located at the level of the individual household, understood also as a 'social safety net', and a broader 'full social services package' that could include 'higher levels of household services and access to public services such as roads, public transport, community services and emergency services' (*op cit*: 4). While the document argues that all municipalities should, through their use of their allocation of the equitable share,[13] provide the essential package of services through indigent management policies, the full social services package should be viewed as an ideal which may be provided by a municipality based on its fiscal strength. Even more significantly, the national indigent framework states:

> An indigent policy will only be fully functional once subsidies are targeted in such a way that the indigent benefit and those who are not indigent pay (DPLG 2005b).

Once again, we see here how the prioritisation of indigent management relates to the overall aim of enforcing the duty to pay for services through the separation of the 'can't pays' from the 'won't pays', the establishment of systems whereby minimal levels of access to basic services are created only for those identified as the 'can't pays' (the poor), and the regulation and monitoring of these systems to ensure that the 'won't pays' are made to pay.

Since 2005, indigent management policies have been crafted in several municipalities (Centre for Development Support 2002), each with the overt aim of separating the 'can't pays' from the 'won't pays'. In this separation, differentiated levels of access to services are entrenched, setting out particular minimums and basic standards for the quality of life acceptable to those identified as indigent, and permitting access to higher standards only to those able to pay for them.

In the 'pro-poor' discourse of the post-apartheid state, then, lie strategies for the governing of the poor under neoliberalism,[14] that population group in society requiring assistance with meeting the basic necessities of life, through indigent management policies that tie accessing such assistance to changing individual ways of living. The evolving policies of the City of Johannesburg illustrate this clearly.

KNOWING AND TARGETING 'THE POOR': The case of Johannesburg

The experience of the City of Johannesburg (CoJ) shows the convergence of several different strategies experimented with in the City's attempts to enforce the duty to pay for basic services, and a logic of conservation, self-restraint and self-discipline around the consumption of those services considered essential for life, in the context of resistance as well as the need to grow into its aspirant role of 'world class city' (Greater Johannesburg Metropolitan Council 1999, 2000, 2001; City of Johannesburg 2005, 2006). The City's evolving indigent management framework, firmly ensconced in the formulation of its human development strategy, is also significant in that it shows so clearly the effects of community resistance on municipal policy, and how paper commitments are ultimately shaped and transformed, through contestation, in their attempted implementation. While it is impossible here to chart the entire evolution of current City policies related to the management of the poor, what follows is a discussion of some of the important policy processes and documents that have unfolded since 1994 in relation to struggles of groups identifying themselves as movements of the poor.

While the CoJ has had an indigent management policy since as early as 1998, it was only in 2002, after a prolonged period of protests and in what the City identified as a fiscal crisis, that there was a serious return to such an approach in the form of the special cases policy, which replaced the City's 1998 indigent management policy and which, significantly, aimed to determine 'special cases *in respect of payment for basic services* provided by local government *to those who cannot afford to pay for basic services*, the elderly and HIV/AIDS patients and orphans' (Palmer Development Group 2004a: 11; [my emphasis]); and 'to enhance credit control measures by providing a safety net for the poorest of the poor and *identifying those using poverty to not pay for basic services*' (*ibid* [my emphasis]).

Its objectives included the provision of subsidies for refuse removal and sanitation for individual households unable to pay for these services (in addition to the universal free basic provisions of water and electricity provided for at national level), and the establishment of a 'poverty register to inform poverty mapping and targeted socio-economic developmental programmes'. This was particularly important because, during non-payment for services under apartheid, many township households would not have signed up as account holders with the City, remaining 'unknown' by the billing systems and therefore unable to be billed for services.

But by 2004 the special cases policy had not met any of these aims, registering a very small number of account holders, and was being criticised in internal CoJ research processes for excluding large numbers of poor people living in backyard shacks and squatter camps as they would usually not be account holders. City-commissioned research argued against the further development of indigent management policies a way of ensuring cost recovery, but City strategists would not heed its advice. Instead, they worked towards improving and extending the reach of the special cases policy, reorienting and restructuring it to fulfil the objective of knowing 'the poor' in order to intervene in their lives in ways that would encourage them to accept the duty to pay for services and make use of targeted assistance to 'help themselves out of poverty' through participation in the market – they had, however, to sign onto indigent registers and accept the prescriptions accompanying indigent management policies. These came in the form of having one's debts written off in exchange for signing onto the indigent register.

As part of the roll-out of prepaid water meters in Operation *Gcin'amanzi* in Soweto, and in the context of heightened resistance to the installation of meters, the City had approved an initiative by Johannesburg Water to progressively write off arrears in deemed consumption areas,[15] on condition that a prepaid meter was accepted and used. In a discussion document of the City's finance and economic development mayoral committee, the following is noted:

> Johannesburg Water advises that the implementation of the project is successful and addresses the affordability and access to water simultaneously whilst a culture of payment is engendered with the incentive of having the historical arrears proportionately written off over an extended period of time on condition that the customer manages his prepaid water meter. To leverage the positive impact of the model and bring holistic relief to

the consumer from the City of Joburg, as the overarching custodian, it is recommended that the total historical debt be brought into the progressive write off programme on exactly the same basis of performance and incentive. Accordingly, the customer will be obliged to accept a prepaid electricity meter to qualify for the progressive write off of the composite debt over the matching period (2005: 1-2).

In the context of increased demands by township communities for the scrapping of the arrears and for the City to become more proactive in addressing the problems of inequality and poverty plaguing it, the key principles, objectives and mechanisms of the special cases policy, the enforcement of prepaid technology and the debt write-off programme were brought together in the crafting of a new indigent management policy. This was the municipal services subsidy scheme (MSSS) and *Reathusa* ('we are helping'). Through these policies, the City introduced 'incentives' for 'customers' to 'rehabilitate' their accounts and be offered 'a second chance' at becoming 'responsible', paying citizens and accepting forms of control such as the prepaid meter. In this way, the City felt it could strengthen its ability to sift out the 'can't pays' from the 'won't pays', and develop a proper system for monitoring 'poverty' and the actions of those identified as 'the poor'.

In May 2005, the MSSS was launched as 'a major incentive to poor communities in Johannesburg to relieve the burden of debts but at the same time create a new culture of payment' (City of Johannesburg, *Press Release*, 6 April 2006). It encouraged residents fitting a particular profile[16] to come forward to have their arrears written off in exchange for signing a binding agreement to pay for services in the future and to install prepaid water and electricity meters for household 'budgeting' within twelve months of being accepted into the scheme. The MSSS would also ensure the delivery of 6 kl of free water and 50 kw monthly of free electricity to households on its register, and would cover refuse removal and sanitation charges. In addition, there would be no charge for assessment rates for properties valued at less than R20 001 (City of Johannesburg, *Press Release*, 9 December 2005).

The obligation to sign onto the prepaid system was explained by a city official, Bongani Nkosi, as a necessary way of enforcing a culture of payment amongst those 'unable to afford debt' (interview, 20 November 2006). In line with the mantra of assuming individual responsibility for one's standard and quality of life, the prepaid meter was proposed as a practical way for 'the poor' to budget efficiently and so to 'live within their means'. And increasingly, a discourse of 'helping' people was mobilised to show that the state was committed to playing a part in making it possible for people to change their habits and become responsible by paying for services.

In February 2006, the City launched what it billed as 'the second phase of its programme of poverty alleviation aimed at assisting the indigent and poor in the city to rehabilitate their municipal accounts and create a culture of payment amongst its account holders' (City of Johannesburg, *Press Release*, 30 January 2006). The *Reathusa* scheme would target municipal account holders with a gross monthly income of R6 500 or less. In the words of the City's revenue department:

> The principles of the Reathusa scheme are that the customer concludes a formal repayment arrangement for half their debt as well as keeping their current account up to date. If they stick to this for the period agreed to and pay their arrears, they will then

have their remaining half of their debt written off (City of Johannesburg, *Press Release*, 30 January 2006).

As with the MSSS, successful applicants to the *Reathusa* scheme were expected to install pre-paid water and electricity meters in their homes within twelve months of acceptance to the scheme. Applications to the scheme were open between 1 February and 31 December 2006.

While the basic principles behind the MSSS and *Reathusa* were similar, it is significant that a separation was made between different levels of poverty. It is also striking that income levels significantly higher than those ordinarily associated with poverty (R6 500) were treated with the same approach as those traditionally identified as 'the poor'. Thus there was an increase in distinctions made between 'those who can pay and won't' ('the won't pays') and 'those who really cannot afford to pay' ('the can't pays'), with one of the aims behind both schemes being the increasing of the City's capacity to separate out 'the can't pays' from 'the won't pays'.

This growing separation of these two categories and its accompanying discourse of responsible citizenship through payment for services, together with the attempt to portray the MSSS as an intervention directed at a minority of the poor, worked together to further reinforce the idea that access to decommodified services should only be possible for the desperate few who are unable to become successful in market society. While the City's own documents state that more than half the city's population[17] earns less than R1 600 a month, its interventions to address their plight target a mere 100 000 households. This alone indicates that the City's commitment to the poor does not lie in any real redistributive desire, but in a concerted effort to entrench a logic of access to different standards of living and qualities of life dependent on one's individual ability to pay for them.

This has most recently been confirmed in the CoJ's responses to struggles undertaken by residents against its rollout of prepaid water meters. In 2007, with the assistance of the Centre for Applied Legal Studies (CALS) and the Coalition Against Water Privatisation, five residents of Phiri brought a class action suit in the Johannesburg High Court against the installation of pre-paid water meters in the township, demanding that the free allocation of water be increased from 6 kl per household per month to 50 kl per person per day; that prepaid water meters be declared unconstitutional; and that normal credit meters be reinstalled in homes. This came after a pro-longed period of protest action in Phiri, during which a new organisation, the Phiri Concerned Residents' Forum (PCRF), was formed. While it is not possible in this short chapter to explore in any detail the nature of the initial period of political unrest in Phiri, it is important to understand that the decision to form the Coalition and adopt a legal strategy that would include the Constitutional Court, came only after struggles on the ground in Phiri were being lost, and through heated debate and discussion within the PCRF, the APF, and later the Coalition[18].

On 30 April 2008, in a landmark ruling, Judge Tsoka declared that prepaid water meters were unlawful and unconstitutional, ordered the municipality to begin providing 50 litres of water per person per day, and allowed all residents of Phiri access to water measured by a normal credit meter. While the Coalition seemed vindicated, the City appealed the ruling, and drew attention to changes it had begun making since 2007. In July 2007, after prolonged struggles in Phiri and greater Soweto against prepaid meters, and in the run-up to the hearing of the case, the city announced its increase in the allocation of free basic water from 6 kl to 10 kl per household per month for all households registered as indigent. In addition, it made available 4 kl of emergency water to all households on the prepaid water system, and established the special needs water application mechanism, by which residents could make special appeal to the municipality for additional water (City of Johannesburg, Mid-term Report, September 2008: 199).

When, on 14 May 2008, Mayor Amos Masondo announced that the city would be appealing the judgment, he claimed that 'the judgment was distorted as the municipality was already providing 50 litres per day to households on the indigence register which had fewer than seven people' (*Business Day* 15 May 2008). In justifying the appeal, Masondo argued that the city's bringing together of prepaid technology, and a targeted system of free basic service provision would enable it to start tackling the plight of poor residents by offering a targeted system of a social safety net as a first step towards realising the benefits of a full social package:

> The amount of water that households get for free is not determined by prepayment meters. It is determined by the City's package of free basic services. We call this our social package. Since 2001 and 2002 this social package has been gradually expanded over time. Residents of Phiri are in a better position than they were in June 2002 (Masondo, statement, 14 May 2008).

He used the increase in the amount of free water provided as an example of how progress was being made. Later on he stated:

> We want to conclude by reiterating that we believe that the introduction of prepayment meters, coupled with a dynamically expanding social package that gives poor households more and more water for free, is the best way to progressively realise the right of access to water on a sustainable basis in our context. We do not think that this approach is unreasonable and unlawful under the circumstances *(ibid)*.

In March 2009, the Supreme Court of Appeal granted the municipality two years in which to change city bylaws in order to make prepaid meters legal, and stipulated that 42 litres of water be provided free to each resident per day. The city argued that its indigent residents were already receiving an amount higher than this. Appealing to the Constitutional Court, residents of Phiri were disappointed by its setting aside of both the previous orders and its finding that the City of Johannesburg's installation of prepaid water meters did not violate national policy or the constitution with regard to the delivery of water. Instead, the final judgement argued that the City's approach to the delivery of water fell within section 27 of the constitution's allowance for the progressive realisation of the right to water. The Court also presented the finding that the quantifying of a sufficient amount of water was not within its jurisdiction, leaving it to government to make such a decision.

It would seem, then, that the careful crafting of an indigent management policy by the City and its representation, as a means towards ensuring the progressive realisation of access to water beyond the bare minimum, was what, after five years of litigation, would finally win it legitimacy in the eyes of the Constitutional Court judges. It is interesting that the Court would choose to speak of the differentiated levels of access prescribed in this policy in terms of progressive realisation, without acknowledging the further entrenchment of inequality through such an approach.

Introduced in July 2009, the latest indigent management policy, named *Siyasizana* ('we are helping each other'), also referred to as 'the extended social package', builds on the principles of targeting and minimal interventions based on need set out in earlier policies, and continues to argue for the assumption by the individual citizen of the responsibility for securing access to resources over and above those minimal amounts provided by the state, primarily through becoming economically productive. Once again mobilising a discourse of 'helping each other', *Siyasizana* put in place a three-tiered system for determining and addressing need on the part of 'the poor'. Significantly, it introduced the means for the targeting of individuals rather than households (as previous policies had done), enhancing the state's ability to register, know, 'rehabilitate', and monitor those identified as the poor. Introducing a new poverty index, *Siyasizana* stipulated the criteria for determining three 'bands of poverty' for all individuals earning a monthly income below R3 366. Band One aimed at helping 'those on the borderline of poverty' and provided the lowest level of subsidy. Band Two was 'those who earn some formal income but whose earnings fall below the survival level defined by the poverty index' and granted a middle level of subsidy. Band Three was 'the highest level of subsidy, aimed at those with no formal income living in the most deprived circumstances (City of Johannesburg, *Social Package* - http://www.joburg.org.za/content/view/3432/168/ [accessed 20 February 2009]).

According to the new classification system, each individual applicant will be given a 'poverty score' out of 100, seventy of these points allocated based on a person's individual socio-economic circumstances, and thirty based on the conditions of the geographical area in which the person resides. While the city had already begun to provide 10 kl of water and 100 kw of electricity free to each household qualifying as indigent during the period of the court action against prepaid water meters, after 1 July 2009 every adult resident earning below R3 366 a month was expected to apply for indigent status, each person being classified according to one of the poverty bands described above. Every household was, thereafter, to be assessed according to the number of indigent individuals residing in it and the allocation of benefits from the extended social package would be determined according to the level of need determined by the overall poverty status of the household, with the maximum allocation to any household remaining 10 kl of water and 100 kw of electricity. City documents state that the determination of such allocations would be dependent on agreements around tariffs, still to be decided at the time of writing.

Two striking differences from earlier indigent management policies are the registration of individuals who are not account holders (that is, who do not reside in a formal dwelling), and the provision of individual benefits over and above household benefits, such as rental and transport subsidies. For non-account holders, then, registration as indigent would not result in access to the subsidies for owning or renting a property (water, sanitation, electricity, refuse removal and rates rebates), but would provide access to subsidies for transport.

In addition, *Siyasizana* establishes an institute called the 'Pathways Centre', which is envisaged as providing contacts to those registered as indigent for accessing employment and/or becoming economically active. While it is not clear whether those registered as indigent will be forced to join the Pathways Centre, *Siyasizana* clearly states that all those coming forward for registration as indigents will be encouraged to join it and to gain access to a social worker to assist them in any special needs they might have in accessing employment and/or becoming entrepreneurs. Social workers are also envisaged as playing the role of determining need among households for accessing 'emergency allocations' of water provided by the City more recently – primarily for households in which HIV-positive people reside.

In this way, individual responsibility and self-reliance have come to be foregrounded in the new indigent management policy, as state interventions that target those unable to provide for themselves have begun to entrench levels of inequality amongst those identified as the poor, with different standards of living prescribed for different groups of the poor based on their ability to pay and/or to be made to pay, whereas the state's own role is cemented as that of providing the minimal levels of resources necessary for the individual to survive. The overt linking of access to jobs and the development of skills for small business development to the status of indigency has also seen greater emphasis on moral attributes of 'the deserving poor', that is, those willing to work and become economically productive, taking responsibility for their own development and the improvement in the lives of their families.

It is also significant that *Siyasizana* requires individuals to re-register every six months. While the CoJ argues that the only requirement for registration and re-registration is the possession of an identity document, it is likely that the administrative burden of the City will be increased through this process. All applicants will also be fingerprinted, to identify and track indigent members of society. Importantly, *Siyasizana* makes the responsibility for registration and re-registration as indigent – and therefore for access to free basic services and other forms of state assistance – that of the individual citizen rather than the state. If individuals do not apply for registration, they simply do not enjoy the 'benefits' of being declared indigent.

In these ways, *Siyasizana* also marks the evolution of policy with regard to the state's ability to know, regulate, target for change, and monitor that population group in society which has historically been seen to present a potential threat to social, political and economic stability – the poor ('the dangerous classes'). Tying access to the basic resources necessary for survival to the process of individual registration as indigent and the acceptance of particular forms of behaviour, *Siyasizana* allows for the increased surveillance of those outside the discipline of wage labour, a group of people increasing as unemployment grows (and who are increasingly unable to provide for their basic needs through the precarious forms of work they are able to find).

STRUGGLES OF THE POOR – SURVIVAL OR LIFE?

> I think people call themselves the poorest of the poor because of our own government. Our government always stresses poverty, we must do some work, have jobs for those people who live in poverty, we must provide jobs for them and do promises... The government always tells people that they are poor and the people themselves become, they give themselves to become the poorest... (Female pensioner living in Orange Farm, participant in focus group discussion, 25 September 2007.)

Government, by promoting this thing of the poorest of the poor, is developing class differences in communities. You can even see with this development. Under apartheid we were fighting against apartheid development, saying that we are being given sub-standard development because we are black people. Today, after this new dispensation, the government says that it builds this same kind of development for poor people because they feel for the poor. Even the words that we use for solidarity as the poor, government also uses to show that it is a government that cares for the poor (Bricks Mokolo, Organiser of the Orange Farm Water Crisis Committee – OWCC, interview, 20 January 2008).

While Johannesburg Water might be receiving accolades for innovation in relation to Operation *Gcin'amanzi* (Madumo 2008), and the Johannesburg municipality celebrating its victory in the courts, the imprint and effects of resistance on the evolution of municipal policy, strategies of cost recovery and neoliberal forms of responsibilisation cannot be denied or wished away, as has been shown above. At the same time, however, struggles of those identifying themselves as the poor and mobilising consciously as the poor have not gone unaffected by the ways in which the state has defined the possibilities for changes under neoliberalism and in the ways it has responded to their demands, forcing political engagement onto a technical plane, centred largely on arguments about what basic needs, those resources considered essential for survival, actually are.

We have seen in post-apartheid South Africa the transformation of struggles demanding the fulfilment of the promise of a better life for all into arguments over the most minimal levels of services necessary for the state to provide free, in order to ensure that those unable to provide for themselves are ensured of survival. While the state of being poor, and the identity of the poor, might have been mobilised strategically by individuals and groups in recognition of the state's proclaimed commitment and responsibility towards the most vulnerable in society (as reflected in the words of the pensioner from Orange Farm), responses from the state have (as suggested by the organiser of the OWCC) resulted in the entrenchment of differentiated levels of access to services and unequal standards of living for – and within – this population group.

The particular experience of Johannesburg, then, confirms Partha Chatterjee's (2004) contention that groups of disadvantaged and marginalised people are able to elicit actions on their behalf from the state by mobilising strategically around and through particular identities (such as that of 'squatters' or 'the poor') in a sphere of political action outside a civil society that, he argues, has come to reflect elite practices and values. The experience of Johannesburg also highlights the ways in which such means of doing politics potentially play into neoliberal forms of government; the moves towards targeted interventions reinscribe inequality and particular ways of living for groups managed as particular populations in ways amenable to the logics of neoliberalism.

As *Siyasizana* is rolled out in Johannesburg, it is unclear what tactics and strategies new social and community movements will adopt. As legal strategies have been pursued and failed, individual residents of disadvantaged areas such as Phiri, Soweto and Orange Farm seem to confront the problems of getting their daily needs for survival and their ways of making better lives for themselves in the strategic realm of the everyday. Acts of illegal reconnection to water and electricity supplies, bypassing of prepaid meters, and negotiations about the prescriptions for indigency are some of these, the subject of which deserves attention in a separate discussion. For now, it is important to acknowledge that while the tactics and strategies employed by organised formations identifying themselves as poor people's movements might have led to the difficulties now confronting the poor in the form of indigent management, struggles still continue as people refuse to accept the status of indigent.

In research conducted by the Coalition Against Water Privatisation (2006: 27) to ascertain how the installation of prepaid water meters had affected residents and struggles in Phiri, it is stated, 'In most cases, where resistance is occurring, it is taking place at a very individualised level, and tactics are emerging on this plane to evade discovery and prosecution'. In Orange Farm, where most residents are unable to afford the cost of a prepaid water meter (R650), signing onto the indigent register is itself proving unaffordable. This has resulted in local councillors and municipal officials agreeing to individual arrangements with residents outside the indigent framework – and even lower levels of service access for that category of the poor referred to as 'the poorest of the poor'. In Orange Farm, then, where access to flush toilets has been made dependent on the installation of a prepaid water meter, large numbers of residents live with toilets that don't flush, and pay as much as they can afford to the municipality each month (usually between R10 and R25). Alternatively, they connect their toilets illegally, choosing the risk of being caught and fined R1 500. In these small ways, alternatives to mere survival are experimented with, and poor people refuse to accept their indigent status. These everyday refusals and reaffirmations of life are where neoliberalism will continue to be challenged.

NOTES

1   This chapter is based on archival work and fieldwork conducted towards my PhD thesis (forthcoming, 2010), and on experiences in the struggles referred to in this work by the Anti-Privatisation Forum (APF). Many of the ideas contained here germinated in collective discussion and participatory research processes that I was involved in as coordinator of the APF research sub-committee between 2002 and 2007. I also owe an inestimable debt to Ahmed Veriava, with and through whom my thinking about these developments has happened. I am also grateful to Dale McKinley for his comments on an earlier draft of this chapter.

2   In the late 1980s, the apartheid regime had to deal with the problem presented by squatter settlements and movements resisting the policies of influx control that sought to confine black people to the 'bantustans' unless they were providing a service in the form of cheap labour to the apartheid economy. This resulted in the policies of 'informal urbanisation' and 'controlled squatting', through which privatisation began to be introduced in the development of low-income black residential settlements on the periphery of the city of Johannesburg such as Orange Farm.

3   Several theorists have shown and debated how neoliberal policies entered South Africa as early as the 1980s under the apartheid regime, but with increased and enhanced force since 1996 and the government's adoption of the Growth, Employment and Redistribution Strategy (GEAR) (Barchiesi 2006; Bond 2000b; Gelb 2004; Marais 2001). While there have been several debates about whether (and what) alternatives to neoliberalism could have been adopted in South Africa (within the ANC alliance, in new social movements, and among left theorists and researchers), it is beyond the scope of this chapter to explore these questions. Rather, this chapter confines itself

to exploring the ways in which neoliberalism has taken root in South Africa through the experience of the delivery of basic services.

4   The discourse in which the BIG emerges is no different from that of encouraging individual responsibility and 'self-reliance' through gaining access to a job and/or participation in the market economy.

5   'Indigent' is defined as 'lacking the necessities of life' in state policy documents that draft policy for the delivery of basic services (DPLG, September 2005a, 2005b & 2005c).

6   In keeping with the neoliberal logic of reducing state spending and corporatising key functions of the state, municipalities would be forced to restructure along the lines of corporate entities, pushing them into contexts where income generation and cutting costs would become priorities in meeting the needs of citizens. As such, the delivery of basic services would become an area through which revenue could be generated, and municipal services would become prioritised as trading services.

7   It has been argued that persistently high levels of unemployment and the introduction of flexible labour make it impossible for large parts of the population to pay for the services they need. Coupled with the historical memory of the refusal to pay in the rent and service boycotts under apartheid, these conditions of life have made it difficult for a culture of payment for basic services to take root in South Africa.

8   While there has been much debate over the validity of statistics related to cut-offs collected by David McDonald and John Pape for the Human Sciences Research Council (HSRC) for the period 1994 to 2002, statistics from the DPLG seem to confirm the extent of the problem – 133 456 water disconnections in the last quarter of 2001 and 256 325 electricity disconnections in the last three months of 2001 (affecting about a million people). (McDonald, *Sunday Independent*, 19 June 2003). In 2003, Minister Ronnie Kasrils admitted that the three largest cities in South Africa were still disconnecting 17 800 households a month (Bond and Dugard 2008:11).

9   Current national policy sets these allocations at a minimum of six kilolitres of water and fifty kilowatts to be provided free by the state to every indigent household. Municipalities are, however, free to provide higher amounts of services as long as their budgets permit.

10 Ruiters (2007: 143) notes that prepaid meters were introduced in black townships because Eskom officials believed that black people had 'the wrong social attitudes' for conventional credit meters, and that prepaid meters were preferred as they ruled out the problems faced by Eskom staff trying to gain access to meters in order to read them.

11 The PCRF was formed in the midst of resistance against the installation of prepaid water meters in Phiri in 2002, with the support of the SECC and the APF. The PCRF, SECC and OWCC are affiliates of the APF, which is an umbrella body, home to over twenty-two community organisations located mainly in Gauteng.

12 Johannesburg Water (JW) is a company that was established in 2001 as part of the CoJ's iGoli 2002 strategy, aimed at restructuring the management of the delivery of water and sanitation services to city dwellers according to business principles.

13 The equitable share here refers to the proportion of revenues collected by national government that are unconditionally transferred to local municipalities to assist them in making up any funding gaps that might exist between their financial resources and their actual operational costs.

14 This governing of 'the poor' has been discussed by other theorists in relation to the early development of capitalism in England (for example Karl Polanyi (1946) and Mitchell Dean (1991)).

15 Under apartheid, certain areas (in particular black townships like Soweto) were considered 'deemed consumption areas', that is, areas in which households were treated as consuming a set amount of twenty kilolitres per month, for which they would be billed. As a result of the payment boycotts, however, these bills were not acknowledged and therefore not paid, resulting in the accumulation of arrears.

16 The MSSS would apply its rules, contained in the Special Cases Policy (approved in October 2004 with amendments adopted in May 2005) to account holders who were pensioners as well as unemployed, self-employed, or employed people with a total family income of less than R1 100 a month;

account holders receiving disability grants who had a total family income of less than R1 100 a month; an account holder whose partner also received a government pension and had a total family income of less than R1 241 per month – the equivalent of two government pensions plus R1; and HIV positive/AIDS breadwinners and/or their orphans (*Joburg City, How It Works? Subsidies,* http://www.joburg.org.za/content/view/724/131/, accessed 10 November 2007).

17   The population of Johannesburg is close to 3.2 million (Census 2001 figures).

18   As JW began to cut off all water to any resident refusing a prepaid meter, and police and private security action intensified against protesting residents, it became increasingly difficult to sustain public, collective refusal and prevention of the implementation of the prepaid system. By the end of the first few weeks of collective resistance, only twenty-seven households were continuing to refuse the installation of prepaid meters in their yards, living with collecting necessary water from neighbours or other parts of Soweto. This number slowly diminished to the five residents finally represented in the court case. This led to debate about the form that the resistance should take. In summary, while some activists felt that attention should be focused on building at community level for greater collective action in the form of the bypassing of meters and refusal of the system in this way, backed up by mass mobilisations against JW and the local authorities, others argued that alternative tactics such as undertaking legal action against the CoJ and JW should be explored. While the former group argued that the adoption of a legal strategy would redirect the movements involved and change their nature by changing their priorities and focus, the latter insisted that the most immediate basic needs of residents had to be met and that illegal actions worked against this. In the end, while it was agreed that a mix of tactics would be employed, the legal approach became the focus of the public campaign, with other forms of resistance continuing at an individual level, in hidden ways. Debate continues in the APF today about the effects of this court case on the movement.

REFERENCES

African National Congress (1994) *The Reconstruction and Development Programme (RDP).* South Africa: Umanyano Publications.

Barchiesi F (2006) *Social Citizenship and the Transformations of Wage Labour in the Making of Post-Apartheid South Africa.* Unpublished PhD dissertation, University of the Witwatersrand.

Bond P (2000a) *Cities of Gold, Townships of Coal: Essays on South Africa's New Urban Crisis.* Eritrea: Africa World Press.

Bond P (2000b) *Elite Transition. From Apartheid to Neoliberalism in South Africa.* London: Pluto Press.

Bond P (2002) *Unsustainable South. Africa: Environment, Development and Social Protest.* Scottsville: University of Natal Press/London: Merlin Press.

Bond P (2008) Macrodynamics of globalisation, uneven development and the commodification of water. In *Law, Social Justice and Global Development Journal,* 9 October. http://www.go.warwick.ac.uk/elj/lgd/2008_1/bond [accessed 10 October 2009].

Bond P and J Dugard (2008) Water, human rights and social conflict: South African experiences. In *Law, Social Justice and Global Development.* 11 February – http://www.go.warwick.ac.uk/elj/lgd/2008_1/bond_dugard [accessed 10 October 2009].

Centre for Development Support (2002) Indigent policy support report. Bloemfontein: Centre for Development Support, University of the Free State.

Chatterjee P (2004) *The Politics of the Governed.* New York: Columbia University Press.

City of Johannesburg Mayoral Committee for Finance, Strategy and Economic Development (2004) Revised methodology for approval of indigency applications.

City of Johannesburg (2005) Human Development Strategy (HDS): Jo'burg's commitment to the poor.

City of Johannesburg (2006) Growth and development strategy.

City of Johannesburg (2008) Mid-term report: Realising the future we choose – A message of progress, September.

Coalition Against Water Privatisation (2003) Nothing for mahala. The forced installation of prepaid water meters in Stretford, Extension 4, Orange Farm, Johannesburg, South Africa.

Coalition Against Water Privatisation and Anti-Privatisation Forum (2004) The struggle against silent disconnections. Prepaid meters and the struggle for life in Phiri, Soweto.

Coalition Against Water Privatisation and Anti-Privatisation Forum (2006) Lessons from the war against prepaid watermeters.

Committee for the Inquiry into a Comprehensive System of Social Security in South Africa (2002) Transforming the past. Protecting the future. Report of the Committee. Pretoria: Department of Social Welfare and Development.

Cottle E and H Deedat (2002) Cost recovery and prepaid water meters and the cholera outbreak in KwaZulu-Natal: A case study in Madlebe. In McDonald D and J Pape (Eds) *Cost Recovery and the Crisis of Service Delivery*. Pretoria: HSRC Press: 81–97.

Dean M (1991) *The Constitution of Poverty: Toward a Genealogy of Liberal Governance*, Routledge: London and New York.

Department of Constitutional Development (1996) Cabinet Memorandum No. 26: Masakhane Campaign.

Department of Social Development (2000) Mobilising for a caring society. People first for sustainable development. Statement by the minister for welfare and population development, Dr Zola Skweyiya, at the launch of a Ten-Point Programme of Action for the Welfare and Development Portfolio, January.

Desai A (2002) We are the poors. Community struggles in post-apartheid South Africa. *Monthly Review Press*.

DPLG – Directorate Free Basic Services (2003) Report on Free Basic Services. Pretoria: DPLG.

DPLG (2005a) Draft Framework for a National Indigent Framework, June. Pretoria: DPLG.

DPLG (2005b) Framework for a Municipal Indigent Framework, September. Pretoria: DPLG.

DPLG (2005c) Guidelines for the Implementation of the National Indigent Policy by Municipalities, November. Pretoria: DPLG.

Everatt D (2008) The undeserving poor: Poverty and the politics of service delivery in the poorest nodes of South Africa. *Politikon* 35 (3): 293–319.

Gelb S (2004) *The South African Economy: An Overview From 1994 to 2004*. Johannesburg: The Edge Institute.

Greater Johannesburg Metropolitan Council (GJMC) (1999) iGoli 2002: Transformation and Implementation Plan.

Greater Johannesburg Metropolitan Council (GJMC) (2000) iGoli 2002: Making Greater Johannesburg Work.

Greater Johannesburg Metropolitan Council (GJMC) (2001) A Vision Statement for the City of Johannesburg 2030.

Hardt M and A Negri (2000) *Empire*. Cambridge: Harvard University Press.

Hardt M and A Negri A (2004) *Multitude*. New York: The Penguin Press.

Hart G (2007) The new poor laws and the crisis of local government. *Amandla*, Pilot Issue 2, October: 5–6.

Harvey E (2005) Managing the poor by remote control: Johannesburg's experiments with prepaid water meters. In McDonald D and G Ruiters (Eds) *The Age of Commodity. Water Privatization in Southern Africa*. London: Earthscan.

Madumo L (2008) Awards are flowing to Johannesburg Water, 16 October - http://www.joburg.org.za/content/view/3069/195/ [accessed 10 October 2009].

Mandela N (1995) Speech at the Launch of the Masakhane Campaign. 25 February, Koeberg, Cape Town.

Marais H (2001) *South Africa: Limits to Change. The Political Economy of Transformation*, Second edition. London: Zed Books/Cape Town: University of Cape Town Press.

Marais H (2007) Getting back to basics: A review of the ANC's social transformation policy discussion document. *Policy: Issues and Actors* 20 (10): 99–106.

Mbeki T (2008) Address to Community Development Worker Indaba, Midrand.

McDonald D and J Pape (Eds) (2002) *Cost Recovery and the Crisis of Service Delivery in South Africa.* Cape Town: HSRC Press.

McDonald D and L Smith (2004) Privatising Cape Town: From Apartheid to Neoliberalism in the Mother City. In *Urban Studies* 41 (8): 1461–1484.

Moosa V (1997) Speech at the National Masakhane Workshop, World Trade Centre, 25-26 July, Johannesburg.

Mosdell T (2006) Free basic services: The evolution and impact of free basic water policy in South Africa. In Pillay R, R Tomlinson and J du Toit (Eds) (2006) *Democracy and Delivery. Urban Policy in South Africa.* Pretoria: HSRC Press: 283-301.

Naidoo P (2010) The making of 'The Poor/s' in post-apartheid South Africa: A case study of the City of Johannesburg and Orange Farm. Unpublished PhD, forthcoming, Johannesburg.

Naidoo P and A Veriava (2005) Re-membering movements: Trade unions and new social movements in neoliberal South Africa. In *From Local Processes to Global Forces, Centre for Civil Society Research Reports Vol.1.* Durban: University of KwaZulu-Natal: 27–62.

Ngwane T and A Veriava (2004) Strategies and tactics: Movements in the neoliberal transition. In *Development Update* 5 (2): 129–146.

Palmer Development Group (2004) Social Services Package. Study commissioned by the City of Johannesburg.

Pillay D (2008) COSATU, the SACP and the ANC post-Polokwane: Looking left but does it feel right? In *Labour, Capital and Society* (41) 2.

Pithouse R (2009) Burning Message to the State in the Fire of the Poor's Rebellion – http://info.inter-activist.net/node/12874 [accessed 18 November 2009].

Polanyi K (1946) *The Great Transformation.* London: Gollanz.

Ruiters G (2005) Knowing your place: Urban services and new modes of governability in South African cities. Paper presented at the Centre for Civil Society (CCS), Durban, October.

Ruiters G (2007) Contradictions in municipal services in contemporary South Africa: Disciplinary commodification and self disconnections. In *Critical Social Policy* 27: 487–507.

South African Local Government Association (SALGA), media release from SALGA Chairperson, 16 June 2004.

Tsoka J (2008) Judgement passed in case no: 06/13885, brought by residents Mazibuko *et al* against the City of Johannesburg, Johannesburg Water and the Department of Water and Forestry Affairs.

United Democratic Front (UDF) (1990) Memorandum on Urban Land and Housing Policies to Hernus Kriel, 16 August. Johannesburg: UDF.

Veriava A (2009) Under the sign of an exception: Post-apartheid politics and the sruggle for water. MA dissertation, forthcoming.

Von Schnitzler A (2008) Citizenship Prepaid: Water, Calculability, and Techno-Politics in South Africa. In *Journal of Southern African Studies* 34 (4): 899–917.

CHAPTER 8

Fear, enervation and the systematisation of disorder: Challenges to reforming the Department of Home Affairs

Colin Hoag

———— ·•· ————

The reputation of the Department of Home Affairs (DoHA) leaves much to be desired. For many South Africans, it represents 'government bureaucracy' at its worst, and use of the term 'horror affairs' (coined by the *Daily Sun* newspaper) has become widespread. Given the shocking stories that emerge in the media, this is understandable: in 2003, a South African citizen whose identity document had been stolen was picked up in Hillbrow as a suspected 'illegal alien' and deported to Zimbabwe (*Pretoria News* 14 November 2006). In 2006, a man took a DoHA official hostage for six hours at a Johannesburg office, demanding that he be issued his national identity document (ID), for which he had been waiting some two and a half years (*Mail & Guardian* 9 July 2008). And in 2009, a twenty-two year-old Durban man who was unemployed for want of his national identity document hanged himself after a Home Affairs official tore up his ID application (*The Citizen* 1-3 September 2009). These cases, though extreme, point to a general atmosphere of disorder and inefficiency at the DoHA.[1] Having spoken with hundreds of people about the Department of Home Affairs since I began researching it in early 2008, I have found that nearly everyone has a personal story of the DoHA's corruption, its inefficiency and/or its disarray, to relate.

To be fair, the Department's notoriety stems in part from the fact that it provides so many important or high-profile services: deporting undocumented non-nationals; processing claims for asylum; and issuing some of the most vital official documents including birth, marriage, and death certificates, national identity documents, passports and work and visitor permits. As officials at various levels in the Department hierarchy told me, the DoHA is with you from the day you are born until the day you die. Additionally, Home Affairs is under heavy scrutiny because, unlike other South African government bureaucracies such as, for example, Agriculture and Land Affairs or Social Services, the DoHA serves people from every walk of life – the wealthy businesswoman in Sandton, the Somali spaza shop owner in Durban, the newborn baby in Mafikeng and the farmer in the Free State are all obliged to make an occasional trip to the DoHA office nearest to them. To carry out this wide range of duties effectively across the country therefore requires a substantial degree of leadership, coordination, technical sophistication and budgetary support. In short, there is considerable margin for error.

But the attention paid to the Department of Home Affairs cannot be explained by its visibility or complexity alone; it points towards very real and consequential shortcomings. In fact, that the DoHA is in need of urgent and sweeping reform is hardly a matter of debate. Even the Department's top officials acknowledge as much.[2] But while it is understood that something should be done, precisely how to go about reforming such a large and complex organisation is a complicated question. In this chapter, I provide a few modest suggestions by identifying several mitigating aspects of what might be called 'organisational culture'.[3] I focus specifically on the Department's Immigration Services Branch (ISB), which deals exclusively with non-nationals.[4]

In relation to previous studies of South African immigration policy and practice (for example Crush and McDonald 2001; Handmaker 2001; Aglotsson and Klaaren 2003; Belvedere 2007; Wa Kabwe-Segatti and Landau 2008), my perspective is methodologically unusual. I did not speak with members of the public who use the services of the DoHA. I did not seek the perspective of the various nongovernmental organisations which analyse or criticise the Department, nor of the politicians or the DoHA's directors general who have traditionally devised plans for reform (although my previous exposure to these perspectives no doubt informed my general understanding). Instead, I spoke with the individual 'street level bureaucrats' who interact with clients and are charged with delivering the important services at issue (Lipsky 1980). Between April 2008 and February 2009, I conducted on-site research at four offices of the ISB's Permitting, Inspectorate and Refugee Affairs sections in the Johannesburg central business district, as well as at a port of entry on the Lesotho border.[5] At these offices, I observed and interviewed street level officials at length, asking what they thought of accusations levelled against them in the media, and what they believed should be done to reform the Department. I worked on the assumption that street level DoHA officials are 'experts' in their own right: that, though they might not be formally educated on immigration policy, budgeting or organisational management, their everyday interactions with policies, procedures, and clientele provide them with valuable insight into the challenges facing the Department.

Such a perspective reveals at least two related and consequential aspects that characterise the Department's organisational culture, both of which foster and derive from an antagonistic relationship with clients and management. I will sketch these aspects briefly here, before discussing them at greater length below. The first aspect is *fear*. Street level officials find themselves constantly at risk of displeasing someone: their managers might discipline them for failing in their duty to protect the Department against clients who cheat the system; human rights organisations might file a case against them and the Department for obstructing migrants or refugees from access to services; and clients might complain about delays that are sometimes out of officials' control. In the light of this, officials[6] find themselves stuck in the middle, as it were, protecting themselves from these threats by exercising a high degree of caution in their work.

Their fear runs parallel with a second notable aspect of organisational culture: *enervation*. Generalised precaution against professional censure in the face of frequent changes in policy and management staff, ambiguous legal guidelines, poor professional development, poor inter- and intra-office communication, and insufficient training mean that officials are often reticent to do anything, much less to think independently and act decisively (if they actually know what they are supposed to do at all).

This inhibition and lack of empowerment results in a hardening of policy practice, with often undesirable outcomes such as corruption and the obstruction of visitors who would otherwise be seen as 'desirable' (for example, wealthy tourists or businesspeople). Inhibited, enervated bureaucrats[7] are discouraged from feeling a sense of ownership and investment in the future of the DoHA, possibly foretelling the long-term underperformance of the Department.

Before discussing these points in more detail, I will consider a few relevant historical aspects, including the DoHA's ongoing 'turnaround strategy'. In conclusion, I will consider the consequences of failure to address the fear and enervation experienced by street level officials, including the systematisation of disorder and corruption.

IMMIGRATION SERVICES BRANCH IN CONTEXT

This section is not a thorough review of the historical context of the Department of Home Affairs,[8] but highlights instead a few important events and processes that inform the Department's current character and capacity, and considers the effectiveness of the recent turnaround strategy, a major departmental reform initiative. The first important historical aspect has to do with the bloated, patronage-oriented state of the apartheid-era civil service, and the human resource challenges posed by the substantial re-staffing of the civil service at the transition to democracy in the 1990s. As has been well documented,[9] the apartheid civil service was a large and sprawling set of institutions, the result of that regime's authoritarian predisposition and its *de facto* affirmative action policies designed to uplift the poor, white Afrikaner population. Individuals who were not white Afrikaners (including white English-speaking South Africans as well as blacks) had, for over three decades after 1948, an exceedingly difficult time finding employment within the civil service, a situation which eased slightly only in the early 1980s when a severe skills shortage stemming from competition from the better paid private sector demanded the hiring of more black staff (Picard 2005: 117).[10] This would ultimately prove detrimental at the transition, when the civil service became a bastion of employment for those previously disadvantaged, and therefore unskilled, persons. Early retirement packages were offered to scores of white officials, many of whom took the offer. Across the civil service, early retirements increased by 180 per cent between 1990 and 1994 (Picard 2005: 113), and this substantial re-staffing undoubtedly disrupted everyday operations.

The operations of the Immigration Services Branch (ISB, formerly the National Immigration Branch) were further complicated at the transition by the ambiguity of the legal documents that were supposed to guide it. After the end of apartheid, South Africa had to wait eight years before new legislation (the Immigration Act of 2002) was enacted. Until that point, the ISB was forced to operate in terms of apartheid-era legislation, the Aliens Control Act of 1991. Known colloquially as 'apartheid's last act', the Aliens Control Act was framed mostly around concerns over security and sovereignty rather than the humane and judicious regulation of people in and out of the country (Wa Kabwe-Segatti and Landau 2008). Furthermore, several key elements of the Act were in contradiction of the 1993 interim constitution and the constitution of 1996, meaning that it was partially redundant very soon after its enactment, leaving a legal void (Wa Kabwe-Segatti 2008).

Complicating matters further still, the ISB has faced extremely high rates of immigration relative to the pre-transition era. As South Africa was opened up to foreign investment once again, the country became the recipient of large numbers of migrants and refugees from throughout Africa and beyond, straining the capacity of the DoHA (Wa Kabwe-Segatti and Landau 2008). Today, becoming legalised in South Africa can be extremely difficult for the non-citizen, a costly process in terms of time, of stress and of money. Restrictions placed on attaining permanent residence flooded the already overburdened temporary residence system (Wa Kabwe-Segatti 2008), and this has pushed thousands of economic immigrants toward application as asylum seekers, overloading that system as well (Landau 2008). The difficulty of obtaining a permit has led to a counterproductive situation for the Department. For planning and budgeting purposes, there are benefits in properly registering those who enter and leave the country, but many people find it easier to apply with another wing of the same Department (for example temporary residence permitting or refugee affairs), or to simply move outside the legal framework altogether by purchasing fraudulent documents or going undocumented. Meanwhile, migrants are taken advantage of by police and other law enforcement officials, who capitalise upon poor oversight and broad public xenophobia (Landau 2008). Such harassment had become so acute that it was termed 'institutionalised' in a report by the Southern African Migration Project (Aglotsson and Klaaren 2003).

Criticism of the DoHA as a whole reached something of a crest in 2003 when former director general Barry Gilder characterised the Department's service delivery as 'a joke'.[11] In 2007, Home Affairs Minister Nosiviwe Mapisa-Nqakula began implementation of the turnaround strategy, a reform measure conceived in 2004 and designed as a fresh start for the Department. That the strategy's title implies the existence of major shortcomings, requiring a Departmental about-face was not lost on outgoing Minister Buthelezi, who stated: 'I feel that [it] has been, somehow, improperly named, and should rather have been styled as a moving forward strategy, for I do not see that it imposes on the Department a new direction'.[12]

The turnaround strategy is a three-year, comprehensive reform strategy, addressing shortcomings in numerous areas of the DoHA's operations.[13] These include improved IT and communications resources; improved training regimens and organisational structures; the implementation of a biometrics-based database called the Home Affairs National Identification System (HANIS) that will integrate a number of existing databases; the streamlining of ID, passport, permit or other document processing; and office renovations. It remains to be seen whether the strategy will be successful in these various goals. In the years since its implementation, the media has reported some definite signs of improvement, including the filling of managerial posts (*The Citizen* 2 March 2009) and the streamlining of processing procedures at the Crown Mines refugee centre (*The Star* 10 November 2008). However, my discussions with officials suggest that more widespread progress is still elusive. Some at the admissions, inspectorate, and port of entry offices had no idea what the turnaround strategy entailed, while others reported only hearing about future reforms. Some of those who had indeed witnessed reforms only experienced them as an increase of or change in production statistics reporting, signifying for these officials not more efficient processes but simply more work.

This was particularly evident at the refugee reception centre at Crown Mines. There, a group of consultants had been hired to evaluate office performance and establish new processes for streamlining. Nearly every official at the centre is required to submit production statistics to demonstrate their performance from the previous day, and these statistics are discussed at daily 'production meetings'. Given the very high numbers of asylum applicants who approach this office, it is understandable that so much focus has been placed on the feeding of applicants through the system, and the office has proven its effectiveness at doing so (*The Star* 10-11 October 2008). Nevertheless, many at the centre are dissatisfied with these reforms. Refugee Status Determination Officers (RSDOs) in particular complain that the demands on processing have made it almost impossible for them to take the time necessary to evaluate properly individual claims for asylum. Most report only having between thirty and forty-five minutes to interview asylum applicants, research their claims and issue decisions. They complain that this amount of time is vastly insufficient if they are to evaluate each claim on its individual merits as they have been instructed, leading many to use shortcuts such as cutting and pasting information from one decision into another. Although the employees at this office were carefully selected for their relatively substantial educational and professional backgrounds (most RSDOs have law degrees of one sort or another, and several have a Master's degree), many told me that they were uncertain how long they would stay with the Department. Churning out decisions was hardly drawing on their skills, they said.

FEAR AND ENERVATION: Challenges to reform

It remains to be seen, therefore, whether or not the turnaround strategy will lead to the types of reforms that would enable the DoHA to operate at a respectable level of performance. It is important to recognise, however, that the difficulties besetting the Department cannot simply be addressed with technical inputs and accounting requirements. The DoHA must understand and work through at least two entrenched, interrelated aspects of organisational culture that complicate and even perhaps preclude these reforms: fear and enervation among its street level officials.

Fear

As I have shown elsewhere (Hoag 2010; Wa Kabwe-Segatti *et al* 2009), whether one considers the practices of the Department of Home Affairs to be incoherent is a matter of perspective.

Anthropologists such as Veena Das (2004) have demonstrated that the unpredictability and arbitrariness of some states can lead members of the public to discern dangerous 'magical' or 'illegible' qualities in the state. But my conversations with immigration services branch officials revealed that, although the public broadly regards the Department to be opaque or unreadable, the reverse can also be true. For officials, it is the public that represents a dangerous, illegible entity the effects of which must be minimised through precaution. Officials said that their precaution against the public is vital, as it protects South Africa from foreign (and domestic) threats, and many expressed pride in their role as 'gate-keepers' to the country. However, this precaution can be excessive. For example, many officials, including one higher-level supervisor, told me that people who enter the country with one type of permit and change it once they arrive are 'abusing the system', despite the fact that this is legally permissible.[14] Unpredictability in service delivery and restrictive interpretations of policy are not always, therefore, the result of 'lazy','corrupt', or 'unintelligent' bureaucrats as one tends to hear on the street (though unfortunately such characters do exist) but can, rather, stem from a response to dangers posed by an 'illegible' public.

Rumours abound at the ISB as to the trickery and untrustworthiness of the public and their 'abuse' of (implicitly, otherwise perfect) state systems. Fraudulent permits, human trafficking, marriages of convenience, well-connected go-betweens, and asylum seekers' sharing of information about lenient offices are merely a few examples. One even learns that it is the public and not Home Affairs officials who are responsible for setting corruption in motion – the public, officials assert, simply want to skirt official procedures to fast-track their applications. When asked about accusations in the media that DoHA officials have taken bribes to marry South African women unwittingly to non-national men seeking to obtain a residence permit (Vigneswaran 2008), officials roundly rejected the assertion. They said that the fault in fact, rests with non-nationals who pay South African women to marry them, and also with those women who enter into this arrangement. Sometimes, officials said, the 'husband' fails to pay the 'wife', and so she cries foul and claims ignorance.

Consider also Refugee Status Determination Officers' perspectives on interpreters. Interpreters are often necessary to the interview process, and can help RSDOs to conclude whether or not claims are legitimate, for example by indicating whether applicants' accents support their stated region or country of origin. However, RSDOs mostly characterised interpreters as dangerous intermediaries with insider knowledge – because interpreters are around the office all day, they form relationships with both clients and officials, allegedly opening up doors for corruption. Additionally, they have first-hand knowledge of which claims are considered 'asylum-worthy', since they are often refugees themselves, and are present during interviews where they witness first-hand which claims are given refugee status. RSDOs argue that interpreters sometimes offer their knowledge as a sellable item to asylum seekers, telling the applicants what to say beforehand, or even providing such information themselves during the interview (RSDOs reported occasions when a short response given by an applicant was translated into a long paragraph by the interpreter, arousing their suspicion). Sometimes, as one RSDO said, they might just want to help out their fellow countrymen by nudging a claim in the right direction, and not even charge a fee.

But the public is not the only entity that officials fear – the DoHA's management also figures as a hard to read actor in officials' everyday activities. According to them, senior management seems to have not the slightest idea of how things work on the ground, disseminating rules and regulations which they claim are sometimes totally out of touch with 'reality'. They noted that many of the people in management positions have little experience working at Home Affairs. Instead of working their way through the ranks from the ground upwards, upper level managers tend to move around from one government department to another, and therefore lack the nuance of understanding required to manage the DoHA's complex responsibilities. Also, they noted that these upper level positions can tend to be politically significant, meaning that upon the exit of the minister or the national president, the character of the Department can change wholesale, including departmental goals, slogans, and even organisational structures.

Street level officials also complained about unpredictability and contradiction in the directives issued by upper management. New directives can be in contrast with existing ones, completely unsupported in terms of resources, or so totally out of touch with circumstances on the ground that they are not implementable. One of the 'production statistics' demanded by upper managemen – that officials create a docket for every suspected undocumented non-national with whom they engage – was completely outside the realm of possibility. In order to comply with this requirement, officials would need to create hundreds of dockets each week, an extraordinarily time-consuming process. Moreover, this requirement is complicated by the fact that it would be difficult – given the chaotic nature of police raids and other common group operations – to say clearly who engaged whom (and even what constitutes an 'engagement'). Further, although officials had been demanding cabinets from head office for many months, the office had insufficient cabinet space at the time of research to store extra dockets. Many officials receive such directives coolly because they are suspicious of the motives of upper management. Some said that upper level managers put their own interests ahead of those of the lower level officials by, for example, demanding time-consuming statistics which appeared to be of little value on the ground, but which could improve that upper level manager's image. Some also saw the statistics as affronts to officials' trustworthiness, as the reporting measures were perceived to be as much about corruption and increased accountability as about production or efficiency.

Enervation

This culture of fear reflects a particular sort of isolation. Instead of seeing head office as a source of support for their work, officials often saw it as undermining or antagonistic, a relationship that compromises the implementation of reform measures, or any measure handed down from head office. Officials have not only become suspicious of policies developed at head office because of their perceived contradictory or unworkable nature, but also on account of debilitatingly poor communication. For example, an admissions official told me how she learned of an important change in policy simply by chancing upon a DoHA circular underneath a pile of papers. The policy change, which stated that asylum applicants could now apply for temporary residence permits while they awaited the outcome of their asylum claims, had gone into effect weeks before, but the official recalled turning away numerous applicants on these grounds.

By poor communication, I also refer to the absence of vertical dialogue across the DoHA hierarchy. Officials at the lower levels feel that they have valuable input to give on the direction and policies of the Department, but that the input is rarely listened to, or even sought. Not only does this mean that officials are made to feel isolated and undervalued, but policies and procedures are drafted which do not take into account officials' intimate knowledge of departmental capacity and limitations on the ground.

This complex of factors shows up in an enervated cadre of bureaucrats, uninformed, unempowered and uninvested in the Department. In the short-term, service delivery suffers. In the long-term, the future success of the DoHA is put in jeopardy. Street level officials' fear of management retribution for failing to exercise sufficient caution against the public means that officials are often reluctant to do anything at all. For example, officials at the admissions offices told me that it was sometimes safer to turn away an applicant rather than accept the application and risk the possibility of inadequate documentation.[15] At the refugee reception centre, RSDOs also told me that to grant refugee status to an asylum applicant can be 'dangerous' in that one's supervisor might suspect the RSDO of having taken a bribe.

Street level officials are also enervated through lack of training. Insufficient training has serious negative short-term effects. Many officials, for instance, are not prepared to apply laws and regulations to the situations that they encounter daily. Many went so far as to state explicitly that they had never been given training on the Immigration Act, the primary document outlining the rights and obligations of visitors to South Africa. Instead, they were trained on the job to know only those specific elements with which they interact on a daily basis. But without a more comprehensive understanding of the Act, it becomes difficult for officials to understand and be guided by the overarching aims of the Department, and the absence of such knowledge is also damaging to the long-term success of the DoHA in that employees who cannot make informed and independent decisions will not develop the leadership skills necessary to inherit tomorrow's management positions. The lack of training indicates to street level officials that upper management is not interested in developing them professionally. This is a serious concern for any official who recognises that professional growth is vital to her or his success in a competitive labour market.

Finally, officials are enervated through under-resourcing.[16] Because Johannesburg receives a large number of immigrants, refugees and visitors relative to the rest of South Africa, its Home Affairs offices are especially busy. The inspectorate office is responsible for one of four zones in the Gauteng West region, covering an area that includes twenty-four police precincts, including areas with some of the highest concentrations of immigrants, such as Hillbrow, Yeoville, and the central business district. Despite this, the office was staffed at the time of research by only twenty-eight immigration officers, later augmented by six trainees. With these new trainees, the office was still twenty-three short of the fifty-seven total approved posts (the temporary residence permitting office was twenty-eight short of the forty-five approved positions). Additionally, at the time of my research, there was no functioning printer, photocopier or fax machine at the inspectorate. The few functioning computers were not connected to the internet, and only one was connected to the movement control system, the primary database with which officials interact in their day to day activities. As a result of this situation, officials were delayed or even completely prevented from carrying out basic duties such as the evaluation of applications and the provision of production statistics to the head office in Pretoria.

CONCLUSIONS: The systematisation of disorder

This chapter has sought to show that a specific historical trajectory and organisational culture has contributed to the underperformance of the Department of Home Affairs. Although the DoHA is generally seen as inscrutable and unpredictable by the public, street level Home Affairs officials have an opposite perspective. For them, it is the public and the DoHA's upper management that appear inscrutable and unpredictable, and the perceived danger this poses is a determinate factor in their everyday actions, causing them to exercise substantial precaution in their work. By failing to train and equip street level officials, the DoHA has created an isolated and unempowered cadre of bureaucrats, uninvested in the future of the Department and sometimes incapable of executing basic responsibilities. Based on these observations, I suggest that fear and enervation have become implicated in a vicious cycle of corruption that still further undermines attempts at reform. The result is that disorder and corruption have become systematised through a combination of what I call 'comfortable underperformance' and an 'economy of access'.[17]

Officials' fears, in combination with upper management's inadequate investment in developing and supporting its employees, have led to a situation whereby street level officials are incentivised to do as little as possible, inaction being safer than action. For example, although accepting an application with an incomplete set of documentation at the admissions section is displeasing to an official's superiors, and could lead to disciplinary action as a reoccurring problem, the non-acceptance of an application will seldom, if ever, result in disciplinary measures. Accepting an application also requires an official to scrutinise each page, receive payment and issue a receipt, whereas turning the applicant away for more or more detailed documentation requires very little in the way of scrutiny and related tasks. As noted above, the Department is currently working towards greater accountability through the production of performance statistics, and upper management has promoted this to officials as a way of determining the distribution of bonuses. The more clients one processes, the larger the bonus. However, officials complain that these performance reviews (the 'performance management development system') rarely happen, and thereby do not motivate them to increase their productivity. Similarly, although RSDOs could risk being admonished for accepting an application for refugee status if their supervisors believe there to be insufficient supporting information, a decision to reject an application never leads to problems. Rejected applications become the responsibility of appeal boards and rarely does an RSDO receive feedback about them.

Ironically, these practices, and the general disorder at the DoHA, deter non-nationals from complying with legal procedure. Although streamlined processes could encourage non-nationals to subject themselves to registration rather than risk going undocumented, a parallel system is encouraged in its stead. Some non-nationals might elect, or be forced, to leave the country. Some potential applicants choose to be undocumented and therefore become invisible to the Department, inhibiting the Department's capacity to make sound policy decisions or to budget accurately. Other organs of state are similarly unable to rely on DoHA data for their own planning.

But the difficulty of accessing the Department's services through proper channels has made the illicit sale of IDs, permits, and other documents a lucrative industry, and the status quo is maintained on account of this internal logic: a symbiotic relationship between 'comfortable underperformance' (non-decision and inaction), and an 'economy of access' (corruption and the commodification of legal status). Failure to deliver services efficiently presents the possibility – or the demand, or sometimes the necessity – of 'fast-tracking' applications.[18] While few officials admitted to taking bribes, most stated plainly that DoHA officials do so out of financial necessity: they are simply not paid enough. If upper management were to eliminate this illicit source of extra income (if this were indeed possible), it would probably necessitate an increase in pay, one that the DoHA might not be able to make.

Corruption has become systemic as a direct result of an organisational culture of fear and enervation. Corruption will only cease, and the Department will only begin to deliver services acceptably, when these 'cultural' aspects are minimised within the organisation. In saying this, I do not absolve any official of corruption, nor do I suggest that those officials who engage in illicit practices are merely victims of institutional deficiency, but I contend that reducing corruption to simple opportunism fails to take into account the broader, complex institutional contexts out of which those practices emerge.[19]

Beyond the promotion of corruption and disorder, however, there are other serious consequences of the poor state of Home Affairs and the Immigration Services Branch specifically. For one, unmanageable permitting procedures can have a negative impact on business and tourism, and in an era of hyper-fluid capital and foreign investment, South Africans should be concerned about unnecessary costs and barriers to doing business. Secondly, by obstructing non-South Africans from legalising themselves in the country, the DoHA promotes xenophobia and the abuse of immigrants. The denial of legal access to the South African body politic relegates (poor) immigrants to the abject spaces of otherness, criminalising them and facilitating their abuse by police, employers and others. As the recurrent xenophobic violence in South Africa demonstrates, steps that can promote equality and social justice – such as the reform of Home Affairs – must be taken to guarantee the dignity and safety of non-South Africans, and to fulfil the 1996 constitutional pledge that South Africa 'belongs to all who live within it, united in our diversity'.

This chapter also demonstrates that efforts at reforming the DoHA must involve substantial and sincere consultation with street level officials and those who represent them (such as the Public Servants Association and the National Education, Health and Allied Workers' Union) if we are to expect such reforms to succeed. As the 'final word' on policy implementation, Home Affairs officials are crucial to the intelligent reform of the Department, ultimately determining how service delivery is enacted on the ground. Their actions, attitudes and inside knowledge of the practice of policy can reveal vital information about the possibility, or impossibility, of a given reform measure. Officials must be seen as part of the solution – not simply as part of the problem.

NOTES

1   In saying this, I do not mean to suggest that the DoHA is always and everywhere disorderly. Thousands of people are successfully served by the Department every day. However, its atrocious reputation, its inability to avoid lawsuits and establish a coordinated legal defence process (Wa Kabwe-Segatti 2008), its widespread condemnation in the human rights community for poor service standards, as well as the findings outlined in the present study, suggest rather extensive disorder.

2   Consider, for example, the implementation of the turnaround strategy. Also consider Deputy Director General for Service Delivery Vusi Mkhize's September 2009 comments at a parliamentary media briefing that corruption is 'endemic' and an 'entrenched culture' at Home Affairs (*Mail & Guardian 15 September 2009*).

3   By 'organisational culture', I am referring to the entrenched values and practices that maintain the *status quo* within the DoHA. In this sense, I am departing from contemporary anthropological usage, which often stresses the complex relational, performative, symbolic and emergent nature of culture. Instead, I highlight, in a specific, narrower sense, the ideological capacity of culture to organise or limit the perceptions of those individuals acting 'within' it. This 'culture' could be thought of as *habitus* in the sense that Bourdieu employs that term (1977).

4   Although it would have been beneficial to speak with officials at branches of the DoHA that handle South African clientele (such as Civic Affairs) in order to determine the extent to which the character of service delivery might be somehow related to the client's country of origin, I unfortunately did not have the time nor the access to do so. I am nevertheless confident that my observations speak to the Department as a whole. Officials regularly transfer from one branch to another, and ultimately work within the same organisational structure and culture as all other DoHA officials, suggesting a degree of homogeneity across branches. Nevertheless, the reader is asked to keep this limitation in mind.

5   The fieldwork was conducted by me while working as a research assistant for the Forced Migration Studies Programme (FMSP). Many thanks to the FMSP and those who provided helpful comments and suggestions to my work on this topic, including David Coplan, Aurelia Wa Kabwe-Segatti, Darshan Vigneswaran, Loren Landau, Kelly Gillespie, Julia Hornberger, Robert Thornton, Eric Worby, and Corinne Hoag. Thanks also to the DoHA and the many DoHA officials who generously offered me their thoughts and time, and to the reviewers and editors of the *New South African Review* for their comments on a draft of this chapter.

6   Unless specified as 'upper level', the term 'officials' refers to 'street level' Home Affairs bureaucrats.

7   I should stress here that by describing ISB officials as inhibited or enervated, I do not intend to suggest that they are powerless. The newspaper stories cited at the beginning of this article, as well as the range of litigation filed by the human rights community, more than attest to officials' ability to affect the lives of individuals both inside and outside South Africa. Instead, I contend that the analyst must disaggregate powerful practices that develop out of a context of perceived threats and un- or mis-information from those pertaining to sheer laziness, opportunism, or obstructionism. Although unscrupulous officials certainly exist, many others are well intentioned, and one must take all types into consideration.

8   See Picard 2005 for a historical overview of the South African civil service; see also Wa Kabwe-Segatti and Landau *et al* 2008 for a review of the DoHA and South African immigration policy since the transition to democracy.

9   See, for example, Evans 1997; Posel 1999; Picard 2005.

10   This excludes workers in menial positions such as cleaners, who were widely employed within the apartheid civil service, as well as blacks who were employed in 'bantustan' offices.

11   'SA immigration service 'a joke'' 2 November 2003. Accessible at <http://news.bbc.co.uk>.

12   'Address by Mangosuthu Buthelezi, MP, Minister of Home Affairs, at the Home Affairs Annual Strategic Planning Workshop, 4 March 2004'. Accessible at <http://www.search.gov.za>.

13   See Wa Kabwe-Segatti *et al* (2009) for a more thorough review of the turnaround strategy and its effects.

14   'Subject to *this Act*, a *foreigner* may change his or her *status* while in the *Republic*' (Immigration Act 2002: 10 (6); emphasis in original).

15   Rarely did I encounter cases where an official was admonished for exercising too much caution, in part because management rarely hears about these cases – the clients often are simply turned away.

16   Although the Refugee Reception Centre is exceptional in this regard, that office is very much an anomaly.

17   A few words of clarification are in order here. In using the phrase 'systematisation of disorder', I evoke the work of Patrick Chabal and Jean-Pascal Daloz (1999) whose thesis on the 'instrumentalisation of disorder' in African states has been widely read and debated. While I draw similar conclusions below – for example, that inadequate training and resources has contributed to a situation whereby illicit practices have become a part of the DoHA's operational logic – I do not suggest that this derivative of some 'cultural' logic particular to Africans or South Africans. Moreover, I hope to complicate their depiction by illuminating the slippage between the 'economy of access' (commoditised legal status) characteristic of a systematised disorder and what I call 'comfortable underperformace', which pertains less to deliberate obstructionism than to the contingent embrace of the comforts of avoiding risk and extra work.

18   David Coplan has written extensively on this and other related points. See, for example, Coplan 2001 and 2008.

19   See Vigneswaran *et al*, forthcoming, for an elaboration of this point.

REFERENCES

Aglotsson E and J Klaaren (2003) Policing migration: Immigration enforcement and human rights in South Africa. *Migration Policy Brief No. 14*. Cape Town: Southern African Migration Project.

Belvedere MF (2007) Insiders but outsiders: The struggle for the inclusion of asylum seekers and refugees in South Africa. *Refuge* 24 (1): 57–70.

Bourdieu P (1977) *Outline of a Theory of Practice*. Cambridge: Cambridge University Press.

Chabal P and JP Daloz (1999) *Africa works: Disorder as Political Instrument*. Oxford: James Currey.

Coplan DB (2001) A river runs through it: The meaning of the Lesotho–Free State border. *African Affairs* 100: 81–116.

Coplan DB (2008) Crossing borders. In S Hassim *et al* (Eds) *Go Home or Die Here: Violence, Xenophobia and the Reinvention of Difference in South Africa*. Johannesburg: Wits University Press.

Crush J and DA McDonald (2001) Introduction to special issue: Evaluating South African immigration policy after apartheid. *Africa Today* 48 (3): 1–13.

Das V (2004) The signature of the state: The paradox of illegibility. In Das V and D Poole (Eds) *Anthropology in the Margins of the State*. Oxford: James Currey.

Evans I (1997) *Bureaucracy and Race: Native Administration in South Africa*. Berkeley: University of California Press.

Handmaker J (2001) No easy walk: Advancing refugee protection in South Africa. *Africa Today* 48 (3): 91–113.

Hoag C (2010) The magic of the populace: An ethnography of illegibility in the South African immigration bureaucracy. *Political and Legal Anthropology Review* 33 (1): 6–25.

Landau LB (2008) Decentralisation, migration and development in South Africa's primary cities. In Wa Kabwe-Segatti A and LB Landau (Eds) *Migration in Post-apartheid South Africa: Challenges and Questions to Policy Makers*. Paris: Notes et Documents Series of the Agence Française de Développement.

Lipsky M (1980) *Street Level Bureaucracy: Dilemmas of the Individual in Public Services*. New York: Russell Sage Foundation.

Picard LA (2005) *The State of the State: Institutional Transformation, Capacity and Political Change in South Africa*. Johannesburg: The Wits Policy and Development Management Governance Series, Wits University Press.

Posel D (1999) Whiteness and power in the South African civil service: Paradoxes of the apartheid state. *Journal of Southern African Studies* 25 (1): 99–119.

Vigneswaran D (2008) Undocumented migration: Risks and myths (1998–2005). In Wa Kabwe-Segatti A and LB Landau (Eds) *Migration in Post-apartheid South Africa: Challenges and Questions to Policy Makers*. Paris: Notes et Documents Series of the Agence Française de Développement.

Vigneswaran D, T Araia, C Hoag and X Tshabalala (forthcoming) Criminality or monopoly? Informal immigration enforcement in South Africa. *Journal of Southern African Studies* 36.

Wa Kabwe-Segatti A (2008) Reforming South African immigration policy in the post-apartheid period (1990-2006): What it means and what it takes. In Wa Kabwe-Segatti A & LB Landau (Eds) *Migration in Post-apartheid South Africa: Challenges and Questions to Policy Makers*. Paris: Notes et Documents Series of the Agence Française de Développement.

Wa Kabwe-Segatti A, C Hoag and D Vigneswaran (2009) The Turnaround Strategy from below: Public sector reform among South African Home Affairs migration officials in Johannesburg. Department of Anthropology and African Studies Working Paper No. 109. Johannes Gutenberg University of Mainz.

Wa Kabwe-Segatti A and LB Landau (Eds) (2008) *Migration in Post-apartheid South Africa: Challenges and Questions to Policy Makers*. Paris: Notes et Documents Series of the Agence Française de Développement.

CHAPTER 9

The mobile nation:
How migration continues to shape South Africa[1]

Loren Landau, Tara Polzer and Aurelia Wa Kabwe-Segatti

MOBILITY SHAPING THE NATION

South Africa's politics, economy, and social formations have been shaped historically by the elaborate regulation of human mobility and resistance to it. From the country's foundation, the majority of its residents – citizens and non-nationals – faced stark limitations on where they could live, and when and how they could move. The system of control was never as absolute or incorruptible as many imagine, but it has left the country with a socially and spatially fragmented population, suspicious of movements within and across its borders (see Crush *et al* 2008; Posel 1997). However, as the apartheid state's power waned in the late 1980s, so too did formal restrictions on movement into and within South Africa, and with the country's first democratic elections in 1994, South Africa's previously forbidden cities became primary destinations for migrants from around the country. Over time, they have also become increasingly important nodes for migrants from around the continent and beyond seeking profit, protection and the possibility of onward passage.

Political events in the past years – not only the continuation of xenophobic violence but a renewed call for 'rural' development – leave little doubt that human mobility, and attempts to reduce or prevent it, remains a potent concern shaping South African development and the self-understanding of the country's citizens and other residents. The language of responses to movement leaves little doubt that officials lack information, policies and capacities which would enable the country to predict and positively address its human mobility. That said, there are signs of change.

The aftermath of widespread violence against foreign nationals in May 2008 has given rise to new political debates about social cohesion and new international perceptions of the country. New policies were announced, and some of them implemented in relation to Zimbabwean migration (Polzer 2009). At long last, local governments have also begun recognising that migration – domestic and international, permanent and temporary – is an issue they cannot ignore.[2]

Despite increased attention to human mobility in all its forms, the country remains without a coherent and shared perspective within government, or between government and the general public, regarding policy aims for South Africa and the region more broadly. A review of the country's laws governing international mobility is underway by the South African Migration Project (SAMP) on behalf of the Department of Home Affairs but there is as yet no clarity as to the direction planned revisions will take. Despite recognising that movements between rural areas, small towns and metropolitan areas are affecting the country's ability to deliver services and alleviate poverty, the knowledge and capacity to address these movements remains elusive. Perhaps most importantly, widespread anti-migration and anti-immigration sentiments among the general population mean that there are few short-term political points to be won by developing an effective policy response to human mobility.

Although there is broad support for severely restricting movement into (and even within) South Africa (Crush *et al* 2008), addressing the challenges mobility brings cannot come from halting migration, whether towards cities or across international borders. Substantially restricting migration is neither possible nor a solution. The country will not meet its short- and long-term development targets without significant migration of skilled and semi-skilled labour. Despite the problems of rapid urbanisation, global evidence suggests that moving out of poor rural areas and into cities is one of the fastest ways of promoting human development (see White 2003). So while government may be unable to alter the number of people who move, or where they go, it can work to develop a more effective response to mobility.

Human mobility, like any process with profound social, economic and political impacts, is not inherently or inevitably positive or negative – whether for migrants, for sedentary communities or for states. Because of mobility's politicised nature, the often-decried 'negative effects' of international and internal migration are often stated as facts, without seeking or taking into account empirical evidence to the contrary. Indeed, many of the actual challenges associated with mobility – whether public health concerns, pressure on public services, urban overcrowding, insecurity or employment competition – arise less from the presence of mobile people *per se* and more from the inability or unwillingness of institutions to respond adequately to mobility.

This chapter explores the trends and tensions associated with movement into and within South Africa in four parts. It begins by providing a broad overview of the demographic and socio-economic data available, appraising the quality of available knowledge on contemporary migration flows to and within South Africa. It then offers an overview of the main policy transformations regarding human mobility, especially in relation to international migration. Third, it looks at what has been termed 'xenophobic violence' as one of the most extreme expressions of a systemic failure to govern a diverse and mobile society. Finally, we discuss the roles and challenges of a largely disregarded set of actors – local government – in addressing the effective governance of mobility.

VOLUMES AND PATTERNS OF MOBILITY

No one knows how many international migrants are in South Africa, how long they have been there, how long they stay, or what they do while they are in the country. The government has largely failed to establish data collection mechanisms that can inform pragmatic migration and development policies. Such weakness is tied to two factors: (1) the difficulty in accurately measuring migration, given the country's extended borders, poor data on the South African population, and mixed migrations within, into, and out of the country; and (2) migration's association with highly politicised issues surrounding nation building, citizenship and belonging. South Africa is by no means unique in this regard, since effectively tracking mobility is a challenge even for the most developed nations. Nonetheless, given South Africa's relatively sophisticated statistical infrastructure compared with other countries on the continent, mobility has received little attention. Consequently, the information presented below provides only rough quantitative estimates of who is coming and where they are going. We complement these with a qualitative overview of migration patterns into, within, and through the country.

While cross-border migration has undeniably increased over the last decade, overall figures are far lower than most South African officials and citizens presume. Moreover, even in the most immigrant-rich parts of South Africa, the number of newly arrived non-nationals is dwarfed by the number of recently arrived citizens from other parts of the country. According to the 2007 Community Survey, a national representative survey conducted by Statistics South Africa (StatsSA), the total number of foreign-born residents is just over 1.2 million or 2.79 per cent of the total population.[3] Although StatsSA has probably undercounted non-nationals – as they have undercounted the homeless and other marginalised groups – there have been no serious or scholarly challenges to findings from the community survey. Based on the probable continuation of increased Zimbabwean migration since 2007, the Forced Migration Studies Programme has calculated a likely overall foreign-born population of just under 1.7 million in 2009. (Approximately 1 to 1.2 million of the total number of foreign-born are likely to be Zimbabwean, an estimate shared by the Department of Home Affairs.) This means that the total number of foreign-born residents is only about 4 per cent of the overall population. That is still higher than many South Africans would like, but is low compared with, for example, Gabon (17.9 per cent), the USA (13.0 per cent), Ivory Coast (12.3 per cent), France (10.6 per cent), the United Kingdom (9.7 per cent), Ghana (7.6 per cent), and Namibia (6.6 per cent). It is even below neighbouring Botswana, although not by much. Furthermore, people counted as foreign-born in the statistics include South Africans born in exile, naturalised citizens, refugees and documented migrants, in addition to undocumented migrants.

Despite such evidence produced by South Africa's official government agencies, there are regular claims by officials, unquestioningly repeated *ad nauseam* in the media, that there are eight to ten million 'undocumented' migrants in the country and two to three million Zimbabweans. Such inflation has fed into feelings of 'helplessness and desperation' among officials (Centre for Development and Enterprise 2008: 8) and discouraged rational and effective responses. False estimates – especially when repeated by officials – have provided a convenient scapegoat for service delivery and economic failures, fuelling fear and anger among the populace.

Part of the common misrepresentation of international migration in South Africa is the focus on undocumented or 'illegal' migration. As in destination countries around the world, the total number of non-nationals living in South Africa is a mix of documented and undocumented migrants, refugees and asylum seekers. The number of temporary work, study, business, and tourist permits[4] granted annually has consistently increased since the end of apartheid, reflecting the reinsertion of South Africa into the international community after decades of isolation. In the same period, permanent immigration permits went from 14 000 a year in 1990 to 4 000 at the end of the 1990s. The number then went back to around 10 000 a year by 2004.[5]

There has been an effort to increase the number of 'exceptionally-skilled' migrants attracted to South Africa through the general work permit, a (skills) quota work permit, an intra- company transfer work permit, treaty permits and corporate permits. There are few statistics available on the numbers of people recruited under these schemes, although it is clear that the numbers fall short of government-set targets.

There is also a relatively small, but expanding, number of refugees and asylum seekers among the non-nationals living in South Africa. The official statistics in this category are also not very helpful in painting a reliable picture, as not all individuals seeking protection from persecution in their home countries are able to gain access to the system (CoRMSA 2009), while many asylum applicants are in the system owing to a lack of more appropriate documentation options, rather than because they are actually fleeing persecution. According to the Department of Home Affairs, 170 865 persons were waiting for their refugee applications to be processed (asylum seekers) at the end of 2007 compared to 36 736 people who had been recognised as refugees.[6]

Since 2007, the number of asylum seekers has increased dramatically, following the acknowledgement by the Department of Home Affairs that Zimbabweans had a right to apply for asylum. However, if a 'special dispensation permit' for Zimbabweans is introduced granting temporary rights to live and work in South Africa (as announced by the Department of Home Affairs in April 2009 but not yet implemented), the asylum seeker numbers are likely to decrease again.

Although international migration attracts the most political attention and popular opprobrium, domestic mobility is far more significant in numeric terms. Research by the South African Cities Network (2006) and others clearly illustrates the spatial dynamics of migration to particular urban centres. In Metsweding, a smaller municipality in Gauteng province, more than 10 per cent of the total population has moved there in the past seven years. In Durban, the figure is less than 1 per cent. And while discussions of urbanisation typically focus on primary cities, the fastest growing municipalities are often smaller communities beyond the 'urban edge'. The most notable and controversial effect of this growth has been the expansion of poorly serviced informal settlements surrounding more established and well serviced formal settlements.

In addition to sheer numbers, and by far outweighing the number of international migrants, shifts within and among provinces are resulting in significant changes in skills levels and social composition. In the Western Cape, the arrival of people from the Eastern Cape, traditionally an ANC stronghold, is not only transforming the province's racial composition, but also threatening the Democratic Alliance's support base. In Gauteng, the enormous diversity fostered by internal migration has proved to be a politically exploitable resource in the past, particularly during the violence preceding the 1994 general elections. As South African politics again become more competitive, there are hints that ethnicity may re-emerge as a dangerous political divide.

Pressures do not only affect places of net in-migration such as large cities. Out-migration is also significantly shifting population profiles of a number of the country's smaller and less prosperous communities. For example, the Chris Hani District Municipality in the central Eastern Cape, a vast area including such small towns as Cradock, Queenstown, Cala and Lady Frere, has lost more than 8.5 per cent of its population over the past decade (Cities Network 2006:18). Many of those who left are young men heading for the Western Cape (Dorrington 2005). Consequently, there are significant distortions in population pyramids in both sending and receiving communities (see Collinson *et al* 2006).

In light of the migration dynamics outlined above, the following section charts the policy frameworks currently in place for international migration, discussing recent challenges and gaps. We will return to considerations of internal migration in the later sections on xenophobia and local government.

TRANSFORMING IMMIGRATION AND REFUGEE POLICY

South Africa's political changes since 1990, including constitutional reforms and an opening of space for political debate, have helped generate a paradox regarding the position of migrants in South African society. Despite legal frameworks guaranteeing international migrants more rights than ever before, migrants remain remarkably vulnerable to socio-economic exclusion, harassment from police, and violence at the hands of state agents and citizens. In official and public deliberation, migration debates often seem caught between complaints about the state's inability to control its border and protect South African jobs, and its incapacity to attract and retain foreign skilled labour and investors. Policies and politics relating to internal migration are much more diffuse, not least because there are no dedicated legal and institutional frameworks relating to internal movement, and because the issue is politically complex. Given the country's history of forcibly restricting movement to the cities and between parts of the country, free movement and the right to settle anywhere are important and valued tenets of South Africa's democracy, as in any liberal democracy. Nonetheless, government actors, and especially urban planners, often remain suspicious of new arrivals to the city and services often remain inaccessible to them.

Tensions in international migration policy are rooted in immigration legislation. The 2002 Immigration Act (amended in 2004) favours highly-skilled labour and investors, providing a number of ways for such people to enter and stay within the country. For everyone else, the Act retains a strong security- and sovereignty-centred agenda reflecting a narrowly defined notion of national interest that bears a strong resemblance to positions held by the apartheid regime. Like many social-democratic governments, the ANC and its migration policy are caught between the acceptance of market rules that include the free circulation of labour and the consequences of South Africa's limited weight in the global economy.

These are among the reasons that the Immigration Act enjoys remarkably limited support in government, business or civil society. The government began a policy review process in 2009 but it remains to be seen whether revisions will build on or counteract some significant recent shifts in South Africa's migration regime. First, after a decade opposing the Southern African Development Community (SADC) Protocol on the Facilitation of Movement of Persons, South Africa was among the first member states to sign the amended protocol in 2005. Even if the 2005 SADC Protocol was largely devoid of its substance compared with the original proposal made by the SADC Secretariat in 1995, this shows South Africa's will to open up to a regional approach. This has also materialised in new agreements with Mozambique (2004) and Lesotho (2007), aiming at progressively lifting border control with these immediate neighbours. Most significantly, in 2009 South Africa introduced a no-cost visa for Zimbabweans, bringing its bilateral arrangements with Zimbabwe in line with all its other neighbouring states. Nonetheless, while these actions hint at regionalism, policy changes continue to be dominated by South Africa's short-term national interests and regionalism moves forward at South Africa's discretion.

There are also uncomfortable, if predictable, intersections between the country's immigration and asylum policy. In many instances, their inadequacies interact in ways that produce vicious synergies, exaggerating the shortcomings of both policy areas. The asylum policy, outlined in the Refugees Act (1998) and subsequent regulations, incorporates international refugee law[7] and offers every individual the right to apply for asylum at any of the country's six refugee reception offices. On application, asylum seekers are granted the right to work, study and access basic public services such as health care, but without specialised social assistance programmes. According to the law, asylum seekers are to receive a decision within six months, although in practice many wait years for a decision. After their cases are decided, they are accorded refugee status (usually for a period of two years), asked to leave the country or told to apply for some other form of documentation such as a work permit. In most instances, people are not eligible for other forms of documentation. Indeed, this is why so many who are in South Africa for work apply for asylum to begin with.

While South Africa's refugee policy is impressively progressive by global standards – as it grants recognised refugees the right to settle, move and work freely in the country rather than constraining people to isolated camps – its implementation has been dogged by administrative inefficiencies and gaps between the immigration and refugee policies. Owing to job seekers' lack of options for obtaining immigration documents within the Immigration Act framework, many use the asylum system as a 'back door' to the right to work. The prevalence of Malawians, Tanzanians and citizens from other peaceful countries attests to this tendency. This has the dual effect of denying protection to many of those who need it while delegitimising the asylum system overall, with few institutions, social services and employers recognising refugee or asylum papers (for more, see Handmaker *et al* 2008 and CoRMSA 2009).

The Department of Home Affairs has repeatedly put in place 'turnaround strategies' aimed at addressing the managerial and administrative challenges faced by the Department overall, including in its migration management functions. Making changes sustainably, however, will require significant changes to human resource management within the status determination process (Wa Kabwe-Segatti *et al* 2009). Realising these demands requires levels of political will and resourcing that have not previously been forthcoming.

The fastest way of reducing the backlog, however, would be to open other avenues for legal migration into South Africa, for without such opportunities asylum will continue to be an attractive option for migrants attempting to regularise their stay in the country. This challenge is especially apparent in relation to Zimbabwean migration, as most Zimbabweans fit neither into a narrowly defined conception of refugee status (over 90 per cent of Zimbabwean asylum applicants are currently being rejected by the Department of Home Affairs), nor can they be treated as 'normal' economic migrants (Kiwanuka and Monson 2009; Polzer 2008). This is due to their reasons for leaving Zimbabwe – high levels of economic and social services collapse – as well as the collective impacts of such high volumes of movement on South Africa.

In 2009 there has been a welcome change from the denialism that has surrounded South Africa's response to Zimbabwe and Zimbabwean migration and the beginnings of a rational and regionalist approach. As noted above, Zimbabweans were granted a free ninety-day visa, and deportations to Zimbabwe were suspended from April 2009 as initial steps toward regularising their position in South Africa. However, the final element of a coherent regularisation policy remained outstanding throughout 2009, even though the minister of Home Affairs announced the introduction of a new 'special dispensation permit' (based on section 31(2)b of the Immigration Act of 2002) in April 2009, which would have granted Zimbabweans the right to reside and work in South Africa for a specified period of time while being able to freely move back and forth across the border.[8]

National level policies and legal frameworks regarding international mobility are important, and ongoing efforts to increase the coherence and appropriateness of such policies in the South and Southern African context are valuable. However, as stated above, there is already a discrepancy between relatively strong and progressive policy frameworks (including the constitution) and widespread rights abuses in practice. Addressing these abuses cannot, therefore, merely rest on revising legal frameworks. The example of widespread 'xenophobic violence', which has been increasing since the mid 2000s, illustrates the need to understand and address a range of structural social and political issues beyond policy and law. While often associated only with international migration, many cases of violence have illustrated broader dynamics to exclude people not considered 'local', including those from provinces or language groups not in the local majority. Through group-based violence, these 'outsiders' are also denied access to resources such as housing or jobs. This suggests that such violence reflects deeper fault lines in South African society, showing the centrality of mobility to many of the country's social and political challenges.

XENOPHOBIA, VIOLENCE AND SOCIAL COHESION[9]

The most extreme expression of the weaknesses in the effective management of mobility and diversity is the rise of anti-outsider violence around South Africa in the late 2000s. Such violence significantly disrupts local and national institutions and economies. Two years after unprecedented levels of violence erupted around the country in May 2008, displacing thousands of people, the threat of further violence remains high. Almost as many people were killed and injured during this violence as in the infamous 1960 Sharpeville attack which galvanised a national and international anti-apartheid movement, yet the xenophobic violence has not attracted the same level of scrutiny or sustained public outrage.

Attacks on foreign nationals continue, even though not always in the form of high profile mob attacks. There were at least twenty-eight separate attacks around the country between June 2008 and July 2009, in locations as diverse as Durban, Boksburg, Port Alfred, Klerksoord, Motherwell, Delft and Darling. Threats of violence and instructions to foreigners to 'get out' of informal settlements also remain common. In May 2009, local businesspeople sent letters to Somali traders in Khayelitsha threatening them if they did not move out within a week. Zimbabweans around Johannesburg report threats from taxi drivers, work colleagues, neighbours or simply strangers passing in the street, and threats of 'just wait until after the [2008] elections' have changed into 'just wait until after the [2010] World Cup, then we will kick all of you out of our country.'(CoRMSA, Crisis in Zimbabwe Coalition, & FMSP 2009).

Representations and analyses of these forms of violence in the media, among politicians and within academia have postulated various causes, including discriminatory attitudes learned under apartheid, structural inequalities such as poverty and unemployment, and too-liberal immigration policies (see Crush et al 2008; Glaser 2008; HSRC 2008; Parliament of the Republic of South Africa 2008, among others). Such analyses naturalise the connection between negative feelings or structural inequalities and violence without addressing the mechanisms and triggers through which one is transformed into the other. While discriminatory attitudes and socio-economic pressures are precursors to violence, they are not enough to explain when and where violence is used (Landau and Misago 2009).

Research by the Forced Migration Studies Programme in locations where violence has occurred identified three common factors leading to group-based violence (Misago et al 2009). First, there is a lack of trusted and effective conflict resolution mechanisms within these locations. Second, there is a culture of impunity that makes people who attack foreign nationals feel that there will be no negative consequences for them. Finally, there is a political vacuum or competition for community leadership so that unofficial, illegitimate and often violent forms of leadership emerge. Such leaders then mobilise residents of the area against foreign nationals in order to strengthen their own power base.[10] Researchers of collective and mob violence in other contexts have come to similar conclusions, suggesting that South Africans are not unique in resorting to violence in such conditions (see Mendoza 2006 on Guatemala). This approach to understanding anti-outsider violence has three implications.

First, it allows violence against foreign nationals to be seen as a continuum with – and, indeed, often something which happens in tandem with – violence against marginalised South

Africans. It is important to remember that of the reported sixty-two people killed during the violence of May 2008, one third were South African. The logic and process of violent mobilisation against groups perceived to be outsiders is similar, whether they originate from across national or provincial borders or from a different political or cultural affiliation (Tilly 2004). This recognition highlights the broader challenge of governing an internally diverse and mobile country, and furthermore it emphasises that the frequent focus on immigration policies and migrant legal status does not go far in explaining 'xenophobic' violence.

Second, seeking to understand concrete local triggers of violence transposes the debate from structural and often intractable relationships between, for instance, poverty, unemployment and violence, to concrete and local political actions and institutions. It helps us distinguish between factors which are actually significantly correlated with the occurrence of violence, and those seemingly commonsensical factors (such as local levels of unemployment) which are not significantly correlated (Wa Kabwe-Segatti and Fauvelle-Aymar 2009). It also enables us to recognise the links between forms of service delivery protests and attacks on foreigners, which often occur simultaneously. Both can be interpreted as expressions of disaffection with unaccountable local governance structures and frustration with government service provision.

Third, we must recognise that should the political interest, imperatives or will exist, it is possible to reduce the likelihood of group-based violence through concrete political and institutional interventions. Mirroring the three key triggers above – lack of conflict resolution mechanisms, a culture of impunity, and political contestation – interventions could include strengthening local conflict resolution mechanisms such as conflicts over scarce resources, maintaining respect for the rule of law and reducing vigilantism by effectively and publically prosecuting perpetrators, and supporting and monitoring accountable local leadership. These three central fault lines in South African society highlighted by the xenophobic violence – competition for access and rights to resources, the rule of law, and accountable local government – have already been recognised by President Zuma's administration as central concerns to be addressed in the interests of poor South Africans. While addressing xenophobia will obviously not be enough to resolve these larger institutional and social challenges for all, the failure to address xenophobia will continue to entrench them.

Before discussing the roles of an important but often overlooked set of actors – local government – in tackling these challenges, we briefly outline the ways in which government and other actors have already responded to xenophobic violence and assess the extent to which these responses deal with the underlying fault lines of resource conflict, respect for the rule of law and legitimate local government.

Some important lessons have been learned since the violence of May 2008. Violence against foreign nationals is now understood by leading politicians to be a threat to the wider stability and reputation of all in South Africa, and not something that can be ignored as a minority issue. But this does not mean there is consensus on the position of foreign nationals in the country. While official and media debates now regularly mention xenophobia as one of the country's ills which must be addressed with urgency, there is still a widespread popular belief that foreign nationals should and could be removed. In spite of a spate of indabas, seminars, workshops and media discussions, there has not been a formal, national debate or position regarding xenophobic violence since the events of May 2008. A formal enquiry by the South African Human Rights Commission was delayed until early 2010, and was given a limited mandate and resources. While the resulting report includes many significant recommendations,[11] the enquiry process did not lead to the development of consensus within government or more broadly in society.

With the economic crisis continuing to hit South Africa in 2010, one hears people in the streets, on the radio and among the political leadership asking whether South Africa can 'afford' to host migrants. Greater government and public awareness of xenophobia has translated into various initiatives to increase 'community cohesion' through dialogues, workshops, school curriculum interventions and religious initiatives. If such interventions build sustained local conflict resolution structures that are considered legitimate by local residents, they may reduce the likelihood that tensions between individuals or groups will become violent. However, such structures often do not or cannot engage with the power relations between local groups and the perceived and real resource constraints that lead to tensions. Although 'social-cohesion dialogues' have mushroomed in the past two years, there have been no independent evaluations of whether such interventions lead to sustained reductions in violence, or what characteristics make such interventions effective in violence prevention.

In relation to respect for the rule of law, vigilantism and impunity, several government departments are developing early warning systems so that threats or early signs of violence can be stopped or prevented from spreading. These initiatives by the Departments of Home Affairs, Intelligence, Disaster Management and the police are still in their early stages of development and not yet integrated with each other or with information flowing through civil society organisations. While they are potentially promising ways of addressing local conflicts and decreasing impunity, these systems will require ongoing commitment and support from government and civil society to become effective.

Then there is still a widespread public perception that none of the May 2008 perpetrators, nor other perpetrators of violence against foreign nationals, were prosecuted. This is not entirely true, as the National Prosecuting Authority reports that out of around 500 cases opened in connection with the attacks, involving 1 500 individuals, eighty-two were found guilty, including at least one murder conviction with a fifteen year sentence (Department of Justice and Constitutional Development 2009). However, a large percentage of cases were withdrawn through 'lack of witnesses' or the loss of dockets, and most of the convictions are for the relatively minor crimes of robbery, housebreaking and public violence rather than for rape and murder. To some extent, this reflects general weaknesses in the criminal justice system, which are also leading to increasing public disaffection and vigilantism with regard to crime targeted at South Africans. In other respects, however, there are particular challenges to addressing the impunity of perpetrators of violence against foreign nationals. One is that in cases of group violence individual perpetrators are often supported by other residents who seek to put pressure on the justice system through political negotiation, such as demanding the release of an accused in return for 'allowing re-integration' of people who were displaced through violence. Second, group based violence is often organised by local leaders (political leaders or businesspersons) but carried out by others, so that the legal system struggles to build strong cases of incitement against the leaders (CoRMSA 2010). This was the case in De Doorns in the Western Cape at the end of 2009, where local counsellors and labour brokers were accused of inciting violence which displaced 3 000 Zimbabwean farm workers (Misago 2009).

Finally, in terms of clear mechanisms to support legitimate local governance and to hold local leaders accountable when threats against foreign nationals are made, local or national elected leaders are yet to play a visible and decisive role in addressing and managing such conflicts. To some extent, this once again mirrors the lacklustre way in which national government has responded to service delivery protests triggered by non-performing or corrupt local government officials (Atkinson 2007). Taking a vocal anti-xenophobia stance carries additional political risks, however, given the widespread anti-foreigner sentiment among much of the electorate, and even at the bureaucratic level there is so far no national policy for preventing or responding to xenophobic violence.

Part of the challenge in effectively and appropriately managing human mobility – where violence is only the most extreme expression of tensions – lies in the fact that the most important institutional level is the least equipped with capacity, and indeed has not even recognised its central role. This institutional level is local government. The following section explores local government's role in responding to migration and some of the challenges associated with developing such a response.[12]

NEW HORIZONS IN GOVERNING MOBILITY: Responses from local government

Constitutionally empowered to be a leading force for development, local governments have nevertheless been wary of addressing migration concerns. This stems partly from a belief among many policy makers (local and national), that immigration is exclusively a national policy concern. Some have yet to realise the degree to which migration is transforming their towns and cities while others naively hope that heightened human mobility is simply a temporary outgrowth of the country's democratic transition. In almost all instances, budgeting and planning exercises have largely excluded extended population projections and as a consequence city leaders continue to plan for a slowly growing and largely stable population.

Our discussion includes national trends with particular attention to the country's two primary cities, Cape Town and Johannesburg, to highlight similarities and critical differences in the political calculus of migration management. As noted above, beyond looking at formal policy frameworks, it is important to pay considerable attention to unofficial and semi-official responses to migration in the form of violence, discrimination and economic exclusion. These include the privatisation of violence and the spreading economies of corruption that are such unfortunate characteristics of countries across the continent.

Some within local government have seen increasing migration and diversity as a positive sign of South African cities' emergence as trading and cultural centres. In response, city planners in both Johannesburg and Cape Town have begun outlining strategies for recruiting and incorporating highly skilled migrants and refugees into the city's socio-economic networks.[13] However, it is also evident that many of the cities' leaders and citizens feel overwhelmed – if not threatened – by migration, and especially the movement of people south from the rest of the continent (Centre for Development and Enterprise 2008). In other places, the out-migration of the cities' skilled and affluent is seen as a precursor of economic decline and an ever-expanding underclass (South African Cities Network 2006). For many, migration is tied to the expansion of drug syndicates, prostitution, and human trafficking, unemployment, crime and a range of other social and economic ills. Apart from a few exceptional cases, elected officials believe that urbanisation and international migration raise the spectre of economic and political fragmentation and urban degeneration (see Beall *et al* 2003).

Most of South Africa's metros are now accepting that new arrivals make up a growing portion of their populations. Part of the shift in policy comes from the slow recognition among some officials in local government that without apartheid-style measures to control movements – measures that even at the time, for reasons of intention and incapacity, never achieved 100 per cent effectiveness – cities can do little to alter regional migration dynamics (Kok and Collinson 2006; Johannesburg Strategic Development Strategy 2006). In the words of one Johannesburg city councillor, 'as much as we might not want them here, we cannot simply wish these people away' (personal communication, 13 July 2005). Research by the Forced Migration Studies Programme reveals similar perspectives among planners and planning documents in Cape Town and elsewhere.

However, this recognition does not come without considerable trepidation, and most local governments have thus far failed to develop empirically informed and proactive policy responses to international migration. Rather than replacing existing divisions with shared rules of economic and social engagement, discrimination against non-citizens threatens further fragmentation and social marginalisation. Exclusion based on nationality or community of origin clearly affects initiatives 'to achieve a shared vision, among all sectors of our society, for the achievement of our goal of improving the quality of life for all citizens' (Gauteng Province 2005:3). Although there are slow changes in government, many officials continue to react to the presence of foreign migrants by implicitly denying their presence, excluding them from developmental plans, or allowing discrimination throughout the government bureaucracy and police.

In both Cape Town and Johannesburg, internal and domestic migrants continue to be seen largely as a drain on public resources (see Provincial Government of Western Cape 2002) rather than as potential resources or, more neutrally, as the people government is dedicated to serve. Even those city officials who wish to more proactively absorb new, often poor and vulnerable populations, face considerable challenges in working out how to do so.

Recognising the imperative to address migration in building inclusive, safe and prosperous cities does not necessarily mean that officials have the information or tools to do this effectively. Perhaps the most fundamental challenge to local governments charged with creating inclusive cities is the elusive meaning of inclusion for South Africa's highly diverse and fragmented urban communities (see Tomlinson *et al* 2003). With the end of apartheid-era pass laws and the country's full reintegration into regional politics and trade, previously 'forbidden' cities have become temporary destinations – if not the terminus – for peoples from throughout South Africa and the African continent. In many instances, these inward movements have been accompanied by the flight of affluent residents from the inner cities; as a result the population of Cape Town, Durban, and especially Johannesburg is a new population and in many neighbourhoods it is difficult to speak of an indigenous community or dominant culture or ethos. This is most visible in central Johannesburg, an area almost completely made up of new arrivals.

For cities that have experienced rapid rates of urbanisation, it is almost impossible to speak about integration or about creating unified urban communities. Multiculturalism is a fact, but without the guarantees that interactions will be peaceful, productive, or characterised by mutual respect. In many instances, the opposite has been true (see the discussion of xenophobia and social cohesion above). The atomisation and fragmentation of South African cities stands in sharp contrast to the vision of a self-identified urban population invested in cities' futures. Negotiating a common basis of belonging is made all the more difficult by the mobile nature of the cities' new populations. Many who come to the city do not expect to stay there for long.

According to Statistics South Africa, 'the temporary nature of rural-to-urban migration in South Africa may add insight into the persistence of overcrowding and poor living conditions in urban townships. Migrants may employ a calculated strategy to maximise the benefits to their household of origin, rather than for their own benefit or the benefit of residential units in the urban setting' (in Johannesburg Development Strategy 2006: 28). Critically, journeys home or onwards often remain practically elusive for reasons of money, safety or social status, which leaves almost two-thirds of Johannesburg's non-national population effectively marooned in the city but not wishing to take root or invest in it. We also see evidence of this extra-local orientation in the levels of remittances being sent out of the city to both rural communities and other countries (see Landau and Freemantle 2009).

A further challenge in responding to migration comes from the little local governments know about the people living in their cities. Whereas national governments have the relative luxury of developing generalised policy frameworks, local governments and service providers are responsible for more focused and context-specific interventions. In almost no instances are city governments able to draw on a nuanced and dynamic understanding of their constituencies. This is generally true regarding the urban poor and all the more so with geo-graphically mobile people. Recent efforts to map 'poverty pockets' (Cross et al 2005) and review both national and localised migration data (Dorrington 2005; Province of the Western Cape 2002; Kok and Collinson 2006; SACN 2006; Landau and Gindrey 2008) represent some of the first concerted efforts to understand South Africa's urban population dynamics.

But many of these studies are based on admittedly incomplete census data – particularly inaccurate regarding foreign-born populations and increasingly unreliable at smaller levels of geographic disaggregation – and are often purely descriptive. While the Department of Cooperative Governance and Traditional Authorities now recognises that there is a need for improving cross-border (across municipal, provincial and national borders) and multi-nodal planning – including a greater consideration of population mobility – planners are effectively unable to understand the 'functional economic geography of the city and its region [and] how the different components relate to each other' (SACN 2006: Section 2–7). In this context, local planners continue to be influenced by stereotypes and the misreading or incomplete readings of data.

The inability to understand and predict urban populations effectively poses significant risks to local governments' ability to meet their obligations and developmental objectives. Perhaps most obviously, the invisibility of large segments of the urban population can result in much greater demand for services than predicted, reducing service quality and outstripping budgetary allocations. In a bureaucratic culture influenced, as elsewhere, by new public management reforms (McLennan 2008), this may even increase officials' perceptions of migrants as an obstacle to their reaching their annual targets, and lead to the additional stigmatisation of mobile populations. In many instances, these are hidden costs to public and private infrastructure, water and other services that are not accessed individually. For example, the degradation to building stock through high-population densities – a consequence of new migrants minimising costs while maximising centrality – also has long-term cost implications for cities that collect taxes on the bases of building values.

Higher populations do not, however, necessarily result in higher costs to local government in receiving areas. Because many of South Africa's internal migrants are young men, they may remain relatively healthy, autonomous and productive in urban areas – and hence levy few costs. Moreover, while they may not invest in property, much of their consumption of food and consumer goods is in urban areas. In such instances, sending communities may lose the benefits of their labour while being saddled with the costs of educating their children and providing for them in their old age. Many of these costs are paid centrally or through the provinces, but others are the responsibility of local government. While both sending and receiving communities are influenced by the significant costs and benefits associated with migration, these calculations have rarely been figured into the distribution of national resources by the South African Treasury. Since the promulgation of the new constitution in 1996, the Treasury has distributed money to the provinces (and subsequently to the metros) based almost exclusively on current population estimates, and such practices are problematic for at least three reasons. First, the population estimates often significantly misrepresent where people actually live; someone may own a house and vote in a rural community but live elsewhere for eleven months of the year (Department of Housing 2006). Second, peoples' presence in a particular locality is not necessarily a good predictor of their costs to local or provincial government. Third, infrastructure and social service planning requires long-term investments based on predictions of population in five to fifteen years' time. Without reliable estimates, cities are unable to prepare for their populations' future needs.

In late September 2006, the South African Fiscal Commission convened a seminar to try to come to grips with these issues in order to better advise the Treasury on resource distribution. In 2008, the Treasury again met – with World Bank support – to discuss resource allocation. However, planning continues to be based on current rather than projected population distributions and all but ignores undocumented migrants and, perhaps most worrying, is that many planners remain unaware of such an approach's frailty in a country with such high rates of mobility. This is likely to become particularly problematic as South Africa begins implementing its national spatial development framework.[14]

The lack of coordination among government departments further exaggerates the partial and often ill-informed responses to human mobility. In discussions, planners in both

Johannesburg and Cape Town repeatedly expressed frustration regarding their efforts to foster collaboration within local government departments and, more importantly, between local government and South Africa's other two governmental 'spheres': provincial and national. However, due to migration's spatial dynamics, effectively responding to human mobility is not something that any single governmental body or sphere can singly address as it requires coordination and planning that transcends the boundaries of metropolitan areas and encompasses a wider area connected by commuter flows, economic linkages and shared facilities.

The paucity of collaboration is visible in a variety of potentially critical areas. Perhaps most obviously, the Department of Home Affairs has been either reluctant or unable to share its data with city planners (this information includes the number of foreigners legally entering the country, and also registered moves, deaths and births). The most probable cause is lack of capacity within the DoHA, although there is undoubtedly also a general reluctance to share information freely. It is, of course, not only the DoHA that has shown a reluctance to work with local government, but the lack of coordination between DoHA and local government is probably the most significant gap.

CONCLUSIONS

This chapter illustrates how human mobility is intricately tied up with two of South Africa's key national challenges: social cohesion and public service provision. The difficulty of adequately managing the impacts of mobility is heightened by the fact that it is not yet widely recognised as something requiring management, and so the requisite information, institutional systems and political support are not available. The first step, therefore, remains to raise awareness among officials and political actors about the centrality of human mobility to South African society, and to overcome the fear and denial which often accompany discussions of migration. Furthermore, while national migration policy revision processes are ongoing, continuous attention is needed on the effective implementation of existing laws and mechanisms for inclusion and non-discrimination.

NOTES

1　This paper draws and expands upon material originally published in more extensive form as Human Development Research Paper 2009/05, Human Development Impacts of Migration: South Africa Case Study by Loren B Landau and Aurelia Wa Kabwe Segatti.

2　In early 2020, the South African Local Government Association began a project to help improve municipal planning for human mobility. Almost simultaneously, the presidency has begun a similar initiative as part of its pro-poor policy development initiative.

3　Many of the 'foreign-born' may in fact be naturalised citizens. Available data on citizenship and legal status is even less reliable than data on place of birth.

4　Temporary residents include entries for reasons of work, study, business, holiday, contract, border traffic, transit and other unspecified categories.

5　Department of Home Affairs, *Annual Reports*, 1990-2004

6　Asylum applications are conducted under the 1998 Refugees Act (implemented in 2001).

7   The South African definition of refugee includes definitions from both the 1951 Convention Relating to the Status of Refugees and the 1969 OAU (now AU) Protocol Governing the Specific Aspects of Refugee Problems in Africa. South Africa is also party to both of these legal instruments.
8   For further discussion of options regarding Zimbabwean migration see Polzer (2008).
9   Much of the following section is drawn from research conducted by Misago *et al* (2009) and from additional analysis by Polzer and Breen (2009).
10 For detailed case studies, see Misago *et al* (2009).
11 SAHRC (2010) Report on the SAHRC Investigation into Issues of Rule of Law, Justice and Impunity arising out of the 2008 Public Violence against Non-Nationals.
12 The introductory paragraphs of this section draw heavily from Götz and Landau (2004) and Götz (2004).
13 In 2005, Cape Town conducted a skills audit of its refugee population so as to better develop policies to capitalise on their presence in the city. Johannesburg has yet to follow suit but has recently officially recognised the potential contributions migrants make to the city.
14 For more on the country's spatial development perspective, visit http://www.thepresidency.gov.za/main.asp?include=docs/pcsa/planning/nsdp/main.html.

REFERENCES

Atkinson D (2007) Taking to the streets: has developmental local government failed in South Africa? In Buhlungu S, J Daniel, R Southall & J Lutchman (Eds) *State of the Nation: South Africa 2007* (pp. 53–77). Cape Town: HSRC Press.

Beal J, O Crankshaw and S Parnell (2003) *Uniting a Divided City: Governance and Social Exclusion in Johannesburg.* London: Earthscan.

Centre for Development and Enterprise (2008) Immigrants in Johannesburg; Estimating numbers and assessing impacts (Indepth No. 9). Johannesburg: Centre for Development and Enterprise.

City of Johannesburg (2006) Johannesburg Strategic Development Strategy 2006.

Collinson M, P Kok and M Garenne (2006) Migration and Changing Settlement Patterns: Multilevel Data for Policypolicy. Report 03-04-01. Pretoria: Human Sciences Research Council.

CoRMSA (2009) Protecting Refugees, Asylum Seekers and Immigrants in South Africa. Johannesburg: CoRMSA.

CoRMSA, Crisis in Zimbabwe Coalition, & FMSP (2009). Is street-level public and institutional xenophobia increasing in Johannesburg? Report on Consultative Forum with Migrant Youth. Johannesburg: CoRMSA, Crisis in Zimbabwe Coalition, FMSP.

CoRMSA (2010) May 2008 Violence Against Foreign Nationals in South Africa: Understanding Causes and Evaluating Responses. CoRMSA, March.

Crush J, DA McDonald, V Williams, K Lefko-Everett, D Dorey, D Taylor *et al* (2008) The Perfect Storm: the realities of xenophobia in contemporary South Africa. SAMP Migration Policy Brief, 50.

Department of Housing (2006) Investigation into Urbanisation Trends in South Africa and the Implications for Housing. Presentation made to the National Finance Commission (Midrand, 29 September 2006).

Department of Justice and Constitutional Development (2009) Progress Report Relating to Cases Emanating from the 2008 Xenophobic aAttacks. Pretoria Department of Justice and Constitutional Development.

Dorrington R (2005) Projection of the Population of the City of Cape Town 2001-2021. Report prepared for the City of Cape Town. Cape Town: Centre for Actuarial Research, University of Cape Town.

Glaser D (2008) (Dis)Connections: Elite and Popular 'Common Sense' on the Matter of Foreigners. In Hassim S, T Kupe and & E Worby (Ed) *Go Home or Die Here: Violence, Xenophobia and the Reinvention of Difference in South Africa* (pp. 53-63). Johannesburg: Wits University Press.

Götz G (2004) The role of local government towards forced migrants. In Landau LB (Ed) *Forced Migrants in the New Johannesburg: Towards a Local Government Response.* Johannesburg: Forced Migration Studies Programme.

Götz G and L Landau (2004) Introduction. In Landau LB (Ed), *Forced Migrants in the New Johannes-burg: Towards a Local Government Response.* Johannesburg: Forced Migration Studies Programme.

Handmaker J, LA de la Hunt and J Klaaren (Eds) (2008) *Advancing Refugee Protection in South Africa.* New York: Berghahn Books.

HSRC (2008) *Citizenship, Violence and Xenophobia in South Africa: Perceptions from South African Com-munities.* Pretoria: Human Sciences Research Council, Democracy and Governance Programme.

Kiwanuka M and T Monson (2009) Zimbabwean Migration into Southern Africa: New Trends and Responses. Johannesburg: Forced Migration Studies Programme, University of the Witwatersrand.

Kok P and M Collinson (2006) Migration and Urbanisation in South Africa. Report No: 03-04-02. Pretoria: Statistics South Africa.

Landau LB and I Freemantle (2010) Tactical Cosmopolitanism and Idioms of Belonging: Insertion and Self-Exclusion in Johannesburg. In *Journal of Ethnic and Migration Studies* 36 (3): 375-390.

Landau LB and V Gindrey (2008) Migration and Population Trends in Gauteng Province 1996-2055. Forced Migration Studies Programme Working Paper, 42. Available at www.migration.org.za.

Landau LB and JP Misago (2009) Who to blame and what's to gain: Reflections on space, state, and vio-lence in Kenya and South Africa. *Afrika Spectrum* 44 (1): 99-110.

Landau LB and A Wa Kabwe Segatti (2008) Human Development Impacts of Migration: South African Case Study. Human Development Research Paper 2009/5. New York: United Nations Develop-ment Programme (December).

McLennan A (2008) The academic/practitioner interface in public administration in South Africa: The early years - 1990 to 2000. Pretoria: DPSA.

Mendoza CA (2006) Structural causes and diffusion processes of collective violence: Understanding lynch mobs in post-conflict Guatemala. Latin American Studies Association San Juan, Puerto Rico, 15-18 March.

Misago JP (2009) *Violence, Labour and the Displacement of Zimbabweans in De Doorns, Western Cape.* Johannesburg: Forced Migration Studies Programme.

Misago JP, LB Landau and T Monson (2009) Towards Tolerance, Law, and Dignity: Addressing Violence against Foreign Nationals in South Africa. Report for the International Organisation of Migration (February 2009). Pretoria: International Organisation of Migration.

Parliament of the Republic of South Africa (2008) Report of the Task Team of Members of Parliament Probing Violence and Attacks on Foreign Nationals. Cape Town: Parliament of the Republic of South Africa.

Provincial Government of the Western Cape (2002) Migration Study in the Western Cape. Compiled by Simon B Bekker. Cape Town: Provincial Government of the Western Cape.

Polzer T (2008) Responding to Zimbabwean migration in South Africa: evaluating options. *South African Journal of International Affairs* 15 (1): 1-28.

Polzer T (2009) Immigration Policy Responses to Zimbabweans in South Africa: Implementing Special Temporary Permits. Background Paper prepared for a Roundtable at Southern Sun Hotel, Pretoria, 9 April 2009. Pretoria: Forced Migration Studies Programme and Lawyers for Human Rights.

Polzer T and D Breen (2009) Xenophobia: Highlighting South Africa's Faultlines. *South African Labour Bulletin.*

Posel D (1997[1991]) *The Making of Apartheid 1948-1961: Conflict and Compromise.* Oxford: Clarendon Paperbacks.

South African Cities Network (SACN) (2006) State of the Cities Report 2006. Johannesburg: South African Cities Network.

Tilly C (2004) Social Boundary Mechanisms. *Philosophy of the Social Sciences*, 34(2), 211-236.

Tomlinson R, RA Beauregard, L Bremner and X Mangcu (2003) The Post-apartheid struggle for an integrated Johannesburg. In Tomlinson R, RA Beauregard, L Bremner, and X Mangcu (Eds), *Emerging Johannesburg: Perspectives on the Postapartheid City.* New York: Routledge.

Wa Kabwe-Segatti A and C Fauvelle-Aymar (2009) Institutions, political participation and violence. Paper presented at Conference Exorcising the Demon Within: Xenophobia, Violence, and Statecraft in Contemporary South Africa (University of the Witwatersrand, Johannesburg, 22 May 2009).

Wa Kabwe-Segatti A, C Hoag and D Vigneswaran (2009) The Turnaround Strategy from below: public sector reform among South African Home Affairs migration officials in Johannesburg, Paper prepared for AEGIS Conference, Panel 20: States, public bureaucracies and civil servants: Organisational fields and actors' practices. Leipzig, 4-6 June 2009: Working Paper no. 109 on http://www.ifeas.uni-mainz.de/workingpapers/AP109.pdf.

White, M (2003) *Cities Transformed: Demographic Change and its Implications in the Developing World*. Washington: National Academy Press.

CHAPTER 10

South African female peacekeepers: An exploration of their experiences in the Democratic Republic of Congo

Maxi Schoeman, Lizle Loots and Kammila Naidoo

MEN ARE THE MILITARY; WOMEN ARE *IN* THE MILITARY[1]

For more than a decade South Africa has been an active participant in international peace-keeping. It is currently the thirteenth biggest troop-contributing country (TCC) to international peace missions, with the largest women's contingent deployed[2] and one of only a handful of countries incorporating women into combat positions in its military.

In 2010, the international community will commemorate the tenth anniversary of UN Resolution 1325 – the women, gender, peace and security resolution – which commits the UN to the mainstreaming of gender in all its peace-related activities. Yet there remains, in the words of Olsson and Tryggestad (2001:3) a 'gap in the knowledge concerning women and peacekeeping – as opposed to men and peacekeeping' (see also Sion 2008). This chapter explores the experiences of a small number of South African female peacekeepers in the Democratic Republic of Congo (DRC), counter balanced by the perceptions of their male colleagues. The research data is supplemented by insights provided by senior decision makers and other experts involved in peacekeeping training, as well as by the comments and discussions of female soldiers involved in the 2007 SANDF Women's Day Conference (WD Conference) organised around the theme Empowering Women for Gender Equity. The purpose is to evaluate the extent to which gender is being incorporated into the training and experience of peacekeepers and to identify the challenges and policy options in this regard in order to contribute to a body of knowledge on best practice, not only for South Africa's involvement in peacekeeping missions, but also for other countries.

In the first section, gender and gender mainstreaming in international peacekeeping is discussed. The second section deals with the methodology applied in this study, as well as with constraints and limitations to it, while section three presents and discusses the research findings based on the themes identified in the first section. A number of recommendations are provided in the conclusion.

GENDER MAINSTREAMING IN INTERNATIONAL PEACE MISSIONS

Resolution 1325,[3] adopted by the Security Council in October 2000, was an indication of the increasing importance at the time attached to the role and position of women in conflict, and in approaches to peacemaking, peacekeeping and peace-building. Although the Resolution is generally perceived to be a product of the Windhoek Declaration of May 2000 which contained the Namibia Plan of Action on Mainstreaming a Gender Perspective in Multidimensional Peace Support Operations',[4] its origins are to be found much earlier in the development sphere of the UN, and specifically in the UN's Decade for Women launched in 1975. In the Forward-Looking Strategies for the Advancement of Women adopted during the Third World Conference on Women, held in Nairobi in 1985, an explicit call was made for mainstreaming in all development programmes and projects. The difference between sex as a biologically defined characteristic and gender as a product of structural relations between men and women in society in terms of which roles and behavioural expectations are created (see Valenius 2007) and, importantly, as having a definitive and often negative impact on women, was one of the key insights that migrated from the development field into broader UN activities.

In the Beijing Report of the Fourth World Conference on Women, held in 1995, gender mainstreaming is presented as the preferred strategy to redress women's inequality and subordination in twelve identified critical areas, including armed conflict. Throughout the Beijing Platform for Action document (1995), reference is made to gender mainstreaming: 'Governments and other actors should promote an active and visible policy of mainstreaming a gender perspective in all policies and programmes, so that, before decisions are taken, an analysis is made of the effects for women and men, respectively'.[5] The ECOSOC definition (1997) of gender mainstreaming cited below became the basis for most institutional commitments, particularly within the UN system:

> Mainstreaming a gender perspective is the process of assessing the implications for women and men of any planned action, including legislation, policies or programmes, in all areas and at all levels. It is a strategy for making women's as well as men's concerns and experiences an integral dimension of the design, implementation, monitoring and evaluation of policies and programmes in all political, economic and societal spheres so that women and men benefit equally and inequality is not perpetuated. The ultimate goal is to achieve gender equality.

By 2000, the concept 'gender mainstreaming' had also made its way into the Security Council and had culminated in the adoption of Resolution 1325 with its twin focuses on women as subjects (its recognition of the contribution of women to conflict resolution and sustainable peace and a call for the inclusion of more women into peacekeeping operations) and as objects (its recognition of the negative impact of war on women – and children). The Resolution stressed the importance of the full participation of women in peace processes, including in decision making positions and peace operations, and urged member states to support gender mainstreaming in all activities related to peace support. However, despite the initial attraction of the concept 'gender mainstreaming' owing to its apparent concreteness (and therefore susceptibility to bureaucratic strategies), attempts at implementation have overall been disappointing when measured against the actual realities of women's lives in many parts of the world.

The idea of gender mainstreaming speaks directly to one of the core paradoxes around women and their status and position in society, 'whether women's rights are best protected through general norms or through specific norms applicable only to women' (Charlesworth 2005:1). Apart from this paradox and, for the purpose of this study, more specifically within the realm of peace and security, the debate is about equality versus difference; that is, whether in this realm gender mainstreaming is or should be about promoting and ensuring gender equality or about 'bringing women in' because as women they have special qualities and needs. It would seem that, at least as far as the UN's approach to the matter is concerned, attention is paid to both. With reference to the former, a senior UN DPKO (Department of Peacekeeping Operations) official commented during a discussion about the inclusion of women in peace operations and with reference to the fact that only 8 per cent of police officers in peace missions are women: 'Do you know of a society that is 92 per cent male?' (UN International Research and Training Institute for the Advancement of Women or INSTRAW 2009a).

The theme of women having some special affinity with peace is, according to some authors, a 'staple of women in peace-building literature' (Charlesworth 2008:349) and is often highlighted by the UN. So, for instance, during the commemoration of the International Day of Peacekeepers in May 2009, the UN Secretary General stressed the 'unique role played by women in peace keeping missions' (INSTRAW 2009b). Yet, in the words of Charlesworth (2005:11), 'almost a decade of gender mainstreaming practice has revealed its limited impact'. This 'limited impact' is best revealed in the number of women involved in peace missions and in the lack of understanding of what gender as a social construct implies.

The number of women peacekeepers internationally has hardly changed since 2000, with the exception of the civilian component of peacekeeping which now boasts 25 per cent (United Nations 2005). The lack of progress in appointing women to leadership and decisionmaking positions is of special concern. By mid-2008 only one out of thirty-seven special representatives of the UN Secretary General was a woman (Ministry of Foreign Affairs of Denmark 2008) and on average only 2.4 per cent of signatories to peace agreements are women – no woman hase been appointed chief or lead peace mediator in UN-sponsored peace talks (United Nations Development Fund for Women or UNIFEM 2009). By late 2008, only thirty-four out of 1 215 staff officers in UN missions were women. This number had increased marginally to fifty-one out of 1 532 by August 2009.

But problems related to gender mainstreaming go beyond head-counting, however important numbers are (as will be argued below). Gender seems to remain inherently linked to – and is 'mistaken' to – refer only to women. The UN secretary general's report on Resolution 1820 (2008) concerning sexual violence against civilians in conflict zones (United Nations Security Council 2009) deals almost exclusively with women and girls as victims of sexual violence: women remain the victims, and objects of concern. Almost more worrying is the lack of understanding that gender mainstreaming entails changes in values and social behaviour and, in the realm of security, a different understanding of what protection means. Nowhere perhaps is this lack of genuine change in understanding and implementation of security better illustrated than in the secretary general's aforementioned report in which he describes one of the 'success stories' in diminishing the threat of sexual violence to women: refugees in Iridimi camp in Chad were provided fuel-efficient stoves, reducing 'the need to leave the camp in search of firewood, thus improving the security of women and girls' (United Nations Security Council 2009: paragraph 50).[6]

Several interconnected reasons for the limited impact of gender mainstreaming in peace and security could be advanced and these constitute the broad themes explored in this study.

- The first is that the main obligation for mainstreaming gender is placed on national governments. As is so often the case with the UN, the organisation's activities are largely constrained by, and dependent on, the extent to which member states implement the various agreements, resolutions and commitments they adopt. Unless member states cooperate and implement their UN commitments and agreements, these will remain in many cases part only of a vocabulary, and not of practice.

- Second, and a pervasive problem, is the fact that gender is regularly equated with women. This leads to an over-emphasis on women, rather than on strategies for change. It tends to 'ghettoise' women as a category of victims with little, if any, agency, and therefore in need of protection. This approach reinforces some of the very stereotypes that gender mainstreaming aims to change: women as passive and as victims; men as violent, but also as protectors.

- Third, despite 'paper commitments', gender activities within peace missions, such as dedicated gender offices, are often under-resourced and marginalised.

- Fourth, 'successful' gender mainstreaming, whether perceived from an equality per spective or a utility perspective (the women's 'affinity to peace' perspective), requires a critical mass of women across all levels of peace operations, including, importantly, decision making positions.

- Fifth, the issue of gender training and awareness raising has received much attention in various UN documents but has remained rather elusive as regards exactly what it should encompass and how progress should be measured.

These broad themes[7] inform this study and the attempt to verify whether and to what extent these problems are reflected in the experiences of South African peacekeepers (specifically female peacekeepers) and relevant decision makers.

METHODOLOGY

This study is exploratory in nature. Little empirical research has been conducted on the experiences of South African peacekeepers and on the gender aspects of such involvement in peacekeeping operations. Pillay's study (2006), based on a comparison between the United Nations Observer Mission to South Africa (UNOMSA) in the early 1990s as the country was preparing for its first democratic elections, and the United Nations Organisation Mission in the Democratic Republic of the Congo (MONUC), is a literature review aimed at examining transformation opportunities for gender equality (as a requirement for a just peace). It provides little empirical information on the issue of gender in peacekeeping or the challenges confronting female peacekeepers in complex missions. Higate's comparative study of gender and peacekeeping in the DRC and Sierra Leone (2004) focuses mainly on the relations of male peacekeepers with local women. Although one of his recommendations is that peacekeeping operations should include more female peacekeepers, especially in military and police components, he does not deal with female peacekeepers as such. More recently, Monica Juma (2009) has published an overview of efforts made to increase the numbers of women and their effectiveness in the defence sectors of African countries, focusing on Southern Africa. Her study does not pay specific attention to peacekeeping though, and deals with South Africa as only one of the countries considered. There is therefore a dearth of information and scholarship regarding the role and experiences, from a gender perspective, of South African peacekeepers. Overall, little is available on female peacekeepers in African defence forces, with the notable exception of the study of the Ghanaian Defence Force by Afrim-Narh (2006).

In order to gather information on the topic we used different sources, focusing mainly on accessing the perceptions and opinions of those most directly involved in peacekeeping – men and women deployed in peacekeeping operations, and senior decision makers involved in gender mainstreaming and the planning of South African participation in peace operations. We employed questionnaires (Loots 2009) and conducted a number of in-depth unstructured interviews. The research data was supplemented with insights and information gathered from official reports and documents and secondary sources with the aim of identifying a number of initial broad themes that would allow for the development of a comprehensive research proposal. The present study is therefore largely an opportunity to open up a field that is under-researched, despite its importance across a spectrum of ideas, ideals and objectives, and one that is poorly understood within the military itself. In fact, the main impression gained from the interviews with senior staff officers was that there was a serious commitment to developing a better understanding of, and to improve, gender mainstreaming across the SANDF as a whole.

The sample group consisted of sixty-three peacekeepers at the Mthatha infantry base in the Eastern Cape (the only base at which recently returned female peacekeepers from the DRC were available); forty-seven were male and sixteen female. This ratio of roughly thirty-three per cent women and sixty-six per cent men was considered adequate, as women make up approximately 21 per cent of the SANDF, and as peacekeepers, less than 5 per cent of those deployed.[8] Given the small number of participants, we do not claim that the findings can be generalised, but that the information gathered does contribute to knowledge about, and an understanding of, the experiences of peacekeepers, while it also serves to open up themes requiring further investigation.

The questionnaires were administered during October 2007. The main problem encountered in the administration of the questionnaires was that fewer respondents were available than had been anticipated because several had been sent to another military base for further training while yet other recently demobilised peacekeepers had returned home. This in itself made it clear that conducting this kind of field research among groups of peacekeepers who had returned from a tour of duty would be very difficult and we aim to conduct further fieldwork within such missions.

Questionnaires were completed anonymously and without any interference from senior officers. From the outset it was decided to include male and female peacekeepers in the questionnaire. The reason was twofold: we wished to avoid the trap of 'gender = women' by exploring their experiences in isolation, and we also wished to gauge male peacekeepers' perceptions of their female colleagues. In this way it is possible to create a fuller understanding of how the issue of gender plays out within a mission and to provide a corrective or balance to the women's perceptions of their experiences. The assumption was that males and females do not necessarily share the same opinions about their experiences and this was to some extent borne out, as will be discussed in a later section.

The first constraint is the fact that the sample group was relatively small. In order to generalise despite the small size of the group, we supplemented the findings with interviews with decision makers, and compared the findings with available literature on the topic. A second constraint was a lack of time and opportunity, given the busy schedules and other circumstances of the peacekeepers who participated in the administration of the questionnaire. Lastly, this study focuses only on the military component of peacekeeping, and not on the police or civilian components, and its findings and recommendations can therefore not necessarily be taken as representative of the full scope of peacekeeping.[9]

FINDINGS AND DISCUSSION

The findings of the study, together with a discussion and interpretation of the data, are presented in this section, structured along the broad themes identified in section one above.

Gender mainstreaming in peace missions as a national obligation, and the question of a critical mass

Even though implementation of the constitutional principles of non-racialism and non-sexism (see following sub-section) in the SANDF has been slow, progress has nevertheless been comprehensive and far-reaching. According to the SANDF Annual Review for 2007/2008, 21 per cent of its uniformed staff are women, showing an initial steady increase over time. However, the 20 per cent level was already reached in 2002 (Heinecken 2002)[10] – moving beyond this ceiling is clearly difficult and seems to pose a serious challenge to the SANDF. Furthermore, the absence of women in senior decision making positions is also generally acknowledged as being problematic: only five out of twenty-nine top management positions were in 2008 occupied by women (Department of Defence 2007/2008:187), although it should be added that cabinet head of the Ministry of Defence is currently a woman, Lindiwe Sisulu, demonstrating the government's commitment to gender equality. Participation of women in peacekeeping deployment is substantially lower than 21 per cent, although well above the international average according to senior SANDF staff interviewed. Unfortunately no hard figures were provided. Worldwide, though, such figures are low. In 2007, less than 2 per cent of the military component of MONUC was female (Hendricks and Hutton 2008). As to overall UN peace missions, 8 per cent of police officers are women and 2 per cent of military personnel are women. Clearly, expanding the numbers of women in peace missions is an international challenge.

That gender mainstreaming has been officially adopted within the SANDF is not least due to the country's obligation vis-à-vis the requirements of Resolution 1325. During the course of 2009, thirty gender officers were appointed and one of them was deployed to the DRC, but the precise objective of these appoitments was unclear, and in answer to the question the researcher was informed that they were 'responsible for gender mainstreaming' and supporting female peacekeepers in particular. However, the detail or 'job description' was not provided, although it was envisaged that these gender officers would provide feedback that would enable the SANDF to mainstream gender throughout the force and particularly in peace missions. It should be pointed out that the purpose of events such as the WD Conference is largely to gather information about the requirements for gender mainstreaming, although it would seem that the emphasis is perhaps largely on women soldiers and peacekeepers, rather than on gender *per se*. The extent to which, and the way in which, gender is being mainstreamed in the country's involvement in peace missions, is a topic that needs investigation in more detail.[11]

In the South African case, and we assume also in many other instances, there are a number of reasons for the apparent lack of success in attracting women to participate in peace missions (keeping in mind that such peace missions usually comprise volunteers).[12] One would be that the perception of women as 'inferior' to men within a military context is a deeply ingrained stereotype and the data collector encountered this attitude throughout informal and background discussions with male soldiers. It was pointed out to her that women were not 'mentally strong' and could therefore not be expected to be deployed in combat or dangerous situations. Female peacekeepers who participated in the WD Conference implicitly confirmed this stereotyped perception of women by complaining about 'anti-retention strategies' ('being expressly discouraged from volunteering for deployment by their senior ranks').

A second reason is the low number of women in the defence force. This means that the pool from which to recruit female peacekeepers is small. Even though South Africa can boast the world's largest contingent of women deployed as peacekeepers, this is still only a small percentage of the total number of peacekeepers participating in peace missions supported by South Africa. Several decision makers interviewed pointed to the problem of recruiting women into the defence force and it is clear that current recruiting strategies are not successful. One of the potential problems, though, is a 'double-edged sword': in order to build the necessary critical mass of women to facilitate genuine gender mainstreaming, an institution loses sight of the purpose of increasing the number of women in its ranks and starts to emphasise 'head counting', which according to Charlesworth (2005:13) can reduce the whole effort to a 'token exercise'. This needs to be pursued further in follow-up interviews and survey research, to find out whether women in the field believe that their status and position (and therefore level and nature of participation in peace missions) would be improved should the number of women increase. Women at the WD Conference emphasised the need for more women in senior positions (officers and warrant officers) and the establishment of 'an acceptable' quota of women for deployment in peace missions.

GENDER EQUALITY WITHIN PEACE MISSIONS

The two core principles on which the South African constitution (1996: article 1) is founded are those of non-racialism and non-sexism. The approach is clearly that of equality as a solution to what is recognised and acknowledged as inherent and structural differences between the sexes. Placing non-sexism on an equal footing with non-racialism recognises the role that South African women played in the anti-apartheid struggle and were expected to continue to play in the trans-formation of the country (see Anderlini 2004), and it also recognises that their status and position in society are influenced and determined by structures of subordination and patriarchy which had been exacerbated by apartheid. By emphasising these values we are not claiming that the country has managed to 'shift society' and to attain a full equality that addresses the inferior status and position of women in a male dominated society. Rather, the argument is that these values are enshrined in the constitution and have been used as guidelines for action and transformation, with increasing attention to the inclusion of women in decision-making positions. In this regard, the following statistics are relevant: 41 per cent of cabinet ministers and 39 per cent of deputy ministers in the current Zuma administration are women. Five out of nine (56 per cent) of provin-cial premiers and 44 per cent of parliamentarians are women. Women occupy a number of key cabinet positions (and not only portfolios traditionally associated with 'soft' issues) such as International Relations and Cooperation (formerly Foreign Affairs), Home Affairs, Defence and Veteran Affairs, and Correctional Services.

These core principles have informed the transformation and democratisation process in South Africa, not least in the country's security sector where, in the case of the SANDF, the past fifteen years have witnessed concerted efforts to transform the defence force into a force characterised by professionalism, and representative of the demographic realities of the country. At the same time, and like many other militaries, South Africa moved from conscription to a professional defence force in the 1990s, also as part of efforts to downscale (or 'right size', in the jargon of the time) the SANDF. This meant that force numbers declined significantly over time: in 2000 the figure was 82 000 but by the end of 2007 it was 75 000. Downsizing has had to be pursued in concert with attempts to increase the number of women in the SANDF.

Do female peacekeepers believe that they are equal to their male counterparts and that they are being treated equally? And how do male peacekeepers perceive the issue of equality? The data obtained from the questionnaires provide mixed results: Only four of the sixteen women peacekeepers indicated that they felt their roles and responsibilities were different from those of their male colleagues; sixteen out of forty-seven male peacekeepers believed that the women were treated differently during deployment. The majority of women and men perceived women's participation as being 'equal', although this might need further probing, for what exactly is understood by equal/different treatment? Here one could contrast some of the responses to an open question in which participants were asked to explain why they thought male/female roles and responsibilities differed or did not differ. One woman answered: 'I was excluded from gaining the experience of driving on difficult and long roads as they said I am female. That held me back from gaining a lot of experience and making me believe more in me and my abilities.' Another woman responded: '... ladies were not allowed to go outside to make peace. We were always in the base and doing base duties like maintenance and guard duty'. There were several similar responses.

From men who participated: 'There were definitely differences because most of the ladies were not going out for operations', and '... female peacekeepers were not available or supplied for patrols and escort duties'. One man noted that 'female peacekeepers were ordered to stay in the base'. The latter comment creates the impression that the difference in treatment was ordered by senior officers, and although this has not been verified it does confirm what one of the interviewees (involved in peacekeeping training) emphasised: that 'everything depends on the leader ... leadership determines how a base is run and who does what and if an officer does not think that women are capable, he will not allow them to become involved.'[13]

As to feelings of acceptance, the majority of the women (fourteen out of sixteen) felt that they had been accepted by their male colleagues, whereas twenty-eight of the male respondents (59 per cent of the male sample) indicated that they found the inclusion of women in their ranks 'acceptable'. There would therefore seem to be some discrepancy between the two groups, though the reasons why women were considered less acceptable by their male colleagues while they perceived themselves to be accepted would have to be probed further, as would the reasons why a relatively large percentage of the male soldiers did not feel that women were acceptable.[14]

Women also felt that their male counterparts did not deal any better with stress than they themselves did, whereas men were rather non-committal on this question. Of interest though is the fact that more than half the male respondents admitted to experiencing fear or threat to their personal safety while on deployment, compared with only six of the women (40 per cent). This might be because men were more exposed to danger than were women , and given the difference in responsibilities discussed above, this would be understandable, but it also points to the fact that these peacekeepers were not treated equally. It would seem that men are still believed to be responsible for dangerous missions, and women for lending 'background' support. During the interviews with senior staff, though, the researcher was informed that women are deployed in exactly the same positions as men, bearing the same responsibilities and facing the same threats as male peacekeepers. Some of these findings need to be explored further.

Two final points regarding equality could be made. During the WD Conference and especially during discussions in breakaway groups, the issue of women's 'special needs', especially in terms of hygiene, was regularly raised and discussed. The general feeling was that in order to encourage women to volunteer for deployment in peace missions, attention should be paid to these needs and to the fact that facilities in bases were not accommodating of them This point is often used to argue that women are not equal to men in the realm of the military and that their presence could create a burden or an obstacle to efficiency and 'getting the job done'. However, this is to miss the point that reaching equality is exactly about levelling the playing field, and making it possible for women to participate equally.

Second, in discussions with social workers and other interviewees, especially at the base in Mthatha, it was pointed out that both male and female peacekeepers experience similar problems 'back home' while they are on deployment and upon their return. Many peacekeepers volunteer for deployment because it is lucrative and their objective is often to strengthen their finances. But many complain that upon return they found that their spouses had used large amounts of this money without their knowledge, and they felt frustrated and helpless. Another problem is that extramarital affairs often develop during deployment (which usually last six months), resulting in problems upon their return, and sometimes ending in divorce. A third problem is that of stress and trauma upon their return, especially for those who had been deployed in complex missions such as MONUC in the Eastern DRC. Again, such experiences place stress on family and marital relations. During interviews with senior officers the possibility of arranging home visits while on deployment was mentioned as one possible option to deal with at least some of these problems. Several respondents pointed out, though, that post-deployment debriefing and counselling were not necessarily efficiently organised and capable of identifying potential problems. Although social workers and psychologists are usually deployed in order to provide emotional and other support and counselling to peacekeepers, these problems often only manifest once the peacekeepers have returned home. A question that springs to mind is whether 'mixed' support groups post-deployment could be useful both in providing opportunities for sharing experiences and advice, and in cultivating a sense of 'similarity' between male and female peacekeepers.

WOMEN'S AFFINITY WITH – AND THEREFORE USEFULNESS TO – PEACE

As discussed in section two, Resolution 1325 rests, at least partly and implicitly, on the assumption that women have a certain affinity with peace, and that their presence in various efforts to resolve conflict peacefully (whether at the peace table, or in peace missions, or in post-conflict reconstruction and development) facilitates such processes. It is in the exploration of this point that the distinction made between women as objects (those who suffer most in war) and women as subjects (those who can 'assist') comes together. It should be pointed out, though, that this is, or should also be, the point at which special attention should be paid to the issue of gender mainstreaming. It should not only be the responsibility of women peace-keepers to bring 'special qualities' to the process, but rather (and especially, given that bringing more women into peacekeeping is proving to be so difficult), that these qualities, where pos-sible, should be instilled in all peacekeepers. This is obviously not a 'blanket recommendation' – available literature on the role of women peacekeepers makes it clear that women peace-keepers are perceived to fulfil at least three specific roles as women (moving beyond an 'add women and stir' approach). The first is that they are required for very specific tasks that also sometimes have a bearing on cultural differences. Some of these tasks involve facilitating investigations of gender-based violence (Gist 2009), performing body searches on women, interrogation of women and intelligence gathering amongst local women. Women are often considered to be 'more approachable and less threatening' by local populations (including local men) (see Hendricks and Hutton 2008).

A second role ascribed to women peacekeepers is that of serving as 'monitors of excessive behaviour among male soldiers' (Hendricks and Hutton 2008:4). As Valenius (2007) points out, the assumption that women can somehow act as 'civilisers' of male behaviour is dubious both in terms of its efficacy, and morally, as it implies a shift of responsibility for men's conduct to women. This issue was not taken up in either the questionnaire or the unstructured interviews, but might be worth investigating, especially as the involvement of male peace-keepers in gender-based violence has increasingly gained international attention. One of the interviewees mentioned that South Africa initially encountered problems in this regard, but that things 'have been improving'. No further information was forthcoming, though, and it was clearly considered a sensitive issue.[15] The researchers are of the opinion that the topic will only be pursued fruitfully if and when a relationship of trust has developed between the research team and senior decision makers in the SANDF.

A third role ascribed to female peacekeepers is that of serving as role models to the local population. Both the first and third roles point to the direct contact between women as subjects and as objects. It could be argued that it is in these spheres in particular, that the inclusion of women in peace missions becomes imperative. If one assumes that changing gender relations is crucial to building lasting peace, then the symbolic presence of women in peace missions ('conquering the ultimate male bastion'), tasked with keeping peace and assisting in post-conflict reconstruction and development becomes crucial to change in conflict and post-conflict societies.[16] Several authors have commented on the fact that the deployment of an all-female police contingent (from India) in the peace mission in Liberia had resulted in a three-fold increase in the number of women applicants to the local police service within the first year of deployment (see Guehénno 2007). The majority of the women respondents in our study indicated that they had had contact with local women. This contact was largely confined to socialising (for instance celebrating public holidays together) and trading, though some were also involved in activities such as handing out books. Their male counterparts confirmed the perception that the women peacekeepers were inclined to interact socially with local women and to form friendships with them. The majority of the women believed that the local population was more trusting of them (nine out of sixteen), yet the majority of the male soldiers did not agree (twenty-eight out of forty-seven). The reason for this difference in perceptions is not clear, though one could entertain the possibility of competition between male and female peacekeepers: males would probably not want to admit to being less trusted and less important to a mission. The different skills that men and women bring to peacekeeping might be something on which pre-deployment training could focus.

Asked about why they thought local women were more trusting of them, it became clear that the women peacekeepers believed that they communicated more easily with local women than their male counterparts.[17] Yet they were much more ambivalent when it came to issues of 'make local women feel safer' and 'control violent tendencies more efficiently': only six out of sixteen felt that their presence made local women feel safer and only four out of sixteen believed that they could control violence more efficiently than male peacekeepers. These results point to a level of uncertainty about, or a lack of confidence in, their roles as peacekeepers and is another issue that should be further investigated. One explanation could relate to their positions within the mission (as has been pointed out, these women were largely confined to base), for by implication there was little expectation that they would play a 'front' role. This raises questions about the extent to which women who are deployed are in fact utilised for the purpose of their inclusion. Nevertheless, ten out of the sixteen women respondents believed that they had made a difference to the lives of those local women with whom they had come into contact, even 'if only' by offering advice. One peacekeeper commented that she had taught local women 'to believe in themselves and being able to fight for their rights and know that women are the flowers of the country so they should be treated with respect, honour and dignity'.[18] Another respondent stated that '[the local women] look up to us now and know that they can also do what their men do'.

There is, however, also a slightly different perspective to the assumption that women have a natural affinity with peace. Asked why they had volunteered, respondents were given four options to choose from: humanitarian, financial, career aspirations and SANDF instruction. The majority of the respondents, male and female, indicated that they had been deployed 'on instruction of the SANDF'. Interestingly though, of the remaining respondents, more men indicated that they had volunteered for humanitarian reasons (fourteen out of forty-seven) than women (three out of sixteen), and more women (five out of sixteen) than men (five out of forty-seven) chose financial reasons. Does this indicate that women are more interested in volunteering for financial gain and that men are more inspired by the 'good that they can do'? As already mentioned, the sample was too small to be used as a basis for generalisation, yet one factor does seem to have some explanatory value: age. In both categories (male and female), the majority fell into the age group twenty to twenty-nine years (thirty-eight out of sixty-three) with more women in this age group (which also contained the more junior ranks such as riflemen). The male respondents who indicated that they had volunteered for humanitarian reasons were largely in the age group thirty to thirty-nine, though not necessarily in higher ranks than the women. Could it be that more mature soldiers are more inclined to volunteer for deployment in peace missions and for reasons directly related to the nature of the work? If so, this might have consequences for recruiting strategies.

Training, learning and awareness issues

Gender mainstreaming is often conceived of as a question of training: building on Resolution 1325 as a point of departure (and justification), a series of training programmes has been developed focusing on gender training or training for gender mainstreaming in peace missions (see for instance DCAF *et al* 2007 and Lyytikinen 2007). Predeployment peacekeeping training is the responsibility of the TCCs while troops usually receive context-specific training upon arrival in the country of mission. As is the case with most TCCs, South African peacekeepers receive gender training as part of their pre-deployment preparation. Preparation for deployment in the SANDF lasts forty-two days, and one week (five days) of this period is spent on a 'training for peace' course which includes half a day on gender issues.

An interesting point about the responses received to questions about gender training and gender awareness was the fact that more males than females seemed to be familiar with the content of Resolution 1325. This gap, and lack of knowledge about a resolution that is crucial to bringing a gender perspective into issues of war, peace and security, was also obvious during discussions at the WD conference of August 2007. Significantly, when asked whether they had been given any information on Resolution 1325 and/or women's issues during the pre-deployment phase, only 35 per cent of the respondents (slightly more males than females) answered 'yes'. The low indication of awareness of Resolution 1325 or of gender issues, or even of women's issues in a peacekeeping setting, might be attributable to a lack of clarity in the questionnaire; the relevant questions would have to be revised for future research. At the same time, the low level of awareness does to some extent correlate with the opinions of some of the interviewees, most notably those involved in pre-deployment training and planning. Apart from noting that too little time was spent on gender issues during training (and then also only as a 'separate' issue – gender as such has not yet permeated training in any way that could be referred to as 'mainstreaming'), one interviewee noted that course material was superficial (the researchers did not have an opportunity to examine the course material, but flagged the issue for future reference). Another interviewee emphasised the importance of focusing on leadership, that is, that decision makers should receive in-depth gender training.

As mentioned, South Africa is one of only a handful of countries to allow women to serve in combat positions and a large part of the pre-deployment training is spent on more 'traditional' training exercises, perhaps indicating the extent to which peace operations are perceived to be a military operation (along the lines of 'war-making') rather than constituting a completely different paradigm. Yet one should perhaps also keep in mind that many peace missions in Africa are complex and call for a measure of 'robust' peacekeeping. What remains clear is that gender awareness and training for understanding the importance of gender – both in the countries of mission and in the missions as such – and promoting gender mainstreaming, receive relatively little attention in terms of scope and depth.

CONCLUSION

The research data clearly points to four areas in which much attention is due: decision making, training, recruitment and debriefing.[19] First, without a strategic plan for increasing the number of women in senior decision-making positions, it is doubtful whether gender can genuinely be mainstreamed in peace operations.

Second, gender as a social construct placing – and keeping – women in an inferior position has been historically pervasive in the vast majority of societies and was further reinforced, and skewed, in the developing world by colonialism and, in South Africa, through apartheid. It would be utopian to expect the power relations constructed through gender to change overnight. Although it has become passé to argue that deep social changes take time, it remains largely true, and one could argue that genuine gender mainstreaming – as a process, policy and end goal – is a long-term process that depends largely on education within a favourable epistemic environment. From this it would follow that specific attention should be paid to the country's education system and the values informing it and transmitted through it. Such a recommendation is, of course, not only pertinent to South Africa, but to the majority of countries, and then especially TCCs . Furthermore, gender training as part of efforts to mainstream gender within peace missions and the military is of crucial importance and could be enhanced through the content and methodology used in training programmes and syllabuses (see Olsson and Tejpar 2009). Of specific importance is training the leadership cadre of peace missions, for in the end, gender mainstreaming succeeds – or fails – on the basis of the attitude and approach of a mission's leadership. Even the appointment of special gender advisers will not contribute significantly to mainstreaming unless the leadership is well-informed, supportive and conscious of the benefits attached to gender mainstreaming.

Third, recruitment strategies to attract more women, both into the SANDF and into volunteering for deployment in peace missions, are crucial for attaining the necessary critical mass that would allow women to contribute to the 'deep' success of peace missions. Profiling women soldiers in the media and conducting targeted recruitment activities at universities are but two ways of attracting more women to the SANDF. Within the armed forces well-communicated efforts to make women soldiers aware of the need for their presence and the ways in which they could contribute to mission success might go a long way in encouraging volunteers.

Finally, something that requires serious attention is the lesson learned: how is knowledge harvested and how is this knowledge, based on the experience of men and women peacekeepers, ploughed back in order to build on it and to improve performance in the widest sense of the word? One of the interviewees commented that 'the big problem' was that there was a system in place, but it was 'not functioning properly'. This is a subject demanding separate study, but what could be mentioned here is that the experience of peacekeepers, both male and female, of their circumstances within the base and the challenges encountered there, and of the environment in which they were deployed, could (and should) be of crucial importance to mission design, planning, training and deployment. As such, the 'lessons learned' component of the peacekeeping process is a *sine qua non* of success, but also of recognising the contribution of women. Talking to them to find out what their experiences are and what can be learned from them is not only a useful way of gathering information and building expertise, but is also a way of showing respect for their contribution. Something that came up several times in discussions with women who had been deployed was how pleased they were to be asked about their experiences. It is worth quoting one of these women: 'Thank you ... it was great and it really made me realise how much I am worth in the world'.

Peacekeeping falls into a paradigm that differs completely from the traditional male-dominated approach to dealing with military affairs and, as such, creates a window of opportunity for the inclusion of women and the development of an ethos that includes all members of society on an equal basis. The very tasks and functions of peacekeepers demand a much bigger and more prominent role for women in all aspects of these missions. Sound and positive recruitment strategies, comprehensive training, the full inclusion of women in all facets of these missions and a debriefing process that would harvest knowledge and pay respect to peacekeepers would contribute not only to more successful peace operations, but in the long-term to more healthy and inclusive societies representative of the needs and aspirations of all their people.

NOTES

1 Comment by a female peacekeeper.
2 The terms 'peace missions', 'peacekeeping' and 'peace support operations' are used interchangeably in this study, as are the terms 'women/men peacekeepers' and 'male/female' peacekeepers.
3 For the full text of Resolution 1325, see www.peacewoman.org/un/sc/1325.html.
4 The Windhoek Declaration and the Plan of Action (2000) were adopted during a seminar of the Lessons Learned Unit of the UNDPKO (Department of Peacekeeping Operations) held in Windhoek, Namibia, in commemoration of the tenth anniversary of the United Nations Transitional Assistance Group (UNTAG).
5 'Beijing Declaration and Platform for Action' in *Report of the Fourth World Conference on Women*, July 1985. www.un.org/womenwatch/daw/beijing/ [accessed 15 September 2009].
6 This incident is illustrative of a broader problem-solving approach in which the *status quo* in terms of gender relations is implicitly accepted and adjusted to solve an immediate problem, not to address the underlying reasons for the existence of these threats and behaviour.
7 These are by no means the only areas of importance, but space constraints prevent a broader exploration in this study.
8 Initially the researcher was informed that 100 peacekeepers would be available as a sample group, but upon arrival in Mthatha it turned out that several soldiers, including women soldiers, had been sent to another camp for further training.
9 The second phase of this project will explore the experiences of South African female police officers deployed in peace missions, with the focus on the mission in Sudan.
10 In 1989, according to Heinecken (2002:719), only 10 per cent of the uniformed staff of the (then) South African Defence Force (SADF) were women, increasing to 13 per cent by 2000 and 20 per cent by 2002.
11 In its *Annual Review* (Department of Defence 2007/2008:70), mention is made of the fact that the Department of Defence (DOD) had participated in the drafting of the Revised White Paper on South African Participation in Peace Support Operations and that this participation 'has resulted in the mainstreaming of gender in peace support operations'. However, the Revised White Paper is not yet available to the public (October 2009) and this was the only reference to gender main-streaming in the Report.
12 Some of the respondents to the questionnaires indicated that they had been 'instructed to volunteer'.
13 Note the 'automatic' use of 'he' in this response – it is assumed that a commanding officer is/would be male.
14 Roughly 40 per cent of the men indicated that women's involvement and participation in peace missions were not 'acceptable'. These findings conform to those of a survey conducted for the SANDF's Equal Opportunities Chief Directorate in 1999 in which 41 per cent of male respondents indicated that they did not believe women had the ability to serve in combat roles, as opposed to only 28 per cent of women respondents agreeing. See Heinecken (2002: 722). This leads to the question whether there has been any change in men's perceptions of women in the defence sector over the past decade.
15 Sexual abuse and violence committed by peacekeepers is a sensitive topic for all troop-contributing countries. See Simic (2009).

16 It is worthwhile to quote at length from the UN DPKO annual review of 2006: 'The increased level of women serving … combined with the establishment of gender offices to ensure the integration of a gender perspective into all aspects of peacekeeping – has contributed to the empowerment of women in countries hosting peacekeeping missions. These gains can be seen in the fact that in these … countries, more women are voting and running for office. Constitutions are being revised to uphold the principle of equal rights of women and girls; discriminatory legislation is being revised; women's advocacy groups are being strengthened; women are becoming increasingly represented in the police and civil service' (UN DPKO 2006).

17 There are various references in the literature to the role of women in peacekeeping, confirming that women are 'better communicators'. See for example Anderlini (2004: 33). However, this literature usually also points to women peacekeepers as having a 'greater capacity to mitigate violence than men' – something not confirmed in this study.

18 This reference to women as the 'flower/s of the country/nation' is one that is regularly used in connection with and by the women who were members of the ANC's military wing, Umkhonto we Sizwe (MK).

19 These issues will be dealt with in more detail in forthcoming publications from this project.

REFERENCES

Afrim-Narh A (2006) Gender integration and international peacekeeping: the case of the Ghana armed forces. Thesis submitted to the Department of Political Science in partial fulfillment of the Master of Philosophy degree in Peace and Conflict Studies, University of Oslo.

Anderlini S (2004) Negotiating the transition to democracy and reforming the security sector: the vital contributions of South African women, August. Women Waging Peace Policy Coalition. www.iav.nl/epublications/2004 [accessed 10 September 2009].

Charlesworth H (2005) Not waving but drowning: gender mainstreaming and human rights in the United Nations. *Harvard Human Rights Journal* 18: 1-18.

Charlesworth H (2008) Are women peaceful? Reflections on the role of women in peace-building. *Feminist Legal Studies* 16: 347-361.

DCAF/INSTRAW/OSCE-ODHR (2007) Good and bad practices in gender training for security sector personnel – summary of a virtual discussion. Vienna: DCAF: 1-19.

Department of Defence (2008) Annual Report 2007/2008. Pretoria: Department of Defence.

ECOSOC (1997) Report of the Economic and Social Council for the year 1997. New York: United Nations.

Gist L (2009) United Nations attempts to recruit additional female peacekeeping police. August www.examiner.com/x -16503- LA County Foreign Policy Examiner-y2009m8d [accessed 21 September 2009].

Guehénno J-M (2007) Statement by the Under-Secretary-General for Peacekeeping Operations, Mr Jean-Marie Guehénno during the Security Council open debate on the implementation of Resolution 1325 (2000) on Women, Peace and Security. www.peacekeepingbestpractices.unlo.org [accessed 7 September 2009].

Heinecken L (2002) Affirming gender equality: the challenges facing the South African armed forces. *Current Sociology* 50 (5): 715–728.

Hendricks C and L Hutton (2008) Defence reform and gender. In Bastick M and K Valasek (Eds) *Gender and Security Sector Reform Toolkit*. Geneva: DCAF, OSCE/ODIHR, UN-INSTRAW 1–36.

Higate P (2004) Gender and peacekeeping: case studies of the Democratic Republic of the Congo and Sierra Leone. Pretoria: Institute for Security Studies Monograph No 91, March.

INSTRAW (2009a) UN official calls for more female peacekeepers. 10 March. www.un-instraw.org [accessed 11 September 2009].

INSTRAW (2009b) Secretary-General highlighted importance of female peacekeepers. 29 May. www.un-instraw.org [accessed 11 September 2009].

Juma M (2009) The return of the Amazons: women in Africa's armed forces, *Africa Insight* 38, 4:59–77.

Loots L (2009) South African women as peacekeepers: experiences in the Democratic Republic of Congo. Short dissertation submitted in partial fulfillment of the requirements for the degree *Magister Societatis Scientiae*: Sociology (Gender Studies). Pretoria: University of Pretoria.

Lyytikinem M (2007) Gender training for peacekeepers: preliminary overview of United Nations peace support operations. New York: INSTRAW Gender, peace and security working paper no 4:1–26.

Ministry of Foreign Affairs of Denmark (2008) 'Thematic debate on women, peace and security: Nordic statement – the Security Council'. 19 June. www.missionfnnewyork.um.dk/en/menu/statements/thematicdebate.htm [accessed on 14 September 2009].

Olsson L and J Tejpar (Eds) (2009) Operational effectiveness and UN Resolution 1325 – Practices and lessons from Afghanistan, pp. 1–152. Stocholm: FOI, Folke Bernadotte Academy, Ministry of Foreign Affairs of Sweden and Ministry for Foreign Affairs of Finland, Norad. May.

Olsson L and T Tryggestad (Eds) (2001) *Women and International Peacekeeping*. London: Frank Cass.

Pillay A (2009) Gender, Peace and Peacekeeping: Lessons from Southern Africa. Pretoria: Institute for Security Studies, paper No. 128: 1–12.

Simic O (2009) Who should be a peacekeeper? *Peace Review*, 21, 3:395–402.

Sion L (2008) Peacekeeping and the gender regime: Dutch female peacekeepers in Bosnia and Kosovo. *Journal of Contemporary Ethnography* 37 (5): 561–585.

UNDPKO (2006) United Nations peace operations year in review 2006. www.un.org/Depts/dpko/dpko/pub [accessed 14 September 2009].

UNIFEM (2009) Facts and figures on peace and security. www.unifem.org/gender_issues/peace [accessed 24 September 2009].

United Nations (1995) Beijing Declaration and Platform for Action. In Report of the Fourth World Conference on Women, July. www.un.org./documents/ga/docs/52/plenary [accessed 15 September 2009].

United Nations (2005) Facts and figures on women, peace and security. New York: United Nations Doc DP/2409 November.

United Nations Security Council (2009) Report of Secretary General pursuant to SC Resolution 1820 (2008). 20 August. http://daccessdds.un.org/doc/UNDOC/GEN/NO9/405 [accessed 24 September 2009].

Valenius J (2007) Gender mainstreaming in ESDP missions. Paris: EU Institute for Security Studies, Chaillon Paper no 101, May:1–77. Windhoek Declaration and Plan of Action (2000) [accessed September 2009].

EDUCATION, HEALTH AND LAND

3

Reform and redress in higher education, health and land

Roger Southall

This section deals with three sectors of South African society – higher education, health and land – which are all widely acknowledged as confronting far-reaching crises. Higher education, perched above a public schooling system which is regularly denounced as failing the nation, is struggling with issues of merger of institutions, rationalisation of resources, and producing qualified graduates from cohorts of students many of whom are desperately underprepared. Public health care – from which a significant minority of better-off South Africans have migrated in favour of a much more highly resourced private health care system – has proved unable to meet the multiple challenges thrown at it during the post-apartheid years, notably that of HIV/AIDS, so that today average life expectancy for South Africans is lower than it was in 1994. Finally, the processes of land reform and restitution have become notorious for having failed to meet their targets and, albeit with important exceptions, for having become ingloriously delinked from the issue of agricultural production. The story in each of these sectors is not, however, nearly as gloomy as the popular media portray it in regular doom-laden reports, for there are silver linings, gleams of light, and promises of positive changes ahead. Nonetheless, the principal worry in each of these sectors is, in essence, South Africa's failure to move significantly away from the divided society of the past; indeed, present policies and processes are, inadvertently, too often reproducing historic inequalities, with all the dangers that holds for the country's already fragile social coherence.

A strong case can be made that, in these and other sectors, many of South Africa's travails are rooted in intellectual failures (to think about radical alternatives): misguided normative assumptions (notably, an uncritical embrace of neoliberal thinking or, indeed, an equally uncritical railing against an often ill-defined evil labelled as neoliberalism); and a post-colonial closing of minds (pursuit of crude 'transformation' agendas without regard to or recognition of their opportunity costs). Peter Vale explores the roots of such failures in his wide ranging survey of the historical development and contemporary currents within the humanities and social sciences in South Africa, although doubtless he would want to argue that the intellectual and normative failures which he discusses have a much wider application across South African society.

Vale sees the present crisis as located in the academy's ultimate failure to confront the challenge represented by the penetration of the logic of the market into the universities – how they are run, how they are organised, and how they have come to see and present themselves. At one level, this has been a local reflection of a much wider international phenomenon, yet inevitably, in this very strange society, it has taken on the image of, and tended to reproduce, past fault lines of racial (and other) inequality. Indeed, he sees the humanities and social sciences in this country as having grown up in the shadow of social policies and problems, of the need to 'make themselves useful'. At one level, this is unexceptional and unobjectionable, yet at another it is highly dangerous, for it has meant that this composite of disciplines has too often come to define their project, not so much as consideration of the condition of humankind, but in relation to policy makers and official policy. He argues that three waves of knowledge-making – Liberal/English, Nationalist/Afrikaner and 'Pan-African' – marked the paths of the human- ities in pre-1994 South Africa, reproducing themselves within three traditions of higher edu- cation defined by race and language, albeit with the Pan-African wave having, perforce, to develop more in exile than amongst home based African scholars. In turn, political struggles within the country as well as international influences led to an important intellectual reaction during the 1970s and 1980s which embraced a 'revisionist Marxism'. This made for what he endorses as the two most exciting decades in South Africa's intellectual history, based upon the imagination of a new society. Thus, by the early 1990s, the humanities and social sciences in South Africa seemed on the verge of a golden age – yet sadly, in his view, it is one whose promise has long been diverted by confusion, lost opportunities, crass materialism, manage- rialism and government pressure. In essence, the end of the Cold War collapsed the Marxist Moment, and installed a discourse of neoliberalism which academia proved unable and perhaps unwilling to confront, as prior South African academic traditions, notably subordination to metropolitan influences, re-asserted themselves. This has seen, *inter alia*, a devaluation by policy-makers of the humanities, consequent financial restrictions, and a marked tendency to insist that their activities should be geared to policy although, more optimistically, he identifies stirrings of revolt which may reassert the value and valuing of humanities within South Africa's national life. One hopes that he may see the present venture, the launch of the *New South African Review* as one such development.

Personally, as a British academic who has worked in the South African higher education sector for some twenty odd years, I find Vale's assessment of the present condition of the humanities a trifle harsh. I think a counter case can be put, certainly in the case of the social sciences (with which I am more familiar than the broader humanities), that academia is more critically engaged with the urgent issues of the society around it than may well be the case in countries in the global North where it is more worn down by financial restrictions and managerial demands than it is here. Yet this is not to deny the heavy weight of the past, which bears down upon the pace of what Kezia Lewins terms 'transformation, equity and social justice' within the country's universities.

Lewins recognises, with Vale, the imposition of managerial and market logic, corporate efficiency and global competition as a major influence upon the restructuring of the higher education sector, although she nuances this by reference to the government's policies of rationalisation and merger of institutions (to make the sector more coherent) and by efforts to make it more accessible, equitable, representative and socially responsive. These latter two influences are by no means incompatible with the first (indeed merger of institutions was an expression of it); yet the attempt at 'transformation' in many ways runs counter to it, although in turn, she proceeds to point out how certain official policies (notably, its restrictive formulas of student financing) work in a contradictory fashion to undermine its objective of 'achieving representivity', for it is poorer, black students who tend to lose out most through lack of resources to pursue their studies.

Lewins points to modest yet important achievements. First, there have been equity improvements in student participation in higher education, and improving rates of black graduation; a small but significant increase in black postgraduate students; and significant feminisation of student cohorts but, echoing Vale, she reports a devaluation of the humanities and social sciences by students themselves. Second, there have been major improvements in total numbers of both black and female academic staff since the early 1990s, although they tend to be employed at lower professional levels. However, this promising development has been countered by a major increase in the proportion of university administrators, most of these in higher managerial positions. While, once again, there have been significant improvements regarding race and gender in this sphere, overall the increase in managers points towards greater bureaucratisation (although it needs to be added that, at departmental/disciplinary level, the student: administrator ratios have hugely weighed in against the latter, subjecting them to immense pressures). Finally, Lewins points to the contradiction between the growth in the size of, and rewards paid to, higher managerial grades, while virtually all universities (Rhodes being an honourable exception) have eschewed a commitment to social justice by having privatised the category of service workers. The mundane tasks of cleaning and maintenance are fundamental underpinnings of universities, yet service workers have had their former permanent conditions of employment converted into jobs that are both insecure and lesser-paid. All this constitutes a mixed and complicated story, yet what comes through is a continuing legacy of racial patterns and hierarchies, within and between institutions.

Racial patterns are far more pronounced in the health sphere. Hein Marais offers an analysis which disabuses us of any notion that the HIV/AIDS epidemic is 'democratic', that is, that it has an equal impact upon South Africa's hierarchies of race, gender and class. The contours of the epidemic fit the contours of race and privilege, and express deeply laid patterns of inequality, although Marais also stresses that there is no straightforward association between poverty and HIV/AIDS . Rather, he depicts the factors that put persons at risk of HIV infection as enmeshed in the circuits and terms on which power, opportunity and entitlements are distributed. These are highly unequal, and a history of systematic dispossession and dislocation of, especially, the African population, the destabilisation of social systems and the disintegration of social cohesion (particularly in the urban peripheries) has helped create a social and ideological context (inclusive of aggressive constructions of masculinity) which seems to favour the spread of HIV and is likely to reinforce those inequalities.

Marais stresses that the HIV/AIDS epidemic is not yet half way through its life cycle, and will define the lives of at least two more generations. It therefore demands a long-term response, yet the reality is that it is threatening to overwhelm an already failing public health system. A major response to HIV/AIDS has been found in the home and community based care system, in which a system of community health workers interlocks into a network of home based (usually female) 'volunteers' who receive training and support from the public health system. Although well meant, in practice the system relapses into a form of cheap family, overwhelmingly female, labour which reduces care demands on the hospital system and financial demands on the state. In any case, Marais observes, the country's health system is highly unequal, and the large majority of financial resources spent on health is funnelled into a private sector which caters only to a small minority of the population and which is staffed by a disproportionately high number of nurses and doctors. The overall impact of the epidemic, he judges, has been to reinforce the huge inequalities within the health sector, even though he acknowledges considerable gains made in the provision of anti-retroviral treatment to those who need it. Yet again such achievements tend to run up against difficulties of implementation and financial restrictions which imply that present gains may be reversed.

Marais' analysis points to the urgent need for the reform of the present two tier system of health care and for the progress towards the establishment of a national health system. This is taken up by Louis Reynolds who seeks to locate the ANC's commitment at its Polokwane national conference in December 2007 to the creation of a national health insurance (NHI) scheme in historical context. Considerable confusion has been created by the elevation of the particular term, 'national health insurance', into something of a mantra for, as Reynolds points out, its aim is to provide affordable and acceptable quality health services to all South Africans, and for health services to be funded in an equitable manner. While the focus of much media debate has been upon NHI as if it were merely a matter of financing, the latter's broader objectives express ambition to establish a genuinely national health system. This, as Reynolds points out, is by no means a new ambition, for it has its origins in new thinking around public health and community medicine which occurred amongst progressive doctors in South Africa in the 1940s and which found institutional form in the appointment of a national health services commission under the Smuts government which advocated reorganisation of the then medical system to provide appropriate health care for the entire population. Recognising the need to tackle the underlying social origins of disease, it recommended the establishment of a community based system whose emphasis would be upon the promotion and preservation of health rather than on curative medicine. Meanwhile, a genuinely national health service would require a uniformity of standards, centralised authority and funding by the exchequer upon the basis of graduated taxation.

These progressive ideas ran up against the vested interests of the majority of the medical profession but, rather more fatally, the hostile thinking after 1948 of the apartheid government. The health centres upon which progressive community oriented primary health care (COPHC) had been founded were transformed into ways merely of providing cheap health care for the poor and marginalised, which increasingly under the National Party meant the black population. Yet, as Reynolds indicates, the ideas that had infused COPHC did not die, for they re-emerged internationally in the 1960s when, following the decolonisation of empires, emphasis upon primary health care re-emerged with recognition that any project of replication of first world health regimes was both inappropriate and unaffordable. This culminated in the Alma Ata declaration in 1978 which required governments, notably in developing countries, to transfer a greater share of health resources to the majority of their populations, to provide universal access to essential health care. Affluent countries were to back this up with their own transfer of resources to the South. Although the radical thrust of Alma Ata was subsequently watered down in country after country for political reasons, its ambitions have remained influential.

These different strands of progressive thought later found expression in the health plan which the ANC put forward in 1994 alongside the Reconstruction and Development Programme. Again, this stressed universal and equitable access to health care, and creation of an integrated national health system whose foundation would be a network of community health centres providing comprehensive care. Yet this soon ran foul of the financial strictures of the 1996 Growth, Employment and Redistribution (GEAR) programme. Implicit in the latter, argues Reynolds, was acceptance of a two tiered health system, private and public, and removal of a unified national health system as a practical reality. Thus although the formally racially segregated health system has been unified, and although significant health gains have been realised through extension of sanitation, water, social grants and welfare, the public health system has remained dysfunctional, collapsing under the weight of HIV/AIDS, tuberculosis, 'old' and 'new' epidemics and, of course, nutritional deficiencies. It is the growing realisation of this that has led to the ANC's resolve to adopt the idea of national health insurance, and of exploring ways of financing a genuinely national health system providing appropriate and adequate health care on a universal basis. Yet while the private health care sector itself is confronting its own crisis in terms of spiralling costs and a declining proportion of the minority who can afford it, the transformation of the present two tier system into a truly national system will meet resistance from vested interests and by implication it is unlikely to be achieved through a single grand reform (as perhaps was initially implied by the ANC's resolution at Polokwane) but will be through a process of both struggle and bridge-building between the public and private sectors over the course of some years.

Progress over years is, apparently, also increasingly the watchword in the spheres of land restitution and reform. The historic inequalities in land ownership, instituted through waves of dispossession of blacks of the vast majority of their land by the white minority under segregation and apartheid, has long been one of the most symbolic markers of colonialism and racial inequality. Thus it was that the ANC came to power with ambitious plans to address the land issue, by restoring land (or equivalent value) to individuals and communities who could prove that they had been deprived of their land after 1913 (the year of the notorious Natives Land Act) and, more generally, of a policy of land reform whereby new black farmers would be assisted to farm productively. However, the government has failed badly in terms of its restitution targets (up to early 2008, only 4.7 million hectares of land out of an envisaged 24.6 million hectares, or 30 per cent of agricultural land, had been transferred to beneficiaries) and, worse, many if not most land reform projects have failed.

Doreen Atkinson provides a summary of four phases of land reform which have occurred since 1994: an experimental period which lasted until 1997; a roll out of small grants to potential farmers to enable them to purchase small farms between 1998 and 2000; a subsequent shift away from this pro-poor focus towards promotion of a class of more commercialised African farmers on somewhat larger plots; and from 2004 a more concerted focus upon the grant of financial and other support to beneficiaries to assist their successful engagement in production. In 2009, as Sam Kariuki outlines, the government broached the Comprehensive Rural Development Programme (CRDP) whose focus is upon sustainable land reform, food security, rural development and job creation linked to skills training and development and which, he avers, is based upon an integrated approach to facilitate integrated rural development and social cohesion through empowerment and popular participation. He views this as a major step forward, and as resulting from official digestion of the reasons for many of the difficulties which land reform has encountered since 1994, and has having been borrowed from a wide range of international experiences. However, as well as acknowledging financial constraints, he also worries about a continuing division of responsibilities between ministries responsible for land reform on the one hand, and agricultural production on the other, while also expressing concerns about what he regards as the incompatibility between the government's passage of the Communal Lands Rights Act of 2004 (which continues to vest considerable authority over communal land in traditional leaders) and realisation of the objectives of the CRDP.

Atkinson, however, is considerably more critical of the entire edifice of land reform, and provides a catalogue of reasons as to why, in her view, it has failed so badly. Fundamentally, her critique revolves round what she regards as the incapacity of the national and provincial ministries responsible for land reform to implement it successfully, and their deliberate exclusion of the commercial agricultural community from the process – indeed, their tendency to regard it (composed as it is largely of white farmers) as hostile and reactionary. Along the way, she explores what she regards as significant flaws in the intellectual justifications for the government's various land reform efforts, driven she argues from a leftist mind-set largely divorced from real experience reinforced by 'politically correct' thinking among bureaucrats, and an urban bias within the ANC. Ultimately, though, she shares a cautious optimism of movement forward with Kariuki: on the one hand, the commercial agricultural community – alarmed by land seizures in Zimbabwe among other developments – has become less fearful and indeed positively disposed to land reform; and on the other, conscious of its own failures, the government itself has slowly edged towards recognition of a need to partner with commercial agriculture if, simultaneously, land reform is to be achieved and food security attained.

Education, health and land: three sectors in which democratic South Africa is struggling to come to terms with its legacy of racial division. Prospects for forward movement in each, as all our authors demonstrate, are highly tenuous. Much will depend upon, not merely clarity of thought and policy in each sphere, but deliberate attempts to 'join up' policy across ministerial and national/provincial boundaries (the fight against poverty and for greater equity should provide common ground in the struggle for improvements across the entire terrain of land, health and education). Ultimately, however, much will depend upon the political determination and the political capacity of the government to realise, in the ANC's time-honoured phrase, 'a better life for all'.

CHAPTER 11

'Silencing and worse … ':
The humanities and social sciences
in South Africa[1]

Peter Vale

⸺•⸺

This chapter – a mix of report and analysis – aims to convey that the 'New South Africa' is not what it once promised. South Africa's experience of change adds force to Max Weber's claim that revolutionary ideas are invariably 'disciplined' by social and political processes. (Abromeit 1994: 27). However, if the rationality which was first projected upon social science by Weber was even-handed, then the sense of loss experienced throughout the humanities in South Africa would be explainable, even perhaps tolerable. But policy in post-apartheid South Africa is increasingly determined by 'experts', few of whom are trained in the humanities, and by a technical language upon which their decisions rest. This has dealt a double blow to the humanities. Their commanding position within the academy has been supplanted by the rise of new ways of both knowing and explaining, and their role in freeing South Africa has been entirely ignored.

The facts and figures in this chapter on the status of the humanities and the social sciences in South Africa cannot be divorced from the profound social and political processes which have completely changed the country but, oddly enough, left many things in place. The necessity of bringing South African society back in line follows upon the near-revolutionary moment which the country had reached in the late-1980s. At that time, the revolt against apartheid was embedded within ideas and interpretations which had to be filtered by, amongst other influences, those of the Cold War. Through this lens, local demands for basic human rights took on a distinct insurrectionary tone which generated anti-enlightenment demands, such as 'no education without liberation', which now seem to have been completely counter-productive. In negotiating this world, the humanities played an enormous role, at times by causing the political sphere to pause, but mostly by creating a language of both struggle and emancipation which helped South Africans to see a world which lay beyond colonialism, apartheid and, indeed, the Cold War. Without understanding this, there is no appreciating the circumstances in which the humanities and social sciences currently find themselves.

And so to a central argument: What has happened to the humanities in South Africa mirrors a global trend. As the American educationalist Sheila Slaughter has suggested:

> [a]cademics in the arts, social sciences and humanities were caught off guard by the rise of neo-liberalism. During the 1960s and 1970s, they had been at the centre of the university, close to the core of the social movements that expanded and changed undergraduate education. However, their … narrative did not compel students, funders, or donors. Undergraduate and graduate students moved to the … professional schools in droves. At many campuses, the arts and sciences became service courses that provided general education courses prior to students' entry into professional schools (Slaughter 2007: 14).

Today the humanities are repeatedly the target of higher education policy-makers and planners as well as managers, who seem preoccupied with promoting the so-called 'knowledge economy'. Understanding this requires attention to four factors: first, the place of the humanities during apartheid. The intention here is to highlight the rise and the efficacy of a critical discourse and political practice which helped to bring apartheid to its end. Thereafter, consideration will be given to the rise of the technical rationality represented by neoliberal economics, especially by the reductionist perspective embedded in the idea of globalisation, a marked feature of public policymaking in the post-apartheid years. Both this political history and rise of the technical end of social science will assist in the understanding of the third: an analysis of the trends within the humanities both across, and within institutions and disciplines. The chapter ends with a consideration of some recent attempts to revive the humanities.

Given the limited space available here, the approach adopted follows a 'thieving magpie' perspective on social analysis (borrowed from the historian Simon Sharma). This technique enables us to draw illustrations from a range of disciplines in order to illustrate the general points driving the argument.

DEFINING THE HUMANITIES AND THE SOCIAL SCIENCES IN SOUTH AFRICA

In contemporary South Africa, the label 'humanities' is inclusive, drawing together the traditionally defined 'humanities', in other words 'social sciences' and the 'arts'. This brand name – to intentionally use the term much loved by the new generation of university administrators – invariably reflects what Ted Schatzki has called 'the contingent facts of institutional, cultural, and educational history' (Schatzki 2009: 31). It is important to note that the use of this name is recent. Until the 1980s, most South African universities used the label the 'arts' to name faculties which included the 'humanities', while some, but not all, of the country's universities organised the 'social sciences' into separate faculties. These definitional issues will highlight the power of the metropolitan – or northern hemisphere – hold on academic organisation, and explain how the social sciences, in particular, were used to serve the purpose of modernity in South Africa as, indeed, they have been elsewhere.

Given that South Africa was founded within a 'network of imperial knowledge' (Dubow 2006: 14), it is not surprising that the separation between the natural sciences and the humanities has been the primary feature of the country's knowledge system. Nevertheless, from the very earliest days the humanities were valued – certainly, early university leadership was provided by those who had trained in the field. An example was Jan Hofmeyr, who was appointed, in 1922, the first principal of the University of the Witwatersrand at the age of twenty-four. After graduating with an MA degree from the University of Cape Town (UCT) at the age of fifteen, Hofmeyr read Classics at Balliol College, Oxford, as a Rhodes Scholar. The post of university principal was to be the prodigy's first real minister of finance and of education. A love of the humanities, however, never left him; when he died, aged fifty-four, he bequeathed money to the University of the Witwatersrand conditional upon the chair of Classics being named after him. Most importantly for this paper, the fact that the university in question was previously called 'The South African School of Mines' suggests that in the 1920s it was thought that the excesses of the 'hard' sciences might need to be tamed by the 'soft' ones.

Towards the end of that decade, it was clear that the American approach to the 'social sciences', with its liberal confidence in the receptiveness of human problems to intervention, would serve as a major influence in the South African context. In 1927, the president and secretary of the Carnegie Corporation of New York visited South Africa, and the Corporation's interest was drawn to the problem of white poverty in the country. Among those who were to join the staff of The Carnegie Commission Report into White Poverty in South Africa was EG (Eddie) Malherbe, son of a Dutch Reformed minister, who had taken a doctorate at Columbia University's Teachers' College. Malherbe was, perhaps, the country's first champion of applied social science and was unafraid of tackling sensitive issues such as ethnicity and race. He would go on to direct the Bureau for Educational and Social Research, a prototype for the Human Sciences Research Council (HSRC), which was established in 1969 and continues in post-apartheid South Africa (see below). But, his lasting contribution may have been profession-alisation of the social sciences in the country, which followed upon this development in the United States and elsewhere. So, the founding of a faculty of social science at Rhodes University in 1930 was a response to a request from the National Council of Women, which had called for the creation of a bachelors' degree in social studies. In the midst of the Great Depression, the goal was training social workers, something that followed upon the professionalisation of this discipline in Britain and the United States. Indeed, the Carnegie Commission's report, which appeared in 1932, recommended the creation of further training sites for social workers. In response, the University of the Witwatersrand began this training in 1937 after an internal university memorandum from the liberal philosopher Professor RFA Hoernlé urging its necessity 'for the development of the scientific study of social problems and the university training of students to deal practically with these problems from a scientific perspective' (Ross 2007: 1).

Professionalisation was only one aspect of the complex goals of social science in what Daniel Lerner later described as 'modernising lands' (Lerner 1959: 32) like South Africa. This reflected what Dubow calls 'the international vogue for expert knowledge, quantification and the pursuit of social efficiency' (Dubow 2006: 7). It is not therefore surprising that Rhodes University, in the early 1960s, was able to claim that the

> scientific knowledge of social phenomena is important for an understanding of the contemporary world. The emergence of social, economic, racial and psychological problems has brought into being specialised services requiring trained personnel with a sound knowledge of the various social sciences such as Sociology, Economics, Anthropology and Psychology, and other fields of a cognate nature (Rhodes University Calendar, 1961: Chapter XX).

Given South Africa's social complexity and the continuous political struggle for the country, it should be no surprise that the social sciences in South Africa reflected this dark side. In intellectual circles, mainly among Afrikaners, the social sciences were often associated with the strengthening of racial ideology. One faux-discipline, known as *Volkekunde*, played a decisive role in what Robert Gordon has called 'the legitimating and reproduction of the apartheid social order on two levels: as an instrument of control and as a means of rationalising it' (Gordon 1988: 536). This approach to anthropology positioned the social category of race at the centre of its epistemology and, with time and the use of official resources, this view of the social cosmos rendered all alternative positions to be outside accepted routines of scholarship sanctioned by people, party and state. Nor was this an isolated case of ideology corroding knowledge. Consider the discipline of International Relations, first taught in a separate academic department at the University of the Witwatersrand in 1963. During the apartheid years, positivist approaches to thinking around 'the international' trapped the discipline within Cold War logic but with time this approach had penetrated the very fabric of national life and extended beyond the country's immediate borders where, mingling with apartheid's racial ideology, it caused death and destruction throughout the southern Africa region.

These two examples highlight the difficulties in describing the humanities (including the social sciences) in a deeply divided society like South Africa. There has been not one but a number of approaches to knowledge within the country – each of which pursued separate epistemological niches, each drawn from (and contributing to) separate cultures.

Three waves of knowledge making – 'Liberal/English', 'Nationalist/Afrikaner' and 'Pan-African' – marked the path of the humanities in South Africa. The first of these descriptors are akin to the standard liberal rendition of apartheid history, and reflect the stance of these categories towards apartheid. So, the liberal or English-medium universities – Cape Town, Witwatersrand, Natal and Rhodes – readily embraced the idea of admitting students of all races. Although their enthusiasm was somewhat uneven, this choice flew in the face of apartheid policy, particularly of two notorious pieces of legislation: the Separate University Education Bill of 1957, and the Extension of Universities Act, No 45 of 1959. Cumulatively, these pieces of legislation made the issue of race the only criterion for admission to higher education.

The cultural roots of the so-called liberal universities drew them towards Oxbridge even though (as with all the country's universities) they were originally dependent on the University of London for the issuing of their degrees. In their academic programmes and their administrative form, however, they were closer to the Scottish university tradition. These affinities strongly influenced the early organisation and the content of the humanities, the arts and the social sciences, and the intellectual hold of the cultural/academic metropole – especially that of the 'golden triangle' of Cambridge, Oxford and London. Arguably, the latter was broken only by the intellectual ferment (and the progressive politics) which followed upon the establishment of the University of Sussex in 1961. A number of South Africans who were to make a deep impression on the humanities in the 1970s and the 1980s did postgraduate work at Sussex; and it was from there that the country's second democratically elected president, Thabo Mbeki, graduated with an MA in Economics from the School of Social Studies.

Lawrence Wright has described South African English-medium universities as instruments for 'transmitting metropolitan knowledge and excitement in a colonial situation' (Wright 2006: 73). The resulting sense of inferiority – the 'cultural cringe' as the Australian AS Philips famously called it – slowed the indigenisation of the humanities in these institutions. Rarely was there any desire to challenge the metropolitan-determined paradigm. A number of inspiring teachers did challenge the *status quo* by instilling what Richard Rorty called 'doubts in the students ... about the society to which they belong' (Rorty 1999: 127). These departures were sometimes less epistemological in their purpose than they were openly political and, interestingly, they drew more from European than British ideas. So, in the early 1970s, the University of the Witwatersrand experienced a strong critical surge in disciplines like Political Studies, African Studies and Anthropology. This exposed students to Habermasian critical theory and French post-structuralism. One particular course, called 'Freedom and Authority' was almost entirely devoted to a consideration of the work of Hannah Arendt. But these dissenting approaches were not readily accepted. Academics and students who pursued them were often censured both within and without the university walls. Some, like Dr Rick Turner, were less fortunate. In early January 1978, the political scientist and labour activist was assassinated in Durban.

By nurturing the idea that the university should offer the fruit of its labour to the building of a nation ('die volk'), the country's Afrikaans-medium institutions faced restrictions of their own epistemological making. However, their success in achieving their political goals may explain why it is that the traditional Afrikaans universities continue to be associated with the legitimacy they offered to apartheid. These are Stellenbosch, Pretoria, Potchefstroom University for Higher Christian Education (now called North West University), Orange Free State (now the University of the Free State) and later the Rand Afrikaans University (now the University of Johannesburg), the University of Port Elizabeth (now the Nelson Mandela Metropolitan University) and Unisa. The oldest of these, situated in the town of Stellenbosch from which it draws its name, began as a theological seminary in 1863. An arts department was added in 1873 when professors were appointed to teach Classics, English Literature, Mathematics and Physical Science. The arts department received its charter from the Cape Parliament and, together with the seminary, became known as the Stellenbosch College. However, in 1877 – the Jubilee Year of Queen Victoria – its name, with royal consent, was again changed – this time to the Victoria

College of Stellenbosch. A University Act, which replaced the latter with the name 'Stellenbosch University', came into effect in early April 1918.

This example confirms that South Africa's Afrikaans-medium universities were in fact also closely tied to the British tradition. As a result (and ironically) their origins were more diverse than those of their English counterparts. The University of Pretoria, for instance, commenced instruction in the English language, switching to the Afrikaans medium of instruction a full twenty-three years after its founding in 1908. But their search for deeper involvement with Afrikaner nationalism, which began in the early 1900s, inexorably drew them on a different trajectory and this change in direction was speeded by their links to European universities. The Dutch were a strong influence; Leiden University graduated successive generations of Afrikaner lawyers, while Utrecht made an early impact on the study of theology. The University of the Orange Free State was founded in 1904; its first principal, Johannes Brill, had graduated in Classics from Utrecht where his father had been a professor.

But the European impact was most strongly felt in the 1930s and 1940s, when the German universities were an important source of succour and support. Of crucial importance to this direction was the idea of a 'volksuniversiteit' – defined by the intellectual, Merwe Scholtz, as 'a university which belongs to the *volk* and must therefore be of the *volk*, out of the *volk* and for the *volk*, anchored in its traditions and fired by the desire to serve the *volk* in accordance with its own view of life' (Degenaar 1977: 152). In this nationalist project, the humanities were to play a crucial role: its sub-disciplines helped to foster the idea that a university education instilled in the student the notion of 'being bound to the people' (*op cit*: 156). As we have already noted Volkekunde was important but so too was the discipline of history: a distinctive feature of this 'scientific historical writing' – almost all of it in the Afrikaans language – was 'that the conception of the past is based on the point of view of the Afrikaner' (Van Jaarsveld 1964: 135). Approaches represented by this perspective on the humanities are drawn together in three volumes entitled *Kultuurgeskiedenis van die Afrikaner*, which were published over a five-year period.

It was through the Carnegie Commission's intervention that the importance of social science in building an Afrikaner nation became clear. The researchers in the investigation were drawn from both language groups, and among them was a young sociologist, HF Verwoerd, who used his involvement in the project to build a career successively in the academy, journalism and politics. Born in the Netherlands, Verwoerd was to become apartheid's leading intellectual and, before his assassination in 1966, was prime minister. To date, Verwoerd has been the only South African head of state to have gained a doctorate.

Given apartheid's grand vision of separating the races, it might be thought South Africa's other university tradition, the black (or in apartheid nomenclature, homeland) institutions, would escape the narrowing strictures of the 'Volksuniversiteit' idea. But this was not to be the case. The oldest of these, the University of Fort Hare (UFH) (initially called The South African Native College), was founded in the enlightenment tradition by Scots missionaries in 1916. In 1946, it gained semi-autonomous status with its degrees issued under the supervision of Rhodes University. But UFH was far more than this mundane and linear account suggests. It was here that Nelson Mandela and other leaders had both studied and honed the politics that would help to free their country. As a student in the humanities, Mandela was expelled by the College's principal during his final year of study, for organising a boycott.

While, the institution's formal academic and intellectual authority was largely destroyed by the 1959 Universities Act, its social and political capital remained intact notwithstanding the state's harrowing assault. The Act established four new universities for 'non-whites', to use the language of the legislation. These were the University of Zululand, the University of the Western Cape, the University of Durban-Westville, and the University of the North. With the attack on UFH came the parallel destruction of a number of revered missionary schools, such as Healdtown, Lovedale, and St Marks, that had fostered a generation of leaders of which Nelson Mandela is undoubtedly the most famous.

As apartheid's grip on these institutions and the newly established universities tightened, Afrikaner Nationalist academics were circulated through these tribal colleges, with the best of these being drawn back into the mainstream Afrikaner universities after a few years. The result was that the reach of the humanities – certainly in the classroom – was narrow and restricted. Syllabuses were somewhat formal and often very contradictory: for example, at UFH in the 1970s, the political science syllabus was uncritically preoccupied with modernisation theory. While this pedagogy was taking place, the institution was 'a cauldron of radical student politics' (Mangcu 2008: 24).

Administratively, too, these institutions were tightly controlled; mostly, ideologues were appointed to leadership positions and their budgets were drawn, not from the national education budget, but from that of the state department designated to deal with black affairs. For almost a decade and a half, these institutions seemed to be formally positioned outside the struggle for their rights in which the other university traditions seemed all too self-righteously engaged. This apparent marginalisation, and whispers over the question of standards, especially in the humanities, denied them the formal voice to defend themselves against their rightfully angry students and the apartheid government.

But outside the country, South African exiles, including the sociologist Ben Magubane and the anthropologist Archie Mafeje, were reinforcing a long-established critical tradition which apartheid simply denied. These scholars not only made deep contributions to both the humanities and the social sciences, but by challenging apartheid policy called into question the western epistemologies that were used in framing the very question of modernity. This work drew on a still to be fully explored intellectual tradition that reached back to the origins of Pan-Africanist thinking with its 'concern for the emancipation of the continent from the ravages of foreign domination and underdevelopment and ... (towards) ... the building of a new Africa' (Mkandawire 2005: 2).

In South Africa, this can be dated to the early 1880s with the founding of the first secular newspaper, *Imvo Zababantusundu,* by John Tengo Jabavu. With an emancipatory impulse at its centre, this trajectory was continued by John Langalibalele Dube (author of the first Zulu language novel), RV Selope Thema (journalist, editor, historian), Pixley ka Isaka Seme (a Columbia and Oxford trained lawyer and journalist), and Solomon T Plaatje (linguist, journalist and author). With other organic intellectuals, these men helped to launch the anti-tribalist New African Movement in 1904-6 and, in 1912, the African National Congress. Although they were a remarkable community, history seems to have judged them harshly for their inability to look beyond the local and the parochial. However, their work continued in the 1940s in the writings and debates of HIE Dhlomo, a major figure in South African literature, Benedict Wallet Vilakazi, novelist, educator and the first black South African to receive a PhD, and Jordan Ngubane, journalist and novelist.

The trifocal lens used in this analysis needs, however, to be drawn together to gain a sense of the contradictory state of South African humanities in the early 1970s. An American political scientist then living in South Africa, John Seiler, offered a depressing assessment of the state of the country's international relations community of those times, which might be viewed as a reflection of the moribund state of some of the social sciences nearly four decades ago. 'The published work' in politics, Seiler wrote:

> [t]ends to be justificatory, rather than analytical; often contains a moralising, or even specifically religious content; and shows a penchant for thoroughness, which is explicable by a notion of 'science', which is often no more than an unquestioning and uncritical search for and regurgitation of authoritative sources. Since the authorities turned to reflect these same characteristics, there is a repetitious resonance (Seiler 1973: 37).

But beneath the arid surface that Seiler described, the ground was shifting, as the facet of the humanities most difficult to pin down – the interface between theory and practice – underwent a profound change. Although John Seiler had read the works of Sol Plaatje, he seems to have missed the shifting ground of which anti-assimilationists would have approved. Provisionally, two possible reasons for this may be suggested. First, state censorship kept much of the emerging literature underground. Second, his positivist instincts (and training) may well have kept his analysis within watertight compartments.

But reflecting later on the changes which were then underway, sociologist Ari Sitas speaks of an 'indigenous hybridity' (1997: 16) which marked the radical intellectual formations of those years. 'What can be traced', he writes:

> as an intellectual formation started being developed outside and despite University 'disciplinarities'. What started from the early 1970s onwards through marginal and harassed groupings of left intellectuals, white and black, was a social discourse which had a normative and political foundation…[This] formation … provided the cultural levers to prize open departments and disciplinary fields of inquiry…[by promoting]… … narratives of emancipation…animated by egalitarian norms (Sitas 1997: 13).

The diversity within this new formation included not just white, left-inclined academics and students, but also intellectuals linked to the Black Consciousness Movement (BCM), which was founded in 1972 by Steven Bantu Biko. These developments were to position the humanities at the centre of the university and the country in the 1980s. But to explain this it is necessary to return to intellectual history.

THE HUMANITIES AND SOCIAL SCIENCE IN PRACTICE

After World War II, liberal interpretations of South Africa's racial quagmire argued that continued white domination undermined capitalist development and stifled economic growth – this, the argument ran, subverted any hope of social emancipation. The approach was exemplified in the two-volume *The Oxford History of South Africa* edited by Monica Wilson and Leonard Thompson. However, as soon as it appeared, a number of scholars, including South African exiles and émigrés, attacked the work of this 'Liberal School' of Southern African Studies. The resulting 'New School' argued that racial domination was integral to the functioning of the South African economy.

The influence of the new thinking was immediately felt in the country's (still largely white) English language universities. Its march, and the simultaneous re-activation of work-based and community-based organisation during the 1970s, enhanced a Marxist explanation of South African events and drew social theory and political practice closer. This was seen in the role played by intellectuals in the formation of black trade union movements in Durban, Johannesburg and Cape Town. The leading figure in this intellectual-activism was the Sorbonne-trained Rick Turner. This is not the occasion to discuss Turner's life's work, but it is necessary to note that long after his death, his ideas continue to inform many South African debates. We must however turn to the influence of the Western Marxism, which inspired him, to appreciate the role of the humanities in South Africa's political change.

Two main perspectives and one theme emerged during early years of this 'Kuhnian revolution in South African studies' (Jubber 1983: 54). The sociologist (and now politician), Wilmot James, called the two sides of the divide 'social history' and 'historical sociology'. The second issue, the thematic focus, was directed towards the study of labour – here the work of the sociologist Eddie Webster stands out. Unfortunately, there is no space here to discuss Webster's work and the profound effect he (and others) have had on the development of labour activism. This work, however, is in the case study mould, in which theory and practice are drawn together in a single emancipatory project.

The 'social historians' were associated with the work of London University's Institute of Commonwealth Studies, which, in the 1970s and into the 1980s, was directed by the South African-born historian, Shula Marks. But the form and influence of this stream is best appreciated through the writing of the historian, Charles van Onselen – especially his two-volume *Studies in the Social and Economic History of the Witwatersrand*. This approach to understanding South Africa's past, its present and its future was widely disseminated by the annual History Workshop organised and held at the University of Witwatersrand whose work stressed social agency, seeking to reconstruct understandings of the country's history through sensitivities to the activities and practices of the country's popular classes.

The other thread of Marxist thinking, as noted previously, was historical sociology: here the leading figure was the exiled Harold Wolpe; other members included the Canadian sociologist Frederick Johnstone and another exile, the historian Martin Legassick. They represented the structuralist tradition in sociology and, with time, their writing was strongly influenced by Nicos Poulantzas, whose impact was evident in the work of a second generation of South African writers.

Generally speaking, South African Marxists were known for their parochialism and for treating racial domination in South African society as exceptional. But it was Belinda Bozzoli who raised the most difficult (if not embarrassing) concerns about South African Marxism by claiming that '[w]hat South African reality could demonstrate to the intellectual world has increasingly been pushed aside in favour of what that world can tell us about South African reality' (Bozzoli 1981: 54). Her critique is a timely reminder of the hold of metropolitan thought over the humanities in the country. Evidence of this was to emerge elsewhere too. Tracing a century of development of the social sciences at UCT, Ken Jubber suggested that, in terms of what was taught, the institution was like a 'displaced British university' (Jubber 1983: 58). But, whatever its lack of local authenticity, the Marxist moment did raise questions far beyond often mundane disciplinary debates. Looking back on those times, Charles van Onselen called them 'the most exciting two decades in the social sciences … [and the humanities] … in this country' (Van Onselen 2004).

But the deep epistemic break – as Foucault called the moment when the unthinkable becomes thinkable – lay in the much-researched but poorly understood issue of race. The question, put in crude terms, was this: Who were South Africans? Were they, as the country's English-speakers claimed, bearers of the liberal heritage of imperial power? Were they, as Afrikaners hoped, an anointed European volk in Africa? Were they, as more crude Marxists often declared, an exploited proletariat on the periphery of a capitalist world? Or were they, as Pan-Africanists might have argued, colonised minds awaiting emancipation in order to contribute to the rise of a new Africa?

South Africans, of course, were all of these, and none of them. The country was a community in the making – to use Benedict Anderson's iconic idea of the nation as an 'imagined community' – and its making was contingent on the assumptions upon which thinking was provided by the humanities. But accepting the inherent instability of this idea was not possible within the scientistic formulations that promised permanence and predictability. Drawing upon the writing of the Martinique intellectual Frantz Fanon, Steve Biko broke the impasse by famously declaring: 'Black man, you're on your own' (Biko 1978: 97). This, the idea of Black Consciousness, was a fresh framing of South Africa's deepest social issue and, as importantly, its framing was not wholly anchored in metropolitan ideas. The body of this approach to social relations was forcefully drawn into an analysis of racism by the psychologist Chabani Manganyi's 1973 book *Being Black in the World*. Its impact outside of its obvious political setting was profound because, as Biko argued:

> The call for Black Consciousness is the most positive call to come from any group in the black world for a long time. It is more than just a reactionary rejection of whites by blacks…The philosophy of Black Consciousness … expresses group pride and determination by blacks to rise and attain the envisaged self. At the heart of this kind of thinking is the realisation by the blacks that the most potent weapon in the hands of the oppressor is the mind of the oppressed (Biko 1978: 149)

This thinking had been brought to the humanities in South Africa by what was later (quite recklessly) called 'global change'. The colonialism which had given birth to the very idea of South Africa was changing, and Pan-Africanism was emerging as a powerful social idea. In the United States a new form of nationalism – which affirmed blackness, black pride, black solidarity, and (in some cases) argued for no alliances with white activists – was on the rise. But other influences were of longer duration: the *Négritude* movement of Léopold Sédar Senghor and Aimé Césaire, Frantz Fanon, and the music of artists like Nina Simone. In South Africa there were clear antecedents for Black Consciousness in Africanist movements of earlier periods which we have already considered, and which were identifiable with figures like Nelson Mandela and Oliver Tambo, and the Pan-African Congress.

As the appeal of Black Consciousness widened, the country's majority – confident of their ownership and power – played an increasing role in setting political and, indeed, intellectual agendas. In the field of English literature, David Attwell points out that the resulting upheaval marked 'a serious rift ... between liberalism and radicalism' (Attwell 2005: 138).

If the rise of Black Consciousness formed one of the strategic wedges that brought apartheid to an end, another came from within Afrikaner ranks where, over time, intellectuals abandoned the ideology. This did great damage to the idea of the *volksuniversiteit* and freed up room for adventure in the humanities – but breaking away was not easy. The acclaimed poet NP van Wyk Louw described how difficult it was to escape the gravitational pull of nationalism. Effective criticism, he argued, 'emerges when the critic places himself in the midst of the group he criticises, when he knows that he is bound unbreakably ... to the *volk* he dares rebuke' (Saunders 2002: 62). Although this '*loyale verset*' – or loyal dissent – was the early form of breakout, eventually Afrikaner intellectuals were more daring. The poet, intellectual and activist, Breyten Breytenbach, jailed for high treason in the early 1970s, was the most famous example of rebellion. But the real revolt by Afrikaners came as apartheid was collapsing in the 1980s, and in this the humanities – in literature, in music, in journalism, especially amongst the young – turned away from all that had gone before.

TOWARDS MARGINALISATION

Although it was plain that the politics which underpinned apartheid were unsustainable, few predicted that a 'New South Africa' would enthusiastically and so quickly embrace a new form of social conformity. Throughout the 1980s, political energy was imagining a new society which was everything that apartheid was not. The form on offer was citizenship free of the fear and discrimination that had marked the country's unhappy past. It is necessary here to point out that at this time there was a deepening nexus between the humanities – especially in their critical form – and the world of policy. This emerging narrative was imbued with the enlightenment values that for two centuries had inspired the growth and the flourishing of the humanities throughout the world and from which South Africa, from the beginnings of apartheid, had increasingly been excluded through academic boycotts and the like.

As the struggle for South Africa intensified, much of the Marxist thought (and its relevance for the country and its future) became acerbic, even debased. In the politically charged atmosphere of the mid- and late-1980s, political rhetoric was heady and frequently by-passed open and free discussion. As a result, not a little vulgar thinking found its way into the curricula in all of South Africa's universities, with the humanities frequently acting as simple vehicles for political struggle. Quite rightly, these distortions were criticised, but it took a decade to realise the damage that was done during these years. But, in responsible places, the drawing together of theory and practice, which had marked the humanities in the 1970s, had reached an interesting point. So, with apartheid on the verge of collapse, and following the release from prison of Nelson Mandela, the American sociologist, Michael Burawoy, visited the country and glowingly wrote that 'everywhere there were sociologists [and other academics] acting as organic intellectuals of the home-grown liberation movements' (Burawoy 2004a: 11). In the early 1990s the humanities in South Africa seemed at the edge of a golden age.

Ten years later, all this had changed, as this research into the 'employment prospects' for graduates attests:

> The employability picture is bleaker for graduates from the faculty of humanities. Commenting on learners' chances of obtaining a job after graduation, deans said: 'not anything significant', 'not with the current programmes' and 'not widespread within the faculty'. They realised that, so far, the programmes offered in their faculties are less demanded by employers and have a lower exchange rate in the market place, which puts students at a disadvantage. University funding for the faculties of humanities is yearly being reduced while funding for faculties that promise to produce more employable graduates is increased, so efforts are being made to turn the situation around. Innovative programmes like communication science and sport development are being introduced and strengthened (Maharasoa and Hay 2001: 144).

Formulating the answer to the question of what had happened provides a window to discuss the humanities post-apartheid. It is a story of confusion, of lost opportunities, of crass instrumentalism and power-point managerialism, of government pressure, and, not surprisingly, of despair. But it is also the story of resistance, of rebirth, of renewal and of rediscovery – placing the humanities at the very centre of the human experience.

The fall of the Berlin Wall paved the way for the collapse of socialism, entirely removing those Archimedean points of reference – east and west – that had dominated thinking about the social world for forty years. In important, though as yet undocumented ways, the apartheid experiment was overshadowed by the Cold War and, as with the teaching of International Relations in the country, individual disciplines often lent themselves to its ideology. In the changing South Africa the contest over ideas about the social world was heightened by increasing violence, which was linked to the deepening political contestation. The holding power of the Marxist moment quickly disappeared for two reasons. First, the collapse of the socialist states compelled political and social discourses to engage with neoliberal social thought, which had been wholly ignored. Secondly, there was a flight of intellectuals from the academy towards policy research, consultancy or into the institutions of the state.

As a result, the increased influence of (what some called) 'the change-industry' used the self-styled ideas around 'freedom', on offer by free market economics, to hone and stabilise an imaginary visioning of a 'New South Africa' based on the idea that history had ended with the fall of the Berlin Wall. This Hegelian-centred argument embraced the idea that liberal democracy had emerged as the most desirable – indeed, only – form of government by finally overcoming the challenge of fascism (of which apartheid was a variant) and communism (which had been embraced by many in the country's liberation movement). Public discourse became dominated by the idea that economics (especially its neoliberal variant) had been at the centre of political change in the country. In this narrative, the humanities, especially the critical ideas that they fostered, were threatening to the 'new order' under construction.

As this idea took hold, the promise of the enlightenment slipped further from its open-endedness towards a future that seemed to rest on market forces alone. These departures from the post-apartheid state's anticipated destination were often sponsored by northern institutions that were keen to see that South Africa should not deviate from the emerging 'global consensu' that there was no alternative to market-driven capitalism. This outcome echoed earlier moments in the country's development. In his book on the history of scientific and social knowledge in South Africa, Saul Dubow repeatedly suggests that science in the country was flattered by 'the glow of metropolitan attention' (Dubow 2006: 14-15). He goes on to argue that the requirements of its science 'were often articulated in terms of the country's international standing or ... (economic) ... competitiveness' (*op cit*: 198). After the end of apartheid, a deepening subservience to homogenising clichés like 'international best practice' in economic practice closed out any possibility that the local could offer anything fresh, or interesting, unless it had been approved by the metropolitan gaze.

This unquestioned appropriation of market fundamentalism was a re-run of the past horror for the humanities, because the approach passively accepted – as apartheid had once done with the question of race – a condition which should have been subjected to intense scrutiny. Instead, through reductionist thinking, the arts, the critical social sciences – the humanities, in general – were increasingly regarded as superfluous to the imperative of exercising 'rational social choice' in the interests of a single outcome: economic growth.

This, of course, was the same intellectual pattern which makes up the popular master narrative called globalisation. Given the intensity of theoretical questioning that had once marked the humanities, it was remarkable that this idea was accepted as a social fact, as the country's only possible destination. By failing to raise questions, the humanities (both in South Africa and elsewhere) have paid a high price for the creation of what Emma Rothschild calls a 'society of universal commerce' (Rothschild 2002: 250). One of these costs Vrinda Nabar has described as the view that 'the humanities and languages are unnecessary indulgences' (Furedi 2004: 3).

This thinking, which has permeated South African society, must now occupy our attention. Consider schooling: private schools report the view that parents assess the education of their young in investment terms, with the idea of 'value for money' playing a strong role; most want their children prepared for a 'lucrative career' and believe that the humanities will not equip their children for this trajectory. At the public end of schooling, the legacy of apartheid continues to blight the lives – and individual prospects – of the majority of the country's population. Teaching in the public sector is poor, facilities inadequate, and access to the social capital essential for higher education is largely lacking. In addition, the school curriculum is prescriptive: every pupil is compelled to do a mathematics course in the final three grades of school. Other compulsory subjects are English, a first additional language and a course called 'life orientation'. This leaves only three subjects to choose from to complete the total of seven. It is, therefore, not always easy to achieve a desirable balance between the natural sciences and the humanities. In addition, because they are considered to be an 'easy option' – even amongst the ranks of university recruiters – the bulk of poorly prepared students enter the humanities.

These issues are exacerbated by a public discourse which is unidirectional. The importance of mathematics, science and technology is a constant theme. Their case is often highlighted by government spokespeople, by the business community and by think-tanks and public policy experts – the last two of which seem entirely dominated by economists. Few examples of humanities trained successes in the everyday world of commercial or industrial work are considered. In addition, television programmes, especially soap operas and sitcoms, depict characters with high-powered careers, usually in the field of business, which guarantee an affluent lifestyle. The value of a humanities education is seldom emphasised.

Within the higher education system, planning has forced the government to use the national purse to steer higher education towards market outcomes. So, for more than a decade, the national subsidy for producing a humanities graduate was less than that of a graduate in other disciplines. The rationale for this decision (only partly based on costs of instruction) was pure public choice theory: a graduate in either science or commerce would help to 'grow the economy' while the value of a graduate in the humanities could not be measured within the logic of economic rationality. This approach, of course, disregarded Edward Ayers's assertion that the 'humanities are intrinsically inefficient' and that training in the humanities did 'not obviously translate into the requirements for a first job' (Ayers 2009: 30). A new funding formula, which came into effect in 2004, changed this evaluative balance somewhat. The subsidy is now calculated according to the field of study (in a simple funding grid where most of the subjects in humanities are in the lowest-yielding category), as well as the level of the degree – so, a bachelor's degree has less weighting than a master's degree, which in turn is less than that of a doctorate. This funding system is based on the input costs of training rather than on the output benefit to the economy. This has certainly increased the 'returns' – to use the accounting term – but the money available for humanities is still much less than it is for science fields.

Within the university funding formula, research outputs are rewarded by a cash pay-out to the author's respective home institution. The greater weighting of these rewards is for research which is published in academic journals, with books and especially book chapters generally yielding lower 'returns'. While some efforts are underway to repair this situation, there is an overall lack of appreciation of the deep scholarship necessary to the writing of a peer-reviewed book, which in turn shows a lack of understanding of the humanities on the part of policy steeped in free market thinking. This said, statistical and bibliometric evidence suggests that the humanities and social sciences (here the definition includes education) account for approximately 40 per cent of all output in accredited journals in South Africa.

However, this work chiefly appears in local journals which are not ISI-indexed and therefore not internationally recognised – interestingly, this outcome is a mirror of that in the natural and health sciences. When measured against ten similar science systems (Argentina, Brazil, Chile, Egypt, Malaysia, Mexico, Portugal, Singapore, Spain and Turkey), South African humanities-authored articles in ISI-indexed journals compared favourably in terms of international visibility, measured as citation rates. Social science articles were ranked in the sample behind Singapore and Brazil in terms of field-normalised citation rates, while the humanities were ranked fourth behind Argentina, Portugal and Egypt.

Complications have also arisen from the way in which research funding is organised and managed. Under apartheid, the chief funding agency, the Foundation for Research and Development (FRD), was devoted to the financing of the natural sciences and technology; around this focus a distinct and quite effective operating culture had developed. At apartheid's end, the FRD went though extensive reorganisation, resulting in the establishment of the National Research Foundation (NRF) through a merger between the FRD and the Centre for Science Development (CSD), the granting arm of the HSRC. By legislation, the NRF became responsible for the promotion and support of research in the humanities and the social sciences. This has not been a happy development for these disciplines. During the time of the FRD, a simple system of 'rated scientists' was deployed, and these scientists were guaranteed access to funding; this system was re-crafted at the birth of the NRF to include the humanities. In its new form, guaranteed funding was removed from the rating, and the system began to operate on the basis of universities competing for the prestige attached to rated scientists. (More recently, however, in another revamp of the system, funding levels have been restored.) Nevertheless, many in the humanities (and some in the experimental sciences) have turned their backs on this 'rating system'.

In a report issued in May 2009, the NRF claimed that the number of humanities and social science researchers had increased 'from 21 per cent to 31 per cent of the total number of rated researchers over the last five years' (NRF 2009: 15). But an earlier report (NRF 2007: 4) indicated that in 2005 only 9.8 per cent of the total number of staff in both the humanities and the natural sciences had been rated. A further obstacle in the relationship between the NRF and the humanities community involved an early effort to direct research into 'focus areas'. These 'exclusionary modes' largely failed to take account of the critical tradition in the humanities. In 2007, John Higgins, one of the country's leading thinkers and himself the recipient of the highest rating of the NRF, published a piece excoriating the NRF for its approach to the humanities (Higgins 2007). The NRF has been responsive to such criticism, and sensitive management of the humanities portfolio may have made the academy more interested in cooperation, although several stumbling blocks remain. One of these has been the creation of government funded research chairs which have been rolled out by the NRF. In these, twenty-four of eighty have been in the humanities and social sciences, including a number in economics, which are not routinely counted in with the humanities.

The humanities, as Edward Ayers (2009: 25) suggests, 'live' in many places and it is to a place other than the universities that attention will briefly turn. The HSRC, the prototype of which (as we have seen) was suggested by Eddie Malherbe in 1921 (Smit 1984), commands a central – if somewhat historically controversial – space in the humanities in South Africa. In the 1980s, as the struggle to end apartheid drew to a close, the HSRC was accused of legitimising the reform initiatives of the apartheid government by offering scientific support for social programmes (White, undated). Its current mandate 'to act as a knowledge hub between research, policy and action; thus increasing the impact of research' reflects the organisation's interest in 'making a difference in people's lives' (www.hsrc.co.za; accessed 16 March 2010). But this is not uncontroversial, since much of the HSRC's work is at the applied end of social *science*, in particular. It certainly has the greatest single concentration of researchers in the country (some 165 professionals in all), who are supported by technical colleagues, and it boasts that its four multidisciplinary research programmes, two cross-cutting research units and three research centres are focused 'on user needs'. These are:

- **Research programmes**: Child, youth, family and social development, democracy and governance, education, science and skills development, and social aspects of HIV/AIDS and health;
- **Cross-cutting units**: Policy analysis and capacity, enhancement unit and knowledge systems;
- **Centres**: Education quality improvement, poverty, employment and growth and centre for service delivery.

The HSRC has been criticised for the high salaries paid to its researchers and for recruiting academics from the university system. It has also not shown deep interest in developing – or, rather, redeveloping – interest in areas like Literature, History, Philosophy, Religion, Art History, Music, Drama and the like. There are, it seems, some discussions within the HSRC to fill this lacuna in its work by directing attention towards the humanities, but ways to achieve this appear still to be at the embryonic stage. It is fair to say that the applied policy direction of the HRSC is understandable in a country where poverty levels are high and where the gap between the richest and poorest is the largest in the world. It is also true that the HSRC has helped to open up space for humanities in the country. Its publishing house, the HSRC Press, operates on an open access system which provides free access to all its publications as part of its public purpose mandate. This is no trifling matter in a country where the selling price of books has greatly increased and in which books are subjected to a value added tax. However, one of its weaknesses has been an unwillingness to engage in debates on the government's macroeconomic policy which has helped to drive the humanities to the margins of intellectual enquiry.

IN SEARCH OF RECOVERY

Once at the centre of the university (and, indeed, in the country), and at the forefront of the struggle to end apartheid, the humanities now face shrinking budgets, economic determinism and managerialism. Of course, the humanities in South Africa are not alone in facing

> declining proportions of students and faculty positions, low funding inside the university, a diminished audience beyond the academy, disorientating shifts in demography of students and faculty, and dislocating theoretical innovations (Ayers 2009: 24).

But in South Africa, this outcome has been subjected to a particular set of circumstances. In the late-1990s, government appeared to encourage the idea that all the country's universities should adopt what was called a 'programme approach' to undergraduate education. This reflected the thinking of planners whose ideal model is that of the (mostly professional) faculties where planned curricula are the norm, but the approach also fitted the modular agenda of the National Qualifications Framework, which was set up by the South African Qualifications Authority. In practice, across the country, the 'programme approach' resulted in long-standing (and often very strong) humanities departments being merged, reorganised or simply disestablished. Some of the 'programmes' have continued, while others reflected instrumentalist 'morphing' into occupational studies like Museum Studies, Tourism Studies and the like. The overall consensus was that the move was a disastrous step for the humanities. A powerful and intellectually rich department of German studies at UCT, for instance, was wrecked by rationalisation and a department of Afrikaans at the University of the Witwatersrand, which was at the cusp of literary studies in the country, was closed. Interestingly, one dean, Rhodes University's Ian Macdonald, faced off the rush into programmes – it never was a directive from the government – by suggesting that all he would do was 'learn the language'. Like all efforts that hope to rupture the crafted balance upon which the humanities rest, this approach was corrosive rather than creative. Notwithstanding this, the temptation to make the humanities 'useful' to the market continues. (One institution has recently out-imagined even the Hegelian ingenuity of Fukuyama by proposing to launch a programme called the Bachelor of Commerce Honours in Peace, Security and Economic Development!)

Individual academics have published thoughts on their own fears for the humanities. This work is often a mix of fear for the future of the established canon mixed with the difficult political issues involved in transformation, especially the consistent pressures to rethink and reconsider the curriculum in the cause of 'Africanisation' (Cornwell 2006). These same issues were dramatically highlighted in a controversy at UCT in 1996 involving the distinguished Africanist, Mahmood Mamdani, who then held the AC Jordan Chair of African Studies, and the university authorities over the development of a syllabus for a foundation course in African studies. Mamdani's proposal, which drew strongly on a Pan-Africanist perspective, so countering the hold of metropolitan thinking, was rejected by his faculty colleagues; he later resigned to take up a chair at Columbia. Undoubtedly, this was but the first salvo in deep and fierce debates that are certain to follow, and indicates why conversations on the epistemologies in the humanities and social sciences are necessary.

There have been interesting moves towards (what are sometimes called) the 'new disciplines' in South Africa. Embryonic interest in film studies has, for example, developed into a healthy and flourishing programme at UCT. The same university has also developed a strongly institutionalised gender programme through the African Gender Institute which publishes the continent's first regional gender studies journal, *Feminist Africa*. A number of other universities have developed programmes in gender or women's studies. Other new disciplines have been developed around HIV/AIDS – an issue in which South Africa has an obvious interest given that it has the highest infection rate in the world. Here, the perennial interface between, in this case, medical sciences and the humanities, has generated many tensions, although an annual HIV/AIDS conference has witnessed interesting areas of cooperation. In this area, the HSRC has developed an international reputation in second generation surveillance of the pandemic.

Studies into water have also seen work done at the interface between the natural and the social sciences; some universities have developed cross disciplinary postgraduate degrees in the field, such as those run through the recently established Institute for Water Studies at the University of the Western Cape (UWC). Equally successful, and at the same institution, has been the development of work dedicated to the sensitive issue of land, its redistribution and agricultural policy through the Programme for Land, Agricultural and Agrarian Studies (PLAAS). Following Thabo Mbeki's championing of the notion, a Centre for African Renaissance Studies was established at Unisa in June 2003. An innovative intellectual development was the establishment of a dedicated institute, called the Wits Institute for Social and Economic Research (WISER), at the University of the Witwatersrand in 2001. In other places, for instance the Centre for the Humanities at UWC and the Centre for Critical Racism at the University of KwaZulu-Natal, newer efforts at developing and strengthening the humanities are underway.

Some disciplines, such as African languages, have had to reinvent themselves. Early settlers were involved in the codification of these languages and, during the apartheid years, the teaching and associated research related to African languages, especially in Afrikaans universities, was mainly aimed at language fluency; in the English universities, a move towards linguistics took these languages away from their moorings in the community. After 1994, most African language departments experienced a decline in students, including mother tongue speakers. This was part of a multifaceted process: the shift towards English as the language of globalisation; the attitude of students towards studying their mother tongue; and the cessation of the teaching of African languages within the schooling system. As a result, new courses were developed for both mother tongue and non-mother tongue students. At Rhodes University this process has involved, ironically, access to foreign funding through the South Africa–Norway Tertiary Education programme (SANTED) which has involved the development of non-mother tongue vocational language courses in isiXhosa and the design of mother tongue courses in isiXhosa which are linked to market related requirements. These offer courses in translation studies, language and technology, language and society, language planning, orthography and writing skills, communication and media studies, as well as the teaching of literature as a discipline which is related to society. While the result has been a marked growth in student numbers, the turn towards the market in this success story seems undeniable.

More concerted efforts are underway to mobilise support for the humanities by organising across universities which are often forced to compete for students and funding. The deans of humanities faculties have recently met and committed themselves to the formation of an organisation called the South African Humanities Deans Association (SAHUDA). Whether these meetings can lead to anything more substantial – or even an organised process of lobbying – is still an open question. Perhaps, the most interesting development was a decision by the Academy of Science of South Africa (ASSAf) to create a consensus panel on the state of the humanities in South Africa. Driven by some of the concerns that have been raised in these pages, the panel hopes to deliver a report (in October 2010) on ways to revive the humanities within academia, and to explore ideas to reassert the centrality of the humanities in South Africa's national life.

The new energy in South Africa's humanities – whatever its funding or institutional base – has the single goal of bringing a deeper understanding of the importance of the humanities in a country still in search of its self. From their commanding places during the long struggle to end apartheid, the humanities seem orphaned by the rise of the 'New South Africa' and by the country's manufactured rejection of what the humanities can offer both the country and humankind.

The title of this chapter, 'Silencing and worse', is drawn from Günter Grass's 1988 Nobel lecture. The challenge which faces the humanities in the country is to break the silence, and this begins, as André Brink has suggested, by recognising that for South Africa and its people the '*reality* ... [of transformation] ... only begins where *information* ends' (Brink 2001: 3-4).

NOTES

1   A version of this paper has appeared as 'The Humanities and Social Sciences "Orphaning the Orphan"'In Roseanne Diab and Wieland Gevers (Eds) *The State of Science in South Africa*. Pretoria: ASSAf. (2009), 211-238. Like the original, this version has benefitted from the comments of two anonymous reviewers.

REFERENCES

Abromeit J (1994) Remembering Adorno. *Radical Philosophy* 124: 27–38.
Anderson B (1991) *Imagined Communities: Reflections on the Origin and Spread of Nationalism*. London: Verso.
Ayers E (2009) Where the humanities live. *Daedalus* 138 (1): 24-34.
Attwell D (2005) *Rewriting Modernity. Studies in Black South African Literary History*. Scottsville: University of KwaZulu-Natal Press.
Biko S (1978) *I Write What I Like: Selected Writings* (Edited by Aelred Stubbs). San Francisco: Harper & Row.
Brink A (2001) Graduation Speech, Rhodes University, Grahamstown, 7 April.
Bozzoli B (1981) Challenging local orthodoxies. *Social Dynamics* 6 (2): 53-59.
Burawoy M (2004) Public sociology: South African dilemmas in a global context. *Society in Transition* 35 (1): 11–26.
Cornwell G (2006) On the 'Africanization' of English Studies in South Africa. *Arts and Humanities in Higher Education* 5 (2): 117–126.
Crary D (1988) A university for alternatives. *Daily Dispatch*, 9 March.
Degenaar J (1977) The concept of a volksuniversiteit. In Van der Merwe HW and D Welsh (Eds) *The Future of the University in Southern Africa*. New York: St Martin's Press.
Dubow S (2006) *A Commonwealth of Learning. Science, Sensibility and White South Africa 1820-2000*. Oxford: Oxford University Press.
Furedi F (2004) *Where Have All the Intellectuals Gone?* London: Continuum.
Gordon R (1988) Apartheid's anthropologists: the genealogy of Afrikaner anthropology. *American Ethnologist* 15 (3): 535–553.
Guilhot N (2008) The realist gambit: postwar American political science and the birth of IR theory. *International Political Sociology* 2 (4): 281–304.
Harpham G (2005) Beneath and beyond the 'crisis in the humanities'. *New Literary History* 36(1): 21–36.
Higgins J (2007) 'It's literacy, stupid!': declining the humanities in the National Research Foundation (NRF) research policy. *Journal of Higher Education in Africa* 5 (1): 95–112.

Jubber K (1983) Sociology and its social context: the case of the rise of Marxist sociology in South Africa. *Social Dynamics* 9 (2): 50–63.

Lerner D (1959) *The Human Meaning of the Social Sciences*. New York: Meridian Books.

Macfarlane D (2007) Education under the axe. *Mail & Guardian Online*, 29 July.

Maharasoa M and D Hay (2001) Higher education and graduate employment in South Africa. *Quality in Higher Education* 7 (2): 139–147.

Manganyi NC (1973) *Being Black in the World*. Johannesburg: SPROCAS/Ravan.

Mangcu X (2008) *To the Brink. The State of Democracy in South Africa*. Scottsville: University of KwaZulu-Natal Press.

McDonald P (2009) *The Literature Police. Apartheid Censorship and its Cultural Consequences*. Oxford: Oxford University Press.

McQuarrie M (2007) Knowledge production, publicness and the structural transformation of the university: an interview with Craig Calhoun. *Thesis Eleven*, 84.

Mkandawire T (Ed) (2005) *African Intellectuals. Rethinking Politics, Language, Gender and Development*. Dakar: CODESRIA Books.

NRF (2007) Evaluation and Rating. Facts and Figures. Pretoria: National Research Foundation, July 2007.

NRF (2009) Trajectories for NRF research support. Pretoria, National Research Foundation, May 2009.

Parenti H (2006) Patricians, professionals, and political science. *American Political Science Review* 100 (4): 499–505.

Rhodes University Calendar (1961).

Rorty R (1999) The humanistic intellectual: eleven theses. In Rorty R (Ed) *Philosophy and Social Hope*. London: Penguin.

Ross E (2007) The History of the Department of Social Work at Wits: 1937–2007. Johannesburg. Emthonjeni Centre, University of the Witwaterstrand.

Ross K (2002) *May '68 and its Afterlives*. Chicago: University of Chicago Press.

Rothschild E (2002) *Economic Sentiments: Adam Smith, Condorcet and the Enlightenment* . Cambridge, MA: Harvard University Press.

Saunders M (2002) *Complicities. The Intellectual and Apartheid*. Scottsville: University of Natal Press.

Schatzki TR (2009) Dimensions of social theory. In Jacklin H and P Vale (Eds) *Re-imagining the Social: Critique, Theory and Post-apartheid Society*. Scottsville: University of KwaZulu-Natal Press.

Seiler J (1973) South African foreign policy and South African perspectives of the world. Paper prepared for delivery at the 1973 Annual Meeting of the American Political Science Association, New Orleans, 4–8 September.

Sharma S (1991) *The Embarrassment of Riches: An Interpretation of the Dutch*. London: Fontana.

Sitas A (1997) The waning of sociology in South Africa. *Society in Transition* 28 (1-4): 12–19.

Slaughter S (2007 Narratives and networks: money and power. Studying the politics of knowledge in a global era. Paper presented at the conference on The Politics of Academic Knowledge in a Global Era: Nationalism, Cosmopolitanism, and Market Values (POAK) organised by the International Centre for Advanced Studies, New York University and the Institute of History, Hungarian Academy of Sciences. Budapest, Hungary 16 to 18 July 2007.

Smit AP (1984) *Staatsondertuende natuur- en geestesweyenskaplike navorsing in Suid-Afrika 1918-1969*, Pretoria: Raad vir Geesteswetenskaplike Navorsing.

Van Jaarsveld FA (1964) *The Afrikaner's Interpretation of South African History*. Cape Town: Simondium Publishers.

Van Onselen C (2004) Address delivered on receiving an Honorary Doctorate from Rhodes University, 2 April.

White C (undated) Research Institutes. Can the HSRC join in the future? *Mimeo*.

Wright L (2006) A research prospectus for the humanities. In Marcus T and A Hofmaenner (Eds) *Shifting Boundaries of Knowledge. A View on Social Sciences, Law and Humanities in South Africa*. Scottsville: University of KwaZulu-Natal Press.

CHAPTER 12

Realising transformation, equity and social justice in higher education

Kezia Lewins

———

South Africa has come from an unequal past in which higher education institutions were designed to confer privilege upon a minority of the population identified through social signifiers of race, gender, and language – an inequality affecting students (how, where and what they could study), staff (who could become academics, administrators and service workers, where and to what occupational level they could ascend); and governance (how institutions were governed and who governed them).

Since 1994, the higher education sector has been moulded in three principal ways. First, through restructuring, whereby institutions were rationalised and merged to make a more coherent higher education system; second, through transformation to render the sector more accessible, equitable, representative and socially responsive; and third, through the implementation of managerial and market logic, corporate efficiency and global competitiveness. The operation of these three processes has often proved to be contradictory, and higher education institutions and their constituencies have found themselves confronting constant crises.

This overview seeks to examine how the sector has fared in terms of transformation, equity and social justice. It acknowledges criticisms that the visionary and expansive nature of transformation as envisaged in the Education White Paper 3 of 1997 has been replaced in practice by a limited focus on equity statistics to gauge student and staff transformation. Jansen (1998 and 2004) has criticised this approach as seldom amounting to more than 'racial accounting', while others (Erasmus 2010 and 2008; Habib 2004) have pondered the complexities of contin-uing to use apartheid categories as indicators to measure post-apartheid change. Nonetheless, the utilisation of equity statistics continues to be a powerful tool, and it is within this light that this chapter uses statistics on student and staff transformation as a proxy for determining progress. An attempt is made here to reflect on both student and staff transformation with the aim of drawing meaningful connections between them.

The chapter relies principally upon data drawn from the Department of Education's Higher Education Management Information Systems (HEMIS). Student data is largely extracted in an already collated format from the South African Survey and various reports of the Council for Higher Education (CHE), while staff data is largely derived from previous work done by the author. It is acknowledged that there are challenges to the utility of the HEMIS database such as the difficulties in conducting temporal and spatial comparisons because of changes in the type of data recorded. Limitations also exist in that demographic data is reported in aggregate (by race or gender and not by intersection of race and gender). Nonetheless it is the most com-prehensive data available and as such is invaluable for evaluating the extent of transformation.

STUDENT TRANSFORMATION

Student transformation can be measured by equity in access, participation and performance within higher education. Equity can be assessed by examining student participation rates, enrolments, graduation rates, degree or programme choices, success rates, and institutional affiliation. A comprehensive review of each of these is beyond the scope of this chapter (but see CHE 2009a and CHE 2009b) although a snapshot analysis will nevertheless be provided to shed light on student transformation.

Cooper and Subotsky (2001) argue that student transformation has occurred organically and represents a revolution when compared with the transformation of staff. However, the data presented here will show that student transformation is still far from complete and that large inequities remain in four specific areas: i) enrolments versus graduates, ii) undergraduate versus postgraduate enrolments and performance, iii) race-based equity versus gender-based equity; and iv) disciplinary and institutional inequities.

Enrolments versus graduation

The reality and continued legacy of the apartheid education system has meant that the pro-portion of the population with higher education qualifications is still highly racially skewed. By 2007, 16.3 per cent of all twenty to twenty-four year-olds were enrolled in higher education (DoE 2008: 124). However, participation rates continued to reflect both racialised and gendered patterns. White females, Indian females and white males continued to have the highest participation rates of over 50 per cent; African males, coloured males and African females continued to have the lowest participation rates of below 15 per cent. While table 1 demon-strates some equity improvements – for example, among coloured and Indian females – it also shows that African males have experienced a minimal increase in participation rates, even though nationally African males are the second largest demographic category. Undoubtedly, the current participation rates of African males are below an acceptable transformatory range.

Table 1: Comparison of higher education participation rates of all 20–24 year-olds enrolled in higher education in 2001 and 2007, disaggregated by race and gender

| Year | Race and Gender | | | | | | | | | |
| | African | | Coloured | | Indian | | White | | Total | |
	Male	Female	Male	Female	Male	Female	Male	Female	Male	Female
2001	9.1%	11.3%	8.3%	8.7%	40.2%	44.3%	57.9%	59.9%	13.0%	15.1%
2007	10.8%	13.8%	11.2%	15.6%	42.3%	54.7%	53.0%	61.5%	14.4%	18.1%
per cent change	+1.7%	+2.5%	+2.9%	+6.9%	+2.1%	+10.4%	-4.9%	+1.6%	+1.4%	+3.0%

(Adapted from Appendix 2 of DoE, 2008: 124))

This skewed participation in higher education is further exacerbated when general participation is compared to output. In 2005 a total of 735 073 students enrolled in higher education, and 120 418 graduated. This represents national participation rates of 26.1 per 1 000 of the national population of twenty to twenty-four year-olds (CHE 2009b: 37 and Statistics South Africa 2005). Meanwhile, master's graduates in 2005 accounted for 0.98 of all twenty-five to thirty-four year-olds and 1.52 of all thirty-five to forty-four year-olds in 2005 with the respective data for doctoral graduates being 0.15 for twenty-five to thirty-four year-olds and 0.23 for thirty-five to forty-four year-olds (CHE 2009a: 41–3). The extent of fallout between initial participation and doctoral graduation shows that only a very small minority graduate the system.

However, this aggregate fallout masks great inequities across various demographic categories. White master's and doctoral graduates amounted to 8.53 and 1.43 per 1 000 white population aged twenty-five to thirty-four in 2005, compared to African master's and doctoral graduates who comprised 0.40 and 0.05 per 1 000 African population aged twenty-five to thirty-four in 2005 (CHE 2009a: 41).

While these inequalities have significant ramifications when it comes to the generalised, scarce and critical skills pools, they should not however obscure the fact that all categories experienced a positive growth of postgraduates between 2001 and 2005 with a growth rate of 15.4 per cent and 9.6 per cent in African master's and doctoral graduates and an increase of 18.6 per cent and 9.4 per cent for coloured master's and doctoral graduates respectively (CHE 2009a: 43).

The extent of access to and participation in higher education is inevitably curtailed by socio-economic inequality, notably ever-increasing tuition and accommodation costs, a declining proportion of the national budget spent on higher education, and an increasing demand for financial aid and the tightening of bursary loan conditions (Lewins and Nieftagodien 2008: 31) In combination, these have meant that while mechanisms have been put in place by the state to widen access to and participation in higher education, the extent and efficacy of the mechanisms leaves much to be desired. Letseka *et al* (2010: 38) argue convincingly that student poverty is the most important issue to be tackled if the student dropout is to be addressed. This clearly highlights the importance of instituting more mechanisms to get and keep black and working class students into and graduating from higher education.

Race and gender: Undergraduate versus postgraduate students

Of all university enrolments in 2007, 59.5 per cent were African, 6.1 per cent coloured, 7.7 per cent Indian and 26.7 per cent white (SAIRR, 2009: 92). Tables 2 and 3 below illustrate the sector-wide enrolments in various types of degrees as well as postgraduate graduations for 2001, 2004 and 2007.

Table 2 shows a relatively small increase in the percentage of black undergraduates (from 65 per cent to 69 per cent), a significant increase in the percentage of black postgraduates (from 50 per cent to 61 per cent of master's students and from 37 per cent to 54 per cent of doctoral students), and most notably an increase in African doctoral students (whose proportion rose from 25 per cent to 39 per cent of all such students). This suggests that although general access by black students to higher education appears to have stabilised in the 2000s, more black students were gaining access to postgraduate programmes and this bodes well for the transformation agenda in terms of the expansion of a professional skills pool for the economy and a skills pool from which future academics may be sourced.

Table 2: Comparison of undergraduate, master's and PhD enrolments by race and gender in 2000 and 2007

Race and gender	Undergraduate degree enrolments		Master's enrolments		Doctoral enrolments	
	2000	2007	2000	2007	2000	2007
African	51%	52%	36%	46%	25%	39%
Coloured	5%	7%	6%	6%	5%	6%
Indian	9%	10%	8%	9%	7%	8%
Total Black	65%	69%	50%	61%	37%	53%
White	35%	31%	49%	36%	62%	47%
Male	53%	55%	-	-	-	-
Female	47%	45%	-	-	-	-

(Adapted from Appendix 2 of DoE, 2008: 124 – 125).

At the aggregate level, the decrease in the proportion of female undergraduate students (from 47 per cent to 45 per cent reflected in table 2) is a potential cause for concern. The CHE (2009a: 26) reports stabilising proportions of female postgraduates; 57 per cent of honours, 45 per cent of master's and 40 per cent of doctoral enrolments in 2005 were of female students. This raises questions about whether female participation is reaching an expected plateau based on population demographics or whether female participation has begun to subside in the second decade post-apartheid. Given the problematisation of female graduation rates (provided later) it would seem as though the claims regarding the successes of the feminisation of higher education are indeed premature and universities as well as the public and private sector need to do more to attract and retain female students particularly in subjects outside of social science and humanities.

Enrolments depict an expansion of access to higher education, but only success, throughput, and graduation rates assess equitable performance and are a fair estimation of the degree of student transformation. In 2007, only white students met the DoE's target of an 80 per cent success rate. The success rate of Indian students was about 78 per cent. Coloured students averaged 71 per cent, and African students experienced a 67 per cent success rate (DoE 2008: 124).

Furthermore, a cohort study of all first-time entering students in 2000 reflected that by 2004 only 24 per cent of African students had graduated compared to 48 per cent of white students; 65 per cent and 41 per cent of African and white students respectively had dropped out of university altogether (DoE 2008: 75). This signifies not only equity concerns but also more generalised concerns about the efficiency of the higher education system. Indeed, of the 2002 cohort, 51 per cent of the entire class had dropped out between initial enrolment and the end of 2007 (SAIRR 2009: 103) suggesting that the majority of undergraduate students, and particularly black students, fail to complete their degrees.

Transformation related questions are raised by these high drop-out rates and whether they are in the main due to academic or financial reasons (for more on this see Letseka *et al* 2010). In part, concerns regarding academic exclusions (self or institutional) might possibly be addressed by diverting such less-academically prepared students into more vocational oriented programmes within the further or higher education sector; the institutional differentiation debate within the sector highlights the anticipated growth of further education in order to meet the economy's vocational skill requirements. However, if this is implemented it will need to be done in such a way so as not to close down the academic route to students who may wish to pursue it but who may require more preparation for higher education. Such an approach is not, of course, a substitute for better preparing students at the primary and secondary levels but attempts to short-cut the comprehensive and long-term change this requires will inevitably be read as the reinforcement of separate and unequal education. However, with financial exclusions, the system is doing a disservice to students who are in fact academically capable and who with better financing could be expected to succeed within higher education.

Race versus gender equity

Of all higher education graduates in 2007, 44.1 per cent were African, 6.3 per cent coloured, 8.7 per cent Indian and 40.6 per cent white (SAIRR 2009: 96). The near to parity proportion between African and white graduates demonstrates very clearly that white students are still more likely to exit higher education with a degree. Nonetheless, there is positive change amongst higher degree holders (table 3), with 13 per cent and 14 per cent increases in the proportions of master's and doctoral degrees respectively attained by black students (with 9 per cent of master's and 12 per cent of doctoral graduations going to African students). This indicates that race-based equity, while not uniform, has in general been positive, although internal blockages and financial considerations appear to be limiting the extent to which students continue with further higher education qualifications on a continuous and full-time basis.

However, the decline of 4 per cent for master's and the recent drop to 2000 levels (that is, 59 per cent) of doctoral degrees going to female students is of potential concern and signals that the surge in the feminisation of the student profile may be beginning to level off. To derive more analytical precision in measurement, it would be helpful if enrolment as well as graduation data was disaggregated by race and gender as a matter of course. Such analysis was begun by Koen (2006) who demonstrated that white women had become the single most populous category graduating with postgraduate degrees. Such analyses are of crucial significance if skills pools and future equity targets are to be addressed in any meaningful way and if we are to get to grips with the intersectional functioning of inequalities in practice.

Table 3: Master's and PhD graduates by race and gender in 2000, 2004 and 2007

Race and gender	Master's			Doctoral		
	2000	2004	2007	2000	2004	2007
African	26%	34%	37%	21%	27%	32%
Coloured	5%	6%	5%	4%	5%	5%
Indian	7%	9%	9%	6%	9%	8%
Total Black	38%	49%	51%	31%	41%	45%
White	61%	51%	49%	69%	55%	54%
Male	42%	44%	46%	41%	38%	41%
Female	58%	56%	54%	59%	62%	59%

(Adapted from Appendix 2 of DoE, 2008: 126).

This data shows generalised improvements in access and graduation by black students, but the analysis still needs to take stock of performance as disaggregated by field of study and institution. Whilst both the Council for Higher Education and individual institutions continue to monitor student progress, many of these analyses continue to use pre-2007 data, hence this analysis will use 2007 data as the most up to date information currently available.

Disciplinary inequalities

Table 4 reflects on the disciplines that attract the largest proportion of all graduates (eleven disciplines collectively accounted for 85.8 per cent of all graduates in 2007). Business, commerce and management science graduated the largest proportion of graduates (24.6 per cent in 2007), followed by education (12.1 per cent), healthcare and health sciences (9.1 per cent), social science and studies (8.3 per cent) and life and physical sciences (5.8 per cent). Table 4 also depicts the relative popularity of each disciplinary category by race. For ease of analysis, the top five most popular disciplines within each racial category are in bold font.

Table 4: The top eleven disciplines in which (bachelor's and higher) degrees were awarded in 2007

Field of study	Race					Total
	African	Coloured	Indian	Black	White	
Business, commerce and management sciences	22.0%	23.2%	36.6%	24.3%	24.9%	24.6%
Education	17.9%	11.6%	4.9%	15.3%	7.5%	12.1%
Healthcare and health sciences	8.4%	11.2%	12.4%	9.3%	8.9%	9.1%
Social science and studies	9.8%	9.7%	7.0%	9.3%	6.9%	8.3%
Life and physical sciences	5.7%	5.4%	6.2%	5.7%	5.8%	5.8%
Law	5.1%	6.1%	5.7%	5.3%	6.4%	5.7%
Engineering and engineering technology	5.0%	4.4%	6.4%	5.2%	6.3%	5.6%
Psychology	3.6%	7.2%	4.9%	4.2%	6.5%	5.1%
Public administration and social services	6.1%	4.5%	1.5%	5.2%	1.1%	3.5%
Computer science and data processing	2.9%	3.4%	3.5%	3.1%	2.9%	3.0%
Languages, linguistics and literature	2.1%	4.0%	2.4%	2.3%	4.0%	3.0%
Percent age of all graduates in top 11 disciplines	88.6%	90.7%	91.5%	90.1%	81.2%	85.8%

(Adapted from SAIRR, 2009: Education Online: 96 - 7)

Business, commerce and management sciences are overwhelmingly the most popular disciplines amongst all graduates. Education, health science and social science are also popular, but what is particularly interesting is the popularity of public administration and social services among African graduates, psychology among coloured and white graduates, and engineering and engineering technology among Indian graduates. This suggests a continued racialisation of specific professional and academic disciplines for some time to come. Furthermore, it emphasises the need for qualitative exploration into the reasons for such racialisation and why efforts to deracialise them have not yielded successes seen in more equitable disciplines.

Examining fields of study by their relative popularity among graduates provides some insight into the element of student self-selection. Table 5 demonstrates that in 2007 above 60 per cent of graduates in public administration and social services, education, computer science and data processing, and health and healthcare sciences, were black. Meanwhile, between 45 per cent and 54 per cent of graduates in languages, linguistics and literature, psychology, engineering and engineering technology, and law were black. In contrast, 88 per cent of public administration and social services graduates and 75 per cent of education graduates were black.

Table 5: The racial composition of the top eleven disciplines for which (bachelor's and higher) degrees were awarded in 2007

Field of study	Race				
	African	Coloured	Indian	Black	White
Business, commerce and management sciences	39.5%	6.0%	13.0%	58.5%	41.3%
Education	65.2%	6.0%	3.6%	74.8%	25.2%
Healthcare and health sciences	40.7%	7.7%	11.9%	60.3%	39.4%
Social science and studies	51.6%	7.4%	7.3%	66.3%	33.4%
Life and physical sciences	43.4%	5.9%	9.4%	58.7%	41.1%
Law	38.9%	6.7%	8.7%	54.3%	45.5%
Engineering and engineering technology	39.3%	4.9%	9.9%	54.1%	45.8%
Psychology	31.2%	8.9%	8.4%	48.6%	51.3%
Public administration and social services	76.1%	8.1%	3.6%	87.8%	12.2%
Computer science and data processing	43.2%	7.3%	10.2%	60.7%	39.2%
Languages, linguistics and literature	30.8%	8.4%	6.9%	46.1%	53.5%

(Adapted from SAIRR, 2009: Education Online: 96)

It is clearly important to reflect upon what makes disciplines popular or not across racial and gender categories as this might help address some of the more qualitative dimensions of student and professional transformation. It would allow for a more sophisticated analysis of supply and demand issues and would also better locate and address blockages within the system. So far, government has identified deficits in the science, engineering and technology sectors which have become a focus for further development. Various initiatives to improve the teaching and learning of maths and science at the school level in particular have been instituted. Koen (2006) began to track differential performance among postgraduates, but as this was exploratory in nature it tended to map trends rather than actually explaining them, or offering solutions. Erasmus and Breier (2009) argue that major improvements to the labour supply through increasing the number of graduates is one basic necessity for most professions but they also argue that improvements in the conditions of work also need to take place to make professions more attractive to potential students and graduates. There are also a number of studies initiated by discipline-based scholars in order to gauge students' perceptions of that particular discipline (such as Wessels and Steenkamp 2009).

However, there has yet to be a comprehensive overview of students' perceptions and experiences across disciplines in South African higher education. In order to assist with this the 2009 CHE report provides data on postgraduate major subject clusters.

Table 6: The proportion of postgraduate degrees awarded to black students in total and African students in 2000 and 2005

Major subject cluster		Honours		Master's		Doctoral	
		2000	2005	2000	2005	2000	2005
Natural and agricultural science	Total black	46%	44%	37%	45%	27%	45%
	African	33%	30%	29%	34%	17%	34%
Engineering and applied technology	Total black	38%	52%	26%	40%	15%	33%
	African	18%	42%	15%	26%	8%	24%
Health science	Total black	36%	37%	32%	46%	31%	42%
	African	26%	20%	20%	30%	19%	25%
Humanities	Total black	56%	44%	40%	42%	34%	39%
	African	47%	32%	29%	30%	24%	29%
Social science	Total black	45%	62%	43%	52%	33%	40%
	African	32%	49%	29%	37%	21%	26%
Total	Total black	47%	57%	39%	48%	30%	41%
	African	34%	44%	27%	33%	19%	29%

(Adapted from Appendix 2 of DoE, 2008: 126).

By 2005, most postgraduate subject clusters had 40 per cent black graduates. Black graduates accounted for 62 per cent and 52 per cent of honours and master's graduates in the social sciences respectively, and 45 per cent of doctoral graduates in the natural and agricultural sciences. In addition, 42 per cent of engineering and applied technology honours graduates, and 49 per cent and 37 per cent of social science honours and master's graduates respectively were black .

At the other end of the spectrum, 63 per cent of health science honours graduates, 58 per cent of humanities master's graduates as well as 61 per cent of humanities, 60 per cent of social science and 67 per cent of engineering and applied technology doctoral graduates were white. All disciplines depict some progress but also indicate that racial skewing is still largely prevalent at the top end of the degree structure. This will have a significant impact on both professional and academic occupational structures and their ability to meet equity targets in the foreseeable future. However, a complicating factor is that in 2005, foreign students contributed significantly to both master's and doctoral registrations at 19 per cent and 25 per cent respectively (CHE 2009a: 38). This indicates that raw statistics may be overstating levels of transformation regarding South African students.

Meanwhile, the importance of gender equity is typically understated in policy and evaluation documents. One reason for this may be the overstated feminisation of higher education represented by aggregate statistics which report that 59 per cent of honours, 45 per cent of master's and 44 per cent of doctoral degrees are awarded to women (CHE 2009a: 29). However, using 2005 data, the CHE reports that 78 per cent of all honours, 45 per cent of all master's and 41 per cent of all doctoral degrees awarded to female graduates were for social science subjects (CHE 2009a: 31). As depicted in table 7, women graduates were 'critically under-represented' in all other major subject clusters (CHE 2009a: 31). Although parity in bachelor's degrees awarded may bode well for the future, urgent interventions need to be made in most subject clusters as the current gender inequity is unacceptable. Such interventions would have to be multifaceted. The knowledge, familiarity and appeal of a variety of disciplines would need to be marketed further at schools, in universities and in the labour market. In particular, gendered stereotypes of what subjects are 'fitting' for men and women as well as 'whose' education should be prioritised when material resources are scarce needs to be seriously tackled. For the most part, these are long-term initiatives which need state and collective public support. In the short-term, targeted bursaries and employer-sponsored internships as well as pre-university partnerships (such as the University of the Witwatersrand's Targeting Talent project) are examples of small-scale interventions that may begin to shift the number and demographic profile of students into both traditional and nontraditional degree choices.

Furthermore, it is from the postgraduate levels that professionals are largely drawn and without more meaningful gender equity, the majority of professions will remain male dominated in numbers and institutional culture.

Table 7: Female graduates by qualification and by major subject cluster in 2000 and 2005:

	Honours		Master's		Doctoral	
Major subject cluster	2000	2005	2000	2005	2000	2005
Natural and agricultural science	8%	8%	5%	6%	10%	9%
Engineering and applied technology	0%	0%	1%	1%	1%	1%
Health science	2%	2%	7%	7%	8%	8%
Humanities	6%	5%	7%	9%	6%	8%
Social science	37%	41%	21%	22%	15%	18%

(CHE, 2009a: 30).

It is also important to examine the average age at which postgraduate degrees are earned. The mean ages at graduation are twenty-nine for honours graduates, thirty-four for master's graduates and forty for doctoral graduates (CHE 2009a: 35). Although these are late peaks in the attainment of educational qualifications, there is considerable differentiation across subject clusters. For example, 75 per cent of natural and agricultural science doctoral students graduated by the age of forty, compared with 65 per cent for engineering and applied technology, 54 per cent for health science, 42 per cent for humanities and 40 per cent for social science doctoral graduates (CHE 2009a: 37). These differential ages at doctoral graduation have a significant impact on the professional development and work-life productivity of academics and researchers in respective fields – and could also indicate a bias in higher degree bursary or grant funding which favours the sciences, engineering and technology.

Institutions

In addition to discipline choice, the historic classification of institutions also shapes experiences of students and staff.

Table 8 refers to the nine universities that each graduate 5 per cent or more of all students at the national level. It demonstrates that the University of KwaZulu-Natal (UKZN), the University of the Witwatersrand (Wits), and the University of South Africa (Unisa) have the most heterogeneous general graduate pool. The three also have the largest proportions of black bachelor's and honour's graduates at 80 per cent, 61 per cent and 58 per cent respectively, as well as the largest proportions of black master's and PhD graduates at 75 per cent, 56 per cent and 53 per cent respectively.

At the other end of the spectrum, the previously Afrikaans medium universities continue to have the least heterogeneous graduate pools; at the Universities of Stellenbosch and Pretoria,

Table 8: Universities that graduate 5 per cent and above of all graduates and the degree type and racial categorisation of graduates.

University	per cent of all national graduates	Racial categorisation of graduates				per cent of all national postgraduates	Racial categorisation of postgraduates			
		African	Coloured	Indian	White		African	Coloured	Indian	White
University of Cape Town	5.5%	25.1%	12.7%	8.1%	52.6%	9.8%	26.1%	9.0%	5.8%	55.7%
University of Free State	4.2%	39.5%	3.3%	1.7%	55.4%	6.1%	39.4%	3.4%	2.3%	54.9%
University of Johannesburg	7.8%	41.7%	3.3%	7.1%	47.9%	4.1%	30.7%	3.4%	7.9%	58.2%
University of KwaZulu Natal	8.5%	38.0%	2.6%	39.3%	20.0%	8.4%	40.8%	1.8%	32.5%	24.6%
North West University	7.8%	40.8%	3.1%	0.9%	55.3%	8.1%	26.1%	2.0%	4.9%	66.8%
University of Pretoria	11.0%	33.1%	1.4%	4.1%	61.5%	13.8%	32.3%	2.7%	6.1%	59.0%
University of South Africa	12.7%	40.2%	5.1%	12.2%	42.3%	7.6%	40.1%	3.6%	8.8%	47.4%
University of Stellenbosch	5.8%	6.0%	11.4%	0.9%	81.7%	11.5%	18.4%	8.8%	3.1%	69.7%
University of the Witwatersrand	5.8%	40.8%	2.9%	17.5%	38.7%	13.3%	42.7%	2.1%	11.7%	43.5%

(Adapted from SAIRR, 2009: 98 – 106).

only 18 per cent and 39 per cent of their bachelor's and honours graduates respectively are black, and at the master's and PhD level the percentages of black graduates at Stellenbosch and North West are only 30 per cent and 33 per cent respectively.

These nine universities graduate just under 70 per cent of all bachelor's and honours graduates and 83 per cent of all master's and doctoral graduates. Consequently, it is important to view their internal dynamics, systems and modes of functioning in order to evaluate the tertiary environment and experience to which students are exposed while within these institutions. That institutions face considerable challenges is due to their provincial location (and immediate feeder pool) as well as language policies which may limit their heterogeneity. This raises key questions of whether all institutions should be held to identical standards and whether a singular ideal type, where all institutions provide students with the same educational and social experience, should be the goal. The national institutional differentiation debate calls for different types of further and higher education institutions to cater for specific academic and vocational needs but little thought has been given to how this may reinforce historical patterns of student differentiation and exclusion. Instead it is assumed that through a few minor modifications institutions will overcome their differences and produce similarly well-equipped citizens who will realise the nation's multicultural and progressive agenda.

It is important to note that many smaller institutions are also fairly racially homogenous and thus do not escape the necessity for redress, as redress is not simply about increasing the proportion of black people and women within institutions but is also about enhancing the diversity of students and staff. Some examples include the Universities of Venda, Limpopo, and Zululand, as well as Walter Sisulu University of Science and Technology (which all have 99 per cent black graduates) and Fort Hare (92 per cent black graduates). In fact, of the universities that were previously designated for black students, it is only the universities of the Western Cape and Fort Hare that have managed to attract and maintain white graduates at a proportion above 5 per cent of all graduates.

Key issues in student transformation

The key issues that emerge from the preceding analysis are that although progress has been made in deracialising the overall student body, significant racial segmentation is still to be found in throughput rates and according to both subject discipline and higher education institution. The effect of race is less significant on completion and graduation amongst those who achieve senior higher education qualifications, but these are a minority and this says nothing of the majority who do not complete, and particularly of those who drop out from undergraduate degrees owing to financial and academic exclusion. Meanwhile, overall enrolments and graduation rates of women appear to be stagnating and there is cause for concern in terms of subject discipline specificities and the reinforcement of a highly gender segmented educational and labour market. The age at which graduation occurs, particularly for postgraduates, is also of concern given the burden this places on many students to do their postgraduate qualifications part-time and the implication this has for reduced years of optimum productivity post-graduation.

The importance of students' socio-economic class position is also of vital significance. Letseka *et al* (2010: 28) report that of institutions studied, 56 per cent of graduates were of low socio-economic status (SES), 21 per cent middle SES and 21 per cent of high SES. Meanwhile 70 per cent of noncompleters were of low SES compared with 16 per cent of middle SES and 12 per cent of high SES.

The Soudien report noted several of these issues without examining the intricate complexities of the system as a whole. It made recommendations to address the skewed nature of throughput to better improve the curriculum and to provide more academic and financial resources, as well as making recommendations to address issues such as problematic and exclusionary institutional cultures, racial and gender discrimination and the development of more progressive curriculum and language policies (DoE 2008: 73, 74 and 102). Such recommendations take the debate beyond the focus on equity statistics. However, the thrust of the argument here is that such recommendations cannot be implemented universally and need to recognise complexities across the entire sector.

STAFF TRANSFORMATION

Staff transformation is important as it speaks to transformation of the university workforce and to universities as worksites. It operates on several levels including staff equity in a range of occupational categories and hierarchies, equity in terms of performance (including the obtaining of doctoral degrees and academic publication), and the provision of funding and mentoring of emerging academics. In addition, transformation entails the fostering of an egalitarian, non-discriminatory, inclusive, and socially just institutional culture.

The extent to which the higher education sector has facilitated and driven staff transformation will be addressed by utilising, in the main, DoE statistics from the HEMIS Database. Data from three years (1987, 1997 and 2007) will be used to provide a series of longitudinal snapshots, although it is important to recognise that this has some considerable limitations. For a start, the dataset is not directly comparable across time because the 1987 data excludes several of what were then called homeland universities. In addition, because of the mergers that occurred during the 2000s, some staff who were included in the 2007 dataset were not reflected in earlier counts. Furthermore, only permanent full-time staff were captured, while contract and/or part-time staff were excluded. Nonetheless, the data has still been utilised as it is the best available.

With these limitations in mind, there are several main trends that can be identified during the twenty year period: i) there has been significant growth of research and instruction professionals (academics) by 136 per cent; ii) there has been an exponential expansion of executive, administrative and managerial professionals by 237 per cent as well as an increase of non-professional administrators by 233 per cent; iii) there has been a shrinkage of the non-professional service sector by 57 per cent; and iv) shifts in staffing demographics have occurred with differential success in regard to race or gender-based equity depending on the occupational type, grade, subject field and institution concerned. These changes bear testament to the increasing bureaucratisation of the higher education sector, the realignment of 'core' functions and the limited extent of equity gains that have been realised.

The irony is that the system reproduces itself in a way that increasingly emphasises the importance of bureaucratic administration at the expense of other essential services such as security, cleaning, maintenance and catering which have all become increasingly outsourced. The effect of this is twofold. First, it provides the new executive management with a seemingly legitimate excuse to shirk a part of the transformation (as social justice) agenda, by arguing that the so-called non-core staff are no longer part of the university. Second, the vital reproduction of university constituencies – workers, staff and students – through the provision of food, health and safety, occupational, learning and residential environment are externalised. Although much of this is done in the name of increasing efficiency, it makes the everyday life of campus increasingly subordinate to market logic.

Aside from whether such regimes have yielded more efficient organisations in practice, there are other transformation related limitations that accompany these structural changes. These include i) the reinforcement of racialised, class-based and gendered segmentation; ii) a failure of social responsiveness which has served to exclude large sections of the poor from being beneficiaries of change; and iii) the growing socio-economic inequality amongst workers on campus with the margin between the highest and lowest paid continuing to increase. As such, many changes occurring within the staffing sector are anti-transformation in both ideology and practice.

Academic staff transformation

The sector has moved from one in which 10 per cent of academics were black and 26 per cent female in 1987 to one which in 2007 was 39 per cent black and 43 per cent female (table 9). This amounts to a crude increase of 262 black academics and an increase of 217 women academics per year. In terms of race-based equity, more change is evident in the post-1997 period as black academics increased by 165 a year prior to 1997 and then increased to 359 a year post-1997. This suggests that for the sector as a whole, increasing race-based equity gains are evident since the implementation of the Employment Equity Act.

For women academics, there have also been significant equity gains, although the rate of change is less impressive. The number of women academics increased by an annual average of 149 a year prior to 1997 to 285 a year post-1997. Undoubtedly some of the differentiation between black and women academics can be explained through the differential starting points of each equity category. Nonetheless, in terms of the generalised academic labour force, both race-based and gender-based equity have gained momentum post-1997 although whether such growth rates are sufficient can only be fairly assessed with more precise and detailed data that reflects on actual recruitment and retention data compared to the recruitment skills pool.

When staffing data is disaggregated by institution (table 10), the proportion of black academics ranges from a high of 89 per cent and 84 per cent at Venda and Walter Sisulu respectively to a low of 15 per cent and 17 per cent at Stellenbosch and Rhodes respectively. The range for women academics among institutions is much smaller, with Unisa and Wits at a high of 52 per cent and 47 per cent respectively, and Venda and the Vaal University of Technology at a low of 31 per cent and 34 per cent respectively.

Table 9: Instruction and research professionals by race and gender in 1987, 1997 and 2007

Year	African		Coloured		Indian		Total Black		White		Other		Total	Male		Female	
	#	%	#	%	#	%	#	%	#	%	#	%	#	#	%	#	%
1987	490	5	193	2	260	3	943	10	8447	90	2	0	9392	6974	74	2418	26
1997	1779	16	290	3	523	5	2592	23	8652	77	2	0	11246	7338	65	3908	35
2007	3966	25	875	6	1344	9	6185	39	9383	59	244	2	15812	9056	57	6756	43

(DoE, 1988, 1998, 2008: Adapted from the HEMIS Database).

Table 10: Proportion of black and women instruction and research professionals in higher education institutions in 2007.

Institution	Black instruction and research professionals		Female instruction and research professionals		Total number of instruction and research professionals
	#	%	#	%	
Cape Peninsula University of Technology	331	50.4	254	38.7	657
University of Cape Town*	172	19.3	322	36.2	889
Cent ral University of Technology	74	33.0	90	40.2	224
Durban Institute of Technology	377	65.7	259	45.1	574
University of Fort Hare*	198	68.0	103	35.4	291
University of Free State	131	18.5	308	43.5	708
University of Johannesburg	243	27.9	382	43.9	871
University of KwaZulu Natal*	830	54.2	667	43.6	1531
University of Limpopo	570	75.3	296	39.1	757
Nelson Mandela Metropolitan University	101	19.1	226	42.8	528
North West University	269	30.3	355	39.9	889
University of Pretoria*	309	19.1	750	46.3	1619
Rhodes University	53	16.6	111	34.7	320
University of South Africa	399	29.9	698	52.3	1335
University of Stellenbosch	129	15.4	339	40.4	840
Tshwane University of Technology	323	39.4	320	39.1	819
University of Venda	248	89.2	87	31.3	278
Vaal University of Technology	221	55.9	134	33.9	395
Walter Sisulu University of Science and Technology	442	84.0	222	42.2	526
University of the Western Cape	312	60.5	238	46.1	516
University of the Witwatersrand	285	28.8	464	46.9	989
University of Zululand	165	71.4	95	41.1	231
Mangosuthu University of Technology	70	72.9	36	37.5	96

(DoE, 2008: Adapted from the HEMIS Database).

[University of Cape Town total also includes 225, that of University of Fort Hare 1, that of UKZN 14, and of Pretoria 4 staff classified as 'other']

According to table 10, three institutions had academic staff complements with over 75 per cent black staff, eight institutions fell within the 50 to 74 per cent range, and six institutions fell within the 49 per cent to 25 per cent range, while a further six had less than 24 per cent black academic staff. Hence the heterogeneity of staffing is to some extent in line with the hetero-geneity seen for students. According to Bezuidenhout *et al* (2008: 45), equity employment data submitted to the Department of Labour indicates that most institutions retain their dominance by overwhelmingly white or African staff with very few reflecting heterogeneity across each of the four specificied racial categories. Further, although the 2006 sectoral average stood at 37.7 per cent for black academic staff, African academic staff averaged at 23.6 per cent compared to 6.2 per cent for coloured academics and 7.9 per cent for Indian academics.

An analysis of academic rank and discipline of tenure are crucial in the analysis of staff trans-formation, but this data is more difficult to come by. Data on the proportion of academics per rank is available but it is not disaggregated by race or gender. From 2007 data, 52.3 per cent were employed in senior positions: 13.9 per cent were employed as professors, 10.6 per cent were associate professors and 27.8 per cent were senior lecturers. In junior positions, 41.2 per cent were employed as lecturers, 5.9 per cent as junior lecturers and 0.6 per cent were employed in positions lower than junior lecturer (DoE 2008 HEMIS Database). From limited institutional data and literature, one can infer that the majority of women and black academics are located in more junior positions within the academic hierarchy and also tend to be employed over-whelmingly within faculties such as humanities, commerce and health science.

The age range of academics is also important given issues such as the loss of senior and experienced academics with high publication output and the ability to mentor younger staff. In 2007, of those whose age was known, only 2.8 per cent of academics were over the age of sixty, while 23.4 per cent were between forty-five and fifty-nine, 72.8 per cent were between twenty-five and forty-four, and 1.1 per cent were below twenty-five (DoE 2008 HEMIS Database). While this does not invalidate the concern over retirees, it does highlight the pro-portion of new and emerging academics and hence makes the issue of mentoring and staff development even more crucial.

Although not disaggregated by rank, data on academic qualifications provides some indi-cation of the skills level within the sector: 80.7 per cent have university qualifications, 9.5 per cent have technikon qualifications, and the remaining 9.8 per cent have qualifications from elsewhere. Of all academics, 71.1 per cent have a higher degree and 56 per cent of these are doctoral degrees or equivalents. This illustrates that although the doctoral degree is seen as the entry qualification for the professoriate, it is not the entry qualification for academia in general. It is the norm for those in senior posts to have doctorates, but the overwhelming majority of junior academics do not; whereas 81.6 per cent of professors and 69.7 per cent of associate professors have doctorates, only 37.0 per cent of senior lecturers and 10.7 per cent of lecturers have doctoral degrees or equivalent (DoE HEMIS Database). This illustrates the extent of staff development required. In this regard, the government has emphasised that staff development must be an integral part of institutional planning, and that earmarked funds will be put aside for staff development, to be matched by equal funding from institutions themselves (DoE 2008: 61-62).

Supervisory load is also a crucial indicator not only of the academic workload burden but also of the conditions under which emerging scholars develop. According to the CHE, the burden of supervision has grown between 2000 and 2005 with the average academic staff member supervising five master's students and two doctoral students. Furthermore, this burden is largely carried by health and social science academics who on average supervise about eleven post-graduate students while academics in the natural and agricultural sciences supervise fewer than five (table 11).

The reality for most academics in South Africa is that they enter the academic labour market post-master's and work as junior lecturers or lecturers while also working on their doctoral degrees. Although this meets the immediate needs of academics and the academic labour markets, it produces systemic inefficiencies such as fewer academic staff being available for doctoral supervision.

Table 11: Supervisory burden: ratio of postgraduate students per academic staff by subject cluster

	Master's		Doctoral		Total	
Subject clusters	2000	2005	2000	2005	2000	2005
All subject clusters	3.8	5.2	1.3	2.2	5.1	7.4
Natural & Agricultural science	2.2	3	1.5	1.8	3.7	4.8
Engineering & applied technologies	4.9	5.3	1.9	2.7	6.8	8.0
Health	7.3	8.5	2	2.8	9.3	11.3
Humanities	3.4	4.8	1.6	2.9	5.0	7.7
Social Science	6.6	8.5	1.7	3	8.3	11.5

(CHE, 2009a: xx).

Differences across institutions and across subject clusters are also significant. Table 12 depicts the average number of master's and doctoral students per supervisor by university although even this level of analysis blurs the differentiation across the sector and across subjects. For example, academics in the natural and agricultural sciences at Wits and Unisa, as well as academics in health science and humanities at RU, supervise the least master's students (at an average of between one and two). At the other end of the spectrum, academics in the health sciences at Wits, Unisa and UKZN, in the humanities at the UL, and in social science at RU, Unisa and UL all supervise in excess of ten students each with health science academics at Wits supervising the most (averaging out at just under thirty master's students per academic staff member) (CHE 2009a: 24).

At the doctoral level, academics in the natural and agricultural sciences at Wits and Unisa, health sciences at UP, and humanities at NMMU and at Wits supervise an average of fewer than one doctoral student per academic. Academics with the heaviest doctoral supervisory loads include those in engineering and applied technologies at NWU and at UJ, in health science at NWU, Unisa and Wits, in humanities at NWU and UP and in social science at NWU,

UJ, UKZN and UP, where there are more than four doctoral students per academic staff member. The case of NWU is particularly alarming as academics in engineering and applied technology, as well as in health science, supervise twenty-three and and just under nineteen doctoral students respectively (CHE 2009a: 24).

The other major indicator of academic productivity is research publication. According to the ISI Web of Science (which captures about three-quarters of all accredited journal articles), South African authored articles have steadily increased and peaked at 8 632 articles in 2008 (CHE 2009b: 47). Over two-thirds of these are authored by academics in the five research universities (CHE 2009b: 48). Furthermore, the post-2004 exponential increase in publication is perceived to be due to the new subsidy framework along with increasing publications by both permanent and contract academic staff, postgraduate students and visiting scholars (CHE 2009b: 48–49). This third stream income has proved to be an important source of funding for both institutions and individual academics, although an analysis of its effects on staffing, teaching, research and writing as well as supervision needs to be conducted.

Only 10 per cent of research output subsidy is derived from monographs, chapters in collective works and published conference proceedings. These are rated highly by academics, although the subsidy system deems the effort put into such publications to be disproportional (CHE 2009b: 51). The subsidy system therefore fails to appropriately reward sustained and rigorous academic work such as book-length publications, instead privileging shorter journal

Table 12: Average master's and doctoral student ratio per academic at the country's universities

	Master's student ratio		Doctoral student ratio	
University	*2000*	*2005*	*2000*	*2005*
Nelson Mandela Metropolitan University (NMMU)	4.3	4.1	1.3	1.5
North West University (NWU)	6.8	6.7	1.3	5.2
Rhodes University (RU)	2.1	2.5	1.5	1.5
Stellenbosch University (SU)	5.1	7.1	1.7	2.3
University of Cape Town (UCT)	4.9	5.6	1.9	2.6
University of Free State (UFS)	4.0	5.2	1.7	1.8
University of Johannesburg (UJ)	5.1	4.7	2.1	2.8
University of KwaZulu-Natal (UKZN)	3.5	5.1	1.3	2.3
University of Limpopo (UL)	2.7	4.4	0.4	1.6
University of South Africa (Unisa)	3.8	7.3	0.2	2.1
University of Pretoria (UP)	4.5	5.6	2.2	2.5
University of Western Cape (UWC)	3.9	3.4	1.0	1.7
University of the Witwatersrand (Wits)	4.5	7.1	1.4	1.9
ALL UNIVERSITIES	3.8	5.2	1.3	2.2

(CHE, 2009a: 24).

length articles thereby encouraging the proliferation of articles – sometimes at the expense of their quality. Such utilisation of market logic to determine the value of academic work is fundamentally anti-transformational, as it reproduces historical and contemporary inequalities.

Some of these inequalities reflect subject bias in existing publishing practice. For example, the natural sciences predominate in journal publishing and account for 36 per cent of all journal articles published. Arts and humanities, as well as medical and health sciences also contribute significantly at 21 per cent and 20 per cent respectively. Chapters and edited works are the publishing medium of choice for academics in the social and economic sciences as well as the arts and humanities which dominate with a 47 per cent and 31 per cent respective share of this form of publishing. Academics in arts and humanities produce 45 per cent of monographs, followed at 37 per cent by social and economic sciences academics (CHE 2009b: 52).

This provides some insight into the publishing trends by subject area, but it is problematic that over 50 per cent of all South African authors publishing in international ISI journals do so in natural and agricultural science journals, and a further 25 per cent publish in health science journals. By contrast, 75 per cent of local non-ISI journal publishing is done by humanities and social science authors (CHE 2009b: 54–55). This skews distribution and collaboration patterns as well as affecting the visibility of South African academics.

The CHE reports that only 10 per cent of academics are National Research Foundation rated researchers and that 13 per cent of these are African, 25 per cent are women and 45 per cent are below the age of fifty (CHE 2009b: 57–58). Although the CHE reports that comparative annual averages cannot be drawn, it does note that publication ranges for black academics are between 4 per cent and 68 per cent; for women academics between 14 per cent and 47 per cent; and that academics under the age of fifty produce between 35 per cent and 62 per cent of all journal articles written at the various institutions (CHE 2009a: 58–59). Some of this data is reflective of the historical inequities in institutional type.

Table 13 below represents patterns of collaboration across academics from different universities and provides a measure of the visibility of South African academics. According to this data, in over 75 per cent of all articles, in 2007 and across the period of 2004–2007, at least one author was in one of the top five research institutions. Over the four-year period, 42 per cent of all articles were of international collaboration, 34 per cent were produced within a single institution and 24 per cent were of national collaboration. This would appear to suggest that academics in the top five research institutions (although this is not limited to these institutions) are internationally visible and the most predominant form of collaboration includes foreign scholars. In terms of international collaboration, the role played by other research productive universities has also begun to increase as seen by comparing 2007 data to data for the 2004–2007 period.

To recap: the most salient issues for academic transformation include the slow rate of race-based and gender-based equity; the nature, shape and size of the postgraduate pool; the skills deficit amongst academics as reflected in low proportions of academics with doctoral degrees and the resultant relatively short optimum productivity span; large and inequitable supervision burdens; and different publishing opportunities across disciplines. Inequalities in both the formal and informal treatment and recognition of academics and exclusionary institutional cultures are also noted as core transformational issues.

Table 13: Research collaboration patterns for research papers:

Collaborative publications (1/+1 author)													Year
Single institution				National institutions				International institutions					
5 most research productive universities	Other research productive universities	3 most productive comprehensives	Total	5 most research productive universities	Other research productive universities	3 most productive comprehensives	Total	5 most research productive universities	Other research productive universities	3 most productive comprehensives	Total	Grand Total	
1204	285	138	1627	943	193	93	1229	1792	346	108	2246	5102	2007
24%	6%	3%	32%	19%	4%	2%	24%	35%	7%	2%	44%	100%	%
4763	1094	478	6335	3548	685	344	4577	6264	1213	430	7907	18819	2004 – 2007
25%	6%	3%	34%	19%	4%	2%	24%	33%	6%	2%	42%	100%	%

(Adapted from CHE, 2009b: 54)

General staff transformation

University administrators have increased exponentially both in number and in terms of their role. Firstly, the proportion of those in management positions expanded by 237 per cent over the twenty year period, with the bulk of the expansion occurring post-1997 when the number of staff in this category grew from 884 in 1997 to 1 562 in 2007. In terms of equity, blacks in this category increased from 6 per cent to 40 per cent over the period, with an annual average growth of approximately fifteen black managers a year prior to 1997 and forty-three post-1997. In terms of gender, the category went from 8 per cent to 34 per cent female, with a pre-1997 increase of ten female managers per year to an annual increase of approximately thirty-eight female managers after 1997.

At this level there has clearly been an increased pace of equity post-1997. However, while this is laudable, the increase in managers points towards greater bureaucratisation and abdication of social justice responsibilities by institutions of higher education.

It is an unfortunate paradox that equity gains occur side by side with more conservative tendencies and that those effecting these policies are increasingly black and women managers who are caught in the contradictory place of being beneficiaries of certain equity gains (typically race and gender-based) while closing down other equity potentials (such as class-based change). As discussed by Modisha (2007), such managers are often caught in multiple contradictions, not least over their own places in the workplace and having to counteract perceptions of their being equity beneficiaries as opposed to having 'earned' their positions and status.

Table 14: Executive, administrative and managerial professionals by race and gender in 1987, 1997 and 2007

	African		Coloured		Indian		Total Black		White		Other		Total	Male		Female	
Year	#	%	#	%	#	%	#	%	#	%	#	%	#	#	%	#	%
1987	24	4	13	2	7	1	41	6	614	93	0	0	658	604	92	54	8
1997	123	14	31	4	35	4	189	21	695	79	0	0	884	727	82	157	18
2007	372	24	133	9	115	7	620	40	933	60	9	1	1562	1030	66	532	34

(DoE, 1988, 1998, 2008: Adapted from the HEMIS Database).

The second category of administrators which has experienced exponential growth is that of the non-professional administrators whose number has increased by 7 532 over the twenty year period. This increase of 233 per cent makes this the second highest growth area in the sector. It is also an occupational category that has undergone significant equity gains (table 15) as in 2007 it was 60 per cent black and 72 per cent female. The average annual increase prior to 1997 was approximately 178 and after 1997 this increased to approximately 375 women administrators a year. However, because this occupation underwent such a huge degree of expansion, the proportion of women administrators remained at 72 per cent in 2007. The proportion of black administrators has increased by 37 per cent over the 20 year period. In the first 10 year period, the average annual increase was of 272 black administrators per year while after 1997, this increased to an average of 412 black administrators per year.

Table 15: Non-professional administrators by race and gender in 1987, 1997 and 2007

	African		Coloured		Indian		Total Black		White		Other		Total	Male		Female	
Year	#	%	#	%	#	%	#	%	#	%	#	%	#	#	%	#	%
1987	751	13	397	7	308	5	1456	26	4209	74	6	0	5671	1651	29	4020	71
1997	2748	33	888	11	544	6	4180	50	4257	50	0	0	8437	2633	31	5804	69
2007	5249	40	2134	16	916	7	8299	63	4856	37	48	0	13203	3645	28	9558	72

(DoE, 1988, 1998, 2008: Adapted from the HEMIS Database).

Much of this expansion has to do with the audit culture that has come to predominate post-apartheid bureaucracies. Thus it is interesting to compare the increases in the research and instruction professionals (the true core of the institution) with the total increase in administrative staff. In 1987, research and instruction professionals totalled 9 392 while both professional and non-professional administrators totalled 6 329. The ratio of academic to administrative staff was 1 to 0.48. By 2007, there were a total of 15 812 academics compared with 14 765 administrators and the ratio of academic to administrative staff had shrunk to 1 to 0.71. This challenges the authenticity of the claim asserted during restructuring that shifts in the workplace and in employment patterns were to prioritise core functioning. Meanwhile, salary differentials between executive managers and academics have caused much strife due to the overpayment of managers and underpayment of academics and workers.

Nonprofessional service workers are the one category of worker which has been almost externalised from the relatively privileged position of institutional employment and now experiences work as increasingly insecure (van der Walt *et al* 2002 and Bezuidenhout & Fabier 2006). These workers represent the full scale of higher education institutions' abdication of their social justice responsibility. Except in one case (RU), institutions of higher education have all outsourced these so-called non-core staff. In most cases, outsourced workers' pay has been halved and, after ten years, outsourced wages are still not comparable to what universities paid when workers were on their own payrolls. Workers' conditions have also deteriorated, with the loss of medical aid benefits, pensions and the vital option of getting staff bursaries for their children to study at higher education institutions. The cumulative effect has been to close off possible upward mobility channels for working class members of university communities.

Between 1997 and 2007, the size of this category of worker shrank by 4 773 workers from a high of 10 512 in 1997 to only 5 739 in 2007 (table 16). The consequence of this for transformation and social justice is significant as this workforce comprises 97 per cent black workers and 40 per cent women workers. From an equity perspective, they have experienced higher education transformation as negative for themselves and their families. Furthermore, they represent another of the contradictions that result from an equity system that prioritises equity for managers and professionals without consideration of a more generalised class-based system of equity and redress.

Table 16: Service staff by race and gender in 1987, 1997 and 2007

	African		Coloured		Indian		Total Black		White		Other		Total		Male			Female	
Year	#	%	#	%	#	%	#	%	#	%	#	%	#	#	%	#	%		
1987	7511	72	2062	20	276	3	9849	95	342	3	211	2	10402	7682	74	2720	26		
1997	8577	80	1548	14	387	4	10512	98	258	2	0	0	10770	6973	65	3798	35		
2007	4956	84	643	11	140	2	5739	97	163	3	2	0	5904	3553	60	2351	40		

(DoE, 1988, 1998, 2008: Adapted from the HEMIS Database).

THE ROLE OF THE STATE AND THE ROLE OF INSTITUTIONS

The state and institutions share joint responsibility for effecting the triple higher education transition. Neoliberal fiscal policies have seen government spending on higher education, and allocation of funding to the national student financial aid scheme, deprioritised prior to 2010. Furthermore, national government remains silent on the issue of outsourcing and the direct worsening of workers' working conditions, despite being now under the direction of Minister Blade Nzimande whose South African Communist Party has been vocal on outsourcing and labour broking. At the national level, there have also been calls for the state to intervene in the set-ting of remuneration for academics, and to curtail the top end of vice-chancellors' salaries. When the state fails to take cognisance of these factors, it fails to appreciate the ways in which the overall system of higher education is constrained by problems which are national and systemic in orientation and therefore require change at the macro or extra-institutional level. Given the current *status quo*, transformation within higher education will inevitably be curtailed.

Secondly, the limited state conception of employment equity policies has meant that higher education institutions have taken their cue from the state and pay almost exclusive attention to race-based change with insufficient attention given to gender and disability equity as well as transformation on the grounds of socio-economic class. The state and institutions also largely focus on equity beneficiaries as mutually exclusive categories, failing to see the cumu-lative disadvantage experienced particularly by black women in higher education.

While demographic reporting is vital for the monitoring and evaluation of equity and transformation, the continued use of identity categories has meant that the state, institutions and individuals have all been complicit in re-entrenching ascriptive apartheid identity labels. Much of this is done without critical forethought or reflection on how it affects both trans-formatory potential and actuality. What is needed is more leadership, recognising where uni-versalised and where differentiated mechanisms are needed to effect substantive change, and implementing these, as well as holding key stakeholders accountable.

REFERENCES

Bezuidenhout A and K Fakier (2006) Maria's burden: Contract cleaning and the crisis of social reproduction in post-apartheid South Africa. *Antipode* 38 (3).

Bezuidenhout A, C Bischoff, S Buhlungu and K Lewins (2008) Tracking progress on the implementation and impact of the employment equity act since its inception. Report produced by Society Work and Development Institute, Wits University, for the Department of Labour, South Africa.

Cooper D and G Subotsky (2001) The Skewed Revolution: Trends in South African Higher Education 1988–1998. Bellville: Education Policy Unit, University of the Western Cape.

Council on Higher Education (CHE) (2009a) Higher Education Monitor No 7: Postgraduate Studies in South Africa: A statistical profile. Pretoria: CHE.

Council on Higher Education (2009b) Higher Education Monitor No 8: The State of Higher Education in South Africa. Pretoria: CHE.

Department of Education (DoE) (2008) Report of the Ministerial Committee on Transformation and Social Cohesion and the Elimination of Discrimination in Public Higher Education Institutions. Pretoria: Department of Education.

DoE. 1988. Excerpts from HEMIS Database for 1987.

DoE. 1998. Excerpts from HEMIS Database for 1997.

DoE. 2008. Excerpts from HEMIS Database for 2007.

Erasmus J and M Breier (2009) *Skills Shortages in South Africa: Case Studies of Key Professions*. Cape Town: HSRC Press.

Erasmus Z (2010) A Future beyond 'race': Reflections on equity in South African higher education. In Hall M, M Krislov and DL Featherman (Eds) *The Next Twenty Five Years? Affirmative Action and Higher Education in the United States and South Africa*. Michigan: University of Michigan Press.

Erasmus Z (2008) Race and 'Race'. In Robins S and N Shepherd (Eds) *New South African Keywords*. Jacana Press: Cape Town.

Habib A (2004) Conversation with a nation: Race and redress in post-apartheid South Africa. In Pieterse E and F Meintjies (Eds) *Voices of the Transition: The Politics, Poetics and Practices of Social Change in South Africa*. Cape Town: Heinemann Publishers.

Jansen JD (1998) But our natives are different! *Social Dynamics* 24 (2).

Jansen JD (2004) Changes and continuities in South Africa's higher education system, 1994–2004. In Chisholm L (Ed) *Changing Class: Education and social change in post-apartheid South Africa*. Cape Town: HSRC Press: 293–314.

Koen C (2006) Challenges facing the education, training and employment of South Africa's scientific workforce. *Higher Education and Work: Setting a New Research Agenda*. Cape Town: HSRC Press: 31–40.

Letseka M, M Breier and M Visser (2010) Poverty, race and student achievement in seven higher education institutions in Letseka M, M Cosser, M Breier and M Visser (Eds) *Student Retention & Graduate Destination: Higher education and Labour Market Access and Success*. Cape Town: HSRC Press.

Lewins K (2010) The trauma of transformation: a closer look at the Soudien report. *South African Review of Sociology* 41(1): 127–136.

Lewins K and N Nieftagodien (1998) Doors of learning not open to all: Struggle to reform higher education. *South African Labour Bulletin* 32 (2): 30–32.

Modisha G (2007) A contradictory class location? The African corporate middle class and the burden of race in South Africa? In Southall R (Ed) *Conflict and Governance in South Africa: Moving Towards a More Just and Peaceful Society*. Lyttelton: The Conflict and Governance Facility: 202–225.

South African Institute of Race Relations (SAIRR) (2009) *South Africa Survey 2008/2009*: Education Online Edition: http://p10.opennetworks.co.za/sairr.org.za/research-and-publications/south-africa-survey-2008-2009/education/Survey%202008-2009%20%20Education%20%28Web%29.pdf: 08/03/10.

Statistics South Africa (2008) Labour Force Survey Statistical Release March 2005. Pretoria: Statistics South Africa.

Van der Walt L, C Bolsmann, B Johnson and L Martin (2002) Globalisation and the Outsourced University in South Africa: the restructuring of the support services in public sector universities in South Africa, 1994-2001. Cape Town. Centre for Higher Education Transformation (CHET).

Wessels PL and LP Steenkamp (2009) An investigation into students' perceptions of accountants. In *Meditari Accountancy Research* 17 (1).

CHAPTER 13

The polarising impact of South Africa's AIDS epidemic[1]

Hein Marais

———•◦•———

What happens when the world's worst AIDS epidemic sweeps through a society already mangled by deep disparities and inequality? Most accounts of the epidemic's impact tell of a scourge that disregards societies' rifts and imbalances and that visits a sort of 'democratic' devastation. In tune with the tenor of our times, much is made of the likely impact on economic growth. Forecasts also warn of decaying institutions and imploding communities, and sketch dark tales of child-headed households, curtailed schooling and deepening poverty. The reality, however, seems less lurid, though more disturbing.

Well into its third decade, South Africa's AIDS epidemic has probably not yet reached its half-life. AIDS will define the lives of at least two more generations. Nowhere in the world – including elsewhere in Africa – has national HIV prevalence reached the levels seen in the hyper-epidemic countries of southern Africa, where at least 15 per cent of the adult population is infected with HIV in Botswana, Lesotho, Namibia, South Africa, Swaziland, Zambia and Zimbabwe. In two more countries in the subregion – Malawi and Mozambique – national adult prevalence is at least 10 per cent. Overall, southern Africa contains about 2 per cent of the world's population but is home to 35 per cent of all HIV-infected persons globally. One in three people who die of AIDS in the world is laid to rest somewhere in southern Africa (UNAIDS 2008).

Figure 1: National HIV prevalence trends among antenatal clinic attendees, South Africa: 1990-2008

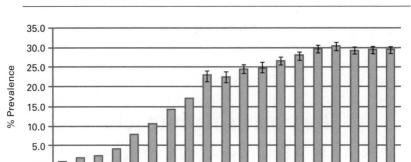

Source: Department of Health

Some 17 per cent of all HIV-infected persons globally live in South Africa, a country with 0.7 per cent of the world's population. In 2008, there were 5.2 million South Africans living with the virus, and more than 250 000 of them died of AIDS in the same year. There were an estimated 1.9 million AIDS orphans in 2009 (Statistics SA 2009).

However, there are a few glimmers of good news. The annual surveys carried out among pregnant women attending antenatal clinics showed HIV infection levels among pregnant women in 2006-2009 were stuck at 29 per cent, indicating an epidemic that has stabilised, but at extraordinarily high levels. Other data, collected in national household surveys, suggest that a substantial decrease in HIV *incidence* among teenagers occurred between 2005 and 2008. That might signal a *slowing* epidemic (HSRC 2009), although it is not clear whether a similar trend is underway among older South Africans. Meanwhile, at least 350 000 adults and around 59 000 children will have been infected with HIV in 2009 (Statistics SA 2009). One in three women aged twenty to thirty-four years is HIV-positive, as is one in four men aged thirty to thirty-nine. Most of them do not know they are infected (Shisana *et al* 2005a).

These statistics paint a fuzzy picture. The epidemic is distributed very unevenly between regions, city and countryside, population groups, genders and income groups. The majority of South Africans living with HIV are poor and African. A national HIV household survey in 2005 found HIV prevalence of 20 per cent among African adults, 3.2 per cent among coloureds, 1.0 per cent among Indians and 0.5 per cent among whites.[2] Infection levels were by far the highest among persons living in urban and rural 'informal' areas, where it was 26 per cent and 17 per cent, respectively (*ibid*).

As in the rest of the African continent, HIV disproportionately affects women: 20 per cent of adult South African women were living with HIV in 2005, compared with 12 per cent of men. Among young people (fifteen to twenty-four years), women were almost four times more likely to be HIV-infected than men (17 per cent versus 4.4 per cent) (*ibid*).

There is geographic variety too. Adult HIV prevalence in 2005 ranged from 26 per cent in KwaZulu-Natal, to 20-22 per cent in the Gauteng, Free State, Mpumalanga and North West provinces, and 8-12 per cent in the Limpopo, Northern Cape and the Eastern Cape provinces (*ibid*). Even within cities, there is great variation. In Cape Town, for example, HIV prevalence increases or decreases several-fold from one suburb to the next. HIV infection levels are consistently higher in urban than in rural areas. Meanwhile, only three countries in the world have more people living with HIV than do the adjacent cities of Johannesburg and Pretoria in Gauteng province. An estimated 1.5 million people with HIV live in predominantly urban Gauteng, more than in the entire Mozambique or Kenya (1.4 million), Tanzania (1.3 million) or Zimbabwe (1.2 million). There are more people living with HIV in Durban than in Brazil or China, and more in Cape Town than in Vietnam or Indonesia. It is estimated that in the next generation two-thirds of people with HIV will be living in South Africa's cities (Van Renterghem 2009). The implications for allocating health resources, and for prioritising *within* HIV programmes, are huge. The epidemic's pattern of distribution seems to fit the contours of privilege and deprivation in South Africa and to express deeply lodged racial, class, gender and spatial patterns of accumulation and dispossession.

AN UNEQUAL EPIDEMIC

Even if HIV infections were evenly distributed across all income groups, close to half of South Africans with HIV could be described as 'poor'. The best estimates indicate that 18-20 million South Africans were living below the poverty line in the mid-2000s (Meth 2006; 2008). The current recession makes it unlikely that those figures improved in 2009. However, there is some evidence in South Africa that HIV prevalence tends to be higher among persons with low skills and incomes (and lower among those with the highest skills and incomes). It is among the more disadvantaged and impoverished sections of society – who are predominantly African, given the country's history of racial discrimination and dispossession – that the highest levels of HIV prevalence are found. Temporary employees of the Buffalo City municipality, for example, were found to have higher HIV prevalence than permanent staff, with infection levels highest in the lowest skills levels (Thomas *et al* 2005). Among health workers surveyed at private and public health facilities in four provinces, HIV prevalence was just under 14 per cent among professionals but exceeded 20 per cent among non-professional staff (Shisana *et al* 2003). A more recent analysis of HIV in twenty-two public and private sector organisations found that HIV prevalence among labourers on average was more than twice as high as among managers (12.4 per cent compared with 5.3 per cent) (Colvin *et al* 2006). Such findings fit with those of successive national household HIV surveys, which found HIV infection levels were highest among residents of informal urban settlements, who generally are unemployed or under-employed (HSRC *et al* 2002: Shisana *et al* 2005).

Yet this does not establish a correlation between poverty and HIV. These studies surveyed employed workers, and therefore have nothing to say about the HIV infection levels among the poorest 20-30 per cent of South Africans. Careful examination of data from demographic and health surveys in eight other African countries has failed to find evidence of a correlation between poverty status and HIV prevalence.[3] In fact, the pattern of association seemed to run in the *opposite* direction than that anticipated, with higher-income individuals experiencing higher HIV risk than their lower-income peers. After controlling for possible confounding factors, the authors concluded that there was no evidence of a consistent and direct relationship between HIV and poverty (Mishra *et al* 2007). However, it seems difficult to detach the epidemic from the unequal distribution of power, opportunity and risk in societies. When Kalichman *et al* (2006) studied three residential settings[4] in South Africa, they found HIV risk to be embedded in a range of 'social ills' that included poor education, unemployment, discrimination, crime and violence. In rural KwaZulu-Natal, researchers found that each additional year of education reduced the risk of acquiring HIV by 7 per cent (Bärnighausen *et al* 2007). The potential interaction between various forms of deprivation and insecurity (poverty among them) and HIV risk is complex and resists flippant conclusions (Piot *et al* 2007; Gillespie *et al* 2007). It seems inescapable, though, that the factors putting persons at risk for HIV infection are enmeshed in the circuits and terms on which power, opportunity and entitlements are distributed and desires and needs are pursued. In South Africa, these are highly unequal. Systematic dispossession and dislocation, the destabilisation of social systems and disintegration of social cohesion (particularly in the urban peripheries) and the entrenching of highly unequal social relations has helped create a social and ideological terrain (including aggressive constructions of masculinity) that seem to favour the spread of HIV. The effects of AIDS morbidity and mortality are likely to reinforce those inequalities.

UNEVEN EFFECTS LAID ATOP AN UNEQUAL SOCIETY

AIDS epidemics arrive in four waves (Whiteside 2008). First, the numbers of new HIV infections (HIV incidence) rise dramatically before eventually peaking. In South Africa, that peak occurred around the turn of the century. Second, HIV prevalence increases before reaching a plateau (as it did in the early 2000s in the case of South Africa). Third, AIDS-related deaths increase. The introduction of antiretroviral treatment (ART) seems to have caused that trend to level off in the mid-2000s. Finally, increasing numbers of children are orphaned by AIDS.

South Africans are dying in unprecedented numbers, and at unusually young ages. Total deaths (from all causes) in South Africa increased by 91 per cent from 1997 to 2008 (from 316 507 to 602 800) (Statistics SA 2009). AIDS was the cause of an estimated 43 per cent of those deaths in 2008. Most deaths are now among people aged thirty to thirty-nine.

The failure to introduce a timely antiretroviral drug treatment programme in the early 2000s cost approximately 330 000 lives, according to modelling (Chigwedere *et al* 2008). Calls to hold former President Thabo Mbeki to account for those delays will come to naught, not least because the denialism propagated by Mbeki appears to have enjoyed significant support or sympathy across the top echelons of government and the ANC at the time (Cullinan and Thom 2009; Govender 2007; Feinstein 2007).

The AIDS epidemic, combined with the closely related TB epidemic (also the worst in the world), has manifestly reversed health gains. Life expectancy in 2008 was twelve years lower than in 1996, child mortality was higher than in Iraq (Kapp 2009), and maternal mortality rates worsened since the early 1990s. The mortality rate for children younger than five years rose from sixty to sixty-nine deaths per 1 000 live births between 1990 and 2006, making South Africa one of only twelve countries in the world where child mortality worsened in that period (Chopra *et al* 2009). AIDS is believed to be the cause of more than half of those deaths,[5] but a properly functioning programme for preventing mother-to-child transmission of HIV could have avoided most of them. Dual therapy (a combination of the antiretroviral drugs AZT and nevirapine) has been shown to cut HIV transmission from mothers to their newborn babies by almost two-thirds, for example (Cullinan 2009).[6]

If the excess mortality caused by AIDS were removed, average life expectancy at birth would be on par with that in other upper middle income countries. Instead, in 2008 it stood at a dismal 53.5 years for men and 57.2 years for women. The rate of population growth in South Africa has fallen from 1.38 per cent in 2001–2002 to 1.07 per cent in 2008-2009 (Statistics SA 2009).

Maternal mortality rose from 117 per 100 000 in 1998 to 147 per 100 000 in 2004, with AIDS responsible for almost half of those deaths (NCCEMD 2009). A government-appointed committee found that more than a third of those deaths 'were clearly avoidable within the healthcare system' (*op cit*:3).

Such statistics paint with a broad brush. Disaggregated, they reveal familiar patterns. Infant mortality amongst the poorest 20 per cent of South Africans was eighty-seven (per 1 000 live births), compared with twenty-two in the richest quintile; among black Africans, it was sixty-four and among whites fifteen (Department of Health 2003). The epidemic's impact is deeply interlaced with South Africa's historical patterns of inequality.

Figure 2: Life expectancy at birth, by region, 1950–55 to 2005–10

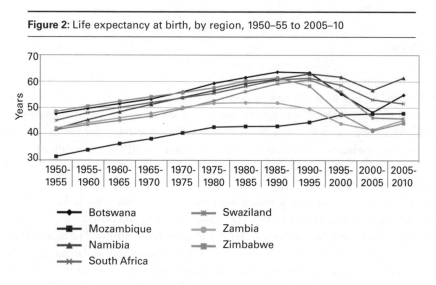

Source: Population Division of the Department of Economic and Social Affairs of the United Nations Secretariat (2008). *World Population Prospects: The 2006 Revision and World Urbanization Prospects: The 2005 Revision.* http://esa.un.org/unpp.

Much has been written about the likely effects of hyper-epidemics on how societies function. Forecasts include dramatic cuts in economic growth, dysfunctional state institutions, 'derailed development' (Feldbaum *et al* 2006; National Intelligence Council 2000), erosion of democratic governance, increasing lawlessness (Youde 2001) and worse. At face value, much of the doomsaying seems overwrought. Nowhere have the epidemics caused any national economy to crash nor have they threatened the viability of any national government (De Waal 2007). But focusing on such spectacular effects alone seems misdirected. In a society as unequal and polarised as South Africa, mishaps are not distributed evenly, nor are their consequences necessarily transmitted neatly from the micro-levels of individuals and households to the macro-levels of national systems and economies. What most accounts of the impact of AIDS neglect are the ways in which risk and responsibility are distributed in society. The burden of care, for example, weighs mainly on women and girls, who perform that labour with remuneration and typically with scant institutional support. The effects of illness and death are not automatically channeled onto the balance sheets of enterprises or into the labour market. Putative workplace related costs often are externalised with the use of HIV screening of workers, retrenchment of ill employees, restrictive or absent health insurance, trimmed worker benefits, and so on (Rosen and Simon 2003). But the evidence does describe an epidemic in which a disproportionate share of the impact is borne by already impoverished and stressed individuals, households and communities – especially those who are unable to deflect and redistribute those costs beyond the confines of their lives. An analysis of the damage done by AIDS requires an understanding of the ways in which the unequal distribution of privilege, risk and responsibility in societies shapes and funnels the epidemic's impact – and how that impact might reinforce those patterns of inequality.

LOCKED UP

The impoverishing effects of AIDS illnesses are well-documented, as is the fact that those effects tend to be most severe in already poor households (Hosegood *et al* 2007; Collins and Leibbrandt 2007). The epidemic robs households of income earners, distorts expenditure patterns, depletes savings and assets and erodes livelihoods (Whiteside 2008; Barnett and Whiteside 2002). Studies of the impact of AIDS on poor households show AIDS compounding the routine distress endured by millions of South Africans, driving an even thicker wedge between the privileged and the deprived.

AIDS illness incurs significant additional expenses, which poor households are least able to bear. Forgone wages and other income, the costs of seeking and providing care (transport expenses, time off from jobs, medicines) all eat into household income. The biggest financial shock usually arrives with death. A study in Diepsloot (Johannesburg), Langa (Cape Town) and Lugangeni (Eastern Cape) showed that funeral costs absorbed up to seven months' worth of income in households suffering an AIDS death (Collins and Leibbrandt 2007). Needless to say, the adversity is most punishing in households with the least resources, lowest incomes, fewest entitlements and the weakest social networks. A loosely woven safety net is available in the form of rationed state grants, but they are too small and are spread too wide in households to remove them from precariousness. Women provide the bulk of care, but those aged between eighteen and fifty-nine are not directly eligible for any social assistance from the state (except for the highly stigmatising indigence grant).

HOME AND COMMUNITY BASED CARE: Passing the buck?

Home and community based care (HCBC) has become a vital part of dealing with the effects of the epidemic. Theoretically, the approach fits neatly in the post-1994 overhaul of the health system, specifically the shift to primary care. In theory, it marshals the respective strengths of households, the communities they constitute and the organisations they spawn, and the resources of the state, thus creating a 'continuum of care' that can boost the quality, scale and sustainability of care without overburdening public hospitals (ANC 2001; Department of Health 2001). Caregivers in the home (typically women) would receive support from community-based 'volunteers' who, themselves, receive training and support from the formal health system.[7] These lay health workers would visit patients in their homes, provide care and counselling, and link them into a functional referral system.

By 2006, there were an estimated 62 000 'community health workers' in South Africa, many of them providing care to persons with HIV and/or tuberculosis. Internationally, the community health worker approach had fallen into disfavour, but the extraordinary demands of the AIDS epidemic saw it revived in the 2000s, especially in southern and east Africa (Schneider *et al* 2008). In an innovative move, these community health workers have been drawn into the ambit of the expanded public works programme, and are paid stipends.

The reality has been less alluring, harking back to some of the early objections to the community health worker approach. Rather than forming the cutting edge of a transformed health system, critics charged, these workers often were 'just another pair of hands' toiling with scant resources, training and back-up (Walt 1990 in Schneider *et al* 2008).

In all countries, women and girls perform the lion's share of social reproduction, raising and nurturing children, schooling them in norms and values, managing their introduction into wider society, performing domestic labour, tending the ill, and much more. Upwards of 90 per cent of caregivers in most African countries are women or girls. In the context of rigid, gendered divisions of labour they usually receive scant support from men (Akintola 2006).[8] South Africa fits that mould (Hunter 2007). In societies defined by extensive labour migration systems women also head a large share of households (more than 40 per cent in the case of South Africa). Home and community based care is melded into this largely invisible and taken for granted labour women perform in the care economy. It is unremunerated, often bereft of institutional support, and very probably contributes to the feminisation of poverty.

HIV caregiving can be highly taxing and time-consuming. Family caregivers in Mwanza, Tanzania, for example, were found to spend three to seven hours a day on care-related activities (Nnko *et al* 2000). Assessments of self-initiated care projects in South Africa report that caregivers often subsidise many aspects of care provision themselves in addition to paying the costs of not receiving the levels of care and support they require. Essential needs, such as food and money for basic necessities, often go unmet (Hunter 2007). Many lack the basic resources they need to safely and efficiently perform their tasks. More home-based care kits have been made available by government departments and donors, but training in care tasks, as well as psychological support and counselling for caregivers have been sorely inadequate. Often care-givers themselves lack sufficient knowledge about AIDS, or are unaware that the person they are caring for is HIV-positive (Campbell *et al* 2004). Basic precautions are neglected, and the caregivers themselves risk becoming infected. The physical demands, and the mental and emo-tional strain are immense (Hunter 2007; Orner 2006; Giese *et al* 2003), and caregivers routinely admit to being wracked by feelings of guilt (Akintola 2006). These burdens were experienced even when support was available from CBOs (*ibid*). On the other hand, interactions with healthcare workers who do provide information, encouragement and emotional support typically have a morale-boosting and empowering effect on patients and caregivers.

HCBC was meant to be a cheap, cost-effective, and flexible means of providing basic symptomatic and palliative care for people living with HIV/AIDS in a heavily-burdened context (Department of Health 2001a). It does this, but mainly by concentrating the bulk of the material and emotional costs of AIDS care within the homes and neighbourhoods of South Africa's poor, saddling women in particular with most of that burden. 'Cost-effectiveness for government appears to be defined as getting family caregivers to carry the bulk of the costs', Nina Hunter (2007:213) concluded from her research in six urban and rural commu-nities in KwaZulu-Natal. Consequently, HCBC intensifies the exploitation of women's labour, financial and emotional reserves – a form of value extraction that subsidises the economy at every level from the household outward, yet remains invisible in political and economic discourse (Marais 2005).

The paucity and erratic and poorly coordinated nature of institutional support has been the single biggest weakness in HCBC. Consequently, the 'continuum of care' has relied heavily on the services of nongovernmental organisations (NGOs) and community-based organisa-tions (CBOs), and on the exertions and resources of individuals – who have operated with uneven and inconsistent support. As late as the mid-2000s in KwaZulu-Natal, for example, the provincial departments of health and social development respectively were allocating 0.3 per cent or less of their total budgets to home- and community-based care. Until very recently, the overall tenor of the HBC system was one of piecemeal support and crisis man-agement (Hunter 2007).

The envisaged system of HCBC can work much better, and efforts are underway to place it on more solid footing. Recent studies suggest that lessons are being learned. Institutional support is improving, enabling community health workers to relieve some of the strain in com-munities. Research by Helen Schneider and her colleagues (2008) in the Free State suggests that these workers are beginning to span the divide between patients and the health system. However, their status as an irregular, support labour force on the margins of the health system still undermines their relationships with professional health workers. Ultimately, though, home- and community-based care only works as well as the health system overall. And in South Africa, that system is a paradigmatic expression of society's inequalities.

AN UNHEALTHY SYSTEM

Health economists have noted that South Africa's health spending as a proportion of GDP is relatively high, compared to other middle income countries, but that the country's health status indicators are far worse than those of most other middle income countries (McIntyre & Thiede 2007). Indeed, South Africans spend a great deal of money on healthcare: the equivalent of close to 8 per cent of gross domestic product in 2008, which is slightly less than Sweden's 8.9 per cent (World Bank 2008). But the spending occurs in a two-tier system, with most of it funnelled into the private sector, which is where most of the resources are also concentrated. Almost 60 per cent of health expenditure each year pays for the health care of about 7 million, typically wealthier South Africans who belong to private medical schemes and who use the well-resourced, for-profit private health system (Statistics SA 2008).[9]

South Africa spent the equivalent of about 3.5 per cent of GDP on its public health system in the mid-2000s, less than many other countries the UNDP classifies as 'medium human development' countries, including Nicaragua (3.9 per cent), Mongolia and Honduras (4 per cent), Namibia (4.7 per cent), Lesotho (5.5 per cent) or Colombia (6.7 per cent) (UNDP 2008). Consequently, at least 23 million South Africans rely entirely on an over-burdened, under-staffed and poorly managed public health system, while about 10 million use the public sector but occasionally pay out of their own pockets to use the private sector (McIntyre and Thiede 2007). The disparities in healthcare access and quality are unconscionable.

There is a major shortage of trained, skilled doctors, and nursing and support staff in the public health system. New nurses are not being trained quickly enough and in requisite numbers,[10] large numbers of doctors and nurses have opted to work abroad, and there is gross misallocation of existing human resources between the public and private health sectors. As the AIDS and TB epidemics crested, the ratio of professional nurses in the public sector shrank, from 149 per 10 000 people in 1998 to 110 for every 10 000 people in 2007. In 1989, 79 per cent of nurses worked in the public sector – a number that dwindled to 59 per cent in 1999 and 42 per cent in 2007, and the percentage of general practitioners employed in the public sector diminished from about 60 per cent in the 1980s to 27 per cent in 2006 (*ibid*). The effects of these shortages are felt most acutely at district level, where clinics and community health centres are meant to function as the backbone of the primary healthcare system. And it is on them that people stricken with AIDS, and those trying to care for them, have to rely.

This dual system is clearly both unjust and inadequate given the scale and nature of South Africa's health crisis. At least as objectionable is the fact that tax revenues are used to subsidise the private medical scheme system. Medical scheme contributions are tax deductible – a handout to the most privileged layers of society worth R10.1 billion in 2005 – equal to about 30 per cent of total government spending on health in that year (McIntyre *et al* 2005). It is vital that these resources be shared equitably. The proposed national health insurance (NHI) plan represents one of several innovations that can help achieve that. But the NHI will not be a panacea. The crisis in the public health system extends beyond financial resources and infrastructure; recuperation requires that systemic dysfunction be overcome.

Meanwhile, the strain on the public health system is increasing. It has been projected that a country with stable 15 per cent HIV prevalence (as in South Africa) could expect to see 1.6 per cent to 3.3 per cent of its health care personnel die of AIDS each year, a cumulative mortality rate over five years of 8–16 per cent (Tawfik and Kinoti 2003). Even before the epidemic death toll peaked, in 1997–2001, AIDS was responsible for an estimated 13 per cent of deaths among health workers, according to HSRC research (Shisana *et al* 2003). A more recent sero-survey in two public hospitals found that 11.5 per cent of health-care workers were HIV-positive, including nearly 14 per cent of nurses (Connelly *et al* 2007). Those who are aware of their HIV-positive status are likely to seek and receive antiretroviral treatment, enabling them to continue working and live relatively normal lives. However, most South Africans with HIV are unaware that they have been infected (Shisana *et al* 2005a), and tend to seek treatment at stages when opportunistic infections have begun ravaging their bodies and treatment efficacy is low, necessitating hospitalisation. The demands placed on public hospitals seems unrelenting, as are workloads and stress borne by their staff, large numbers of whom cite burn-out, low morale and ramshackle systems as chronic problems (Von Holdt and Murphy 2007).

FAILING THE TEST?

Access to education has widened substantially since 1994, and there are many examples of excellent educational practice in the country's 26 000 public schools. But the overall quality of schooling is sub-standard. Numeracy and literacy levels are poor. South Africa was the worst performer in a forty-country reading literacy study carried out in 2006,[11] and the department of education's own study of Grade 6 learners nationally described their achievement as 'generally poor' in mathematics, language and natural science. The verdict was generous. In fact, only 19 per cent of learners could do mathematics, and only 37 per cent could read and write in the language of instruction at the appropriate grade level (Department of Education 2005:75).

Matric (Grade 12) pass rates improved to 65 per cent in 2007 (Presidency 2008), though few would celebrate a system in which one third of learners fail to pass their final exams. In reality, the picture is grimmer. A Western Cape province study tracked learner enrolment from 1995 to 2008, and found that only 44 per cent of those who had enrolled in Grade 1 reached Grade 12 (de Jager 2009).[12] Earlier, national data suggested that only about 40 per cent of black African students complete twelve years of schooling (Louw *et al* 2006). The reasons for such poor performance are complex.[13] But the costs are immense. For one, the employment prospects for young South Africans who have not completed or, better, continued beyond secondary school, are doleful.

Not only are overall education performances poor, but the prospects of receiving a good quality education are distributed along highly discriminatory class and racial lines. Schools in wealthier areas routinely outperform the rest. In a survey in 2009, some 11 000 of the 17 000 learners in the country's 'top one hundred schools' were white.[14] In reality, the public school system comprises two parallel education systems (Bloch 2008). One dispenses an education of reasonable quality that serves as a launch pad for successful tertiary education employment and career advancement. A small minority of learners benefit from that system.

The other provides sub-par education or, especially in the case of many rural and township schools, does little more than 'warehouse' learners.

AIDS almost certainly is compounding that inequality. The epidemic's effects on schooling in South Africa are poorly researched. There is some evidence that school attendance is lower in households affected by AIDS. Among 'AIDS-affected' households surveyed in the Free State, Gauteng, KwaZulu-Natal and Mpumulanga provinces, about 5 per cent of boys and 10 per cent of girls were out of school. The main reason was lack of money for school fees, uniforms and books (Steinberg *et al* 2002).[15] But the epidemic's effects probably penetrate much deeper than revealed in such studies. There are many thousands of communities in South Africa where infection levels exceed 20 per cent. In such settings, the epidemic's effects, naked or otherwise, are ubiquitous.

It is not known how many school learners are living with HIV, but it has been estimated that more than 300 000 primary school learners are HIV-infected (Jansen 2007). Since almost all of them will have acquired HIV during their births six or more years earlier, it is likely that they will be experiencing complicated health problems that will handicap their learning abilities. At the same time, HSRC research indicates that approximately 13 per cent of educators are HIV-infected (Shisana *et al* 2005b).[16]

Attrition was a problem for the public education system even before the epidemic peaked, with poor pay, increased workloads, lack of career advancement prospects, and dissatisfaction with work policies typically cited as reasons for leaving the profession. Between 1997–1998 and 2003–2004, the system was losing about 21 000 educators each year. At the beginning of that period, deaths accounted for a small percentage of the attrition (about 7 per cent in 1997–1998 (HSRC 2005). By 2003–2004, however, almost one in five teachers (18 per cent) lost to the system had died. The increase is almost certainly due to the AIDS epidemic (*ibid*). At the turn of century, before the AIDS mortality peaked fully, already 58 per cent of teachers dying were younger than forty years of age (Jansen 2007). It has been estimated that about 30 000 educators have to be trained annually to maintain current staffing levels. Demand far outstrips supply, with management and administrative skills especially short in numbers.

If the public schooling system's capacity to provide quality education suffers, the springboard for higher education and skills training weakens. Channels for quality educational advancement would be available but they would be tightly rationed, expensive and available to a privileged few. It is estimated that learners in township schools on average benefit from one-third as much instructional time as their counterparts in former 'white schools' enjoy (*ibid*). Limited in number and imposing high school fees, the latter are schools of privilege and are inaccessible to all but a few. The vast majority of learners have to cope with learning environments riddled with routine dysfunction,[17] and where AIDS adds exceptional difficulties. The odds are that, in most schools, at least one educator is living with HIV and a large proportion of learners are either themselves infected or living in households with at least one HIV-infected person. Not all of them will be subjected to the trauma and panic of severe AIDS-related illnesses. But those that are will find teaching or learning an even more gruelling experience.

What might this mean for inter-generational social mobility? If the quality of public school education deteriorates further against a backdrop of continuing marginalisation of the poorest households and of overall polarisation, social mobility will be hobbled further, trapping more people in a dismal cycle of poor education, paltry employment prospects and precarious livelihoods.

COLLATERAL DAMAGE

Similarly, AIDS appears to be corroding other institutions' capacities to provide predictable, consistent and acceptable standards of service. Already saddled with heavy workloads and compromised capacity, the police, correctional and judicial services, as well as managerial and administrative services at local government level, are especially vulnerable. In South Africa, 233 local councillors in the twenty-two to forty-nine age group died in office between early 2001 and the end of 2007 (Chirambo and Steyn 2009). Community-based organisations that play important welfarist roles at local level, and are often heavily reliant on the work of a few key individuals, are similarly vulnerable.

THE BOTTOM LINE

That South Africa's epidemic will affect the economy at large seems beyond dispute but it is less obvious what the extent of that damage might be. Some estimates trivialise the effect of AIDS by suggesting a minor effect on national economic output, while others foresee severe damage. The disagreements stem from the fact that the estimates rest on different assessments of the epidemic's demographic impact, about the channels along which AIDS affects the economy, and about the nature of those effects. The direct costs of AIDS to organisations and businesses tend to register in the form of higher healthcare costs and more expensive workers' benefits, while the indirect costs take the form of reduced productivity, loss of skills, experience and institutional memory, as well as (re)training and recruitment time and expenses. Indirect costs are significantly higher for skilled workers, as are employee benefit costs (Whiteside and O'Grady 2003). In a serious AIDS epidemic, those costs can add up to a hidden employment or payroll tax (De Waal 2007). Some corporations have introduced high-profile antiretroviral treatment (ART) programmes for some of their employees, and several more have added prevention activities. Most companies, though, seem to be taking AIDS in their stride. In bids to achieve greater flexibility in production and employment, companies continue to shift the terms on which they use labour, a trend that predates AIDS. The adoption of labour-saving work methods and technologies, the outsourcing and casualisation of jobs, and the whittling of worker benefits have a huge effect on working South Africans' abilities to cushion themselves against the epidemic's repercussions.

By the early 2000s, only one-quarter of workers in the private sector had access to subsidised medical care (Torres *et al* 2001). For workers with such access, medical benefits are now often capped at levels far too low to cover the costs of serious ill health or injury. Companies have been cutting death and disability benefits too, as well as limiting employer contributions and requiring that workers pay a larger share of the premiums for the same benefits. In addition, a huge shift occurred from defined-benefit retirement funds to defined-contribution funds (the latter offering scant help to workers felled, for example, by disease in the prime of their lives). These sorts of adjustments enable many companies to sidestep the worst of the epidemic's impact. The net effect has been a paring of real wages and benefits for those South Africans with formal employment at a time when they and their families are at increased risk of severe illness and premature death. Left to fend for themselves are the masses of 'casual' and 'non-permanent' workers and the unemployed. The costs of AIDS are being 'socialised', channelled back into the lives, homes and neighbourhoods of the poor in a massive and regressive redistribution of risk and responsibility.

A POLARISED SOCIETY

The same dynamics that govern the distribution of wealth, opportunities, resources and power in society also filter, dissipate and redistribute a good deal of the impact of South Africa's AIDS epidemic. This is not a 'democratic' epidemic. Alan Whiteside (2008) seems correct in arguing that the inequalities that shape the social and economic architecture of a hyper-endemic country like South Africa also act as barrier and filter preventing the effects of AIDS from snowballing into systemic collapse. Thus a great deal of mayhem wrought by AIDS is compressed and contained within the lives and communities of the poor; the more privileged and powerful sections of society seem capable of 'gating' themselves, to a considerable extent, against the worst of the impact.

Yet, in some respects the impact *does* travel to macro realms in ways that are likely to further aggravate inequalities. In highly stratified labour markets (such as South Africa's) that are marked by shortages of highly-skilled workers and a surplus of low and unskilled workers, attrition in an already limited pool of skilled and highly skilled labour pushes up those wages and salaries. Meanwhile, the surfeit of labour available at the 'low' end of the market continues to depress wages. At the least, this will undermine attempts to narrow income gaps, which currently are wider than in any other country. In the mid-2000s, the poorest 5 million South Africans received about 0.2 per cent of national income (through wages and social grants), while the richest 5 million pocketed 51 per cent of national income, according to the latest income and expenditures survey (Statistics SA 2008).

All this underlines the prospect for heightened marginalisation of the very poor, and especially of women in those ranks. The ability to participate in networks of reciprocity, entitlement and responsibility is an essential tool of survival and advancement in impoverished settings. But participation depends on whether a person can marshal the time, energy and other means for remaining a part of the social circuitry of reciprocity (Pieterse 2003). The poorest households, especially those headed by women, find themselves pushed back in the queue of entitlement and claims-staking. The effects feed into a loop. The more impoverished and marginalised sections of society are least equipped to manage or overcome the effects of these corroded capacities, while the more privileged sections have the means to sidestep or vault those obstacles. Inequality deepens.

HEADWAY

The most obvious first step for cushioning this impact is the provision of antiretroviral treatment (ART) to all who need it. The Department of Health states that about 370 000 people were receiving ART in the public sector in 2008. Record-keeping and monitoring systems are poor, however, making it difficult to gauge the accuracy of that claim.[18] After examining various data sources for both the public and private sectors, Adam and Johnson (2008) estimated that 568 000 people were getting ART in 2008 in both the public and private sectors. If accurate, that means a little more than one-third of the 1.5 million adults and 106 000 children in need of ART were receiving the drugs in 2008 (Statistics SA 2009).

Government's stated target is to have 1.4 million people on treatment by 2011–2012 (about 80 per cent of those in need of ART), an improbable outcome on current trends. It is highly doubtful whether ART access can be expanded and sustained in the medium-term unless health systems and resources are strengthened considerably (Barnighausen et al 2007). The infrastructure, systems and staff required to properly monitor treatment retention and loss are increasingly inadequate, as programmes are expanded. When the Free State's health department ran short of ARVs in mid-2009, for example, officials blamed funding shortfalls. In reality, though, the problem appeared to have arisen from poor governance and accountability systems, and poor budget planning and management (Parker 2009).

There is a danger that a scale-up which compromises the quality of treatment and care could decrease programme benefits in the long-term and could result in the growth of viral resistance (Hirschhorn and Skolnik 2008). Already early treatment mortality is a major problem, partly because of late HIV diagnosis, late initiation of therapy, and inequitable access to healthcare. This limits the overall impact of ART programmes (Hallet et al 2008). Tracking and monitoring ARV provision is weak, and pharmacovigilance is poor. There is growing concern about patient retention, which elsewhere in sub-Saharan Africa averages at about 60 per cent after two years. The main causes of attrition appear to be failure to follow up and death (Rosen et al 2007).

Looming, meanwhile, is the future affordability of ARV drugs. Given the lifelong need for treatment, the volume of people requiring ARVs will continue to grow, and increasing numbers of them will at some stage need to shift to second-line regimens. It costs between R6 000 and R8 000 a year to provide each patient with ARVs, with drug expenses comprising about two-thirds of total cost (Parker 2009). Significant further price reductions for first-line antiretroviral drugs are still possible, but most second-line drugs (such as abacavir, lopinavir/ritonavir, nelfinavir, saquinavir) remain under patent and are exorbitantly priced.[19] As a hyper-epidemic country, South Africa has the right to issue compulsory licenses for the cheaper manufacture of such life-saving medications. So far it has recoiled from using that right for fear of retaliation from its major trading partners. But government's fundamental duty to safeguard the lives of citizens means it will have to cross that line at some stage soon – and it is only likely to do so with success if simultaneously pressured and backed by popular mobilisation, at home and abroad.

Government took several useful steps in late 2009. TB and HIV are to be treated under one roof, an overdue move that might be tripped up by inefficiencies in the health system, but which can save many lives. South Africa accounts for more than one-quarter (28 per cent) of the world's people with both HIV and TB and 33 per cent of all cases in sub-Saharan Africa (WHO, UNAIDS, UNICEF 2008). Patients presenting with both TB and HIV infections will also be eligible for earlier ARV treatment. Also significant is the decision to provide all HIV-positive pregnant women with ARVs if their CD4 counts (a measure of the strength of their immunity) fall below 350. All children younger than one year will also be provided with ART if they test HIV-positive.

Treatment alone, though, will not save the day. Modelling indicates that even if 2.1 million South Africans were receiving ART by 2011, nearly 1.5 million people would still die of AIDS between 2007 and 2012 (Walensky 2008). The biggest challenge ultimately is to radically reduce the rate at which HIV spreads from person to person.

There are tentative grounds for encouragement. More young people are using condoms, for example. But achieving consistent and correct condom use (especially in long-term relationships) is massively difficult (Simbayi and Kalichman 2007; de Walque 2007; Chimbiri 2007). Even among young South Africans with concurrent partners, condom use declines rapidly with a 'main' partner, and is inconsistent even with 'other' partners (Parker *et al* 2007). Condom promotion remains an important cornerstone for HIV prevention, but reducing multiple sexual partnerships, especially concurrent partnerships, can have an even more dramatic effect on HIV transmission (Shelton 2007; Halperin and Epstein 2007). Uganda's 'zero-grazing' campaign is credited with a reduction of more than 50 per cent in the number of people with multiple partners between 1989 and 1995 (Shelton *et al* 2004) and helped reverse the country's HIV epidemic. The problem is that a replicable approach for reducing multiple concurrent partnerships still eludes us (Potts *et al* 2008).

King Goodwill Zwelithini's support for a male circumcision campaign among Zulus could have telling positive effects within a decade. There is strong evidence that male circumcision dramatically reduces the risk of HIV acquisition in men during *heterosexual* intercourse by up to 60 per cent, according to randomised controlled trials in Kenya (Bailey *et al* 2007), Uganda (Gray *et al* 2007) and South Africa (Auvert *et al* 2005). Modelling suggests that large-scale male circumcision could avert up to 5.7 million new HIV infections and 3 million deaths over the next twenty years in sub-Saharan Africa, including among women and non-circumcised men (Williams *et al* 2006). Evidence from Botswana and Swaziland suggests male circumcision services are acceptable and desired (Westercamp and Bailey 2007). But gender dynamics must be factored in. Overall, at population level, women would gain some protection against HIV infection (via the 'herd immunity' effect) (Hallett *et al* 2008; Williams *et al* 2006) even though it still is unclear what, if any, protective effect male circumcision may have on individual women (Gray *et al* 2000; Turner 2007; Wawer *et al* 2008).[20] And there are concerns that some circumcised men, aware that their risk of acquiring HIV is reduced, might be disinclined to practice safe sex, thus putting their female partners at risk. So male circumcision is not a 'magic fix', but is potentially one of the most powerful interventions available to SA to help protect men and women from infection – and, in the long-term, to help reduce AIDS deaths and the need for ART, and to cushion the overall impact of the epidemic.

It is generally accepted that HIV responses that focus exclusively on behaviour change (such as condom use) are inadequate in hyper-epidemic settings like South Africa. The choices they promote are often short-circuited by powerful underlying factors that lie beyond the immediate, direct control of individuals (JLICA 2009; Wellings *et al* 2006). Comprehensive approaches to HIV prevention therefore focus also on tackling the social relations and structural factors that shape people's sex lives and choices. The most promising approach is one that resolutely promotes 'conventional', behaviour-focused interventions in the context of society-wide egalitarian strategies. South Africa's record on the latter front is spotty and invites rampant improvement. A wider and stronger social protection system that significantly and directly benefits women in impoverished communities is an essential, intermediate requirement. In the meanwhile, the cleaving effect of the AIDS epidemic will continue to offset efforts at loosening the grip of poverty and precariousness on many millions of South Africans. This is an epidemic that meshes savagely with the social relations that reproduce inequality and deprivation, generating a glacial, miserable crush. It unmasks the society we live in, but also broadcasts the need for drastic changes that favour the dispossessed.

NOTES

1   This chapter is a version of a more detailed discussion of the AIDS and TB epidemics in South Africa which appears in my forthcoming (2010) book 'South Africa Pushed to the Limit: The Political Economy of Change'.
2   The survey sample of whites and Indians was very small and probably led to an underestimation of HIV prevalence in those population groups. However, other survey data suggest that the error is slight.
3   Burkina Faso, Cameroon, Ghana, Kenya, Lesotho, Malawi, Tanzania and Uganda. Wealth status was gauged using an improvised asset index.
4   An African township impoverished overall, an economically impoverished but fairly well serviced and racially integrated township, and a relatively wealthy urban neighborhood.
5   About 300 000 HIV-positive women give birth to infants each year in South Africa; see Patrick and Stephen (2007).
6   The findings emerge from a study among 38 000 mothers in KwaZulu-Natal's six largest urban areas.
7   According to the Department of Health's guidelines (2001: 1), this approach entails 'the provision of health services by formal and informal caregivers in the home, in order to promote, restore and maintain a person's maximum level of comfort, function and health including care towards a dignified death'. Those guidelines were drafted before government relented to popular pressure and introduced an antiretroviral treatment programme through the public health system.
8   These divisions of labour are enforced by both women and men. Akintola's (2006) qualitative research in peri-urban parts of KwaZulu-Natal, for example, found many female caregivers were dismissive of men's caregiving abilities.
9   Almost 70 per cent of white households belong to medical schemes, compared with just 8 per cent of Africans (and 22 per cent of coloureds and 39 per cent of Indians). The proportion of households with medical aid membership actually dropped to 14 per cent in the mid-2000s before rising slightly.
10   Between 2003 and 2005, for example, the total number of nurses registered with the South African Nursing Council rose by less than 5 per cent (Matsebula and Wilie 2007).
11   The 2006 Progress in International Reading Literacy Study, reported in 'Girls reading achievement', *BBC News*, 28 November 2007. See http://news.bbc.co.uk/2/hi/uk_news/scotland/7117675.stm.
12   Cited in Idasa (2009). Using Western Cape data, where the matric rate in 2008 was 79 per cent, this means that once drop-outs are factored in, the actual pass rate was 35 per cent.
13   These are examined in some detail in Marais (forthcoming, 2010).

14   So 65 per cent of the learners in those top performing schools were white, whereas whites comprise 9 per cent of South Africa's population. In some of the Afrikaans-medium schools, fewer than 10 per cent of the learners were not white. See Govender, (2009).

15   It's likely that once one controls for pregnancy, the gender discrepancy in school attendance found in this study would narrow.

16   But 22-24 per cent of female educators aged twenty-five to thirty-four were HIV-infected, as were 17-19 per cent of their older male peers (aged thirty to thirty-nine) (Shisana *et al* 2005b).

17   Jansen (2007:26) locates many of these 'routine factors' in 'the deeply ingrained culture of black schooling made visible since the 1976 uprising', in which 'dedicated teaching, managerial discipline, parental involvement in schooling and learner commitment have been irretrievably lost'. The outcome, he laments, is 'the inertia of black schooling'.

18   Official data do not reflect patients who are lost to follow-up, who deregister or who died after commencing treatment.

19   In low and middle income countries, the average price per person per year in 2007 of the most commonly used second-line regimen (didanosine, abacavir and ritonavir-boosted lopinavir) was USD 1,214. Prices vary, though: South Africa was paying an average USD 1600 for that regimen in 2007, while El Salvador was paying USD 3448 (WHO, UNAIDS, UNICEF 2008).

20   If fewer men become infected with HIV, all else being equal, the numbers of HIV-positive men capable of transmitting to women decreases, and the number of women who become infected should then also decrease – hence the 'herd immunity' effect.

REFERENCES

Adam M and L Johnson (2009) Estimation of adult antiretroviral treatment coverage in South Africa. *South African Medical Journal* 99 (9): 661–667

Akintola O (2006) Gendered home-based care in South Africa: more trouble for the troubled. *African Journal of AIDS Research* 5 (3): 237–247.

Altman M (2005) The state of employment. In Daniel J, R Southall and J Lutchman (Eds) (2005) *State of the Nation: South Africa 2004–2005.* Cape Town: HSRC Press.

ANC (2001) A national guideline on home-based care and community-based care. African National Congress. Johannesburg.

Auvert B, D Taljaard, E Lagarde, J Sobngwi-Tambekou, R Sitta and A Puren (2005) Randomised, controlled intervention trial of male circumcision for reduction of HIV infection risk: the ANRS 1265 trial. *PLoS Medicine* 2 (11): 1112–1122.

Bailey RC, CB Parker, K Abot, I Maclean, JN Krieger, CF Willaims, RT Campbel and JO Ndinya-Achola (2007) Male circumcision for HIV prevention in young men in Kisumu, Kenya: a randomised controlled trial. *Lancet* 369: 643-656.

Barnett T and A Whiteside (2002) *AIDS in the 21ˢᵗ Century: Disease and Globalization.* London: Palgrave MacMillan, London.

Bärnighausen T, V Hosegood, IM Timaeus and ML Newell (2007) The socioeconomic determinants of HIV incidence: evidence from a longtitudinal, population-based study in rural South Africa. *AIDS.* 21. Suppl.7: S29-38.

Bloch G (2008) The complexity of systems change in education. In Maile S (Ed) *Education and Poverty Reduction Strategies: Issues of policy Coherence.* Colloquium proceedings, Cape Town: HSRC Press: 125–135.

Campbell C, Y Nair and S Maimane (2004) Home-based careers: A vital resource for effective ARV roll-out in rural communities? *AIDS Bulletin* 14 (1): http://www.mrc.ac.za/aids/march2005/homebased.htm.

Chigwedere P *et al* (2008) Estimating the lost benefits of antiretroviral drug use in South Africa. *Journal of Acquired Immune Deficiency Syndrome* 49 (4): 410–415.

Chimbiri AM (2007) The condom is an 'intruder' in marriage: evidence from rural Malawi, *Social Science and Medicine* 64 (5): 1102–15.

Chirambo K and J Steyn (2009) *AIDS and Local Government in South Africa: Examining the Impact of an Epidemic on Ward Councillors.* Cape Town: Idasa.

Chopra M, E Daviaud, R Pattinson, S Fonn and JE Lawn (2009) Saving the lives of South Africa's mothers, babies and children: can the health system deliver? *Lancet* 374 (9692): 835–846.

Collins DL and M Leibbrandt (2007) The financial impact of HIV/AIDS on poor households in South Africa. *AIDS*, 21 Suppl.7: S75–81.

Colvin M and C Connolly (2006) The epidemiology of HIV in South African workplaces, Presentation to UCLA Business & AIDS in South Africa seminar, 21-23 June, Zimbali, South Africa.

Colvin M, C Connolly and L Madurai (2007) The epidemiology of HIV in South African workplaces, *AIDS*, 21 Suppl.3: S13–S19.

Connelly D, Y Veriava, S Roberts, J Tsotetsi, A Jordan, E DeSilva, S Rosen and MB DeSilva (2007) Prevalence of HIV infection and median CD4 counts among healthcare workers in South Africa. *South African Medical Journal* 97 (2): 115–120.

Cullinan K (2009) AIDS-free generation within grasp, 8 December, *health-e.*

Cullinan K and A Thom (Eds) (2009) *The Virus, Vitamins and Vegetables: The South African HIV/AIDS Mystery.* Johannesburg: Jacana.

De Jager L (2009) The South African education system, 2009 and beyond, Discussion paper. Cape Town.

Department of Education (2005a) Grade 6 Intermediate phase systematic evaluation report, December, Department of Education, Pretoria. Available at http://www.education.gov.za/dynamic/imgshow.aspx?id=1343.

Department of Health, South Africa (2001) An enhanced response to HIV/AIDS and tuberculosis in the public health sector: Key components and funding requirements, 2002/2003-2004/2005, Department of Health, Pretoria.

Department of Health, South Africa (2003) South Africa demographic & health survey 2003. Department of Health, Pretoria.

Department of Health, South Africa (2006) The national HIV and syphilis prevalence survey, South Africa, 2005, National Department of Health, Pretoria.

Department of Health, South Africa (2009) The national HIV and syphilis prevalence survey, South Africa, 2008, National Department of Health, Pretoria.

de Waal A (2007) *AIDS and Power.* London: Zed Books.

de Walque D (2007) Sero-discordant couples in five African countries: implications for prevention strategies. *Population and Development Review* 33 (3): 501–523.

Feinstein A (2007) *After the Party: A Personal and Political Journey Inside the ANC.* Johannesburg: Jonathan Ball Publishers.

Feldbaum H, K Lee and P Patel P (2006) The National Security Implications of HIV/AIDS, *PLoS Medicine*, 3.6, e171.

Giese S *et al* (2003) Health and social services to address the needs of orphans and other vulnerable children in the context of HIV/AIDS, Report submitted to the National HIV/AIDS Directorate, Department of Health, January, Cape Town.

Gillespie S, S Kadiyala and R Greener (2007) Is poverty or wealth driving HIV transmission? *AIDS*, 21 Suppl.7: S5–S16.

Govender P (2007) *Love and Courage: A Story of Insubordination.* Johannesburg: Jacana.

Govender P (2009) Exclusive: We reveal SA's top schools, *Sunday Times*, 17 October.

Gray RH, G Kigozi, D Serwadda, F Makumbi, S Watya, F Nalugoda, N Kiwanuka, LH Moulton, MA Chaudhary, MZ Chen, NK Sewankambo, F Wabwire-Mangen, MC Bacon, CF Williams, P Opendi, SJ Reynolds, O Laeyendecker, TC Quinn and MJ Wawer (2007) Male circumcision for HIV prevention in young men in Rakai, Uganda: a randomized trial. *Lancet* 369: 657–666.

Gray RH, N Kiwanuka, TC Quinn, NK Sewankambo, D Serwadda, FW Mangen, T Lutalo, F Naluqoda, R Kelly, M Meehan, MZ Chen, C Li and MJ Wawer (2000) Male circumcision and HIV acquisition and transmission: cohort studies in Rakai, Uganda. *AIDS* 14 (15): 2371–81.

Hallett TB, K Singh, JA Smith, RG White, LJ Abu-Raddad and GP Garntett (2008) Understanding the impact of male circumcision interventions on the spread of HIV in Southern Africa. *PLoS ONE*, 3, 5: e2212.

Halperin DT and H Epstein (2007) Why is HIV prevalence so severe in southern Africa? *The Southern African Journal of HIV Medicine* 8 (1): 19–25.

Hirschhorn LR and R Skolnik (2008) Making universal access a reality – what more do we need to know? *Journal of Infectious Diseases* 197: 1223-5.

Hosegood V, E Preston-Whyte, J Busza, S Moitse and IM Timeaus (2007) Revealing the full extent of households' experiences of HIV and AIDS in rural South Africa. *Social Science and Medicine* 65 (6),: 1249-1259.

HSRC (2002) Nelson Mandela/HSRC study of HIV/AIDS: South African national HIV prevalence, behaviour risks and mass media household survey 2002. Pretoria HSRC, MRC, CADRE, ANRS.

HSRC (2005) Survey gives hard facts about the lives of educators. *HSRC Review* 3 (2): 12–15.

HSRC (2009) South African national HIV prevalence, incidence, behaviour and communication survey, 2008: A turning tide among teenagers? Cape Town: HSRC.

Hunter N (2007) Crises in social reproduction and home-based care. *Africanus*, November, University of South Africa.

Idasa (2009) What should we be discussing at we head to the polls? Background paper, 20 March, PIMS. Cape Town: Idasa.

Jansen J (2007) Bodies count: AIDS Review 2006. Centre for the Study of AIDS, University of Pretoria.

JLICA (2009) Home truths: Facing the facts on children, AIDS and poverty. Final Report of the Joint Learning Initiative on Children and HIV/AIDS. JLICA. Available at http://www.jlica.org/resources/publications.php.

Kalichman SC *et al* (2006) Associations of poverty, substance use and HIV transmission risk behaviors in three South African communities. *Social Science and Medicine* 62 (7): 1641–9.

Kapp C (2009) South Africa heads into elections in a sorry state of health. *Lancet*, 373, 24 January.

Louw M, S van der Berg and D Yu (2006) Educational attainment and intergenerational social mobility in South Africa, Working paper no. 9, Department of Economics, University of Stellenbosch.

Marais H (2005) Buckling: The impact of AIDS in South Africa, Centre for the Study of AIDS, Pretoria University. http://www.sarpn.org.za/documents/d0001789/index.php.

Marais H (2007) The uneven impact of HIV in a polarized society, *AIDS*, 21, Suppl 3: S21–9.

Marais H (2010) *South Africa Pushed to the Limit: The Political Economy of Change*. Forthcoming. Cape Town and London: University of Cape Town Press and Zed Books.

Matsebula T and M Willie (2007) Private Hospitals. In Harrison S, R Bhana and A Ntuli (Eds) *SA Health Review 2007*, Health Systems Trust, Durban: 159–174.

McIntyre D and M Thiede (2007) Health care financing and expenditure. In Harrison S, R Bhana and A Ntuli (Eds) *SA Health Review 2007*. Durban: Health Systems Trust: 35–46.

McIntyre D, H McLeod and M Thiede (2005) Comments on the National Treasury. discussion document on the proposed tax reforms relating to medical scheme contributions and medical expenses. Cape Town: Health Economics Unit.

Meth C (2006) Income poverty in 2004: A second engagement with the recent van der Berg et al figures, Working Paper 47 (September), School for Development Studies, University of KwaZulu-Natal.

Meth C (2008) The (lame) duck unchained tries to count the poor, Working Paper No. 49, School of Development Studies, University of KwaZulu-Natal, Durban.

Mishra V, SB Assche, R Greener, M Vaessen, R Hong, PD Ghys, JT Boerma, A Van Assche, S Khan and S Rutstein (2007) HIV infection does not disproportionately affect the poorer in sub-Saharan Africa. *AIDS*, 21 Suppl. 7: S17–S28.

National Committee on Confidential Enquiries into Maternal Deaths [NCCEMD] (2009) Saving mothers 2005-2007: Fourth report on confidential enquiries into maternal deaths in South Africa, Expanded Executive Summary, Department of Health, Pretoria.

National Intelligence Council (2000) Global Trends 2015: A Dialogue About the Future with Non-government Experts, December. Washington, DC: National Intelligence Council.

Nattrass N (2002) AIDS, growth and distribution of South Africa, Centre for Social Science Research, University of Cape Town Working Paper No 7.

NnKo S, B Chidano, F Wilson, W Masuya and G Mwaluko (2000) Tanzania: AIDS care – Learning from experience. Review of African Political Economy 27 (86): 547–557.

Orner P (2006) Psychological impacts on caregivers of people living with AIDS. AIDS Care 18 (3): 236–240.

Parker F (2009) AIDS policy: 'Systemic problems need to be addressed', Mail & Guardian, 3 December.

Parker W, B Makhubele, P Ntlabati and C Connolly (2007) Concurrent sexual partnerships amongst young adults in South Africa. Johannesburg: CADRE. Available at http://www.comminit.com/en/node/269915/36.

Patrick M and C Stephen (2007) Saving children 2005: a survey of child healthcare in South Africa. Cape Town: Medical Research Council Unit for Maternal and Infant Health Care Strategies.

Pauw K, M Oosthuizen and C van der Westhuizen (2006) Graduate unemployment in the face of skills shortages: A labour market paradox. Presented at the conference on Accelerated and Shared Growth in South Africa: Determinants, constraints and opportunities, Trade and Industrial Policy Strategy (TIPS) & Development Policy Research Unit, Johannesburg & Cape Town.

Pieterse E (2003) Rhythms, patterning and articulations of social formations in South Africa, In Everatt D and V Maphai (Eds) The Real State of the Nation: South Africa After 1990. Development Update special edition. Johannesburg: Interfund.

Piot P, R Greener and S Russell (2007) Squaring the circle: AIDS, poverty and human development, PLoS Medicine 4 (10): 1571-1575.

Potts M, DT Halperin, D Kirby, A Swidler, E Marseille, JD Klausener, N Hearst, RG Wamai, JG Kahn and J Walsh (2008) Reassessing HIV prevention. Science 320: 749–50.

Presidency (2008) Development Indicators. Pretoria: Government of South Africa.

Rosen S, M Fox and C Gill (2007) Patient retention in antiretroviral therapy programs in sub-Saharan Africa: a systematic review. PLoS Medicine, 2007, 10:e29.

Rosen S and J Simon (2003) Shifting the burden: The private sector's response to the AIDS pandemic in Africa. Bulletin of the World Health Organization 81 (2): 133–137.

Schindler J (2005) Access to education in South Africa 2001. Edusource Data News, No. 49, October.

Schneider H, H Hlope and D van Rensburg (2008) Community health workers and the response to HIV/AIDS in South Africa: tensions and prospects. Health Policy and Planning 23: 179–187.

Shelton JD (2007) Ten myths and one truth about generalised HIV epidemics. Lancet 370 (9602): 1809–11.

Shelton JD, JD Halperin, V Nantulya, M Potts, HD Gayle and KK Holmes (2004) Partner reduction is crucial for balanced 'ABC' approach to HIV prevention. British Medical Journal 328 (7444): 891-3.

Shisana O, E Hall and HR Maluleke (2003) The Impact of HIV/AIDS on the Health Sector: National Survey of Health Personnel, Ambulatory and Hospitalised Patients and Health Facilities 2002, HSRC, Medunsa and MRC. Cape Town: HSRC Press. http://www.hsrcpress.ac.za/index.asp?areaid=4.

Shisana O, T Rehle, L Simbayi, W Parker, K Zuma, A Bhana, C Connolly, S Jooste and V Pillay (2005a) South African National HIV Prevalence, HIV Incidence, Behaviour and Communication Survey, Human Sciences Research Council, Pretoria. Available at http://www.hsrc.ac.za/media/2005/11/20051130_1.html.

Shisana O, K Peltzer, N Zungu-Dirwayi and J Louw (2005b) The Health of our Educators: A Focus on HIV/AIDS in South African Public Schools. Cape Town: HSRC Press.

Simbayi LC and SC Kalichman (2007) Condom failure in South Africa. South African Medical Journal 97 (7): 476.

Statistics SA (2008) General Household Survey 2007, Statistical release P0318, September, Statistics South Africa, Pretoria.

Statistics SA (2009) Mid-year population estimates 2009, Statistical Release P0302, July, Statistics SA, Pretoria. http://www.statssa.gov.za/publications/P0302/P03022009.pdf.

Steinberg M, S Johnson, S Schierhout and D Ndegwa (2002) Hitting home: how households cope with the impact of the HIV/AIDS epidemic. Henry J Kaiser Foundation & Health Systems Trust. October. Cape Town.

Sundararaman T (2007) Community health workers: scaling up programmes. *Lancet* 369 (9579): 2058–2059.

Tawfik L and KN Kinoti (2003) *The Impact of HIV/AIDS on Health Systems in sub-Saharan Africa with Special Reference to the Issue of Human Resources.* Washington, DC: USAID Bureau for Africa.

Thomas EP, M Colvin, SB Rosen, C Zuccarini and S Petze (2005) HIV prevalence study and costing analysis undertaken for the development of an HIV/AIDS workplace strategy for Buffalo City Municipality. Cape Town: Medical Research Council & South African Cities Network.

Torres L, D Drury, L Eldring, P Lewis and J Vass (2001) Mesebetsi Labour Force Survey, Topline Report, Cape Town.

Turner AN (2007) Men's circumcision status and women's risk of HIV acquisition in Zimbabwe and Uganda. *AIDS* 21: 1779–89.

UNAIDS (2008) *Report on the global AIDS epidemic 2008.* Geneva: UNAIDS.

UNDP (2008) Human Development Report 2007/2008. Fighting climate change: Human solidarity in a divided world. New York: UNDP.

Van Renterghem H (2009) AIDS and the city: Intensifying the response to HIV and AIDS in urban areas in sub-Saharan Africa. Working paper. Johannesburg: UNAIDS Regional Support Team.

Von Holdt K (2009) The South African post-apartheid bureaucratic state: Inner workings, contradictory rationales and the developmental state. In Edigheji O (Ed) *Constructing a Democratic Developmental State in South Africa: Potential and Challenges.* Cape Town: HSRC Press [in press].

Von Holdt K and M Murphy (2007) Public hospitals in South Africa: stressed institutions, disempowered management. In Buhlungu S, J Daniel, R Southall and J Lutchman *State of the Nation: South Africa 2007.* Cape Town: HSRC Press: 312–341.

Walensky RP (2008) Scaling up antiretroviral therapy in South Africa: the impact of speed on survival. *Journal of Infectious Diseases* 197 (9): 324–32.

Walt G (1990) *Community health workers in national programmes: just another pair of hands?* Philadelphia Open University Press.

Wawer M, G Kigozi, D Serwadda, F Makumbi, F Nalugoda, S Watya, D Buwembo, V Ssempijja, L Moulton and R Gray (2008) Trial of circumcision in HIV+ men in Rakai, Uganda: effects in HIV+ men and women partners. Fifteenth Conference on Retroviruses and Opportunistic Infections, Boston. Abstract 33LB.

Wellings K *et al* (2006) Sexual behaviour in context: a global perspective. *Lancet* 368: 1706–1728.

Westercamp M and RC Bailey (2007). Acceptability of male circumcision for prevention of HIV/AIDS in sub-Saharan Africa: a review. *AIDS Behavior* 11 (3): 341–55.

Whiteside A (2008) *HIV/AIDS: A Very Short Introduction.* Oxford: Oxford University Press.

Whiteside A and M O'Grady (2003) AIDS and private sector: Lessons from Southern Africa. In Sisask A (Ed) One step further: Responses to HIV/AIDS. Stockholm & Geneva: Sida & UNRISD.

WHO, UNAIDS, UNICEF (2008) Towards Universal Access: Scaling up priority HIV/AIDS interventions in the health sector. Progress report 2008. Geneva: WHO.

Williams BG, JO Lloyd-Smith, E Gouws, C Hankins, WM Getz, J Hargrove, I de Zoysa, C Dye and B Auvert (2006) The potential impact of male circumcision on HIV in sub-Saharan Africa. *PloS Medicine*, 3:e262.

World Bank (2008) World development indicators. Washington, DC: World Bank.

Youde J (2001) All the voters will be dead: HIV/AIDS and democratic legitimacy and stability in Africa. Research paper, University of Iowa.

CHAPTER 14

Health for all?
Towards a national health service in South Africa

Louis Reynolds

At its landmark conference in Polokwane in December 2007, the African National Congress (ANC) adopted a resolution to implement a National Health Insurance (NHI) as part of a broader ten point plan to address the key challenges facing the health system.

In the Government Gazette of 11 September 2009, Health Minister Aaron Motsoaledi established a ministerial advisory committee to advise on the development of policy, legislation and implementation of the NHI. The Gazette declares: 'The introduction of a National Health Insurance System is founded on three principles. Firstly, that it is a Constitutional right that the public has access to affordable and acceptable quality health services; secondly, that it is the responsibility of the State to ensure the progressive realisation of the right to health for all South Africans that is premised on the objective of universal coverage; and thirdly, that it is important for health services to be funded in an equitable manner that promotes social solidarity' (Department of Health 2009).

Motsoaledi said the committee would release a draft white paper on the NHI for public comment in due course but by mid-March 2010 the white paper had not been released, and very little is known about the proposed NHI apart from the three fundamental principles outlined above.

The available information indicates that the NHI will pool all the money currently spent on health into a single National Health Insurance Fund (NHIF). This includes money allocated through the health budget, together with a 'mandatory contribution' from everyone over a certain income threshold. The mandatory contribution will increase progressively according to income but the unemployed and those below a defined income threshold will be exempt. The NHIF will pay for all health care services in South Africa. Citizens and permanent residents will be able to choose either a public or a private health care facility. There will be no user fees or co-payments for health care (Department of Health 2009).

The rationale for the NHI is made clear in the Gazette: 'The South African health care system is ... fragmented and inequitable ... due to ... huge disparities ... between the public and private health sectors with regards to the accessibility, funding and delivery of health services ... To address these imbalances in access and utilisation of health services as well as health outcomes ... the health care system requires the creation of a National Health Insurance System that transforms the health system into an integrated, prepayment-based health financing system that effectively promotes the progressive realisation of the right to health care for all' (Department of Health 2009).

In addition to the NHI, the proposed ten point plan includes the following:
- Stronger leadership (the number one priority)
- Improving quality of care
- Upgrading health system management
- Increasing human resources for health
- Revitalising infrastructure
- Accelerating an anti-AIDS strategy
- Creating mass mobilisation for better health
- Tackling policies on access to medicines
- Strengthening South Africa's research and development community.

Thus the proposals for the NHI are envisaged as located within a broader thrust to promote an affordable national health care system which be equally accessible to all South Africans.

The highly respected journal, *The Lancet*, has taken a special interest in these developments, and recently commissioned a special series of articles on health in South Africa, written by researchers, physicians, and public health specialists with intimate knowledge of the situation (Kleinert and Horton 2009).

An accompanying editorial expresses a mixture of caution and optimism:

> Is Motsoaledi's strategy deliverable? The past decade has seen Nelson Mandela's Rainbow Nation stripped of some of its brightest colours: thanks to escalating unemployment, deepening inequalities within the black population, emigration of some of the country's most skilled professionals, rapid declines in domestic food production, regressive tax policies, the collapse of the education system, a bloated welfare dependency culture, falling life expectancy, violence and social instability, and eroded standards of public service provision. Worse, The Economist has put South Africa at the top of a league table of vulnerable emerging market economies. The global financial crisis has severely limited the country's room for reform.
>
> Despite these broader economic uncertainties [there is a sense of] unprecedented opportunity. A new coalition for national health renewal – between government,

professionals, scientists, and activists – has been born. There are outstanding examples of excellence across South Africa's health service to learn from. And despite the past, as Aaron Motsoaledi pointed out, there is no predetermined future ahead. The outlook for South Africa can be different. As *The Lancet* continues to follow South Africa's progress, we believe it will be different – and better (*The Lancet* 2009).

The Lancet is correct: there is a palpable sense of optimism among a wide range of health professionals, civil society actors, scientists and health department officials.

However, excellent proposals and plans to improve health and health care have cropped up in the past in South Africa and internationally. Some have been inspirational, filling people with enormous enthusiasm and goodwill and commitment, only to falter and fail because of lack of political will and the power of vested interests. Three examples are particularly relevant to the NHI.

The first emerged in South Africa in 1944 when a national health services commission recommended the establishment of a single tax-funded national health service for all citizens irrespective of race or class. It was inspired by the concept of Community Oriented Primary Health Care (COPHC), developed under the leadership of doctors Sydney and Emily Kark in the 1930s and 1940s. COPHC based itself firmly in local contexts, provided comprehensive promotive, preventive and curative care through a team-based approach, and relied on a continuing cycle of local epidemiological research to guide practice. This departed from existing health care models, and was later to influence public health understanding internationally, notably in the USA and Israel. The second example was the almost universal adoption by many countries of the 1978 Declaration of Alma Ata with its commitment to health as a fundamental human right and its vision of 'Health for All' by the year 2000. Finally, in 2004, the Reconstruction and Development Programme and the ANC's national health plan for South Africa provided a vision for a just and equitable health system for the new democracy. All three, however, failed to meet their potential, largely because of a deadly combination of a lack of political will and the power of vested interests.

This article gives an overview of why and how these historic opportunies emerged and why they failed. Against this background, it then explores what it would take for the NHI and associated reforms to contribute to making universal health care for all South Africans a real possibility. It argues that unless the lessons of history are learned, powerful vested interests grounded in neoliberal orthodoxy may attempt to shape the NHI in their favour. If they succeed, the NHI is unlikely to contribute to the transformation of the health system in a way that effectively promotes the progressive realisation of the right to health care for all.

SOUTH AFRICA IN THE 1940s: Community Oriented Primary Health Care and the National Health Services Commission

An experiment with social medicine in South Africa six decades ago provides particularly trenchant lessons for today's attempts to improve the country's health and establish an excellent and equitable health system. In the late 1930s and early 1940s, new thinking around public health, community medicine and family practice emerged in South Africa, challenging prevailing ideas and creating great excitement. Progressive pioneering doctors, notably Raymond Dart, Eustace Cluver, Harry Gear, George Gale, David Landau, and Sidney and Emily Kark, developed a highly sophisticated and holistic understanding of the causal influences and roots of disease. They recognised the need for community participation and intersectoral coordination in health promotion and actively ensured that health and agricultural workers, for example, worked closely together to reduce malnutrition in people, animals and the soil (Yach and Tollman 1993).

At Pholela, along the Umkomaas river valley, the Karks employed and trained local community health workers who compiled detailed maps drawn from the local population. These maps provided a basis for the first population census in the area. The resulting report, compiling information gleaned from 887 inhabitants of the 130 homes adjacent to the centre, stressed the need for village planning in the areas of basic sanitation, soil erosion and nutritional status.

There was, therefore, early recognition of the importance of the environmental and agricultural sectors, and of community involvement. Annually thereafter, the initial defined area was expanded and served as a practice site for more intensive study and service. An annual household health census, administered by the health assistants, was introduced. 'In this way,' Kark wrote, 'we hope[d] to lay the foundation for accurate epidemiological studies, for measuring movements of the population, and for assessing the influence of various environmental factors on people' (Yach and Tollman 1993). These steps laid the basis for what later became known as community oriented primary care which strives to link community wide interventions with primary medical care, using community epidemiology as its base.

The results were remarkable: crude mortality rate decreased from 38.3 in 1942 to 13.6 per 1 000 in 1950; infant mortality dropped from 275 to 100 per 1 000; and the incidence of severe malnutrition declined sharply. These improvements were accompanied by increasing interest and active cooperation on the part of the people served by the project (Kark and Cassel 1952).

In 1942, the South African government under the prime minister, Jan Smuts, appointed the National Health Services Commission (NHSC). Its task was to make recommendations for an organised national health service to ensure 'adequate medical, dental, nursing and hospital services to all [sic] sections of the people' (Jeeves 2005).

The Commission's chair was Dr Henry Gluckman, United Party MP for Yeoville. Gluckman had been prominent in parliamentary debates on South Africa' poor health status in the late 1930s. Sydney Kark was appointed the commission's technical adviser (Yach and Tollman 1993: 1043-1050).

The Commission proceeded with a comprehensive survey of the health conditions and needs of 'the people as a whole' and tabled its report two years later. It declared that the health of the people was 'far below what it should be and could be', and blamed this upon the poverty of the black population and large sections of the white population, as well as on the primitive health and educational facilities then available. It further argued that the medical system was not using its resources effectively. Its services were not available to large sections of the population, not organised on a national basis, and not up to modern standards. It needed a complete reorganisation.

The NHSC made it clear that reform of the health system on its own could achieve little unless the country addressed the underlying social origins of much of the preventable disease affecting it. Furthermore, rather than relying on individual doctors, health care should be delivered by teams made up of doctors, nurses and auxiliary personnel. Their mandate would be the 'promotion and preservation of health', rather than reliance on curative medicine (Jeeves 2005: p.91).

Over three and a half months of fieldwork the commissioners gathered evidence and testimonies from more than 1 000 witnesses. They described how service provision was disjointed, haphazard, provincial and parochial, and thus 'very inadequate'. Services did not conform with 'the modern conception of health' but were curative rather than promotive, and were 'poorly supplied to the under-privileged sectors who require them most'.

The Commission insisted that a national health authority's efforts should be directed not towards 'the provision of more and more hospital beds, but towards the provision of more and more health centres with periodic examination of all members of the population'. It therefore proposed the establishment of 400 health centres under twenty regional health organisations, each looking after roughly 25 000 people. These centres would provide 'personal health services for all sections of the people as a citizens' right . . . according to needs rather than means'. They were to be 'the basic unit' in the national health scheme where 'the actual personal health service will be rendered'. The entire country would be served, and every family would have a health centre to which it would look for health services which would replace the system of uncoordinated private practice (Digby 2008).

It concluded that adequate health services for all sections of the population required national uniformity under a centralised authority. This implied a single national health service that would reach all the people of South Africa, and would be paid for by a graduated tax assessed as part of general taxation.

The pioneering work of Sidney and Emily Kark and their colleagues at Pholela served as a model for the centres. The healthcare team there developed an intensive family health service in which the home visit, and not the clinic, was seen as the basis for activity. Health assistants acted as field workers in compiling detailed records of domiciliary visits. Preventive and curative healthcare gradually merged into 'a more comprehensive outlook best described by the title of social medicine'.

The future work of staff in Gluckman's health centres more generally was envisaged as being 'to act as the practitioners of social medicine'. Training the personnel who would practice social medicine in health centres had started at Pholela. In 1945 Kark and others established the Institute of Family and Community Health at Clairwood in Durban. The Rockefeller Foundation helped the Institute with generous funding. The Institute offered public health training to a wide range of professionals from doctors to community workers.

The NHSC's innovative idea of health centres challenged the existing order, both in South Africa and Britain. As a doctor, Gluckman was well aware of the medical profession's sensitivities. Anticipating opposition, the Commission spelled out patients' rights to a free choice of doctor in the new health centres, as well as the fact that there would be no compulsion for medical practitioners to enter the national health service. In its turn, the Medical Association of South Africa (MASA) made it clear that its 'preparedness to cooperate wholeheartedly in a national health service for the prevention and treatment of disease' was conditional on the preservation of personal relationships between doctors and patients, and on the right of doctors to engage in private practice.

The Commission decided to make 'a practical beginning' by rolling out the health centres, before 'delicate and important negotiations' had been accomplished and a 'comprehensive solution' had been reached. Meanwhile, the Smuts government, which turned out to be luke-warm about the Commission's recommendations, was signalling that reform would be intro-duced by a series of measures and not by major legislation as was to be the case in Britain with the establishment of the National Health Service in 1948.

The first 'Gluckman' health centre began in December 1945 at Grassy Park, in Cape Town, followed by Lady Selborne and Tongaat in 1946. Cradock and White River were set up in 1947. By 1953 there were more than thirty centres, and by 1960 the number had grown to more than forty. Most stressed promotive health education (through ante-natal clinics, mother and baby clinics or the examination of schoolchildren), as well as preventive measures (through improved nutrition, immunisation and vaccination), but the importance of curative medicine in the treat-ment of disease (through the outpatient clinic or district nursing station) varied considerably.

The extent to which health centres offered curative care threatened private medical practice. When Gluckman became minister of health in November 1945, he had thought it necessary to reassure the profession by stating that those receiving curative care at health centres would not have been able to afford a private doctor, and that centres had only been set up 'in those areas where there are large numbers of people so poor that they cannot afford to engage the services of private practitioners' (Digby 2008).

When the National Party (NP) won the elections in 1948, the political environment changed drastically, closing 'the window that had briefly opened for a more innovative approach' (Jeeves 1998). The multiracial health teams embedded in the health centres were antithetical to the NP's programme of apartheid. Staffing problems became endemic since more than one in five staff left, were transferred or had their services terminated, whilst major difficulties were expe-rienced in staffing rural or remote centres. Within a few years, peripheral centres closed or had been handed over to provincial administrations. Discouraged by hostile government policies, the Karks, and many of South Africa's most progressive doctors, emigrated.

But, as Shula Marks has pointed out, the hostility of the apartheid state to the health centre movement and what it stood for was not the only, or even the main, reason for the ultimate failure of the health centre approach. The Smuts government had been lukewarm to the proposal, and allowed the powerful authorities of the then provinces (Transvaal, Orange Free State, Cape and Natal) to retain control over publicly funded curative services and hospitals. The direct tax by which the system was funded was unpopular, and the government agreed to refund 50 per cent of provincial expenditure. Ironically, the provinces used this subsidy to provide free hospital services. However, the result of the political failure to bring all publicly funded health services under unified administrative control was that from the outset the health centres were starved of resources and the hospitals were favoured. In 1944/45, for example, the vote for health centres was only £50 000 – less than 4 per cent of the state health budget. This set up a vicious cycle (not unlike that being experienced today) in which the neglect of preventive and local curative services led to an urgent demand for hospital beds from a growing number of desperately ill people, driving up health care costs (Marks 1997: 456).

Furthermore, with the changed political climate and because the medical profession became more hostile to any notion of 'social medicine', district surgeons and private doctors also felt encroachment on their territories. Health centres became located only in areas where local authorities were unable to provide personal health services or where people were too poor to pay for private health care. Contrary to the original intention, the health centre idea became associated with the poor and progressively marginalised (*ibid*).

This shift of the health centres from the centre to the margins undermined the non-racial vision of the NHSC. By the early 1950s, when the apartheid government was implementing increasingly rigorous racial segregation, the majority of the centres were located in black areas. In 1952 the standing committee of the Commission resolved that 'the time has come for the official acceptance of the health centre as the means for improving the health of the non-European population and reducing the costs of health care.' As Marks points out 'health centres were finally reduced to being a cheap option for black health care' (*ibid*).

THE 1978 DECLARATION OF ALMA ATA

The concept of primary health care re-emerged in the late 1960s when it became clear that western-based colonial models of 'development' foisted on the colonies and based on the idea of modernisation and progress and of 'helping them be like us' were failing. This included the transplantation of hospital-based health care systems that had evolved in England and Europe to the colonies with their vastly different climates, cultures and health environments.

Cueto (2004) has reviewed the historic strands and events that led to the establishment of the global goal of 'Health for All' by the year 2000 (HFA2000). The main historic strands were the work of missionary doctors in poor communities in different parts of the world, the success of 'barefoot doctors' during the cultural revolution in China, and the emergence of strong anticolonialist movements in Africa and elsewhere.

Missionary doctors working among poor people in underdeveloping countries discovered the value and importance of involving local people actively in their own health care. In the late 1960s they established the Christian Medical Commission (CMC), a specialised organisation under the auspices of the World Council of Churches and the Lutheran World Federation. The CMC emphasised the training of village workers at the grassroots level, equipped with essential drugs and simple methods. In 1970, it created the journal *Contact*, which probably used the term 'primary health care' for the first time. The offices of the CMC in Geneva were close to the WHO headquarters, and there were personal links between John Bryant and Carl Taylor of the CMC and Halfdan Mahler, then director general of the WHO. In 1974, collaboration between the CMC and the WHO was formalised. Influential books such as Newell's *Health by the People* (Newell 1975), cited examples of CMC programmes, while others were brought to the attention of the WHO by commission members (Cueto 2004).

Meanwhile, news had spread from communist China of enormous health gains achieved by 'barefoot doctors'. The barefoot doctors, whose numbers increased dramatically between the early 1960s and the cultural revolution of 1964–1976, were a diverse array of village health workers who lived in the communities they served – thus rural rather than urban health was stressed (Cueto 2004).

While the progressive health community debated PHC, a new political context favourable to it emerged with the spread of national, anti-imperialist, and leftist movements in decolonised African nations and other underdeveloping nations. These changes led to new proposals on development made by some industrialised countries. Modernisation was no longer seen as the replication of the model of development followed by the United States or Western Europe (Cueto 2004).

In 1975, the WHO and UNICEF produced a widely discussed joint report, Alternative Approaches to Meeting Basic Health Needs in Developing Countries. The term 'alternative ' underlined the shortcomings of traditional vertical programmes concentrating on specific diseases. According to the document, the principal causes of morbidity in developing countries were malnutrition and vector-borne, respiratory, and diarrheal diseases, which were 'themselves the results of poverty, squalor and ignorance' (Djukanovic and Mach 1975). The report also examined successful primary health care experiences in Bangladesh, China, Cuba, India, Niger, Nigeria, Tanzania, Venezuela and Yugoslavia to identify the key factors in their success. Again, the assumption that the expansion of 'Western' medical systems would meet the needs of the common people was highly criticised (Cueto 2004).

The landmark event for primary health care was the international conference on primary health care that took place at Alma Ata, the capital of the Soviet Republic of Kazakhstan, from 6 to 12 September 1978 – more than three decades after the Karks pioneered the concept at Pholela.

The conference was attended by 3 000 delegates from 134 governments and 67 international organisations from all over the world. Its main document, the Declaration of Alma Ata, which was already known by many participants, was approved by acclamation (Cueto 2004). However, despite the initial enthusiasm, it was difficult to implement primary health care after Alma Ata. About a year after the conference took place, a different interpretation of primary health care appeared, and once again the concept challenged vested interests.

Werner and Sanders have described the strong socio-political implications of the Alma Ata concept of PHC (Werner and Sanders 1997). First, it explicitly stated the need for a comprehensive health strategy that not only provided health services, but also addressed the underlying social, economic, and political causes of poor health. Specifically, it called for a more equitable distribution of resources. Political commitment to primary health care implied more than formal support from government and community leaders. For developing countries in particular, it implied the transfer of a greater share of health resources to the under-served majority of the population. It therefore recognised that there was a need for increases in national health budgets until entire populations had access to essential health care. Furthermore, it required affluent countries to commit themselves to a more equitable distribution of international health resources to enable poor countries, and especially the least developed, to apply primary health care. Finally, Alma Ata also emphasised the close link between health and development of the poorer sector of the community (although, unfortunately, to make the declaration palatable to the politically diverse governments represented at the gathering, a precise statement of just how 'development' was to be achieved was omitted) (Werner and Sanders 1997).

In line with three decades of experience, the Declaration also called for participation of the people affected, asserting that 'self-reliance and social awareness are key factors in human development', and emphasising the importance of 'community participation in deciding on policies and in planning, implementing, and controlling development programmes'. Strong community participation had clearly been a common feature of the successful community-based programmes which had been studied in the process of formulating the Declaration. The participants at Alma Ata recognised that PHC itself can contribute to development and serve as an arena for awareness raising and organised action. At the same time, they realised that the dynamic unleashed by greater awareness and mobilisation was potentially revolutionary, and was therefore likely to meet with opposition from those wanting to maintain the *status quo* (Werner and Sanders 1997).

This realisation of the socio-political implications of PHC may have been the reason for the imprecise language of the Declaration and for its subsequent reinterpretation to suit a range of agendas and interests. At a meeting at the University of the Western Cape in 1992, Dr Ofosu-Amaa of UNICEF acknowledged this lack of clarity: 'Unfortunately the use of the term 'primary health care' for so many themes and features of the basic idea has been the source of endless confusion'. This lack of clarity is arguably one of the reasons for the failure of the Declaration to lead to HFA2000 (Reynolds 2009).

In the narrowest interpretation, PHC was merely a place of health care delivery, the site of first contact between people and the health service, usually the local clinic. This, and the fact that local primary care facilities had for many years been functioning inadequately (mainly because disproportionate amounts of money were being spent on central hospitals) gave the impression that PHC was a cheap and inferior form of health care. However, others saw PHC as a changed philosophy of health care delivery, a reform of the health sector to provide comprehensive care at all levels 'from the small health post to hospitals and even the ministry of health'. This broader view included all levels of health care, but it ignored the necessity for inter-sectoral collaboration and community participation.

What, then, was the basic idea? The themes mentioned above are part of it, but there is more. The missing theme, implied in the document but perhaps not stated clearly enough, is often spoken of as '*the spirit of PHC*'. The spirit of PHC is its premise that health is a social, economic and political issue, and above all a fundamental human right. It addresses the underlying determinants of health and is based on the concepts of equity, sustainability, and community empowerment (see, for example, Spirit of Alma Ata 1978; Caucus 2006). The Alma Ata Declaration states that ' … primary health care is *essential health care* based on practical, scientifically sound and socially acceptable methods and technology *made universally accessible* to individuals and families in the community through their *full participation and at a cost that the community and country can afford* to maintain at every stage of their development in the spirit of self-reliance and self-determination. It forms an integral part *both of the country's health system*, of which it is the central function and main focus, and of the *overall social and economic development* of the community. It is the first level of contact of individuals, the family and community with the national health system bringing health care as close as possible to where people live and work, and constitutes the first element of a continuing health care process. People have the right and duty to participate individually and collectively in the planning and implementation of their health care [italics added for emphasis]'. PHC 'requires and promotes maximum community and individual self-reliance and participation in the planning, organisation, operation and control of primary health care, making fullest use of local, national and other available resources'.

In essence, the PHC approach seeks to empower people through a bottom-up notion of human development, controlled by people at the community level. Starting with local knowledge and resources, it promotes self sufficiency, and should be sustainable.

These ideas imply redistribution not only of resources but also of power and control. Instead of being at the top of a hierarchy, doctors would work in teams with other levels of health workers, including community health workers. They would learn to avoid professional jargon and to demystify technology and other aspects of care, seeking to empower people to understand more and take more responsibility and control over their lives. The voices of previously marginalised people would be heard and respected. They would become central actors in their own health and development (Reynolds 2009).

The most serious reinterpretation of PHC came with the emergence of *selective* PHC (SPHC). In 1979 the prestigious *New England Journal of Medicine* published a paper by Julia A Walsh and Kenneth S Warren under the title 'Selective Primary Health Care: an interim strategy for disease control in developing countries' (Walsh and Warren 1979). The idea behind SPHC was that better health outcomes would be achieved more quickly in poor countries if groups of people who were at risk from major diseases were targeted with well chosen and cost-effective preventative measures and treatments. This shifted the focus from the overall social and economic development and empowerment of the community as a means of achieving health to technical interventions aimed at the prevention and cure of diseases.

The cartoon encapsulates the arguments that led to the advent of SPHC (Werner and Sanders 1997, with permission).

This narrow focus on disease was a fundamental departure from the values of the comprehensive PHC approach of Alma Ata, and to many it represented the demise of PHC. Where comprehensive PHC necessitated changes not only in the health sector but also in other social and economic sectors and in community structures and processes, SPHC involved the health sector on its own, leaving out other government sectors that are important for health. Furthermore, it ignored the emphasis on the overall social and economic development of the community and on social justice. More fundamentally, it ignored the all-important principle of involving the community in the planning, implementation and control of PHC. This depoliticised PHC, stripping it of its potential to transform people's lives and their place in the world (Reynolds 2009: 309-336).

But to others selective PHC was an attractive idea. Some public health experts felt that the broad, comprehensive PHC approach did not have clear targets. Selective PHC, on the other hand, made it possible to set clear, attainable short-term targets and to measure progress relatively easily. And because it removed the political dimension of health care it was attractive to governments closely allied to privileged minorities, elites with vested interests and corporate groupings (Reynolds 2009).

As an example of SPHC, UNICEF adopted the 'Child Survival Revolution' in 1983, with the goal of reducing by half the number of children in the Third World who die before their fifth birthday by the year 2000, at a cost that poor countries could afford. To meet this goal it prioritised four important health interventions under the acronym 'GOBI':

1. Growth monitoring – weighing growing children regularly to identify those at risk of malnutrition.
2. Oral rehydration therapy – to prevent children with diarrhoea from dying of dehydration by giving them a carefully prepared mixture of water, sugar and salt to drink.
3. Breastfeeding – because of its many beneficial effects on child health.
4. Immunisation – to prevent some of the major infectious diseases.

Responding to criticism that the programme was too narrow, UNICEF expanded it to 'GOBI-FFF' by including in the package the three Fs: Family planning, Food supplements and Female education.

Governments that had shown little support for comprehensive PHC welcomed GOBI enthusiastically. USAID and the World Bank pledged major financial support. By the mid-1980s, many poor countries were promoting some or all of the GOBI interventions. These interventions are excellent in themselves, and there have been many successes since the Alma Ata Declaration. Immunisation and oral rehydration have saved many children's lives and will continue to do so. Around the world, mothers and children are, on average, healthier than they were thirty years ago. But SPHC did not prove to be the interim programme it was supposed to be. In most poor countries it failed to transform into a broad comprehensive approach with universal coverage, intersectoral collaboration and community participation. As a result, the improvements in health it delivered were not sustainable.

This is not difficult to understand. Although immunisation prevents some of the major infectious diseases, it does not prevent other common diseases that flourish in poor socioeconomic conditions: gastroenteritis, pneumonia, tuberculosis, malaria, HIV/AIDS and malnutrition. Countless children whose lives were saved by oral rehydration became sick again and many died because they continued to live in conditions that made them sick, and because many were malnourished (Reynolds 2009). The health measures of the child survival initiative can only realise their full potential to save children's lives in a sustainable way if health is seen as a fundamental human right and the underlying social and economic conditions in which poor people live change.

HEALTH CARE UNDER THE ANC: A road to crisis

In the run-up to the first democratic election in April 1994, the ANC adopted the Reconstruction and Development Programme (RDP) as its election manifesto in return for the support of the Congress of South African Trade Unions (Cosatu) in the elections. Through the RDP, labour hoped to commit the state to 'beginning to meet the basic needs of people: jobs, land, housing, water, electricity, telecommunications, transport, a clean and healthy environment, nutrition, health care, and social welfare' (Visser 2004: 6).

In May 1994, five decades after the NHSC had tabled its report, the ANC published its national health plan for South Africa, drawn up with the technical support from the WHO and UNICEF (ANC 2004). The plan stated clearly that:

> A single comprehensive, equitable and integrated National Health System (NHS) will be created and legislated for. A single governmental structure will coordinate all aspects of both public and private health care delivery and all existing departments will be integrated. The provision of health care will be coordinated among local, district, provincial and national authorities. Authority over, responsibility for, and control over funds will be decentralised to the lowest level possible that is compatible with rational planning, administration, and the maintenance of good quality care. Rural health services will be made accessible with particular attention given to improving transport.
>
> Within the health system, the health services provide the principal and most direct support to the communities. The foundation of the National Health System will be Community Health Centres (CHCs) providing comprehensive services including promotive, preventive, rehabilitative and curative care. Casualty and maternity services will be available as 24-hour services. Community health services will be part of a coordinated District Health System, which will be responsible for the management of all community health services in that district.

However, the RDP soon ran into trouble. It had considerable success in social security and welfare as well as access to healthcare, but there were huge backlogs in housing and access to basic services. Then, in 1996, the ANC-led government effectively abandoned it and replaced it with GEAR – the neoliberal Growth, Employment and Redistribution macroeconomic policy.

GEAR was not the product of consultation with Cosatu and the ANC's own broader constituency but was developed by a technical team of fifteen policy makers made up of officials from the Development Bank of Southern Africa, the South African Reserve Bank, three state departments, academics and two representatives of the World Bank.

The ANC health plan did not last long either. Although it was never explicitly changed, the emphasis on private health care implicit in GEAR totally removed the vision of a national health plan from practical reality.

Nevertheless, it is important to acknowledge that there has been substantial progress since the dawn of democracy, notably in access to sanitation, water, and social grants and welfare. The proportion of households with access to sanitation increased from 50 per cent in 1994 to 73 per cent in 2007. In 2007, 60 per cent of all households had access to a flush or chemical toilet (an increase from 51 per cent in 1996). Households with access to the RDP standards of a minimum of 25 litres of potable water per person per day within 200 metres increased from 62 per cent in 1994 to 87 per cent in 2007. But the largest gains have been in the area of social grants. Between 1996/07 and 2007/08, beneficiaries of social grants increased from 2.4 million to 12.4 million. The new child support grant reached 8.2 million beneficiaries; recipients of the disability grant, which is payable to people with AIDS, doubled to 1.4 million, and old age pensioners rose from 1.6 million to 2.2 million (Coovadia *et al* 2009). Meanwhile, the government has provided the poorest households with free minimal access to water and electricity to meet their most basic needs, although many households are still unable to afford adequate access to either (Coovadia *et al* 2009: 817–834).

In the health sector, the aim has been to reduce inequities in health and health services through free primary care for pregnant women and children and a one-year community service programme for newly graduated health professionals. The racially segregated and fragmented homeland health care systems have been drawn into one national public health care system. Anti-tobacco legislation has been promulgated in spite of resistance from the tobacco industry. The Choice on Termination of Pregancy Act of 1996 has resulted in a reduction in abortion-related deaths of between 51 and 96 per cent. There has been a reorientation of services towards primary care, and more than 1 300 clinics have been built (Chopra *et al* 2009) .

Concurrently, the government has had to resist the vested interests of corporate companies in South Africa and worldwide that could cause harm to health, especially the tobacco and pharmaceutical industries. User fees were removed for maternal and child primary health care services, and abortion was legalised. Government policy to remove discrimination and promote wealth redistribution has led to improved pensions, a burgeoning number of social grants, and a social expenditure programme to build houses, and provide clean water, sanitation, and electricity (Chopra *et al* 2009; Harrison 2010).

Despite these gains, in 2010 the South African health system remains divided into public and private sectors, and the distribution of resources is inequitable. For example, using 2006 data from PERSAL, PCNS and Statistics South Africa, Wadee and Khan calculated that the number of people per doctor was 4 219 in the public sector and 601 in the private sector. The number of doctors per 100 000 dependents was 23.7 and 166.3 in the public and private sectors respectively (Wadee and Khan 2007).

Furthermore, both systems are in a crisis. As health economist Gavin Mooney points out, 'the public sector is grossly underfunded and overworked; the private sector is grossly inefficient and inequitable. This is a disastrous combination for health and for health care' (Mooney 2009).

The public health system is facing arguably its deepest crisis in history. It is fragmented, inequitably distributed across and within the new nine provinces, and even between sub-districts at local level. It remains hospital and doctor centred, and concentrated in the larger urban areas and cities. It is plagued by chronic staff shortages, low morale and a persistent brain drain. On the other hand, the private sector is plagued by spiralling costs of technology and medicines, a shrinking client base, now exacerbated by increasing unemployment arising from the global crisis of capitalism, and an ageing population.

This dysfunctional health system has to deal with one of the largest disease burdens in the world, including an estimated 4.9 to 6.6 million people living with HIV infection (making South Africa the country with the highest proportion of infected people in the world) (UNAIDS/WHO Working Group on Global HIV/AIDS and STI Surveillance 2008); rampant and uncontrolled tuberculosis with growing numbers of patients with multi- and extreme drug resistant strains; the emergence of new epidemics such as avian influenza and the H1N1 virus; the re-emergence of 'old' epidemics such as measles; persistent childhood malnutrition; and a creeping epidemic of non-communicable disease including high levels of homicide and violent trauma, predominantly affecting poorer communities. Nutritional deficiencies and maternal and child health problems continue to affect large numbers of poor people.

Alarmingly, life expectancy at birth is estimated to have declined from 57 in 1996 to 50.5 in 2004. In 2004, life expectancy still showed significant racial differences. For example, the lowest life expectancy was for African males (47.8) and the highest was for Indian females (66), followed by white females (65.6) (Day and Gray 2008). The disease profile (and therefore life expectancy) reflects the socio-economic situation in the country, where the more affluent live a healthier and longer life and the economically disadvantaged have a lower life expectancy (Day and Gray 2008; SAIRR 2008/9: 483).

South Africa is very unlikely to achieve the health-related Millennium Development Goals (MDGs). With respect to MDGs one and four (eradicate extreme poverty and hunger; reduce deaths in children under five years old) the country is showing 'reversal of progress'. Goal five (reduce maternal deaths) shows 'no progress', while goals two and six (achieve universal primary education; combat HIV, AIDS, malaria and other diseases) show 'insufficient progress' to meet the goals (Chopra *et al* 2009).

The massive burden of disease stems largely from neoliberal orthodoxy and the failure under GEAR, with its focus on growth rather than employment and redistribution, to deal effectively with the underlying social determinants of health, including growing inequality, deep poverty, inadequate housing, sanitation and domestic water in the home. South Africa has one of the largest burdens of disease in the world.

It is as true today as it was in the 1940s that realising the right of all South Africa's inhabitants to health cannot be achieved without dealing adequately with the underlying social and economic determinants of health.

THE NHI AND THE TEN POINT PLAN: Towards health for all?

Whether implementation of the ANC's proposed NHI and its accompanying Ten Point Plan will lead to the progressive realisation of the right to health, as envisaged by the PHC experiment of the 1940s, Alma Ata and indeed, the country's constitution, depends fundamentally on the nature of the society we want to build. More specifically it depends on the model of health care that the Ministerial Advisory Committee (MAC) agrees to promote and particularly on the human resource policy it adopts.

It is clear that attempting to extend the doctor-centered, hospital-based system focused on curative care such as that currently operating in the private sector to a wider section of people will be unaffordable. Yet unfortunately this seems to be the assumption that underpins current thinking as shown, for example, by the recent Econex study, commissioned by the Hospital Association of South Africa (HASA), a body representing the private hospital industry (Van der Berg *et al* 2010). The study finds that the healthcare sector is performing poorly by international standards and that there is growing dissatisfaction with the service. It points out that free care at the point of service delivery will increase demand for doctors' services, especially among those who currently cannot afford such care. Demand for private visits and hospital services will increase, while demand for public facilities will fall.

Then it examines 'the supply side' and concludes that about 10 000 extra general practitioners and 7 000 to 17 000 specialists will be needed to meet the increased demand. It shows that apart from the costs of employing such a large number of extra doctors, the country is simply not training enough doctors and nurses to meet the demand 'in the short- term'. It argues that South Africa's large disease burden means that utilisation of services will be higher under a NHI than most other countries. In addition, a properly designed system for South Africa should 'take cognisance of ... the high unemployment rate, the prevalence of poverty, the shortage of doctors and the relatively small tax base'. After considering a range of scenarios, the report concludes that the NHI is simply unaffordable (Van der Berg *et al* 2010).

Although it has been criticised by the unions, there is no reason to doubt the quality of the Econex report. Rather, its major problem is that it assumes a doctor-centered, hospital-based model, which, it has shown, is manifestly unaffordable. The argument that the NHI is 'unaffordable' favours those that benefit from the *status quo*. Though it has dominated the NHI debate, it is essentially a red herring. A country needs a health system that it can afford. According to Alma Ata, 'Primary health care is *essential health care* based on practical, scientifically sound and socially acceptable methods and technology *made universally accessible* to individuals and families in the community through their *full participation and at a cost that the community and country can afford* to maintain at every stage of their development in the spirit of selfreliance and self-determination'. Mooney points out that 'all countries can afford an NHI if they place enough weight on social cohesion and equity'. He estimates that an NHI will increase health care costs by about 15 to 20 per cent.

An alternative conception of how a South African health system should function, and the human resources it would need, has been provided by Sanders and Lloyd (2010) in a study for the National Health and Allied Worker's Union. In this, they are critical of the continuing focus on the medical model, and argue for a much wider concept of health worker than the one currently in favour. In essence, they go back to many of the ideas which were originally put forward in this country in the late 1940s.

Sanders and Lloyd argue that Community Health Workers (CHWs) can assist in service delivery at the community level. While there are thousands of Community Based Health Workers (CBHWs), there is no defined scope of practice, standardised training or model of working. Many are working on single issue or vertical programmes; there is no career progression; and despite carrying out essential health services, the CHWs (who are most often women and usually from the most disadvantaged communities), are often paid a stipend, or expected to volunteer.

The health system should focus on 'task shifting' and proper recognition of existing and new cadres of health workers; redefining their scope of practice and ensuring that there is no duplication of roles; revising the training curriculum of health professionals; increasing production of all categories of health workers (old and new); and initiating effective mechanisms to ensure retention of health professionals in the public sector.

Comparing Brazil and Sweden, Sanders and Lloyd feel that the success of the Brazilian model offers lessons for South Africa. The Brazilian government takes responsibility for health service delivery, including prevention and promotion, and uses teams of professionals, which include paid CHWs, as essential members of the health teams. Doctor-centered curative services such as that offered in Sweden would cost significantly more than the family health team model of Brazil.

In South Africa, where a relatively small number of people would be contributing to the NHI fund relative to the number of people using it, it is very unlikely that a doctor-centred curative model would be able to address the broader health needs of the majority of the population. Extreme maldistribution of doctors results in large sections of the population being unable to access their services. Moreover, even if an NHI scheme could enrol the services of doctors currently working in the private sector, it is highly unlikely that they would relocate to rural or peri-urban areas.

By contrast, lower level health workers, CHWs and mid level workers (MLWs) are much more likely to remain in rural and peri-urban areas and are capable of undertaking many of the functions of doctors in dealing with common illnesses and injuries. They require to be supported by nurses and must be able to refer complicated cases to higher levels of the health system. In the short-term, the skills gap must be primarily filled by CHWs and MLWs while simultaneously the training of nurses and doctors must be accelerated and their skills base adapted to low-resource settings.

CONCLUSION

Without knowing more about the thinking of the Ministerial Advisory Commission (MAC) on the NHI about the nature of South Africa's health service it is not possible to know whether the NHI will help bring about health for all. Although the members of the committee are there in their capacity as experts and not organisational representatives, it is inevitable that they will bring considerations related to their own backgrounds and prejudices, their occupations, lifestyles, preoccupations and other extraneous considerations to bear on the proceedings.

It is dangerous to speculate, but it is reasonably safe to say that given the diversity of their backgrounds, it is likely that the members of the MAC will not see eye to eye on some of the issues on which they must deliberate. Those who benefit from the current system will defend it, and it is highly likely that a range of vested interests will come to bear on the proceedings of the MAC. Apart from essential arguments about the distribution and mix of human resources, there will be disagreements about the right to health and universal access to equitable services versus health as a marketable commodity. What is clear, however, is that meeting the constitutional requirement of the progressive realisation of the right to health will require learning the lessons of South Africa's rich history of innovations in health care and a shift away from the current biomedical hospital- and doctor-centered system.

The underlying socio-economic inequality and underdevelopment that spawned community oriented PHC in the 1940s and made the PHC approach necessary in the 1970s still exist. A growing number of progressive health workers and activists in civil society believe that now, more than ever, a comprehensive and progressive PHC approach adapted to the South Africa of today is the key to health for all. It will require community participation and intersectoral action to tackle the social and economic determinants of health. Improving the health service on its own is not enough.

REFERENCES

African National Congress (2004) A National Health Plan for South Africa. http://www.anc.org.za/anc-docs/policy/health.htm.

Chopra M, JE Lawn, D Sanders, P Barron, SS Abdool Karim, D Bradshaw, R Jewkes, Q Abdool Karim, AJ Flisher, BM Mayosi, SM Tollman, GJ Churchyard and H Coovadia (2009) Achieving the health Millennium Development Goals for South Africa: challenges and priorities. *Lancet* 374 (9694): 1023–1031. doi:10.1016/S0140-6736(09)61122–3.

Coovadia H, R Jewkes, P Barron, D Sanders, D McIntyre (2009) The health and health system of South Africa: historical roots of current public health challenges. *The Lancet* 374 (9692): 817-834. doi:10.1016/S0140-6736(09)60951-X.

Cueto M (2004) The Origins of Primary Health Care and Selective Primary Health Care. http://www.ncbi.nlm.nih.gov/pmc/articles/PMC1448553/.

Day C and A Gray (2008) Health and related indicators. In Barron P and J Roma-Reardon (Eds) *South African Health Review*, 2008. Durban: Health Systems Trust.

Department of Health (2009) Establishment of the National Health Insurance Advisory Committee. *Government Gazette* 32564. Pretoria: Government Printer. 11 September.

Digby A (2008) Vision and vested interests: National Health Service reform in South Africa and Britain during the 1940s and beyond. *Social History of Medicine* 21(3): 485–502.

Djukanovic V and EP Mach (1975) Alternative approaches to meeting basic health needs in developing countries. A joint UNICEF/WHO study. http://openlibrary.org/b/OL4940962M/Alternative_approaches_to_meeting_basic_health_needs_in_developing_countries.

The Global Health Council (2006) Spirit of Alma Ata 1978 Caucus. Available from: http://www.global-health.org/docs/caucuses/summary_first_mtg_053006.doc [accessed 2 May 2010].

Jeeves A (1998) Public health and rural poverty in South Africa: Social medicine in the 1940s and 1950s. Unpublished paper, Wits Institute for Advanced Social Research, 1–11. Cited in: (Digby 2008: 489.)

Jeeves A (2005) Delivering primary care in impoverished urban and rural cmmunities: The Institute of Family and Community Health in the 1940s. In Dubow S and A Jeeves (Eds) *South Africa's 1940s: Worlds of Possibilities.* Cape Town: Double Storey: 87–107.

Kark SL and J Cassel (1952) The Pholela Health Centre; a progress report. *South African Medical Journal* 26 (6): 101-104 (cited in: van Rensburg H and D Harrison 1995).

Kleinert S and R Horton (2009) South Africa's health: departing for a better future? *Lancet* 374 (9692): 759-760.

The Lancet (2009) South Africa steps up [Webpage]. *Lancet*, 374 (9692 Page 757), 5 September. http://www.thelancet.com/journals/lancet/article/PIIS0140-6736 per cent2809 per cent2961572-5/fulltext

Marks S (1997) South Africa's early experiment in social medicine: Its pioneers and politics. *American Journal of Public Health* 87: 452–459.

Marks S (2001) Doctors and the state: George Gale and South Africa's experiment with Social Medicine. In Dubow S (Ed) *Science and Society in South Africa.* Manchester: Manchester University Press: 188–210.

Mooney G (2009) SA healthcare in desperate need of reform – health economist [Webpage]. *Health-e News Service,* 8 June. Available from: http://www.health-e.org.za/news/article.php?uid=20032330 [accessed 2 May 2010].

Newell KW (1975) *Health by the People.* 1st Edition. Geneva: World Health Organization.

Reynolds L (2009) The future of primary health care. In McClellan M (Ed) *Primary Health Care. Fresh Perspectives.* Pinelands, Cape Town: Pearson Education and Prentice Hall: 309-336.

Sanders D and B Lloyd (2010) National Health Insurance: Human Resources Requirements. 2010. Unpublished.

South African Institute of Race Relations (SAIRR) (2008/9) *South Africa Survey 2008/09.* Johannesburg: SAIRR.

Van der Berg S, R Burger, N Theron, C Venter, M Erasmus and J van Eeden (2010) Financial implications of a national health insurance plan for South Africa. Study commissioned by the Hospital Association of South Africa. [PDF]. Econex, March. http://www.econex.co.za/images/stories/Econex_NHI per cent20Final per cent20Report_March2010.zip.

Van Rensburg HC and D Harrison (1995) Chapter 4: History of health policy. In *South African Health Review, 1995.* Health Systems Trust, Cape Town.

Visser W (2004) Shifting RDP into GEAR. The ANC government's dilemma in providing an equitable system of social security for the 'new' South Africa. Proceedings of the 40th ITH Linzer Konferenz, 17 September 2004. Stellenbosch: University of Stellenbosch.

Wadee H and F Khan (2007) Human resources for health. In *South African Health Review 2007.* Cape Town: Health Systems Trust: 141–149.

Walsh J and K Warren (1979) Selective primary health care: an interim strategy for disease control in developing countries. *New England Journal of Medicine* 301 (18): 967–974.

Werner D and D Sanders (1997) *Questioning the Solution: The Politics of Primary Health Care and Child Survival.* [Online book]. Palo Alto CA 94301: Healthwrights. http://www.healthwrights.org/books/QTSonline.htm.

Yach D and S Tollman (1993) Public health initiatives in South Africa in the 1940s and 1950s: Lessons for a post-apartheid era. *American Journal of Public Health* 83 (7): 1043–1050.

CHAPTER 15

The Comprehensive Rural Development Programme (CRDP):
A beacon of growth for rural South Africa?

Samuel Kariuki

This chapter discusses two key interrelated themes underpinning South Africa's renewed attempt to develop and implement a Comprehensive Rural Development Programme (CRDP). First, a brief outline of the CRDP programme is presented, inclusive of its three sub-programmes agrarian reform, land reform and rural development, as well as a discussion of its institutional framework. Second, an evaluation of the CDRP is offered against the backdrop of international experiences with rural development (notably the changing paradigms of rural development from the 1950s to the present and the lessons thereof) and South Africa's own experiences with rural development. Finally the customary challenges facing South Africa's land question as one of the key pillars of the CRDP programme are examined. These three levels of discussion are used to question some of the underlying assumptions the CRDP makes about rural development.

The cardinal argument made here is that notwithstanding the institutional, legislative and fiscal limitations that will encumber the CRDP, one of the primary challenges is to rehabilitate failed land reform projects and to institute reforms that will generate viable sustainable livelihood outcomes to augment the broad developmental mandate of the programme. It is proposed that the CRDP potentially heralds a beacon of growth for rural South Africa despite the fragility of the socio-economic and institutional milieu in which it is embedded.

THE COMPREHENSIVE RURAL DEVELOPMENT PROGRAMME

The CRDP framework document sees rural development as a process '…enabling rural people to take control of their destiny, thereby dealing effectively with rural poverty through the optimal use and management of natural resources' (DRDLR 2009: 4).

The envisaged outcome of the process is the creation of 'vibrant, equitable and sustainable rural communities' (DRDLR 2009: 3). Four key outcomes are proposed: sustainable land reform, food security, rural development and job creation linked to skills training and development. A range of complex and often overlapping distinctions are made with regard to the distinction between a 'vibrant' and 'sustainable' community (DRDLR 2009: 10) in terms of expected outcomes envisaged in rural communities. Each of six such distinctions demarcates what constitutes 'vibrance' and 'sustainability' in the targeted communities. For instance, one of the key features of a vibrant community is 'a high work ethic and industrious character'. Achieving sustainability in this regard will entail promoting 'a savings and investment culture' (*ibid*).

The strategic objective of the CRDP is to 'facilitate integrated development and social cohesion through participatory approaches in partnership with all sectors of society' (*ibid*). To achieve the broad objectives of rural development, the CRDP uses a three pronged strategy: agrarian transformation, rural development and land reform. The framework document stipulates a range of ambitious and very specific programme activities that make up each of the three pillars of the CRDP. The first pillar, agrarian transformation, is conceptualised as the rapid, fundamental change in the relations of land, livestock, cropping and community. It will include the establishment of agro-industries, cooperatives, use of appropriate technologies, strengthening rural livelihoods and enhancement of food security. The second pillar, rural development, is defined as increasing the capabilities of rural people's capacities to control their destiny through optimal utilisation and management of natural resources. Key components of rural development will include capacity building initiatives, building strong organisational and institutional capabilities and investments in a range of social, economic, and institutional infrastructure.

The third pillar of the CRDP is enhancement of the land reform programme (land tenure, restitution and tenure reform) as enshrined in the South African constitution (section 25, subsection 4). Within the framework of the CRDP, the land reform agenda will focus on reviewing the restitution, redistribution and tenure reform programmes. In relation to restitution, the focus will be on expediting the processing of settled claims and the settlement of outstanding claims, whilst that on redistribution and tenure reform will be to develop less costly alternative models of land redistribution while reviewing legislation and policies that apply to both.

The design of the programme is predicated on lessons learnt from pilot sites across the nine provinces selected through socio-economic profiling, community participatory processes and intergovernmental cooperation. The first two initial pilot sites were in Riemvasmaak in the Northern Cape, and Muyexe Village in Giyani in the Limpopo province. Pilot sites have been initiated across all other provinces, and it is envisaged that by 2014 the department will have rolled pilots out to at least 160 wards, with at least 60 per cent of rural households per site meeting their own food requirements (DRDLR 2010: 3). These broad targets are a clear recognition of the development lethargy (for example in infrastructure development and job creation) that has marked rural South Africa in the last sixteen years despite notable growth within its urban localities.

This is despite the fact that a substantial number of people live in the rural areas. Some 45 per cent of South Africa's population lives in non-urban areas, depending on the definition used. Of these, some 85 per cent live in the former homelands and the rest on commercial farms and in small towns (May and Norton 1997). Rural areas carry a disproportionate burden of poverty. The imprint of apartheid spatial geography is still much evident as manifested in the levels of socio-economic disparities between rural and urban areas. Inequality of land ownership and attendant poverty patterns are stark reminders of this past. In terms of land inequality, in 1996, less than 1 per cent of the population owned and controlled over 80 per cent of farmland. This 1 per cent was part of the 10.9 per cent of the population classified as white, whilst 76.7 per cent of the population that is classified as African had access to less than 15 per cent of agricultural land, with less secure tenure rights. Added to this, an estimated 5.3 million black South Africans live with almost no security on commercial farms owned by white farmers (Wegerif 2004: 1). A recent report clearly noted the spatial dimensions that mark the rural/urban dichotomy in South Africa with regard to under development:

> While formal policies of spatial separation by race are long gone, a lingering legacy remains in the rural-urban marker of inequality and poverty (Leibbrandt *et al* 2010: 9).

The challenge of the CRDP broad outcome, 'sustainable, vibrant and equitable' rural communities is an acknowledgement of this historical legacy and its assessment will invariably take place against the backdrop of the historical burden of rural underdevelopment bequeathed to South Africa's democracy.

APPRAISING THE CRDP

Implementation mechanism – the institutional challenge

A workable rural development strategy must be based on multi-pronged, coordinated and effective government initiatives that are decisive enough to make a real difference in the capacity of disadvantaged rural people (Delius and Schirmer 2001: 26). The Department of Rural Development and Land Reform's (DRDLR) central role is to ensure it initiates, facilitates, coordinates and acts as a catalyst (DLDLR 2009: 12) in enabling rural development implementation. A key concern is whether a single line department has the capacity and legislative authority to enforce the type of coordination, integration and participation expected from an array of stakeholders both within and outside government. In the medium- to long-term, a rural development agency will be formed with responsibility for coordination, planning and resource mobilisation, monitoring and evaluation, and developing reporting systems and accountability measures (*op cit*: 31). Given the fact that agrarian transformation is one of the three pillars of the CRDP, the division of responsibilities between the DRDLR from the Department of Agriculture, Forestry and Fisheries raises doubts about the potential of the

CRDP to achieve an integrated development outcome. Since 1994, this has compromised the attainment of a seamless integrated land reform programme as the two departments have historically perceived themselves as autonomous from one another in fulfilling their mandates. This tension was aptly captured in an unofficial status report on land reform in 2004:

> Land affairs is a national competency based in a national department, whereas agriculture is a 'concurrent' competency, with policy direction coming from a national department, while provincial departments are partly funded by and answerable to provincial legislatures (Hall 2004: 4).

This separation has made coordination and integration of land reform in relation to post settlement support difficult to achieve. The expectation that line departments such as the Department of Agriculture will provide the required support as stipulated in the policy has not been forthcoming. The fact that the Department of Agriculture has been merged with Forestry and Fishing, further calls into question whether this was a strategic attempt to respond to the demands of a well established and vocal agricultural constituency (Agri-SA). The institutional silo approach to land reform and rural development may accentuate the separation of core departments (that is, land and agriculture). It may also aggravate the divide between commercial agriculture, which is seen as a preserve of established agricultural interests mediated by the Department of Agriculture, Forestry and Fisheries, and smallholder pro-poor farming options emerging from land reform that will be seen as a preserve of the new department, Rural Development and Land Reform. The CRDP (DRDLR 2009: 13) lists the Department of Agriculture, Forestry and Fisheries as one of the critical stakeholders. In essence, the Department of Rural Development and Land Reform is tasked to drive the broad development mandate of rural development.

Enforcement of coordination, integration and seamless delivery of the CRDP outcomes is contingent on the efficacy of legislative regimes that will underpin the rollout of the programmes as an inter-departmental process. In anticipation of possible coordination challenges, the CRDP framework states:

> In playing its coordinating role it is important that the Department of Rural Development and Land Reform recognise the principles of cooperative governance and the provisions of the Intergovernmental Relations Framework Act, 2005. Partnering protocols will also be initiated so that clear roles and responsibilities are defined. The protocols will also ensure joint accountability for the implementation of the CRDP priorities (DRDLR 2009: 13).

Beyond the coordination role, sustaining the local sphere of government as the coalface of CRDP delivery presents other new challenges. Against the backdrop of the inefficiencies and incapacity experienced by local government, this calls for a rethink on institutional and legislative precursors that must precede the rollout of CRDP. Some of these concerns are noted in the CRDP document:

In the implementation of the CRDP there will be overlaps with local government functions but section 151 of the Constitution (status of municipalities) provides in ss. (3) 'that a municipality has the right to govern, on its own initiative, the local government affairs of its community, subject to national and provincial legislation, as provided for in the Constitution.' Schedule 4 also provides for national government 'when it is necessary to maintain national security, economic unity or essential national standards, to establish minimum standards required for the rendering of services… (DRDLR 2009: 6)

A national department can only oblige another department at national, provincial or local authority level to do something if there is a legally enforceable agreement and funding to execute a task that falls within its area of competence. Instead of strengthening the capacity of the department to implement land reform (as its line function) and to ensure better linkages to agriculture, the department will be tasked to undertake a coordinating role to oversee the implementation of rural development across three spheres of government (Pienaar 2009). The CRDP document states that the DRDLR will improve and develop economic infrastructure. These functions fall under other provincial, national and local authorities which must attend to these issues in accordance with their own legally determined priorities. The proposed drafting of the rural development legislation will, it is hoped, respond to these anomalies.

Given the wide ranging cross sectoral initiatives outlined in the CRDP, the programme will require a coordinated strategy to meet the diverse needs of the communities and consequently the participation of various departments across the different spheres of government, non-governmental organisations, research institutions and communities is vital. Central to the three-pronged CRDP is a job creation model in which community members will be employed for a minimum of two years using the expanded public works programme principles. The refinement of the CRDP will continue through the pilot sites nationally. The pilot phase is expected to run for a minimum of two years until the proposed rural development agency is able to assume management of the initial projects and other initiatives that arise from the CRDP.

The CRDP framework document further notes that the minister of rural development and land reform will be the national political champion of the CRDP, but at the provincial level, the premier is the CRDP champion. The premier will appoint an MEC with a rural development function to be the driver of the CRDP in the province. The premier is required to assist the DRDLR in getting the commitment of all stakeholders to ensure an integrated implementation of the CRDP. In addition, a council of stakeholders will be formed. This will be made up of community-based organisations and forums, school government bodies, government (national, provincial and local), community policing and ward committees. The council of stakeholders will primarily be expected to enforce compliance with agreed codes of conducts in pursuit of CRDP objectives, to identify community needs and to play an oversight and monitoring role. The CRDP technical committee will implement the decisions taken by the council of elders. These committees will be made up of provincial sector departments which will primarily play a project management role.

The CRDP framework document will lead to the formulation of a green paper on agrarian transformation, rural development and land reform. Related draft legislation was scheduled for submission to the Cabinet by January 2010 and thereafter it will follow the white paper process, for approval by Parliament in 2011 (DRDLR 2009: 31). However, the deadline was not met and was subsequently extended to the end of May 2010. The CRDP is an ambitious project, given its broad developmental mandate to revitalise the rural economy. An assessment of its ability to succeed can be contextualised within the international and South Africa experiences of rural development programmes. Such a review will reveal some common trends and lessons that underpin programmes of rural development.

The CRDP and international experiences with rural development paradigms

Rural development has proved to be a contested and multi-dimensional concept. In essence:

> The definition of rural development has evolved through time as a result of changes in the perceived mechanisms and/or goals of development. A reasonable definition of rural development would be: development that benefits rural populations; where development is understood as the *sustained* improvement of the population's standards of living or welfare (Stamoulis and Anriquez 2007: 2).

The literature on rural development has seen changes in paradigms from the 1960s, when the focus was on modernisation, through to the 1970s when it shifted to state intervention, to market liberalisation in the 1980s, and to participation and empowerment in the 1990s (Ellis and Biggs 2001: 437). The CRDP development paradigm is a combination of a variety of features that have marked all these models across the entire period. As argued by Shepherd (1998: 10), these broad shifts are notable in both the 'theory and practice of rural development'. Earlier attempts at rural development were expressed through the community development approach that was in place in the 1950s and which focused more on interacting with communities within geographical boundaries. As a concept, community development adopted a multidisciplinary approach to development aimed at improving the welfare and productivity of the rural populace. The community development approach gained prominence in more than sixty countries in Asia, Africa and Latin America in the 1950s before its decline in the 1960s, and failed to achieve its goals largely through its inability to bolster the growth of vibrant grassroots democratic institutions and to nurture the participation of targeted communities. The approach also failed to prioritise agricultural development and to improve food security and alleviate poverty among its intended beneficiaries (Ruttan 1984).

In the 1960s, the modernisation of agriculture was viewed as a central engine of rural development. The expected outcome was greater integration of a commercialised, mechanised agricultural sector within the national and international economy (Shepherd 1998). In the 1970s, the efficacy of small farm growth as a constituent element of the integrated development approach gained prominence. The period from the late 1970s to the 1990s witnessed a shift from a top down approach to rural development characterised by external technologies and national level policies to a bottom up, grassroots approach which conceived rural development as a participatory process that empowers rural dwellers to take control of their priorities for change (Ellis and Biggs 2001: 443). A key aspect of the CRDP is its embrace of the participation and empowerment of communities. Government is viewed as an 'enabler' to help rural communities meet their development aspirations as articulated through a community-led participatory process.

The 1990s have increasingly witnessed the adoption of a rural territorial approach to development whose emphasis is on what rural areas can achieve for themselves. Support and assistance is geared towards enabling local economic growth (Quan 2008). In this model, rural development is analysed as a multi-level, multi-actor and multi-faceted process that seeks to incorporate the farm and non-farm sector and respond to development needs of specific territorial areas.

The overall approach of the CRDP is essentially to mainstream rural development as a strategy for poverty reduction. Elements of previous epochs of rural development are discernable within the CRDP process: a focus on community participatory processes, a focus on land and agricultural reform and infrastructural investment, and involvement of a range of stakeholders in programme implementation. This focus reflects a historical approach to understanding the relational dimension to South Africa's crisis of rural underdevelopment. Despite implementing various development efforts in rural areas, the outcome hitherto has not changed forms of structural inequality that have hindered economic prosperity but has rather reinforced existing modes of domination and economic marginalisation. This form of marginalisation has found its expression in the concept of the second economy (Kate 2009: 1) which best describes rural areas. As aptly put by Cousins (2004: 6):

> The vast bulk of rural dwellers, as well as of the urban unemployed, are not so much excluded as included on highly adverse terms in the functioning of the economy.

Mainstreaming rural development as a poverty reduction strategy is a key phase that has underpinned the practice of rural development since 2000 (Ellis and Biggs 2001: 444). Prior to this, in the 1990s, the sustainable livelihoods framework was predominant. It is from this that the CRDP draws its multisectoral, community participatory approach to rural development. Rural development policy today expects that local communities are in a position to identify solutions to challenges arising in their area and to participate in activities that address them. However, the participation of citizens in local level decision-making through active involvement in formal structures, or through organised pressure groups, as part of civil society, is something that is difficult to achieve and to sustain. The achievement of genuine participation is difficult because local elites monopolise power and are often hostile to widespread participation (Roodt 2001: 479). Nonetheless, emphasis on the participation of rural people and the creation of enabling conditions for them to undertake self help initiatives affirms the 'people centeredness' of the CRDP and its bottom-up approach in driving local development initiatives. The ability of the CRDP to respond to development needs as identified through community participatory processes will be contingent on the resource and institutional endowment in which the programme is embedded.

Owing to the limitations noted in models of rural development, recent approaches that place emphasis on effective models of governance have increasingly gained prominence (McAreavey 2009: 138). This is due to the recognition that the cross-sectoral and multioccupational diversity of rural livelihoods should become the cornerstone of rural development policy if efforts to reduce rural poverty are to be effective (Ellis and Biggs 2001: 445). A focus on the requisite institutional and governance models has emerged as a key area of concern for CRDP, given the complex array of development activities and stakeholders it stipulates.

The CRDP and the national context: Rural development experience in post-1994 South Africa

After 1994, rural development became an important issue in policy discourse. The new government implemented three successive strategies that overlapped. A key feature that marked all the strategies (the Reconstruction and Development Programme of 1994, the Rural Development Strategy of 1997, the Rural Development Framework of 1997 and the Integrated Sustainable Rural Development Programme of 2001) was an almost exclusive focus on former homeland areas (Atkinson 2007: 69).

The Reconstruction and Development Programme (RDP) explicitly recognised the inextricable link between apartheid and landlessness, its attendant poverty patterns in the rural areas, the emergence of a dual agricultural regime, and the insecurity of land tenure experienced by rural black citizens. Based on this prognosis, the RDP clearly advocated the need for land as the 'most basic need for rural dwellers' (ANC 1994: para 2.4.1). The urgency with which the RDP approached the land question was evident in the timeframes it scheduled for the implementation of the programme, namely the transfer of 30 per cent of agricultural land within five years (ANC 1994: 2.4.14). However, sixteen years into the implementation of the land reform programme, none of the broad delivery objectives has been achieved, as exemplified in the fact that only close to 6.7 per cent of such land had been transferred by 2009. Beyond the attainment of the targets, the RDP had also envisaged a significant economic renewal of rural areas as an outcome of a successful land reform project. It acknowledged that a comprehensive rural development programme must raise incomes and productivity, increase agricultural production and ensure security of tenure for all South Africans. The provision of rural infrastructure, support services, training, water provisioning, and health care were deemed crucial markers to define rural development. As did the CRDP, the RDP focused on the need to invest both in the on-farm and off-farm economy in the rural areas.

Within two years of the 1994 RDP white paper, however, the government's macroeconomic policies were revised, the RDP office was closed and its task-teams disbanded. The responsibility for the implementation of the RDP was now devolved to various national and provincial departments (Harrison 2001), with the Department of Land Affairs being delegated the responsibility for rural development. In place of the RDP, policy development towards rural development was guided by the 1995 rural development strategy (RSA 1995) which proposed mechanisms by which rural people and their elected representatives on rural district councils and local councils could begin to identify local development priorities (RSA 1995).

The rural development strategy (RDS) outlined the new government's vision for rural areas over the next twenty-five years. Like the broader principles of the RDP on land and agrarian reform, it adopted a broad and functionalist view towards land reform and rural development. The strategy called for better tenure security, restitution and farmer support measures. In addition to land reform, the RDS called for wide ranging programmes of land reform and infrastructure investment to be made in the rural areas, the strategy explicitly acknowledging the primacy of supporting smallholder agriculture as part of a poverty allevi- ation measure. In this regard, the strategy argued against maintaining the then current bias in land reform which sought to sustain a large scale farming sector that had traditionally been seen as pivotal to the attainment of national food production.

The implementation of the programme was to happen at the local government level (RDS 1995). However, the strategy did not enunciate a systematic plan of action for integrated rural development with clearly defined objectives, timelines, budgets or monitoring/evaluation pro- cedures. In short, it ended up as another broad statement of intent. The aim of government was to publish a white paper on rural development based on public comment on the RDS. However, this never occurred. Instead of the white paper, another process ensued, namely the drafting of the Rural Development Framework (RDF) in 1997. The RDF's primary focus was on rural infrastructure, public administration and local government, although it also stressed the need for the coordination of rural development in the country. However, the framework was not confirmed as the government's strategy for rural development. The responsibility for updating and finalising the RDF was with the Department of Land Affairs (DLA). However, like the RDS, the RDF failed to develop detailed implementation plans and procedures and by the DLA's own admission it was not a strategy document on rural development. The DLA's mandate did not extend to acting as the government's inter-departmental coordinating author- ity in the production of the RDF (Greenberg 1999). Current institutional concerns with regard to CRDP hinge on whether the newly created department of rural development and land reform will marshal the required authority, resources and capacity once the necessary legislation (that is, rural development legislation) is enacted to allow for effective execution of its tasks.

Following the effective demise of the RDF, land reform proceeded in the absence of a wider rural development framework until the Integrated Sustainable Rural Development Programme (ISRDP) was launched in 2001 (Hall 2004: 9). This was aimed at poverty allevi- ation in both rural and urban areas through robust mobilisation of the resources of all three spheres of government in a coordinated manner. Its objective was to 'attain socially cohesive and stable rural communities with viable institutions...' (DPLG 1999: vi). Through the ISRDP, rural development was to be realised at a district level through coordination of state and other agency functions – rather than through dedicated funds – to improve infrastructure and service delivery. Thirteen 'nodal' districts were identified. Its effect was the creation of a number of priority projects through which funds and support were to be channelled (Hall 2004: 9). The ISRDS (DPLG 1999: 23) viewed rural development as a multidimensional and sectoral process encompassing improved provision of socio-economic infrastructure.

This approach was, however, subjected to considerable criticism for attempting to fast- track development, which makes the strategy vulnerable to failure for being too reliant on the Integrated Development Programme (IDP), and for not setting out clear priorities and sequences which would make change possible. In addition, the programme was criticised for not offering rural regeneration by accepting the established contours of policy and for not challenging the deep inequalities characteristic both of wider South African society and of rural communities (Hemson et al 2004). As a result:

This led to a prognosis that what is required is 'integrating' rural areas into the economy, 'comprehensive regional development', and 'strengthening rural-urban linkages' ie. on inclusion into the larger economic structures – without adequate recognition of the need to address structural inequalities of wealth and power, the redistribution of assets and economic opportunities, and the radical restructuring of various economic sectors, including agriculture (Cousins 2004: 13).

In many ways, the CRDP broad development approach does not delve into questions of inequities of power relations nor does it probe the broader economic strategy it relies upon to complement its programmatic areas. The broad national economic system, largely responsible for the duplication of unbalanced development outcomes between the rural and urban areas, remains largely unaddressed, since the key thrust of CRDP is one of integrating rural areas into the broader national economy. This is also reminiscent of the modernist approach that informed rural development in the 1960s where modernisation and commercialisation of rural agricultural systems was viewed as the bedrock of reforms required to integrate rural economies into regional, national and international economies.

CRDP and the challenge of land and agrarian reform

After 1994, the newly democratic state formulated land and agrarian policies that would fundamentally alter the skewed relations of production, property rights and their attendant uneven patterns of poverty. However, these policies were also meant to create enabling political and economic conditions that would spur prosperity, alleviate deepening poverty, enhance confidence in land markets, create equitable outcomes in land ownership, deal with historic injustices and create sustainable outcomes in the use of land-based natural resources. The policy broad agenda to enforce a progressive social and economic transformation in rural South Africa created a constitutionally sanctioned three-pronged programme of land reform: restitution, tenure reform and redistribution.

The formulation of policies and laws on land reform found expression in the publication of the white paper on land reform policy in April 1997 which addressed questions of redress, equity, security of tenure, nation building and national reconciliation and sustainable land use patterns (DLA 1997: 18). It noted:

> We envisage a land reform which results in a rural landscape consisting of small, medium and large farms; one which promotes both equity and efficiency through a combined agrarian and industrial strategy in which land reform is a spark to the engine of growth.

From a policy perspective, the provisions of the 1997 white paper were ambitious and from the outset created an overburdened expectation that land reform was able to accord redress on the one hand, whilst conterminously dealing with the crisis of underdevelopment and economic growth on the other. Despite the acknowledgement of the links between land and agrarian reform, rural development and poverty alleviation, the implementation of the policy has come to be measured in terms of transfer of land, often expressed by reference to the target of 30 per cent of agricultural land in black ownership by 2014. However, a key feature of the land reform question over the last sixteen years has been the dissonance between policy objectives, institutional framework, fiscal and human resources, and the support infrastructure put into place. This disjuncture is evident in the rate of land delivery achieved since the inception of the programme, and the limited impact these programmes have had. In sum, the limitations of the land reform programme are two-pronged, that is, they are quantitative (inability to meet targets), and qualitative (inability to create sustainable livelihood impact, and multiple effects on local and national economy). These limits call into question the extent to which issues around historic injustice, reconciliation and nation building as objectives of these programmes can be realised.

Appreciation that land reform was failing to meet its objectives of historical redress and economic growth led to the adoption of a view that policy should embrace a renewed focus on land reform and rural development. As a result, the national policy conference of the ANC, held in June 2007, proposed a resolution on economic transformation to be considered for adoption at the 52nd National Conference later in the year:

> Land reform has not been located within a broader strategy of rural development or a commitment to supporting smallholder farming on a scale that is able to improve rural livelihoods. As a result, changes in land ownership have not realised their full potential to transform social relations, combat rural poverty and promote rural development (ANC 2007: 25).

The programmes of rural development, land reform and agrarian change were to be integrated into a clear strategy that would seek to empower the poor, particularly those who already derive all or part of their livelihoods from the exploitation of productive land.

It is against this background that it can be appreciated that the success of CRDP depends to a large extent on improving the pace and quality outcomes of the land and agrarian reform programme, namely redistribution, restitution and tenure reform. This is against the backdrop of poor performance of land reform delivery averaging 6.7 per cent (5.5 million hectares) in 2009 against expected targets of 30 per cent of agricultural land in 2014. Of this, 3 million hectares of land has been transferred through the redistribution and tenure reform programmes combined and 2.5 million hectares have been transferred to claimants through the restitution programme. The DRDLR plans to transfer the remaining 19.1 million hectares (23.3 per cent shortfall of the 30 per cent target of agricultural land), by 2014 (PLAAS 2009: 1). However, recent media reports have pointed to the department's need to adopt a more pragmatic approach that does not necessarily target 2014, but focuses on sustainable development outcomes on the redistributed farms. Attempts by the department to allocate budget towards the rehabilitation of failed land reform farms clearly affirms a new pragmatism.

The overall budget for the Department of Land Affairs has declined between 2008/09 and 2009/10 by 8 per cent, driven by a precipitous decline in the capital budget allocated for the land restitution programme (PLAAS 2009). In the 2010 budget, the new Ministry for Rural

Development and Land Reform was allocated only an extra R860 million over three years. Given the comprehensive nature of the CRDP, the budgetary outlay signals a conservative and cautious approach to rural development despite the political prominence this has received since 2009. Indeed, recent pronouncements by the Ministry appear to indicate that the government is considering extending the deadline of 30 per cent to 2025 given the budgetary shortfalls. However, the shift in policy has not formally been made with regard to the change in deadline (*Mail & Guardian Online* 18 November 2009).

Indeed, as noted in the CRDP document, only 25 per cent or R500 million of the land reform budget during the 2009/10 financial year had been set aside for rural development, enabling the DRDLR to deliver only 2 369 863 hectares as opposed to a scheduled 8 100 000 hectares by 2011. Additional resources were therefore urgently needed to finance the CRDP in its entirety (DRDLR 2009: 26). Clearly, the wide ranging programmes defined in the CRDP will require a massive increase in budgeted funds, although given shortfalls in government recorded in 2009/10 it seems unlikely that this will eventuate.

The land reform programme, through the rights-based approach, has thus far focused predominantly on the transfer of land or natural capital at the expense of deficient financial, human, social and physical resources which are all interdependent and necessary to generate sustainable livelihoods (Hall 2007). This is despite the fact that the broad developmental thrust envisaged in the RDP and the 1997 White Paper demands a significant paradigm shift in the policy models pursued thus far. The CRDP reaffirms the need to accelerate the rate of delivery while simultaneously improving on the sustainable outcomes of land reform projects. For it to succeed in its land reform and agrarian objectives, a significant shift in policy instruments, resource endowments, and institutional systems is needed. Retaining land and agrarian reform – as two of the three critical pillars of the CRDP – is based on the assumption that these teething problems will be dealt with. For instance, the need to rehabilitate failed land reform projects and adopt a developmental approach to the outstanding restitution cases (estimated at 4 500) is acknowledged in the CRDP. Other key initiatives are reviews of existing models of land reform such as the willing buyer willing seller approach, and the DRDLR's securing of major increase in budget for settlement of land restitution and acquisition of land through the existing market-based approach to land reform.

Progressive bias in land reform beneficiary selection model

With regard to land reform beneficiaries targeting, Hall avers:

> Experience with land reform elsewhere in Africa has shown that efforts to redistribute rural land to 'the disadvantaged' or to the 'rural landless' have tended to reinforce existing forms, and given rise to new dimensions of inequality within beneficiary communities. The gap between vision and reality is a regular and patterned trend in rural development and land reform programmes. It appears to be a systemic problem (1998: 451).

The CRDP proposes a new hierarchy of beneficiaries beyond the traditional bifurcated 'subsistence' and 'commercial' strata the Land Reform for Agricultural Redistribution (LRAD) had widely propounded. The central thesis of the LRAD vision was the production of a stratum of black commercial farmers, although in policy, provision was made for support to subsistence production. Programme outcomes from LRAD indicated a bias towards support for projects geared towards commercial farming. This marked a shift from the pro-poor/welfare based approach pursued from 1994 to 1999. A focus on the progressive farmer/black commercial farmers has preoccupied the discourse around land redistribution despite the failure of the state to accord substantial support to augment their growth. This trend is reminiscent of previous attempts towards rural development. One of the traditional criticisms levelled at programmes of rural development centred on the idea of 'elite capture' is that the rural poor seldom gain from the dividends of rural development. In his trenchant critique three decades ago of Kenya's rural development and land reform programme, Christopher Leo made the following remarks:

> One of the most widely accepted assumptions in the literature on rural development during the past two decades has been the belief that 'favoring the progressive farmer' is prudent policy. The safest way of investing rural development funds, it has been argued repeatedly, is to allocate them to those who have already succeeded in farming or business, or who have had relevant training or education … The policy of 'favouring the progressive farmer', therefore means, in effect, that the government should intervene in the economy to offer extra advantages to an already privileged minority. It is not an idea which is easy to harmonise with any of the widely-accepted political ideologies (Leo 1978: 619).

In Kenya, the bias towards progressive farmers was expressed through the 1954 Swynnerton plan that aimed to create individual freehold rights as an inducement to produce successful black commercial farming. Although the Swynnerton plan was initiated to counter the rural insurgency of Mau Mau (the guerrilla challenge to colonial rule that emerged in 1950) by creating a bulwark of landed gentry, the economic success it envisaged was never achieved. Swynnerton aimed at transforming customary land rights to individual freehold through the process of adjudication, consolidation and registration. However, the programme proved to be a failure insofar as protecting the rights of women was concerned because the statutory registration of title did not replace customary law. Rather, customary and statutory strategies were used in tandem to secure rights to land and control the disposal of land at inheritance. The recreation of components of customary law led patrilineal groups to exclude women's claims to land lest this lead them to lose land to others (William and Francis 1993; Gertzel 1970). This explains why women accounted for less than 5 per cent of the total registered landholders. Those who gained were heads of households, who in many communities were adult males (Kibwana 1990). The development impetus that individual freehold rights was envisioned to hold never materialised. The logic behind these schemes exemplifies a long held tradition in studies of rural development where a 'safe and sound' investment is regarded as that which concentrates on building a class of 'progressive farmers' to the exclusion of the 'poor and less able' farmers. Through the programme of individualisation:

... the government appeared implicitly to have abandoned the idea of community control in favour of a 'slow individualisation' benefitting those who were considered 'progressive farmers' – notably chiefs and other loyalists and civil servants (Kanyinga 2000: 42).

Consequently, the reform initiative led to an increase in land disputes rather than resolving them and it decreased people's security in land (*op cit*: 44). Leo's claims of 'elite capture' and marginalisation of the rural poor have relevance for South Africa three decades later. The CRDP proposes six categories of beneficiaries under the aegis of land reform: landless households; commercial-ready subsistence producers; expanding commercial smallholders; well established black commercial farmers; financially capable aspirant black commercial farmers; and established businesspeople. This hierarchy seeks to suggest that subsistence production is the permanent preserve of the non-market realm whilst acknowledging the growth potential of capable, resourced and skilled individuals to succeed in commercial farming.

Significantly, these rigid categorisations obfuscate a precarious category of South Africa's rural population that should significantly inform beneficiary targeting: farm workers, labour tenants, farm dwellers and residents of former homelands who bear the brunt of rural poverty, tenure insecurity, lack of infrastructure, poor service delivery and ineffective governance systems. Creating such rigid categorisation steeped in favour of commercialisation clearly ignores some of the most basic and pressing land rights needs that require urgent attention. At an operational level, the criteria for selecting participants are not stated in the CRDP framework document. As Kenya's experience with land reform suggests, targeting of beneficiaries along preconceived notions ('qualifying criteria'), and with no actual strategies to ensure their inclusion, inadvertently leads to their exclusion. A key prerequisite for CRDP success in achieving its targets is to clearly state how the various strata of its beneficiaries will be targetted through specified accountability mechanisms.

Land tenure in freehold farming areas and the CRDP

A key limitation of the renewed focus on rural development and land reform is the marginal status accorded to land tenure. The CRDP acknowledges the need to advance the socio-economic rights of the farm dweller community, and the need to formalise communal tenure. However, there is limited analysis of tenure reform within the CRDP. The CRDP acknowledges the need to enforce the rights of farm workers and labour tenants, inclusive of the provision of decent jobs and socio-economic services to them (DRDLR 2009: 18–19), but no comprehensive programme of how this will be achieved is articulated. Approximately, 2.8 million people live on commercial farmland, many without secured tenure.

One of the achievements of the government was the Extension of Security of Tenure Act, 62 of 1997 (ESTA), which aims to prohibit the illegal eviction of farm workers. The Act applies in all rural areas (anywhere outside a proclaimed township) and creates a procedure to be followed when applying for an order to evict people. In practice, many people continue to be illegally evicted by owners who resort to extra-judicial means such as threats and intimidation (Hall 2003 *et al*: 18–19; Atkinson 2007: 84). Overall, the law is seen to be strong in terms of procedural rights – defining the procedures one needs to follow to enforce a legal eviction – but exceptionally weak in defining the substantive rights of the farm workers and labour tenants.

The Nkuzi Development Association undertook an eviction survey to establish baseline data for the prevalence of eviction over a twenty year period, from 1984 to 2004. This survey found, *inter alia*, that between 1994 and 2004 about 1 million people were evicted and only 1 per cent received some form of legal representation (Wegerif *et al* 2005). This crisis was captured in the White Paper on Land Reform (1997: 33):

> ... the systemic violation of their rights is exacerbated by the lack of access to legal resources, awareness of their rights, and the unequal power relations that pervade rural South Africa.

Given the above, part of the CRDP mandate is to advance a clear strategy on how the proposed reforms of legislation will complement the objectives of rural development. Reform of ESTA and LTA are currently underway by the DRDLR. The precarious status of farm dweller communities clearly manifests the difficulties CRDP will have in attaining its broad vision of securing tenure and economic development in freehold farming areas.

The Communal Land Act (CLARA) and the CRDP

Tenure reform in the former homelands has been the least successful aspect of the land reform programme. Key issues of concern in these areas relate to the *de facto* land rights residents hold under the jurisdiction of tribal authorities. Ineffective management of these rights, coupled with the legacy of underinvestment, congestion and high incidence of chronic poverty, provide a compelling case for urgent reforms.

During 1994-99, an effort was made to develop a communal tenure bill to secure land rights in the former homelands. However, immediately following the second general elections in June 1999, the proposed Land Rights Bill was shelved. The ostensible reasons for this change in direction were to place greater reliance for land administration on the traditional authorities and thus reduce the burden on the state (Ibsen and Turner 2000). Part of the controversy centered on the Bill's silence on the role traditional authorities should have in land management systems in the former homelands. In place of the Land Rights Bill, the Communal Land Rights Act (CLARA 2004) was formulated and signed into law by the then president, Thabo Mbeki, on 14 July 2004. The objective of the Act was to legalise security of tenure in the former homelands, home to some 21 million South Africans. The provisions of the Act give effect to the constitutional pronouncements (section 26, subsection 6) which oblige the state to legislate reforms that will secure land tenure security.

The core of CLARA deals with the transfer of land title from the state to traditional communities, the registration of individual land rights within 'communal owned' areas and the use of traditional council or modified tribal authority structures to administer the land and represent the 'community' as owner (Cousins 2008: 39). In ensuring alignment to the broader outcome of rural development, the CRDP acknowledges the role of CLARA as follows:

> In order to stimulate economic growth in traditional communities ... the Department ... has an obligation to ensure that its measures ultimately result in the broader socio-

economic development of the communal areas ... people will be able to use the newly acquired title to land as surety in order to participate effectively in the markets for the factors of production ... (DRDLR 2009: 19).

This corroborates current debates on formalisation of communal tenure as the basis for economic growth, modernisation and productivity in much of rural Africa. This approach is essentially an 'economic reductionist' view (Kanyinga 2000) that identifies freehold tenure security as a precursor to agricultural growth. From a purely economic perspective, the upgrade of land tenure rights is seen as an impetus to greater economic efficiencies, growth and prosperity within the agricultural sector. A more recent argument advocated in this front, in support of tenure formalisation, is best captured by the view of Hernando De Soto, whose focus is formal recognition of 'extra-legal' property (informal property) to allow the use of formal assets as collateral for a loan (De Soto 2000). However, formalising communal tenure into freehold tenure systems does not always guarantee economic dividends. From an international perspective, Kenya's formal individual titling systems failed to completely replace informal systems, with informal systems often cropping up as a response to individual titling and the confusion surrounding status. Formal titling never fully replaced those systems which carried social legitimacy and indeed greater utility (Adams *et al* 1999: 11; Kariuki 2004).

Beyond the model of rights conversion proposed (freehold tenure conversion), civil society organisations argued forcefully for the democratisation of land administration, often referring to the key white paper principle that rights holders should be free to choose which local institution should be responsible for land administration (Cousins 2008: 14). Apart from concerns levelled at the capacity of government to implement the provisions of the Act, and the wide discretionary powers the Act vests on the minister of rural development and land reform, the main criticism related to the power traditional authorities have in managing formal rights in communal areas at the expense of democratically elected structures. In addition, the success of CLARA is contingent on the success of the Traditional Leadership and Governance Framework (TLGF) Act. The essence of the latter is to provide for the formal recognition of traditional communities and to provide for the establishment and recognition of traditional councils that will conduct the affairs of its subjects in accordance with customary law and practice and in compliance with the values and principles enshrined in the constitution (Kariuki 2004). As a result of these controversies, a court challenge to the Act was instituted.

The challenge was launched by public interest law firm, the Legal Resources Centre (LRC) and Webber Wentzel on behalf of four communities: Kalfontein, Makuleke, Makgobiestad and Dixie in Limpopo, Mpumalanga and North West provinces. On 6 November 2009, the North Gauteng High Court judge, Aubrey Ledwaba, declared fourteen sections of the act unconstitutional in that they gave unelected traditional leaders and the minister of land reform and rural development powers to impose decisions that undermined existing property and tenure rights instead of protecting them as required by the constitution (*Business Day* 2 November 2009). In his ruling, Judge Aubrey strongly objected to section 21.2 of the Communal Land Rights Act, which accords traditional authorities the opportunity to take over management functions of land administrative committees in their respective jurisdiction:

...in terms of section 21.1 the community has no choice when the traditional council is in existence' (High Court of South Africa, North Gauteng High Court, Case No. 11678/2006. Section 34).

Furthermore:

On careful analysis of section 21(2) of CLARA the act conferred powers on the traditional council to do the functions of the land administration committee and that may undermine the tenure security of the other community... In my view some of the existing traditional council have not been democratically elected and the interest of women, children, elderly and youth may not be represented in such council. For that reason provisions of section 9 of the Constitution are infringed *(ibid)*.

The ruling has now been referred to the Constitutional Court for confirmation. This is a huge setback to the CRDP process. The proposed CLARA would, if comprehensively implemented, have the potential to affect 892 communities currently occupying roughly 13 per cent of the former homeland. The reform of communal tenure has been a primary pillar of the land reform programme but it has also been the least successful given that no implementation has taken place.

CONCLUSION

Census data reveal that 46 percent of South Africa's population of 40.6 million people lived in rural areas in 1996 – the areas where 70 percent of the country's poor live. Despite the dramatic political and social reforms that have taken place, rural areas seem to have benefitted less than urban areas from the policy changes introduced after 1994 (Van den Brink *et al* 2007: 165). Will the CRDP vision accentuate the rural/urban divide which South Africa's development trajectory has created? As noted, CRDP hinges on three interrelated regimes of reform: land reform, agrarian reform and rural development. A review of some of the customary problems facing land reform indicates the potential limitation this aspect of reform will have on the overall outcome of the programme. Of particular significance is the land tenure reform in the freehold areas and the former homelands which has been the least successful thus far.

Through the CRDP, the department aims to link the implementation of land reform to the broad objectives of rural development. The CRDP is therefore different from past government strategies because it is based on proactive, participatory, community based planning as opposed to state-led approaches to rural development. The CRDP is aimed at being an effective response to poverty and food insecurity by maximising the use and management of natural resources to create vibrant, equitable and sustainable rural communities (DRDLR 2009: 2-3).

Beyond the obvious challenges of institutional and fiscal limitations that may compromise the viability of comprehensive rural development, its key conceptual assumptions remain unexplored in this framework. The CRDP should be preceded by a broader understanding of what ails South Africa's development trajectory, and what economic and governance reforms are needed to define a new development path that does not duplicate the spatial imprints of the structural inequality that bedevils rural South Africa. As a result, CRDP emerges as a set of localised development initiatives responding to development needs based on community participatory processes. These demands range from infrastructure and service delivery issues aimed at bridging the backlog that underpins underdevelopment in rural South Africa.

Perhaps of greater significance is the need to refine our understanding of what constitutes 'rural' in South Africa, and what criterion to use in crafting an operational definition of 'rural' as argued by Wiggins *et al* (2001: 427):

> … what constitutes rural, peri-urban and urban has often been a subject of debate in the development discourse. There is no exact definition of the term 'rural', either conceptually or empirically.

These are over-arching frames of reference from which the CRDP is currently de-linked and which herald great potential in redefining CRDP as a beacon of growth for rural South Africa.

REFERENCES

Adams M, T Sibanda and G Thomas (1999) The Institutional Arrangements for Land Reform: The South African Case, Presented at the Stakeholder Workshop on the National Land Policy, 14-15 June, Harare, Zimbabwe.

ANC (1994) *The Reconstruction and Development Programme: A Policy Framework*. Johannesburg: Umanyano.

African National Congress (ANC) (2007) 52nd National Conference 2007 – Resolutions.

Atkinson D (2007) *Going for Broke: The Fate of Farm Workers in Arid South Africa*. Cape Town: HSRC Press.

Cousins B (2004) Not rural development, but agrarian reform: Beyond the neo-liberal Agenda. Cape Town: Programme for Land and Agrarian Studies (PLAAS), University of the Western Cape (Paper first presented at a national conference on land tenure, Department of Land Affairs, Durban, November/December 2001).

Cousins B (2008) Contextualising the controversies, dilemmas of communal tenure reform in post-apartheid South Africa. In Claassens A and B Cousins (Eds) *Land, Power & Custom: Controversies Generated by South Africa's Communal Land Rights Act*. Cape Town: UCT Press: 3–32.

De Soto H (2000) *The Mystery of Capital: Why Capitalism Triumphs in the West and Fails Everywhere Else*. New York: Basic Books.

Delius P and S Schirmer (2001) Towards a workable rural development strategy. Trade and Industrial Policy Secretariat (TIPS) Working Paper 3. University of the Witwatersrand.

Department of Land Affairs (DLA) (1997) *White Paper on South African Land Reform Policy*. Pretoria: Government Printer.

Department of Land Affairs (2004) *Communal Land Rights Act 11*. Pretoria: Department of Land Affairs.

Department of Rural Development and Land Reform (DRDLR) (2010) Speech by the Minister of Rural Development and Land Reform, Mr G Nkwinti (MP). National Assembly, Parliament, Cape Town.

DPLG (Department of Provincial and Local Government) (1999) Integrated Sustainable Rural Development Strategy.

DRDLR (2009) Comprehensive Rural Development Programme (CRDP), Framework Document. Pretoria: DRDLR.

Ellis F and S Biggs (2001) Evolving themes in rural development 1950s-2000s. Development Policy Review 19 (4): 437–448.

Gertzel C (1970) *The Politics of Independent Kenya 1963-1968*. London: Heinemann Educational Books.

Greenberg S (1999) Building a people driven rural development strategy: Lessons from the Rural Development Initiative. Paper presented to the Land and Agrarian Conference, 26-28 July 1999.

Hall R (1998) Design for equity: Linking policy with objectives in South Africa's land reform. *Review of African Political Economy* 77: 451–462.

Hall R (2004) A political economy of land reform in South Africa. *Review of African Political Economy* 31: 213–227.

Hall R (2007) Transforming rural South Africa? Taking stock of land reform. In Ntsebeza L and R Hall (Eds) *The Land Question in South Africa*. Cape Town: Human Sciences Research Council: 87–106.

Hall, R (2009) Another countryside? Policy options for land and agrarian reform in Southern Africa. Programme for Land and Agrarian Studies (PLAAS), University of the Western Cape.

Hall R, P Jacobs and E Lahiff (2003) Evaluating land and agrarian reform in South Africa. Final Report. Programme for Land and Agrarian Studies (PLAAS), University of the Western Cape.

Harrison P (2001) The genealogy of South Africa's Integrated Development Plan. *Third World Planning Review* 23: 1–18.

Hemson D, M Meyer and K Maphunye (2004) Rural development: the provision of basic infrastructure services. HSRC, Integrated Rural and Regional Development, Position Paper, January 2004, Pretoria, South Africa.

Ibsen H and S Turner (2000) Land and agrarian reform in South Africa: A Status Report. University of Western Cape, Programme of Land and Agrarian Reform.

Kanyinga K (2000) *Re-distribution from Above: The Politics of Land Rights and Squatting in Coastal Kenya*. Uppsala: Nordiska Afrikainstitutet.

Kariuki S (2004) Failing to learn from failed programmes? South Africa's Communal Land Rights Act 2003. *Stichproben, Vienna Journal of African Studies* 7 (4): 49–66.

Kate, P (2009) Second economy strategy: Addressing inequality and economic marginalisation. A strategic framework. Trade and Industrial Policy Strategies, Pretoria.

Kibwana K (1990) Land tenure. In Ochieng W (Ed) *Themes in Kenyan History*. Nairobi: Heinemann Kenya.

Leibbrandt Woolard I, A Finn and J Argent (2010) Trends in South African income distribution and poverty since the fall of apartheid. OECD Social, Employment and Migration Working Papers No. 101.

Leo C (1978) The failure of the 'Progressive Farmer' in Kenya's million-acre settlement scheme. *The Journal of Modern African Studies* 16 (4): 639–656.

May J and A Norton (1997) A difficult life: The experience and perceptions of poverty in South Africa. *Social Indicators Research*, 41(1-3): 95–118.

McAreavey R (2009) *Rural Development Theory and Practice*. New York: Routledge.

Pienaar K (2009) Draft 1: Comments and reference documents on the concept/visions of a Comprehensive Rural Development Programme (CRDP). Legal Resource Centre, Cape Town.

Programme for Land and Agrarian Studies (PLAAS) 2009 'Umhlaba Wethu 7' A Quarterly bulletin tracking land reform in South Africa.

Quan J (2008) Land reform and rural territories, Experiences from Brazil and South Africa. International Institute for Environment and Development (IIED).

Roodt M (2001) Land restitution in South Africa: An overview. In JK Coetzee, J Graaff, F Hendricks and G Wood (Eds) *Development, Theory, Policy and Practice*. Cape Town: Oxford University Press: 305–329.

Ruttan VW (1984) Integrated rural development programmes: A historical perspective. *World Development* 12(4): 393–401.

RSA (Republic of South Africa) (1995) Rural Development Strategy of the Government of National Unity. Government. Gazette # 16679 of 3.1.95 Notice 1153 of 1995.

Shepherd A (1998) *Sustainable Rural Development*. Basingstoke: Macmillan.

South Africa (1996) Constitution of the Republic of South Africa. Pretoria: Government Printer.

Stamoulis K and G Anriquez (2007) Rural development and poverty reduction: Is agriculture still the key? ESA Working Paper No. 07-02. Agricultural Development Economics Division. The Food and Agriculture Organization of the United Nations.

Van den Brink R, G Sonwabo and H Binswanger (2007) Agricultural Land Redistribution in South Africa: towards accelerated implementation. In Ntsebeza L and R Hall (Eds) *The Land Question in South Africa*. Cape Town: HSRC Press: 152–201.

Wegerif M (2004) A critical appraisal of South Africa's market-based land reform policy: The case of the Land Redistribution for Agricultural Development (LRAD) Programme in Limpopo. Research Report 19. Programme for Land and Agrarian Studies (PLAAS), University of the Western Cape.

Wegerif M, B Russel and I Grundling (2005) Still searching for security: The reality of farm dweller eviction in South Africa. Nkuzi Development Association, South Africa.

Wiggins S and S Proctor (2001) How special are rural areas? The economic implications of location for rural development. *Development Policy Review* 19 (4): 427–436.

William G and E Francis (1993) The land question. *Canadian Journal of African Studies* 27 (1): 380–403.

CHAPTER 16

Breaking down barriers:
Policy gaps and new options in South African land reform

Doreen Atkinson

In March 2010, the new minister of rural development and land affairs, Mr Gugile Nkwinti, declared: 'Food security and economic growth are being undermined by the collapse of more than 90 per cent of the farms that the government [has] bought for restitution or redistribution to victims of apartheid' (*Times Live* 2 March 2010).

This is a serious indication that all is not well with land reform. This chapter will argue that black farmers have been set up for failure by a government bureaucracy which is out of its depth when it comes to implementing a vast programme of social engineering. There are significant blind spots in land reform policy which can no longer be ignored. These are attributable to theoretical assumptions which have become so sacrosanct that they now block consideration of alternative solutions. The intention here is not to allocate blame, for in fact the tortuous process of land reform over the last fifteen years was a necessary precursor to reassessing the naive assumptions which informed the policy at its inception. The stage is now set for a new debate on agricultural and developmental realities, stripped of the ideological straitjackets which have thus far constrained policy makers. This chapter will argue that, counter to much current thinking on land reform, the commercial agricultural sector needs to be regarded as a partner in land reform design – at policy design level as well as the implementation of projects. South Africa's commercial farming sector is a major asset in terms of knowledge, networks, markets and capital investment. A resource-poor, developmental state will be short-sighted if such resources are not harnessed for the purposes of social change.

It is commendable that the land reform process has been so exhaustively monitored and evaluated (Hall 2007: 88, 90). But there remains a major blind spot – the institutional mechanisms by which government bureaucracy functions. This chapter will reflect on the institutional weaknesses of the land reform machinery in South Africa.

The gist of the argument is as follows: South Africa inherited a 'master narrative' which encapsulated a set of values regarding the political and symbolic importance of land (Walker 2008). This narrative emphasises the loss of access to land by the black population, before and during the apartheid years, and the need to restore racial balance regarding land ownership. The need for land reform is therefore based on racial and equity arguments.

This normative dimension to the land question has created an additional set of dynamics. It has effectively prevented a coherent partnership between the state and the most significant agricultural stakeholder, the commercial farmers. This is because the narrative is preoccupied with the putatively reactionary values of commercial farmers, and has construed them as being intrinsically opposed to land reform. For most land reform analysts, white commercial farmers are *the problem*, and therefore cannot be instrumental in a solution.

This discussion will draw on political science literature to show that collaboration between states and peak economic organisations – so-called 'corporatism' – is now an accepted element of modern governance architecture. It will propose that a much greater degree of collaboration between government departments, parastatals and 'peak organisations' representing commercial agriculture and agri-business will be necessary for significant land reform to succeed.

LAND REFORM IN SOUTH AFRICA: From small beginnings to large-scale implementation

South Africa's post-apartheid land reform programme can be divided into four phases. The first phase was explicitly experimental: a land reform pilot programme was initiated in 1995 to enable the Department of Land Affairs (DLA) to test and refine land reform policies. By April 1997, 372 projects had been approved (SAIRR 1998: 327). This came to an end in 1998; presumably government felt that sufficient lessons had been learned, and that the time was ripe to move to more extensive land reform implementation.

With hindsight, it would seem that a longer window period was required to assess the effectiveness of land redistribution projects. However, the political and symbolic importance of land reform meant that the process had to be hurried. Evaluations of the pilot programme raised the key issue of 'aftercare' – the practical assistance which should be provided to new farmers to negotiate the rocky road to sustainable farming. Project evaluations repeatedly showed that the land transfer process had to be accompanied by meaningful farmer support. However, the main concern of the DLA remained land transfer. Productive land use was regarded as the responsibility of the national Department of Agriculture (NDA) and its provincial counterparts, and thus the pilot phase only addressed the DLA's administrative procedures of land transfer, and not the much longer process of agricultural support.

The second phase was the extensive rollout of land reform, master-minded by the then minister of land affairs, Derek Hanekom, between 1998 and 2000. This phase had a strong pro-poor focus. In terms of the Settlement/Land Acquisition Grant (SLAG), government distributed small grants (around R15 000 per person) as widely as possible, to enable poor people to purchase land.

Unfortunately, this policy coincided with a post-democratisation property boom, and land became increasingly unaffordable, especially with such small subsidies. Land prices had been artificially depressed under apartheid and after 1995 they increased to levels which began to bear some semblance to land prices in more developed countries. Four factors contributed to property price increases: first, black South Africans could now invest in land; second, the state was purchasing land for land reform; third, South Africans and foreigners began to invest in farms, often as lifestyle purchases; and fourth, there was a shift away from food production towards game farming, eco-tourism and hunting, which are land-extensive activities.

At the same time, the government removed virtually all agricultural marketing supports, including agricultural price stabilisation, tariff protection and agricultural subsidies. This was at a time when South Africa's international competitors were still committed to protecting their own agriculture. The budget for the agricultural sector in the 2001/2002 financial year was approximately R2 billion, a 50 per cent reduction compared with the 1988 allocation (Tregurtha 2005: 2). Consequently, 'emergent' black farmers were caught in a squeeze between rising land prices and declining farm-gate prices, and faced increasingly stiff competition with foreign imports. Many black farmer representatives have pointed longingly at the agricultural supports that were in place when white commercial agriculture was consolidated in the early twentieth century. New black farmers, by contrast, are expected to succeed with very little government support and, unsurprisingly, many new black farmers have turned to commercial farming organisations for technical and marketing support, thereby creating a new economic solidarity across racial lines. This has been particularly evident in the wine, fruit, sugar, grain, wool and red meat sectors (Hall 2009c: 129), thereby indirectly promoting the deracialisation of the rural economy.

A consequence of the SLAG programme was that groups of poor people had to pool their subsidies ('rent-a-crowd'), in order to afford land. Beneficiaries now also had to manage agricultural enterprises collectively, which caused many projects to fail (Hall 2009a: 26). Collective farming is very problematical, because of the complex management and social cohesion problems which result from any group-based economic enterprise.

The third phase of land reform was launched under Thoko Didiza, who took office in 2000. This featured a more commercial approach. Under the Land Reform for Agricultural Development (LRAD) programme, beneficiaries could now access up to R100 000 per adult household member, according to a sliding scale of capital contributions made by the beneficiary. This enabled a greater degree of family farming, which entails a more effective decision-making unit. The intention of the policy was to transfer 30 per cent of agricultural land to black farmers by 2014 – a target total of 24.6 million hectares (SAIRR 2007: 386). Over time, DLA budgets have steadily increased, from around R650 million in 1996/1997 (SAIRR 1998: 326), to about R3,4 billion in 2005/2006 (Hall 2007: 102). Land reform budgets have now stabilised at about R4 billion per annum. At times, DLA was unable to spend its full budget, and in 2005/2006, the

Department had to return R1 billion of its R3.9 billion budget to Treasury. A vacancy figure of 1 020 posts (compared to 850 filled posts) contributed to the problem.

By March 2008, DLA had transferred 4.7 million hectares (Parliament 2009). The rate of transfers was increasing every year: during 2008/2009, the combined land reform programmes had yielded transfers amounting to 443 600 hectares, in a total of 501 projects (DLA 2009: 34). Thus far, DLA's progress has been measured primarily in terms of 'hectares transferred', a yardstick which has given rise to concerns that other key deliverables are being neglected.

In 2004, the NDA introduced the Comprehensive Agricultural Support Programme (CASP), to assist land reform beneficiaries with agricultural production. Allocations to CASP rose from R200 million in 2004/2005 to R415 million in 2007/2008. This was projected to increase to R758 million in 2010/2011. By 2008, CASP had assisted 3 270 projects and 218 000 beneficiaries. In 2006, the MAFISA Agricultural Loan Scheme was introduced to assist emergent farmers with farming credit (NDA 2008). However, the optimal use of these allocations was constrained by administrative difficulties.

After 2006, several more innovations to address critical government shortcomings were introduced under a new minister, Lulu Xingwana. A major assessment of land reform was conducted by the Sustainable Development Consortium in 2007 and made valuable recommendations to the DLA and NDA. The resultant Settlement and Implementation Support (SIS) strategy reflected critically on the poor ability of government departments to implement land reform and provide support for beneficiaries. This was due to a host of reasons, including poor interdepartmental coordination, unenthusiastic municipal involvement in land reform, deficient integration of land reform with other social services, and weak agricultural extension services (SDC 2007).

After this landmark report, three significant trends emerged: a recognition of the importance of post-transfer land use; a new focus on spatial dynamics; and a new appreciation of rural development. These are dealt with in more detail below. But a fourth factor was hinted at in the extensive text of the SDC report: the tacit acknowledgement of the state's incapacity to implement any of its strategies on its own, and the need to find suitable partners. However, where since 1994 this need has been acknowledged, it has focused on institutions such as parastatals, universities and NGOs. Seldom, if ever, has the central role of the commercial agricultural sector been identified as key to making land reform work.

TREND 1: From equity to production – transcending the 'hectare fetish'

The SDC report reflected the growing importance of *utilitarian* considerations – the ability to use the land productively – instead of an exclusive focus on racial equity in land ownership. This corroborates international evidence that agricultural skills are critical when selecting beneficiaries (Kinsey and Binswanger 1996: 122). In 2007, this policy shift coincided with the ASGI-SA (Accelerated and Shared Growth Initiative for South Africa) programme under President Mbeki. ASGI-SA exhibited a greater appreciation that land reform was an investment that had to yield agricultural results and represented a significant shift away from the quantitative obsession with hectare transfer.

The SDC Report (2007: 22) was the first to critique 'the primary emphasis on meeting quantitative targets as the measure of success for land reform – settling all claims by March 2008 and transferring 30 per cent of agricultural land by 2014 ... Prioritising the attainment of quantitative targets is having the unintended consequence of undermining the quality of programme delivery'.

The dominant paradigm of hectare transfer took a while to recede. DLA's 2008 Annual Report still referred to the 1,5 million hectare target for that financial year (DLA 2008: 33). Despite the growing awareness of the inappropriateness of the 30 per cent target, there has been constant criticism of the slow pace of land reform and the inadequate budgets provided for it. DLA budgets remain miniscule in comparison with the estimated R72 billion to achieve a transfer of 30 per cent of agricultural land by 2014 (Nkwinti 2010).

Increasingly, however, DLA is focusing its concerns on the creation of jobs, livelihoods, and improving agricultural productivity. The director general of land affairs, Tozi Gwanya, stated in 2007 that the land reform target set for 2014 is too steep. 'Let's reflect as a nation on land reform driven by targets versus quality ... We have only delivered four million hectares, which against a target of 25 million hectares is admittedly very slow. But if we are to give another 25 per cent of our agricultural land to the previously disadvantaged, we must ensure that they can participate in the commercial agricultural economy...' (*Farmers Weekly* 23 November 2007).

The shift in focus from hectare transfer to agricultural production culminated in the contentious 'use it or lose it' approach of minister Xingwana. In a few controversial cases, she insisted that certain land reform beneficiaries be evicted from their land on the grounds that they were not productive. Such heavy-handed tactics elicited criticism, because beneficiaries had received inadequate post-transfer support from government. Agricultural unions and land activists denounced this as a pre-election ploy aimed at diverting attention from the Department's bungles (*Business Day* 27 May 2009).

The key question is *how* sufficient support will be provided to land reform beneficiaries. Will the provincial departments of agriculture have sufficient staff and skills to assist beneficiaries with the complex task of becoming productive?

TREND 2: Towards spatial dynamics in land reform

The second sea change in land reform policy was a greater emphasis on spatial issues. From 2007 onwards, a new system of 'proactive land acquisition' (PLAS) was instituted, which enabled government to purchase land and rent it to a selected beneficiary, until the beneficiary is able to take transfer. This policy means that government can acquire well situated and appropriately priced land when it becomes available on the market.

The significance of spatially based land reform can hardly be overstated. It enables government to proactively identify the land needs of a wide variety of constituencies such as farm dwellers, labour tenants, landless livestock owners, users of overstocked commonage land, residents of informal settlements, evictees from farms, and people encroaching on public or private land (Hall 2009b: 70). It will enable suitable land, particularly around towns, to be identified. Such land can be then divided into suitably sized land parcels, ranging from small-holdings to small farms. This will encourage existing land owners to sell, whether at market prices or expropriation price levels. It will also enable government authorities, including municipalities, to provide integrated services to support the agricultural, economic, social and infrastructural needs of the land reform beneficiaries.

But once again there is an underlying conundrum: will the state have sufficient capacity to integrate these complex economic, marketing, and infrastructural issues?

TREND 3: From land reform to rural development and 'agrarian transformation'

Land reform has become increasingly associated with broader rural and agrarian development. In 2007, the Land and Agrarian Reform Programme (LARP) was launched as a partnership between DLA, NDA and provincial departments of agriculture. For the first time, land reform was conceived of as part of a bigger programme of rural and agrarian development. Its goals were to: a) redistribute 5 million hectares of white-owned agricultural land to 10 000 new agricultural producers; b) increase the participation of black entrepreneurs in agri-business; c) provide universal access to agricultural support services to target groups; d) increase agri-cultural production by the target groups; and e) increase agricultural trade by the target groups. Target groups were defined as 'farm dwellers; new producers in rural, peri-urban and urban areas; new primary producers; farm dwellers; communal farmers; new and existing black agri-business entrepreneurs in rural, peri-urban and urban areas' (DLA 2008).

The culmination of this sea change in land reform thinking came with Nkwinti's appointment of the new Department of Rural Development and Land Reform (DRDLR) and constituted a welcome inclusion of non-land issues into the land reform context. The discourse has now shifted to 'agrarian transformation', defined as including, but not limited to, increased agri-cultural production, local economic development, local infrastructure and sustainable use of natural resources (DRDLR 2009). In addition, the DRDLR emphasises improved social infra-structure such as savings clubs, cooperatives, sanitation facilities, clinics, sports and recreation, rural libraries, schools, community halls, museums, non-farm livelihoods, adult education, leadership training, municipalities, and social cohesion – all of which are supplementary rural factors needed to add value to agriculture.

This theoretical shift has however not engaged with the question of *who* will assist munic-ipalities, government departments and land reform beneficiaries to explore their various pro-ductive options, and how to integrate these into local and regional markets.

THE MISSING LINK: The question of state capacity

The three trends all neglect the growing evidence of the sheer incapacity of the state to under-take land transfers and simultaneously provide adequate support for subsistence or newly commercial farmers. Thus far, the DLA and the NDA have relied largely on their own in-house capacity to promote land reform. Given the scale of the task, the lack of experience with large-scale social engineering, the rapid 'transformation' of these departments in terms of mandates and staff, and the rapid changes affecting the international economy, this is formidable.

There has been growing concern about the viability of many land reform schemes. This includes the widespread problem of inadequate aftercare or post-transfer support for beneficiaries. In 2005, one study showed that 44 per cent of land reform projects in North West Province were not producing, or were in major decline (Kirsten *et al* 2005). The most frequent reasons were: no long-term supply contracts; no commercial farming experience; no mentorship; no support from suppliers; no marketing training; communal management; no working capital; no implements; no support from the agriculture department; collapsed farm infrastructure; and conflict among members. 'Bad advice from the agriculture department' was cited in 36 per cent of the cases.

One of the reasons for poor after-care is the dwindling skills, knowledge and experience of the agricultural extension service. While land reform has been picking up speed, the Department of Agriculture has conducted its own transformation and affirmative action process. Many experienced white extension officers have left the service, and have been replaced by young and inexperienced black staff with very limited agricultural training or business acumen (Duvel 2004). In areas where skilled white extension officers have remained, and skilled new black staff have been employed, such as the south-west Free State, the pace and sophistication of land reform has been impressive.

Private sector critics of government have repeatedly pointed out the weak management systems of the DLA and the NDA. But there are structural issues too, for land reform requires coordination between two government departments, one of which (Rural Development and Land Reform) is a 'national competency' and one (Agriculture) which is a shared national-provincial competency. It also requires collaboration with district and local municipalities, in terms of drafting integrated development plans (IDPs), local economic development strategies, and spatial development frameworks. Steering such a complex institutional machinery is demanding. A key unresolved question is the relationship between agricultural extension officers (employed by provincial departments of agriculture) and local municipalities. Poor linkages between municipalities and extension officers have greatly exacerbated planning difficulties (Duvel 2004).

The capacity problems of government surface in many ways. A growing problem is that the two land reform programmes, land redistribution and land restitution, are increasingly at odds with one another. Particularly in Limpopo, Mpumalanga and KwaZulu-Natal, land restitution claims have blocked viable land redistribution opportunities. Once a restitution claim has been lodged or gazetted, the land cannot be sold or transferred to emergent black farmers. The gazetting of land claims also acts as a disincentive to maintenance or investment in infrastructure, with the result that farming deteriorates, and banks do not accept gazetted land as collateral (CDE 2008: 16).

In many cases, government regulations are poorly designed, and have the unintended effect of undermining beneficiaries' economic interests. For example, land reform beneficiaries are not allowed to sell their land because this would reflect poorly on departmental statistics on 'hectares transferred' and these restrictions prevent the black beneficiaries from benefitting from capital growth with the result that failed farming operations lead to land left idle. This is unfortunate for both beneficiaries who have 'outgrown' the land they received, and need to sell it to raise capital for larger land purchases and those beneficiaries who are not successful and who need to exit farming altogether. Such strictures fly in the face of international lessons. 'Constraints on sale, leasing and other forms of land reallocation should not be imposed since they create idle land and other inefficiencies' (Kinsey and Binswanger 1996: 131).

Agri SA has repeatedly criticised the DLA's poorly drafted regulations, weak management capacity, inadequate communication channels, and critical skill shortages (see for example *Farmers Weekly* 18 February 2008). In numerous cases, the media have reported on delays in land redistribution and restitution projects. Delays have been estimated at an average of forty-six months (*Farmers Weekly* 23 January 2009).

There have been many reports of deserving black farmers who were not assisted by DLA or NDA officials because their projects were not defined as a cooperative or they were not land reform subsidy recipients (*Farmers Weekly* 24 April 2009). In some cases, DLA's preferential relationship with certain consultants (*Landbouweekblad* 5 October 2007) appeared to hamper land reform, because these consultants were not adequately skilled, or their performance was less than conscientious. The demise of the flagship company, SA Farm Management (SAFM) in 2008 also raised concerns about the awarding of contracts to specific consultants who benefitted from political links with provincial politicians without going through an open tender process (*Farmers Weekly* 12 December 2008).

For its part, the DLA has become increasingly candid about its own capacity limitations, including a lack of financial controls (*Farmers Weekly* 24 October 2008); a 'lack of legal skills to draft agreements or the skills to understand valuations' (*Farmers Weekly* 27 June 2008); poorly trained extension officers; a shortage of 5 500 extension officers (*Landbouweeekblad* 16 May 2008); administrative red tape; a chronic lack of staff (*Farmers Weekly* 11 April 2007); frequent departmental restructuring; high staff turnover; and poor alignment between DLA and the NDA (*Farmers Weekly* 6 July 2007).

GROWING CONTROVERSIES AROUND LAND REFORM

The slow pace of land reform has caused considerable political controversy. Critics on the left have ascribed it to the recalcitrance of white farmers to sell their land at reasonable prices. The principle of 'willing-buyer-willing-seller' (WBWS) has become increasingly controversial, and the DLA has now proposed a land tax to reduce the price of land and bring more white land onto the market. In response, the commercial agricultural sector has blamed the bureaucratic ineptitude of the DLA. Agri SA, representing the commercial farming sector, frequently argues that there is more land available on the open market, at reasonable prices, than government can buy or manage.

All this reflects an unresolved ideological stalemate, which originates in two factors. Firstly, there was a time lag of several years after 1995, while the commercial agricultural lobby made a fundamental ideological shift from being indifferent or negative about land reform, to becoming an enthusiastic advocate. Secondly, there is the tendency of leftist critics to regard the business sector as intrinsically reactionary and opposed to land reform. This stalemate plays itself out at various levels.

Some commercial farmers believe that DLA officials are implicitly hostile towards them. Reports abound of the shoddy treatment received by commercial farmers at the hands of government officials. Repeated offers of land to DLA have been met with indifference (*Farmers Weekly* 31 August 2007). A major consequence of stalled projects has been the deterioration of infrastructure, business operations and the environment, particularly in eco-tourism enterprises (*Farmers Weekly* 7 November 2008; 19 September 2008). This has led to the loss of jobs, for example, 12 500 farm workers in Magoebaskloof, 915 in Trichardsdal, and 1 150 in Letsitele Valley (*Farmers Weekly* 26 September 2008). The arrogance and heavy handedness of officials have also drawn criticism (*Farmers Weekly* 8 September 2006). According to Agri SA, 'Land Affairs employs young, inexperienced people in senior positions who don't have a clue as to the urgency and importance of their work. There is nepotism and corruption and employees find it more important to enrich themselves than to empower the country' (*Farmers Weekly* 23 January 2009). Reports also abound of sellers being subjected to intimidation.

On the left, there are typically four assumptions about commercial agriculture. Firstly, there is the view that commercial agriculture operates as a 'powerful lobby' influencing government (see for example Andrews, Zamchiya and Hall 2009: 187). This view, often drawing on an implicit neo-Marxist explanatory framework, describes commercial agriculture as 'agrarian capital' which 'has deployed a range of strategies to protect and advance its interests … [and] to block meaningful land reform' (Jara and Hall 2009: 214). By contrast, Agri SA is constantly bemoaning its *lack* of effective access to policy-makers, and feels aggrieved that its practical knowledge base is undervalued by officials.

A second issue is the standpoint of commercial agriculture towards land reform. Agri SA's fervent expressions of support for land reform have seldom been recognised in academic discussions. Jara and Hall (2009: 215), for example, maintain that 'agrarian capital undertakes and initiates land reform projects that nurture a thin layer of emerging black commercial farmers and, while actively resisting policy or legislation that veers in a radical direction, readily shifts the blame to a failing state for delays'.

Such neo-Marxist *ideologie-kritik* is not helpful. Modern society is simply too complex to 'read off' the ideas or interests of a group of people from the place they occupy in society. Political ideas and values have a potency of their own, which often transcend narrow class interests and can include a concern for the welfare of others (Reich 1988). In many cases, normative ideas or interests emerge because of different types of institutional failure, and these failures require combined interventions by the state, the market and civil society (Frodin 2008).

The third issue is that of land prices. Critics of commercial agriculture remain convinced that land sellers inflate their prices. Even when farmers ask realistic market prices, those prices are seen as too high for a viable programme of land reform. Expropriation therefore becomes the obvious solution, a standpoint which alarms commercial agriculture. The concept which has elicited the most ideological heat is that of 'market-led' land reform, which refers to the

WBWS principle. The government has been constrained by the property clause in the constitution, to avoid resorting to more assertive, non-market methods such as expropriation. But
the threat of such methods is constantly uttered, by government as well as leftist critics, creating
an atmosphere of impending confrontation with commercial agriculture. The apex of confrontation took place at the National Land Summit in July 2005, where popular organisations
representing 'the landless' pushed through a decision that WBWS be rejected, and that the
state should have the right of first refusal on all land sales.

In contrast, Agri SA maintains that there is more than enough land on the market, and
that market prices invariably reflect future opportunities for capital growth. The real problem,
as seen by commercial agriculture, is DLA's insistence that government is only prepared to
purchase land, and does not acquire farms as going concerns. This means that farmers are
not reimbursed for infrastructural investments, goodwill or market share, often built up over
many years (*Farmers Weekly* 5 September 2008).

A fourth point of contention is smallholder farming. Some critics remain convinced that
commercial agriculture is committed to large-scale, capital-intensive production, which is said
to clash directly with small-scale, labour-intensive land reform (Kleinbooi 2009: 194, 201). In
fact, it is almost impossible to find any evidence for a preference for large-scale farming on the
part of commercial agriculture. In fact, Agri SA has publicly and repeatedly declared itself to be
in support of any viable and sustainable type of land reform, and many commercial farmers
want to subdivide their land too, due to new rural trends such as the rise of rural tourism.

There is currently an awkward stand-off between leftist (Bernstein 2007; Moyo 2007) and
pragmatic proponents of land reform (CDE 2008). This stalemate has far-reaching consequences for land reform. It devalues collaborative efforts between established (white) commercial agriculture and black farmers; it undermines the search for common understandings
and mutually acceptable solutions between intellectuals and experts affiliated to land reform
organisations and commercial agriculture; and it exaggerates ideological differences. Most
importantly, it has deprived the government of a set of conceptual tools to identify and justify
options for collaboration with the private sector. Yet without key partners in the private sector,
government is setting itself up for failure.

In this impasse, leftist critics have assumed that the slowness of land reform is due to ideological pressure placed on the state by commercial agricultural interests. This assumption
needs to be critically examined.

White farmers have their own powerful symbolisms that need to be overcome: 'The dominant
picture [of land reform] is one of destruction – homesteads being stripped, infrastructure being
demolished and sold as scrap, productive orchards being allowed to die and then used for firewood
and rangeland being degraded' (*Farmers Weekly* 14 September 2007). But this view is frequently
countered in the farming trade magazines by stories of successful black farmers.

Organised agriculture has repeatedly emphasised its support for land reform, which denotes a
marked shift in ideological position from its original standpoint in 1994. Zimbabwe's destructive
land reform process and economic implosion has focused the minds of the leaders of commercial
agriculture on the need for extensive land reform. This is not simply rhetoric. It is based on a
profound appreciation of the tinderbox quality of the land question, and the realisation that

pre-emptive and orderly land reform is urgently needed to avoid more radical approaches which will destroy the rural economy. In many cases, there is a growing acceptance of the justice of black people's desire to return to the land, to use the land, and to own the land. Many white farmers believe that their workers should have their own land, and are accordingly prepared to offer practical assistance (Atkinson 2007). Increasingly, the official position of commercial agriculture is that the restitution and land redistribution processes need to be implemented quickly and efficiently to ensure that they do not have a negative impact on food production, national food security and investor confidence.

THE MULTIPLE DISCOURSES OF LAND REFORM IN SOUTH AFRICA

The government's policy agenda remains fundamentally unclear. Commercial agriculture lobbies remain anxious about what the real goal of land reform may be. According to Agri SA, 'No one is clear on how the 30 per cent target is calculated. First it was 30 per cent of land, then 30 per cent of agricultural land, and now 30 per cent of commercial agricultural land' (*Landbouweekblad* 18 April 2008). In 2008, the director general of DLA claimed that its 30 per cent target would *exclude* the private sector's contribution to land reform and BEE activities, and would only include government funded land transfers. By 2010, the 30 per cent target is much less evident in policy statements, but this has been overtaken by a new and often undefined discourse about 'agrarian transformation'.

These shifting goalposts may well be due to the underlying ideological debates in leftist circles about land reform: is it about poverty alleviation (Hall and Ntsebeza 2007:4), or agrarian restructuring to transform large-scale commercial farming into more small-scale farms (Van den Brink *et al* 2007; Cousins 2007)? Is it about 'class and popular struggles' and 'an agrarian question of labour' (Bernstein 2007); or about 'race, class and nationality' and a challenge to 'hegemonic neoliberal ideology' (Moyo 2007)? Or is it about a challenge to the constitution's property clause to address 'the history of colonial conquest and land reform', or even 'whether the land should be privately owned or not' (Ntsebeza 2007)? Or is it about mobilising 'progressive social forces ... to contest the social and economic power, influence and interests of agrarian capital' (Jara and Hall 2009: 225)?

If this is the emotional, symbolic and ideological substance of land reform, it is no wonder that Agri SA has retreated into defensive mode, insisting on the 'rule of law', the sanctity of private property and WBWS models of land reform. In this context, it is remarkable that the beginnings of consensus between government and commercial agriculture have emerged at all, and are slowly becoming more prominent. This is largely because of an appreciation by government of more realistic rural development outcomes and the need to promote food production, whether for the market or for subsistence. This finds resonance in the thinking of commercial farmers.

In fact, there is great scope for collaboration between commercial agriculture (white and black), farm workers' groups, and organisations representing landless people (Atkinson 2007). The substance of such collaboration could be pragmatic issues such as job creation, training, peri-urban land reform, underutilised land in the former homelands, market access, farm worker agri-villages, and the involvement of land reform beneficiaries in the whole agricultural value chain, including agro-processing, marketing, transport and eco-tourism These issues potentially create a platform of common discourse between DLA, provincial departments of agriculture, emergent farmers' associations, commercial agriculture, and urban businesses.

At an official level, a strategic plan was drawn up for agriculture in 2001, which was a collaborative effort of commercial agriculture, the National African Farmers Union (NAFU), and the NDA. This recommended 'fast tracking the programme of land redistribution for agricultural development and processes of empowerment for targeted groups' (NDA 2001). The NDA, Agri-SA and NAFU established a joint mechanism to supervise the process of implementing the national plan. However, this plan has remained largely unimplemented.

In the years following the agreement, there was a break in relations between commercial agriculture and government. Initially, various overtures to government were rebuffed (*Farmers Weekly* 28 March 2008), but there has been growing awareness of the potentially positive contribution by the commercial farming sector. Dirk du Toit, the then deputy minister of land affairs, made conciliatory remarks about 'an unheard of spirit of cooperation to make land reform succeed' (*Landbouweekblad* 30 April 2004). Minister Didiza referred to the sugar industry's Inkezo initiative (creating a database of sellers and buyers, and providing a skills base to DLA to prepare business plans and secure loan finance) as a viable model of a possible partnership (*Farmers Weekly* 28 October 2005). Minister Xingwana acknowledged in 2007 that there were 'local areas where white commercial farmers have assisted previously disadvantaged communities and helped to alleviate poverty'. Tozi Gwanya, DLA director general, pointed out in 2008 that land reform cannot succeed without strategic partners. In the Polokwane Agreement of July 2008, the NDA and various agricultural unions agreed to join forces to support land reform (*Farmers Weekly* 17 October 2008).

In 2008, a high level ANC delegation met Agri SA in Johannesburg, as part of a drive by Gwede Mantashe, secretary general of the ANC, to respond to frequent requests by Agri SA for such a meeting (*Farmers* Weekly 26 September 2008). The fact that it took so long for a top-level meeting suggests the extent to which commercial agriculture, as an economic lobby, had been marginalised during the previous decade. Significantly, the new minister, Tina Joemat-Petterson, may be the first ANC minister to be quite comfortable with the commercial farming sector.

In several cases, practical partnerships have developed at local level. In 2007, a partnership was created in KwaZulu-Natal, with DLA, the provincial Department of Agriculture, the KZN Agricultural Union, NAFU and the Landless People's Movement, who collectively created a joint forum (*Farmers Weekly* 5 October 2007). In northern KwaZulu-Natal, the Council of Churches facilitated a partnership between the local Landless People's Movement and the district agricultural union, in reaction to bureaucratic delays in DLA (*Landbouweekblad* 19 September 2008). Ladysmith in KwaZulu-Natal also featured a joint plan between land tenants and the local farmers' union (*Landbouweekblad* 7 September 2007). Increasingly, provincial agricultural structures pride themselves on their nonracial membership (*Farmers Weekly* 28 March 2008).

But what still stands in the way of an effective multistakeholder partnership is the emotional history of injustice, associated with black people's loss of access to land during the last century. As Walker (2008: 38) has noted, 'Popular expectations have been shaped by a 'master narrative' of quintessentially rural dispossession and restoration'. This narrative is typically based on the oft-repeated claim that whites have occupied 87 per cent of the land, a statistic which ignores the fact that this percentage includes all urban areas, all state-owned public land (such as natural parks), and vast areas of unproductive semidesert land (Walker 2008: 43). But this narrative remains powerful, and is responsible for a constant flow of mixed messages.

On the part of many government officials, there remains a deep suspicion of the motives of white commercial agriculture. In particular, the sheer fact of white land ownership, which was secured at a time of great political inequality in South Africa, remains an emotional hurdle which is difficult to overcome. The belated government response to the overtures of commercial farmers, whether black or white, may be related to the fact that the ANC has historically been an urban party. There is, as yet, no real ANC lobby representing commercial agriculture. This, in turn, may be due to the fact that many middle class black people who have acquired farmland have in fact secured their incomes from their involvement in urban jobs, politics or the state, and not because they have grown from the ranks of commercial agriculture.

Meanwhile, many middle level government officials have remained locked within the 'master narrative'. This is not an unusual phenomenon. Public policies very often rest on the beliefs and perceptions of those who help make them, whether or not those cognitions are accurate: 'Policies reproduce whatever people have been socialised to perceive and believe, rather than analysing the range of alternative symbolic evocations' (Edelman 1977: 15). Social ties and group identifications within organisations help to shape patterns of belief (Schein 1985). Language devices such as phrases and metaphors elicit stock responses. Consequently, words such as 'agrarian capital' and 'neoliberal ideology' evoke dominant images of an exploitative, oppressive economic class, bolstered by racial privilege, holding out against sharing scarce resources, and set on capturing the state for its own self-interested purposes. Any idea that such economic agents could become *partners* in land reform therefore becomes almost unthinkable. It is scarcely surprising that the dominant approach of the state is to 'go it alone', in a context where South Africa's economic competitors have long ago institutionalised the need for effective and ongoing state-society relations in agriculture.

Commercial agricultural lobbyists are frequently confused by government's mixed messages. On several occasions, ANC politicians have expressed a willingness to work with commercial agriculture. But this sentiment typically does not filter down into the administrative system where real decisions are made. For their part, commercial agricultural lobbies are not value neutral either. They are animated by the ethics of pragmatism and production, by middle class values of achievement, investment and advancement, by the sanctity of private property, and by the legitimacy of competition, profit and material gain for themselves, their families, their descendents and their communities. They want to share this world with a new generation of black farmers, whether large-scale, small-scale or subsistence producers. For them, the world of historical materialist theoreticians and neo-Marxist class analysts remains totally opaque and incomprehensible.

MODERN GOVERNANCE: The role of policy networks and corporatist relations

In order to understand why land reform has been so difficult to implement, we need to consider what theoretical resources have been made available to policy makers. In this process, it becomes evident that DLA has been insulated from several analytical trends which characterise governance in modern societies.

The chasm between government, commercial agriculture and left-wing theorists flies in the face of modern government practice, and in particular a new generation of state-society relations. Arguing the case that social interests affect governments is nothing new, but what is new, since the Second World War, is the perception that governments cannot actually govern without the active support and participation of social interests – typically, but not exclusively, capital and labour. Relations between states and social interests can vary between more 'pluralist' forms (where interest groups compete for influence), to more 'corporatist' relations. 'Corporatism' refers to institutionalised and shared patterns of policy-making (Eising 2008: 1170).

In the agricultural sector in the European Union, for example, such state-society relations have taken the form of permanent and formalised relationships, where an interest group (representing the agricultural sector) functions as a natural partner in policy implementation (Eising 2008: 1173; Coleman and Chiasson 2002). Such relationships do not exclude interactions with other interests. Typically, there is space, at various levels in the governmental system, for diverse interests to be part of 'corporatist' arrangements. Government-society relationships are often a shifting terrain, responding to new and critical policy challenges in ways that resolve and accommodate competing social interests. Significantly, 'government capacity' is a characteristic of governments found *in relation to* social actors, and not in splendid bureaucratic isolation:

> Of central importance is the state's ability to use its autonomy to consult and to elicit consensus and co-operation from the private sector … Through its linkages with key economic groupings, the state can extract and exchange vital information with producers, stimulate private-sector participation in key policy areas, and mobilise a greater level of industry collaboration in advancing national strategy (Weiss 1998: 39).

At the heart of the problem is the changing understanding of 'state', 'market' and 'civil society'. These terms are now recognised as theoretical ideal-types (Frodin 2008: 20). They are not three distinct spheres characterised by mutually differentiated norms, modes of decision-making and logics of action. The notion of 'state capacity' is increasingly being defined as 'the ability of policy-making authorities to pursue domestic adjustment strategies that, *in cooperation with organised economic groups*, upgrade or transform the industrial economy' (Weiss 1998: 5 in Frodin 2008: 20, italics added). 'State capacity' is increasingly defined as the ability to mobilise a range of government and non-government resources. Public and private actors need to agree on strategies to transform the economy, and then coordinate their actions to reach them. Similarly, the concept of 'governance' refers to the capability of a central state authority to coordinate a multitude of societal actors operating within the realm of the state (Pierre 2000, cited in Frodin 2008: 26). At the same time, the distinction between 'public sphere' and 'private sphere' is breaking down, with governments behaving increasingly like corporations and corporations taking on public-good functions.

In South Africa, there is virtually no systematic corporatist relationship between state and commercial agriculture. Until now, the ANC's disregard of commercial agriculture is evident in every aspect of its policy. Agriculture is the major producer of food and fibre, the major employer of unskilled labour, the major underpinning of rural towns, and the major economic reason for maintaining rural infrastructure. Yet South African departments of agriculture provide virtually no support to commercial farmers, whether in terms of finance, infrastructure or research and technical support. South African farmers' lot compares very unfavourably with their pampered equivalents in Europe and the United States who are key competitors in agricultural markets. In South Africa, it is now accepted, virtually as an article of faith, that only black emergent farmers can expect support from government. Commercial farmers – white and black – face the cold winds of global competition on their own.

The removal of all kinds of market protection for commercial agriculture has made South Africa one of the most vulnerable agricultural economies in the world (Tregurtha 2005). Financial subsidies to agriculture have not been seen since the late 1980s. When compared to the support received by farmers in the US, UK, Brazil, Germany and France, it is astonishing that so many South African commercial farmers have survived globalisation. In fact, the number of commercial farm owners in South Africa has declined by about a third in the last ten years, with no effort by government to stem the tide. The number of farming units has declined by 31 per cent, from 57 987 in 1993 (SAIRR 2007: 377) to 39 982 in 2007 (SAIRR 2009: 554). Commercial farmers who are not hyper-efficient are likely to simply go out of business. When they cannot sustain their businesses, they sell their land to other farmers who are generally more capital intensive and financially resilient. In fact, the difficulties of commercial agriculture are prompting a growing stream of commercial farmers to opt for investment in other African countries. South African food production now relies fundamentally on a network of privately owned agricultural support organisations, which operate with a high degree of technical sophistication.

Given the government's lack of engagement with commercial agriculture, the issue of land reform (defined as 'land transfer') has remained virtually the only key deliverable. Consequently, land reform has generally failed as a contribution to rural development, because of its poor links to the agricultural, agro-processing and and non-farm sectors.

There is an urgent need to reconsider economic and political linkages. It is impossible to have a rural development policy, or a land reform policy, or an agricultural empowerment policy without understanding and supporting the commercial agricultural sector as an inalienable partner in the design and implementation of the process. As Thabo Mbeki recognised, it is crucial to create new links between the 'first' and 'second' economies.

Ultimately, the issue is not simply the type of land reform required. The underlying question is the way that the state can and should govern. Should it continue to try to 'go it alone', excluding commercial agriculture from a land reform partnership? Or should it focus on getting its capacity to govern in place, in partnership with established economic interests? In the process, new rural development opportunities are being overlooked, at least partly because so much of the public discourse is distracted into hoary ideological debates.

NEW-GENERATION PARTNERSHIPS FOR RURAL DEVELOPMENT

Rural development is now defined by government in terms of land reform and 'agrarian transformation'. This section reflects on new rural trends and opportunities which demand much more innovative and creative responses.

Government has failed to identify and capitalise on new rural dynamics such as lifestyle land purchases (by urban South Africans and foreigners), the transition to game farming, and the rise of eco-tourism and agri-tourism, as valuable adjuncts to food production. These form part of the rise of the 'post-productivist rural economy', a phenomenon which is widespread in Europe, Australia and the United States (Halfacree 2006). Furthermore, a growing number of rural dwellers are involved in non-farm livelihoods, which require us to look beyond the issue of agricultural land ownership.

The issue of changing rural livelihoods has far-reaching implications for land reform. Until now, land reform in South Africa has been based on the premise that beneficiaries can make a living from full-time agricultural production. Provincial departments of agriculture still focus on the 'full-time farmer'. This often sets land reform beneficiaries up for failure. Increasingly, in South Africa and internationally, farmers are farming part-time, and bolster their livelihoods with urban incomes. Expecting poor people to make a living from agriculture is often possible *only* if it is a part-time activity, and there are other income streams not linked to agriculture. This also has an implication for land use planning. If part-time farming is the key route, then there should be a focus on peri-urban agricultural land for land reform beneficiaries, where other family members can have non-agricultural income streams (Hall 2009b: 84). Significantly, this trend towards part-time farming characterises commercial farming too.

A further oversight is the equation of land reform with land *ownership*, instead of 'access to land'. It is, in fact, perfectly possible to farm successfully on rented land, whether rented from government or private owners. Using rented land can mean that farmers can rapidly acquire more land. They can also quickly abandon inappropriate land (for instance, if they want to change the types of products, or change localities). Many commercial farmers *only* use rented land, because of its flexibility. By farming for a few years on rented land, new farmers can build up sufficient capital (finance and livestock) to position themselves for land purchase. In both commercial and former homeland farming areas, land rental can facilitate land reform. In commercial areas, municipal commonage land is a potentially very valuable resource for start-up black farmers. In traditional areas, land rentals can mean an important revenue stream for land owners.

Furthermore, land reform requires flexible land parcels. For many years, a debate has raged about the intrinsic profitability of small farms versus large farms. Binswanger and Deininger (1996: 64) have argued that family farms are more productive, because family members share risk and management overheads (Van den Brink *et al* 2007). As Cousins (2010) has argued, there needs to be a new appreciation of the merits of smallholder farming. In contrast, there are analysts who have expressed scepticism about small-scale agriculture (Palmer and Sender 2006; Sender and Johnston 2004). In many provinces, the departments of agriculture have opposed the division of farms, to the detriment of land reform as well as commercial farmers (Hall 2009b).

A rural development strategy could be combined with programmes to encourage large-scale farmers to promote employment, for example by skills training and placement. In other areas, new eco-tourism enterprises could create opportunities for new skills such as tracking and guiding, hospitality services, transport services and craft-making.

There is a great need for research to uncover practical rural development opportunities, which will include the 'first' and the 'second economy'. Do we have statistics regarding the various dimensions of farm employment – labour broking, part-time work, skills development, wages, job advancement and tourism-related work? Do we have sufficient understanding of the nature of agricultural processing and tourism in local towns? Do we understand the nature of employment creation? Are new black farmers employing black labour, and if so, on what terms? What happens to rural matriculants? Who attends agricultural high schools and colleges, and what happens to them after matriculation? Is there a demand for agricultural and technical training? Are the graduates of rural high schools employable in rural areas, or are they condemned to urbanise? Do we know the extent and nature of share equity schemes? Do we understand the rapid shifts in rural products, from small livestock to large livestock, from livestock to game, from maize and wheat to niche (high-value) crops, and from food production to bio-fuels? How can the changing relationships between large processors and outgrowers be used to promote rural development? Can we promote private sector-led empowerment programmes, such as the wool industry which has transformed sheep production in the former homelands? Do we understand the need for rural housing, whether on-farm or off-farm? Do we have sufficient information on the functioning of rural markets? How do towns and rural areas interact?

Modern agriculture and rural development raise far-reaching new questions. An 'old question' may be the racial identity of the land owner; the new question may be whether we want to promote a mix of agri-business, family farms or peasant farming. An 'old question' may be whether the land reform beneficiary makes productive use of the land; the new question may be whether land reform beneficiaries will survive climate change or not, or will survive an international recession. Until now, land ownership has been regarded as the key to rural development but now, we need to ask whether land rentals and agro-business may not be more useful interventions. These are all very practical questions, for which strong ideological pitches may be inappropriate.

In all these cases, a partnership between land reform beneficiaries, emergent farmers and established commercial farmers, based on an almost infinite variety of mutual support mechanisms, becomes possible. The creation of such partnerships should be addressed at national level. Promoting collaboration between state and economic agencies does not obviate the need for critical thinking about the nature and content of such collaboration, including the need to constantly broaden the collaborative partnership to include other interests such as organised labour, NGOs, and organisations representing the landless. This should be the framework for inclusive 'corporatist' arrangements to promote the land reform and rural development agendas.

REFERENCES

Agri SA (2009) Agricultural policy statements. Accessed at www.agrisa.co.za.

Andrews M, P Zamchiya and R Hall (2009) Piloting alternatives in the Breede River Winelands. In Hall R (Ed) *Another Countryside? Policy Options for Land and Agrarian Reform in South Africa*. Bellville: PLAAS, UWC: 165–190.

Atkinson D (2007) *Going for Broke: The Fate of Farm Workers in Arid South Africa*. Cape Town: HSRC Press.

Bernstein H (2007) Agrarian questions of capital and labour: Some theory about land reform (and a periodisation). In Ntsebeza L and R Hall (Eds) *The Land Question in South Africa*. Cape Town: HSRC Press.

Binswanger H and K Deininger (1996) South African land policy: the legacy of history and current options. In Van Zyl J, J Kirsten and HP Binswanger (Eds) *Agricultural Land Reform in South Africa: Policies, Markets and Mechanisms*, Oxford: Oxford University Press: 64–103.

Centre for Development and Enterprise (2008), Land reform in South Africa: Getting back on track, Research Report no. 16, Johannesburg.

Coleman WD and C Chiasson (2002) State power, transformative capacity and adapting to globalisation: An analysis of French agricultural policy, 1960-2000. *Journal of European Public Policy* 9 (2): 168–185.

Cousins B (2007) Agrarian reform and the 'two economies': Transforming South Africa's countryside. In Ntsebeza L and R Hall (Eds) *The Land Question in South Africa*. Cape Town: HSRC Press.

Cousins B (2010) What is a smallholder? Working Paper no. 16. Bellville: PLAAS, University of the Western Cape.

Cousins B and I Scoones (2010) Contested paradigms of 'viability' in redistributive land reform: Perspectives from southern Africa. *Journal of Peasant Studies* 37: 31–66.

Department of Land Affairs (2007) Report to Parliamentary Portfolio Committee, Acting Deputy-General, Mr T Gwanya. Accessed at: www.pmg.org.za/docs/2007/071107dla.ppt.

Department of Land Affairs (2008) The Land and Agrarian Reform Project (LARP): Concept Document, Pretoria.

Department of Land Affairs (2009) *Annual Report*. Pretoria.

Department of Rural Development and Land Reform (DRDLR) (2009b) The concept/vision of a comprehensive rural development programme (CRDP), Notes from a DRDLR meeting, 17 June 2009. Accessed at http://www.dla.gov.za/Comprehensive_rural_dev/Pilots.htm.

Duvel GH (2004) Developing an appropriate extension approach for South Africa: Process and outcome. *South African Journal of Agricultural Extension* 33: 1–10.

Edelman M (1977) *Political Language: Words that Succeed and Policies that Fail*. New York: Academic Press.

Eising R (2008) Clientelism, committees, pluralism and protests in the European Union: Matching patterns? *West European Politics* 31 (6): 1166–1187.

Frodin O (2008) Synergies, stalemates and social dilemmas: Governance, development planning and state-in-society relations in Eastern Cape, South Africa. Department of Sociology, Lund University.

Halfacree K (2006) From dropping out to leading on: British counter-cultural back-to-the-land in a changing reality. *Progress in Human Geography* 30: 309–335.

Hall R (2007) Transforming rural South Africa? Taking stock of land reform. In Ntsebeza L and R Hall (Eds) *The Land Question in South Africa*. Cape Town: HSRC Press.

Hall R (2009a) Land reform for what? Land use, production and livelihoods. In *Another Countryside? Policy Options for Land and Agrarian Reform in South Africa*. Bellville: PLAAS, UWC: 165–190.

Hall R (2009b) Land reform: How and for whom? Land demand, targeting and acquisition. In *Another Countryside? Policy Options for Land and Agrarian Reform in South Africa*. Bellville: PLAAS, UWC: 63–91.

Hall R (2009c) Dynamics in the commercial farming sector. In *Another Countryside? Policy Options for Land and Agrarian Reform in South Africa*. Bellville: PLAAS, UWC: 119-131.

Hall R and L Ntsebeza (2007) Introduction, Transforming rural South Africa? Taking stock of land reform. In Ntsebeza L and R Hall (Eds) *The Land Question in South Africa*. Cape Town: HSRC Press.

Jara M and R Hall (2009) What are the political parameters? In Hall R (Ed) *Another Countryside? Policy Options for Land and Agrarian Reform in South Africa*. Bellville: PLAAS, UWC: 207–230.

Kirsten J, C Machethe and A Fischer (2005) Appraisal of land reform projects in North West Province. Report for the National Department of Agriculture, March 2005.

Kleinbooi K (2009) The private sector and land reform. In Hall R (Ed) *Another Countryside? Policy Options for Land and Agrarian Reform in South Africa*. Bellville: PLAAS, UWC: 193–205.

Land Claims Commission (2007) *Annual Report 2006-7*, Pretoria.

Moyo S (2007) The land question in Southern Africa: A comparative review. In Ntsebeza L and R Hall (Eds) *The Land Question in South Africa*. Cape Town: HSRC Press.

National Department of Agriculture (NDA) (2001) *Strategic Plan for South African Agriculture*, Pretoria. Accessed at: http://www.nda.agric.za/docs/sectorplan/sectorplanE.htm.

National Department of Agriculture (NDA) (2008) Report to Parliamentary Committee on Agriculture.

Nkwinti G (2010) Budget vote speech to Parliament, 24 March. http://www.pmg.org.za/briefing/20100324-minister-rural-development-and-land-reform-budget-speech.

Ntsebeza L (2007) Land redistribution in South Africa: The property clause revisited. In Ntsebeza L and R Hall (Eds) *The Land Question in South Africa*. Cape Town: HSRC Press.

Palmer and Sender (2006) Prospects for on-farm self-employment and poverty reduction: An analysis of the South African Income and Expenditure Survey 2000. *Journal of Contemporary African Studies* 24 (3): 347–376.

Parliament of the Republic of South Africa (2009) Report of the Portfolio Committee on Rural Development and Land Reform, on the Annual Report of the Department of Land Affairs for 2008/9, 4 November.

Pierre J (2000) Introduction: Understanding Governance. In Pierre J (Ed) *Debating Governance: Authority, Steering and Democracy*. Oxford: Oxford University Press.

Schein EH (1985) *Organizational Culture and Leadership*. San Francisco: Jossey-Bass.

Sender J and D Johnston (2004) Searching for a weapon of mass production in rural Africa: Unconvincing arguments for land reform. *Journal of Agrarian Change* 4 (1 & 2): 142–164.

South African Institute of Race Relations (SAIRR) (1998) *South African Review 1997-1998*. Johannesburg: SAIRR

SAIRR (2007) *South Africa Survey 2006-7*. Johannesburg: SAIRR.

SAIRR (2009) *South Africa Survey 2008-9*. Johannesburg: SAIRR.

Sustainable Development Consortium (2007) *The Settlement and Implementation Support (SIS) Strategy*, Commission on Restitution of Land Rights, Department of Land Affairs.

Tregurtha N (2005) South Africa's new agribusiness and land reform policy regime: A case study of the wine industry. Policy Brief no. 44, Commark Trust, Johannesburg.

University of Pretoria (2005) Appraisal of Land Reform Projects in North West Province. Report submitted to National Department of Agriculture, Pretoria.

Van den Brink R, G Thomas and H Binswanger (2007) Agricultural land redistribution in South Africa: Towards accelerated implementation, in Ntsebeza L and R Hall (Eds) *The Land Question in South Africa*. Cape Town: HSRC Press.

Walker C (2008) *Landmarked: Land Claims and Land Restitution in South Africa*. Athens, OH: Ohio University Press.

Weiss L (1998) *The Myth of the Powerless State: Governing the Economy in a Global Era*. Cambridge: Polity Press.

CRIME AND SEX

4

Introduction: Signs of social decline?
Crime, prisons, child trafficking and transactional sex

Prishani Naidoo

———·•·———

When all the balance sheets are tallied and the sums done, it is still the nature and quality of the everyday lived experiences and interpersonal relationships, in particular of the most vulnerable, that speak to the character of a society. This section presents a glimpse into the fractured and fragile nature of a society trying to grapple with the entrenched divisions and inequalities left by apartheid in a context in which first-world, consumerist aspirations, values and standards are becoming the norm. The character of the South African transition and post-apartheid society has been shaped both by the ways in which apartheid influenced (and continues to influence) the nature of social relations and experiences of the everyday, as well as by the demands (made on people and institutions) of re-entry into a global economy and society in which neoliberal principles and values have gained dominance. This is reflected in various ways in this section, from a sobering account of the continuing occurrence of violent crime (Bruce), to the deplorable conditions of awaiting trial prisoners and the broader problems of the South African criminal justice system (Gordin), to the largely uncharted terrain of child trafficking across the Zimbabwe-South Africa border (Kropiwnicki), and an exploration of the ways in which young men and women in an urban South African township relate to each other in the form of 'transactions' (Selikow and Gibbon).

Beginning with an overview of violent crime, David Bruce provides us with evidence that a culture of violence continues to define everyday life in South Africa. Bruce cites official statistics

of over 328 000 murders (homicides), over 750 000 incidents of rape, close to 1.6 million incidents of aggravated robbery, and 3.6 million incidents of assault with intent to inflict grievous
bodily harm as having occurred since 1994. Disaggregating national crime statistics from various
sources according to race, gender and age, Bruce shows several continuities in racialised trends
consistent with apartheid, and points to other significant differences with regard to gender
and age. While he focuses on murder and the three other major forms of violent crime
(assaults related to arguments, anger and domestic violence; rape and sexual assault; and robbery and other violent property crime), Bruce's chapter nevertheless highlights the many
nuances and differences that exist in law, policy and academic literature with regard to defining
and categorising different forms of violence, suggesting the need for greater debate, discussion
and clarification amongst those working to understand and intervene in this already massive
and still growing problem in South African society.

While Bruce's chapter sets out to clarify the nature of violent crime in South Africa at a
macro level, providing a broad understanding of its extent, it also inadvertently speaks to the
texture of social relations in the everyday. Understanding homicide in South Africa to be classified into the categories 'argument type' and 'crime type,' Bruce goes further to show that if
the argument type category were to be understood broadly to include various interpersonal
disputes and conflicts such as those related to domestic violence and 'love triangles,' then, on
a national level 'argument type' homicides are the most predominant, with a recent SAPS
study indicating that these account for 63.6 per cent of all homicides. That the majority of
deaths resulting from violent crimes in South Africa result from or are related to arguments
between individuals, speaks to just how deeply ingrained violence is in the fabric of society,
and to the lack of nonviolent, social means whereby everyday conflicts between neighbours,
co-workers, lovers, husbands and wives, parents and children … might be resolved.

On the flipside of this close analysis of violent crime, Jeremy Gordin then explores the
results of an approach to crime that prioritises prison as punishment – that is, the growing
problem of awaiting trial detainees (ATDs) in South Africa. An already overcrowded prison
system, and a prison population growing from just below 120 000 in 1995 to more than 180
000 by 2004, lead Gordin to reflect on the problems and injustices of the current system of
ATDs in which approximately one-third of the entire prison population of South Africa is
being held in custody without trial. Surprisingly, South Africa is not exceptional in this regard.
Citing evidence of cases known to go on for as long as nine years, and noting that two in five
ATDs will eventually be acquitted, Gordin argues that keeping any potentially innocent person
incarcerated for a prolonged period of time without trial is unjust. Presenting the lived experiences of some ATDs in South Africa, Gordin opens a lid on the inhumane conditions under
which ATDs are expected to survive in South African jails, and portrays the awaiting trial system
as denying people (including the potentially innocent) their basic needs, rights and dignity. Of
significance is Gordin's lament that it is often poor people who cannot afford the bail set for
petty crimes (sometimes as little as R200) who end up sitting in jail for extended periods of
time as their cases are continuously postponed. This is made worse by the fact that a South
African Law Reform Commission study (2000) showed that only 6 per cent of serious and
violent crimes that were tracked resulted in conviction.

A significant portion of Gordin's chapter is dedicated to the failures of the legal and criminal justice systems, and the need for alternative systems to deal with the very real problem of crime (of various types) in a context of high unemployment, declining sources of welfare support and growing poverty, as well as the immediate problems of prison overcrowding and the lack of resources to properly cater for the growing ATD and general prison population. He offers several suggestions as solutions, including the immediate release on bail of as many ATDs as possible, starting with those who are not accused of violence and those who have already served more than any sentence they could possibly receive. In general, however, Gordin argues that there needs to be a move away from prioritising 'fighting crime', in which there is a tendency to measure progress according to the ability to produce statistics of increasing numbers of arrests and incarcerations. While Gordin has chosen to focus on the problem of ATDs, his chapter just touches on the related problems of the general prison population in South Africa, an area of work that demands as much attention as the issues of ATDs. Conditions in South African prisons, for both the guilty and those potentially innocent, are notoriously atrocious. It is, then, the prison and criminal justice systems *overall* that demand transformation.

Writing from within an international non-governmental organisation seeking to effect change in the lives of some of society's most vulnerable, Zosa de Sas Kropiwnicki, reflects on the trafficking of children from Zimbabwe to South Africa through the border town of Musina. Noting that there is very little documented information about trafficking to South Africa, De Sas Kropiwnicki's chapter is an important start in trying to understand a serious problem affecting some of society's most vulnerable, and also a reflection of the future potentials for society's development. Based on a preliminary study conducted towards the purposes of more comprehensive research, legal and policy interventions, the chapter only skims the surface of a complex and growing problem for the southern African region, emphasising the need for further research on this issue. In this chapter, we get a sense of the extent of South Africa's social problem, reaching beyond its national borders, the people spewed out by the wars and economic and social problems plaguing neighbouring countries, such as Zimbabwe, seeking refuge in its border towns and crossings where they become vulnerable to the evil intentions of organised groups of criminals. De Sas Kropiwnicki argues that although many migrants are at risk of being trafficked, unaccompanied minors are particularly at risk, and she shows that trafficking does indeed occur for, *inter alia*, the purposes of sexual exploitation, sexual slavery, labour exploitation, sale of illegal substances and goods, and forced criminal activity. In many cases, individuals are lured into being trafficked by 'wolves in sheep's skin', men who feed off the desperation of migrants by offering them false promises of employment in Johannesburg and/or safe transport across the border. She also highlights the fact that few migrants are aware of immigration procedures and/or the dangers involved in crossing the border illegally.

Outlining the international juridical framework governing trafficking, and child trafficking in particular, De Sas Kropiwnicki shows that there are several confusing and contradictory aspects of the laws and their definitions that, she argues, often make the prosecution and prevention of trafficking difficult, and that therefore require further clarification. She also believes that in spite of the confusions related to the laws and definitions, which can constantly be contested by different interests, particular attention must be given to the agency of children in each case. In the case of such severe political turmoil and socio-economic deprivation, such as in Zimbabwe, children, just as much as adults, are forced to make decisions (sometimes difficult and unexpected) about their lives in relation to their families and communities. In taking the best interests of the child into consideration, then, De Sas Kropiwnicki argues that the law must be further refined and implemented with the understanding that the child is an active participant in the situation under investigation. Such an approach to agency must nevertheless consider the specific context in which the child acts or chooses not to act in a particular way, and the influence of social, political and economic factors on his or her ability to act in any way.

In the final chapter, Terry-Ann Selikow and Graham Gibbon provide an excellent illustration of the claim that the logic of the market touches all aspects of life today. Through the voices of young South African men and women living in an urban township, Selikow and Gibbon show how the most intimate aspects of life are commodified today, and relationships between young men and women are viewed and approached as vehicles for the exchange of sex for material (and other) favours. The authors show how, with the rise of conspicuous consumption, a discourse of exchange has developed in which young men are classified and rated by young women according to their ability to provide materially and financially, and young women are treated as subordinates in a 'hierarchy of lovers' by their male partners. Known as 'transactional sex for conspicuous consumption' (TSCC), this 'exchange of sex for luxury gifts or services from a man', Selikow and Gibbon point out, is different from the phenomenon of 'transactional sex' (TS), identified in an earlier period to refer to the exchange of sex for money and other necessities for survival. This is indeed distressing as it suggests that this kind of exchange occurs not only in circumstances of extreme need, but is becoming a general, defining characteristic of relationships between young men and women today.

Selikow and Gibbon illustrate how the changing aspirations of young men and women, influenced by global consumer culture, are increasingly met through engaging in TSCC, the latter entrenching inequalities between them and enforcing commodified ways of relating as men and as women. Not only has this resulted in the enhancement of conditions for the abuse of women but, as the authors show, it has also fuelled the practice of multiple concurrent partners (MCPs) in a context of socio-economic deprivation where a single partner might not have the material means to fulfil all one's desires. They go on to show how this, in turn, contributes to the spread of HIV/AIDS, as the potential for condom use decreases because women are less likely to negotiate condom use in situations of powerlessness or where their status in a relationship stands to be questioned. The authors also, nevertheless, highlight that TSCC affords some women the opportunity to exercise their agency, sometimes making demands of their partners and setting the terms and conditions of their relationships. What seems most significant, however, is that all matters of choice and agency are in the final instance constrained by the market logic that seems to have taken root in the minds and hearts of the youth surveyed by Selikow and Gibbon.

It is significant that any analysis of South African society today cannot ignore the related issues of crime and sex. In the lives of rich and poor, sex and crime feature variously as means to pleasure, as fears, as means of survival, as means of escape, and so on. In a highly commodified yet economically deprived society, meanings of sex and relationships are relegated to or mixed up in the realm of exchange for money. And crime features in the fears of all South Africans, while at the same time presenting the only means of survival for many of the poor and unemployed. While the prison population and the number of ATDs grow, crime still increases. In spite of existing legislation, social injustices continue to be perpetuated in the form of the ATD system and the experience of child trafficking. The stories and incidents explored in this section point to old and new social problems facing South Africa today, problems that demand new attempts at solutions; solutions that acknowledge that so-called victims each participate in their circumstances in ways that they choose or are coerced into. This section also highlights the need for further research and analysis related to questions still unanswered about the various issues explored here, suggesting that there is much work for those attempting to understand society in order to change it.

CHAPTER 17

Our burden of pain:
Murder and the major forms
of violence in South Africa

David Bruce

In the fifteen years since 1994, official statistics record over 328 000 murders, over 750 000 incidents of rape, close to 1.6 million incidents of aggravated robbery, and 3.6 million incidents of assault with intent to inflict grievous bodily harm. Numerous other incidents, of common assault, indecent assault and robbery, are also included in official statistics. Taking into account the fact that statistics under-represent (particularly nonfatal) violence, it is apparent that South Africa is a country seriously brutalised and traumatised by violence.[1]

Most South Africans are inclined to agree that the problem of violent crime is a serious one. But a continuing feature of contemporary debates about crime is a question about whom it affects (Pharoah 2009; Silber and Geffen 2009). These debates are partly racialised. Many white South Africans, for instance, hold the view that crime, and violent crime, primarily involves young black men targeting whites (Myburgh 2009; 2010), and many perceive women as the primary victims of violence. Meanwhile, the recent outbreaks of xenophobic violence have led to suggestions that much of the violence in South Africa is directed at foreigners, while alternatively, the view is often expressed that it is poor people who are the principal victims (Silber and Geffen 2009).

The problem with all of these views is that while violent crime has common features and underlying causes it is not a uniform phenomenon. Murder, for instance, is probably best understood as a manifestation of a number of different forms of violence. But murder itself, and each of these different forms of violence, affects different groups within South Africa's population in different ways. In understanding the impact of violent crime on people in South Africa, it is necessary to take a differentiated view of violence.

This chapter is therefore largely descriptive in its focus. It aims to describe how murder and the related 'major forms of violence', the primary contributors to the overall problem of violent crime in South Africa, manifest themselves. It engages not only with questions about the various groups of victims affected by different aspects of the problem of violence, but also some of the other key commonalities and differences. In so doing it hopes to contribute to establishing a firmer basis for understanding what we are talking about in South Africa when we discuss violent crime.

GENERAL CHARACTERISTICS OF VIOLENCE IN SOUTH AFRICA

Violent deaths in South Africa[2]

Available data on homicide[3] indicates that it is young, black (particularly coloured and African) men who are most affected by violent death. Data from the National Injury Mortality Surveillance System (NIMSS) for 2004, 2005 and 2007 on the age distribution of homicide consistently shows between 38 and 39 percent of homicide victims to be in the twenty to twenty-nine age category, with 65 to 67 per cent of homicide victims being between twenty and thirty-nine years of age (table 1).[4]

Table 1: Contribution of five-year age bands in 10–49 year age group to overall homicide rate for 2004, 2005 and 2007

	10-14	15-19	20-24	25-29	30-34	35-39	40-44	45-49	Other age groups	All murders
2004	50	650	1620	1650	1460	1040	750	470	885	8575
per cent	0.6	8	19	19	17	12	9	5	10	100
2005	57	643	1580	1626	1421	928	708	434	826	8223
per cent	0.7	8	19	20	17	11	9	5	10	100
2007	82	919	2172	2271	1671	1257	923	627	1392	11314
per cent	0.7	8	19	20	15	11	8	6	12	100
Total	189	2212	5372	5547	4552	3225	2381	1531	3103	28112
per cent	0.7	8	19	20	16	11	8	5	11	100

Source: *NIMSS 2005, 2006, 2008.* (Figures for 2004 are estimates based on a bar graph provided in the NIMSS report for that year. There is no NIMMS report for 2006. The 'other age groups' column refers to those victims nine years and under, and fifty years and over.)

Since 1994, agencies involved in collecting data on crime have mostly avoided collecting data relative to racial categories so such data is relatively hard to come by. The available information is therefore somewhat dated but there are no apparent grounds for believing that the trends reflected in this data have changed substantially since then. NIMSS data for 2000 and 2001, for instance, indicated that homicide accounted for 50 to 51 per cent of non-natural deaths amongst coloureds, and 48 to 49 per cent of such deaths amongst Africans, while the proportions amongst Indians (26 to 27 per cent) and whites (17 to 18 per cent) were significantly lower (table 2). Unless Indians and whites had substantially higher levels of non-natural death overall, which is not demonstrated by the data (Statistics SA data, cited in Myburgh 2010), this indicates that there are more homicide victims among coloureds and Africans. A study of murders of women in 1999 indicated that intimate femicides of coloured women (18.3 per 100 000) were substantially higher than those for Africans (8.9 per 100 000), Indians (7.5 per 100 000) and whites (2.8 per 100 000) (Mathews *et al* 2005.)

Table 2: Percentage of non-natural deaths linked to homicide by racial categories

	African	Asian	Coloured	White
2000	49 %	26%	50%	17%
2001	48 %	27 %	51 %	18%

Source: *NIMSS*

Table 3: NIMSS data on gender of victims of death by violence (homicide), 2000–07[6]

	2000	2001	2003	2005	2007
Male victims	7 268	9 700	9 014	7 933	10 306
Female victims	1 073	1 463	1 371	1 143	1 598
Total male and female	8 341	11 163	10 385	9 076	11 904
per cent female	13	13	13	13	12

Source: *NIMSS*

A distinctive feature of murder in South Africa is the high proportion of male victims. Statistics provided over the last decade by the national injury mortality surveillance system consistently indicate that male victims have accounted for 87 to 88 per cent of homicide victims. The proportion of male homicide victims in South Africa is far higher than global averages as well as averages for poor and African countries (Altbeker 2008: 129–130). Homicide victims are marginally less likely to be male in rural or small towns than in metropolitan areas, partly reflecting differences in patterns of homicide between these areas as well as the greater concentration of women in rural areas.[5]

Data on the profile of perpetrators of murder is by its nature more difficult to come by. In a study of murder in six areas conducted by the Centre for the Study of Violence and

Reconciliation (CSVR) (2008a), the proportion of suspects and victims of thirty-five and older was 22 per cent. However, suspects who are identified tend to be associated with specific types of homicides (for example argument-type homicides, often occurring between acquaintances – see further below) and cannot be generally taken to be representative of the age distribution of perpetrators. As a general rule, however, it seems that while both suspects and victims are likely to be young adults, in the age band twenty to thirty-nine, and particularly twenty to twenty-nine, more suspects than victims are younger and more victims than suspects are older than these age categories. For instance, 20 per cent of suspects were younger than nineteen whilst 11 per cent of victims were in this age category.[7]

Murders are, overwhelmingly, perpetrated by males. For instance, in the CSVR study of murder in six urban areas with high rates of murder, 94 per cent of suspects were male and 6 per cent female. However, the proportion of arrests of women in argument-type murders is much higher; in the CSVR study 9 per cent of the arrests for argument-type murders were of women; argument-type murders accounted for 310 (48 per cent) of the 641 identified suspects and 28 (78 per cent) of the 36 arrests of women, although they accounted for only 26 per cent of the murders overall.[8] In most other categories there were proportionately fewer arrests (relative to the total number of cases) but also few or no arrests of women. Thus all the suspects arrested for killings committed in the course of another crime (80 per cent of which were robberies), for killings carried out in self-defence (the victims in these cases had allegedly been involved in carrying out crimes), and for killings related to rivalry between groups (such as taxi associations) were male (CSVR 2008a: 93). This suggests that if the sex of all perpetrators in all categories of murder had been known, the proportion of male perpetrators would probably have been even greater than 94 per cent (in a 2009 SAPS docket analysis the figure is 95.1 per cent).

For all murders in which male suspects were identified, 15 per cent of victims were female and 85 per cent were male (*op cit*: 93-94). Victims were female in 32 per cent of cases and male in 68 per cent of the relatively small number of cases where suspects were female.

The paucity of data on issues of race relative to violent crime is even greater in relation to perpetrators than to victims. It appears reasonable to conclude that the overall patterns of homicide victimisation in terms of which coloureds and Africans are most vulnerable are also reproduced for perpetration, with some evidence, once again, that coloureds are even more strongly represented, relative to population numbers, than are Africans.

NIMSS data also suggests that firearms were previously the most commonly used weapons in incidents of homicide but that sharp instruments (mostly knives) have now displaced firearms (table 4). Changes in the profile of mortuaries in the NIMSS system are, however, likely to change the picture presented here: firearms are more likely to be associated with homicides in urban and particularly metropolitan areas, and so the predominance of firearm homicides in early NIMSS data might partly be a reflection of the continuing urban/metropolitan bias of the NIMSS system, which was particularly strong in its earlier years – although it appears possible that implementation of the Firearms Control Act (60 of 2000) has also contributed to a reduction in the number and relative proportion of homicides committed by means of firearms.[9]

Table 4: Weapons used in homicide, 2000–07[10]

	2000	2001	2002	2003	2004	2005	2007
Number of mortuaries	15	32	34	36	35	21	39
Firearms	4 372	6 104	5 572	5 387	3 953	3 487	3 929
Sharp force	2 547	3 168	3 151	3 220	2 992	3 204	4 408
Other method (blunt instrument,strangulation, burn)	1284	1653	1447	1727	1524	1177	2692
Total by weapons	8 203	10 925	10 170	10 334	8 469	7 868	11 029
per cent firearms	53	56	55	52	47	44	36
per cent sharp instruments	31	29	31	31	35	41	40

Source: *NIMSS*

Table 5: Types of murder in South Africa by gender of victim[11]

Type	Sub-type	Male victims	Female victims	All victims (per cent)
Argument type	Misunderstanding /argument general	47.9	3.7	51.6 (50.4)
	Domestic related	3.2	4.3	7.5 (7.3)
	Jealousy/love triangle	2.9	1.7	4.6 (5.5)
	Sub-total	54	9.7	63.7 (63.2)
Crime type	Consequence of another crime	12.7	3.1	15.8 (15.9)
Other	Vigilantism	5.0	0.0	5.0 (4.8)
	Self-defence	3.6	0.2	3.8 (4.5)
	Other	10.4	1.4	11.8 (11.5)
	Total	85.6 per cent	14.4 per cent	100

Source: *SAPS 2009; 2010*

Homicide in South Africa is largely differentiated between 'argument-type' and 'crime-type'. If these categories are understood very broadly (so that the argument-type homicides are understood to include a variety of interpersonal disputes and conflicts such as those related to domestic violence and 'love-triangles'), then it appears that on a national level 'argument-type' homicides are the most predominant, with a recent South African Police Service (SAPS) study indicating that these account for 63.6 per cent of homicides. Crime-type homicides accounted for a quarter (15.9 per cent) of this figure (table 5).

As indicated in table 5, killings categorised by the SAPS as 'domestic related' (a category which may be equated with that of 'fatal intimate partner violence') make up over 7 per cent of murders in this study. It is notable here that while female victims predominate (accounting for roughly 60 per cent of victims), there are also substantial numbers of male victims. The proportion of male victims here is comparable to that in the CSVR murder study (2008a: 90) where 31 per cent of intimate partner killings involved the killing of a man by a female. Intimate partner homicides account for 30 per cent of homicides of women. This figure is similar to that recorded in the CSVR study (31 per cent), though lower than that recorded in a major study of 'intimate femicide' which, based on an analysis of the murder of women in 1999, found that the killings of female intimate partners by men accounted for 50.2 per cent of killings of women where the relationship between victim and perpetrator could be determined, and 41 per cent of killings of women overall (Mathews *et al* 2005: 2). These killings are presumably distinguished from the SAPS category of 'jealousy/love triangle' killings also used in table 5 by the fact that the latter involve the killing of a rival rather than an intimate partner – although there are murder incidents where both a rival and partner (or former partner) are killed and jealousy plays a role in intimate partner violence and killings more generally.

There are certain factors which should be borne in mind in interpreting this type of data. The first is that the data does not differentiate between different types of locations. Aggravated robbery (robbery committed with weapons such as guns or knives) is the primary driver of 'crime type' murders and is heavily concentrated in and close to South Africa's metropolitan areas. Crime-type murders are therefore a far more significant phenomenon in metropolitan South Africa. For instance, the CSVR report on murder in six areas (focused on areas within metropolitan South Africa), found that crime-type murder constituted roughly a quarter, and argument type murders roughly half, of murders in known circumstances. In one of the areas, KwaMashu, crime-type murders in fact exceeded the number of argument-type murders (CSVR 2008a: 43).[12]

The use of the designation 'crime-type' also masks significant gender differences. The male victims of crime-type murders would overwhelmingly have been killed during incidents of robbery. The SAPS report indicates that 2 per cent of victims had been raped and murdered and these victims may be assumed to have been mainly (if not exclusively) female. This suggests that over 60 per cent of the female victims of crime-type murders (or 13 per cent of female victims overall) were women who had been raped (this may have included some incidents involving both rape and robbery).[13]

A further critical point which should be taken into account in referring to this data, is that it is only a representation of murders in 'known circumstances'. A 2004 SAPS report found that 37 per cent of murders were, however, in circumstances described as unknown while in the study of murder in six areas, murders in circumstances which were 'unknown or unclear' accounted for a full 53 per cent of cases (*op cit*: 31). The latter report also concludes that murders in unknown circumstances are more likely to be crime-type than argument-type murders and that the picture which we have of murder would be slightly different if we had data on the murders in unknown circumstances. The consequence would probably be that the proportion of argument-type murders would be somewhat less than the above data suggest, and the proportion of crime-type murders would be slightly greater. Nevertheless, the available evidence would appear to support the above picture in general terms and particularly the conclusion that argument-type murder is the major type of murder in South Africa.

Major forms of violence

As indicated above, murder is not a single discrete phenomenon. Often it takes place in the context of an argument or a robbery or rape. Though it is regarded as the most serious type of violent crime, it is not the most common. If we are to understand the overall problem of violent crime in South Africa, it is necessary to understand how violence usually manifests itself. For this purpose it is helpful to think of violent crime as mostly constituted by three major forms of violence:

1. *Assaults linked to arguments, anger and domestic violence*: In crime statistics, these incidents are reflected as offences such as murder, assault with intent to inflict grievous bodily harm (assault GBH), common assault, and others.
2. *Rape and sexual assault*: In crime statistics these incidents are reflected in offences such as murder, rape, indecent assault and others.[14]
3. *Robbery and other violent property crime*: These are linked to offences such as murder, aggravated robbery (primarily involving robberies of civilians in public space but also including vehicle hijacking and residential robbery), common robbery and others.

While it is difficult to quantify violence, and specific forms of violence, the available evidence would suggest that it is reasonable to regard these three 'forms' of violence as making up the bulk (at least two-thirds) of violence or violent crime in South Africa. Addressing the problem of violence in South Africa is therefore principally about addressing these three forms.

It should be noted that the system of classification used here, by which violence is described in terms of forms, might appear to resemble the offence categories which are reflected in crime statistics. However, examples of other forms, which appear to be less significant, illustrate the fact that these are not synonymous with offence statistics. For instance, the form of violence associated with the wave of attacks on foreigners which took place in South Africa in May 2008 might be classified as another form of violence (possibly 'xenophobic violence' or as a sub-form of collective violence) though individuals prosecuted for involvement in this violence would be prosecuted for offences such as murder, assault GBH or common assault or in some cases rape (other forms of violence are discussed briefly later in this chapter).

Related to this, as already indicated, murder, though a separate offence category, is not regarded as a separate form of violence. Instead murder is understood as usually related to one of the forms of violence, whether one of the three 'major' forms or another form of violence. The argument-type murders are therefore regarded as part of the first form listed above, while crime-type murders are mostly related to the third, and to a lesser degree the second, of these forms.

Assaults linked to arguments, anger and domestic violence

It appears reasonable to take as our point of departure that all the major forms of violence can be imagined as distributed within 'violence pyramids'. In the case of assaults, this implies that less severe assaults (that would be prosecuted as common assault) occupy the bulk of the pyramid at the bottom, more serious assaults (that would be prosecuted as assault GBH) occupy a band across the middle, with assault related murders (that is, argument-type murders) at the top. Although for present purposes actual physical violence or the threat thereof is seen as defining the parameters of the term 'violence', abusive verbal behaviour and other forms of violence are clearly interconnected, sometimes being part and parcel of an incident of violence and in other cases, merely expressing the hostile feelings which in other circumstances are expressed in violence.

It would appear possible that the number of male and female victims is similar, the total number of males slightly outnumbering that of female assault victims. In three major victim surveys conducted in 1998, 2003 and 2007 the number of male assault victims has been 51 per cent, 57 per cent, and 59 per cent, suggesting also that the proportion of female assault victims may have declined over this period (Pharoah 2008: 9).[15] The sex of victims is also not uniform across the violence pyramid. For instance a docket analysis conducted by the SAPS some years ago indicated that 54 per cent of victims of common assault, 40 per cent of victims of assault GBH and 18 per cent of victims of attempted murder were female (SAPS 2003: 33). In the CSVR study of six areas with high rates of murder which differentiated between different forms of murder, women similarly constituted 18 per cent of victims of argument-type murders (CSVR 2008a: 45). Women therefore suffer proportionately less from the more severe forms of assault at the upper levels of the assault pyramid. However, insofar as violence against them is linked to domestic violence, it is often related to a pattern of repeat victimisation and ongoing intimidation. In the worst cases this means that they live out their lives in circumstances which are continually tarnished and constrained by the fear and trauma of violence.

As already illustrated in relation to murder, women make up a small but significant minority of perpetrators of this form of violence. Their involvement as perpetrators is far more significant in relation to assaults (the equivalent to argument type-murders) than to any of the other major forms. In a small-scale study of violent crime dockets conducted in 1998, women made up 10 per cent of perpetrators of incidents of violence in Mamelodi and 4 per cent in Randburg. For female victims in Mamelodi, 17 per cent of perpetrators were female while for male victims, 7 per cent of perpetrators were female. For Randburg, the comparable figures were 3 per cent for male victims and 4 per cent for female victims (South African Law Commission 2001 quoted in CSVR 2007: 74).[16] As indicated, in the study of areas with high murder rates, 9 per cent of suspects in cases of argument-type murder were female.

Linked to questions about the sex of the participants are questions about how to identify the persons involved in these incidents. Insofar as violence is equated with 'crime', people may be inclined to assume that the participants can readily be identified as either 'perpetrators' or 'victims' but, particularly in incidents involving two or more males who actively contribute to the escalation of an argument into violence, it may be more appropriate to identify them as 'opponents' who are simultaneously both victims and perpetrators.

This form of violence is often a way of provisionally resolving issues that are a source of interpersonal conflict or of expressing the emotions emerging from it. Assaults are therefore a means of maintaining control or power or obtaining cooperation in situations where the people feel unable otherwise to do so, or of expressing anger related to this inability to maintain control. The people involved are usually known to each other, although available data does not demonstrate that this violence takes place predominantly within the inner circle of intimate or family relationships. Much violence involves people in 'intermediate relationships' such as those between neighbours, roommates, or colleagues – and many who are simply known by sight'. Although in the minority, assaults sometimes involve strangers, one example being road rage assaults (including killings).

In terms of the circumstances giving rise to violence of this nature, it appears that many conflicts are related to mundane disputes of one kind or another, such as over money or possessions or alleged insults, with jealousy also prominent as a factor, particularly in incidents of male violence against women. The reason why such disputes become violent in some circumstances but not others may be an expression of various factors including cognitive patterns, feelings of humiliation or threatened self-esteem. It would nevertheless also appear that many people experiencing these emotions avoid actual physical violence, so that dynamics specific to the situation, the social setting and the individuals involved are also important in understanding these incidents. Participants may already, for instance, have developed a familiarity with the use of violence. Many perpetrators are highly selective about the people that they choose to aggress against and will often only engage in actual violence where they (perhaps subconsciously) have judged the other person to be weaker or less capable of inflicting harm (Collins 2008). Those who aggress against others irrespective of these considerations would be people who are already severely hardened or brutalised by violence.

The approach to categorisation of violence used here is fairly loose. The category of 'assaults linked to arguments' used here is a broad category which some may wish to define as incorporating different types of violence. For instance, a study in the United Kingdom identifies one category of homicides as 'confrontational homicides' in which 'the offender and victim engaged in a form of honour contest or face-to-face encounter' which 'shared the fundamental common feature of the victim and offender actively engaging in an altercation together' (Brookman 2003: 39). Another category of homicide is identified as 'revenge homicide'. Although these are also related to 'a history of ongoing strife (albeit sometimes fairly recent) between the relevant parties', they are also all 'planned to some extent' and characterised by the 'lethal intent' of one of the participants (op cit: 43).[17]

Similarly, domestic violence is often classified as a distinct form of violence. Although domestic violence incidents often have specific distinguishing characteristics (such as the association with repeat victimisation), there are also many such incidents which share features in common with other argument-type assaults. Furthermore, not all incidents of violence, or argument related assaults, in which women are victims, whether at the hands of men or other women, are incidents of domestic violence.

There is obviously not one single satisfactory system of classifying violence. The approach taken here is to see incidents of violence in which some form of argument or conflict gives rise to an assault of some kind as constituting a single form. Related to its all-encompassing character, therefore, this form is by far the largest form of violence, as well as the principal driver of the murder rate. Though some are inclined to emphasise that victimisation by violence affects people of all classes, it appears fairly clear that assaults are more prevalent, and also are far more likely to involve extreme or serious violence in poorer or working-class communities.[18] As is the case elsewhere, in South Africa most violence 'has been found to be both intra-class and intra-race, partly reflecting lifestyles in which males engage in honour contests or domestic oppression' (Levi and Maguire 2002: 807).

Rape and sexual assault

Rape, and (in a short while) robbery will be discussed far more briefly mainly to emphasise some of the ways in which they may be differentiated from assaults as a form of violence. As with assaults, sexual assaults may be assumed to have a pyramid-like distribution with acts of 'sexual harassment' and 'indecent assault' accounting for the largest volume of incidents at the bottom of the pyramid, rape a band across the upper middle section of the pyramid, and rape related murders occupying the apex of the pyramid. Apart from the – by definition – sexual nature of acts of sexual assault, the most obvious way in which rape may be differentiated from assaults as a form of violence is the fact that women (particularly young women) predominate overwhelmingly among victims, and the virtual total absence of the phenomenon of female perpetration. The victimisation of men has primarily been documented in prisons (Gear 2007). However, a recent study based on interviews with young men in areas of KwaZulu-Natal found that 2.9 per cent of respondents reported rape of a man, as opposed to 27.6 per cent who reported rape of a woman (Jewkes et al 2009: 24).[19] Although acquaintances are prominent as perpetrators, rape is also distinct from assaults in that the phenomenon of predatory crime, linked to perpetration by strangers, is far more significant. In a study of rape in Gauteng based on cases reported in 2003, 39 per cent of rapes were committed by a perpetrator described as a 'stranger' or 'known by sight' (Vetten et al 2008: 34).[20]

Many rapes are in part sexually motivated. For reasons to do with political contestation over how to understand rape, this is regarded by some as a controversial statement,[21] although the observation is not incompatible with explanations which emphasise that rape is often facilitated by patriarchal ideas which privilege male sexual entitlement and male authority over women more generally. Rape may also be punitive in motivation (in the context of group conflict this may be punishment of the rival group rather than just the individual) or a means of self reassurance or reassurance of others (where it is perpetrated in a group for instance) about the masculinity or worth of the perpetrator.

As in robbery, physical coercion or threats of physical harm are therefore often a means of overcoming the victim's resistance, many victims apparently submitting to rape for fear of being hurt with a weapon or otherwise physically assaulted.[22] However, in addition to the rape itself, other harm is sometimes inflicted on victims even where they do not resist. Thus in the Gauteng study referred to above, 39 per cent of adult victims had non-genital injuries (injuries unrelated to the act of forcible penetration itself) (op cit: 41). While some of those who had injuries were women who had resisted the rape or tried to escape, others who had such injuries had apparently not done so (CSVR 2008b: 45-49).

As indicated above, a substantial proportion of crime-type murders of women are related to incidents of rape, and rape homicides may account for as many as one in six homicides of women. However homicides take place in less than 0.5 per cent of rape incidents.

Rape has a similar class distribution to that of assaults but since it is sometimes predatory in nature it sometimes involves men from poorer backgrounds specifically targeting more affluent women, including incidents where there is a racial component to such targeting. This is sometimes related to the fact that acts of robbery (including those carried out across the class and racial divide in South Africa) are sometimes accompanied by rape. In a small study of residential robbery, rape occurred in 4 per cent of incidents (Newham 2008:11). Vehicle hijackings have sometimes also been accompanied by acts of rape.

Robbery and other violent property crime

Robbery is differentiated from the other forms of violence by overtly acquisitive motives, which characterise it as violent property crime. In most robberies the victims are threatened with violence or violence is used to overcome their physical resistance, but violence is not used to harm them other than in this respect.[23] Some incidents of property crime, which start off as 'not-violent', also turn into incidents of violent crime. Thus, some criminals break into people's homes or businesses with the intention of escaping undetected with stolen goods. They may nevertheless be armed. Sometimes employees or residents return to the business or home, catching them in the act, thus precipitating a murder or other violence intended to prevent the returning person from raising the alarm or identifying the criminals to the police.

Robbery is also differentiated from the other major forms of violence by being far more consistently a stranger crime.[24] The fact that robbery is an acquisitive crime also has major ramifications in terms of the class (and racial) distribution of robbery victimisation, the potential gains from robbery of more affluent victims (including private citizens, businesses, banks, trucking companies and the cash-in-transit industry) making these the most desirable targets. However, it does not necessarily follow that affluent people are more likely to be targeted by robbers, as wealthy people and formal businesses are better able to finance the installation of security devices and the hiring of private security companies to protect them, and poorer people are more physically vulnerable to attack partly when, as pedestrians, they are present in public spaces.

It is unclear whether women or men are more likely to be robbery victims, but the factors shaping the gender distribution of victims of robbery have some resemblance to those already identified. Men are more likely to be income earners, (and more likely to be high income earners), and therefore more likely to be in possession of the kinds of goods which robbers target and may also be more likely to walk in places or at times where there is a greater risk of robbery. But if one assumes that men are in general physically stronger than women, and more likely to be armed with weapons such as firearms, they may be 'harder' targets (the possibility that they may be armed with a firearm may however be a motivation for targetting them, as the acquisition of firearms is sometimes a principal motivation for robbery). Whatever the overall distribution of robbery victimisation by gender, it appears that men are far more likely to physically resist a robbery, or be expected to do so by the robbers, contributing to the fact that men constitute a far higher proportion of victims of murder during the course of robbery than do women (women are far more likely, however, to be the victims of robbery related rapes). In the study of murder referred to above, men accounted for 92 per cent of crime (mostly robbery) related murder victims (CSVR 2008a:45). Where victims don't cooperate with the robbery, such use of violence might partly serve to punish the victim for not accepting the perpetrator's control of the situation and is not necessarily purely a means of overcoming victim resistance (*op cit*: 70–73).

Official statistics on robberies differentiate aggravated robbery (robbery with a weapon such as a gun or a knife) and common robbery (where the robber does not use a weapon, for instance 'bag-snatching' or 'smash and grab' incidents). Aggravated robbery statistics in turn differentiate between seven sub-categories: vehicle hijacking, residential robbery and business robbery (these are sometimes called the 'trio' robberies), bank robberies, cash-in-transit heists and truck-hijackings and 'street robberies', the last-mentioned being an omnibus category for robberies which do not fall into the first six categories and which mostly take place in public spaces. In a report on violent crime in South Africa, the first six of these were labelled the 'high profile six' related to the fact that they are given much prominence in the media and in public and official discourse around violent crime (CSVR 2009). The prominence given to them is related partly to the fact that they are the forms of robbery and violent crime which have the biggest impact on the formal business sector and middle class, the groups which have the greatest power to shape official discourse around violent crime.[25] Aggravated street robberies, however, account for a clear majority (and possibly more than two-thirds) of incidents of robbery and may be assumed to be the form of robbery that makes the greatest contribution to the murder rate.

Robberies as a contributor to murder are particularly significant in metropolitan and other urban areas because it is in these areas (notably in South Africa's 'multi-metropolitan' Gauteng province) that robbery, particularly armed or aggravated robbery, is most entrenched.

Other forms of violence

There is no single way of defining the forms of violent crime and there are potentially multiple ways of doing so. One attempt at providing a comprehensive list of forms of violence, for instance, differentiates twelve different forms of violent crime (CSVR 2007: 57). Examples of other categories of violence based on this list might include:

- Conflict between groups over territory, markets, or power (such as conflict within the taxi industry or related to conflict between gangs).
- Vigilantism and excessive use of force by law enforcement personnel.
- Violence related to resistance to law enforcement action.
- Hate crime including xenophobic violence, racial violence or anti-gay violence.

As illustrated in table 5 it appears that both vigilantism (4.9 per cent of murders) and self-defence (3.6 per cent) related killings are small but significant contributors to official murder statistics. As indicated in the discussion related to that table, available data also puts rape homicide at roughly 2 per cent of all homicides, indicating that these are fewer than vigilantism related and self-defence related homicides. However, this should not by any means be understood to imply that vigilantism, for instance, is more widespread than sexual violence, but merely that a very high proportion of incidents of vigilantism have a fatal outcome, while rape homicides make up a much smaller proportion of rapes.

The series of violent attacks against foreigners in May 2008, and other events of this kind, have given some prominence to the issue of xenophobic violence, raising the question about the relative significance of this kind of violence in contributing to overall levels of violence in South Africa. However, there is no reason to believe that xenophobic violence, or other hate crime, is anywhere near as significant as the 'major forms of violence' referred to above.[26]

The issue of violence involving foreigners also illustrates some of the difficulties in defining 'forms' of violence. For instance in some incidents of violence related to arguments where foreigners and South Africans are involved, some reference might be made, in a disparaging way, to the foreigners' identity. However, the incident might be a dispute over money or other property, or motivated by jealousy and more appropriately classified as an 'argument related assault' than an incident of 'hate crime', notwithstanding that a foreigner is involved and xenophobic prejudices are manifested in the incident.

The occurrence of violence in the lives of children

There are important differences in the victimisation of children (defined in different studies as those under eighteen or those under twenty-one). In general, it seems that children suffer higher levels of victimisation from violence. This violence, whatever the form it may take, is mostly at the hands of their peers or people known to them. Thus youth respondents (aged twelve to twenty-two) in a 2005 national youth victimisation study experienced assault at a rate 7.5 times greater than those responding to a 2003 victimisation survey of adults (over sixteen years) (Leoschut and Burton 2006: 47).[27] In a study of violence at schools, those at primary schools (roughly six to twelve years of age) were even more likely than those at high schools (roughly thirteen to eighteen) to have been assaulted at school, though the opposite applied in relation to robbery (Burton 2008: 18). However, the high level of violence in the lives of children is not strongly associated with fatal or other serious injury. As shown in Table 1, the number of deaths recorded in the twenty to twenty-four age group is more than double that in the fifteen to nineteen year age group, and this in turn is more than ten times greater than that in the ten to fourteen age group. In addition, as indicated, looked at in per capita terms the homicide rate in the fifteen to nineteen age bracket is substantially lower than that that in each of the succeeding five-year age bands, up to and including the forty to forty-four year age bracket.

Table 6 indicates that this dramatic increase in violent mortality between older children and young adults is partly related to an increasing level of firearm fatalities, with the number of these types increasing far more dramatically than those related to the use of sharp force between the fifteen to twenty-five and the twenty-five to thirty-four age bands.

Table 6: Number of youth victims of firearm and sharp force fatal injuries (derived from NIMSS data)[28]

	Firearms	*Sharp force*
2004		
15-24	1022	885
25-34	1586	1057
per cent increase	55	19
2005		
15-24	889	1000
25-34	1371	1158
per cent increase	54	16
2007		
15-24	989	1452
25-34	1497	1576
per cent increase	51	9

While the incidence of homicide appears to peak in the twenty-five to twenty-nine age band (see table 1), the age band which is most affected by rape victimisation is somewhat younger. The study of Gauteng 2003 rape dockets indicated that girls and young women in the thirteen to twenty-two year age band accounted for 45 per cent of rape victims. By comparison those in the twenty-three to thirty-two year age band accounted for 22 per cent of victims (CSVR 2008b: 54).[29]

CONCLUSION

This chapter has sought to present a picture of violent crime in South Africa focusing firstly on the crime of murder, and then on the three major forms of violence. More could be said about the characteristics of these types of violence: for instance, as in relation to the characteristic times at which and localities in which they occur, the degree to which they are associated with alcohol use, or the involvement of individuals and groups in their perpetration. Other debates around the characterisation of violence also concern questions such as to what extent and in what way violence is linked to the problem of organised crime.

A further key issue in characterising violence concerns questions about the apparent high degree of violence in South Africa. Not only is violence widespread, but many people believe that many of the perpetrators are particularly malevolent, engaging in violence gratuitously 'for the sake of violence' rather than for any other overt purpose. Though it appears to be true that violence of this kind is part of the overall problem, as noted above, much violence is in many ways 'instrumental'. For instance, many robbers do not inflict deliberate harm on victims who cooperate with them though they may not hesitate to kill or otherwise seriously harm those who resist or otherwise obstruct the robbery.

Another major issue, which has not been addressed in this chapter, concerns the quantification of violence. Internationally it is broadly accepted that crime statistics do not provide a full picture of the extent of crime owing to the problem of under-reporting which is believed to affect all offence categories with the exception of murder. Crime statistics therefore represent not all crime but merely reported crime. Nevertheless, where they are recorded by the police in a reliable way, they may often be regarded as indicators of underlying crime trends, though they are also affected by changing patterns of reporting. But there is good reason to doubt that current South African statistics pertaining to categories of violent crime can be understood in this way. This is related to the fact that since 2003-2004, government has committed itself to reducing violent crime in each year by 7 to 10 per cent. This and other factors have fed into a widespread problem within the SAPS of deliberate non-recording of offences by police at police stations. Non-recording is concentrated in certain categories of violent crime. It is therefore not merely the case that violent crime statistics do not tell us the full story about levels of violence, but also that they cannot be regarded as providing reliable indicators of violent crime, or reporting trends (Bruce 2010).

The mechanism that has been developed within crime research to compensate for the deficiencies of crime statistics is the victimisation survey. Three major national victimisation surveys (of persons sixteen and over)[30] have been conducted in South Africa in 1998, 2003 and 2007 (Household Surveys Unit 1998; Burton *et al* 2004; Pharoah 2008) However, it would appear that the outcome of these surveys can also not be taken at face value as providing a full picture of violent, and other, crime in South Africa. In other countries it has been found that there are often systematic ways in which victimisation surveys distort the crime picture,[31] and this phenomenon is probably more extensive in South Africa due to its linguistic and cultural diversity and the very substantial stratifications, not just of class and race but also of life experience, which characterise it. Attempts at understanding the extent and nature of violence therefore need to use the results, not only of crime statistics, but also of victimisation surveys, with some caution. Although not all of these sources are reflected here, this chapter has engaged with South African crime statistics and victimisation survey data and has attempted to present as 'true' a picture as is possible taking into account what is known about the limitations of these types of data sources.

A third area, which has not been addressed in this chapter, is the important question about why South Africa is so violent. Many efforts to engage with this type of question focus on specific aspects of the problem of violence. Some of the more in-depth work on explaining violence in South Africa, for instance, focuses primarily on sexual violence. But the problem of violence is obviously one which goes far beyond this. The chapter then takes us towards accounting for violence by providing a profile of the main manifestations of violence that we must account for if we are to provide meaningful explanations. Explaining why South Africa is so violent is obviously also part of developing responses to the problem of violence, and such responses need to address the overall problem of violence rather than selective aspects of it. Finally, it should be emphasised that the concept of forms of violence has been used here to illuminate our understanding of the nature of the problem of violence in South Africa. This is not intended to imply that there are rigid boundaries between these categories of violence. Research on violence against women, for instance, demonstrates that there are various ways in which incidents of assault related to arguments and sexual violence overlap with each other. Perpetrators of rape are frequently involved in other argument or assault type violence against women, particularly their female partners. Thus a recent study found that 52 per cent of men who admitted to having perpetrated acts of rape against women also admitted to involvement on more than one occasion in intimate partner violence (for those who said they had not raped the figure was 20 per cent). Sometimes intimate partner violence is intended to coerce a female partner into agreeing to sexual intercourse or to punish her for being unwilling (Wood and Jewkes 2001). As indicated above, incidents of robbery are sometimes accompanied by acts of rape. The distinction between robbery or violent property crime and assaults related to arguments is also blurred somewhat if one takes into account that many of these arguments are about money or items of property. In the CSVR study of murder, arguments over money or other material goods accounted for 39 per cent of the cases where the motivation for the argument was apparent (CSVR 2008a: 62).

Related to this is the fact that many perpetrators of violent crime are linked to a number of different forms of violence. Though available statistics indicate that, on average, less than 20 per cent of suspects in cases of serious violent crime have previous convictions[32] this is partly a reflection of the relative inefficiency of the criminal justice system in obtaining convictions against perpetrators. A more telling figure is provided in a recent study in which, among men who indicated that they had at some point been involved in rape, 58 per cent also indicated previous involvement in stealing or robbery on more than two occasions, 44 per cent had on at least one occasion been involved in a fight with knives, and 26 per cent indicated that they had at some point had possession of an illegal gun (for those who indicated that they had not perpetrated rape the figures were 24 per cent, 20 per cent and 6 per cent respectively) (Jewkes *et al* 2009: 23).[33] Another study involving interviews with perpetrators of violent crime noted that:

> [R]ather than taking place in discrete arenas, either as violence in the public domain against strangers, or violence in the 'private' domain against intimate partners ... many of these individuals are implicated in a wide range of violent or coercive interactions, whether with girlfriends, 'friends' or the 'strangers' they explicitly go to rob and hijack (HSRC 2008: 103).

Violence in South African society is a multifaceted phenomenon, but the core of the problem is a culture of violence and criminality, which is most concentrated in metropolitan areas and which involves young men who are engaged in active criminal lifestyles, although their violence or coercion may also be targeted at people who are known to them. Within the peer networks in which they are situated, credibility is partly earned by demonstrating the readiness to resort to extreme violence with a weapon, and this culture is therefore strongly linked to South Africa's problem of armed violence. Understanding why South Africa is so violent is therefore about understanding how it is that South Africa has produced, and continues to sustain, this culture.

NOTES

1   The terms 'violence' and 'violent crime' are used interchangeably. This chapter focuses on physical violence and not other kinds of violence such as 'structural' or 'symbolic' violence.

2   At law, homicides may be distinguished as either cases of murder (the intentional and unlawful killing of a human being), culpable homicide (the criminally negligent killing of another human being) and justifiable homicide (intentional but lawful killings as in cases where people are judged to have acted reasonably in self-defence against a threat of death or serious injury). Where it appears that a death has been caused by the actions of another person the SAPS opens either a murder docket or a culpable homicide docket (it is possible that the latter are usually opened in cases where people are killed by a vehicle driven by another person). The main sources of data on fatal violence which are used in this article are statistics from the National Injury Mortality Surveillance system on deaths from violence, SAPS murder statistics and studies of murder in South Africa, usually based on SAPS murder dockets. It may be noted that all of these sources of data deal with deaths resulting from violence, including many which at law would be classified as cases of murder, but also some which may be classified as cases of justifiable or culpable homicide. Related to this, the terms 'homicide' and murder are to some degree used interchangeably in this chapter.

3   The National Injury Mortality Surveillance System and a number of docket studies undertaken by SAPS provide the two major sources of homicide data. The former, which collects data on non-natural deaths at mortuaries, has an urban, particularly metropolitan, bias. SAPS reports

consistently lack information on sampling procedures.

4   Translated into per capita figures the picture looks quite different. Mapped against population data on size of each age band this indicates that during these three years those most at risk of homicide victimisation were in the 25-29 age band, followed by the 30-34, 20-24, 35-39, 40-44 and 15-19 year age bands. From this perspective the 40-44 group is victimised at more than double the rate of 15-19 year-olds.

5   In 2005, NIMSS data indicated that women were 11.2 per cent of homicide victims in the metros and 15.1 per cent outside them. Differences were slightly smaller in 2003 and 2007.

6   The totals for gender of victims are slightly higher than those for weapons (see table 4) as data on gender is more consistently recorded than that on weapons. Data on the overall gender profile of homicide victims and on the profile of deaths in the metros was not provided in some years.

7   The figure of 22 per cent cited earlier is from the same study cited in Graham, Bruce and Perold 2010: 63. The age distribution reflected here is specific to murder and is not common to all forms of violence.

8   Male suspects in argument related cases constituted 48 per cent of all male suspects. The high proportion of male and female suspects in this category reflects the fact that suspects are more often identified in argument related murders .

9   NIMSS data on the four major metropolitan areas indicates that there were decreases in firearm homicides in each of these areas between 2003 and 2007, though in Cape Town the number of firearm homicides increased from 2004 onwards after decreasing dramatically between 2003 and 2004. Trends in Pretoria and Johannesburg were also not uniform. Cape Town and Pretoria, however, recorded more homicides in 2007 than in 2003, related to increases in sharp force homicides (CSVR 2009: 25).

10   Figures do not add up to 100 per cent as percentages for other weapons/methods are not provided in this table. 'Other' figures for 2005 exclude data on burn victims as this was not provided in that year. The 'other method' category here excludes data in NIMSS reports headed 'other' as this was not provided in most years.

11   Table 5 has been constructed using data provided in the 2009 SAPS crime report (SAPS 2009: 10-11) based on an analysis of a representative sample of 1 348 murder dockets linked to cases reported nationally from 1 April 2007 to 31 March 2008 and a supplementary report (SAPS 2010) which indicates that female victims constituted 14.4, and male victims 85.6 per cent. The totals reported are not identical to those in the SAPS report which appear in brackets in the right hand column. This table should therefore be seen as a close approximation of the SAPS data. The categories in the left column are those applied by the author of this chapter. Those in the second column are from the SAPS reports.

12   Vigilantism type murders accounted for 7 per cent of murders in known circumstances, a figure comparable to the 5 per cent in table 5. Though self-defence also accounted for 4 per cent in the CSVR study there may be differences in the way in which the category is applied.

13   See also Abrahams et al 2008, which estimates that 16 per cent of female homicide victims in South Africa are victims of rape. If female victims constitute roughly 15 per cent of all victims, 16 per cent of the latter figure provides a figure of 2.4 per cent.

14   Child sexual abuse is understood here as part of the overall problem of sexual violence.

15   The paper compares the results of the national victimisation surveys conducted by the Institute for Security Studies in 2007 and 2003 with one conducted by Statistics South Africa in 1998. Note that both women and men might under-report assaults for various reasons.

16   More than three quarters (77 per cent) of the cases where women were victimised were assault GBH (65 per cent) or attempted murder (12 per cent) cases, though the proportion was much lower in Randburg (45 per cent) which is also a CBD area where robbery is prevalent, than in Mamelodi (73 per cent).

17   Arguably this distinction is not purely relevant to homicides but to assaults generally, though the term 'lethal intent' would need to be substituted with, for instance, 'assaultive or lethal intent'.

18   Data on per capita rates of murder for instance indicate that specific African and Coloured communities have far higher murder rates than any of the middle class areas (for instance the communities selected in CSVR 2008a were selected on the basis of per-capita murder rates). This assertion is not supported by the data from victimisation surveys in Pharoah 2009 (at 9 and 11) but it is assumed here that the latter data is not reliable. This should also not be taken to imply that it is the poorest communities (such as those in rural areas) that suffer most from violence, though it appears, for instance, that informal settlements in township areas often suffer much higher rates of violence than the rest of the townships.

19   Figures in the report indicate that 49 respondents indicated that they had raped a man of whom 43 were amongst the 27.6 per cent (466) who had been involved in the rape of a woman and 6 were amongst the 1220 respondents (72.4 per cent) who indicated that they had not. Until the Sexual Offences Act, 32 of 2007 came into effect, South African law only recognised rape as an offence which could be perpetrated by a man against a woman. Along with anal rape of women, rape of men was regarded as 'indecent assault'.

20   Other data on this issue is presented in CSVR 2008b. Note that stranger rapes, and predatory stranger crimes more generally, are probably more common in urban and metropolitan areas. In addition, the proportion of stranger rapes varies substantially by the age of victims, contributing to 48 per cent of rapes of women of 18 years and over.

21   The origins of this controversy lie in the feminist politics of recent decades which have partly focused on achieving acknowledgment of rape, including for instance marital rape, and date rape, as a serious crime. The rhetorical formulation that 'rape is a crime of violence and not of sex' (precluding the possibility that rape may be a crime of both violence and sex) may be seen to have been deployed towards this end.

22   Data from studies of this kind do not indicate how many women were able to successfully resist rape. As with robbery, resistance might enable a person to defeat the attempt at victimising them, but simultaneously carries a risk of increasing the degree, and/or likelihood, of physical harm.

23   It is also assumed here that robbery can be imagined within a pyramidal type of structure with robbery murders at the top, aggravated (armed robberies) across a band in the middle, and 'common' (unarmed) robberies at the bottom. It is possible though that, in South Africa in particular, there is a tendency for robbers to be armed so that, compared to the assault pyramid for instance, the base of the pyramid is narrower. Whether this is true or not the data from the 2007 victimisation survey (Pharoah 2008: 7), indicating that in 2007 robbers were unarmed in fewer than 4 per cent of cases, is unlikely to be plausible. Common (unarmed) robbery is likely to be reported at much lower rates than aggravated (armed) robbery. But even 2008–2009 SAPS crime statistics indicate that common robberies make up at least 33 per cent of robberies. This, notwithstanding the fact that these statistics probably reflect the impact of systematic non-recording by the police of reported common robbery over several years (Bruce 2010).

24   Note however that the National Youth Victimisation Survey indicated that in cases of robbery involving young people perpetrators appear to be frequently known to the victim and included 'known community members' (38 per cent), learners at school (21 per cent) and other friends or acquaintances (11 per cent) (Leoschut and Burton 2006: 57-58).

25   This does not necessarily imply that the majority of businesses which are robbed are in the 'formal sector' or that the majority of homes which are robbed are in middle class areas.

26   The violence in May 2008 killed 62 people (International Organisation for Migration 2009:2), less than 0.5 per cent of all people killed in incidents of violence in South Africa that year.

27   Note the reservations expressed about victimisation survey data in the conclusion of this chapter. One can only speculate as to whether the factors contributing to the limited reliability of these surveys have different effects on youth and adult surveys.

28   The number of victims is calculated here by multiplying raw figures on the number of homicide victims in each age band (see table 1) with figures for the percentage of youth victims of firearm

and sharp force homicide in each age category provided in NIMSS data. The latter percentages are only provided in the NIMSS reports for these ten-year age bands.)

29   Sexual crimes against children by adults are more likely to involve deception or manipulation or the threat of violence as opposed to the actual use of physical force. The proportion of male victims of sexual abuse (relative to the proportion amongst other age categories) may be greatest amongst young (eleven years and younger) children.

30   Figures from a national youth victimisation survey (Leoschut and Burton 2006) and a survey of violence at schools (Burton 2008) have also been referred to in this article.

31   For instance Silber and Geffen (2009: 38) cite a 1985 article indicating that 'a study in the United States showed that people with university degrees recalled three times as many assaults as those with high school education'.

32   In a SAPS murder docket study (2004) 14 per cent of suspects had criminal records of whom roughly a third had criminal records for violent crime (CSVR 2007: 126–127). In a more recent murder docket study 19 per cent of suspects had a criminal record (CSVR 2008a: 101). In a study of rape in Gauteng in 2003, 18 per cent of suspects had previous convictions of whom just over half (52 per cent) had convictions for offences involving some form of violence (CSVR 2008b: 97-98).

33   Note that 13 per cent of rape perpetrators and 6 per cent of those who said they had not perpetrated rape indicated that they had been imprisoned at some point.

REFERENCES

Abrahams N, L Martins, R Jewkes, S Mathews, L Vetten and C Lombard (2008) The epidemiology and the pathology of suspected rape homicide in South Africa. *Forensic Science International.* Doi:101016/j.forsciint.2008.03.006.

Altbeker A (2008) Murder and robbery in SA: A tale of two trends. In Van Niekerk A, S Suffla and M Seedat (Eds) *Crime, Violence and Injury Prevention in South Africa: Data to Action.* Cape Town: Medical Research Council.

Brookman F (2003) Confrontational and revenge homicides among men in England and Wales. *The Australian and New Zealand Journal of Criminology* 36 (1): 34–59.

Bruce D (2010) 'The ones in the pile were the ones going down' – the reliability of current violent crime statistics. *SA Crime Quarterly (31).* Pretoria: Institute for Security Studies.

Burton P (2008) *Merchants, Skollies and Stones – Experiences of School Violence in South Africa.* Cape Town: Centre for Justice and Crime Prevention.

Burton P, A du Plessis, T Leggett, A Louw, D Mistry and H van Vuuren (2004) National victims of crime survey: South Africa 2003. Monograph No. 101. Pretoria: Institute for Security Studies.

Centre for the Study of Violence and Reconciliation (CSVR) (2007) The violent nature of crime in South Africa: A concept paper prepared for the Justice, Crime Prevention and Security Cluster. Johannesburg: Centre for the Study of Violence and Reconciliation & Department of Safety and Security.

Centre for the Study of Violence and Reconciliation (CSVR) (2008a) Streets of pain, streets of sorrow: The circumstances of the occurrence of murder in six areas with high rates of murder. Johannesburg: Centre for the Study of Violence and Reconciliation & Department of Safety and Security.

Centre for the Study of Violence and Reconciliation (CSVR) (2008b) A state of sexual tyranny: The prevalence, nature and causes of sexual violence in South Africa. Unpublished report. Johannesburg: Centre for the Study of Violence and Reconciliation & Department of Safety and Security.

Centre for the Study of Violence and Reconciliation (CSVR) (2009) Creating a violence free society: Key findings and recommendations of the study on the violent nature of crime in South Africa. Unpublished report. Johannesburg: Centre for the Study of Violence and Reconciliation & Department of Safety and Security.

Collins R (2008) *Violence – A Micro-Sociological Theory*. Princeton: Princeton University Press.

Gear S (2007) Behind the bars of masculiinity: Male rape and homophobia in and about South African men's prisons. *Sexualities* 10 (2): 209–227.

Graham L, D Bruce, H Perold and others (2010) Youth violence and civic engagement in the SADC region. Unpublished report prepared for the Southern African Trust, 17 March.

Household Surveys Unit (1998) Victims of Crime Survey. Pretoria: Statistics South Africa.

Human Sciences Research Council (HSRC) (2008). Case studies of perpetrators of violent crime. Unpublished report. Pretoria: Human Sciences Research Council and the Centre for the Study of Violence and Reconciliation.

International Organisation for Migration (2009) Towards tolerance, law, and dignity: Addressing violence against foreign nationals in South Africa. International Organisation for Migration (IOM), Regional Office for Southern Africa.

Jewkes R and N Abrahams (2002) The epidemiology of rape and sexual coercion in South Africa: An overview. *Social Science & Medicine* 55 (7): 1231–1244.

Jewkes R, Y Sikweyiya, R Morrel and K Dunkle (2009) Understanding men's health and use of violence: Interface of rape and HIV in South Africa. South African Medical Research Council, University of KwaZulu-Natal and Emory University.

Leoschut L and P Burton (2006) How rich the rewards? Results of the 2005 National Youth Victimisation Study. Cape Town: Centre for Justice and Crime Prevention.

Levi M and M Maguire (2002) Violent crime. In Maguire M, R Morgan and R Reiner (Eds) *The Oxford Handbook of Criminology* (3rd Edition). Oxford: Oxford University Press.

Mathews S, N Abrahams, LJ Martin, L Vetten, L van der Merwe and R Jewkes (2005) Every six hours a woman is killed by her intimate partner: A national study of female homicide in South Africa. Cape Town: South African Medical Research Council.

Myburgh J (2009) Did 142 academics & others get it wrong on crime? Politicsweb, 15 September. http://www.politicsweb.co.za/politicsweb/view/politicsweb/en/page71619?oid=143475&sn=Detail [Accessed 18 January 2010].

Myburgh J (2010) On race and crime: A reply. Politicsweb, 17 January http://www.politicsweb.co.za/politicsweb/view/politicsweb/en/page71619?oid=156282&sn=Detail [Accessed 18 January 2010].

National Injury Mortality Surveillance System (NIMSS) (2000) A profile of fatal injuries in South Africa 2000: Second annual report of the National Injury Mortality Surveillance System. Medical Research Council and UNISA Institute for Social and Health Sciences. Available at: http://www.sahealthinfo.org/violence/nimss2000parti.pdf.

National Injury Mortality Surveillance System (NIMSS) (2001) A Profile of fatal injuries in South Africa: Third annual report of the National Injury Mortality Surveillance System 2001. Medical Research Council and UNISA Institute for Social and Health Sciences. Available at: http://www.sahealthinfo.org/violence/nimssannual2001.htm.

National Injury Mortality Surveillance System (NIMSS) (2002) A profile of fatal injuries in South Africa: Fourth Annual Report of the National Injury Mortality Surveillance System 2002. Medical Research Council and UNISA Institute for Social and Health Sciences. Available at: http://www.sahealthinfo.org/violence/nimss.htm.

National Injury Mortality Surveillance System (NIMSS) (2003) A profile of fatal injuries in South Africa: Fifth Annual Report of the National Injury Mortality Surveillance System 2003. Medical Research Council and UNISA Institute for Social and Health Sciences. Available at: http://www.sahealthinfo.org/violence/injury2004.htm.

National Injury Mortality Surveillance System (NIMSS) (2004) A profile of fatal injuries in South Africa: Sixth Annual Report of the National Injury Mortality Surveillance System 2004. Medical Research Council and UNISA Institute for Social and Health Sciences. Available at: http://www.sahealthinfo.org.za/violence/2004injury.htm.

National Injury Mortality Surveillance System (NIMSS) (2005) A profile of fatal injuries in South Africa: Seventh Annual Report of the National Injury Mortality Surveillance System 2004. Medical Research Council and UNISA Institute for Social and Health Sciences. Available at: http://www.sahealthinfo.org/violence/2005injury.htm.

National Injury Mortality Surveillance System (NIMSS) (2007) A profile of fatal injuries in South Africa: Ninth Annual Report of the National Injury Mortality Surveillance System 2004. Medical Research Council and UNISA Institute for Social and Health Sciences. Available at: http://www.mrc.ac.za/crime/nimms_rpt_Nov08.pdf.

Newham G (2008) Reclaiming our homes: Tackling residential robbery in Gauteng. *SA Crime Quarterly* 23: 7-12. Pretoria: Institute for Security Studies.

Pharoah R (2008) The dynamics of crime: Comparing the results from the 1998, 2003 and 2007 National Crime and Victimisation Surveys. ISS Paper 177. Institute for Security Studies.

Pharoah R (2009) Who is most at risk? Victimisation trends in the 2007 national crime and victimization survey. ISS Paper 182. Institute for Security Studies.

Silber G & N Geffen (2009) Race, class and violent crime in South Africa: Dispelling the Huntley thesis. *SA Crime Quarterly (30):* 35-43.

South African Law Commission (SALC) (2001) Sentencing: A compensation scheme for victims of crime in South Africa. Discussion Paper 97. Available at: http://www.doj.gov.za/salrc/index.htm. Retrieved on 4 November 2004.

South African Police Services (2003) Annual report of the South African Police Services for 2002/2003. Pretoria: SAPS Strategic Management (Head Office).

South African Police Service (2004) Murder analysis RSA. Unpublished report. Pretoria: Crime Information and Analysis Centre.

South African Police Services (2006) Annual Report of the South African Police Services for 2008/2009. Pretoria: SAPS Strategic Management (Head Office).

South African Police Service (2009) Crime Situation in South Africa. Pretoria: SAPS Strategic Management (Head Office). http://www.saps.gov.za/saps_profile/strategic_framework/annual_report/2008_2009/2_crime_situation_sa.pdf [accessed 22 January 2010]. (Note that this publication is part of the SAPS 2009 Annual report.)

South African Police Service (2010) Murder: an analysis. Unpublished document received by author from Crime Information Management, South African Police Service, 19 January 2010.

Vetten L, R Jewkes, R Sigsworth, N Christofides, L Loots and O Dunseith (2008) Tracking Justice: The attrition of rape cases through the criminal justice system in Gauteng. Johannesburg: Tshwaranang Legal Advocacy Centre, the South African Medical Research Council and the Centre for the Study of Violence and Reconciliation.

Wood K and R Jewkes (2001) Dangerous love: Reflections on violence amongst Xhosa township youth. In Morrel R (Ed) *Changing Men in Southern Africa*. Scottsville: University of Natal Press.

CHAPTER 18

Waiting for Godot:
Awaiting trial detainees in South Africa

Jeremy Gordin[1]

———

*What is that world like? It is one of repression and of baseness where the lowest instincts
prevail; it is a world of humiliation and whore's values ... it is a world with its own culture –
language, customs, laws, myths, structures; it is a world of promiscuity, of closeness
in fetid cells, of living in the clothes and beds of others, of greyness,
of losing all sense and appreciation of beauty ...*
(*The True Confessions of an Albino Terrorist*, Breyten Breytenbach, 1984)

Yet, in many parts of Africa, significant gaps exist between the state's de jure *and* de facto
compliance with international standards in respect of pre-trial detention.
(Martin Schönteich, 2008)

*The reality is that many unsentenced prisoners [in South Africa] spend long periods awaiting
trial and many of them will be acquitted*
(Lukas Muntingh, 2009a)

THE CARCERAL ARCHIPELAGO

It was in 1975 that Michel Foucault (1999: 297) famously suggested that we live in 'what one
might call [a] carceral archipelago'. He was perhaps influenced by the haunting title of
Alexander Solzhenitsyn's *The Gulag Archipelago*, his opus on the Soviet forced labour and
concentration camp system (*Gulag* being the Russian acronym for the whole system) which

had been published in the West a year before. During the forty-six-year long apartheid era, countless South Africans were made familiar with a similar sort of carceral archipelago.

It was of course not only political prisoners who knew about the local archipelago. Hundreds of thousands of 'ordinary' African men and women, even if they eschewed politics, knew all about the inside of jails because of the pass (*dompas*) laws.

With the ending of apartheid, that ghastly reality has ended and the local situation is of course different. Or is it? The country has a democratic government and there are no political prisoners or, at least, political detainees. Yet we still have inside our borders a prison archipelago although it is not as secret or murderous as that which existed before 1994. In South Africa there were in 2009 about 166 000 people 'behind bars', so to speak (Mashele 2009: xvi). That said, it would be wise to remember the caveat issued by Martin Schönteich:[2] that criminal justice statistics, like all statistics, need to be treated with caution, particularly in Africa, where in some countries data is manually collated … while '[o]thers collect data at irregular intervals, [and] while some do not consistently gather any quantitative data at all' (Schönteich 2008: 99). Nonetheless, there is little doubt that South Africa's prisons are filled to the brim.

SHOULD WE CARE ABOUT OUR PRISONS AND WHAT IS HAPPENING INSIDE THEM?

A plaque on the wall of Number Four, that part of the notorious old Fort Prison in Johannesburg which housed black prisoners under apartheid, apparently taken from the auto-biography of Nelson Mandela, *Long Walk to Freedom,* suggests that we should: 'It is said that no one truly knows a nation until one has been inside its jails. A nation should not be judged by how it treats its highest citizens but its lowest ones …'

Breyten Breytenbach, the poet jailed for underground anti-apartheid activities in 1975, published *The True Confessions of an Albino Terrorist* in 1984.[3] He wrote:

> Any society – so Winston Churchill declared on occasion – can be measured by its atti-tude to its prisoners.
>
> At the risk of emitting a series of platitudes and pious wishes I'd still like to make the following simple remarks.
>
> Prisons serve only to create prisoners. If society views prisoners as its outcasts, its anti-social elements, then they will indeed become and remain that. Penal reform, the treatment of prisoners – these are not the problems of specialists but of concern to everybody. The solution to crime is one of social consciousness to be solved by the whole of society (Breytenbach 1984: 314).

According to Muntingh (2009a: 195)[4] South Africa's imprisonment rate 'is calculated at 342 per 100 000 of the population, placing it in the top ten countries in the world, excluding non-democratic states'. This high incarceration rate, he adds, 'is achieving exactly the opposite of creating a safer society: it continues to fuel conditions for crime and re-offending'.

In 1995, South Africa had a prison population of just below 120 000. After ten years of democracy this had grown to more than 180 000, an increase of around 50 per cent. More significantly, the number of prisoners serving sentences longer than seven years (primarily for crimes of violence in contrast to the apartheid era during which the majority of prisoners were held for crimes of property such as housebreaking, theft and shoplifting) had increased from fewer than 30 000 in 1995 to nearly 69 000 by the end of 2008. The number of prisoners sentenced to life imprisonment increased from approximately 400 in 1995 to more than 8 000 by 2008 As noted earlier, at the end of 2009 there were some 166 000 people behind bars although, again as noted, the statistics are imprecise and also fluctuate (Muntingh 2009b: 203).

AWAITING TRIAL DETAINEES (ATDs)

A major grouping in the South African carceral archipelago is that commonly referred to as ATDs or awaiting trial detainees. Penal Reform International, a London-based NGO, describes awaiting trial detainees:

> Prisoners in pre-trial detention, or on remand, are those who have been detained without a sentence and are awaiting legal proceedings. They are also known as untried or unconvicted prisoners. The excessive length and use of pre-trial detention is a major cause of overcrowding in prisons. In some countries the majority of the prison population comprises detainees awaiting trial. In Nigeria, for example, more than 25 000 prisoners are currently detained in prisons without conviction due to delays in the justice system, missing files, absent witnesses and prison mismanagement. In India, as many as seven out of ten Indian prisoners are pre-trial detainees ...Articles 9 and 14 of the *International Covenant on Civil and Political Rights (ICCPR)* require that prisoners must be brought to trial and the proceedings completed within 'a reasonable time' or be released on bail. This reflects other principles, namely that everyone charged with a crime has the right to be presumed innocent until proven guilty and that the deprivation of liberty must be an exceptional measure. The UN Human Rights Committee has stated that: "What constitutes 'reasonable time' is a matter of assessment for each particular case. The lack of adequate budgetary appropriations for the administration of criminal justice ...does not justify unreasonable delays in the adjudication of criminal cases.[5]

ATDs, then, are people who have been arrested and charged, but whose trials either have not started or not been completed, for a variety of reasons. In other words, they have not been found guilty and are therefore 'innocent'. Yet in South Africa they are held in custody because either they cannot afford bail or they have been refused bail.

In 1995, the South African ATD population numbered 23 783. By 2000 it had increased to 57 811. In 2005, it came down to 47 305. But it then started climbing again – and in March 2008 there were, according to Ngconde Balfour, the then minister of correctional services, 52 662 awaiting-trial detainees in correctional facilities across the country (Kharsany 2008).[6]

To put it another way, roughly one-third of the entire prison population of the country is being held in custody *without trial*. By the end of 2008, nearly 45 per cent of the ATD population had been in custody, waiting for their trials to be finalised, for three months and longer; 26 percent had been in custody for longer than six months; about 6 000 had been incarcerated without a finalised trial for more than one year; there are an unknown number who have been held in custody for more than two years; and there are cases of ATDs who have been held for up to nine years (Muntingh 2009b: 204; Pauw 2009: Yaso and Gordin 2009).[7]

It has been calculated that two in five ATDs will eventually be acquitted. In other words, of the men, women and youthful teenagers presently awaiting trial in SA's badly overcrowded facilities, in many cases for years, about 22 000 are likely to be set free (Mashele 2009: xvi; Kharsany 2008). They are held in captivity although they are technically 'innocent' of any wrongdoing, deprived for weeks, months and sometimes years of liberty, education, and/or the opportunity to make a living. Even worse, scores of ATDs remain incarcerated only because they cannot afford to pay bail amounting sometimes to as little as R200.

Some caveats are now in order, in advance of a more detailed discussion of ATDs. First, the focus of this chapter is ATDs – people waiting for completed trials, who have not been convicted. This should not, however, be construed to strengthen the view that convicted prisoners 'deserve all they get' and that we need only be concerned about awaiting trial prisoners: prison conditions in South Africa are unacceptable for all who must stay in our jails, convicted or not, innocent or guilty, and for whatever the duration. The important issue here is not the guilt or innocence of any detainee, but the availability of a fair trial (which includes a trial within a reasonable time) and the humane treatment of all those detained by the state.

A second caveat is that the number of South African ATDs expressed as a percentage of the total prison population is, relatively-speaking, unexceptional, even low. It is 31.2 per cent, just above the world average of 30 per cent.[8] The percentage of ATDs versus total prison population in Italy is 48.3 per cent; in Denmark 35.5 per cent; in the Netherlands 34.7 per cent. In some of the sub-Saharan African states and India, it is high enough to make South Africa look good by comparison: in Nigeria 70 per cent of prisoners are awaiting trials; in Uganda 56 per cent of the prison population has been awaiting trial for more than three years; in Kenya it is 43.3 per cent. In India, 66.6 per cent of the prison population, about 250 000 people, are awaiting trial (World Prison Brief).[9]

So South Africa's ATD population, which hovers between 25 per cent and 30 per cent of the total number of prisoners, is neither uncommon nor especially shocking. Nonetheless, ATDs are of concern for at least three reasons.

No one should be subjected to even one night of detention in a local prison, given the conditions, especially the conditions for awaiting trial prisoners, prevailing in them. Second, it is undesirable for prisoners who are entitled to bail to be detained simply on grounds of poverty. Third, a spell, even a short spell, in a South African prison can be a death sentence owing to the high incidence of rape and consequent HIV/Aids infection.[10]

Why don't we care? Why, relatively-speaking, do we know so little about awaiting trial detainees (and about convicts in general)? In a country in which crime and, to a lesser extent, the justice system, are continually if not obsessively discussed, why is the issue of ATDs and indeed of all prisoners not front-of-mind?

Writer Michiel Heyns has remarked (2005) that '[a] nation that locks up some of its finest minds is at least assured of an impressive body of prison literature' and, in addition to the book he was reviewing (*Make A Skyf, Man!* by Harold Strachan), he goes on to name such books as HC Bosman's *Cold Stone Jug*, Hugh Lewin's *Bandiet*, and Breytenbach's *True Confessions of an Albino Terrorist*. But with the exception of Jonny Steinberg's *The Number*, there is, after 1994, virtually nothing to be found about or by individual prisoners and nothing at all about ATDs.

The reason is that the people written about before 1994, or who themselves wrote about prison, were political activists, freedom fighters, 'heroes of the struggle'. Most of the ANC's leaders and government officials present and just past (Mandela, Zuma, Kgalema Motlanthe, Siphiwe Nyanda, Jeremy Cronin and many many others) 'did time'; it was almost *de rigueur*, the red badge of courage for those involved in the struggle. Such people were generally literate, intelligent and committed. As for the books about jail in the pre-1994 days, they described and analysed a reprehensible system used as a means of oppression.

Today, however, our jails do not hold any political prisoners. They hold those who were in the majority before 1994, but to whom no one paid much attention: ordinary criminals. And those awaiting trial, ATDs, are simply people *accused* of ordinary, even if appalling, crimes. More often than not, ATDs, like convicts, emanate from the lowest and most miserable of society, and in addition they are generally only partially literate, if not illiterate. This means of course that there is no reporting about ATDs by ATDs, which is why there are no books or articles about them. One of the main reasons for ATDs being in prison longer than they should be is, ironically, also banal: a dysfunctional legal system. Their story is thus neither 'sexy' nor 'romantic' since it is not 'political'. It is not even related to something about which a conscientious citizen might feel indignant, such as a pass offence.

There is another reason why the situation of nonpolitical criminals is not a favourite cause. Steinberg hit the proverbial nail on its head in his book on prison gangs, *The Number*, when he underlined the abyss-like split between left-wing social histories on the one hand, and left-wing political histories on the other.

> It is as if the South African masses rose above their wretched circumstances and found an essential nobility which transcended time and place. The morbidity and violence of social life *which finds such lucid expression in the left's social histories finds no expression in its political histories* [my emphasis] (Steinberg 2004: 10–11).

Yet,

> [t]he reality, of course, is both more complicated and less comforting than that. Twentieth-century South Africa bore witness to a host of political and social movements that will never find a place in the lexicons of political orthodoxy; movements both politically articulate and chillingly anti-social; movements enraged by, and yet symptomatic of, the psychological damage inflicted by South African industrialization.

> Prison gangs are precisely that. They are a century old, avowedly political and yet horribly pathological … As such, they get too close to the bone. They show us why generations of young black men lived violent lives under apartheid, and why generations more will live violently under democracy *(ibid)*.

But, to be perhaps less literary about the matter, the main reason why so few people are interested in ATDs is that we live in a society in which crime is rampant and extremely frightening (Russell 2009; Altbeker 2007; Butler 2009). According to the 2008/09 Annual Report of the South African Police Services (SAPS), about fifty individuals are murdered every day in South Africa. In 2007, there were more than 50 000 reported rapes (Rape Crisis suggests only one in twenty rapes is reported) and in 2007 the 18 000 or so people who were robbed violently included thousands whose cars were hijacked (Russell 2009: 110). House and business robberies, often violent, are rife – the former having climbed by 13.5 per cent between 2006/7 and 2007/8, the latter having increased by 47.4 per cent during the same period (Mashele 2009: xiv). In addition, Mashele, formerly of the Institute of Security Studies, has pointed out that:

> A study conducted by the South African Law Reform Commission in 2000 found that only six percent of serious and violent cases of crime that were tracked resulted in a conviction; three-quarters of the cases did not make it to court; and of those that did get to court, prosecutors withdrew half. The other half of these cases went to trial and only one quarter of them resulted in convictions (2009: xvi).

And there is no reason to think that the conviction rate has improved. In short, although South Africans might be obsessed by crime – and, given the data, it is not surprising that they are – there is for obvious reasons precious little sympathy from anyone for those perceived to be criminals, no matter that they are awaiting trial and have not been charged (and even less, of course, for those convicted).

Imagine for a moment that Nadine Gordimer were to respond today about the prevalence of crime in the same way she did in 1999. She wrote then:

> If you move about in our cities you don't need to be a sociologist or a criminologist to identify the reason for the prevalence of crime. And it is not a bleeding-heart apologist response when the answer is: unemployment. To me, [Johannesburg's innumerable minibus taxis] are symbols of the immeasurable influx of people to the city since freedom was confirmed at the ballot box in 1994, the trek of many thousands who come to find work, and for whom there will be little possibility of finding it. When the humiliation of begging fails, desperation offers one way to survive – crime (quoted in Steinberg 2001: 1).

Were Gordimer to write that now, she would be howled down. The fate of ATDs is neither of burning concern to the public nor is it high on the priority list of human rights groups. The presumption of innocence is one – or is supposed to be one – of the fundamental principles of justice in a democratic society. Yet most South Africans assume – again, perhaps understandably – that prisoners, whether sentenced or not, are behind bars for a reason. While this may be the case for many, it is also not so for many others.

In summary, there is not much that is heroic or appealing about the terrain of the post-1994 prison archipelago and 'the criminal justice system'. Those outside looking in are suspicious and frightened of those inside, whether they are convicts or ATDs; and those inside, especially long-term ATDs without money or connections, feel lost, trapped and voiceless.

WHY SO MANY ATDs?

Where do ATDs come from? Why are so many held in jails for such long periods? To begin with, many people – accused of relatively petty crimes – often do not get bail. This is because the constitution requires that accused people have to be brought before a court without unreasonable delay. But when such people are brought before the court, they often come up against the chronic dysfunctionality of the prisons and judicial systems. The court cannot consider bail in a judicious manner without knowing certain information, such as an individual's correct identity, address, his or her previous criminal record, and whether he or she is facing any other criminal matters.

But in South Africa, where the state agencies continue to operate in different silos, and seem to suffer from information technology difficulties, '[g]etting hold of these records within a short time often poses a challenge', as Jerome Chaskalson and Ynze De Jong put it (2009: 90-1). Bail hearings are invariably postponed. In terms of the Criminal Procedure Act, this must be for a period not exceeding seven days. But it sometimes takes seven *months* before the necessary information is obtained, and the bail hearing is postponed time and time again. The court cannot make a 'balanced' bail decision – it cannot, for example, give bail to someone who is, unbeknown to the court, actually facing so serious a charge that she or he will run if freed – so the accused ends up in custody until the court feels confident that it can make a 'judicious' decision.

A second category of ATDs are those who have been granted the option of paying bail but remain in custody because they simply cannot afford bail, even when the amount is as low as R250.

Interestingly, the legislation governing bail and related issues (section 63A of chapter 9 of the Criminal Procedure Act 51 of 1977, as amended) makes provision for a head of a prison to request the court to reconsider the release, or the amendment of bail conditions, for ATDs charged with less serious offences – if prison conditions warrant this. But, as Chaskalson and De Jong tell us (2009: 92), notwithstanding the fearsome overcrowding of prisons, the provision is seldom used. Of those from the category who might be given bail – if the court felt confident that it knew something about them or that they could actually be found at some address if necessary – the problem often is partial literacy coupled with ignorance of how the system works. They are of course 'given' public defenders who work for Legal Aid SA (previously the Legal Aid Board) but these people are themselves overburdened. Sometimes they appear for people whose court files they had only seen for the first time a minute before appearing. Often they do not even have time to consult with a defendant as the presiding magistrate and pro-secutor try to keep the 'sausage machine' rumbling onwards. Often the ATD's case file will have disappeared. Sometimes she will not have heard her name being called early in the morning in whichever lock-up she is – and so misses her appearance in court. There are in many magistrate courts independent attorneys who can be found wandering the corridors, looking to make money – and some are experienced, sharp, and known to the court – but their *modus operandi* is money upfront.[11]

Another, major, category of ATD is those charged with a 'serious' crime – murder, rape, hijacking – and to whom the court cannot therefore grant bail. Their trial – which becomes many trials – is plagued by much the same difficulties as those faced by other ATDs: initial ignorance of the system; poor or venal representation; a lack of the proper documentation (as discussed above) and also lost documents, a problem endemic to the South African justice system; and long postponements of various kinds – due to an overburdened police force and an over-burdened court system. In summary, and to generalise: that ATDs are in custody for so long is due to what Shakespeare referred to as 'the law's delay'. The system is clogged and, as more people are arrested but fewer trials completed, it becomes ever more clogged.[12]

In his presentation to the portfolio committees on Justice and Constitutional Development, and Safety and Security, on 5 August 2008, former deputy minister of justice Johnny de Lange said *inter alia* that across the country regional courts had a 35 per cent backlog; the hours spent in court were 'low' (courts closing on average at 15h30 daily); and the average number of finalised cases by each regional court per month was only seven (Mashele 2009: xvi). As Mashele commented, 'This is a criminal justice system that has a lot in common with a ter-minally ill patient in need of emergency treatment.'

Sed quis custodiet ipsos custodes? (But who is to guard the guards themselves?)[13]

As noted above, the custodial system suffers from some serious information-sharing problems. State agencies do not or are unable to share information – thus *inter alia* delaying countless bail hearings. There is another sort of information dearth. Chaskalson and De Jong suggest (2009: 92) that, given that 78 per cent of ATDs have been denied bail, it might be useful, for example, for someone to find out on what basis this happened. Were all of the 78 per cent accused of serious offences and thus unable to convince the courts that it was in the interests of justice that they be released? Or are there large numbers of ATDs who have simply been refused bail for less serious offences? And if so, why? Knowing the answers to these questions 'will help shed light on both how the courts are applying the bail legislation and the impact of the legislation itself' (*ibid*).

Various components of the criminal justice system have a knock-on effect on one another. For example, taking a long time to finalise a trial obviously contributes to the size of the ATD prison population. And the large and increasing numbers of unsentenced people in prisons impose massive pressure on the Department of Correctional Services (DCS) in terms of infra-structure – staff, food, buildings, electricity, water, clothing, bedding – and of course, in terms of finance.

According to the Inspecting Judge of Prisons (IJOP), overcrowding has a significant impact on conditions of detention and adherence to human rights standards. And that last sentence hides a multitude of sins. Persistent overcrowding has been targeted by the IJOP as one of the major causes of the problems in prisons.

Having to house ATDs while simultaneously holding convicted prisoners has been, as Muntingh puts it (2009b), the source of many challenges for the Department of Correctional Services (DCS). For example, Muntingh suggests that the DCS has opted to distance itself from ATDs in the sense that it feels a greater responsibility towards sentenced offenders than those awaiting trial, 'regarding the latter [ATDs] essentially as a nuisance inherited from the previous regime' (*ibid*). Previously, the Department of Prisons was administered under the Ministry of Justice and was perceived to have a single 'custodial mandate'. As Muntingh points out, 'there is a policy gap in relation to the responsibility for awaiting-trial detainees' (2009b: 214).

To put it bluntly, the DCS is not enormously interested in ATDs and looks on them as an 'overcrowding problem' rather than a DCS responsibility. This is why ATDs receive little or no training, education or anything but housing and food (I shall return to this point below). Incidentally, of sentenced prisoners, those with sentences of less than two years in duration have also had their services curtailed. What this means, in effect, is that nearly 75 per cent of released offenders will not have had the benefit of a programme aimed at assisting them 'to lead crime-free and socially responsible lives after imprisonment as required by section 36 of the Correctional Services Act – they will simply have been locked up' (Muntingh 2009b: 202-3).

The DCS employs 42 000 staff members but 'staff in general [do not] possess the skills and knowledge to … ensure compliance with the Correctional Services Act'. There is also a serious shortage in the Department of professionals – social workers, educators, nurses, doctors and psychologists (Muntingh 2009b: 204-5). And HIV/AIDS has had a marked impact on DCS staff (*ibid*).

The DCS is not numerically short-staffed, except for professionals, but according to the IJOP, the real problems are poor production levels, absenteeism and low efficiency levels (Muntingh 2009b: 205).

The Correctional Services Act was promulgated in October 2004. In March 2005, the White Paper on Prisons and Correctional Services was released. As Muntingh explains, the Act has a retributionist approach, albeit restrained, to corrections: offenders should be punished and prison is the place to do that. The White Paper, however, has a rehabilitationist approach: offenders are people whose behaviour can be changed, and prison is the place to do that. The difficulty is that the vision of the White Paper is at odds with the reality of South African prisons, which remain fundamentally retributive; the policies derived from the White Paper have not been translated into new standing orders and job descriptions. New recruits have no idea therefore how to implement the rehabilitationist vision into daily activities. 'Older member remains untrained in, and sceptical of, rehabilitation' and the prisons remain in practice places of excessive retribution without a rights-based agenda (Muntingh 2009b: 206).

Budget increases for the DCS have been handsome since 1994. But the budget allocation has gone to security and infrastructure development, not to staff training, rehabilitation services, and post-release support for offenders. Explaining this irrational budgeting,

Muntingh (2009b) suggests that it is simply easier for the DCS to spend its money on large capital works and technologically advanced security systems rather than on rehabilitation and social reintegration programmes, which require unusual skills and high motivation.

It is also common cause that capital projects are more vulnerable to tender corruption. The 2006 Jali Commission – set in motion after countless complaints were raised about prisons, prisons administration and prisoners, and which issued a voluminous report after many years – found that the Department was fraught with corruption and not adequately under the control of the state. Financial management has been a disaster – there have been five qualified audit reports from the auditor general. The powers of the IJOP have been weakened by a 2002 amendment that removed reporting on corruption and fraud from the inspectorate's mandate. Moreover, mandatory reporting to the IJOP by the DCS is limited and restricted to such incidents as deaths in custody. In 2006, the United Nations Committee Against Torture noted that it was 'concerned at the high number of deaths in detention … [and] at the lack of inves-tigation of alleged ill-treatment of detainees and with the apparent impunity of law enforcement personnel (UN Report 2006: 5).

As regards conditions in prisons, in his report of 2007/8, the Inspecting Judge of Prisons observed that:

- Prisoners at 21 prisons were required to eat with their hands and were not issued with utensils and containers;
- At several prisons, prisoners were required to sleep on the floor, share beds, or were issued with inadequate bedding;
- Searches were conducted in a dehumanising manner and male prisoners are required to strip naked in front of staff and other prisoners with no privacy afforded;
- There were no facilities in 94 per cent of prisons to separate prisoners with contagious diseases;
- Only 56 per cent of prisons were equipped with classrooms;
- Only 40 per cent of prisons were equipped with workshops – and only 2 per cent of sentenced prisoners were involved in production workshops;
- 72 per cent of prisons had dining halls, but the majority of the halls were not used for this purpose and meals were taken in cells;
- More than 40 per cent of prisons were without libraries, although access to adequate reading material is a constitutional requirement (JIOP *Annual Report* 2007/8).

WHAT IS IT LIKE TO BE AN ATD?

This section narrates some of the harrowing stories about ATDs that I uncovered in research on the court system in 2009. They are not, of course, typical cases but they are tragic and reveal what can happen to detainees who literally get lost in the wheels of a dysfunctional system.

First, the case of Prince Molefe, 29, an alleged car hijacker who was in New Lock for nine years. New Lock is an assortment of single and communal cells in the heart of Pretoria Central Prison where thousands of ATDs are held. It was designed to house 2 400 ATDs but it is the norm that twice that number are held there. Violent criminals share beds with petty thieves; young offenders are in close proximity to older, hardened criminals. The DCS provides ATDs with no rehabilitation, training, educational or recreational programmes, or any social work or psychological services. 'We just sit here and rot,' said Molefe to journalist Jacques Pauw (2009). Every afternoon at three o'clock, after dinner, Molefe told Pauw, prisoners were locked into their overcrowded cells until early the next morning. Only a skeleton staff of warders remained on duty, leaving prisoners to their own devices and to those of the prison gangs and rapists.

Molefe was locked in a communal cell, which he said he shared with up to sixty prisoners, though the cell was supposed to house only twenty. He said the cell had one shower and two toilets. Molefe and four co-accused, allegedly part of a gang operating in Soshanguve and Ga-Rankuwa, were arrested in August 2000 and charged with robbery with aggravating circumstances. They were denied bail. Nine years after their arrest, in July 2009, the state had yet to call another three witnesses; the case could easily have lasted until July 2011. Molefe said he had been in and out of court more than a hundred times. The trial has been repeatedly postponed over the decade because witnesses were missing, one of the accused pleaded guilty (and was sentenced to fifteen years in jail), and another escaped, was re-arrested and transferred to Pretoria Central's C-Max.

Molefe was repeatedly denied bail, one magistrate saying that the seriousness of the charges against Molefe outweighed his right to liberty. Finally, however, in November 2009, partially as result of newspaper coverage, and a friend's hiring a reputable Pretoria attorney, Molefe was given bail.

Serge Christiano, an Angolan refugee, was held in New Lock for eight years before being found not guilty. He was apprehended in 1999 and charged with robbery, rape, attempted murder, assault, malicious damage to property and kidnapping. His arrest followed an attack on a house outside Pretoria during which a woman was raped and residents robbed at gunpoint (Pauw 2009; Yaso and Gordin: 2009). None of the residents could implicate Christiano – with the exception of a sole eyewitness who also happened to be Christiano's former girlfriend. Christiano claimed he had been framed, legal experts cautioned that his ex-girlfriend's testimony needed corroboration, Christiano had an alibi, his fingerprints were not found at the scene of the crime, and he was not found in possession of stolen goods. Yet the state went ahead with his prosecution for eight years. He was refused bail because he was considered a flight risk.

At one point – four years into his saga – he was so distraught that he slashed himself in open court with a razor and tried to swallow sleeping pills. Even after this incident (in 2004), he was found mentally fit to stand trial, and sent back to New Lock for another four years. 'It's hell being a foreigner in a South African prison. There was no end to my case. Postpone, postpone, postpone. I was desperate.' At the end of Christiano's trial, the regional court prosecutor conceded that only one state witness could identify Christiano and that there existed 'certain discrepancies' in the witness's evidence. The magistrate acquitted Christiano on all charges.

But he had lost everything – including his son (sent overseas to relatives), his car, and clothing shop.

Laurence Cramer was arrested for contempt of court on 16 July 2008 and taken to Diepkloof Prison, also known as Sun City, as an ATD (Cramer 2009). Cramer, who claimed to be a former special forces operative, was initially not too concerned as he thought going to prison would be like army basic training but with fewer weapons. In the admissions area, a warder said to him: 'You will be locked up with career criminals, murderers, rapists and gangsters. You will be attacked, stabbed, sodomised – and you can try and fight, but when five men come at you, in the night, in the yard, every day, you will give in to what they want: being tough isn't what it takes to survive Sun City. Get a lawyer to get you out of here.'

Cramer was given an orange overall, no socks, no jersey (this was in winter and it was freezing). A warder told him he would get a jersey, blanket, toothbrush and soap but he received none of those things. Though an ATD, he was put into a cell with men who had been sentenced that morning. They gave him useful advice, such as: "Wear plastic bags over your feet in the shower – these guys like to shit in the shower. Ask your family to send cigarettes and phone cards. You can use these to trade with – a place to sleep, a blanket, protection.' On his first night Cramer found himself in a cell designed for twenty; there were fifty-six prisoners in it. The cell was about 20m by 5m, with a toilet area to one side. The open-plan toilet consisted of a toilet (no toilet paper), urinal, two shower heads and two basins. The men showered from two o'clock to five o'clock in the morning. Of course, wrote Cramer, everyone, having been fed at the same time, wanted to use the one toilet at the same time.

Once they were locked in, in the late afternoon, out came the dagga, mandrax and tik. Thirty-four of the fifty-six slept on the icy floor, so jammed in that they could not sleep on their backs. Cramer had no cup or bottle so could not access water – and all around him men heaved and coughed. The smell of the cell with the smoke, stale sweat and bad breath was nauseating. In the middle of the night, Cramer was woken by an emissary of a bunch of lifers gathered in the toilet area. Cramer realised this could be trouble for him, that he was in all likelihood about to be raped. He attacked the man, and luckily his cell mates helped him. The group of men in the toilet area did not intervene.

Cramer's family had him released urgently and he was out by six in the evening, on the day after he went in. Most other ATDs do not have such luck, or families with money and knowledge.

SOLUTIONS?

South Africa's post-apartheid correctional system is seriously dysfunctional. 'The law's delay is tantamount to an assault on the spirit of human beings. 'The system can squeeeze the life out of the young, especially if they are also illiterate, resulting in a deadening frustration and lassitude. One can be stripped naked and humiliated, even if not made to do so literally – and in some jails prisoners are made to do so literally.

The number of people held so long in custody without trial in post-apartheid South Africa bespeaks the crumbling of an important part of the criminal justice system, which is one of the major pillars on which a constitutional democracy is founded. It is in addition illegal in terms of our own constitution as well as international standards and guidelines (Schönteich 2008: 94–9).

The incarceration of ATDs costs the taxpayer R2.2-million a day (Chaskalson and De Jong 2009). The longer a prisoner has to wait for his or her trial, the less likely it is that the trial will end in a conviction, yet the more likely it is that he or she will leave jail as a hardened, brutalised person, whether found guilty or not. Many youngsters – many people in general – are raped and contract HIV.[14]

WHAT ARE THE SOLUTIONS TO THE PROBLEM OF ATDs?

Certain avenues seem obvious and commonsensical. For example, it would make sense to release on bail as many ATDs as possible. Provided that the detainees are not accused of having used violence, or if they have already been in detention for as long as any prison sentence they would likely get if convicted, this would be one way of alleviating a number of problems. Apart from any issues of humanity or legality, it also makes sense given the cost to the state of keeping people in detention.

Minister of Justice Jeff Radebe commented on 4 March 2010 at a parliamentary media briefing given by the justice, crime prevention and security cluster[15] that a newly-appointed ministerial task team in the DCS would conduct an audit of certain categories of offenders so as to alleviate overcrowding.[16] Furthermore, he said, DCS officials had been mandated to put into action the 'controlled release' of ATDs who had been given bail of R1 000 or less but had been unable to pay it. Radebe also said that the Cabinet had resolved that the DCS would indeed be responsible for ATDs. Whether all or any of these changes will indeed happen, and how quickly, in an environment in which the amelioration of harsh conditions for ATDs and other prisoners is not a government or ANC priority – and in which 'fighting crime' *is* one – remains to be seen.

Besides releasing ATDs, who have not been accused of serious crimes, and of making the DCS responsible for ATD welfare, numerous, more specific suggestions have been made by numerous specialists in criminological issues like Schönteich (2008: 111-115), Chaskalson and De Jong (2009: 93-5), and Muntingh (2009b: 210-12).[17] Chaskalson and De Jong have recommended that there needs to be a powerful push to have justice cluster government departments share 'timeous and accurate digital information relating to the identity, previous criminal history and pending charges' of individuals who have come into conflict with law. At the same time, a strategy should be developed 'to enable the wider availability of pre-trial reports'. They also recommend that accurate information on bail data be shared by the various departments so that there is a better understanding of who is being refused bail, or who is not taking up bail, and why. If those not taking bail are predominantly people who cannot afford it, but who are not serious offenders, then decisions need to be made about whether people should be locked up merely because they are poor.

Muntingh has pointed to the dire need for reframing 'the purposes of imprisonment to give effect to the values of the Constitution'. This is because the country's sentencing regime has resulted in the over-utilisation of imprisonment and the neglect of noncustodial sentencing options, which has in turn been exacerbated by the minimum sentencing legislation. He also noted that the 2005 White Paper on Corrections has little to do with daily prison realities such as the physical conditions of detention, staff morale, poor accountability and human rights violations. There is, for example, no evidence from any reliable research that imprisonment reduces recidivism. In short, there has to be the proverbial paradigm shift among legislators in terms of which all policy development would be based both on evidence and on the aims of the constitution – and not just on locking people up.

Muntingh's second main recommendation is that the size of the prison population should be aligned to available physical resources (buildings and infrastructure) and human resources (staff and skills in the prison system). He stresses that studies have shown that 'prison population size has less to do with the rate of crime *than the policies and ideologies of governments with regard to incarceration* [my emphasis].'

One way of reducing overcrowding and massive imprisonment, Muntingh has argued, is for there to exist clear legislation for non-custodial sentences (where the offender is punished in some other way than prison – correctional supervision, restitution orders, suspended and postponed sentences, community service orders), especially if the court is contemplating a sentence of less than twenty-four months.

Muntingh also argues for the sharpening of the teeth of the judicial inspectorate of prisons, especially when it comes to being able to compel the commissioner of correctional services to take disciplinary action against officials. Muntingh believes too that the DCS's budget needs to be re-directed away from hi-tech infrastructure, private prisons, and so on, and be used to attract scarce skills, set up rehabilitation and education programmes, improve existing infrastructure, and to finance compliance with basic human rights.

Muntingh has also recommended (as have Chaskalson and De Jong) a proper pre-trial service that offers 'verified information' before an accused's first appearance and that would include SAPS supervision. Second, he suggests that SAPS avoid unnecessary arrests for minor offences, and third, that cases be properly screened to verify that there is a *prima facie* case, thus avoiding months of postponements for further investigation. With regard to ATDs specifically, Muntingh suggests that a monitoring and liaison mechanism should be established in prisons. He believes that such a mechanism could 'facilitate communication' between prison management, unsentenced prisoners, Legal Aid SA, and prosecutors and magistrates. He also argues that establishing a 'mechanism' that would enable and facilitate plea bargaining soon after the prosecutor has made a decision to prosecute, would help cut down on the time that cases are taking.

We all live in hope, but none more so, and perhaps none more in pathetic vein, than the awaiting trial prisoners languishing for years in various parts of democratic South Africa's prison archipelago. Palpable steps need to be taken to bring the whole sector into line with our constitution and a humane and just approach. As noted, as many ATDs as possible should be released on bail and the habit of postponing cases 'for further investigation' needs to end. The authorities have indicated that a ministerial task team is looking at the plight of ATDs. But given that the government, justice department and DCS are frighteningly sluggish in everything that they undertake and that the present administration seems caught up in internal political squabbling, there does not, alas, seem to be an imminent solution for those languishing in various parts of democratic South Africa's prison archipelago.

NOTES

1   The author wishes to thank Anthony Butler of the University of the Witwatersrand and an unidentified reviewer, an attorney, for their comments on an earlier draft.

2   Schönteich is senior legal officer: National Criminal Justice Reform at the Open Society Justice Initiative in New York.

3   Breytenbach recently returned to the subject of his prison time in an essay, 'You Screws!', pp 135–156, in *Notes from the Middle World: Essays by Breyten Breytenbach* (Chicago: Haymarket Books, 2009).

4   Muntingh is project coordinator of the Civil Society Prison Reform Initiative of the Community Law Centre at the University of the Western Cape.

5   http://www.penalreform.org/pre-trial-detention-2.html, accessed 7 March 2010.

6   These appear to be the best 'formal' figures currently available. According to Balfour, or according to the newspaper report, it cost the state 'R169 a day to keep *each* [ATD] imprisoned, and awaiting-trial detainees are kept in prison for 170 days on average' [my emphasis].

7   Much more research is needed to find out what percentage of ATDs have been in jail for specific periods of time - in other words, how many have been inside for longer than two years, three years, four years, and so on. This information does not seem to be available at the moment.

8   The largest awaiting-trial populations in the world (as a percentage of prison populations) are in the United States, China and India (www.worldmapper.org/posters/worldmapper_map294, accessed 7 March 2010).

9   www.kcl.ac.uk/depsta/law/research/icps/worldbrief, accessed 7 March 2010.

10   I have not touched on the prison conditions in many other sub-Saharan African countries – which are often deplorable owing to severe overcrowding, abuse, disease, and lack of food – because other African countries are not my subject. But *vide* Sarkin 2008.

11   Observations from the days spent by author in Hillbrow Magistrates' Courts, November 2009, following case of ATD, Loyiso 'Victory' Nzwana.

12   On 3 March 2010, in answer to a question for written response from ID president Patricia de Lille, a question given to her by Wits journalism's Justice Project, Minister of Justice Jeff Radebe confirmed that a total of 281 cases in the South Gauteng High Court were unable to go to appeal as a result of problems with [lost] transcripts. Radebe also said that: 'An audit of 54 cases out of the 281 cases revealed that the average waiting period since the date of lodging leave to appeal by applicants/prisoners in respect of the cases, is ± 2 years.' *National Assembly, Question for written reply, Q no. 5.*

13   Much of this section is based on Muntingh: 2009b.

14   'I am told the "punishment" of a recalcitrant gang member or the induction of a fresh arrival is now to be gang-raped and thus infected with HIV. Why should the innocent be allowed to live?' (Breytenbach 2009: 128).

15   www.info.gov.za/speeches/2010/10030410451001.htm, accessed 5 March 2010.

16   According to former minister of correctional services, Ngconde Balfour, in July 2008, 73 per cent of the country's 237 prisons were overcrowded. According to Balfour, South Africa's 237 prisons provide for the accommodation of 114 559 prisoners; however, 165 987 prisoners were in custody on 31 January 2008, 51 428 too many. This amounted to a national average overcrowding level of 45 per cent (Kharsany 2008).

17   Unless otherwise indicated, the recommendations that follow in the next paragraphs are taken from the pages indicated.

REFERENCES

Altbeker A (2007) *A Country at War with Itself: South Africa's Crisis of Crime.* Johannesburg: Jonathan Ball Publishers.

Beckett S (1965 2e). *Waiting for Godot: A Tragicomedy in Two Acts*. London: Faber and Faber.

Breytenbach B (1984 2ri). *The True Confessions of an Albino Terrorist*. Johannesburg: Taurus.

Butler A (2009 2e). *Contemporary South Africa*. Basingstoke: Palgrave Macmillan.

Chaskalson J and Y de Jong (2009) Bail. In Gould C (Ed) *Criminal (In)Justice in South Africa: A Civil Society Perspective*. Pretoria: Institute for Security Studies: 86–97.

Cramer L (2009) Time to kill. *Mail & Guardian*, 14-20 August 2009: 14–15.

Foucault M (1991) (1977; in French 1975). *Discipline and Punish: The Birth of the Prison*. Translated by Alan Sheridan. London: Penguin.

Gould C (Ed) (2009) *Criminal (In)Justice in South Africa: A Civil Society Perspective*. Pretoria: Institute for Security Studies.

Heyns M (2005) A multilingual potpourri of witty invective: *Make a skyf, Man!* by Harold Strachan: Review, *The Sunday Independent*, 23 January 2005.

Kharsany Z (2008) R1,5bn to keep suspects behind bars. *Mail & Guardian*, 17 July 2008.

Lewin H (1989) (reprint; new edition). *Bandiet Out of Jail: Seven Years in a South African Prison*. Cape Town: David Philip.

Mashele P (2009) Preface to Gould C (Ed) (2009) *Criminal (In)Justice in South Africa: A Civil Society Perspective*. Pretoria: Institute for Security Studies: xiv–xvii.

Muntingh L (2009a) Sentencing. In Gould C (Ed) (2009) *Criminal (In)Justice in South Africa: A Civil Society Perspective*. Pretoria: Institute for Security Studies: 178–200.

Muntingh L (2009b) The Prison System. In Gould C (Ed) (2009) *Criminal (In)Justice in South Africa: A Civil Society Perspective*. Pretoria: Institute for Security Studies: 201–216.

Office of the Inspecting Judge of Prisons *Annual Report of the Judicial Inspectorate of Prisons 2007/8*.

Pauw J (2009) We just sit here and rot: Awaiting-trial prisoners can spend 10 years behind bars with no protection from rape or violence. *Mail & Guardian*, 24-30 July 2009: 10.

Radebe, Mbalula defend Section 59 changes. Transcript of crime prevention and justice cluster media briefing. Government Communications, 05 March 2010. http://www.politcsweb.co.za/politcsweb/view/politicsweb/en/page71656?oid=16420 Accessed 7 March 2010.

Russell A (2009) *After Mandela: The Battle for the Soul of South Africa*. London: Hutchinson.

Sarkin J (Ed) (2008) *Human Rights in African Prisons*. Pretoria: HSRC Press.

Schönteich M (2008) Pre-trial detention and human rights in Africa. In Sarkin J (Ed) *Human Rights in African Prisons*. Pretoria: HSRC Press: 93–116.

Steinberg J (Ed) (2001) *Crime Wave: The South African Underworld and Its Foes*. Johannesburg: Witwatersrand University Press.

Steinberg J (2004) *The Number: One Man's Search for Identity in the Cape Underworld and Prison Gangs*. Johannesburg: Jonathan Ball Publishers.

UN Committee against Torture, Consideration of Reports Submitted By States under Article 19 of the Convention: Conclusions and Recommendations of the Committee against Torture – South Africa. Geneva.

Yaso M and J Gordin (2009) Nine years in a cell – still not convicted: Prince Molefe is just one of 50 000 prisoners – of a total prison population of 164 000 – who rot in South African jails while waiting trial. *The Sunday Independent*, 23 August 2009.

CHAPTER 19

Wolves in sheep's skin:
Trafficking of children in Musina,
Limpopo Province

Zosa de Sas Kropiwnicki

There is a dearth of accurate information about the incidence and prevalence of child trafficking in South Africa. It is held that South Africa is the site of internal trafficking whereby people are moved from rural and peri-urban areas to urban centres, tourist locations and sites of infrastructural development or agricultural growth. In addition, various reports state that South Africa is a source, transit and destination country for the trafficking of children and adults for the purposes of labour and sexual exploitation, and that children are trafficked from countries in the southern African region and elsewhere in Africa including Angola, Botswana, Democratic Republic of Congo, Lesotho, Mozambique, Malawi, Namibia, Swaziland, Tanzania, Zambia and Zimbabwe (International Organisation for Migration (IOM) 2003; 2006). Few reports, however, provide an in-depth analysis of trafficking along the South Africa-Zimbabwe border, the subject of this chapter.

Anecdotal evidence and the high level of migration of people from Zimbabwe into South Africa suggest that trafficking in persons may be taking place in Musina, where economic migrants, unaccompanied minors, asylum seekers and others wait in abhorrent conditions for the possible regularisation of their legal status. These migrants may be vulnerable to trafficking.

This chapter is based on the findings of a rapid assessment commissioned by the International Organisation for Migration (IOM), which sought to 'understand and tailor responses to the vulnerabilities and characteristics of trafficking in the Musina border area of

South Africa' (IOM 2009d). In addition to a literature review, data was collected over a period of fifteen days, from 29 July 2009 to 15 August 2009, in Musina and in Beitbridge, a border town in Zimbabwe. Focus group discussions and interviews were conducted with 140 key state and non-state informants and migrants (on the streets, in brothels, in shelters, on farms and at the border).[1] The focus is on the vulnerabilities of migrants in Musina and the mechanisms by which they may be trafficked.

DEFINITIONS AND CONCEPTS

In the sparse literature on trafficking in human beings, discussions about definitions and concepts are often lacking in depth and nuance. For instance, conceptual debates often overlook the fact that the international definition of child trafficking is distinct from the definition of trafficking of persons. Trafficking is also often conflated with kidnapping or smuggling, which affects incidence and prevalence estimates.

This chapter adopts the definition of trafficking in persons outlined in the Protocol to Prevent, Suppress and Punish Trafficking in Persons, especially Women and Children, supplementing the UN Convention against Transnational Organised Crime – otherwise known as the Palermo Protocol (UN 2000):

> (a) 'Trafficking in persons' shall mean the recruitment, transportation, transfer, harbouring or receipt of persons, by means of the threat or use of force or other forms of coercion, of abduction, of fraud, of deception, of the abuse of power or of a position of vulnerability or of the giving or receiving of payments or benefits to achieve the consent of a person having control over another person, for the purpose of exploitation (Article 3).

In the Palermo Protocol, consent is irrelevant if it is obtained by means of coercion, deceit[2] and abuse of power without the exercise of physical force. This applies to cases when individuals consent initially (for example, to migrate or work) but are then subject to exploitation. If there is no realistic possibility of free fully-informed consent or refusal, it amounts to trafficking. In Article 3(c) of the Palermo Protocol, the question of consent is irrelevant in the case of a child, who is defined as a person under eighteen years of age (Article 3(d)).

According to the Protocol, exploitation may include sexual exploitation (including the prostitution of others, pornography and forced marriages); forced labour or services; slavery; practices similar to slavery; or the removal of organs.[3] If the intent is discovered, the exploitative outcome need not be fulfilled for the act to constitute a case of trafficking. In Article 3, border crossing is not included as a constituting element of 'trafficking in human beings', as trafficking may also occur *within* a country.

The South African government signed the Palermo Protocol on 14 December 2000 and ratified it on 20 February 2004. Although a comprehensive discussion of policy frameworks is beyond the scope of this chapter, it is important to note that the South African Law

Commission into Trafficking in Persons finalised the draft text for comprehensive legislation against trafficking in persons in June 2007 and recommended it to the Department of Justice in 2008 (IOM 2008a). The proposed bill against trafficking in persons does not provide a specific definition of trafficking of children, but defines trafficking in persons in line with Article 3a:

> …the recruitment, sale, supply, procurement, capture, removal, transportation, transfer, harbouring or receipt of persons, within or across the borders of the Republic
> 1) by any means, including the use of threat, force, intimidation or other forms of coercion, abduction, fraud, deception, abuse of power or the giving or receiving of payments or benefits to achieve the consent of a person having control or authority over another person; or
> 2) by abusing vulnerability, for the purpose of exploitation.

In addition to the Combating of Trafficking in Persons Bill, the following pieces of legislation refer directly or indirectly to child trafficking and exploitation: Children's Act No. 38 of 2005; Basic Conditions of Employment Act 57 of 1997; Criminal Law (Sexual Offences and Related Matters) Amendment Act No. 32 of 2007; Immigration Act 13 of 2002; Refugee Act 130 of 1998 and the Films and Publications Act, 65 of 1996 as amended in 2004. Although there has been an increased awareness at an institutional level of trafficking in persons,[4] a number of gaps in implementation exist, many of which relate to definitional and conceptual confusion.

For instance, there has been a tendency to subsume all forms of 'children on the move' under the category of 'child trafficking' (Bissel 2008; Reale 2008) whereas it is important to note that the expression 'children on the move' refers to a wide range of children, including those who have been trafficked, child migrants, asylum-seeking children, children who seek family reunification, and children seeking employment and educational opportunities. These categories are not mutually exclusive as children's situations may change over time and/or children may fall into two or more groups at the same time. The manner in which the experiences and needs of children across these categories differ should be subject to in-depth analysis (Cantwell 2007).

It is difficult to determine the 'intention to exploit' when a child is moved by an individual or third party, particularly since power dynamics within these relationships are constantly shifting (De Sas Kropiwnicki 2007). Not all traffickers rely on physical abuse, but some actively manipulate notions of 'trust' to fulfill their intentions, especially when traffickers are family members, relatives or friends (Dottridge 2006; Shuteriqi et al 2007: 24; Surtees 2005). Trust may be associated with contextually-specific notions of reciprocity, duty and obedience, often linked to constructions of gender, childhood and maturity, and buttressed by socio-economic dependency (Dottridge 2006: 19). In order to understand the mechanisms and processes by which trafficking occurs, it is therefore necessary to look at the nature of the child-trafficker relationship, as perceived by children, their families and communities.

When determining a case of child trafficking it is also necessary to distinguish between child work and child exploitation in line with the International Labour Organisation's International Programme on the Elimination of Child Labour (ILO/IPEC) conventions. Child work includes activities in the home or the commercial setting that stimulate children's development, skills and expertise and helps them to fulfill their roles and responsibilities in their homes and communities while not detracting from their school attendance or violating their rights and physical and mental development. Labour is exploitative when it involves health hazards, enslavement, separation from families and, in general, proves to be harmful to children's physical and mental development (http://www.ilo.org/ipec/facts; accessed 10 January 2010).

Although such classifications are contextually specific, ILO/IPEC has set minimum standards related to the child's age, the nature of the work and the type and hours of the work in the Minimum Age Convention No. 138 of 1973 and the Worst Forms of Child Labour Convention No. 182 of 1999. It is important to note that many people do not understand or use the notion of 'exploitation', because they are not aware of this concept, do not have alternative options or believe that they are able to exercise high levels of choice and power over their working conditions (De Sas Kropiwnicki 2008). This will have a significant effect on the identification of trafficking, which, by definition, rests on the intention to exploit.

In order to prevent child trafficking, it is important to understand why children may believe and/or go with a trafficker even when coercion is not present (De Sas Kropiwnicki 2007 and 2009a). This decision is influenced by highly contextual macro, interpersonal and individual risk factors. Although it is difficult to determine a single causal pathway to being trafficked, given the resilience of certain children in certain families and communities, research has found that HIV/AIDS orphans, children who are subjected to maltreatment, migrant children, working children, children living on the streets and children in institutions may be tempted by what turn out to be false offers of transportation, shelter and employment. Even though children's choices may lead to a range of unwanted and negative consequences, their decision-making processes cannot be ignored. It is therefore necessary to adopt a framework that foregrounds agency when trying to understand how children find themselves in a trafficking or exploitative situation.

This chapter refers to identified or presumed cases of human trafficking or sale as *reported* by migrants, service providers and law enforcement officials. Some professionals prefer to refer to victims as 'survivors' in order to emphasise the resilience they have exhibited, the risks that they have overcome and the role that they can personally play in overcoming them. The chapter recognises that, despite their suffering, these 'victims' are 'agents' who, through their decision-making and action, develop various strategies and use self-defined 'weapons' to exercise power, escape and survive adverse experiences (Honwana 2005).

TRAFFICKING IN MUSINA

There is little quantifiable information on the trafficking of persons between Zimbabwe and South Africa. The United Nations Office on Drugs and Crime (UNODC) (2009) states that three South African victims were repatriated from Zimbabwe and the Middle East. Four victims of trafficking from Zimbabwe and seven from the Congo were assisted by IOM in South Africa from 2005 to 2006 (*op cit*: 128). Despite these relatively low figures, reports suggest that trafficking from Zimbabwe has increased as 'Zimbabweans flee a desperate situation at home'

(Molo Songololo 2009). Their vulnerability is exacerbated by their lack of documentation and what has until recently been an irregular legal status in South Africa (IOM 2008a). IOM's (2008a) report on internal trafficking in South Africa does not discuss Musina as a source or destination site for human trafficking although, by map and graph, it notes that Polokwane is a destination city along internal trafficking routes. These reports have highlighted the role played by criminals, collectively known as 'Magumagumas', who operate along the Limpopo River, and the 'Malaisha', who provide taxi and smuggling services to migrants (IOM 2009a and b).

A 2007 report on the situation of Zimbabwean migrants in South Africa highlighted the potential that exists for smuggling to turn into trafficking:

> ... there are reports of smuggling scenarios turning into trafficking once in South Africa. The Malaisha sometimes request additional money for transporting migrants and keep them in servitude until additional payments have been made or the women are sold into prostitution (IOM 2007: 5).

The sexual exploitation of Zimbabweans has been raised in various reports. For instance, the IOM stated: 'there are reports of South African employers demanding sex from undocumented Zimbabwean workers under threat of deportation' (IOM 2006: 23). It is held that migrants are trafficked from rural Limpopo to Johannesburg for the purposes of sexual exploitation (*op cit*: 41) or exploitation in the agricultural sector (IOM 2008a: 51): the Musina Legal Advice Office (MLAO) reported that it received cases where people had been deceived into travelling to a farm where they were exploited under 'slave-like conditions' (MLAO 2009: 5). The report also mentions that children, especially females, seem to be 'disappearing without a trace' (*op cit*: 6). The authors of the report do not, however, link this to potential trafficking.

With regard to 'children on the move', a number of reports discuss risk factors that increase children's vulnerability to violence and exploitation, including their socio-economic status, undocumented status and age, but they do not address the issue of trafficking (Save the Children UK and Norway 2008: ix; Save the Children UK 2009a). While the 2008 report describes how the Magumagumas and Malaishas prey on children's vulnerability and powerlessness through robbery, physical violence, rape and kidnapping, no mention is made of trafficking.

A recent United Nations Children's Fund (UNICEF) review found that unaccompanied minors in particular are vulnerable to exploitative working conditions, violence and denial of basic rights (Palmary 2009: 3). A Forced Migration Studies (2007) report states that 10 per cent of the child migrants interviewed were forced against their will by a parent to come to South Africa, and 8 per cent were advised by a relative or friend. Other than this, no reference is made to deception or coercion as being factors behind children's decision to migrate to South Africa or to work under exploitative conditions.

While there is information about trafficking in persons from Zimbabwe to South Africa, and some reference to labour and sexual exploitation in Limpopo generally, these reports do not contain any specific information about the situation of Musina and the particular experiences of vulnerable children and adults in the context of trafficking. Although there are reports about children's vulnerability to abuse, violence and exploitation, there is no indication of child trafficking. Similarly, reports on adult migration refer to violence and exploitative practices, but do not examine whether deception or coercion are factors in the recruitment or transportation of migrants into exploitative circumstances. While the importance of moving beyond a narrow focus on trafficking to broader protection issues faced by adults and children is supported, it is also important not to lose sight of the fact that trafficking may be occurring and that targeted responses to prevent and combat it are needed.

Map 1: Limpopo Province, South Africa

'ANYTHING SOUNDS BETTER THAN THAT SIDE'

Economic migrants and refugees from Zimbabwe, the Democratic Republic of Congo (DRC), Rwanda, Somalia and elsewhere[5] seek work, prosperity and safety in South Africa, which they enter through Musina. Political violence, poverty and the collapse of the social welfare and education systems have enhanced the vulnerability of Zimbabwean migrants to false promises such that 'anything you say to them sounds better than that side' (NGO worker, Musina, 30 July 2009). Their movement is facilitated by the porous geopolitical border between South Africa and Zimbabwe; as the fence is damaged in many sections, cigarettes, drugs (dagga, cocaine and tik), diamonds and gold (from Zambia and northern Zimbabwe) and humans are smuggled through it – and potentially trafficked (farm manager, Musina, 2 August 2009). People can hide (or be hidden) in cars and trucks, and overwhelmed immigration officers are unable to detect them at the official border crossing point. Joint Zimbabwean police, South African National Defence Force (SANDF), Immigration and South African Revenue Service (SARS) patrols are unable to patrol all border points, particularly at night, owing to human resource shortages and safety concerns (law enforcement officer, Musina, 14 August 2009; immigration officer, Beitbridge, August 2009). Allegations of corruption continue to plague law enforcement and immigration officers (law enforcement officer, Musina, 13 August 2009).

Against this backdrop, the visa regime has fuelled smuggling and trafficking practices. Since May 2000, Zimbabweans who obtain section 11 asylum permits in South Africa cannot be deported for a period of ninety days (government official, Musina, 12 August 2009). Migrants do not require a passport and visa to enter South Africa but can travel with an emergency travel document (ETD), which is valid for six months. These changes are a source of protection for many migrants, who no longer need to enter South Africa through dangerous non-official border crossing routes in the bush and across the Limpopo River (law enforcement officer, Beitbridge, 4 August 2009).[6] In the words of a farmworker interviewed on 31 July 2009, 'If you have a work permit, it's no problem. Only the border jumpers have problems. They stop and rape you.' Despite these changes in visa requirements, many migrants continue to cross through unofficial border points because the passport (US$190) and ETD (US$50) fees are too high for the average person. Furthermore, many migrants do not possess birth registration documents, a requirement for an ETD, so in order to avoid fees, bureaucracy and other delays, they continue to bypass the official border point (government official, Musina, 12 August 2009). Even if adults have ETDs or corporate working permits, their children may not have the correct documents and therefore continue to cross through unofficial border points.

Many migrants are not aware of these changes in visa requirements or of the dangers lurking by the bush or river; information about risks is rarely shared with others. This was explained as a 'coping mechanism to block things' (international non-governmental organisation (INGO) worker, Beitbridge, 4 August 2009). Others attributed it to competition over employment and success: 'If you spread the news, they think you are jealous and lying and don't want them to come. Information is not reaching every corner of the country' (migrants, Musina, focus group, 1 August 2009).

'PUTTING THEIR LIVES AT RISK'

The ignorance and desperation of migrants is exploited by criminal networks such as the Magumagumas. In Beitbridge, Malaisha transport migrants to unofficial border point crossings at the river, where they are left to wait for the Malaisha who will collect them on the South

African side of the river. It is at this point that they are subjected to violence from Maguma-gumas who lie in wait.

Those who appear to be confused, lost, and stranded in Beitbridge are targeted. According to a male migrant, 'People need to know about the bad route. Even if they know the Magumagumas are there, they do not know who they are. They come like a *wolf in sheep's skin*. They say, "my brother you are in trouble". People cannot distinguish. So men are raped, and brothers made to rape sisters.' A Malaisha in Beitbridge admitted that some drivers deceive migrants by promising them transport, employment, and/or asylum documents.

Many migrants are aware of the dangers of believing promises of transportation and employment. For instance, a female farm worker in Musina stated: 'Inside Zimbabwe, the man says he has a job for you in Johannesburg. You go with him but then he rapes you.' While females fear sexual violence, male migrants tend to fear being 'cheated' by someone. A male farm worker stated: 'When things are not good in Zimbabwe, everyone is forced to come here for a better life. So you will cheat him like say you will do something good, but then you do something wrong.' Despite these fears, many migrants continue to accept such offers and either travel transnationally, across the border into South Africa, or internally, from Musina to Johannesburg or Cape Town. A nurse on a farm stated: 'There are plenty of stories of people going to Johannesburg but we don't see them again.'

'IN THE DISGUISE OF HELPING, THEY ABUSE THEM'

The majority of migrants cross the border voluntarily but may be subjected *en route* to violence. As there is no deception or coercion in the process of movement, they are not victims of trafficking, but a number of reported cases suggest that this notion of 'voluntary' movement must be interrogated, as false promises of safe entry, transportation and employment are used to obtain consent from migrants.

It is very difficult to determine whether a case is one of human smuggling or trafficking. In 2007, police officers found people from the DRC hidden under the tarpaulin of a truck. They were unable to determine the intention of the driver, and classified it as a case of attempted smuggling; the driver was fined approximately R2 000 for carrying illegal migrants and the migrants were sent to a detention centre in Polokwane (law enforcement official, Musina, 7 August 2009).

By contrast, a similar case was classified by law enforcement officials as attempted trafficking: in August 2009, eleven Congolese and Burundian women were discovered with ten Congolese men sitting behind a petrol station on the South African side of the border. The women claimed that they had left the DRC to escape the effects of war and had used public transport to travel to Zimbabwe where they met the Malaisha who promised them safe passage to Cape Town – which, they were told, was only one hour away from Musina (paralegal, Musina, 14 August 2009). Officers classified this as trafficking because of its clandestine nature. No reference to the means by which they were moved (deception, coercion or an abuse of power) or the intention to exploit them, was made.

According to IOM in Beitbrige, two Zimbabwean women were employed by a man from Burkina Faso who ran a cleaning service in Johannesburg. One of the women disappeared when she tried to resign. Her sister opened a docket for kidnapping on 17 September 2006. The outcomes of this case are unknown and it is therefore impossible to know if the victim has been abused or exploited; only the latter would constitute trafficking.

These cases suggest that it is very difficult to distinguish between trafficking, kidnapping and smuggling if there is no information about the outcome of the movement, or the intention of the person who transported the victims. It is, however, not very useful to focus only on the means by which they are moved in order to establish whether a particular case constitutes trafficking. As adult victims *en route* may themselves not be aware that they have been deceived, it may *appear* as though they have consented to this movement and are therefore being smuggled, and not trafficked.

Key informants also found it difficult to distinguish between trafficking, smuggling and kidnapping of children, particularly since they were not aware that children's consent is irrelevant when identifying a case of trafficking, according to the Palermo Protocol. Workers in Musina and Beitbridge (in government departments, law enforcement agencies and INGOs) were very concerned about 'unaccompanied' children on the move, many of whom travel with relatives or people who claim to be their relatives, and a key informant, a paralegal interviewed in Musina in August 2009, stated: 'There are cases of children at SMG [Soutpansberg military grounds][7] who say that they are travelling with their uncle but the "uncle" does not know the child's last name and does not have proof that he will deliver the child to his mother.' Officers suspected that these children are possibly kidnapped or trafficked.

The involvement of the extended kin network in transporting or facilitating the transportation of children poses particular challenges in identifying cases of trafficking. Research from West Africa and other parts of Southern Africa suggests that the extended kin network is an essential source of support for children who in many cases are orphaned or left to fend for themselves because their parents are economic migrants or have abandoned them; however, there are many reports of relatives who, instead of caring for these children, restrict their school attendance and subject them to various forms of exploitation (De Sas Kropiwnicki 2009a and b).

The key challenge encountered by law enforcement officials lies in determining the intention to exploit. Two cases of children who were suspected of having been kidnapped in South Africa were intercepted trying to cross the border into Zimbabwe. In June 2009, a six-year-old girl was reportedly taken from Johannesburg by two men who were stopped at the border. Officials questioned the girl in Beitbridge and found that she did not know the two men with whom she was travelling. They brought the child to the Victim Empowerment Unit, a Department of Social Development initiative based at the police in Musina. The men claimed that the child was an orphan and that they were asked by her uncle to take her to her grandmother in Zimbabwe. The two men were released when the uncle confirmed their story and, as the children were so young, the officers did not know how to consult them (law enforcement officer, Musina, 4 August 2009).

In May 2009, officials at SMG found that a woman travelling with a two-year-old child had used the birth certificate of another child to enter South Africa; she lied about the birthplace and birthdate of the child but was insistent that this was her biological offspring. Staff felt that they could not remove this very young child from her care, and two days later she ran away with the child. The next week officials encountered a similar case; a woman travelling with two children under the age of four had no proof that they were her children. While officials were trying to trace her family, she managed to run away with the children. Key informants were very suspicious given that these two cases were discovered in such close proximity to each other (paralegal, Musina, 14 August 2009; government official, 12 August 2009).

In July 2009, key informants discovered a woman at SMG who had four children, of whom only one was her biological child. She claimed that the children's mother had asked her to collect them from Zimbabwe. Officials also questioned a man with a child aged six. The child was kept at the boy's shelter until the mother came to collect him. In August 2009, two women travelling with five children who were not related to them (apart from one step-son), were brought to the Uniting Reform Church (URC) Women's Shelter. They claimed that relatives had asked them to bring the children to South Africa. During their two-day stay at the URC shelter, Lawyers for Human Rights verified the story by contacting their parents, who faxed the children's birth certificates. The parents, who travelled to Musina to collect their children, were apparently 'mad' (angry) that they had been stopped (paralegal, Musina, 14 August 2009).

On 3 August 2009, South African Police Services (SAPS) intercepted fourteen Zimbabwean children aged from five to fifteen who were travelling with two Malaisha. The Malaisha claimed that they had been asked by the children's parents to bring them to South Africa as schools had closed that week. In this case, officials called the parents to collect their children, but this is not always possible for many parents, who are difficult to locate in rural outlying areas and/or do not have the means to travel to collect their children (paralegal, Musina, 14 August 2009; social worker, Musina, 13 August 2009).

Front-line development workers providing assistance to migrants are concerned that these children are at risk of abuse, exploitation and trafficking. An INGO worker in Musina explained that children are told to lie about their relationship to the Malaisha, which makes it difficult for the police to detect: 'When police ask, I tell you to pretend that you are my child. So if we get to a destination, it will be a better life'. This secrecy suggests that the Malaisha may have other motives. A law enforcement official interviewed in August 2009 classified this as trafficking or posing a risk of trafficking: 'Malaisha are taking children to their mothers in Johannesburg. That's trafficking. Small children are taken to their parents, but what about the girls and young ladies – what do they do with them? And the bigger boys, they might use them for work.' As they are *en route*, it is difficult to determine whether the Malaisha intend to exploit the children or whether they are just offering a transportation/smuggling service. This is exacerbated by the fact that immigration officials do not have the training required to consult children about their relationship with a suspected perpetrator.

'FEAR STOPS THEM FROM LEAVING': Trafficking for sexual exploitation

Migrants are subject to various forms of violence *en route*, which in addition to sexual and gender-based violence might contain an element of exploitation and may leave migrants at risk of further exploitation or trafficking. Both men and women are victims of this sexual violence: men and women are raped, and men are forced to rape women. Although difficult to quantify, sexual and gender based violence is highly prevalent. It is perpetrated in the bush, or victims are taken to a place called Makakavhule, twenty kilometres outside Beitbridge. Other men are brought on site to rape these women. A staff member of a women's shelter recounted the case of three women who were kept in this house and continually raped for up to a month. They are not free to leave: 'Even if the door is not locked, fear stops them from leaving. In most cases, people do not know much about Beitbridge and are afraid to move. They do not know who is a part of the group. They are afraid of people monitoring them.'

A sixteen-year-old girl in the women's shelter, interviewed in August 2009, described her experiences at Makakavhule:[8]

> 'On twentieth January 2009 I travelled with my sister from Harare to Beitbridge. We arrived at four a.m. At eight a.m I was caught by the Magumagumas. They offered me a lift to SA for three hundred rands. At first we were scared, but because of the way they were talking, we thought that they were good guys. They put me in a place called Makakavhule. They said we must stay there. The girls who were there were raped and cut. Many people who were cheated were taken there. We ran away. They caught us and cut me. I managed to run away. Another woman carried me to hospital. They stitched me and then I crossed the border.'

It is unclear whether men who visit Makakavhule pay a fee to the Magumagumas for sex with the women. If the Magumagumas do receive benefits or payments from facilitating the transportation and rape of these children and adults, it would constitute trafficking. This is likely, given their power and women's relative position of vulnerability:

> 'When in the Magumaguma's control, anything can happen. They can rape you or make you rape your colleague in front of them. They have that power. There is every reason to think that if a recruiter comes to take people to Johannesburg, they are at their mercy. There is a high possibility that the recruiter can approach and pay Magumagumas for girls' (paralegal, Musina, 3 August 2009).

If the Magumagumas transport, deceive/coerce *and* exploit migrants, they can be described as traffickers.

Cases recounted by several key informants suggest that trafficking for the purposes of sexual exploitation does occur: women are transported from their homes of origin to other communities under the false promises of transportation and employment. On arrival they are held in confinement and raped repeatedly. They become trapped in slave-like situations where they lose power over their own decision-making and movement. An eighteen-year-old Zambian girl arrived at the offices of an INGO on 8 May 2009. She claimed that instead of fulfilling a promise of work in Johannesburg, a woman forced her to engage in prostitution (practitioner, Musina, interview, 6 August 2009). In another case, a woman was brought into

Musina with a Malaisha early in 2009. He took her to a house where she was raped repeatedly. She managed to escape out of a window and hitchhiked to Pretoria where she reported the case to the police (law enforcement official, Musina, 7 August 2009). An INGO worker from IOM described the case of a seventeen-year-old waitress in Beitbridge who was offered a job in South Africa in 2005. On arrival in Pretoria she was raped, beaten and her movement restricted. When she threatened to run away the man stated that 'he did not care as he would find other easy targets in Zimbabwe'.

There is evidence of sexual exploitation on the farms, although many describe these practices as a survival strategy for female migrants rather than as exploitation. As a male farm worker explained: 'Some people call young ladies and say that they have a job for them, but when they cross the border they ask you to become a wife for them. The ladies do not know where they are going. They do not know anyone. They are forced by the man to live with them for accommodation or food'. In other words, they are deceived into believing that there is shelter and work for them, but this would only amount to trafficking if the person who deceived the woman intended to turn her into his own 'sex slave', or accepted payment from another man for this purpose, or sought to exploit her in another way – for instance, through domestic work. A female farm worker expressed the belief that this was normal: 'It's obvious that she becomes a wife when there is no accommodation'.

Many of the adolescent sex workers in Beitbridge were aware of the dangers of trafficking, especially when they travel with their clients. Many are dropped in outlying areas without clothes or money: 'Some go with truck drivers on a journey. If you do not give them enough attention they dump you on the way. You agree on the amount but they do not give you the same amount. Sometimes you do not know the attitudes. There are many pretenders, but you think that they are a good person' (sex worker, Beitbridge, focus group, 4-5 August 2009). They provided the example of a girl they knew who had trusted three men enough to go off with them and two other girls in a truck. The men slept with each of the girls and then dumped them when they reached Johannesburg. One of the girls (seventeen years old) was helped to return by a relative after she had spent a week on the streets, but nothing more had been heard of the others.

It is debatable whether adolescent sex workers who 'voluntarily' travel with truck drivers and other clients can be considered trafficked persons. As they are below the age of eighteen the Palermo protocol dictates that their consent is irrelevant, and as they are moved and exploited for prostitution their cases should be classified as trafficking. There is an obvious tension between this classification and a perspective that focuses on adolescents' decision-making and agency in the context of prostitution (De Sas Kropiwnicki 2008).

'BEING TREATED LIKE ANIMALS': Trafficking for labour exploitation

Countless children, men and women have been deceived by false promises of employment. Boys are particularly vulnerable to labour exploitation because they more readily accept abhorrent working conditions to support themselves, their friends and families as a means of fulfilling socially constructed notions of masculinity and maturity.

A nurse in Beitbridge gave the example of a fourteen-year-old Zimbabwean boy who was promised a job in Johannesburg. When he arrived he was dumped and picked up by someone else. She told of how he had endured sex, drug and alcohol abuse because he 'had no way of saying no' as 'Zimbabwe is far away'. In order to pay for their transportation back to Zimbabwe, children may become vulnerable to abuse and exploitation – but it does not constitute trafficking unless they are exploited by the person who transported them or by arrangement with this person. Nevertheless, it is important to bear in mind that some migrants may be 'dropped' by people whose plans to exploit them are thwarted. According to the Palermo Protocol, such cases would still be considered trafficking, although they are very difficult to prove. Even so, those who have been dropped may be at risk of being trafficked by people who exploit their desperation for transportation and employment. As a farm worker in Musina stated, 'they see you are stranded and they say "come, you will get work". But when you get there, there is nothing like that'.

There was no clear evidence that farmers were trafficking labourers from Zimbabwe. Some key informants stated that farmers (particularly from small commercial farms) use agents to recruit and transport labourers from Musina. According to a paralegal in Musina:

> Agents recruit people to work on farms. They promise them accommodation, salary, everything. But when they arrive they become a victim of violence and torture. Under the pretext of work, they come with trucks but it is the opposite from what is promised: they become slaves. Not every employer is like this but there are serious cases with farmers. The situation is not what they have been told.

For some, this constitutes trafficking in persons. To support this claim, the same paralegal described the case of a farmer in Dendron, 120 kilometres south-west of Musina, who allegedly recruited and transported Zimbabwean workers in Musina to his farm. Working conditions were not as he had promised and the workers were physically abused. Two female workers and some men, including a boy of fourteen accused the farmer of forcing workers to stand between the two fences which separate lions from the public. This case is currently under investigation. As a migrant stated,

> Some people come here and want people for certain jobs. They are taking us for a ride. When they get there, they are treated like animals … People threatened that if they didn't do the job, they will be thrown in with the lions. So if people come and say they have a job, we don't believe that they are serious. We try to ask more questions about the conditions. But some are desperate so they just go (migrant, Musina, focus group 1 August 2009).

The Palermo Protocol includes the 'abuse of power' as a means by which people can be trafficked. Although socio-economic inequities can inform this abuse of power such that migrants feel that they have no choice but to travel and work for someone, it is difficult to classify all Zimbabwean migrants as trafficked persons.

Similar arguments are employed to say that by virtue of a child's age, there is a *de facto* imbalance of power that can be abused. On this basis, children's consent is deemed irrelevant in international protocols, despite the fact that many are making conscious decisions to migrate and work to ensure their own survival and that of others. A seventeen-year-old boy left the boys' shelter on 18 June 2009 to find employment on a tomato farm near Musina. He slept on the floor in a large room with other children and was told that money for his food, blankets and clothing would be deducted from his salary. In another case, a sixteen-year-old boy was not paid for his work on a citrus farm. As these boys travelled of their own accord to the farm, this constitutes a case of labour exploitation, but not trafficking for the purposes of labour exploitation (INGO practitioner, Musina, 3 August 2009), but if these children are recruited and transported by a farm manager, foreman or agent to the farm, and then exploited, it would constitute trafficking according to the Palermo Protocol, even if the children went voluntarily.

'THEY CAN PASS THROUGH EASIER': Trafficking for the sale of illegal substances and criminal activity

Evidence suggests that children are being recruited and transported to assist with the sale of illegal goods and substances. A social worker in Beitbridge stated:

> They are used in illicit dealings like tobacco smuggling at the border. Children are used because they are likely to pass through easier. Some get something little but others get nothing. If the child complains or requests payment, they would threaten the child.

In this account, physical coercion is used to force children to travel across the border to sell cigarettes for an adult person. This would amount to trafficking if the money earned by the children from the sale of the cigarettes was appropriated by the person under whose duress they had smuggled the goods.

A nurse in Beitbridge told of a sixteen-year-old Zimbabwean boy who was smuggled into South Africa with some men but, on arrival, was left with strangers in a small town where he was forced to sell drugs: 'He had no food and no clothes. They wanted him to sell drugs – small packets. One day when he wanted to run away he was cut with a knife'. These cases suggest that the trafficking of illegal substances is linked to the trafficking of persons in that Zimbabwean migrants may be physically coerced to traffic illegal substances, for which they receive little or no benefit.

In terms of criminal activity, a man in his mid-twenties told an INGO worker in Beitbridge that when he arrived in Johannesburg, the men who provided him with transport enclosed him in a room and would only let him out to 'rob and kill'. He managed to escape and found his way back to Musina where he was deported by the South African authorities and later assisted by IOM Beitbridge.

'PAYMENT ON ARRIVAL': Trafficking and debt bondage

Most Malaisha insist on a small payment for transportation, shelter and food prior to departure to South Africa, and the rest on arrival. Upon arrival, the requested amount may change in accordance with what one Malaisha described as 'logistical costs': paying for food and shelter on the journey, paying bribes to police, dealing with car trouble, and so on.

Migrants are not told in advance that the rate will change, but *en route* they are suddenly asked for more and more money, which many cannot afford. In order to cover these fees, the Malaisha contact relatives or people whom their passengers know, and ask them to pay the outstanding amount. In some cases, migrants are confined to a house for many days, waiting for someone to collect them and pay their debt. They are not allowed to leave and do not receive adequate food and shelter. If no one collects them, they may be forced to work to repay the Malaisha. Alternatively they are left in Johannesburg because the Malaisha cannot afford to bring them back to Musina and Beitbridge (Male migrant, Musina, focus group, 1 August 2009; Malaisha, Beitbridge, focus group, 4 August 2009).

In July 2009, a sixteen-year-old Zimbabwean boy from Chipinge was offered transportation and employment in South Africa, which he accepted because his parents were unemployed and he wanted to be 'self-sufficient'. The Malaisha charged him R400, which he paid from his piece-job earnings. They locked him in a house in Beitbridge for three days while they went to find fuel and additional customers. They returned with other young boys and girls. He was then asked for an additional R100, the last of his money. When they left through the main border, money was paid to a policeman at the bridge. Upon arrival in Johannesburg he was locked in a room while they tried to reach his relatives to pay the outstanding fee. As relatives could not help him, he was locked up for seven days. He did not receive food and was physically abused. Eventually they sent him out to find work under the threat of more physical abuse. When he failed to find work, they brought him back to Musina and left him at the showgrounds, where he was referred to a boys' shelter. He did not know what had happened to the other fourteen children with whom he had travelled (INGO worker, Musina, interview, 1 August 2009).

This study suggests that the Malaisha are perpetrators of debt bondage, deceiving their desperate victims into these situations, but whether this constitutes trafficking or smuggling and then kidnapping and extortion, requires further investigation.

POLICY AND PRACTICE

Without the space to provide a comprehensive analysis of the field of policy and practice with regard to child trafficking, what follows are a few challenges that are currently faced.

With regard to the identification of trafficking cases, training has been identified as an area deserving attention. SAPS officers and front-line workers in the Department of Social Development and NGOs identified the need for more training, and refresher training, on how to employ gender and child-sensitive techniques to identify cases of human trafficking. Service providers such as school teachers, social workers and health practitioners, who are in contact with children, should be trained on how to identify, report and refer children who are at risk of being trafficked and/or those who have been trafficked. Even when there is a suspected case of trafficking, if the intention of the person that migrants are travelling with is unknown, it is difficult to determine with certainty whether it is in fact a case of trafficking. Victims themselves may not know that they have been trafficked. Furthermore, they may have been instructed to give false information, or may not trust those who question them.

Once a victim of trafficking has been identified, there is no clear standard operating procedure or referral protocol that functions across departments and agencies. When referrals are made it is unclear which agency will take responsibility for following up on the case and ensuring that the rights are protected and the well-being of the suspected victim is ensured. As there is no regional referral protocol involving both state and non-state actors, referral of non-nationals is hindered by poor cross-border communication and collaboration.

This extends to investigation and prosecution, where cross-border jurisdiction issues thwart timely and effective police and border patrol action. Allegations of corruption and sexual harassment at the main border and at irregular border crossing points, together with a perceived inertia on the part of the police in arresting the Magumagumas and other perpetrators, have led to a loss of faith in law enforcement and in the law itself. Investigation and prosecution is hindered by an overall perception that the South African police are not fulfilling their duties, and this has a negative effect on reporting patterns. In addition, many migrants do not report the violence either because they are afraid of the repercussions, both physical threats and fear of being ostracised, or because they do not know where to find a police station. According to a law enforcement official, language constraints also hinder in-depth investigations. Furthermore, border patrols do not have specialised personnel who can respond to cases involving children or cases of rape where victims are too traumatised to talk. It is often difficult to find witnesses who can confirm the complainant's statement, as people do not want to get involved in 'private matters', especially when this involves the police. Additional delays are caused during the judicial process. Police officers complained that victims who make these claims cannot be found when cases finally come to court: 'Victims think it's better to find something to eat than wait for a court date. So when it finally comes to court, you can't track them. These are foreigners in transit, so you can't locate them' (law enforcement official, Musina, interview, 7 August 2009).

In Musina there are shelters for migrants who may or may not have experienced various forms of violence. The Victims Empowerment Unit (VEP), is a DSD initiative based at the South African police office, which has space for five adult or child victims of violence; Soutpansberg Military Grounds, a former detention facility, is used to shelter undocumented migrants for no longer than forty-eight hours prior to being taken to the Department of Home Affairs. Shelters for boys at the Uniting Reform Church and Save the Children UK have space for approximately 200 and 50 children respectively. The Uniting Reform Church's MG Matsao Women's Shelter provides accommodation for vulnerable women who have survived sexual and gender based violence, are pregnant or disabled. The 'I Believe in Jesus' shelter caters for 350 male migrants. Although each shelter faces specific challenges, a few important observations can be made. First, most staff are not trained to identify a case of trafficking and do not know how to provide specialised support and care. Second, cases that have not been identified by the police may initially be classified as smuggling or as yet another case of undocumented migration. As a result, potentially traumatised victims may be placed in shelters which are unable to offer adequate health and psycho-social care. Third, protection of women at the shelters was raised as a concern, as practitioners have observed women leaving the shelters with men who promise them jobs. Fourth, there is no shelter that caters specifically for girls who, practitioners argue, should not be housed with adult women victims of violence. This, they contend, encourages relationships in which young girls rely on older men in the community for food and shelter in exchange for sexual and/or other favours. Fifth, although there is shelter for children in Beitbridge, the absence of a shelter for women who have been raped in transit has resulted in women who are stranded and feel that they have nowhere to go turning to sex work to survive. Sixth, victims of sexual and gender based violence, are often denied access to health care due to unnecessary bureaucracy and the absence of clear procedures and protocols that should prioritise their free and immediate medical treatment and confidentiality.

The return and reintegration of child victims of violence, including trafficking, is hindered by a number of factors. Some children do not want to return to Zimbabwe because they feel that they have failed their parents by not succeeding in South Africa. There are also logistical challenges – a shortage of vehicles and human resources – as well as difficulties locating caregivers in South Africa or Zimbabwe. Even when caregivers are found, the fact that pre- and post-placement assessments are rarely done poses a number of child protection risks as children may be placed back into situations of abuse and exploitation.

Various workshops have been facilitated by UNICEF, IOM, UNHCR (the office of the UN High Commissioner for Refugees), and others on child trafficking and some training has been provided by IOM staff to local officials in Musina. However, more work should be done in the area of prevention: instead of separate disjointed campaigns, there should be greater interagency coordination around the messages that are relayed to migrants and the reporting and referral protocols that are displayed.

Awareness-raising campaigns should focus not only on definitions of trafficking but should actively equip communities, parents and children with practical advice on how to report suspected cases of trafficking, and how to ensure their own safety and security in risky circumstances. Adults and children should be empowered to protect themselves and make informed decisions. This should be part of broader awareness-raising initiatives about human rights and an attitude of zero tolerance to all forms of abuse, sexual and gender based violence, and exploitation.

CONCLUSION

While there is little documented information on the incidence and prevalence of human trafficking in Musina, this study suggests that trafficking in persons does occur there. Evidence was found of trafficking for the purposes of sexual exploitation, sexual slavery, labour exploitation, sale of illegal substances and goods, forced criminal activity, extortion and other forms of exploitation. These crimes are perpetrated by those referred to by a migrant, as 'wolves in sheep's skin', men who exploit migrants' desperation through false offers of safe transportation and employment.

While many migrants are at risk of being trafficked because they are trying to escape from dire socio-economic circumstances and political violence, are inexperienced and not informed of immigration procedures and the dangers of travelling through unofficial border post crossings, the research found that unaccompanied minors are at particular risk of being trafficked. There are high levels of confusion around the definition of trafficking, which rests on conceptual debates around issues pertaining to consent and abuse of power, specifically in relation to children. Despite this confusion, in order to prevent trafficking it is important to understand children's agency and why they may decide to migrate, work and engage in practices such as prostitution. This will inform an understanding of why children may believe a false offer and agree to travel with a person who turns out to be a trafficker. Children's decisions are constrained by factors such as the visa regime in South Africa, socio-political instability in Zimbabwe and high levels of socio-economic deprivation, which affect their relationships with their families, peers and wider communities. In this context, children – like adults – make decisions in order to ensure their survival and that of their friends and families. These decisions may have unintended consequences, such as placing them at risk of violence, exploitation and trafficking.

The assessment found that there is a protection system in Musina to support undocumented Zimbabwean adults and children by providing shelter, food and medical assistance. However, there are a number of gaps in this system and it is not adequately geared to combat human trafficking and provide assistance to victims. Interventions should be targeted at children and adults who may be at risk of being trafficked. Although they should focus on the specific needs of individual victims, holistic approaches are needed that involve the victim, family and wider community and should rest on a systems model of protection, whereby trafficking is seen as a cross-cutting issue that is either causally related or linked with other protection risks. These interventions will require high levels of collaboration and communication between a range of actors. As a first step, officials need to show a clear commitment to these issues as affirmed at a legal and policy level. However, in order for the law to have a deterrent effect on would-be exploiters and to protect those at risk, more investments must be made in developing coordinated, inter-departmental and inter-agency strategic frameworks informed by evidence and supported by adequate financial and human resources, to ensure that law is translated effectively and meaningfully into policy and practice.

NOTES

1   A snowballing sampling technique was employed to access a wide range of respondents in these communities.

Respondents in Musina	No.
Government officials	11
INGO respondents	18
NGO respondents	4
CBOs (e.g. church organisations)	4
Farm managers	4
Migrants (see breakdown below)	53
Malaisha	1
Total	95

Migrant Respondents in Musina	No.
Male migrants (shelters, farm workers)	19
Female migrants (shelters, street sellers, prostitutes)	14
Girl migrants (shelters)	4
Boy migrants (shelters, street children)	16
Total	53

Respondents in Beitbridge	No.
Government official	4
INGO	11
NGO	1
Brothel (x4 – focus groups)	23
Malaisha	6
Total	45

2   Deception can relate to the nature of the services to be performed as well as the conditions under which the person will be forced to perform such services.

3   While the Palermo Protocol does not mention the recruitment of children for hazardous work or illegal adoption, the ILO Convention No. 182 on the prohibition and immediate action for the elimination of the Worst Forms of Child Labour and the Hague Convention on the Protection of Children and Cooperation in Respect of Inter-country Adoption provides for the protection of children by states from such circumstances.

4   A national intersectoral task-team was formed by the National Prosecuting Authority in December 2003. It is chaired by the Sexual Offences and Community Affairs Unit (SOCA). Its multisectoral response centres on awareness-raising, capacity building and development, victim support and

integration, legislation and policy development, liaison and consultation, and monitoring and evaluation. A number of other departments have made counter child trafficking and exploitation their responsibility.

5   Over the April-June 2009 period, MLAO assisted people in Musina from the following countries: Bangladesh, Burundi, DRC, Ethiopia, Ghana, India, Malawi, Nigeria, Mozambique, Rwanda, Somalia, Zambia and Zimbabwe.

6   Children reportedly cross the Limpopo River at Beitbridge, Chikwalakala, Dete, Thohoyandou, Sango Border Post, Crooks Corner Mahenye (Save the Children UK, and Save the Children Norway in Mozambique 2008).

7   Migrants are placed temporarily (no longer than forty-eight hours) at the SMG, a detention facility that caters for 90 to 110 migrants.

8   This homestead was also mentioned in IOM (2009b: 2).

REFERENCES

Bandura A (2001) Social cognitive theory: An agentic perspective. *Annual Review of Psychology* 52: 75–78.

Bissell S (2008) Protection of children on the move – applying lessons learnt from child trafficking research. Florence: Innocenti Research Centre, UNICEF.

Cantwell N (2007) Draft report of the UNICEF workshop meeting 'Children on the Move'. Zurich, 29-30 November.

De Sas Kropiwnicki Z (2007) Children speak out: Trafficking risk and resiliency in South East Europe. Tirana: Save the Children Norway, Child Trafficking Response Programme.

De Sas Kropiwnicki Z (2008) The sex trade hierarchy: the interplay of agency and structure in the decision-making processes of female adolescent prostitutes in Cape Town, South Africa. Unpublished PhD/ DPhil thesis, University of Oxford.

De Sas Kropiwnicki Z (2009a) The trafficking of women and children in Mozambique. Maputo: Save the Children in Mozambique.

De Sas Kropiwnicki Z (2009b) 'Because we are suffering, we will trust our children with anyone'. A situational analysis of human trafficking, especially women and children in Liberia. Monrovia: UNICEF and the Liberian Department of Labour.

Dottridge M (2006) Action to prevent child trafficking in South Eastern Europe: A preliminary assessment. Geneva: Terre des Hommes and UNICEF Regional Office for CEE/CIS.

Forced Migration Studies Programme (2007) The unaccompanied minors study. Johannesburg: University of the Witwatersrand.

Honwana A (2005) Innocent and guilty: Child soldiers as interstitial and tactical agents. In Honwana A and F De Boeck (Eds) *Makers and Breakers: Children and Youth in Postcolonial Africa*. Oxford: James Currey: 31–52.

International Labour Organisation (2007) Child trafficking – The ILO response through IPEC. Geneva: ILO.

International Organisation for Migration (2003) Seduction, sale and slavery. Pretoria: IOM.

International Organisation for Migration (2004) HIV/AIDS vulnerability among migrant farm workers on the South African–Mozambican border. Researched for Japan International Cooperation Agency (JICA). Pretoria: IOM.

International Organisation for Migration (2006) Breaking the cycle of vulnerability: responding to the health needs of trafficked women in East and Southern Africa. Pretoria: SIDA.

International Organisation for Migration & United Nations (2007) Joint assessment report on the situation of migrants from Zimbabwe in South Africa. Pretoria: IOM Regional Office for Southern Africa.

International Organisation for Migration (2008a) No experience necessary: The internal trafficking of persons in South Africa. Pretoria: IOM Regional Office for Southern Africa.

International Organisation for Migration (2008b) Migrants' right to health in Southern Africa. Pretoria: IOM Regional Office for Southern Africa.

International Organisation for Migration (2009a) Migrants' needs and vulnerabilities in the Limpopo Province, Republic of South Africa: Report on Phase One, November–December 2008. Pretoria: IOM Regional Office for Southern Africa.

International Organisation for Migration (2009b) Migrants' needs and vulnerabilities in the Limpopo Province, Republic of South Africa. Report on Phase Two, February–March 2009. Pretoria: IOM Regional Office for Southern Africa.

International Organisation for Migration (2009c) Baseline assessment: Preparing for the implementation of IOM's health promotion projects. Pretoria: IOM Regional Office for Southern Africa.

International Organisation for Migration (2009d) Terms of reference – Research consultant: Rapid assessment of human trafficking and related health concerns at the Musina Border. Pretoria: IOM Regional Office for Southern Africa.

International Organisation for Migration (2009e) Trainings on human trafficking: July 2008-March 2009, Limpopo Region. Pretoria: IOM Regional Office for Southern Africa.

International Organisation for Migration (2009f) Victims assistance standard operating procedures. Pretoria: Southern African Counter Trafficking Assistance Program (SACTAP).

Matope T (2006) 'I was kidnapped and abused on camera, says girl (16)'. In *The Herald*, 15 July 2006, Harare.

Médecins Sans Frontières (2009) No refuge, access denied: Medical and humanitarian needs of Zimbabweans in South Africa.

Molo Songololo (2009). Rapid assessment on impact of 2010 FIFA World Cup on abuse, exploitation and trafficking of children. Cape Town: Molo Songololo.

Musina Legal Advice Office (2009) Migrant Rights Protection Project: Final report to International Organisation for Migration, April–June 2009.

Palmary I (2009). For better implementation of migrant children's rights in South Africa. Pretoria: UNICEF.

Reale D (2008) Away from home: Protecting and supporting children on the move. London: Save the Children UK.

Save the Children UK (2007) Children on the move: protecting unaccompanied migrant children in South Africa and the region. South Africa. Pretoria: Save the Children UK.

Save the Children UK (2009) *Our Broken Dreams: Child Migration in Southern Africa*. Harare: Weaver Press.

Save the Children UK (2009) Report on children's participation in the regional seminar on children who cross borders in Southern Africa. Johannesburg 25-27 May.

Shuteriqi M, D Pippidou and D Stoecklin (2007) Transnational protection of children: The case of Albania and Greece 2000-2006. Terre des Hommes, Transnational Action against Child Trafficking Project.

Surtees R (2005) Other forms of trafficking in minors: Articulating victim profiles and conceptualizing interventions. NEXUS Institute to Combat Human Trafficking and International Organisation for Migration.

United Nations (2000). Protocol to prevent, suppress and punish trafficking in persons, especially women and children, supplementing the UN Convention against Transnational Organised Crime.

United Nations Children's Fund, The Office of the United Nations High Commissioner for Refugees and International Organisation for Migration (2009) Minutes of the workshop to address child smuggling and possible child trafficking, Musina, 8-9 July 2009.

United Nations Educational, Scientific and Cultural Organisation (UNESCO) (2007) Human trafficking in South Africa: Root causes and recommendations, *Policy Paper Poverty Series* 14 (5).

United Nations Office on Drugs and Crime. 2009. Global report on trafficking. Policy, Analysis and Research Branch.

United States State Department for Trafficking in Persons (2009) Trafficking in persons report. http://www.state.gov/documents/organisation/123357.pdf.

CHAPTER 20

Relationships of exchange amongst South African youth in an age of conspicuous consumption

Terry-Ann Selikow and Graham Gibbon

―――――

*'... but I need his help, or might need it later on – there is, after all, that invisible institution
called the Favour Bank, which I have always found so very useful.'*
'What is this Favour Bank?'
'You know. Everyone knows.'
'Possibly, but I still haven't quite grasped what you're saying.'
*'It was an American writer who first mentioned it. It's the most powerful bank in the world,
and you'll find it in every sphere of life.'*
(Paulo Coelho, *The Zahir*, 2006)

'Selling sex' is said to be the oldest profession in the world. However, starting in the 1990s, a new term, transactional sex (TS) emerged to describe particular forms of the exchange of sex by women for money and other necessities for survival. Distinctive to TS was that the inter-action was not framed as a 'sex for sale' exchange and women who engaged in this process did not construct themselves as sex workers. In the early 2000s, however, researchers began to challenge assumptions that sexual exchange was merely an economic survival strategy (Hunter 2002, 2007; Leclerc-Madlala 2002, 2004; Selikow *et al* 2002; Thorpe 2002), hence the term transactional sex for conspicuous consumption (TSCC) emerged.

This term encompasses an exchange where women provide one 'favour', sex, in return for luxury gifts or services from a man. Unlike TS for survival, it does not involve the exchange of resources for subsistence needs but is driven primarily by the pressures of modernity and codes of consumer culture. Within this globalised culture TSCC is becoming more common-place in Africa and in South Africa (Hunter 2002, 2007; Kaufman and Stavrou 2002; Leclerc-Madlala 2004; Luke 2003). To understand the workings of day to day gift giving and sexual relationships, it is necessary to locate them within the context of consumerism, modernity and globalisation and other broader structures and processes. It is also important to note that not all gift giving is based on expectations of sex; indeed giving or receiving a gift does not necessarily imply any sexual transaction (Kaufman and Stavrou 2002), and the boundaries between gift giving for sex and other forms of gift giving are blurred.

Moreover, while we draw primarily on TSCC as it occurs in an urban township in South Africa, the practice of TSCC is not limited to South Africa, or indeed to Africa. It is in fact a worldwide phenomenon, particularly noticeable in countries that experience extreme socio-economic disparities. This may be accentuated as young people share a globalised culture that emphasises materialism and consumerism in the context of a worldwide recession.

A NOTE ON METHOD AND TERMINOLOGY

Like most qualitative research, the aim here is not to make sweeping generalisations, but to develop rich and detailed explanations. Young people are not a homogenous group and, as they are affected differently by the unique and complex interplay of material and cultural factors, we limit our empirical focus to young people in an urban township in South Africa. This focus allows for depth and nuance. Seventy youths were interviewed either individually or in focus group discussions (FGDs) (Selikow 2005). Furthermore, we locate this data in similar studies to substantiate our argument. Where an asterisk appears, the quotation is drawn from the study by Selikow. We have presented lengthy verbatim quotes to allow the youth to tell their own stories in their own words (Root 1987), so that their voices are not lost in academic analysis. In this regard it is imperative to present original, authentic voices of actors in everyday life to capture lived experiences. However, this type of qualitative in-depth data, which allows for a focus on the symbolic and on meanings, perceptions, semantics and practices, does not lapse into extreme interpretism as these are located within systems and structural relations. This approach, termed structural hermeneutics (Chouliaraki and Fairclough 1999; Sayer 2000), begins with the actors' understandings, often located in a case study, and connects the micro level of sex for exchange to the macro level of large-scale social structures and processes such as patriarchal norms, glob-alisation, a capitalist ethic and a widespread culture of consumerism (Neuman 2000).

As has been argued (Selikow 2004), the language that young people use is partly constitutive of the social world. Indeed young people have devised their own terminology. In the urban town-ship studied, as in many other townships, metaphors and specific vocabularies are used to refer to categories of lovers. For example in Oxlund's research in Limpopo (2007) popular phrases were 'taste and pass', 'takeaways' and 'side kicks', and in Pattman's study in Botswana (2005a) 'cats' and 'Ugandans' were used to refer to categories of men. In our study, the hegemonic masculinity of the 'real man' was embodied in the phrase *ingagara*. The ingagara was defined by his sexual prowess, the visibility of a number of beautiful girlfriends at any given time and his material wealth. The permanent girlfriend of the ingagara was dubbed a *regte* – she was the 'right one', suitable to be the mother of his child. The part-time girlfriends were termed 'cherries', and the ingagara would have a number of cherries whom he would regularly swap. Although the relationship with the cherrie was not a permanent one, as with that of the regte, it was based on some affection. In most cases the regtes and cherries were dependent on the ingagara for a number of reasons, the primary one being material rewards. Some cherries believed that they were regtes, while others were aware of their cherrie status. Still others knew they were cherries but were hoping to be promoted. It appears therefore, that a hierarchy of lovers exists.

The TSCC interaction has a number of characteristics, some of which overlap with, and some that differ from, other sexual interactions, such as those of a sex worker, one night stands and main girlfriend/boyfriend relationships, making it a distinctive interaction and one that is conducive to high risk sex and HIV infection.

While the sex worker generally has sex with a man outside the context of a relationship, and one night stand sex is a 'once off' outside a relationship, TSCC is characterised by the fact that the sexual relationship with 'part-time' cherries lasts for a number of months (Leclerc-Madlala 2004; Luke 2003). In contrast to the relationship with a main girlfriend, however, it is seen by men as a temporary relationship. Also, TSCC, while primarily seen as a relationship of exchange, is constructed as a girlfriend/boyfriend relationship that involves some emotions. Then again, it is not money, but rather gifts and favours, which are usually given by men as the tokens of exchange. This detracts from a 'cold cash', monetary exchange, further cementing the idea of a girlfriend/boyfriend relationship (Hunter 2007; Leclerc-Madlala 2004). This, and the duration of the relationship undermine condom usage as they place the relationship within narratives of love and trust. Ironically, despite such discourses, many women view men primarily as providers of gifts and favours and because of the exchange, men view women as 'prostitutes of a special kind', and believe that their 'investment' in women entitles them to dividends in the form of sex. Moreover, as they have 'paid' for sex, they believe that they should control the conditions of sex, and often this means condomless sex. Condomless sex is also frequently promoted by women, as condoms are symbolic of a lack of trust and monogamy. Not using a condom is therefore seen as an affirmation of 'special' status in a relationship that often involves multiple and concurrent partners (MCP).

To understand TSCC, it is necessary to locate it within post-apartheid modernity and relate it to a globalised consumer culture. As Meekers and Calves (1997) argue, in sub-Saharan Africa sexual relations at a younger age are increasing with exposure to western values through mediums such as television, novels and magazines. Writing about globalisation in contemporary urban South Africa, Salo and Davids (2009: 39) assert that:

> … the impact of globalisation on youths' popular practices is taken for granted or naturalised. In most urban South African contexts, the smell of perfume brands a la Estee Lauder, the beat of Nike or Reebok sports shoes on the street, the low cut jeans displaying the requisite naked band of midriff as part of seasonal fashions, even the glossy covers of the women's magazines on the coffee tables, in the bathrooms or on the magazine stands in the supermarkets could be anywhere in Suburban Mall, Smallsville, USA.

TSCC is one way of enabling young people to perform these 'popular practices', centred on the acquisition and public display of material goods. In this regard, Dineo* (a cherrie who is aware of her position but hoping to be promoted to that of a regte) emphasised the status she derives from being seen in her boyfriend's car:

> '… He's very financially able … when you see his car, you know automatically. If I'm with him driving the BMW or the M Coupe, then everybody wants to see, "Who's the girl on his left side?" … Every girl … would like to be in that car, you know …'

Dineo, like many young women, attests that it is common to exchange sex to enable the personal display of material goods. Writing about South Africa, both Hunter (2007) and Leclerc-Madlala (2004) argue that materialism is a defining feature of modernity. One way for young women to accumulate material goods is through sex, so the commoditisation of sex has intensified and there is an ' … inextricable intertwining of sexuality and consumer culture' (Radner 2008: 98). Although this goes against the idealistic and romantic relationships of young people, such as those described by Harrison (2008), TSCC is not necessarily devoid of emotion.

It has long been argued that young women's self-evaluation depends partly on the degree to which their bodies and sexuality are publicly valued and that fashion can become a resource for girls through which they can assert their independence (McRobbie 2000). However, in the context of globalisation and modernity, there is an even fiercer need to 'dress to impress: marking the body as part of the new femininity' (Salo and Davids, 2009: 87). The public visibility of the trappings of globalisation and modernity, such as branded cars, designer clothes and glamorous hairstyles, thus become increasingly important markers of feminine identity (Radner 2008; Salo and Davids 2009), and are also some of the key indicators of masculine identity. Indeed, Radner (2008: 3) argues that for a woman to be desirable (and thus to identify herself as a 'woman'), she must be adept at 'manipulating and presenting herself according to the strict codes of consumer culture'.

Fashion and attractiveness are directly associated with being a successful heterosexual being (Salo and Davids 2009). It is not only women who have to abide by the 'strict codes of consumer culture'; men also use fashion and other resources to 'make visible' their masculinity. The dominant notions of heterosexual masculinity have been influenced by a complex shifting of social and cultural landscapes, and a confluence of tradition and globalisation, and this calls for men to constantly renegotiate the signifiers of their masculinity. Part of performing their manhood and securing their status as 'real men' in ways that are visible to both women and to other men is sexual prowess. Many studies have indicated that sexual prowess is a highly regarded masculine attribute and that perceived insufficient male sexual experience carries a negative stigma for young men, both within their male peer groups and among women and young girls (Lindegger and Maxwell 2007; Pattman 2005b; Reddy and Dunne 2007; Selikow et al 2002, 2009; Thorpe 2002; Walsh and Mitchell 2006). Sexual experience can be made visible by being seen with multiple women, and if these women are beautifully packaged, the status of the man is further increased. Thus, 'looking after a woman's wardrobe', benefits men not only sexually but also in the symbolic domain as described by Dineo*:

'... most of us, we don't really have money, you need a six hundred rand jeans ... so you get a boyfriend who's going to deal with your wardrobe specifically, because you get those guys, who say "I want you to wear this and that, you look good in this and that", and just buy you anything, like Nike shoes. Money's not a problem to them, you know. And you find that you don't really like him, it's just that you're doing it for the money and end up sleeping with them.'

In this scenario, women are 'gatekeepers' not only to sex, but also to the desired masculine identity (Mooney-Somers and Usher 2008: 8).

As being seen with beautiful, well-dressed women contributes towards young men exhibiting their masculine identities, young women become the consumables of the 'real man' as Tebogo* attested when explaining the significance of material belongings and the relationship of 'wealth' to 'love':

'You know why you are respected? It's money! ... Now obviously if you dress well, smartly, drive a good car, a Z3W, and you've got money, your job is three quarters done. Sometimes they [girls] might just fall into you, because they don't like you but they like your lifestyle, so they would automatically fall in love with you.'

Thus in post-apartheid urban South Africa, in a contradictory context of both limited economic resources and increased materialism, the commoditisation of sex has intensified and TSCC is becoming increasingly normative (Kaufman and Stavrou 2002; Hunter 2002; Leclerc-Madlala 2002, 2004; Selikow *et al* 2002; Selikow 2005). With women's growing demands for consumables, Thorpe (2002) has argued that the formerly desirable characteristics of a man such as love, caring and compassion have been replaced by the three Cs: cash, car, cellphone (and clothing of course would make up the fourth 'c'). In order to have these, as well as a range of other consumables, it is 'necessary' to have more than one boyfriend, and often concurrently (Hunter 2002; Luke 2003).

While some women claim that they are lucky and have an 'all-in-one', (a man who can meet all of a woman's needs), most women need to rely on a number of men, and TSCC thus involves both an increased number of sexual partners and concurrent sexual relationships. This practice has been termed 'multiple concurrent partners' (MCP) (UNAIDS 2008) and has been identified as a key driving factor in the heterosexual transmission of HIV/AIDS in Africa (SADC 2006; UNAIDS MCP 2008/9) and in South Africa (Dunkle *et al* 2004; HSRC 2009; Parker, Makhubele, Ntlabati, and Connolly 2007).

While men have the bulk of multiple concurrent partnerships, the overall rate for both men and women in South Africa of having concurrent partners is high. In the latest HSRC study on HIV/AIDS (2009), 45 per cent of men and 28 per cent of women aged between fifteen and nineteen, and 36 per cent of men and 21 per cent women aged between twenty and twenty-four reported being involved in MCP.

Although many young women accept that their boyfriends have multiple partners, it is common for women, especially regtes, to be beaten if their boyfriends discover that they have another partner (Jewkes *et al* 2003; Wong *et al* 2008).

THE CHICKENS IN THE CABINET/MINISTRY

In our study, as well as in others (Kaufman and Stavrou 2002), terms such as minister of transport, minister of entertainment, minister of fashion, minister of education and so on have become part of the shared lexicon in South Africa. However, in this context they do not refer to actual members of parliament. In the framework of TSCC, a minister is a man who meets a particular need of a woman as elucidated by a male respondent in a focus group discussion (FGD):

> 'Minister, it's one of the names that they give us. Maybe I am having a girlfriend only to find out that she has three boyfriends. The other one is called the minister of finance because he has got money. The other if he has a car he is called the minister of transport because she is using him for transport. The other one maybe for studies, if she got a problem with her studies she contacts that one, eish, the minister of education, he has got brains.'

Other identities constructed by young people in the arena of TSCC signify that men are often seen in terms of what they can provide for women, and may be dubbed as an *automatic teller machine (ATM)* and/or *chicken*. Thandi* described a chicken in the following way:

> 'You just say he [the man you are sleeping with for material benefits] is "inkukhu yami". You just say, "That one is my chicken". Maybe you have your real boyfriend, then you have the other boyfriend, that is the chicken. He is called a chicken because all you want to do with him is get him to give you whatever you want. We say "uyamcutha" [skinning the chicken]. You just want his money or his stuff and you do not love him.'

Innocentia* elaborated on the symbolic chicken:

> 'You see those feathers of chickens? Yah, even though you don't put the boiling water on, they just come out. So, it's like every time you ask them for the money he just, he doesn't ask you for what or why or I don't have it, he just takes it out.'

Young people have developed an extensive vocabulary to describe categories of lovers in terms of the resources that can be extracted from them, despite the fact that they construct their relationships as girlfriend/boyfriend to distance themselves from sex workers. For example Oxlund (2007) describes how, in Limpopo, university students use the term 'cheese boys' to refer to men with numerous girlfriends and cash to spend on them, and in their study Cameroon, Meekers and Calves (1997) describe how women use the term 'milking the cow' to describe how they extract money from men.

Thus women are not necessarily passive victims in TSCC relationships and the chicken dis-course is an interesting example of how women exert agency by (re)inventing their sexuality and subverting the dominant patriarchal discourse. By defining men as chickens, they linguistically redefine their relationship to men – from that of passive objects of men ('cherries' or 'regtes' who are 'fucked' or made love to and provided for) to agents who do something to men (extract money from them in the same way that a chicken is plucked) (Selikow 2004). Moreover, such discourses illustrate that although there are social expectations that girls are passive and deferential (Pattman 2005b; Varga 1997), norms about gender roles are rapidly changing.

The concept of 'men for money' is not hidden, but is part of public discourse. In fact, most men are aware that some women are after money and they are proud of their status as providers, a visible signifier of masculinity. Kwena* articulates this consciousness:

> 'Kutluane, she likes money [laughing] … She sees me sometimes, maybe once in a month or twice or thrice in a month … whenever I speak to her, she must ask for something. So, then I begin to analyse that, no, she wants something from me. Money, as to be specific, not exactly love and stuff like that. Because of, whenever I call her she has to say something that, "Oh my hair, I'm with my friends. I need to go somewhere with my friends. I don't have money" [imitating a woman's voice]. Even if there's a trip at school, "There is a trip at school a hundred and fifty rands, I don't know what to do … I know that she likes money more than me. Eish, no, I am proud.'

While Kwena is proud that he can provide for his cherries, he also feels entitled to view them as 'prostitutes'. Indeed a number of men and women argued that 'there are many types of prostitutes', and that cherries 'sell sex in a polite-mannered way', or as Dali* claimed:

> 'They are prostitutes of a special kind. Look, she expects you to bring money home, okay. Yah, if you don't, if I get paid tomorrow and I don't give her money it's gonna be war … That means I'm not going to have sex with her because I didn't give her money. She's trading with sex.'

Similarly, Vusi* claimed that 'they are prostituting but they are making it indirectly, because if you don't have anything they won't fall in love with you'. Dineo* views many women in the township where she lives as prostitutes, despite the fact that they do not use the term 'prostitutes'. Rather, they call the men with whom they exchange sex 'boyfriend':

> 'Basically, it's just that now you tell yourself that he's some kind of a boyfriend, it's not like it's a one night stand or anything. That's where they get their bucks. Basically, it doesn't really differ, you sleep with a guy who gives you money, tomorrow morning, it's like hey.'

As will be explained below, while some men call women prostitutes, they differentiate between an interaction with a conventional prostitute (generally a one-off emotionless event) and a cherrie, where there is some emotion, 'feelings' being a key defining characteristic of TSCC. Witness, for example, Kwena*:

'I call them, all girls, prostitutes. [But] prostitutes it's just that you need to pop up money and give her straight, but girls, they are a bit of a different but they are doing the same. Because of for example, if I'm saying I'm going to a party. So I take my girl there. So when I go with my girl there I need to organise her some food, liquor and stuff like that. It's all about spending and then at the end of the day I sleep with her. Which is just the same with prostitutes because if you just give a prostitute forty rand then you go to bed. So the difference with a girl is just that you talk, I mean you get closer and you just discuss some other things but they are just the same according to me. And you might find that you even spend more in girls than in prostitutes because of, I mean, going to a party and getting thirty rand plate and drinking five, which is cost about ninety rand. So, in a prostitute, you just give a prostitute fifty rand and then you go to bed. So that is to me, and I want to be open, to me all girls are prostitute, to me.'

Hence Kwena compares the price of a prostitute and a cherrie and although the cherrie is 'more expensive than the prostitute', as Kwena continued, even though both involve a monetary exchange for sex, there is a difference between prostitutes and cherries:

'… when you propose a cherrie, it means that there is a certain feeling so going to a prostitute and buying [sex] in the same day, it's not a problem, but then it's not some-body that you feel and think of at some other time. So that is the reason for us to propose ladies, for me in fact to propose ladies. If, if I did not have feelings for someone I mean I'll go straight to prostitutes.'

Kwena, and other youths, make it clear that there are some emotions involved in relations of exchange. 'Love'and money are clearly not mutually exclusive, so having 'some feelings' for a cherrie does not exclude the fact that ultimately the relationship is part of a 'deal'.

'THE DEAL' AND 'THE INVESTMENT'

A defining feature of a sex-work relationship is that the 'deal' is up front and negotiated by both parties (Hunter 2007; Leclerc-Madlala 2004; Selikow *et al* 2002). This is in contrast to the TSCC relationship in which this is a tacit, rather than articulated, understanding, although both parties are aware that the relationship is part of an exchange as illustrated in a mixed sex FGD*:

Male: I'm looking for sex, you looking for money, it just happens.
Female: You don't discuss it but in your mind it just happens. But you don't say, 'You want those new Levi's, give me sex, you want five hundred rand … but there is an understanding.

Dineo* says that although women and men do not speak about 'a deal', they both 'know':

'You sleep with him, [you say] "Eric, I've seen these nice boots and I, why don't we go shopping tomorrow?" Then that guy wants sex, that guy is obviously going to buy you something. Then it's like, OK, that's how it's going to be for your whole relationship, you know. That's it. Or, the brother himself might say, "I like that girl's body, if I can just give her and all that, if I can just bed her, I'll give her five hundred bucks and all that." You don't speak about it, but its like, you both know.'

Leclerc-Madlala (2004) has contrasted TS with sex work, arguing that the chance of negotiating a condom is diminished in TS because TS is tacit and there is no discussion and upfront deal making. Thus, talking about using a condom does not occur, in contrast to the explicit, upfront and pre-negotiated 'business' conditions of sex work. Despite these differences, the idea of 'pay back' in exchange for sex is common to both self-identified sex workers and women in TS relationships. Dali* explained it in the following way:

'… obviously if you have sex with a particular person, you must pay back. One must pay back in one way or the other. It's either you buy her something, a gift or something, maybe shoes or maybe, give her money to go and do her hair … When you get a cherry first thing you have to think about, being a man, is her hair. Whatever she wants to do with her head. Well it starts from hundred rands upwards. Then, the next thing that you talk about – cell phones, buy her these new cell phones 3310, and she's happy. She feels, "Yah, I've got a man who looks after me".'

Indeed, most youth believe that, although it is implicit, a deal has been struck. Part of this deal is that the woman is an investment and the dividend is sex or, as Kaufman and Stavrou (2004: 377) note, gift giving 'entitles' men to the physical rights to the receiver's body, and these 'rights' include whether or not to use a condom. Themba's* comments draw attention to the fact that men feel entitled to sex and to decide on the conditions of sex if they have spent money on a woman:

'If I buy something for my girlfriend she's not independent. I buy something. I buy! I buy! I buy! If I want to have sex with her I'll have sex. She'll never tell me that she don't want to have sex with me because she knows that I'm buying something for her. Buying some clothes, some food, everything … you can give her money to make hairstyle, to buy some food, to buy some clothes. You see, that's where you control the girl … If I don't want to use a condom I will never use a condom.'

Nokuthula* echoed the above view:

'Some of the ghetto guys will say, "OK, I took you to the movies, we went for supper, we went for this, blah, blah, blah, and now why you wanna go home? No, don't go home" and everything, "We're going to my place". Fine, you go to his place and after that, all of a sudden he wants to have sex with you. He's like, "No, I did this and that for you so now why you don't give me something in return?" and all stuff like that, you know, and then still he refuses a condom.'

Under these circumstances, and in the context of widespread gender based violence (GBV) in South Africa (Dunkle *et al* 2004, 2007; Shefer *et al* 2008; Wong *et al* 2008), where a woman's request that a condom be used may result in a beating, it is highly unlikely that a condom will be used (Luke 2003). To be sure, common to all research on TS, with regard to condom use, women lack negotiating power (Dunkle 2004; Leclerc-Madlala 2004; Luke 2003).

BEYOND THE TRANSACTION

A defining feature of TS is that while there is an exchange of sex for a resource, the exchange goes beyond this to embrace some type of relationship. Notions of love, intimacy, affection and trust are often interwoven into the exchange. Receivers of gifts in TSCC do not label themselves as sex workers, but are rather constructed by themselves as 'girlfriends' despite the fact that they say how they manipulate men to obtain money. Similarly, 'givers of gifts', who are the receivers of sex, are often (but not always) constructed as 'boyfriends' (Hunter 2002; Leclerc-Madlala 2004), although, as will be recalled, this does not mean that boyfriends are not also seen as providers. These constructions of girlfriend/boyfriend introduce a degree of intimacy to the exchange, cemented by the fact that the medium of exchange is sex for gifts and favours and not 'cold cash'. Ironically, the fact that TSCC goes beyond an economic exchange makes it a very high risk sexual interaction as discourses of love and trust undermine the use of a condom.

'Feelings' for cherries may range from 'declarations of love' (although the cherrie still remains second best to the regte), to 'a little bit of feeling'. With regard to 'feelings', cherries are contrasted with 'prostitutes' and one night stands since, as Kwena* proclaimed ' … with the cherries there is that little bit of feeling you know, like with a prostitute is just someone you meet on the street'.

Moreover, as cherries may be regtes-in-waiting, their characteristics should be appealing to a man, and not only sexually as with a sex worker or a one night stand. Indeed, in the market language of the young people, a cherrie can apply to become a regte and can be promoted, as explained by a man in an FGD*:

> 'Sometimes cherries become real ones. We are always judging them, comparing them, check their qualities, their behaviour and maturity … Maybe the girlfriend acts otherwise [in a way you don't like], only to find the cherrie is behaving sharp [ok, good], so the cherrie becomes the girlfriend and the girlfriend becomes a cherrie. Cherries apply to become girlfriends.'

Men feel that even though, as Mpho* stated, a cherrie is ' … just somebody who's like maybe second best in your relationship', it is important that, as expounded in two male FGDs*, a cherrie has certain qualities that men appreciate in the event of the need for a 'back-up'.

> Male 1: It's [the idea of having a cherrie] like a bucket, you cannot depend on one bucket to carry water, any mistake can happen to that bucket.

Male 2: You need to have a spare wheel, meaning that if something goes wrong, you know that maybe your car has a puncture, you know that I have a spare wheel, I need to take off that tyre, I have another tyre. That is why guys do have a spare wheel … it's like with the cherrie, so she is like the spare wheel … you know that I guarantee, if the car punctures, you know you'll just put another tyre.

Cherries are clearly more than an exchange and are part of a broader relationship that includes complex issues such as love and intimacy (Dunkle 2007; Hunter 2002; Leclerc-Madlala 2004). As Dali* explained:

'[I have a regte but also] I do have a girlfriend … What I think we exercise with her is the best of love, you know. And for me, the woman that I am talking about, being the other woman in my life, is very affectionate … She [the other woman] knows, she knows [about his regte] and we are still going out.'

While Dali* says that he intends to have a very long-term relationship with his 'other women', most men have short-term relationships with cherries (unless the cherries are promoted to regtes), as Kwena* describes:

'… can I call it a temporary relationship because of I'm definitely sure we won't last. I mean before I had Kutluane I had Lindiwe, I had Candys, I had Phindi … I mean it's not something serious … I can't have a girl [cherrie] whom I can waste time with [spend time with] for about two years. Hey, I can't. We do it for months.'

The above vignettes underscore the fact that key to the definition of a cherrie in TSCC, unlike a regte, is that the relationship is not viewed as temporary. Unlike that of the sex worker and the one night stand, the exchange of resources is more than a one-off exchange.

Although Kwena* labels his relationships as 'temporary', each partnership does last for months and it does have features of a relationship, both of which undermine condom use. Condom use declines with the length of a relationship by virtue of the fact that the longer the relationship lasts the more trust is established (Leclerc-Madlala 2004; Thomson and Holland 1998). On this score, a young man from an FGD* claimed:

'… we don't use a condom. Sometimes you can be in a relationship with a girl maybe for six months using condom. After six months you told yourself "I trust this girl now" and you say "this girl is good girl now".'

Condoms are not neutral objects and decision-making about condoms is partly based upon the symbolic meanings attached to condom use. Condoms are associated with certain types of sex: sex outside a serious relationship, illicit sex and casual sex; and with certain groups of people – people who have sexually transmitted diseases, people who sleep around and who have casual relationships (Weiss et al 1996). Thus using a condom places the relationship outside of a girlfriend/boyfriend construction and the request to use a condom may be seen as an accusation of a lack of trust in your partner or an admission that you are not to be trusted (Hunter 2002; Leclerc-Madlala 2004; Varga 1997). The word 'trust' is used to justify not using a condom in a relationship and many young people take it as a given that if you love your partner, she or he should be trusted. Tebogo's* testimony illustrates how the word 'love' has become intertwined with the notion of 'trust':

> 'Trust is a, you know, trust is a very, very, big, big, big word … Like I said, when I use the word love, I really mean the word love, because I respect the word love, I understand the word love. What does it mean? Love means trust.'

As affirmed by women in an FGD*, the 'marrying' of love and trust has undermined condom use:

> Female 1: So mostly they [males] say 'We don't want to use a condom'.
> Female 2: And they'll [males] make you feel guilty for using the condom, the guys.
> Female 3: [To make us feel guilty they will say] 'Like you don't trust me. Now you think I've got other girlfriends, but now you know [I haven't]', and they'll make you feel insecure. So the next time they come what you gonna do? You not gonna use a condom.

Thandi's* account further attests to such insecurities and she expands on the difficulties in negotiating use of a condom in the discourse of trust, as this means the risk of 'losing' one's boyfriend:

> 'Sometimes you can you say you want to use condoms but when your partner forces you not to use it, or maybe he will say, you are not faithful to him or you do not trust him, why do you want to use condoms and such stuff. He will come with the saying of "Don't you trust me?" Eish, what can you say? … You end up accepting sleeping with him without using condoms …You sleep with him even then [if you know you could become infected]. Maybe if you love the guy, if you refuse to sleep with him without using a condom, maybe you will lose him.'

While it has been shown globally that men are decision-makers when it comes to whether a condom will be used, and that they are usually resistant to condom usage (Weiss *et al* 1996), it should not be assumed that it is only men who are resistant to condom use. As the primary motive for the relationship is a gift or favour, young girls view their sexual activity in terms of keeping their relationships rather than in terms of their physical health. Because insisting on a condom may jeopardise their relationships, and hence their economic goals, it becomes 'unsafe' (in another sense) to insist on using a condom (Dunkle 2007; Hunter 2002; Leclerc-Madlala 2004; Reddy and Dunne 2007). Not only is there the fear of losing a relationship, but many young girls believe that unprotected sex will strengthen the intimacy and bond in a relationship. Thus 'the discourse of love is clearly contradictory to the discourse of safe sex' (Reddy and Dunne 2007: 164).

Sex without a condom is a symbolic demonstration of trust and loyalty employed by young women either to retain or to advance their position in the hierarchy of lovers. Condomless sex '[c]an in itself become a euphemism for monogamy or love' (Thomson and Holland 1998: 67). Regtes do not insist on condoms in order to retain their status as 'the only one'. For cherries, condomless sex is viewed as opening the door for the possibility of love and long-term relationships (Reddy and Dunne 2007). Finally, satisfying the needs of male partners is often considered by young women to be more important than their own pleasure (Reddy and Dunn 2007; Varga 1997), and it is believed that sex with a condom may reduce male pleasure.

Hence, 'love' and condom usage become contradictory in relations of exchange. While 'love' and 'trust' are expressed through unprotected sex, wearing a condom is perceived as related to infidelity and lack of trust (Wilton 1997). Ironically, as argued by Murray *et al* (2006), intimacy is usually associated with love, trust and affection, but these positive connotations mask the fact that perceived relationship intimacy is also associated with unprotected sex.

CONCLUDING THOUGHTS

A growth in the culture of consumerism, spurred on by globalisation and modernity in post-apartheid South Africa, and the accompanying pressure on young people to acquire and publically display material goods, are some of the factors that have led to an increase in the commoditisation of sex.

Fashion and attractiveness are increasingly important markers in the construction of femininity. However, it is not only women who have to visibly construct their sexuality. Men, too, are under pressure to make visible the signifiers of masculinity. Like women, one way they are able to do this is through globalised fashion statements and, more importantly, to secure their status as 'real men' they need to demonstrate sexual prowess. This can be done by displaying 'beautifully packaged' multiple sexual partners, usually in the form of one regte and a number of cherries. MCP arises when men have enough money to invest in a number of women and when a woman may need more than one partner to meet all her needs. Despite the fact that cherries primarily view the men with whom they have relations of exchange as providers, they also construct them as boyfriends. This contradiction is also seen where men often view their cherries as 'prostitutes of a special type', while at the same time proclaiming some affection for their cherries. The introduction of a degree of fondness in the exchange, and the intimacy and discourse of trust derived from the constructions of girlfriend/boyfriend means that the use of condoms is undermined, with cherries often being reluctant to use a condom as they strive for regte status. Further, while both men and women understand that resources are exchanged for sex, the 'deal' is tacit and therefore the opportunity to communicate about condom use is diminished.

With regard to TSCC, a debate has arisen as to whether TSCC gives women agency and power within the confines of heterosexual relationships or whether, ultimately, women are victims of economic limitations, peer pressure and patriarchal norms. We speculate that there is no either/or answer to this question and that, regardless of whether women are labelled as 'victims' or 'vixens', TSCC ultimately leads to high risk sex. Indeed, according to the codes of the culture of consumerism, TSCC enables both men and women to be 'winners' but, with regard to engaging in high risk sex and increasing the chances of becoming HIV positive, both are losers.

REFERENCES

Chouliaraki L and N Fairclough (1999) *Discourse in Late Modernity: Rethinking Critical Discourse Analysis.* Edinburgh: Edinburgh University Press.

Coelho P (2006) *The Zahir.* New York. Harper Collins.

Dunkle KL, RK Jewkes, HC Brown, GE Gray, JA McIntyre and SD Harlow (2004) Transactional sex among women in Soweto, South Africa: Prevalence, risk factors and association with HIV infection. *Social Science & Medicine* 59. (8): 1581–1592.

Dunkle KL, RK Jewkes, M Nduna, N Jama, J Levin, Y Sikweyiya and M Koss (2007) Transactional sex with casual and main partners among young South African men in the rural Eastern Cape: Prevalence, predictors, and associations with gender-based violence. *Social Science & Medicine* 65: 1235–1248.

Harrison A (2008) Hidden love: Sexual ideologies and relationship ideals among rural South African adolescents in the context of HIV/AIDS. *Culture, Health & Sexuality* 10 (2) 175-189.

Human Sciences Research Council (2009) *South African National HIV Prevalence, Incidence, Behaviour and Communication Survey, 2008: A Turning Tide Among Teenagers?* Cape Town: HSRC Press.

Hunter M (2002) The materiality of everyday sex: Thinking beyond prostitution. *African Studies* 61 (1): 99–120.

Hunter M (2007) The changing political economy of sex in South Africa: The significance of unemployment and inequalities to the scale of the AIDS pandemic. *Social Science and Medicine.* 64: 689–700.

Jewkes RK, JB Levin and LA Penn-Kekana (2003) Gender inequalities, intimate partner violence and HIV preventive practices: findings of a South African cross-sectional study. *Social Science and Medicine* 56: 125-134.

Kaufman CE and SE Stavrou (2004) 'Bus fare please': The economics of sex and gifts among young people in urban South Africa. *Culture, Health & Sexuality* 6 (5): 377–391.

Leclerc-Madlala S (2002) Youth, HIV/AIDS and the importance of sexual culture and context. *Social Dynamics* 28 (1): 20–41.

Leclerc-Madlala S (2004) Transactional sex and the pursuit of modernity. *Social Dynamics* 29 (2): 1–21.

Lindegger G and J Maxwell (2007) Teenage masculinity: The double bind of conformity to hegemonic standards. In Shefer T, K Ratele, A Strebel, N Shabalala and R Buikema (Eds) *From Boys to Men: Social Constructions of Masculinity in Contemporary Society.* Cape Town: UCT Press.

Luke N (2003) Age and economic asymmetries in the sexual relationships of adolescent girls in sub-Saharan Africa. *Studies in Family Planning.* Vol. 34. Iss. 2. pp. 67–86.

McRobbie A (2000) *Feminism and Youth Culture* (2nd ed.). Basingstoke: Palgrave.

Meekers D and A Calves (1997) 'Main' girlfriends, girlfriends, marriage, and money: The social context of HIV risk behaviour in sub-Saharan Africa. *Health Transition Review* 7 (suppl.): 361–375.

Mooney-Somers J and J Usher (2010) Sex as commodity: Single and partnered men's subjectification as heterosexual men. *Men and Masculinities* 12 (3): 353–373.

Murray DAB (2006) Who's right? Human rights, sexual rights and social change in Barbados. *Culture, Health and Sexuality* 8: 267–281.

Murray L, L Moreno, A Rosario, J Ellen, M Sweat and D Kerrigan (2006) The role of relationship intimacy in consistent condom use among female sex workers and their regular paying partners in the Dominican Republic. *AIDS Behaviour* 11 (3): 463–470.

Neuman L (2000) *Social Research Methods: Qualitative and Quantitative Approaches* (4th ed). Boston: Allyn and Bacon.

Oxlund B (2007) Of cheese-boys, course–pushers, ministers and the right ones: Love, sex and relationships in a South African university campus. *Paper presented at the Past, Present and Future Conference,* June, Umeå, Sweden.

Parker W, B Makhubele, P Ntlabati and C Connolly (2007) Concurrent sexual partnerships amongst young adults in South Africa. Johannesburg: CADRE. Available at http://www.comminit.com/en/node/269915/36.

Pattman R (2005a) 'Ugandans', 'cats' and others: constructing student masculinities at the University of Botswana. In Ouzgane L and R Morrell (Eds) *African Masculinities: Men in Africa from the Late 19th Century to the Present.* pp. 221–237. New York/Scottsville: Palgrave Macmillan/University of Kwa-Zulu Natal Press.

Pattman R (2005b) 'Boys and girls should not be too close': Sexuality, the identities of African boys and girls and HIV/AIDS education. *Sexualities* (8): 49–516.

Radner H (2008) Compulsory sexuality and the desiring woman. *Sexualities* 11: 94–100.

Reddy S and M Dunne (2007) Risking it: Young heterosexual femininities in the South African context of HIV/AIDS. *Sexualities* 10 (2): 159–172.

Root M (1993) *Philosophy of Social Science.* Oxford: Blackwell Publishing.

Salo E and B Davids (2009) Glamour, glitz and girls: The meanings of femininity in high school matric ball culture in urban South Africa. In Steyn M and M van Zyl (Eds) *The Prize and the Price: Shaping Sexualities in South Africa.* Cape Town: HSRC Press.

Sayer A (2000) *Realism and Social Science.* London: Sage Publications.

Selikow T, B Zulu and E Cedras (2002) The *Ingagara*, the *regte* and the cherry: HIV/AIDS and youth culture in contemporary urban townships. *Agenda* 53: 22–32.

Selikow T (2004) 'We have our own special language'. Language, sexuality and HIV / AIDS: A case study of youth in an urban township in South Africa. *African Health Sciences* 4 (2): 102–108.

Selikow T (2005) Youth, sexuality and HIV/AIDS in South African urban township: A critical realist approach. PhD dissertation. Department of Educational Policy Studies, University of Alberta.

Selikow T, AJ Flisher and C Matthews (2009) I am not 'Umqwayito': A qualitative study of peer pressure and sexual risk behaviour among young adolescents in Cape Town, South Africa. *Scandinavian Journal of Public Health* 37 (Suppl. 2): 107–112.

Shefer T, M Crawford, A Strebel, L Simbayi, N Dwadwa-Henda, A Cloete, M Kaufman and S Kalichman (2008) Gender, power and resistance to change among two communities in the Western Cape, South Africa. *Feminism & Psychology.* 18 (2): 157–182.

South African Development Community (SADC) (2006) Expert think-tank meeting on HIV prevention in high prevalence countries in southern Africa. Maseru, Lesotho.

Thomson R and J Holland (1998) Sexual relationships, negotiating and decision making. In Coleman J and D Roker (Eds) *Teenage Sexuality.* pp. 59–79. Australia: Harwood Academic Publishers.

Thorpe M (2002) Masculinity in an HIV intervention. *Agenda* 53: 61–68.

UNAIDS (2008) Report on the Global AIDS epidemic. Annex 2: Country Progress Indicators, South Africa.

UNAIDS MCP (2008/9) Multiple concurrent partnerships campaigns and communications: Towards a coordinated regional response. Meeting of HIV Prevention Communications Practitioners 17-18 September, Johannesburg, South Africa.

Varga CA (1997) Sexual decision-making and negotiation in the midst of AIDS: Youth in Kwazulu-Natal, South Africa. *Health Transition Review* 7 (Suppl. 3): 45–67.

Walsh S and C Mitchell (2006) 'I'm too young to die': HIV, masculinity, danger and desire in urban South Africa. *Gender and Development* 14 (1).

Weiss E, D Whelan and G Rao Gupta (1998) Vulnerability and opportunity: Adolescents and HIV/AIDS in the developing world. Findings from the Women and AIDS Research Program. *International Centre for Research on Women*. Washington, DC: USAID.

Wilton T (1997) *EnGendering AIDS: Deconstructing Sex, Text and Epidemic.* London: Sage Publications.

Wong FY, Z Wong, J Huang, J DiGangi, EE Thompson and ED Smith (2008) Gender difference in intimate partner violence on substance abuse, sexual risks and depression among a sample of South Africans in Cape Town, South Africa. *AIDS Education and Prevention* 20 (1): 56–64.

Contributors

Doreen Atkinson is Professor of Development Studies, University of the Free State.

David Bruce is a Senior Researcher at the Centre for the Study of Violence and Reconcilaition, University of the Witwatersrand.

Anthony Butler is Professor of Political Studies at the University of the Witwatersrand.

Scarlett Cornelisson is Associate Professor of Political Science at the University of Stellenbosch.

John Daniel is Academic Director of the programme in Social and Political Transformation of the School for International Training, Durban.

Graham Gibbon is studying for his Master's degree in Sociology at the University of the Witwatersrand.

Jeremy Gordin is Director of the Justice Project in the School of Journalism, University of the Witwatersrand.

Colin Hoag is a Ph D student in Anthropology at the University of Santa Cruz, California.

Samuel Kariuki is Senior Lecturer in Sociology, University of the Witwatersrand.

Zosa de Sas Kropiwnicki is Research Manager for Health and Development Africa, an NGO based in Johannesburg.

Loren Landau is Director of the Southern African Migration Programme at the University of the Witwatersrand.

Lizle Loots recently completed her Master's degree in Sociology at the University of Pretoria.

Kezia Lewins is a Lecturer in Sociology, University of the Witwatersrand.

Neva Makgetla was until recently Lead Economist, Development Planning Division, Development Bank of Southern Africa and is now Deputy Director General in the Department of Economic Development.

Hein Marais is an independent writer and author, *inter alia*, of *South Africa: Limits to Change: The Political Economy of Transition*.

Seeraj Mohamed is Director of Corporate Strategy and Industrial Development in the School of Economic and Business Sciences at the University of the Witwatersand and teaches in the Economics Department and the Global Labour University Master's programme.

Mike Muller is a visiting Adjunct Professor at the Wits University Graduate School of Public and Development Management. He was Director General of the Department of Water Affairs and Forestry from 1997 to 2005.

Kammila Naidoo is an Associate Professor in Sociology, University of Pretoria.

Prishani Naidoo is an Associate Lecturer in the Department of Sociology, University of the Witwatersrand.

Devan Pillay is Associate Professor of Sociology, University of the Witwatersrand.

Tara Polzer is Senior Researcher in the Forced Migration Studies Programme, University of the Witwatersrand.

Maxi Schoeman is Professor of Political Science, University of Pretoria.

Aurelia Wa Kabwe-Segatti is a Senior Research Fellow in the French Institute for Development on attachment to the Forced Studies Migration Programme, University of the Witwatersrand.

Terry-Ann Selikow is a Lecturer in Sociology, University of the Witwatersrand.

Louis Reynolds is Senior Specialist and Associate Professor in the Department of Paediatrics and Child Health, University of Cape Town and at the Red Cross War Memorial Children's Hospital.

Roger Southall is Professor of Sociology, University of the Witwatersrand.

Mark Swilling is Division Head, Sustainable Development in the School of Public Management and Policy, University of Stellenbosch.

Peter Vale is the Nelson Mandela Professor of Political Studies, Rhodes University.

Index

Tables and illustrations are indicated in italics. Prepositions in subheadings are not used in alphabetical ordering.